THE NINETEENTH-CENTURY
CONSTITUTION
1815-1914

THE
NINETEENTH-CENTURY
CONSTITUTION
1815-1914

DOCUMENTS AND COMMENTARY

EDITED AND INTRODUCED BY

H. J. HANHAM

PROFESSOR OF HISTORY
HARVARD UNIVERSITY

CAMBRIDGE
AT THE UNIVERSITY PRESS
1969

Published by the Syndics of the Cambridge University Press
Bentley House, 200 Euston Road, London N.W.1
American Branch: 32 East 57th Street, New York, N.Y.10022

© Cambridge University Press 1969

Library of Congress Catalogue Card Number: 69–11148

Standard Book Number: 521 07351 0

Printed in Great Britain
at the University Printing House, Cambridge
(Brooke Crutchley, University Printer)

PREFACE

As the fourth volume in a series this book inevitably reflects the character of its predecessors. The presentation is by subject rather than by period, text and commentary are closely related, and there is little about the British Empire. There are, however, some major shifts of emphasis. There is more than in the earlier volumes about constitutional theory, because during the nineteenth century men were consciously remoulding the character of institutions. There is much more about the party system, because nineteenth-century parliamentary government meant in practice government by party. And there is also much more about the development of the career civil service and of the central departments of government. Space has been found for these additions by reducing the amount of attention given to the church and to the law, and by omitting a good deal of case law which may be found in text-books in constitutional law. Overlap with other collections of documents has been kept to a minimum.

There is alas no general history of nineteenth-century political thought to which the reader can be referred in order to follow up the more theoretical issues raised in the following pages. There are, however, three very useful general text-books which may be consulted with profit. Alpheus Todd's *On Parliamentary Government in England: its Origins, Development and Practical Operation*, first published in 1867–9 and re-issued posthumously in a revised and expanded version in 1887–9, is a storehouse of miscellaneous information. Abbot Lawrence Lowell's *The Government of England*, first published in 1908, gives an unrivalled account of the operation of the constitution in the years before 1914. And Sir William Holdsworth's *History of English Law* may be consulted on a wide variety of topics with great profit.

H.J.H.

Edinburgh
January 1968

CONTENTS

CONTENTS

TABLE OF DOCUMENTS

C   The Cabinet and the Ministry

The Recording of Cabinet Proceedings

The Unity of the Administration

Cabinet Committees

The Cabinet and Military Policy

CHAPTER 3: PARLIAMENT

A   Government and Parliament

Government and Opposition

B   The House of Commons

The Character of the House

C The House of Lords

TABLE OF DOCUMENTS

C   The franchise and the electoral system

C The central departments

D The management of the armed forces

ACKNOWLEDGMENTS

The Author is indebted to the following for permission to reproduce copyright material in the documents indicated. George Allen & Unwin Ltd. and Oxford University Press, New York (256), Beaverbrook Newspapers Ltd. (89), Ernest Benn Ltd. (67, 99, 143, 199), Cassel & Co. Ltd. (147, 198), Chatto & Windus and Frank Eyck (17, 18), The Clarendon Press, Oxford (196, 206), The Clarendon Press, Oxford and Miss A. Ramm (183, 304), The Controller of Her Majesty's Stationery Office (137), Constable & Co. (23, 35, 59, 95, 96), Cromwell-Collier and Macmillan Inc. (179, 197), Curtis Brown Ltd. (81, 128, 148, 149), The Bulletin of the Institute of Historical Research and Professor F. W. Bealey (207), His Grace the Duke of Devonshire (83), The present Lord Esher (263), The Executor of the late Mrs E. M. Dicey (10), Eyre & Spottiswoode (publishers) Ltd. and Oxford University Press, New York (25, 150, 285), The Hansard Society (153), Mrs Jenifer Hart and the Royal Institute of Public Administration (271), Hodder & Stoughton and the Owner of the Copyright (44, 194), Hodder & Stoughton and Margery, Lady Pentland (63), Hutchinson Publishing Group Ltd. (24, 38, 39, 64, 131, 172, 173), The Librarian, Warrington Municipal Library (132), Longman's, Green & Co. Ltd. (239, 243), Macmillan & Co. Ltd. (52, 54, 79, 94, 157, 176, 228, 305, 306, 308), Methuen & Co. (145), John Murray (91, 146, 188, 190, 297), The National Trust (93), The present Lord Newton (166, 171), James Nisbet & Co. Ltd. (284), The Public Record Office (118), Routledge & Kegan Paul Ltd. and the University of Toronto Press (37), The Royal Historical Society and A. Aspinall (71), The Royal Historical Society and Miss A. Ramm (20, 31, 92, 160, 161), The Marquess of Salisbury (80), The Trustees of the British Museum (57), The Trustees of the Goodwood Collection at the West Sussex County Record Office (283).

Documents in this collection numbered 29, 30, 32, 33, 36, 43, 48, 60, 66, 68, 84, 85, 114, 117, 139, 162, 163, 165, 298, 299, 302 (published by John Murray) appear by gracious permission of Her Majesty the Queen, as does number 164. Documents numbered 69, 78, 82, 86 and 141 are reproduced from photographic copies in the Public Record Office of original letters in the Royal Archives and made available also by the gracious permission of Her Majesty the Queen.

ABBREVIATIONS

CJ	Journals of the House of Commons
EHD XI	Aspinall and Smith, *English Historical Documents*, XI, *1783–1832*.
EHD XII(1)	Young and Handcock, *English Historical Documents*, *XII(1)*, *1833–1874*.
GG1	Ramm, *Gladstone–Granville Correspondence, 1868–76*.
GG2	Ramm, *Gladstone–Granville Correspondence, 1876–1886*.
Kebbel	Kebbel, *Selected Speeches of the Earl of Beaconsfield*.
LQV	*Letters of Queen Victoria*.
PGS	*Public General Statutes* or *Public General Acts*.
SCOS	*Report from the Select Committee on Official Salaries*.

CHAPTER I

THE THEORY OF THE
CONSTITUTION

The British constitution during the nineteenth century was not simply a British institution. It was the yardstick and exemplar for liberals all over the world, the pattern of a constitutional monarchy and a liberal state. In France, in Germany, in Holland and Belgium, in far-away Japan and Siam, quite as much as in Britain itself or the self-governing British colonies, there was an active debate as to the precise nature of British institutions and the extent to which they could be exported to other lands. Such men as Thiers, Guizot, Gneist and Redlich became devoted scholars of English constitutional development because they wished to apply the lessons of English history in their own homeland.

The consciousness that Britain had something of value to give to the world in the form of political institutions encouraged British statesmen and scholars to become constitutional theorists. For the most part they were theorists in what we should now call the Whig tradition. That is to say, they believed both in the progressive evolution of institutions from the primitive to the refined, and in the leadership of men of education, character and social position, rather than in the politics of interests and groups. Most of them were prepared to accept the extension of the franchise to responsible working men, but all alike were opposed to 'socialism' if it meant a challenge to existing political institutions, and to the sort of primitive priestly politics which they believed to be common to Spain, Portugal and Ireland. Some of them were driven to support Home Rule for Ireland, but what they wanted to see was a liberal Irish state on the British model, not a Rome-dominated theocracy.

The most widely accepted statement of the underlying theory of the constitution was that contained in John Stuart Mill's *Representative Government*, where it is argued that freedom of discussion, free elections, and a parliamentary system can only flourish in advanced societies such as the British. Other societies, like those of India and Africa, must pass through a period of liberal tutelage before acceptance into the comity of advanced nations. True liberals accepted the implication of this 'white man's burden', strove to equip India with the institutions which Indians would need if they were to enter into full membership of modern society, and encouraged the growth of middle-class Indian political movements. But most of those who in general accepted Whig constitutional doctrines were not prepared to go so far, and looked forward to a long period of imperial tutelage. They, like the jingoistic Tories, spoke of Britain's imperial mission, and were prepared to enjoy Lord Salisbury's uninhibited comparison between the Irish and the Hottentots which suggested that neither were likely to be capable of managing their own affairs for a long time.

It had long been customary for Whigs to argue that in Britain representative institutions had sprung up spontaneously in Anglo-Saxon England and were somehow inseparable from the English soil and climate. This view was attacked by many of the nineteenth-century historians of the Middle Ages, but it found an ardent defender in E. A. Freeman (8), and continued to form part of the stock-in-trade of Chartist, radical and country politicians for most of the nineteenth century. More cautious writers preferred to attribute the origins of contemporary institutions first to the efforts of the seventeenth-century Puritans and subsequently to those of the architects of the 1688 Revolution to establish the rights of the people. The Revolution in particular became the subject of a cult which, thanks to Macaulay's *History*, dominated British thought down to 1914. The Glorious Revolution was held to have established a new system of government: constitutional monarchy, which had subsequently been distorted by corrupt and self-seeking politicians and very nearly subverted by the machinations of King George III, but had finally been restored and renewed by the Whig ministry of Lord Grey which had carried through the Reform Act of 1832 and a host of other beneficient measures which had in good time been supplemented by further reforms.

The main features of the constitution as it is outlined in the works of writers of the Whig/liberal school down to 1865 were 1. a pervasive atmosphere of civil and religious liberty whose fundamental importance was emphasised by Sir James Mackintosh in a famous speech—'Liberty, the parent of commerce; the parent of wealth; the parent of knowledge; the parent of every virtue!', 2. a drastic limitation of the powers of the monarch, who as a constitutional ruler was held to be bound always to accept the recommendations of such ministers as could command a majority in the House of Commons, 3. a balance between the powers of the monarch and the two houses of parliament but subject always to the supremacy of parliament, 4. the existence of free elections at regular intervals to enable the people to express their judgement, 5. the freedom of members of parliament to act as spokesmen of the national interest rather than as delegates from particular districts or spokesmen of particular interests, 6. the independence of the judiciary, whose function it was to safeguard the liberties of the subject, 7. the restriction of government expenditure to the lowest possible level, 8. the limitation of the army, except in India, to a largely ceremonial role and to occasional assistance for the civil magistrates, 9. the recognition of the Church of England as a branch of the state subject to regulation by the state.

Nineteenth-century writers gradually abandoned the eighteenth-century view that the main feature of the constitution was its checks and balances. Influenced no doubt by James Mill, Whig writers, headed by Earl Grey, argued that the executive and the legislative powers were in Britain 'virtually united' (6). Lawyers still occasionally argued that a 'balance of powers' was the main characteristic of the constitution,[1] but this old-fashioned view was not accepted by either of the two most influential late nineteenth-century writers, Bagehot in his *English Constitution* (1867) and A. V. Dicey in his *Lectures Introductory to the Study of the Law of the Constitution*, which first appeared in 1885.

The main features of Whig constitutional theory were evolved by Charles James Fox and his circle from a study of Blackstone, and enshrined in the works of Sir James Mackintosh, Henry Hallam and their contemporaries. They were subsequently taken up and popularised by a group of younger Whig politicians of whom the most notable were Lord John Russell, Sir George Cornewall Lewis, Thomas Babington Macaulay, and the third Earl Grey, all of whom were more or less influenced by John Austin, the jurist.[2] Refined and developed for the use of lawyers and scholars, the Whig view of the constitution subsequently passed into general currency through the work of Sir Thomas Erskine May, W. E. Hearn, Alpheus Todd and other text-book makers.

Nineteenth-century writers and politicians assigned to parliament the chief role in the British system of government. Parliament, according to the Duke of Devonshire, could do anything it chose (11). The key problem was therefore how to secure a good parliament through a good electoral system. The classical exposition of the Whig view on this subject is contained in an article by Sir James Mackintosh published in the *Edinburgh Review* of 1818 (3). In it are set out all the main features of the Whig point of view, including the characteristic Whig emphasis on the importance of landed proprietors as upholders of the constitution. The next generation of Whig writers after Mackintosh were chiefly concerned to come to terms with the type of parliamentary government established by the Reform Act of 1832. The supremacy of the reformed parliament was now recognised, and the defects of parliamentary government were becoming apparent. The leading Whig theorist of this generation was the third Earl Grey, himself a leading politician. His *Parliamentary Government*, published in 1858 (6, 105, 123), attempts to strike a balance between the virtues and defects of the constitution, and suggests the outlines of a new scheme of parliamentary reform. Grey is however markedly uneasy about the future. For him, much of the merit of

---

[1] E.g. Homersham Cox, *The Institutions of the English Government*, 77.

[2] Austin's *A Plea for the Constitution* is, however, virtually a restatement of the views of the third Earl Grey.

the post-1832 constitution derived from the diversity of parliamentary life (**123**), and this he felt to be threatened. Like Bagehot he regarded England as a deferential society (**7**) and feared that the progressive extension of the franchise would undermine the balance of society and of the constitution.

The Whig view of the constitution, or at least its main features, was accepted by the great majority of people in political life down to the 1880s. Queen Victoria (coached by Lord Melbourne), Prince Albert, Peel, Grey, Russell, Melbourne and Palmerston all belonged to recognisably the same political tradition. Moreover, even the Conservatives after 1846 were for the most part Whigs at heart. Derby had served in Lord Grey's Reform ministry and Disraeli's hero, Lord George Bentinck, came of an old Whig family and had voted for the Reform Bill. Disraeli, indeed, makes this amply clear in his life of Bentinck: 'In politics, he was a Whig of 1688...He wished to see our society founded on a broad basis of civil and religious liberty. He retained much of the old jealousy of the court, but had none of popular franchises. He was for the Established Church, but for nothing more, and very repugnant to priestly domination.'[1] Even Disraeli himself, after a good deal of hesitation, opted for a romanticised version of the Whig constitution, to be based, however, on a Tory rather than a Whig landed aristocracy.

The course of events also suggested for many years that the Whigs had history on their side. Gladstone, a reluctant convert from high-church Toryism, came round to this point of view and as late as 1884 is to be found arguing that Whig liberalism possessed a permanent majority in Britain (**176**). Indeed Gladstone's indignation at the abandonment of the masses by the classes (**178**) largely arose from the feeling that the Whigs of his day were betraying the Whig tradition and destroying the Whig constitution. As it was, the events of the 1880s undermined the foundations of classical Whig theory. Liberal intellectuals continued to talk the language of the Whig constitution down to 1914, but there were no new Whig theorists after 1885.

Instead it became the fashion to talk in terms of the elaboration of the constitution in a democratic direction. The reforms of the 1830s were rightly seen by Macaulay as essentially the work of what he called 'the middle class of England' (**4**). After 1885, the electoral reforms of 1867 and 1883–5, the creation of county councils in 1888 and of district and parish councils in 1894, were seen as part of a consistent pattern of democratic evolution. Radicals took political democracy for granted and began to turn their attention to social reform and international problems, while spokesmen of the old Whigs and the Utilitarians threw up their hands at the prospect of government by the masses and of collectivism, and talked of democracy as the enemy of progress. For most purposes the Whig position as exponents of the constitution was now occupied by the Fabians. Like the old Whigs the

---

[1] Disraeli, *Bentinck*, p. 28.

Fabians had little faith in the people *en masse* and like the old Whigs they were prepared to praise the constitution. Indeed the celebrated Fabian Tract No. 70 is almost chauvinistic in its emphasis on the capacity of the British constitution to form the basis of a democratic socialist commonwealth (**12**).

The constitution still had its critics, but they were now less concerned with the reform of institutions than with a change in social patterns. Whereas the Chartists had committed themselves to the view that a change in the electoral and registration system (the central feature of the People's Charter) would lead to major structural changes, the Radicals of the 1880s and 1890s could see that electoral reform need not bring social reform and might indeed lead to a long period of Conservative government. Critics now attacked 'the system' rather than its institutions. Yet they made very little impact. Socialists and syndicalists who attacked the whole structure of parliamentary democracy were in a tiny minority. The normal theme of the critics, voiced by Hilaire Belloc and Robert Wallace in the nineties (**13, 126**), was that British politics was a closed system, run for the benefit of the two rival teams of political leaders in the Commons, who constituted a self-perpetuating oligarchy. This was to be the cry not merely of pre-1914 tracts like Belloc and Chesterton's *The Party System* but of successive generations of Radical writings from the Left Book Club's *Tory M.P.* in the 1930s onwards.

1. A Radical questions the merits of the constitution, 1816

It is impossible either to deny or disguise the fact that the perpetual misconduct of government during the present reign; the misfortunes and miseries by which it has been characterised; its follies, its vices, and its crimes, have given occasion to a new and very serious investigation of the principles of the British constitution; and amongst men of philosophic reflection may be discerned a great abatement of that enthusiastic ardour with which they were once in the habit of thinking and speaking of a form of government, which has been found, by fatal experience, not incompatible, for a long series of years, with the grossest neglect or perversion of those ends for which government is alone instituted. Amongst the most palpable and pernicious of the existing abuses, must undoubtedly be reckoned the enormous and overwhelming influence of the crown; the inequality of the national representation; the long duration of parliaments; the rapid and monstrous increase of the national debt; and of the civil and military establishments; the oppression, absurdity, and iniquity, connected with the present ecclesiastical system; the municipal tyranny exercised over the poor, under cover of the poor laws, originally intended for their relief and protection; the amazing number of superfluous places, pensions, sinecures, and lucrative appointments, by which individuals are aggrandized and enriched at the expense and impoverishment of the public. When these evils are remedied, the constitution of Britain will have a fair trial, and the beneficial effects it has in itself to produce, will be fully ascertained. But until this happy period arrives, all reflections can only be applicable to the present deformed and destructive system of administrative government. Oldfield, *Representative History*, I, 507–8

2. Hallam on the beauty of the constitution, 1818

No unbiassed observer, who derives pleasure from the welfare of his species, can fail to consider the long and uninterruptedly increasing prosperity of England as the most beautiful phaenomenon in the history of mankind. Climates more propitious may impart more largely the mere enjoyments of existence; but in no other region have the benefits that political institutions can confer been diffused over so extended a population; nor have any people so well reconciled the discordant elements of wealth, order, and liberty. These advantages are surely not owing to the soil of this island, nor to the latitude in which it is placed; but to the spirit of its laws, from which, through various means, the characteristic independence and industriousness of our nation have been derived. The constitution, therefore, of England must be to inquisitive men of all countries, far more to ourselves, an object of superior interest; distinguished, especially, as it is from all free governments of powerful nations which history has recorded, by its manifesting, after the lapse of several centuries, not merely no symptom of irretrievable decay, but a more expansive energy. Hallam, *Middle Ages*, ch. VIII, pt. I

3. Sir James Mackintosh on representative government, 1818

The object of Government, is security against wrong. Most civilized governments, tolerably secure their subjects against wrong from each other. But to secure them, by laws, against wrong from the Government itself, is a problem of a far more difficult sort, which few nations have attempted to solve,—and of which it is not so much as pretended that, since the beginning of History, more than one or two great states have approached the solution.

6

It will be universally acknowledged, that this approximation has never been effected by any other means, than that of a Legislative Assembly, chosen by some considerable portion of the People. The direct object of a popular representation, is, that one, at least, of the bodies exercising the Legislative Power being dependent on the people by election, should have the strongest inducement to guard the interests, and to maintain the rights of the people.

For this purpose, it is not sufficient, that they should have the same general interests with the people; for every government has . . . the same interests with its subjects. It is necessary, that the more direct and palpable interest, arising from election, should be superadded. In every legislative senate, the modes of appointment ought to be such, as to secure the nomination of members the best qualified, and the most disposed, to make laws conducive to the wellbeing of the whole community. In a Representative assembly this condition, though absolutely necessary, is not of itself sufficient. To understand the principles of its composition thoroughly, we must divide the people into classes, and examine the variety of local and professional interests of which the general interest is composed. Each of these classes must be represented by persons who will guard its peculiar interest, whether that interest arises from inhabiting the same district, or pursuing the same occupation,—such as traffic or husbandry, or the useful or ornamental arts. The fidelity and zeal of such representatives, are to be secured by every provision, which, to a sense of common interest, can superadd a fellow-feeling with their constituents. Nor is this all. In a great State, even that part of the public interest which is common to all classes, is composed of a great variety of branches. A statesman should indeed have a comprehensive view of the whole: But no one man can be skilled in all their particulars. The same education, and the same pursuits, which qualify men to understand and regulate some branches, disqualify them for others. The Representative assembly must therefore contain,—some members peculiarly qualified for discussions of the Constitution and the Laws, others for those of Foreign Policy;—some for the respective interests of Agriculture, Commerce, and Manufactures;—some for Military affairs by sea and land, and some also who are conversant with the colonies and distant possessions of a great empire. . . .

It is obvious, that as long as this composition is insured, it is . . . a matter of secondary importance whether it be effected by direct or indirect means. To be a faithful representative, it is necessary that such an assembly should be numerous; that it should learn, from experience, the movements that agitate multitudes; and that it should be susceptible, in no small degree, of the action of those causes which sway the thoughts and feelings of assemblies of the people. For the same reason...it is expedient that its proceedings should be public; and the reasonings on which they are founded, submitted to the judgment of mankind. These democratical elements are indeed to be tempered and restrained by such contrivances as may be necessary to maintain the order and independence of deliberation: But, without them, no assembly, however elected, can truly represent a people.

Among the objects of representation, two may...deserve observation:—the qualifications for making good laws, and those for resisting oppression. Now, the capacity of an assembly to make good laws, evidently depends on the quantity of skill and information of every kind which it possesses. But it seems to be advantageous that it should contain a large proportion of one body of a more neutral and inactive character—not indeed to propose much, but to mediate or arbitrate in the differences between the more busy classes, from whom important propositions are to be expected. The suggestions of every man relating to his province, have doubtless a peculiar value: But most men imbibe prejudices with their knowledge; and, in the struggle of various classes for their conflicting interests, the best chance for an approach to right decision, lies in an appeal to the largest body of well-educated men, of leisure, large property, temperate character, and who are impartial on more subjects than any other class of men. An ascendancy, therefore, of landed proprietors must be considered, on the whole, as a beneficial circumstance in a representative body.

For resistance to oppression, it is peculiarly necessary that the lower, and, in some places, the lowest classes, should possess the right of suffrage. Their rights would otherwise be less protected than those of any other class...They also often send to a representative assembly, members whose character is an important element in its composition. Men of popular talents, principles, and feelings; quick in suspecting oppression; bold in resisting it; not thinking favourably of the powerful; listening, almost with credulity, to the complaints of the humble and the feeble; and impelled by ambition, where they are not prompted by generosity, to be the champions of the defenceless....

In all political institutions, it is a fortunate circumstance, when legal power is bestowed on those who already possess a natural influence

8

and ascendant over their fellow-citizens.... Where law and nature coincide, government is most secure; and the people may be most free.... But in a representative assembly, which exercises directly no power...the security and importance of the body...depend on the natural influence of those who compose it. In this respect, talent and skill, besides their direct utility, have a secondary value of no small importance. Together with the other circumstances which command respect or attachment among men—with popularity, with fame, with property, with liberal education and condition—they form a body of strength, which no law could give or take away. As far as an assembly is deprived of any of these natural principles of authority, so far it is weakened, both for the purpose of resisting the usurpations of government, and of maintaining the order of society.

An Elective system tends also...to secure that free government, of which it is the most essential member. As it calls some of almost every class of men, to share in legislative power, and many of all classes to exercise the highest franchises, it engages the pride, the honour, and the private interest as well as the generosity, of every part of the community, in defence of the Constitution. Every noble sentiment, every reasonable consideration, every petty vanity, and every contemptible folly, are made to contribute towards its security....

Popular representation thus...tends to make governments good, and to make good governments secure. These are its primary advantages: But free, that is, just governments, tend to make men more intelligent, more honest, more brave, more generous....

These effects of free government on the character of a people...will perhaps be better shown by a more particular view of the influence of popular elections on the character of the different classes of the community.

To begin with the higher classes. The English Nobility, who are blended with the gentry by imperceptible shades, are the most opulent and powerful order of men in Europe.... They have attained almost all the objects of human pursuit. They are surrounded with every circumstance which might seem likely to fill them with arrogance, to teach them to scorn their inferiors,—and might naturally be supposed to extinguish enterprise, and to lull every power of the understanding to sleep. What has preserved their character?...Where all the ordinary incentives to action are withdrawn, a free constitution excites it, by presenting Political Power as a new object of pursuit. By rendering that power in a great degree dependent on popular favour, it compels the highest to treat their fellow-creatures with decency and courtesy; and disposes the best of them to feel, that inferiors in station may be superiors in worth, as they are equals in right. Hence chiefly arises that useful preference for country life, which distinguishes the English gentry from that of other nations. In despotic countries they flock to the Court, where all their hopes are fixed. But here, as they have much to hope from the people, they must cultivate the esteem, and even court the favour of their own natural dependants. They are quickened in the pursuit of ambition, by the rivalship of that enterprising talent, which is stimulated by more urgent motives....

The effects of the Elective franchise upon the humbler classes, are, if possible, still more obvious and important. By it the peasant is taught to 'venerate himself as a man'; to employ his thoughts, at least occasion-ally, upon high matters; to meditate on the same subjects with the wise and the great; to enlarge his feelings beyond the circle of his narrow concerns; to sympathize, however irregularly, with great bodies of his fellow-creatures; and sometimes to do acts which he may regard as contributing directly to the welfare of his country.... The judgments of the multitude are never exact, and their feelings often grossly mis-applied: but, after all possible deductions, great benefits must remain. The important object is...that they should contemplate extensive consequences as capable of arising from their own actions, and thus gradually become conscious of the moral dignity of their nature. Among the very lowest classes, where the disorders of election are the most offensive, the moral importance of the Elective franchise is, in some respects, the greatest. As individuals, they feel themselves of no con-sequence;—hence, in part, arises their love of numerous assemblies, the only scenes in which the poor feel their importance. Brought to-gether for elections, their tumultuary disposition...is gratified at the expense of inconsiderable evils. It is useful that the pride of the highest should be made occasionally to bend before them; that the greatest objects of ambition should be partly at their disposal: It teaches them to feel that *they* also are men. It is to the exercise of this franchise, by some bodies of our lowest classes, that we are to ascribe that sense of equality—that jealousy of right—that grave independence, and calm pride, which has been observed by foreigners as marking the deport-ment of Englishmen. *Edinburgh Review*, XXXI, 174–80

4. Macaulay on reform, revolution, and the middle classes, 16 December 1831

It is difficult, Sir, to conceive any spectacle more alarming than that which presents itself to us, when we look at the two extreme parties in this country; a narrow oligarchy above; an infuriated multitude below; on the one side the vices engendered by power; on the other side the vices engendered by distress; one party blindly averse to improvement; the other party blindly clamouring for destruction; one party ascribing to political abuses the sanctity of property; the other party crying out against property as a political abuse. Both these parties are alike ignorant of their true interest. God forbid that the State should ever be at the mercy of either, or should ever experience the calamities which must result from a collision between them! I anticipate no such horrible event. For, between those two parties stands a third party, infinitely more powerful than both the others put together, attacked by both, villified by both, but destined, I trust, to save both from the fatal effects of their own folly. To that party I have never ceased, through all the vicissitudes of public affairs, to look with confidence and with a good hope. I speak of that great party which zealously and steadily supported the first Reform Bill, and which will, I have no doubt, support the second Reform Bill, with equal steadiness and equal zeal. That party is the middle class of England, with the flower of the aristocracy at its head, and the flower of the working classes bringing up its rear. That great party has taken its immovable stand between the enemies of all order and the enemies of all liberty. It will have Reform: it will not have revolution: it will destroy political abuses: it will not suffer the rights of property to be assailed: it will preserve, in spite of themselves, those who are assailing it, from the right and from the left, with contradictory accusations: it will be a daysman between them: it will lay its hand upon them both: it will not suffer them to tear each other in pieces. While that great party continues unbroken, as it now is unbroken, I shall not relinquish the hope that this great contest may be conducted, by lawful means, to a happy termination. But, of this I am assured, that by means, lawful or unlawful, to a termination, happy or unhappy, this contest must speedily come. All that I know of the history of past times, all the observations that I have been able to make on the present state of the country, have convinced me that the time has arrived when a great concession must be made to the democracy of England; that the question, whether the change be in itself good or bad, has become a question of secondary importance; that good or bad, the thing must be done; that a law as strong as the laws of attraction and motion has decreed it.   Macaulay, *Works*, VIII, 71–2

5. Macaulay accounts for the absence of an 1848 revolution in Britain
[Speech at Edinburgh, 2 November 1852]

...The madness of 1848 did not subvert the British throne. The reaction which followed has not destroyed British liberty.

And why is this? Why has our country, with all the ten plagues raging around her, been a land of Goshen? Everywhere else was the thunder, and the fire running along the ground,—a very grievous storm,—a storm such as there was none like it since man was on the earth; yet everything tranquil here; and then again thick night, darkness that might be felt; and yet light in all our dwellings. We owe this singular happiness, under the blessing of God, to a wise and noble constitution, the work of many generations of great men. Let us profit by experience; and let us be thankful that we profit by the experience of others, and not by our own. Let us prize our constitution: let us purify it: let us amend it; but let us not destroy it. Let us shun extremes, not only because each extreme is in itself a positive evil, but also because each extreme necessarily engenders its opposite. If we love civil and religious freedom, let us in the day of danger uphold law and order. If we are zealous for law and order, let us prize, as the best safeguard of law and order, civil and religious freedom.

Yes, Gentlemen; if I am asked why we are free with servitude all around us, why our Habeas Corpus Act has not been suspended, why our press is still subject to no censor, why we still have the liberty of association, why our representative institutions still abide in all their strength, I answer, It is because in the year of revolutions we stood firmly by our Government in its peril; and, if I am asked why we stood by our Government in its peril, when men all around us were engaged in pulling Governments down, I answer, It was because we knew that though our Government was not a perfect Government, it was a good Government, that its fault admitted of peaceable and legal remedies, that it had never inflexibly opposed just demands, that we had obtained concessions of inestimable value, not by beating the drum, not by ringing the tocsin, not by tearing up the pavement, not by running to the gunsmiths' shops to search for arms, but by the mere force of reason and public opinion. And, Gentlemen, preeminent among those pacific victories of reason and public opinion, the recollection of which chiefly, I believe, carried us safely through the year of revolutions and through the year of counter-revolutions, I would place two great reforms, inseparably associated, one with the memory of an illustrious man, who is now beyond the reach of envy, the other with the name of another illustrious man, who is still, and, I hope, long will be, a living mark for detraction. I speak of the great commercial reform of 1846, the work of Sir Robert Peel, and of the great parliamentary reform of 1832, the work of many eminent statesmen, among whom none was more conspicuous than Lord John Russell.   Macaulay, *Works*, VIII, 418–19

6. The third Earl Grey on parliamentary government, 1858

...since the establishment of Parliamentary Government, the common description of the British Constitution, as one in which the executive power belongs exclusively to the Crown, while the power of legislation is vested jointly in the Sovereign and the two Houses of Parliament, has ceased to be correct, unless it is understood as applying only to the legal and technical distribution of power. It is the distinguishing characteristic of Parliamentary Government, that it requires the powers belonging to the Crown to be exercised through Ministers, who are held responsible for the manner in which they are used, who are expected to be members of the two Houses of Parliament, the proceedings of which they must be able generally to guide, and who are considered entitled to hold their offices only while they possess the confidence of Parliament, and more especially of the House of Commons.

By this arrangement the Executive power and the power of Legislation are virtually united in the same hands, but both are limited,—the executive power by the law, and that of legislation by the necessity of obtaining the assent of Parliament to the measures brought forward, so that even the strongest administrations do not venture to propose the passing of laws to which public opinion is decidedly opposed. The exercise of this high authority is also placed under the check of a strict responsibility and control, and its possession is made to depend on the confidence placed by the Representatives of the People in the Ministers to whom it is committed....

On comparing Parliamentary Government as it now exists in this country with other Representative Governments, the following seem to be the chief advantages belonging to the former.

First.—It enables the different powers of the State to work together with harmony and energy, and provides for the systematic direction of the measures of the Legislature to objects of public good, more perfectly than Representative Constitutions of a different kind. In the latter, the executive power and the power of legislation are lodged in separate and independent authorities, while under the system of Parliamentary Government, those to whom the executive authority is entrusted, have also the duty of recommending to the Legislature the measures it should adopt, and must retire if their advice is not generally followed. By this arrangement the Executive Government is able to act with the vigour which the assurance of having its policy supported when necessary by Legislation, can alone give to it. We cannot read a page, either of our own history, or of that of other countries, without perceiving how constantly the Executive Government of a great nation is compelled to apply to the Legislature for new powers, or new laws to meet new exigencies that arise; and how greatly its action would be crippled, if it could not depend upon obtaining the assistance of this kind which it requires.

This remark applies more particularly to financial arrangements. The imposition of taxes, and the appropriation of the revenue to the public service, constitute one of the chief duties of Representative Legislatures, as well as the source of their power. In the performance of this part of their duties, it is of the utmost importance that they should act in strict concert with the Executive Government, or rather under its direction. Without this there can be no security for efficiency and economy in conducting the public service....

Secondly.—Closely connected with the advantage I have just described as belonging to Parliamentary Government, is that which it derives from the manner in which it brings the policy of the Executive Government under the review and control of the Legislature. Parliament does not interfere directly in carrying on the Executive Government; and it is right that it should abstain from doing so, since experience has demonstrated the unfitness of large deliberative assemblies for this function. But every measure of the Ministers of the Crown is open to censure in either House; so that, when there is just or even plausible ground for objecting to anything they have done or omitted to do, they cannot escape being called upon to defend their conduct.

By this arrangement, those to whom power is entrusted are made to feel that they must use it in such a manner as to be prepared to meet the criticisms of opponents continually on the watch for any errors they may commit, and the whole foreign and domestic policy of the Nation is submitted to the ordeal of free discussion.

The discussion of the measures of the Executive Government in Parliament contributes to keep the Nation well informed as to its own concerns, and to throw light upon what are its duties, and its true interests, with regard to the various questions with which the Government has to deal. This is more especially useful with reference to the relations of the State with foreign Powers. The policy pursued in this important branch of public affairs is explained by the debates which take place in Parliament, not only to the public at home, but to the civilized world; and the opinion of the world is thus brought to bear upon the Nation and on its rulers. At the same time, as the Crown is invested with large executive powers, which are exercised by its Ministers without requiring the previous sanction of Parliament, so long as they possess its general confidence, the vigorous action of the Government is not impeded, as it would be if Parliament were called upon to concur more directly in conducting it....

Thirdly.—It is another great advantage which may, I think, justly be attributed to Parliamentary Government, that it renders the contests of men for power as little injurious as possible, and furnishes what seems on the whole the best solution hitherto discovered of the great problem, how to provide some safe mode of determining to what hands the principal direction of public affairs shall be entrusted....

Fourthly.—It is another advantage of Parliamentary Government, that, by causing the inevitable contests among men for power to assume the form of debates on the policy by which the Nation is to be governed, and on measures affecting its most important interests, it has tended to raise these contests above those of a mere selfish and personal character. No doubt selfish and personal interests have often really governed the conduct of Parliamentary leaders and their followers; but the motives publicly appealed to have been of a far higher order; and though the practice of politicians has fallen lamentably short of their theory, the habit of Parliamentary debates, in which high principles of right and wrong have been recognized, and unworthy conduct meets with severe reprobation, has tended to raise by degrees the standard to which men are expected to conform in public life, and to render ambitious men less unscrupulous in their conduct in this than in other countries. If we compare our own political contests with those of other times and of other nations, I think we may fairly take credit to ourselves to this extent. At the same time, we have little reason to boast; and we must acknowledge and lament, that the improvement made in our own political morality, during the last century, is very small as compared to what is wanted. It is still common for improper means, such as corruption and immoral compliances with the prejudices and passions of the day, intrigue, or abuse of the great power of the Press, to be employed for the purpose of securing victory in Parliamentary contests, and of recommending individuals and parties to the favour of the Nation and of its Representatives.

Fifthly.—The mode in which our Parliamentary contests have been carried on, has had the further and great advantage of contributing much to instruct the Nation at large on all the subjects most deeply concerning its interests, and to form and guide public opinion. If men's passions and feelings were not so much excited by political struggles, it is not likely they would read, as they do, the debates in Parliament in which these subjects are discussed, and in which, amidst all the trash and sophistry that disfigure them, the keen encounter of intellects seldom fails in the end to lead to the discovery of truth and to the triumph of sound reason over error. The value of Parliament as an instrument for the instruction of the Nation, and for enabling it to arrive at just and wise conclusions on matters affecting its welfare, is hardly less than that which belongs to it as the organ for expressing and enforcing the national will when it has been deliberately formed. The former function our Parliament discharges much more perfectly than the Congress of the United States,—probably, in part, because the debates in Congress are not read with the same interest, from their having no immediate effect on the tenure of power by those to whom the Executive Government is entrusted. Grey, *Parliamentary Government*, pp. 4–5, 16–17, 20–2, 33–5

7. Bagehot argues that the English constitution works because England is a deferential society, 1867

...The English constitution in its palpable form is this—the mass of the people yield obedience to a select few; and when you see this select few, you perceive that though not of the lowest class, nor of an unrespectable class, they are yet of a heavy sensible class—the last people in the world to whom, if they were drawn up in a row, an immense nation would ever give an exclusive preference.

In fact, the mass of the English people yield a deference rather to something else than to their rulers. They defer to what we may call the *theatrical show* of society. A certain state passes before them; a certain pomp of great men; a certain spectacle of beautiful women; a wonderful scene of wealth and enjoyment is displayed, and they are coerced by it. Their imagination is bowed down; they feel they are not equal to the life which is revealed to them. Courts and aristocracies have the great quality which rules the multitude, though philosophers can see nothing in it—visibility. Courtiers can do what others cannot. A common man may as well try to rival the actors on the stage in their acting, as the aristocracy in *their* acting. The higher world, as it looks from without, is a stage on which the actors walk their parts much better than the spectators can. This play is played in every district. Every rustic feels that his house is not like my lord's house; his life like my lord's life; his wife like my lady. The climax of the play is the Queen: nobody supposes that their house is like the court; their life like her life; her orders like their orders. There is in England a certain charmed spectacle which imposes on the many, and guides their fancies as it will. As a rustic on coming to London finds himself in the presence of a great show and vast exhibition of inconceivable mechanical things, so by the structure of our society he finds himself face to face with a great exhibition of political things which he could not have imagined, which he could not make—to which he feels in himself scarcely anything analogous.

Philosophers may deride this superstition, but its results are inestimable. By the spectacle of this august society, countless ignorant men and women are induced to obey the few nominal electors—the £10 borough renters, and the £50 county renters—who have nothing imposing about them, nothing which would attract the eye or fascinate the fancy. What impresses men is not mind, but the result of mind. And the greatest of these results is this wonderful spectacle of society, which is ever new, and yet ever the same; in which accidents pass and essence remains; in which one generation dies and another succeeds, as if they were birds in a cage, or animals in a menagerie; of which it seems almost more than a metaphor to treat the parts as limbs of a perpetual living thing, so silently do they seem to change, so wonderfully and so perfectly does the conspicuous life of the new year take the place of the conspicuous life of last year. The apparent rulers of the English nation are like the most imposing personages of a splendid procession: it is by them the mob are influenced; it is they whom the spectators cheer. The real rulers are secreted in second-rate carriages; no one cares for them or asks about them, but they are obeyed implicitly and unconsciously by reason of the splendour of those who eclipsed and preceded them.

It is quite true that this imaginative sentiment is supported by a sensation of political satisfaction. It cannot be said that the mass of the English people are well off. There are whole classes who have not a conception of what the higher orders call comfort; who have not the prerequisites of moral existence; who cannot lead the life that becomes a man. But the most miserable of these classes do not impute their misery to politics. If a political agitator were to lecture to the peasants of Dorsetshire, and try to excite political dissatisfaction, it is much more likely that he would be pelted than that he would succeed. Of parliament these miserable creatures know scarcely anything; of the cabinet they never heard. But they would say that, 'for all they have heard, the Queen is very good'; and rebelling against the structure of society is to their minds rebelling against the Queen, who rules that society, in whom all its most impressive part—the part that they know —culminates. The mass of the English people are politically contented as well as politically deferential.

A deferential community, even though its lowest classes are not intelligent, is far more suited to a cabinet government than any kind of democratic country, because it is more suited to political excellence. The highest classes can rule in it; and the highest classes must, as such, have more political ability than the lower classes. A life of labour, an incomplete education, a monotonous occupation, a career in which the hands are used much and the judgement is used little, cannot create as much flexible thought, as much applicable intelligence, as a life of leisure, a long culture, a varied experience, an existence by which the judgement is incessantly exercised, and by which it may be incessantly improved. A country of respectful poor, though far less happy than where there are no poor to be respectful, is nevertheless far more fitted for the best government. You can use the best classes of the respectful country; you can only use the worst where every man thinks he is as good as every other. Bagehot, *English Constitution*, pp. 236–9

8. Freeman traces the constitution to Anglo-Saxon origins, 1872

For my own part, my object has been to show that the earliest institutions of England and of other Teutonic lands are not mere matters
of curious speculation, but matters closely connected with our present
political being. I wish to show that, in many things, our earliest institutions come more nearly home to us, and that they have more in
common with our present political state, than the institutions of inter-
mediate ages.... the holders of Liberal principles in modern politics
need never shrink from tracing up our political history to its earliest
beginnings. As far at least as our race is concerned, freedom is everywhere older than bondage; we may add that toleration is older than
intolerance. Our ancient history is the possession of the Liberal...not
of the self-styled Conservative....

The primitive Teutonic constitution...is democratic, but it is
not purely democratic.... Democracy...demands that every freeman
shall have a voice in the affairs of the commonwealth; it does not
necessarily demand that every freeman should have an equal voice.
It does not forbid the existence of magistrates clothed with high
authority and held in high reverence, nor does it forbid respect for
ancient birth or even an attachment to an hereditary line of rulers.
The older school of English constitutional writers delighted to show
that the English Constitution contained a monarchic, an aristocratic,
and a democratic element, the three being wrought together in such
true and harmonious proportion that we could enjoy the good side
of all the three great forms of government....there is no doubt
that, in every glimpse we get of old Teutonic politics, we see what
we may fairly call a monarchic, an aristocratic, and a democratic
element....

Here we have a picture of a free commonwealth of warriors, in
which each freeman has his place in the state, where the vote of the
general Assembly is the final authority on all matters, but where both
hereditary descent and elective office are held in high honour. We see
also in a marked way the influence of personal character and of the
power of speech; we see the existence of local divisions, local assemblies, local magistrates; in a word, we see in this picture of our forefathers in their old land, seventeen hundred years ago, the germs of all
the institutions which have grown up step by step among ourselves
in the course of ages...The continued national life of the people, not-

withstanding foreign conquests and internal revolutions, has remained unbroken for fourteen hundred years....

Changed as it is in all outward form and circumstance, the England in which we live, has, in its true life and spirit, far more in common with the England of the earliest times than it has with the England of days far nearer to our own. In many a wholesome act of modern legislation, we have gone back...to the earliest principle of our race.... We have reformed by calling to life again the institutions of earlier and ruder times, by setting ourselves free from the slavish subtleties of Norman lawyers, by casting aside as an accursed thing the innovations of Tudor tyranny and Stewart usurpation.

Freeman, *The English Constitution*, pp. vii–viii, 10–11, 17–21

9. Herbert Spencer attacks the sovereignty of parliament as 'the great political superstition', 1884

The great political superstition of the past was the divine right of kings. The great political superstition of the present is the divine right of parliaments. The oil of anointing seems unawares to have dripped from the head of the one on to the heads of the many, and given sacredness to them also and to their decrees....

The tacitly-asserted doctrine, common to Tories, Whigs, and Radicals, that governmental authority is unlimited dates back to times when the law-giver was supposed to have a warrant from God; and it survives still, though the belief that the law-giver has God's warrant has died out. 'Oh, an Act of Parliament can do anything', is the reply made to a citizen who questions the legitimacy of some arbitrary State-interference; and the citizen stands paralyzed. It does not occur to him to ask the how, and the when, and the whence, of this asserted omnipotence bounded only by physical impossibilities.

Here we will take leave to question it. In default of the justification, once logically valid, that the ruler on Earth being a deputy of the ruler in Heaven, submission to him in all things is a duty, let us ask what reason there is for asserting the duty of submission in all things to a ruling power, constitutional or republican, which has no Heaven-derived supremacy....

When that 'divinity' which 'doth hedge a king,' and which in our day has left a glamour around the body inheriting his power, has quite died away—when it begins to be seen clearly that, in a popularly-governed nation, the government is simply a committee of management; it will also be seen that this committee of management has no intrinsic authority. The inevitable conclusion will be that its authority is given by those appointing it; and has just such bounds as they choose to impose. Along with this will go the further conclusion that the laws it passes are not in themselves sacred; but that whatever sacredness they have, is entirely due to the ethical sanction—an ethical sanction which, as we find, is derivable from the laws of human life as carried on under social conditions. And there will come the corollary that when they have not this ethical sanction they have no sacredness, and may rightly be challenged.

The function of Liberalism in the past was that of putting a limit to the powers of kings. The function of true Liberalism in the future will be that of putting a limit to the powers of Parliaments.

Contemporary Review, vol. 46, pp. 24–5, 48

10. A. V. Dicey on the sovereignty of parliament, 1885

The principle of Parliamentary sovereignty means neither more nor less than this, namely, that Parliament...has, under the English constitution, the right to make or unmake any law whatever; and, further, that no person or body is recognised by the law of England as having a right to override or set aside the legislation of Parliament. A law may, for our present purpose, be defined as 'any rule which will be enforced by the Courts'. The principle then of Parliamentary sovereignty may, looked at from its positive side, be thus described; any Act of Parliament, or any part of an Act of Parliament, which makes a new law, or repeals or modifies an existing law, will be obeyed by the Courts. The same principle, looked at from its negative side, may be thus stated; there is no person or body of persons who can, under the English constitution, make rules which override or derogate from an Act of Parliament, or which (to express the same thing in other words) will be enforced by the Courts in contravention of an Act of Parliament.

Dicey, Law of the Constitution, p. 36

11. The Duke of Devonshire on parliamentary supremacy, 5 September 1893

In the United Kingdom, Parliament is supreme not only in its legislative but in its Executive functions. Parliament makes and unmakes our Ministries; it revises their actions. Ministries may make peace and war, but they do so at pain of instant dismissal by Parliament from Office, and in affairs of internal administration the power of Parliament is equally direct. It can dismiss a Ministry if it is too extravagant, or too economical; it can dismiss a Ministry because its government is too stringent or too lax. It does actually and practically, in every way, directly govern England, Scotland and Ireland.... That is the nature of the Government and the supremacy of Parliament in the United Kingdom; it is the direct government of these Islands by Parliament through a Committee.

4 *Hansard* XVII, 33–4

12. The Fabian view of the constitution, 1896

FABIAN DEMOCRACY

Democracy, as understood by the Fabian Society, means simply the control of the administration by freely elected representatives of the people.... When the House of Commons is freed from the veto of the House of Lords and thrown open to candidates from all classes by an effective system of Payment of Representatives and a more rational method of election, the British parliamentary system will be, in the opinion of the Fabian Society, a first-rate practical instrument of democratic government....

FABIAN SOCIALISM

Socialism, as understood by the Fabian Society, means the organization and conduct of the necessary industries of the country, and the appropriation of all forms of economic rent of land and capital by the nation as a whole, through the most suitable public authorities, parochial, municipal, provincial, or central.

The Socialism advocated by the Fabian Society is State Socialism exclusively. The foreign friends of the Fabian Society must interpret this declaration in view of the fact that since England now possesses an elaborate democratic State machinery, graduated from the Parish Council or Vestry up to the central Parliament, and elected under a franchise which enables the working-class vote to overwhelm all

others, the opposition which exists in the Continental monarchies between the State and the people does not hamper English Socialists....
The difficulty in England is not to secure more political power for the
people, but to persuade them to make any sensible use of the power
they already have. *Fabian Tract No. 70, p. 5*

13. Belloc on the usurpation of the rights of the people, 1897

The history of England since the Middle Ages is the history of a slow
and successful usurpation of the rights of the people on the one hand,
and of the Crown upon the other, by a large territorial class. Until the
period of that industrial revolution which has so signally increased the
wealth, the population, and the perils of England, this class was supreme.
During even our own time its influence has been modified rather than
destroyed, and the country is still ruled by a legislature, a judicature,
an armed force and an executive drawn from an upper class of which
the territorial interest supplies the main element and direction. And
you will find but a very small proportion of judges, officers, ministers
or representatives abroad who are not connected with or descended
from this ring of families. And this assertion is in proportion truer as
we regard the higher and more powerful positions; for while it would
be easy to discover a second-rate consul or curate, or an urban magistrate who has no link with the country houses, to find a series of ambas-
sadors, judges, or bishops in this position would amount to a stupendous
miracle. Hilaire Belloc in *Essays in Liberalism*, p. 25

CHAPTER 2

CABINET GOVERNMENT

A THE MONARCHY

During the greater part of the nineteenth century the proper role of the monarchy in British society was a subject of controversy. Since the Revolution of 1688 Whig theory had insisted that the monarch was the servant rather than the master of the people, even though the language of the lawyer and the courtier implied that the monarch was something very much more important than the first servant of the people. But this doctrine left undecided the extent to which the monarch was free to play an active part in politics. Most nineteenth-century writers in the Whig tradition assumed that a 'constitutional monarchy' should keep clear of the everyday turmoil of party politics. And this view, enunciated in its most coherent form by Walter Bagehot, was ultimately to become, in the twentieth century, the official orthodoxy accepted alike in Buckingham Palace (23) and in Fleet Street. Yet when Bagehot, in a famous passage, remarked that 'the sovereign has, under a constitutional monarchy such as ours, three rights—the right to be consulted, the right to encourage, the right to warn. And a king of great sense and sagacity would want no others (19), he was setting up a yardstick, not describing the monarchy as it in fact functioned. Bagehot, like Palmerston and Gladstone, wanted the monarchy to become a sort of mystic museum piece, to be brought out on state occasions to remind us of the continuities of past, present and future; 'Its mystery', he wrote, 'is its life. We must not let in daylight upon magic.' Yet this was only one view of the role of the monarchy. It was not the view of George IV or William IV or Victoria or Edward VII. Nor was it the view of the majority of statesmen and text-book writers. These latter felt that the monarch's role as head of state in a popular parliamentary system had still to be satisfactorily defined. On some points they were prepared to stretch the powers of the monarchy— Dicey and Anson, the leading authorities of the day, wanted the monarch to insist on a dissolution over Home Rule in 1913[1]—whereas on others they felt that the monarch might well give way.

As it was, whatever theories might be put forward by outside observers, the monarchy operated under Queen Victoria and King Edward VII much as it had operated under George IV and William IV. Victoria was quite as wilful as her uncles, but she was better educated, more prudent, and better

---

[1] Jennings, *Cabinet Government*, pp. 436–43.

advised than they were, and she also ruled much longer, so that she learned to come to terms with a wide variety of political situations. In her later years the growing importance of organised political parties gave her less room to manœuvre than her predecessors had enjoyed. But the role of the monarchy was still something that depended very much on the character of the monarch, and each monarch was still in a position to set the style of politics during his reign. Politics had a different flavour under George IV from politics under George III; the amiable and eccentric William IV set an entirely different tone from his predecessor; Queen Victoria lived to become the matriarch-symbol of British imperial greatness; and even Edward VII was set down in the books as 'Edward the Peacemaker' and the lynchpin of the Edwardian age. Not until the sailor-king George V succeeded was there a monarch who deliberately set out to be politically and socially neutral, in the style which Bagehot prescribed. This does not mean that George IV or William IV or Victoria or Edward VII habitually got their own way. Like William III and the first three Georges, they had to accept the fact that they were often unable to find ways of carrying out their objects, and that the weight of organised opinion against them was too great to be overborne. But every monarch from George IV to Edward VII had policies of his own, and wished to play a distinctive part in the shaping of political decisions.

The popularity of the monarchy changed dramatically over the course of the century. George IV as prince regent was regarded with the deepest contempt by a large proportion of the public, and began his reign as king with an unprecedented dispute with his wife, designed to prevent her from becoming Queen. Parliament and the ministry were divided by the issue: the London mob backed the Queen, and public respect for the monarchy reached its lowest ebb. The Duke of Wellington despised the man, and so did educated opinion, as George IV's obituary notices were to show. Yet even George IV could be sensible on occasions, and his state visit to Edinburgh in 1822 was a major success, though it smacked of burlesque and of the antics of minor German princes. William IV was generally liked, but his fits of impatience and irresolution lost him the respect of his subjects, and he died unlamented. Victoria, who entered into an uncertain heritage at the age of 18, had the advantage of being able to give her undivided attention to Britain, because the personal union of the crowns of the United Kingdom and Hanover ended with William IV. But there were few who expected her reign to be a success, and some who expected it to end in disaster. Victoria's marriage to Prince Albert of Saxe-Coburg-Gotha—the subject of many hostile cartoons—gave Victoria the sort of support she needed and in fact constituted a sort of joint monarchy, but neither Albert nor the young Queen was much liked. Nor did matters improve during the long period of royal mourning which followed Albert's death. The government grew restive at the Queen's seclusion. The Prince of Wales became the subject of much malicious gossip. Gladstone began to wonder whether the monarchy could survive (20). A republican movement sprang up, and there was a great deal of hostility against the annexation to the crown of the title Empress of India in 1876. But Disraeli knew what he was doing when he made the Queen the Empress of India. He seems to have sensed by 1872, when he championed the monarchy in his speech at Manchester (22), that the tide had turned. His object now was to ensure that some of the coming glamour of the monarchy should rub off on the Conservative party. The monarchy ranked as the chief symbol of the new cult of imperialism. And by the 1880s the monarchy had attained a new popularity. For the remainder of her reign, Queen Victoria was to be the mother of her people, universally accepted as the symbol of the national greatness, and commemorated as such during the two great jubilee celebrations—the golden jubilee in 1887 and the diamond jubilee in 1897. Upon her death in 1901 the whole nation went into mourning. The monarchy had clearly re-established itself and it was left to Victoria's elderly son, Edward VII, to let some light and air into a court life grown stuffy and old-fashioned, and to come to terms with the new social forces which his mother was so loath to recognise.

The revival of the monarchy was accompanied by a steady tightening up of the ceremonial side of state affairs. Royal occasions under George IV and William IV lacked dignity and organisation. Queen Victoria's coronation was rather huddled and the Queen herself had no taste at all for display. The funeral procession of the Duke of Wellington in 1851 was much more impressive than any royal function for generations, and it was a long time after the Prince Consort's death before the Queen was willing to take part in great state processions. But the taste for reviews of volunteers, the improvements in London which opened up new processional ways like the Embankment, and the succession of state visits by foreign monarchs and heads of state which marked Queen Victoria's later years, created a new role for the monarch as ceremonial head of state. Queen Victoria in her widow's weeds might refuse to dress up for the part, but her increasingly professionalised household and the Office of Works became adept at staging ceremonies which had an immense popular appeal. The two jubilees, the funeral of the Queen, the coronation of Edward VII, and the great parades which Edward VII delighted in, entirely changed the public image of the monarchy, and made public ceremonials one of the central features of British life.

The central political problem of the monarchy during the period was how to ensure that the monarch was sufficiently well informed to be capable of playing a useful part in the shaping of policy and administration. Here there were two main problems: 1. the need to develop at court a body of well-informed advisers, to act as an antidote to the banalities and jealousies of court life and society gossip, and to provide a liaison between the court and the politicians; 2. the need to provide a steady supply of information about the day-to-day work of government in a form which enabled the monarch to participate meaningfully in the discussion of issues.

Under George IV and William IV little was done to solve either problem. George IV was notoriously susceptible to the influence of favourites and to gossip and he relied, perhaps too heavily, on his secretary, until the two men fell out and the office of secretary was formally abolished. Thereafter the king relied on his doctor, Sir William Knighton, who became a focus of dislike and jealousy. William IV was, if anything, even less well organised than his brother, but he secured the services of an experienced secretary, Sir Herbert Taylor. Queen Victoria's accession raised in a new form the question of providing the monarch with close advisers. Young and inexperienced, Victoria needed both a mentor and a secretary capable of managing her affairs. Lord Melbourne became her mentor, teaching her the mysteries of Whig constitutional theory, and a variety of arrangements were made to supply her with help and assistance. But these arrangements were perforce changed out of all recognition by Victoria's marriage. In Albert she found a companion, part guide, part secretary, part master, whose constitutional position at once became a subject of controversy. In law, the Queen's husband had no status at all, whatever precedence she might accord him (Albert as Prince Consort ranked immediately after the Queen), but in fact he was a sort of court prime minister. The role was an uneasy one, satisfactory neither to Albert nor to the ministers with whom he did business on the Queen's behalf, but the nobility of Albert's motives in the end got him over the worst difficulties. After Albert's death, the Queen was forced to rely on her staff for the assistance she needed. First General Grey (Prince Albert's secretary, who was at last gazetted as the Queen's secretary in 1867), then Sir Henry Ponsonby and Sir Arthur Bigge (Lord Stamfordham) took charge of her political business. And Edward VII followed her example by appointing Lord Knollys as his secretary.

The problem of keeping open channels of communication with the government was a difficult one. After each Cabinet meeting the Prime Minister sent an account of what had been done to the monarch—down to 1839 often in the form of a minute, subsequently in the form of a letter (65). But these minutes and letters were of very variable quality. Some Prime Ministers—notably Peel, Aberdeen and Disraeli—liked the monarch to get the feeling that she really knew what was happening; others, notably Palmerston and Gladstone, preferred to present a formal account, giving little information about disputes in the Cabinet. This had the effect of keeping the Queen at arms' length, a practice she resented because it tended to make the decisions of the government incomprehensible. In addition there were ministers in every government who were on especially friendly terms with the Queen, through whom she could make enquiries about the way business was being done—such as Sir Charles Wood and Lord Granville who for many years sent unofficial reports on Cabinet business (66) to her. The main source of detailed information about affairs of state was the circulation of Cabinet papers and diplomatic and colonial despatches to the monarch as well as to members of the Cabinet. Queen Victoria rightly emphasised that these documents should be sent to her in time, so that she could if she wished make observations on them. She also insisted that she must be consulted in advance about all matters concerned with the royal prerogative—notably appointments, honours and the commutation of sentences. Ministers sometimes felt that the seemingly excessive preoccupation of royalty with these rituals of preliminary consultation was to be condemned; but it is clear that without attention to detail a monarch could easily drift away from the centre of the political stage. Certainly Queen Victoria would have found it difficult to play the active role in diplomatic negotiations with the royal families of Europe which was expected of her (43-4) without such consultation. From this point of view, Queen Victoria was quite right to lay down precise rules relating to both the Foreign and India Offices (41-2), and to demand Lord Palmerston's dismissal when she was convinced that he had broken the rules. Nor did Palmerston dispute this exercise of the royal prerogative, although he blamed Russell, the Prime Minister, for misrepresenting his actions.

Whether the monarch was free to consult whomsoever he wished about political matters was always a disputed question. The leaders of the government in the Lords and Commons were required to send in daily reports on parliamentary business (29), and the monarch had, of course, other means of enabling him to follow the course of political events. Whenever there was a crisis, it was natural for the monarch to turn to leaders of the Opposition for help. Sometimes Queen Victoria asked the Opposition to drop a particular line of attack (162). Occasionally she urged the party leaders to get together. And, very occasionally, she made it quite clear to the Opposition that she would like to be rid of her ministers.

The monarch was also, of course, entitled to his or her own political views. The vagaries of George IV and his brothers were such that their views carried little weight, and ministers were prone to write them off as little more than a public nuisance (14-16). But George IV was able to prevent Catholic emancipation for very many years, and William IV in 1834 went so far as to dismiss ministers whose views he disapproved of, being the last monarch to do so (26). Queen Victoria and Prince Albert were active in promoting a number of projects, including the Great Exhibition. And Queen Victoria, after Albert's death, frequently expressed to her ministers very strong views both on foreign policy (notably over the Danish duchies in 1864, and the Eastern question in 1880) and on the Irish question. Queen Victoria's negotiations with the Unionists in 1886 have been condemned by Sir Ivor Jennings on the ground that the monarch is not entitled to identify himself with a particular set of measures or a particular set of party politicians.[1] But right or wrong, this is just what every monarch in our period did, with more or less skill, tact and determination, though, as the years went by, with progressively less effect.

More prone to misunderstanding than flirtations with the Opposition or the expression of strong views, was the inevitable reliance of the monarch on unofficial advisers, who worked behind the backs of the politicians of all parties. These men aroused jealousies and were liable to poison the atmosphere, however good their intentions. Lord Brougham, once he had been excluded from the Woolsack, made himself desperately unpopular as a backstairs politician; so did Baron Stockmar, King Leopold of the Belgians, and various members of Queen Victoria's family; and so did even that very mild man, Lord Esher, Edward VII's friend and military adviser, who deliberately refused to take Cabinet office because he preferred backstairs influence.[2] And lower down the scale there was a considerable number of diplomats, soldiers, sailors, colonial officials, civil servants and minor politicians, from whom the monarch was accustomed to seek advice occasionally. This made for a well-informed monarch, but led to a good deal of irritation in Whitehall.

The influence of the monarch was directly proportional to the strength of the largest party in the House of Commons. When a party had a safe majority and a clearly designated leader, the monarch could make his influence felt in only three ways: in the selection of individual ministers and of bishops and other crown nominees, in the conduct of foreign and colonial policy, and in facilitating or discouraging administrative reform. A strong party leader like Disraeli could afford to laud the role of the monarch in traditional Tory style (22) because he knew that in the last resort he could always get his own way. At such times the monarch was, indeed, more a colleague than a rival to the politicians. It was only when the party situation was more fluid that the monarch really came into his own. Lord Liverpool and his successors down to 1837 were always in danger of being turned out by the sovereign, simply because their support in the House of Commons was extremely unstable. George IV frequently talked of dismissing his ministers: William IV actually did dismiss his in 1834: and Queen Victoria in 1839 made it virtually impossible for Peel to form a government by refusing to change the Whig ladies of her household—a matter of only minor importance (27). Thereafter Prince Albert's influence served to restrain the Queen's Whig prejudices ('The Whigs', she wrote in 1840, 'are the only safe and loyal people.' (28)) But the Queen still retained the right to dismiss a ministry. Gladstone on

---

[1] Jennings, *Cabinet Government*, p. 237.   [2] Esher, *Journals*, II, 14–23.

several occasions feared that Queen Victoria would dismiss Liberal governments (31), although such an action would have endangered the monarchy. The monarch also retained a good deal of freedom in the choice of a Prime Minister in certain circumstances—Aberdeen in 1852 and Rosebery in 1894 were royal selections—and could influence the trend of politics both as a peacemaker and intermediary and as wielder of the power of dissolution.

It was agreed after 1815 that the monarch should be kept out of party politics. What was not so clear was how to preserve this neutrality in times of crisis. Queen Victoria always regarded herself as *above* politics, ready to intervene if required. But when it became clear that royal intervention was likely to be of a conservative character, Liberal politicians began to have second thoughts on the matter. As a result in 1911, with Queen Victoria and King Edward VII safely dead, Asquith went so far as to lay down the principle that 'it is not the function of a Constitutional Sovereign to act as arbiter or mediator between rival parties and policies' (24). He did this because it suited his party to argue that the king must always accept the advice of the government in office, which meant on that occasion that the King must agree to the creation of enough peers to carry the Parliament Bill through the House of Lords. But too much should not be read into Asquith's words. He did not mean that the King could not arrange a meeting of party leaders in order to secure an agreement in time of crisis, as over the Parliament Bill or the Home Rule Bill. All he meant was that the monarch could no longer lay down a line of behaviour to be followed and that it was very dubious whether he any longer possessed the power to dismiss a ministry.

GEORGE IV AND HIS BROTHERS

14. Wellington on the royal family, 1828

[Duke of Wellington to Robert Peel, 26 August 1828]

Between the King and his brothers the Government of this country is become a most heart-breaking concern. Nobody can ever know where he stands upon any subject. Parker, *Peel*, II, 42

15. Lord Campbell on George IV and William IV

(a) *John Campbell to George Campbell, 26 April 1830*

The new reign will produce no change in the Government. The Duke of Clarence (I must say) magnanimously forgave the Duke of Wellington for turning him out of his office of Lord Admiral. The danger is that the Duke of Clarence will become deranged before he has been long on the throne. He was very nearly upset by his High Admiralship; and the excitement of a crown will be too much for him to bear. He will be difficult to manage for, though very good-natured, he is fond of meddling, and is very 'bizarre' in many of his notions. George IV is the model of a constitutional King of England! And when he is missed he may be mourned. *He has stood by and let the country govern itself.*

(b) Autobiography of Sir John Campbell

On the 20th of June 1837 died his Majesty King William IV. Without education or much natural shrewdness, he had the good qualities of sincerity and honesty, and as King he had upon the whole performed the part more reputably than had been expected by those who knew him as Duke of Clarence.   Hardcastle, *Campbell*, I, 466–7; II, 99–100

16. Wellington on the Duke of Cumberland, 1836
[Duke of Wellington to Sir Robert Peel, 11 February 1836]

There is no person who feels more than I do the inconvenience of the Duke of Cumberland. I feel it every day, and all day. Others feel it only occasionally. But I can't see a remedy. His whole business is to pass the time. His amusement is mischief, preparing for it, hearing parties about each other, and talking of it afterwards. But I never could discover that he felt any real interest in any question, or entertained any serious opinion.   Parker, *Peel*, II, 323

THE CONSTITUTIONAL MONARCHY
17. King Leopold of the Belgians on the popular character of the British monarchy, 1841
[Memorandum by George Anson, 14 July 1841]

The Monarchy of this Country has its sole foundation in the will of the people. Without that will it cannot stand and from that will it derives every prerogative and power. The Commonwealth has shown that the Country can exist and flourish without a monarchy and the Sovereign should be reminded forcibly by this fact, that the Sovereign of a free people cannot be the Sovereign of a party.   Eyck, *Prince Consort*, p. 29

18. Prince Albert on the moral responsibility of the monarchy, 1850
[Memorandum by Prince Albert, 11 July 1850]

I had often heard it stated as the nature of the English constitution and the Royal Prerogatives, that the Sovereign could not interfere with the Government or the management of Parliament which are left to the sole control of the responsible Ministers, but that he was absolutely free in the choice of his Minister. Now I differed completely from that doctrine, I held the Sovereign to have an immense moral responsibility upon his shoulders with regard to his government and the duty to watch and control it, and *no* choice almost in the selection of his Ministers, if he understood his duties. The circumstances which led to a change of Ministry almost always pointed out also the men to succeed, public opinion and parliamentary position designated the candidates and there hardly was an instance in History, where, the Sovereign following the bent of his own inclination, had chosen another man than the one who had been brought forward by the circumstances, it had not produced the greatest difficulties to the Sovereign and danger to the Country. A sagacious Sovereign therefore would look forward and take his share in the preparatory arrangements of Party organisation even, when he could, in order to have those presented to his choice in times of emergency, who he had before recognised as eligible. Lord John knew, I continued, that the leader of the Majority in the House of Commons will always have the strongest claim.

Eyck, *Prince Consort*, p. 138

19. Walter Bagehot on the powers of the monarch, 1867

To state the matter shortly, the sovereign has, under a constitutional monarchy such as ours, three rights—the right to be consulted, the right to encourage, the right to warn. And a king of great sense and sagacity would want no others. He would find that his having no others would enable him to use these with singular effect. He would say to his minister: 'The responsibility of these measures is upon you. Whatever you think best must be done. Whatever you think best shall have my full and effectual support. *But* you will observe that for this reason and that reason what you propose to do is bad; for this reason and that reason what you do not propose is better. I do not oppose, it is my duty not to oppose; but observe that I *warn*.' Supposing the king to be right, and to have what kings often have, the gift of effectual expression, he could not help moving his minister. He might not always turn his course, but he would always trouble his mind.

Bagehot, *English Constitution*, p. 67

20. Gladstone doubts whether the monarchy can survive, 1870

[W. E. Gladstone to Earl Granville, 3 December 1870]

For our time as a Government, and my time as a politician, Royalty will do well enough in this country, because it has a large fund to draw upon, which was greatly augmented by good husbandry in the early and middle part of this reign, and which is not yet exhausted.

But the fund of credit is diminishing, and I do not see from whence it is to be replenished as matters now go. To speak in rude and general terms, the Queen is invisible, and the Prince of Wales is not respected. With the Queen, who abounds beyond all necessity in private and personal kindnesses to those having relations with her, it is a matter of great and ever increasing difficulty to arrange for any part of those formal ceremonial duties to the public, which in an ordinary state of things would go as matters of course. These parts of business are among the most difficult, and are the most painful, of the duties of my place; and it would be a relief to me if I could lay the blame upon the unhandy manner in which I perform them. The Queen's reluctance grows, and will grow, with age. And even if it did not, her influence dwindles with the deaths of those who have felt it, & who are not replaced; while we live in a time in which the personal influence of the Sovereign is among the main props of the Crown. The Prince of Wales is now in his thirtieth year. He has, I think, that average stock of energy, which enables men to do that which they cannot well avoid doing, or that which is made ready to their hands: but he has not the rare supply of it, which enables a man to make duty, and so to win honour and confidence. When this negative position as to duty is combined with the highest activity of the appliances and stimulants of pleasure, the position is, for the formation of character, the most dangerous in which a human being can be placed; and perhaps, all things considered, we ought to be thankful even that matters are no worse than they are.

But the outlook for ten, twenty, thirty, forty years hence is a very melancholy one. And, in these circumstances, the only remedial measure of which I can think is, to try and frame some plan under which the

Prince, before the habits of his mind and life become so to speak rigid, shall be provided with some fair share, not of political responsibility, but of public duty.

G.G.1, I, 170–1

21. A moderate republican's view of the monarchy, 1872

...the serious arguments for monarchy all resolve themselves into this—that it is there. And this is a very strong argument indeed; in truth, it is a conclusive argument against any wanton meddling with it. It is the old argument which has so long saved Temple Bar. There it is. No one would now put it there; no one can see any particular use in it; every one can see we should be better without it. But still the associations round it are so great, and the shock its absence would cause is so grave, that it is as well to let it stand. The monarchy, although a political nullity, is indeed associated with every phase of English society. It is the embodiment of the *status quo*. It is the keystone of our social system. Thus, though of very small account in itself, it is a most potent symbol. To the governing classes it is the sign of their right to govern. It is more than the sign, it is their consecration, the holy oil with which they are anointed. To them, it is what the Sacrament of the mass is to the Catholic priesthood. As the priest is sanctified to his congregation, who 'see God made and eaten all day long,' so the governing orders fresh from the actual presence of Majesty seem to acquire a power to rule the common.... In fact, the governing orders in England could no more manage the plebeians without the mystical rites of monarchy than the Roman aristocracy could have ruled without augurs and sacred chickens.

To the wealthy orders, again, the monarchy is the symbol of respect for wealth, respect for luxury, and respect for an idle class. Not that it is itself very rich, or very luxurious, or at present at all idle. Personally, the sovereign now drudges like a head examining clerk at dull, though perfectly useless, tasks.... But a society which still maintains a purely sinecure monarchy consecrates dignity without responsibility, wealth without toil, and display for its own sake....

To the entire middle class, in a word, from the capitalist down to the smallest tradesman, the monarchy at present represents prosperity because it represents the existing order of things.... It is true all this is not because it is a monarchy: not because it at all produces that prosperity, but simply because it is there. In the United States the republic is just as much the palladium of the existing state, and...even more favourable to the art of making fortunes. There the entire industrial and money-making class rallies round the republic with an even deeper jealousy than does our moneyed class round the throne as the symbol of the *status quo*; and it has the advantage of being entirely in harmony with all their other tendencies and interests, which cannot be said for the monarchy here.

Monarchy, in a word, is the social *status quo*. Politically it has no tangible importance, socially it is the consecration of the present. The monarchy is therefore not a political question at all, but a social question. And since social questions cannot be settled by external revolutions, any violent attack on the monarchy as an institution would fail to secure its object. It would be like attempting to abolish luxury or suppress wealth by Act of Parliament or popular plebiscite....

This high attribute of monarchy to elevate the vulgar to the adoration of wealth ought not to blind responsible persons to facts. Now, whilst there is a general desire in England to maintain public order, and a general acceptance of the monarchic form as a convenient *status quo*, there is a very wide and deep republican feeling more or less definite and conscious. In London and the great cities the bulk of the working-classes are republican by conviction, unless where they are perfectly indifferent. There are a score of towns in the north and centre where the republican feeling is at fever-heat, as honourable members may soon be somewhat 'surprised to learn.' Through the body of the smaller shopkeeping class, loyalty to the throne finds its highest expression in royal footmen and portraits of a princess: nor is it likely to take a more solid form. The heir to the crown is 'popular,' but he is just as popular in the United States, where huzzaing a notability can hardly be mistaken for political principle. And popularity is a vague term. It may be applied to the 'Claimant,' to a comic singer, and to a race-horse. In Ireland they are raising a statue to a beloved greyhound.

As we all know, amongst the educated classes there is a quiet pooh-poohing of monarchy as a living institution, with a tacit understanding to keep things as they are.... An effective faith in hereditary monarchy as a reality, and not an etiquette, would, in fact, be an effective repudiation of modern civilisation. Our whole cast of action and of life is now so essentially republican, that to any thoughtful mind hereditary monarchy as a principle can present itself only as a conspiracy or a mummery.

As to the *tableau vivant* which sentimentalists are pleased to call our English monarchy, we can take off our hat decently when it passes our way, as judicious Voltaireans do to the Host. We must all allow that it seldom gives us that trouble....

...The cramped and obsolete notion of loyalty to the crown chokes the abiding sense of loyalty to the public. There were ages once, and there are States now, where loyalty to a king has power to ennoble and strengthen the entire governing machine. But only is this possible in times, or in nations, where that governing body is crowned with a living and conscious head. Where, in place of a conscious head there is only a symbolical figure-head, it is impossible. ...In the true republic ...the nation is the visible ever-present and ultimate master: from the president to the meanest functionary, from the highest function of government down to every button on every policeman's coat, there is visibly, indelibly imprinted the nation, and duty to the nation, employment only to those worthy of the nation. From top to bottom of the social scale runs the instinct of merit; and office held in trust for the common weal....

England is amongst the first of nations simply because it is in essence republican—because it has long passed into that stage in which public opinion is the foundation of power, and capacity its true qualification—because it has long passed out of that stage in which allegiance is an accident of birth, and government a piece of property. England is, in heart, republican, because it has asserted in all material things, past question and past change, the principle that the public good is the sole standard, and personal fitness the real criterion of civil power. Most imperfectly and half-consciously republican it must be said. The *débris* of privilege and of feudalism through which the republican ideal has forced its way encumber it still on all sides. The ennobling reality of loyalty to the nation is choked at every turn by the obsolete fiction of loyalty to a family—loyalty to a pageant—loyalty to a sinecure. The social might which should clothe all office is bedimmed whilst the highest is the nominal appanage of a noble house. It is in the republic alone that the true loyalty is possible or that true monarchs exist....

Frederic Harrison, *Fortnightly Review*, new ser. XI, 632–6, 639, 641

22. Disraeli makes party capital out of the monarchy, 1872

[Speech at Manchester, 3 April 1872]

Gentlemen, the programme of the Conservative party is to maintain the Constitution of the country. I have not come down to Manchester to deliver an essay on the English Constitution; but when the banner of Republicanism is unfurled—when the fundamental principles of our institutions are controverted—I think, perhaps, it may not be inconvenient that I should make some few practical remarks upon the character of our Constitution—upon that monarchy, limited by the co-ordinate authority of Estates of the realm, which, under the title of Queen, Lords and Commons, has contributed so greatly to the prosperity of this country, and with the maintenance of which I believe that prosperity is bound up.

Gentlemen, since the settlement of that Constitution, now nearly two centuries ago, England has never experienced a revolution, though there is no country in which there has been so continuous and such considerable change. How is this? Because the wisdom of your forefathers placed the prize of supreme power without the sphere of human passions. Whatever the struggle of parties, whatever the strife of factions, whatever the excitement and exaltation of the public mind, there has always been something in this country round which all classes and parties could rally, representing the majesty of the law, the administration of justice, and involving, at the same time, the security for every man's rights and the fountain of honour. Now, gentlemen, it is well clearly to comprehend what is meant by a country not having a revolution for two centuries. It means, for that space, the unbroken exercise and enjoyment of the ingenuity of man. It means, for that space, the continuous application of the discoveries of science to his comfort and convenience. It means the accumulation of capital, the elevation of labour, the establishment of those admirable factories which cover your district; the unwearied improvement of the cultivation of the land, which has extracted from a somewhat churlish soil harvests more exuberant than those furnished by lands nearer to the sun. It means the continuous order which is the only parent of personal liberty and political right. And you owe all these, gentlemen, to the Throne.

There is another powerful and most beneficial influence which is also exercised by the Crown. Gentlemen, I am a party man. I believe that, without party, Parliamentary government is impossible. I look upon Parliamentary government as the noblest government in the world, and certainly the one most suited to England. But without the discipline of political connection, animated by the principle of private honour, I feel certain that a popular Assembly would sink before the power or the corruption of a minister. Yet, gentlemen, I am not blind to the faults of party government. It has one great defect. Party has a tendency to warp the intelligence.... It is, therefore, a great merit in our Constitution that before a minister introduces a measure to Parliament, he must submit it to an intelligence superior to all party, and entirely free from influences of that character.

I know it will be said, gentlemen, that, however beautiful in theory, the personal influence of the Sovereign is now absorbed in the responsibility of the minister. Gentlemen, I think you will find there is great fallacy in this view. The principles of the English Constitution do not contemplate the absence of personal influence on the part of the Sovereign; and if they did, the principles of human nature would prevent the fulfilment of such a theory.... From the earliest moment of his accession that Sovereign is placed in constant communication with the most able statesmen of the period, and of all parties. Even with average ability it is impossible not to perceive that such a Sovereign must soon attain a great mass of political information and political experience. Information and experience, gentlemen, whether they are possessed by a Sovereign or by the humblest of his subjects, are irresistible in life. No man with the vast responsibility that devolves upon an English minister can afford to treat with indifference a suggestion that has not occurred to him, or information with which he had not been previously supplied. But, gentlemen, pursue this view of the subject. The longer the reign, the influence of that Sovereign must proportionately increase. All the illustrious statesmen who served his youth disappear. A new generation of public servants rises up. There is a critical conjuncture in affairs—a moment of perplexity and peril. Then it is that the Sovereign can appeal to a similar state of affairs that occurred perhaps thirty years before. When all are in doubt among his servants he can quote the advice that was given by the illustrious men of his early years, and though he may maintain himself within the strictest limits of the Constitution, who can suppose when such information and such suggestions are made by the most exalted person in the country that they can be without effect? No, gentlemen; a minister who could venture to treat such influence with indifference would not be a Constitutional minister, but an arrogant idiot.

Gentlemen, the influence of the Crown is not confined merely to political affairs. England is a domestic country. Here the home is revered and the hearth is sacred. The nation is represented by a family—the Royal Family; and if that family is educated with a sense of responsibility and a sentiment of public duty, it is difficult to exaggerate the salutary influence they may exercise over a nation. It is not merely an influence upon manners; it is not merely that they are a model for refinement and for good taste—they affect the heart as well as the intelligence of the people; and in the hour of public adversity, or in the anxious conjuncture of public affairs, the nation rallies round the Family and the Throne, and its spirit is animated and sustained by the expression of public affection.   Kebbel, II, 491–4

23. The future King George V learns about the monarchy, 1894

[The Prince was set by his tutor, J. R. Tanner, to précis Walter Bagehot's account of the monarchy: what follows is his précis]

MONARCHY

1 The value of the Crown in its *dignified* capacity
  (a) It makes Government *intelligible* to the masses.
  (b) It makes Government *interesting* to the masses.
  (c) It *strengthens* Government with the *religious* tradition connected with the Crown.
      After the accession of George III the Hanoverian line inherited the traditional reverence of Stuart times.
  (d) The *social* value of the Crown.
      If the high social rank was to be scrambled for in the House of Commons, the number of social adventurers there would be incalculably more numerous and infinitely more eager.
  (e) The *moral* value of the Crown.
      Great for good or evil.
      Compare the Courts of Charles II and George III in their influence on the nation.
  (f) The existence of the Crown serves to *disguise* change & therefore to deprive it of the evil consequences of revolution, e.g. The Reform Bill of 1832.

2 The value of the Crown in its *business* capacity. The Crown is no longer an 'Estate of the Realm' or itself the executive, but the Queen nevertheless retains an immense unexhausted *influence* which goes some way to compensate for the formal *powers* which have been lost; this influence can be exercised in various ways:

(a) In the *formation* of Ministries; especially in choosing between the Statesmen who have a claim to lead party.

(b) During the *continuance* of Ministries. The Crown possesses *first* the right to be consulted, *second* the right to encourage & *third* the right to warn. And these rights may lead to a very important influence on the course of politics, especially as under a system of party government, the Monarch alone possesses a *continuous political experience*.

(c) At the *break up* of a Ministry (but this can be treated best in connection with the House of Lords).

Thus, though it would be possible to construct a system of political machinery in which there was no monarchy, yet in a State where a monarchy of the English type already exists, it is still a great political force & offers a splendid career to an able monarch; he is independent of parties & therefore impartial, his position ensures that his advice would be received with respect; & he is the only statesman in the country whose political experience is continuous.

Nicolson, *King George V*, pp. 62–3

24. Asquith on the functions of the monarch, 1910

[Memorandum for the King on relations with the Opposition]

The part to be played by the Crown, in such a situation as now exists, has happily been settled by the accumulated traditions and the unbroken practice of more than 70 years. It is to act upon the advice of the Ministers who for the time being possess the confidence of the House of Commons, whether that advice does or does not conform to the private and personal judgment of the Sovereign. Ministers will always pay the utmost deference, and give the most serious consideration, to any criticism or objection that the Monarch may offer to their policy; but the ultimate decision rests with them; for they, and not the Crown, are responsible to Parliament. It is only by a scrupulous adherence to this well-established Constitutional doctrine that the Crown can be kept out of the arena of party politics.

It follows that it is not the function of a Constitutional Sovereign to act as arbiter or mediator between rival parties and policies; still less to take advice from the leaders on both sides, with the view to forming a conclusion of his own. George III in the early years of his reign tried to rule after this fashion, with the worst results, and with the accession of Mr. Pitt to power he practically abandoned the attempt. The growth and development of our representative system, and the clear establishment at the core and centre of our Constitution of the doctrine of Ministerial responsibility, have since placed the position of the Sovereign beyond the region of doubt or controversy.

It is technically possible for the Sovereign to dismiss Ministers who tender to him unpalatable advice. The last instance of such a proceeding was in 1834, when William IV compelled the resignation of Lord Melbourne and his colleagues. The result was, from the King's point of view, singularly unsatisfactory. The dismissed Ministers found an adequate majority in the new House of Commons. The King was compelled to take them back again, and they remained in power for another 6 years. During the long reign of Queen Victoria, though she was often in disagreement with the Ministry of the day, she never resorted to this part of the prerogative. She recognised that, so long as a Ministry possessed the confidence of the House of Commons, she had no alternative but to act on its advice. The reason is plain. The House of Commons, by reason of its power over Supply, has every Ministry at its mercy. The King cannot act without Ministers, and Ministers are impotent to carry on the government of the country without a majority in the House of Commons.

The position becomes exceptionally clear and simple, when—as the case is now—a ministry has appealed to the country upon the specific and dominating issue of the day, and upon that issue commands a majority of more than 100 in the House of Commons.

Spender and Asquith, Asquith, I, 305–6

The Monarch and the Ministry

25. Liverpool on the monarch's power to exclude individuals from the government, 1821

[Earl of Liverpool to Earl Bathurst, 27 June 1821]

...Upon the abstract question whether a King should be allowed to exclude an individual from his Cabinet, it is very difficult to give any general opinion. There are circumstances which might certainly justify such a decision: strong discordance of opinion on political events actually depending; belief of disloyalty; the moral character of a man materially tainted—may all sufficiently account for such exclusion.

There may likewise be many other cases which I do not at this moment contemplate, but I am quite sure a King should be most cautious in acting on such a principle, for the effect of it will generally be to exalt the individual and to lower the King.

I speak not without experience on this subject. I was the person in 1806 to advise the late King to waive his exclusion of Mr. Fox. I had then seen the evil effects of such exclusion. A few months before Mr. Pitt was sent for in 1805 [1804] by the King, no man could stand lower in reputation, character and credit than Mr. Fox. You will recollect that he had been termed by Windham the pander of all the base passions of the people, and yet the day after he had been proposed by Mr. Pitt as a colleague and personally excluded by the King, his character stood higher in the eyes of the country than it had ever stood at any former period of his political life.

In the present case it is to be observed that there is no pretence for any discordance of opinion between Mr. Canning and the King's Government on any material public question, foreign or domestic. He is known to agree on every point as much as we agree one with another; and since the termination of the discussion on the Queen's business, he has, when in England, regularly attended the House of Commons and supported the Government much more steadily than many of those who are considered as their decided friends....

It is not *Mr. Canning out of office*, but Mr. Canning *out of office by the personal exclusion of the King, agreed to by his Government*, which is the question. Can anyone doubt that he would become an object of compassion in the first instance, and afterwards of popularity—that his case would be taken up by all who on any account oppose the Government, and that we should be accused of meanness and servility in abandoning a man to the personal resentment of the Sovereign, whom we had thought it right to propose as one of his Ministers? I feel this perhaps the more strongly because I have reason to know that there will remain after this a further stock of humiliations in store for us, and yet of humiliations of such a nature that I do not see how we can do otherwise than submit to them.

It is said that the exclusion is only temporary. Ought we not to know what is meant by temporary? Kings may have said that they never would admit particular individuals into their Cabinet. Public men may have said that they never would sit in a Cabinet with this or that individual, but such declarations have always been justly considered as ebullitions of passion. No man can be proscribed for ever, and the temporary exclusion may operate therefore with exactly the same effect as a professed permanent one.... *EHD* xi, 149–50

26. William IV contemplates the failure of his attempt to replace the Whigs by a Tory government, 1835

[King William IV to Sir Robert Peel, 22 February 1835]

His Majesty considers that the confidence, the countenance, and the support of the Sovereign are indispensable to the existence and the maintenance of the Government, so long as the Constitution of the country is monarchical; and he can confidently appeal to all those whom he has called to his councils since Providence has placed him on the throne, whether he has not uniformly made this the rule of his conduct.

If unfortunately the present factious Opposition should carry their purpose to the length of refusing the supplies, and his Majesty's confidential servants should not consider it advisable to recommend to his Majesty to make a further appeal to the country, his Majesty would consider it his duty to yield to their advice, although he might have been led to believe that the result of such appeal would offer proof of a further reaction in the public feeling.

In such event, however, his Majesty would be placed under difficulties which attach more peculiarly to his own station, and as combined with it to the interests of the monarchy; and it behoves him to consider well what might be the course to which he would be reduced.

The last change of Administration was his own immediate and exclusive act. He removed Ministers whom he considered no longer capable of carrying on the business of the country with advantage, and he called to his councils others whom he considered deserving of his confidence.

The proceeding which is threatened would be a direct censure passed upon his Majesty's conduct, by a party avowing its determination to force itself upon him, and into his councils, in opposition to his declared principles and sentiments, his wishes, and his conscience.

Imperious circumstances, and the apprehension of throwing the country into confusion, may oblige his Majesty to sacrifice feeling, comfort, and rooted opinions, and to bow under the overpowering weight of this evil.

But it is impossible that he can give his confidence to men so introduced to his councils. They cannot expect it, nor can they claim a support to which their proceedings would have so little entitled them. His Majesty might be obliged to *tolerate* them, but he could not meet them cordially, nor communicate with them as with friends. They may become his Ministers, but never his *confidential* servants. He would receive all their advice with jealousy and suspicion. He could not bring himself to affect that which he cannot feel. Parker, *Peel*, II, 287–9

27. Peel writes to the Queen during the Bedchamber Crisis, 1839

[Sir Robert Peel to Queen Victoria, 10 May 1839]

Sir Robert Peel presents his humble duty to your Majesty, and has had the honour of receiving your Majesty's note of this morning.

In respectfully submitting to your Majesty's pleasure, and humbly returning into your Majesty's hands the important trust which your Majesty had been graciously pleased to commit to him, Sir Robert Peel trusts that your Majesty will permit him to state to your Majesty his impression with respect to the circumstances which have led to the termination of his attempt to form an Administration for the conduct of your Majesty's service.

In the interview with which your Majesty honoured Sir Robert Peel yesterday morning, after he had submitted to your Majesty the names of those whom he proposed to recommend to your Majesty for the principal executive appointments, he mentioned to your Majesty his earnest wish to be enabled, with your Majesty's sanction, so to constitute your Majesty's Household that your Majesty's confidential servants might have the advantage of a public demonstration of your Majesty's full support and confidence, and that at the same time, as far as possible consistently with that demonstration, each individual appointment in the Household should be entirely acceptable to your Majesty's personal feelings.

On your Majesty's expressing a desire that the Earl of Liverpool should hold an office in the Household, Sir Robert Peel requested your Majesty's permission at once to offer to Lord Liverpool the office of Lord Steward, or any other which he might prefer.

Sir Robert Peel then observed that he should have every wish to apply a similar principle to the chief appointments which are filled by the Ladies of your Majesty's Household; upon which your Majesty was pleased to remark that you must reserve the whole of those appointments, and that it was your Majesty's pleasure that the whole should continue as at present, without any change.

The Duke of Wellington, in the interview to which your Majesty subsequently admitted him, understood also that this was your Majesty's determination; and concurred with Sir Robert Peel in opinion that, considering the great difficulties of the present crisis, and the expediency of making every effort in the first instance to conduct the business of the country with the aid of the present Parliament, it was essential to the business of the commission with which your Majesty had honoured Sir Robert Peel, that he should have that public proof of your Majesty's entire support and confidence which would be afforded by the permission to make some changes in that part of your Majesty's Household which your Majesty resolved on maintaining entirely without change.

Having had the opportunity, through your Majesty's gracious consideration, of reflecting upon this point, he humbly submits to your Majesty that he is reluctantly compelled by a sense of public duty, and of the interests of your Majesty's service, to adhere to the opinion which he ventured to express to your Majesty.

Parker, Peel, II, 396–7

28. Queen Victoria a Whig partisan, 1840

[Queen Victoria to Prince Albert, 21 January 1840]

The Tories really are very astonishing; as they cannot and dare not attack us in Parliament, they do everything that they can to be personally rude to me.... The Whigs are the only safe and loyal people, and the Radicals will also rally round their Queen to protect her from the Tories; but it is a curious sight to see those, who as Tories, used to pique themselves upon their excessive loyalty, doing everything to degrade their young Sovereign in the eyes of the people.

LQV 1st ser. I, 268

29. The Queen to be informed of proceedings in parliament, 1841–93

(a) George Anson to Sir Robert Peel, 9 September 1841

The Queen would wish you [Sir Robert Peel] always to send after the debates, or other business of interest, a short report of what has taken place. Her Majesty would wish the Duke of Wellington to do the same thing in the House of Lords. I do not know whether this has been usual in former days with you, but it has always been her Majesty's habit to receive this early intelligence from the leader in each House.

Parker, *Peel*, II, 525

(b) Queen Victoria to the Earl of Derby, 8 May 1867

The Queen wishes to remind Lord Derby of continuing, as he formerly used to do, his habit of reporting what passed in the House of Lords.

LQV, 2nd ser. I, 425

(c) W. E. Gladstone to Sir Henry Ponsonby, 17 January 1893

I have in mind the established usage under which, when I first became Prime Minister and thereafter, I made known by a letter written nightly and forthwith to Her Majesty the purport of the proceedings of the House of Commons during the sitting just expired. I am under the impression that under other Governments during the last twenty years, or part of that period, some change has taken place, and that the proceedings of the House have been made known during the sitting from time to time by telegraph. I do not know how far if at all, the change altered the practice, or the character of the nightly letter. I am afraid that I personally can no longer look forward to that regularity of personal attendance until towards the virtual close of business which was the basis of my old reports. Nor would a report based habitually upon information from others be the same thing, whenever written, as the old report. I have thought that under the circumstances I might ask you to be so kind as to let me know, subject to the Queen's permission, what the practice has been under the Governments of Lord Beaconsfield and Lord Salisbury as this knowledge might afford me some light with a view to any request or proposal I might humbly submit for the immediate future. But I should state that in no case could I submit any request or proposal which would exempt me from the duty of keeping Her Majesty duly informed upon all matters of importance or special interest.

(d) Sir Henry Ponsonby to Gladstone, 18 January 1893

There has been no change in the custom which has existed I believe since the time of Sir Robert Peel, that the leader of the House of Commons furnished The Queen with a short report of the proceedings in the House.

There have been a few occasions when, if there were nothing of special interest going on, the Prime Minister has not written.

In Lord Salisbury's late Government Mr. Smith and Mr. Balfour wrote regularly.

Your reports have always been most valuable—but The Queen observed a short time ago that she could not expect a continuance of these nightly letters from you and asked me whether you would entrust the duty to Sir W. Harcourt or some other member of your Government. I imagine she will readily agree to any suggestion you may make.... Guedalla, *Queen and Mr. Gladstone*, II, 458–9

30. The Queen and the Opposition, 1879

[Queen Victoria to Lady Ely, 21 September 1879]

I wish it were possible for Sir H. Ponsonby [the Queen's Private Secretary] to *get at some* of the *Opposition*, and to point *out* the *extreme danger* of binding themselves by foolish, violent declarations about their policy beforehand. I hope and trust the Government will be able to go on after the Election, as change is so disagreeable and so bad for the country; but, if it should *not*, I wish the *principal* people of the Opposition should *know* there *are certain* things which *I never can* consent to. 1. Any lowering of the position of this country by letting Russia have her way in the East, or by letting down our Empire in India and in the Colonies. This *was* done under Mr. Gladstone, quite *contrary* to Lord Palmerston's *policy*, which, whatever faults he had, *was always* for *keeping up England*, which of late years had *quite* gone down, so that we were *despised abroad*. 2. That I would never give way about *the Scotch Church*, which is the real and true stronghold of Protestantism.

These are points which I *never* could *allow* to be *trifled with*, and I could have *no* confidence in any men who attempted this. Our position in India, and in the Colonies, *must* be *upheld*. I wish to *trust my* Government whoever it is, but they should be *well aware* beforehand I never could if they intended to *try* and *undo* what has been done.

In the same way I never could take Mr. Gladstone or Mr. Lowe as my Minister again, for I never COULD have the slightest *particle* of confidence in Mr. Gladstone *after* his violent, mischievous, and dangerous conduct for the last three years, nor could I take the *latter* after the very offensive language he used three years ago against *me*.

Sir H. Ponsonby has so many Whig friends that he might easily *get* these things *known*. In former days *much* good was done by Baron Stockmar and Mr. Anson paving the way *for* future arrangements and *preventing* complications at the moment, like Sir R. Peel's failure in '39 about the Ladies. Ever yours affectionately, V.R. & I.

I never *could* take Sir C. Dilke as a *Minister*.   LQV, 2nd ser. III, 47–8

31. Gladstone contemplates the possible dismissal of his ministry by the Queen, 1880

[W. E. Gladstone to Earl Granville, 20 September 1880]

I may mention now a few words which I found occasion to use in the quasi-Cabinet after the Prorogation Speech about the Candahar Telegram. They were to this effect 'Depend upon it that in all our discussions upon serious and critical matter there is one thing that we should not wholly exclude from our minds: namely that H[er] M[ajesty] may turn round upon us and say she has no further occasion for our services; a most serious affair. I am far from saying this will happen, but it is a point which should not be left wholly out of view in our thoughts'.

I need not say that, rightly or wrongly, this was not spoken in haste.

The present case [relations with Turkey] carries us back to George III and the pledge he demanded from the Whigs not to stir the R.C. question.   GG2, I, 180

32. The Queen's speech, 1881

[Earl of Beaconsfield to Queen Victoria, 11 January 1881]

The principle of Sir W. Harcourt, that the Speech of the Sovereign is only the Speech of the Ministers, is a principle not known to the British Constitution. It is only a piece of Parliamentary gossip.

The Speech from the Throne must be approved in Council by the Sovereign, but to be so approved, it should be previously considered by the Sovereign. Ample time ought to be secured to the Sovereign for this purpose, so that suggestions may be made, and explanations required and given.

The degree of resistance which the Crown may choose to make against any expressions which the Crown disapproves must depend upon circumstances. If, for example, there was a proposal to surrender Malta under an alleged engagement of the Treaty of Amiens, the Sovereign would, in all probability, be supported by the nation in resisting such a counsel. The unfortunate state of parties at this moment limits the power of the Throne, but that is no reason why the constitutional prerogative of the Crown should be treated as non-existing. Even under the present circumstances, your Majesty has a right, which it would be wise always to exercise, to express your Majesty's opinion on every point of the policy of your Ministers, and to require and receive explanations....

I think it right to state that there are instances in which the Speech from the Throne has been altered after it was approved in Council, but, so far as my experience can guide me, they were always instances in which news from abroad or the Colonies had affected the statements of fact. Then no change was made without obtaining the previous sanction of the Sovereign, and if the Cabinet could not be assembled, the Prime Minister took the responsibility of the change....

LQV, 2nd ser. III, 181-2

33. Queen Victoria a Conservative partisan, 1882
[Queen Victoria to the Prince of Wales, 27 May 1882]

The state of affairs—this dreadfully Radical Government which contains many thinly-veiled *Republicans*—and the way in which they have truckled to the Home Rulers—as well as the utter disregard of all my opinions which after 45 years of experience ought to be considered, all make me very miserable, and disgust me with the hard, ungrateful task I have to go through and weigh on my health and spirits. You as my eldest son, and so intimate as you are with Lord Hartington, *might* and *should* I think speak strongly to him, *reminding* him *how* HE *asked you to tell me in '80 that if I took Mr. Gladstone I should certainly* NOT *have to take these violent and dangerous Radicals*, instead of which, *two* days after, I had *most unwillingly* taken this most dangerous man; *all the worst men* who had no respect for Kings and Princes or any of the *landmarks* of the Constitution *were put into the Government in spite of me.*

The mischief Mr. Gladstone does is *incalculable*; instead of *stemming* the current and downward course of Radicalism, which he could do *perfectly*, he *heads and encourages it* and alienates all the true Whigs and moderate Liberals from him. Patriotism is nowhere in their ranks. How differently do the leaders of Opposition in the House behave to the disgraceful way in which in times of great difficulty the *Liberal Opposition* opposed Lord Beaconsfield and tried to injure him! You and all of you should *speak* to *those* who *might and ought*, to act *differently* to what they do! Lord Granville behaves miserably; he is the only one *I know well* and he never *even answers* my remarks!! *LQV*, 2nd ser. III, 298–9

34. The Queen urges the party leaders to meet to deal with the franchise question, 1884

[Queen Victoria to W. E. Gladstone, 31 October 1884]

The Queen thinks that it would be a means of arriving at some understanding if the leaders of the parties in both Houses could exchange their views personally. The Duke of Argyll or any other person unconnected for the present with the government or the opposition might be employed in bringing about a meeting, and in assisting to solve difficulties. The Queen thinks the government should in any project forming the basis of resolutions on redistribution to be proposed to the House, distinctly define their plans at such a personal conference. The Queen believes that were assurance given that the redistribution would not be wholly inimical to the prospects of the conservative party, their concurrence might be obtained. The Queen feels most strongly that it is of the utmost importance that in this serious crisis such means, even if unusual, should be tried, and knowing how fully Mr. Gladstone recognises the great danger that might arise by prolonging the conflict, the Queen *earnestly* trusts that he will avail himself of such means to obviate it. Morley, *Gladstone*, III, 135

35. Harcourt argues that the monarch can appeal to the Cabinet against a minister's decision, 1889

[Memorandum by Sir W. V. Harcourt, 12 July 1889]

[It] is the right of the Sovereign to demand the opinion of the Cabinet as a court of appeal against the Prime Minister or any other minister in his general or departmental action. As a general rule the foreign dispatches are settled between the Prime Minister and the Foreign Secretary, and are submitted to the Queen, but if she dissents she has the practical right to demand the opinion of the Cabinet on the dispatch. This power was extensively used in the years 1859–61 by Albert acting through the Queen in German affairs, and I remember Sir G. Lewis telling me at the time when almost weekly Cabinets were called at the instance of the Queen that the dispatches were almost invariably modified.

This is really a very practical power in the hands of the Crown, especially where there is a strong Cabinet.

I think you know that the recognition of the South in the American Civil War was prevented by the majority of the Cabinet against the opinion of the Prime Minister, the Foreign Minister and the Chancellor of the Exchequer.

We had several instances in the 1880 Government where the Queen especially required that the Cabinet should be consulted as distinguished from the Prime Minister and the Foreign Secretary upon views stated by herself. Of course the decision of the Cabinet in such a case is final. I also take it that a Minister who is at issue with the Prime Minister has a right if he chooses to insist on the case being brought before the Cabinet.   Gardiner, *Harcourt*, II, 611

36. Queen Victoria suggests a different arrangement of Cabinet posts, 1895

(a) Queen Victoria to the Marquess of Salisbury, 26 June 1895 (Cypher)

While fully appreciating your difficulties in selecting the exact person for the particular post, cannot help being anxious regarding your nominee for Admiralty. Lord Spencer has been very successful, not only as an Administrator, but from his personal and social position, which had lent prestige to what is our national service. My wish is that your Government should be no less fortunate. Fear Mr. Goschen was not altogether popular in same capacity from 1871–1874.

As to India, I am not quite confident in Lord G. Hamilton. Without questioning his ability, doubt whether personally he will be a power in that important post.

(b) The Marquess of Salisbury to Queen Victoria, 26 June 1895

Lord Salisbury with his humble duty respectfully submits that having had an audience in which he had submitted Mr. Goschen's name, he at once directed that notice to move his writ should be given. He very much regrets if in doing so he misunderstood your Majesty's pleasure. Mr. Goschen, however, was resolved not to go back to the Exchequer; and if he had refused to take any office, except the Admiralty, and he were excluded from that, the Government could not have been formed. With respect to Lord George Hamilton, the case is this. Last time the extreme inconvenience of having no Secretary for India in the Commons was much felt. The case of Manipur was a striking example. But Lord George is the only man of Cabinet rank in the Commons, who knows anything about India. He served for four years under Lord Salisbury at the India Office.   *LQV*, 3rd ser. II, 527–8

37. The exercise of the Royal Prerogative of Mercy, 1903

[A. Akers-Douglas to King Edward VII, 26 September 1903]

Mr. Secretary Akers-Douglas with his humble duty begs leave to enclose a Memorandum which he has prepared at Your Majesty's desire on the Royal Prerogative of Mercy—or rather on the constitutional practice as to the exercise of the prerogative.

Mr. Douglas thinks it is most important that the practice of the last 80 years at any rate, should not be departed from. He would particularly emphasize the three following points.

(1) There are from 5000 to 6000 petitions every year against convictions and sentences. If Your Majesty is to deal personally with any of them, you ought to deal personally with all. It would be invidious to pick and choose.

(2) If Your Majesty is to deal with death sentences your attention must be available at all times from sentence to final decision. The practice of the S[ecretary] of S[tate] is to deal not only on the evidence at the trial: but on evidence which accumulates until the last moment.

(3) The power of reprieve involves the power, and duty to refuse to reprieve. This latter power is sometimes bitterly attacked, and public opinion is lashed up by an unscrupulous partisan press. For instance the Radical Press took up Lipski's case—in Mr. Secretary Matthews's time—and if my memory serves me Mr. Stead in one of his papers said, 'So an innocent man is to be sent to the gallows to gratify the wounded vanity of the Home Secretary.' Such cases may always arise from time to time—and it must be borne in mind that 'yellow journalism' is on the increase. It would be intolerable that Your Majesty's

name should be dragged into the mire to serve the temporary purposes of some wretched newspaper.

Again suppose a man of good position is reprieved strictly according to the traditional exercise of the prerogative (say great temptation and sudden passion) a section of the Press would not hesitate to attribute it to personal influence and raise the cry of 'one law for the rich and another for the poor'. It is in Mr. Douglas's opinion the Home Secretary's duty to bear the brunt of such attacks, and to defend himself if necessary in Parliament.   Chilston, *Chief Whip*, p. 310

38. The King decides to approach the Opposition to secure a settlement of the budget question, 1909

[H. H. Asquith to Margot Asquith, 6 October 1909]

I saw the King immediately on my arrival. He entered almost at once on the subject of the Budget and the Lords.

He asked me whether I thought he was well within constitutional lines in taking upon himself to give advice to, and if necessary put pressure upon, the Tory leaders at this juncture.

I replied that I thought what he was doing and proposing to do, perfectly correct, from a constitutional point of view; that the nearest analogy was the situation and action of William IV, at the time of the Reform Bill; in both cases the country was threatened with a revolution at the hands of the House of Lords.

He said that, in that case, he should not hesitate to see both Balfour and Lansdowne on his return to London.   Spender and Asquith, *Asquith*, I, 257

39. The King insists on a dissolution before creating peers, 1909

[Memorandum by Vaughan Nash for H. H. Asquith, 15 December 1909]

Lord Knollys asked me to see him this afternoon and he began by saying that the King had come to the conclusion that he would not be justified in creating new peers (say 300) until after a second general election and that he, Lord K., thought you should know of this now, though, for the present he would suggest that what he was telling me should be for your ear only. The King regards the policy of the Government as tantamount to the destruction of the House of Lords and he thinks that before a large creation of Peers is embarked upon or threatened the country should be acquainted with the particular project for accomplishing such destruction as well as with the general line of action as to which the country will be consulted at the forthcoming Elections.

Spender and Asquith, *Asquith*, I, 261

THE MONARCH AND FOREIGN AND INDIAN AFFAIRS
40. William IV requires to see foreign despatches, 1832

[Sir Herbert Taylor to Earl Grey, 19 April 1832]

The King proceeded to say that, in expressing his wish to see the instructions to his Ministers at Foreign Courts before they were dispatched, he meant nothing offensive, nor expressive of suspicion: nor did he mean that it should apply to the general course of the communications; but that he could refer your Lordship and Lord Palmerston to his communications with reference to the Polish and the Italian questions, for proofs of the anxiety with which he contemplates them, and the possibility of their committing this country in a manner, and in the support of interference, and of opinions which he deprecates; and, with this feeling, he has been particularly desirous of preventing the issue of instructions, or the use of expressions, which might not accord with his view of the subject, and which it would be difficult to cancel or recall.

The King is persuaded that there never has been any intention to send instructions of any importance, or upon which it might be conceived that a doubt would arise, without previously submitting them to His Majesty; but there may have been instances in which such doubt has not been anticipated; and, adverting to the date of those addressed to Mr. Seymour, and the day on which received, the King might have presumed that they had been dispatched before they were submitted to him; and yet a perusal of His Majesty's letter respecting these to Lord Palmerston will show that he strongly objected to many parts, as the answer from Lord Palmerston will show that the soundness of many of the objections was admitted. Grey, *Reform Act, 1832*, II, 376–7

41. The Royal sanction required for the Foreign Secretary's policies, 1850

[Queen Victoria to Lord John Russell, 12 August 1850]

With reference to the conversation about Lord Palmerston which the Queen had with Lord John Russell the other day, and Lord Palmerston's disavowal that he ever intended any disrespect to her by the various neglects of which she has had so long and so often to complain, she thinks it right, in order *to prevent any mistake* for the *future*, shortly to explain *what it is she expects from her Foreign Secretary*. She requires: (1) That he will distinctly state what he proposes in a given case, in order that the Queen may know as distinctly to *what* she has given her Royal sanction; (2) Having *once given* her sanction to a measure, that it be not arbitrarily altered or modified by the Minister; such an act she must consider as failing in sincerity towards the Crown, and justly to be visited by the exercise of her Constitutional right of dismissing that Minister. She expects to be kept informed of what passes between him and the Foreign Ministers before important decisions are taken, based upon that intercourse; to receive the Foreign Despatches in good time, and to have the drafts for her approval sent to her in sufficient time to make herself acquainted with their contents before they must be sent off. The Queen thinks it best that Lord John Russell should show this letter to Lord Palmerston.　　　　　　　*LQV*, 1st ser. II, 315

42. The Queen to be consulted on Indian affairs, 1858

[Queen Victoria to Lord Stanley, 4 September 1858]

The Queen sends to Lord Stanley a Memorandum embodying her wishes with respect to the transaction of business between herself and the new Secretary of State.[1] He will find that she has omitted any reference to Military appointments, as Lord Stanley seemed anxious to defer a settlement on this point; she expects, however, that in all cases in which her pleasure was taken by the Commander-in-Chief, even during the administration of the East India Company and Board of Control, the same practice will be continued unaltered....

[1] The Secretary of State for India, for whom see below (253).

[MEMORANDUM]

The Queen wishes the practice of the Office with reference to submissions to her to be as nearly as possible assimilated to that of the Foreign Office.

All despatches, when received and perused by the Secretary of State, to be sent to the Queen. They may be merely forwarded in boxes from the Office without being accompanied by any letter from the Secretary of State, unless he should think an explanation necessary. No draft of instructions or orders to be sent out without having been previously submitted to the Queen. The label on the boxes of the Office containing such drafts to be marked 'For Approval'.

In cases of Civil appointments the Secretary of State will himself take the Queen's pleasure before communicating with the gentlemen to be appointed.

Copies or a *précis* of the Minutes of the Council to be regularly transmitted to the Queen.

The Secretary of State to obtain the Queen's sanction to important measures previously to his bringing them before the Council for discussion.
LQV, 1st ser. III, 379–80

43. Queen Victoria and the German Emperor, 1896–9

(a) *Queen Victoria to the Emperor William II of Germany, 5 January 1896*

My Dear William,...As your Grandmother to whom you have always shown so much affection and of whose example you have always spoken with so much respect, I feel I cannot refrain from expressing my deep regret at the telegram you sent President Kruger. It is considered very unfriendly towards this country, which I feel sure it is not intended to be, and has, I grieve to say, made a very painful impression here. The action of Dr. Jameson was of course very wrong and totally unwarranted; but considering the very peculiar position in which the Transvaal stands towards Great Britain, I think it would have been far better to have said nothing. Our great wish has always been to keep on the best of terms with Germany, trying to act together, but I fear your Agents in the Colonies do the very reverse, which deeply grieves us. Let me hope that you will try and check this....

I hope you will take my remarks in good part, as they are entirely dictated by my desire for your good. VICTORIA R.I.

(b) Queen Victoria to the Emperor William II, 12 June 1899

Your other letter, I must say, has *greatly astonished* me. The tone in which you write about Lord Salisbury I can only attribute to a temporary irritation on your part, as I do not think you would otherwise have written in such a manner, and I doubt whether any Sovereign ever wrote in such terms to another Sovereign, and that Sovereign his own Grandmother, about their Prime Minister. I never should do such a thing, and I never personally attacked or complained of Prince Bismarck, though I knew well what a bitter enemy he was to England and all the harm he did.

I naturally at once communicated your complaint against him to Lord Salisbury, and I now enclose a memorandum he has written for my information, which entirely refutes the accusations, and which will show you that you are under a misapprehension.

LQV, 3rd ser. III, 8–9, 381–2

44. Salisbury's view of Queen Victoria's role in foreign policy making

As a collaborator in his [Lord Salisbury's] own particular business of foreign affairs, he continually affirmed her value. Her unrivalled experience in all the intricacies of international affairs, made presently available by her remarkable memory, was interpreted in the light of a strong common sense. Lord Salisbury used to express his approval, ungallantly, by saying that talking over public affairs with her was like talking with a man. She had certain strong partialities and antagonisms, but they did not cover a large field. The most prominent was her dislike and distrust of Russia....But he found reasoning with her a satisfactory process, even when it failed to persuade. Her judgment, when aroused, acted dispassionately and on large lines; she did not adhere to opinions simply because she had expressed them, or refuse to admit conviction when it came. And, above all, there were no secondary motives, no hidden or half-conscious purposes to stumble against in the darkness.

There was one department of knowledge in which her assistance was peculiarly useful to him. Drawing her facts from her large private correspondence, illuminated by old experience, she would discuss the characters and motives of the sovereigns and statesmen of Europe much in the same way that an intelligent and observant country gentleman's wife might discuss those of her country neighbours.... It was a point of view outside the reach of official diplomats.   Cecil, *Salisbury*, III, 184-5

THE POSITION OF PRINCE ALBERT AND THE PRINCE OF WALES

45. Prince Albert reviews his position, 1841

[Memorandum by George Anson, 27 July 1841]

The Prince went yesterday through a review of the many steps he had made to his present position—all within eighteen months from the marriage. Those who intended to keep him from being useful to the Queen, from the fear that he might ambitiously touch upon her prerogatives, have been completely foiled; they thought they had prevented Her Majesty from yielding anything of importance to him by creating distrust through imaginary alarm. The Queen's good sense, however, has seen that the Prince has no other object in all he seeks but a means to Her Majesty's good. The Court from highest to lowest is brought to a proper sense of the position of the Queen's husband. The country has marked its confidence in his character by passing the Regency Bill *nem. con.* The Queen finds the value of an active right hand and able head to support her and to resort to for advice in time of need. Cabinet Ministers treat him with deference and respect. Arts and science look up to him as their especial patron, and they find this encouragement supported by a full knowledge of the details of every subject. The good and the wise look up to him with pride and gratitude as giving an example, so rarely shown in such a station, of leading a virtuous and religious life.   *LQV*, 1st ser. I, 371

46. Queen Victoria on the lack of a constitutional status for her husband, 1856

[Memorandum by Queen Victoria, May 1856]

It is a strange omission in our Constitution that while *the wife* of a *King* has the highest rank and dignity in the realm after her husband assigned to her by law, the *husband* of a *Queen regnant* is entirely ignored by the law. This is the more extraordinary, as a husband has in this country such particular rights and such great power over his wife, and as the Queen is married just as any other woman is, and swears to obey her lord and master, as such, while by law he has no rank or defined position. This is a strange anomaly. No doubt, as is the case *now*—the Queen *can* give her husband the highest *place* by *placing* him *always near her person*, and the Nation would give it him as a *matter of course*. Still, when I first married, we had much difficulty on this subject; much bad feeling was shown, and several members of the Royal Family showed bad grace in giving precedence to the Prince, and the late King of Hanover positively resisted doing so. I gave the Prince precedence by issuing Letters Patent, but these give no rank in Parliament—or at the Council Board—and it would be far better to put this question beyond all doubt, and to secure its settlement for *all future Consorts of Queens*, and thus have this omission in the Constitution rectified. Naturally my own feeling would be to give the Prince the same title and rank as I have, but a Titular King is a complete novelty in this country, and might be productive of more inconveniences than advantages to the individual who bears it. Therefore, upon mature reflection, and after considering the question for nearly *sixteen years*, I have come to the conclusion that the title which is now by universal consent given him of 'Prince Consort', with the highest rank in and out of Parliament immediately after the Queen, and before every other Prince of the Royal Family, should be the one assigned to the husband of the Queen regnant *once and for all*. This ought to be done before our children grow up, and it seems peculiarly easy to do so *now* that none of the old branches of the Royal Family are still alive.   *LQV*, 1st ser. III, 244–5

47. The title Prince Consort created by Order in Council, 25 June 1857

Whereas there was this day read at the Board the draft of Letters Patent, conferring upon His Royal Highness Prince Albert the title and dignity of Prince Consort, Her Majesty, having taken the same into consideration, was pleased, by and with the advice of Her Privy Council, to approve thereof. . . .   *London Gazette*, 26 June 1857

48. The Prince of Wales excluded from policy making, 1864
[General Grey to Earl Russell, 4 June 1864]

The Prince of Wales seems to be under some misapprehension about the communication of despatches from the Foreign Office; for he seems to think you would have no objection to communicate them to him direct, and thus to keep him acquainted with the policy of her Majesty's Government.

As I have already said, the Queen entirely sympathises in this wish on his part, and thinks it should be gratified as far as possible; and, regulated and controlled, as it would be, by you, there might probably be no great harm in the direct communication his Royal Highness wishes to establish.

But the Queen cannot help objecting to the *principle*, which would be thus admitted, of separate and independent communication between the Prince of Wales and her Government. The principle once admitted, it would be exceedingly difficult to limit the extent to which it might be acted upon.

Were the Prince of Wales to be cognisant of the confidential discussions between the Queen and her Ministers, as to the course to be pursued by this country; and were he to take antagonistic views on any important question (as he probably would have done on this Danish question), great inconvenience, not to say injury, might be occasioned to the public service. *LQV*, 2nd ser. I, 210–11

A Council of State Created
49. A Council of State to act during the King's absence in India, created by Order in Council, 10 November 1911

His Majesty in Council was, this day, pleased to declare His intention of going out of the Kingdom for the purpose of celebrating in His Indian Dominions the solemnity of His Coronation, whereupon the Draft of a Commission making provision for the summoning and holding of the Privy Council and for the transaction of other matters and things on behalf of His Majesty during His absence was this day read at the Board and approved; and His Majesty was further pleased to nominate His Royal Highness Prince Arthur Frederick Patrick Albert of Connaught...the...Archbishop of Canterbury...Earl Loreburn... Lord High Chancellor of Great Britain, and...Viscount Morley of Blackburn... Lord President of the Council, for the purposes therein mentioned, and to declare that they should be designated under the style and title of Counsellors of State.

London Gazette, 10 November 1911

B THE PRIME MINISTER

The office of Prime Minister first took on its modern character under Pitt the Younger, although the Prime Minister was not formally recognised as such until 1905 (**56**). The Prime Minister was charged with three main responsibilities: the management of Cabinet, parliament and party; the conduct of foreign affairs in association with the Foreign Secretary; and the handling of those crises and those great measures which marked the life of every ministry. Lord Liverpool showed how men of discordant views and temperaments might be induced to pull together as an efficient team, and every successive Prime Minister looked back upon Liverpool's long period of office with a certain nostalgia. Peel, for most of his contemporaries, was the paragon of premiers; hard working, thoroughly trained in administrative techniques, and capable of running every department of government simultaneously. But each Prime Minister had to work with a different set of men and in different conditions, and for most of them even to survive was a triumph. Each man developed his own characteristic way of managing a government, and few Prime Ministers found that they could manage things in the way they would have preferred.

After Peel's 1841–6 ministry, which was dominated by Peel, Graham, Goulburn and Gladstone, the idea got about that all cabinets should form a tightly knit team working under the direction of a strong Prime Minister. But most other Cabinets were, in fact, very unlike the Peel Cabinet. Russell and Palmerston both had great difficulty in managing their ministerial team. Aberdeen had disconcertingly little control over his colleagues. And even supposedly strong Prime Ministers like Gladstone, Disraeli, Salisbury and Asquith were criticised by colleagues and civil servants for letting their colleagues get out of hand (**53–4, 81**). Indeed, the criticisms Salisbury made of Disraeli in 1880 were to be made in very similar language by Hicks Beach of Salisbury, after Salisbury's death. Clearly very much depended on the personality of the Prime Minister and his general political position. A Prime Minister in the Commons was always more likely to get his own way than a Prime Minister in the Lords, because the Leader of the House of Commons was in a position to impose a sort of veto on legislation of which he disapproved. But a Prime Minister in the Lords had the advantage of more time free for public business, and a more dispassionate view of current crises: Lord Salisbury was quite as effective a Prime Minister as Gladstone, even though his range of electoral activities was limited because he was a peer. The major danger was lest a Prime Minister should become tired and slack, as happened with Disraeli, Salisbury and Asquith.

The monarch's choice of Prime Minister was an easy one only when each of the major parties had a clearly designated leader and one of the parties possessed a majority in parliament. In 1841 there was no doubt that Peel was, in effect, chosen by popular acclamation (50), and the same thing happened in the case of Gladstone in 1868 and 1880. In 1868 Disraeli underlined the fact that the people had opted for his opponents, by resigning before parliament met. And in similar circumstances in 1874, 1880 and 1886 this precedent was followed (108).

But the state of politics was rarely as simple as in 1841, 1868 and 1874, when the Queen had simply to send a straightforward invitation to the leader of the Opposition to take office. Even in 1880 there were complications, because although Gladstone's Midlothian campaign dominated the conduct of the general election, Gladstone was not himself the leader of the Liberal party. The Queen was, therefore, bound to turn to the Liberal leaders in Lords and Commons (Granville and Hartington) before asking Gladstone to take office. The choice of Prime Minister was naturally most difficult in those cases when there was no single statesman to whom the monarch could entrust the promotion of a government in the sure knowledge that he would be able to form a ministry. On Liverpool's resignation in 1827, on Canning's death in 1827, on Derby's defeat in 1852, and on Gladstone's resignation in 1894, the choice of a Prime Minister was particularly difficult.

Where the monarch had some freedom of choice the decision as to which man should be invited to form a ministry depended largely on the circumstances of the time. It was customary for the monarch to take the advice of the outgoing Prime Minister, if it were possible, but the monarch was not bound to ask for such advice, nor to take it if given. Gladstone was affronted when he retired in 1894 at not being consulted by the Queen about the choice of his successor, but he recognised that the Queen was entitled to dispense with his advice. Usually there was a good deal of negotiation between the monarch and leading statesmen (61-4).

In theory, at least, the most important powers possessed by the Prime Minister as an individual were the right to form and reorganise a ministry in the way he chose. Offices were normally filled by the Prime Minister after discussion with those whom he wished to become his leading colleagues and with the Chief Whip in the House of Commons (90-6), but appointments might be vetoed by the monarch. The leading ministers usually chose themselves because of their proved efficacy; the remaining places were filled up on the recommendation of the Prime Minister's friends, after taking into account the stream of applications that every Prime Minister received. Some ministers were allowed to choose their own under-secretaries; others were asked to accept people who had to be found a place. The royal veto was rarely an absolute one, since a man the King or Queen disliked could usually be placed in an office which did not require much personal contact with the sovereign. But the royal review of appointments was never a formality, and many Prime Ministers welcomed the opportunity to talk over the character of potential ministers with a well-informed professional of a different type—the monarch.

Curiously enough, there was a good deal of uncertainty as to whether the Prime Minister had the right to dismiss ministers he had appointed. Even in 1873, when experience had demonstrated that four leading ministers, Lowe, Bruce, Ayrton and Monsell, were a serious liability to the government, Gladstone felt bound to keep three of them in the ministry, but in different posts, while the fourth, Monsell, was given a peerage as a compensation for loss of office. In 1884 when Gladstone wanted a place in the Cabinet for Rosebery, he found it impossible to dislodge Lord Carlingford, who refused to give up his place in the Cabinet and become an ambassador. Sir William Harcourt argued that Carlingford should be dismissed (95), but Gladstone felt that he lacked the authority to dismiss a minister. His failure to act in this case made it practically impossible for Salisbury to dismiss a bad Home Secretary (Matthews), for as Salisbury said, 'There is no instance of dismissal; and it would require some open and palpable error to justify it.'[1] Right down to 1914 it was felt that ministers had a prescriptive right to retain their office until the government came to an end or until they were offered some compensation. Indeed, even elderly ministers proved singularly hard to get rid of, and the failing eighty-year-old Lord Wolverhampton was persuaded to resign in 1910 only with the greatest difficulty, although he was quite unable to perform the work of his office.[2]

One of the most difficult of all the responsibilities borne by the Prime Minister was that of keeping up the morale of the ministry, even when things were going badly. This was something that no Prime Minister during the nineteenth century did better than Palmerston. He spent a great deal of time in discussing matters with back-bench members of the House of Commons, and he was astonishingly fertile in devising little speeches that heartened his followers. Above all, he was always available when he was wanted, even though this meant working immensely long hours (106).

THE CHARACTER OF THE OFFICE

50. The people choose a Prime Minister, 1841

[J. W. Croker to Sir Robert Peel, 20 July 1841]

The elections are wonderful, and the curiosity is that all turns on the name of Sir Robert Peel. 'Tis the first time that I remember in our history that the people have chosen the first Minister for the Sovereign.

[1] *LQV*, 3rd ser. I, 646
[2] FitzRoy, *Memoirs*, II, 40–56.

Mr. Pitt's case in '84 is the nearest analogy; but then the people only confirmed the Sovereign's choice; here every Conservative candidate professed himself in plain words to be Sir Robert Peel's man, and on that ground was elected. *Parker, Peel, II, 475*

51. Gladstone on the Cabinet and the Prime Minister, 1878

The nicest of all the adjustments involved in the working of the British Government is that which determines, without formally defining, the internal relations of the Cabinet. On the one hand, while each Minister is an adviser of the Crown, the Cabinet is an unity, and none of its members can advise as an individual, without, or in opposition actual or presumed to, his colleagues. On the other hand, the business of the State is a hundredfold too great in volume to allow of the actual passing of the whole under the view of the collected Ministry. It is therefore a prime office of discretion for each Minister to settle what are the departmental acts in which he can presume the concurrence of his colleagues, and in what more delicate, or weighty, or peculiar cases, he must positively ascertain it. So much for the relation of each Minister to the Cabinet; but here we touch the point which involves another relation, perhaps the least known of all, his relation to its head.

The head of the British Government is not a Grand Vizier. He has no powers, properly so called, over his colleagues: on the rare occasions, when a Cabinet determines its course by the votes of its members, his vote counts only as one of theirs. But they are appointed and dismissed by the Sovereign on his advice. In a perfectly organised administration, such for example as was that of Sir Robert Peel in 1841–6, nothing of great importance is matured, or would even be projected, in any department without his personal cognisance; and any weighty business would commonly go to him before being submitted to the Cabinet. He reports to the Sovereign its proceedings, and he also has many audiences of the august occupant of the Throne. He is bound, in these reports and audiences, not to counterwork the Cabinet; not to divide it; not to undermine the position of any of his colleagues in the Royal favour. If he departs in any degree from strict adherence to these rules, and uses his great opportunities to increase his own influence, or pursue aims not shared by his colleagues, then, unless he is prepared to advise their dismissal, he not only departs from rule, but commits an act of treachery and baseness. As the Cabinet stands between the Sovereign and the Parliament, and is bound to be loyal to both, so he stands between his colleagues and the Sovereign, and is bound to be loyal to both.

...The Prime Minister has no title to override any one of his colleagues in any one of the departments. So far as he governs them, unless it is done by trick, which is not to be supposed, he governs them by influence only. But upon the whole, nowhere in the wide world does so great a substance cast so small a shadow; nowhere is there a man who has so much power, with so little to show for it in the way of formal title or prerogative. Gladstone, *Gleanings*, I, 242–4

52. John Morley on Gladstone and the Cabinet of 1880–5

In common talk and in partisan speeches, the prime minister was regarded as dictatorial and imperious. The complaint of some at least among his colleagues in the cabinet of 1880 was rather that he was not imperious enough. Almost from the first he too frequently allowed himself to be over-ruled; often in secondary matters, it is true, but sometimes also in matters on the uncertain frontier between secondary and primary. Then he adopted a practice of taking votes and counting numbers, of which more than one old hand complained as an innovation. Lord Granville said to him in 1886, 'I think you too often counted noses in your last cabinet'.

What Mr. Gladstone described as the severest fight that he had ever known in any cabinet occurred in 1883, upon the removal of the Duke of Wellington's statue from Hyde Park Corner. A vote took place, and three times over he took down the names. He was against removal, but was unable to have his own way over the majority. Members of the government thought themselves curiously free to walk out from divisions. On a Transvaal division two members of the cabinet abstained, and so did two other ministers out of the cabinet. In other cases, the same thing happened, not only breaking discipline, but breeding much trouble with the Queen.

*   *   *

In fact Mr. Gladstone found that the ministry of which he stood at the head was a coalition, and what was more, a coalition of that vexatious kind, where those who happened not to agree sometimes seemed to be almost as well pleased with contention as with harmony. The two sections were not always divided by differences of class or station, for some of the peers in the cabinet often showed as bold a liberalism as any of the commoners. This notwithstanding, it happened on more than one critical occasion, that all the peers *plus* Lord Hartington were on one side, and all the commoners on the other. Lord Hartington was in many respects the lineal successor of Palmerston in his coolness on parliamentary reform, in his inclination to stand in the old ways, in his extreme suspicion of what savoured of sentiment or idealism or high-flown profession. But he was a Palmerston who respected Mr. Gladstone, and desired to work faithfully under him, instead of being a Palmerston who always intended to keep the upper hand of him. Confronting Lord Hartington was Mr. Chamberlain, eager, intrepid, self-reliant, alert, daring, with notions about property, taxation, land, schools, popular rights, that he expressed with a plainness and pungency of speech that had never been heard from a privy councillor and cabinet minister before, that exasperated opponents, startled the whigs, and brought him hosts of adherents among radicals out of doors. It was at a very early stage in the existence of the government, that this important man said to an ally in the cabinet, 'I don't see how we are to get on, if Mr. Gladstone goes'. And here was the key to many leading incidents, both during the life of this administration and for the eventful year in Mr. Gladstone's career that followed its demise.

Morley, *Gladstone*, III, 5, 3

53. Salisbury on Disraeli as Prime Minister

[Arthur Balfour records a conversation with Salisbury, 8 May 1880]

As the head of a Cabinet his fault was want of firmness. The chiefs of Departments got their own way too much. The Cabinet as a whole got it too little, and this necessarily followed from having at the head of affairs a statesman whose only final political principle was that the Party must on no account be broken up, and who shrank therefore from exercising coercion on any of his subordinates. Thus it became possible that the Transvaal should be annexed—not indeed against the wish of the Cabinet, but actually without its knowledge. Lord Carnarvon wished to do it. Lord Beaconsfield was persuaded that it was an excellent thing to do: *i.e.*, the responsible head of the Department told him, and he believed, that it was an excellent thing to do, and it was done.

Again—Bartle Frere should have been recalled [from the Cape] as soon as the news of his ultimatum reached England. We should then have escaped in appearance, as well as in reality, the responsibility of the Zulu War. So thought the majority of the Cabinet, so thought Dizzy himself. But the Queen was strongly opposed to it; and Hicks-Beach was strongly opposed to it; and the Prime Minister was unable to resist his Sovereign and the Colonial Secretary together. Again, it was decided in Cabinet that the invasion of Afghanistan should take place only through one Pass. Lytton [Viceroy of India] objected. Because Lytton did, Hardy [Secretary of State for India] did. Because Hardy did, Dizzy did: for was not Hardy at the head of the India Office? And so the plans were altered.

The Eastern policy of the Government suffered much through having at the head of affairs a man who, with all his great qualities, was unable to decide a general principle of action, or to ensure that when decided on it should be carried out by his subordinates. When Lord S[alisbury] was going to Constantinople for the Conference he constantly urged upon his colleagues that it was little use his going unless it was previously decided exactly what should be done in the event of the Turks refusing the proposition of the Powers. 'Oh, but they won't refuse,' was the only answer he could ever get; and with that he had to be content. At a later period a clear line of action should have been decided on, respecting the Russian advances on Constantinople. It might have been possible (though probably not expedient) to stop them at the Danube. With the help of Austria it might have been possible *and* expedient to stop them at the Balkans. Dizzy's natural policy would probably have been the first. But with a man like him at the head of affairs who *could* not look far ahead, and with a man like Derby [Foreign Secretary] who *would* not look far ahead, we naturally drifted.

Lord Derby indeed would never have consented to fixing on any determinate line of policy which would, or might, end in serious and decided action; and Dizzy shrunk to the last from insisting on anything to which Lord Derby would have refused his consent.

Balfour, *Chapters of Autobiography*, pp. 113–15

54. Hicks Beach on Salisbury as Prime Minister

I think his kindness sometimes amounted to a fault: I feel sure that on more than one occasion it led him to give office to persons who ought to have been left out, because he could not hurt their feelings. There was much in what we call public life that was distasteful to him. He kept aloof from the Carlton and political society, and cordially despised 'honours' and the men who sought them. I think this feeling may have made him sometimes a little careless about his recommendations in such matters. He hated wire-pulling, self-advertisement, and all the meaner arts of politics; nor do I think that he liked a political career for its own sake. I once ventured to say in a speech that I believed it was only a strong sense of duty to his country that dragged him from scientific pursuits and home interests to the work of a Prime Minister; and from the way in which he thanked me I believe I was right. On the leading questions of Home politics of the time, such as the constitution of Parliament, Local Government, or Irish Land, he was more Tory than his colleagues; but, though certainly no 'Tory Democrat', he was keen about the housing of the poor and sanitary improvement. He had small respect for the opinions of the House of Commons, and constantly chafed against his obligation as Prime Minister to support in the Lords proposals to which his colleagues in the Commons had been obliged to agree.

Partly, perhaps, on this ground, partly on account of the engrossing nature of the Foreign Office work in which he was so long engaged, he seemed less interested in home than in foreign politics; and certainly as Prime Minister he did not exercise the control over his colleagues, either in or out of Cabinet, that Lord Beaconsfield did. I have known Lord Beaconsfield enforce his own view on the Cabinet after all of its members but one had expressed a different opinion; Lord Salisbury frequently allowed important matters to be decided by a small majority of votes, even against his own opinion. Lord Beaconsfield kept a very watchful eye on the proceedings of all his colleagues. When I was Irish Secretary in 1874, the *Daily News* had an article charging me with a new departure in Irish Education. On the next morning a letter came to Dublin from Mr. Disraeli asking for an explanation. Lord Salisbury left his colleagues very much to themselves, unless they consulted him. . . .

In my opinion, Lord Salisbury's record as Prime Minister and Foreign Secretary would have gained if his nature had been harder and more self-assertive; but this might possibly have detracted from his personal charm, which is no small asset in the conduct of affairs.

His was a fine character. Wise, patient and courageous; possessed of very high intellectual, oratorical and literary powers. Never thinking of his own position, or courting popularity, he devoted himself, often at the sacrifice of his own opinions and inclinations, in the true spirit of duty to 'carrying on the Queen's Government'....

Hicks Beach, Sir Michael Hicks Beach, II, 360–1, 363

55. The office of Prime Minister revived, 1900

[Sir H. Campbell-Bannerman at Dundee, 16 November 1900]

In the first place, let me congratulate you, as men really interested in the welfare of your country and this great Empire, on this—that the Government have thought fit to revive an ancient and time-honoured office, which we have always found useful in this country in past years—I mean the office of Prime Minister which has been completely in abeyance and under eclipse for the last five years [while Lord Salisbury was Foreign Secretary as well as Prime Minister]. I say it has been in abeyance because every one knows it is absolutely impossible for any man who conducts the foreign affairs of this country, at the same time to supervise and take charge of the general action of the Government. I hope, therefore, that in the future there may be a little more consistency in their action and a little more care in their legislation, and, above all, a little more care and prudence and better supervision over their foreign, their external, policy, and, above all, their colonial policy. Lord Salisbury will bring to bear on these great purposes the cynical wisdom which is his characteristic, and which evokes from his fellow-countrymen a correspondingly and sympathetically cynical confidence in it. Campbell-Bannerman, Speeches, p. 51

56. The office of Prime Minister officially recognised by King Edward VII, 4 December 1905

Know ye...that in the exercise of our Royal Prerogative We do hereby declare Our Royal Will and Pleasure that in all times hereafter the Prime Minister of Us, Our Heirs and Successors, shall have place and precedence next after the Archbishop of York.

London Gazette, 5 December 1905

A Prime Minister in the Lords and the Leader of the House of Commons

57. Gladstone accepts Russell's invitation to lead the House of Commons, 1865, but makes his own terms

[W. E. Gladstone to Earl Russell, 23 October 1865]

You having thought fit to propose that I should lead the House of Commons, I felt it necessary first to be assured that Sir Geo Grey, who was in constructive possession of that office, and under whom I should have served with perfect satisfaction, could not be induced to accept the duty. Of this your letter seemed to contain sufficient proof.

Next, I felt it to be necessary that some arrangement should be made for relieving me of a considerable & singularly disabling class of business, consisting of the cases of real or supposed grievance, at all times arising in connection with the collection of the public revenue under its several heads. The effectual mode of doing this, and of providing at the same time for much other good, would be a reorganisation of the Board of Treasury. For prudential reasons I do not propose this at the present moment: but will endeavour to suggest some less disturbing expedient, at least for the time.

The third difficulty which I named to you in the way of my accepting your proposal, is what I venture to call the lop-sided condition of the Government, with the strain & stress of administration in the H. of Commons, and nearly all the offices about which the H. of Commons cares, represented by Heads in the House of Lords.

This difficulty will even be aggravated, when Ld. Clarence Paget, who has so long managed several matters in chief, & with so much tact & ability, quits the government.

It weighs very seriously on my mind, and I beg you to *consider* it.

The introduction of at least one naval member of the Board of Admiralty at this juncture into Parliament, seems on its own grounds quite necessary. . . .   Gladstone Papers. Add. MS. 44, 292, fos. 198–9

58. Gladstone on the difficulties of a peer Prime Minister, 1878

The overweight. . .of the House of Commons [in Parliament] is apt, other things being equal, to bring its Leader inconveniently near in power to a Prime Minister who is a Peer. He can play off the House of Commons against his chief; and instances might be cited, though they are happily most rare, when he has served him very ugly tricks.

Gladstone, Gleanings, I, 242

59. Harcourt lays down the terms on which he will lead the Commons, 1894

[Memorandum by Sir William Harcourt, 2 March 1894]

I must, however, express a very distinct opinion that no man could attempt to lead the Liberal Party in the House of Commons with the smallest chance of success who was not armed, and known to be armed, with the authority essential to such a position.

Among the particulars of such authority, the following seem to be obvious:—

I. He must have power and discretion upon emergencies arising in the House of Commons to act upon his own judgment upon the spot, as the occasion appears to require, and it must not be understood that he has to await directions to be obtained *aliunde*.

II. In relation to foreign affairs he must stand in the same position in respect of communication and consultation beforehand upon all important decisions before they are adopted as that which belongs to the Prime Minister. It is plain that upon no other condition could he be responsible for the defence of foreign policy in the House of Commons.

III. He should be consulted on appointments, as the opinion of the House of Commons in such matters greatly affects the stability of an administration.

IV. It should be understood that upon his request a Cabinet should be summoned to consider questions which he regards as material.

V. The practice of direct communication by the Leader of the House of Commons with the Queen upon questions of general policy is already recognized.

Gardiner, Harcourt, II, 627–8

60. Rosebery laments his fate as Prime Minister, 1894

[Earl of Rosebery to Queen Victoria, 14 May 1894]

He is as Prime Minister more unfortunately situated than any man who ever held that high office. He has inherited from his predecessor a policy, a Cabinet, and a Parliament; besides a party of groups, one of which is aimed against himself. All this is kept in existence by a narrow majority which may at any moment break away. He himself is only able to guide this tumultuous party through a leader, bitterly hostile to himself, and ostentatiously indifferent to the fate of the Government.

Lord Rosebery in the meantime is shut up in a House almost unanimously opposed to his ministry, and, for all political purposes, might as well be in the Tower of London.

Under these circumstances, though he hates making speeches anywhere, he has no course open to him but to speak in the country. Otherwise, little known as he is, he would be completely eclipsed by the leader of the House of Commons, and obliterated as Prime Minister.

As to policy, he is pledged to the policy of Mr. Gladstone's Government, having formed part of that Government. He has no power (even had he the desire) to dissociate himself from it. He did not indeed take an active part in the framing of the measures of that Government, but he is none the less responsible for them. LQV, 3rd ser. II, 399

THE PRIME MINISTER AND THE CHOICE OF HIS SUCCESSOR
61. Melbourne advises the Queen to send for Wellington, 1839
[Viscount Melbourne to Queen Victoria, 7 May 1839]

The present circumstances have been for some time so probable, or rather so certain, that Lord Melbourne has naturally been led to weigh and consider maturely the advice which, if called upon, he should tender to your Majesty when they did arrive. That advice is, at once to send for the Duke of Wellington. Your Majesty appears to Lord Melbourne to have no other alternative. The Radicals have neither ability, honesty, nor numbers. They have no leaders of any character. Lord Durham was raised, one hardly knows how, into something of a factitious importance by his own extreme opinions, by the panegyrics of those who thought he would serve them as an instrument, and by the management of the Press, but any little public reputation which he might once have acquired has been entirely dissipated and destroyed by the continued folly of his conduct in his Canadian Government. There is no party in the State to which your Majesty can now resort, except that great party which calls itself Conservative, and of that party, his rank, station, reputation, and experience point out the Duke of Wellington as the person to whom your Majesty should apply.

Lord Melbourne therefore advises that your Majesty should send for the Duke of Wellington, and should acquaint him, provided your Majesty so feels, that you were entirely satisfied with your late Government, and that you part from them with reluctance; but that as he and the party of which he is the head have been the means of removing them from office, you naturally look to him to advise you as to the means of supplying their places and carrying on the business of the country.

If the Duke should be unwilling to form the Government himself, and should desire to devolve the task upon Sir Robert Peel, Lord Melbourne would advise your Majesty to accede to that suggestion; but Lord Melbourne would counsel your Majesty to be very unwilling to suffer the Government to be formed by Sir Robert Peel without the active assistance in office of the Duke of Wellington.

With respect both to measures and appointments, your Majesty should place the fullest confidence in those to whom you entrust the management of affairs, exercising at the same time, and fully expressing, your own judgment upon both.

Your Majesty will do well to be from the beginning very vigilant that all measures and all appointments are stated to your Majesty in the first instance, and your Majesty's pleasure taken thereon previously to any instruments being drawn out for carrying them into effect, and submitted to your Majesty's signature. It is the more necessary to be watchful and active in this respect, as the extreme confidence which your Majesty has reposed in me may have led to some omission at times of these most necessary preliminaries.   *LQV*, 1st ser. I, 195–6

62. Derby and Prince Albert on the selection of a new Prime Minister, 1852

[Memorandum by Prince Albert, 18 December 1852]

Yesterday evening Lord Derby arrived from Town formally to tender his resignation.... He felt that after having failed to obtain the confidence of Parliament himself, he could do nothing else than retire at once, and he advised the Queen to send for Lord Lansdowne, who knew better than anybody the state of Parties, and would give the best advice. He did not advise the Queen to send for Lord Aberdeen at once, because, if it were reported that he had given this advice, many of his Party—who had already been distressed at his declaration to

them that if he was defeated he would withdraw from public life—
would think it necessary to join Lord Aberdeen as their new appointed
leader; and then the other half, which felt the deepest indignation at the
treatment they had received from the Peelites, would throw themselves
into a reckless alliance with the Radicals, to revenge themselves upon the
new Government, so the great Conservative Party would be broken up,
which it was so essential for the country to keep together and moderate.

I interrupted Lord Derby, saying that, constitutionally speaking, it
did not rest with him to give advice and become responsible for it,
and that nobody therefore could properly throw the responsibility of
the Queen's choice of a new Minister upon him; the Queen had thought
of sending for Lord Lansdowne and Lord Aberdeen together. This,
Lord Derby said, would do very well; he knew that, strictly speaking,
the Sovereign acted upon her own responsibility, but it was always said
on such occasions, for instance, 'Lord John advised the Queen to send
for Lord Derby,' etc., etc.   *LQV*, 1st ser. II, 500–2

63. Edward VII prepares the way for a change of government, 1905
[Sir Henry Campbell-Bannerman (Leader of the Opposition) to J. B.
Smith, 11 September 1905]

The King is gone [from Marienbad] and we have some peace.
I saw a great deal of him and was treated with the utmost friendliness
and confidence: this was done openly and frankly, and I as well as
every one saw in it a desire to show that he would be on very good
terms with a Liberal Government. But though he discussed public
questions with me with the utmost frankness, he never even referred
to the actual political position and the question of dissolution, etc., etc.
So that he was perfectly loyal to his Ministers.

Spender, *Campbell-Bannerman*, II, 178

64. Asquith succeeds Campbell-Bannerman, 1908
(a) *H. H. Asquith to Margot Asquith, 4 March 1908*

I had quite a pleasant interview with the King after the Privy Council
yesterday. He talked sensibly about the Licensing Bill and other such
matters, and said generally that he thought the offices in the present
Government were very well filled, and that he would be sorry to see
anything in the nature of a general shuffling of the cards....

He said he had quite made up his mind to send for me at once in the event of anything happening to C.-B., or of his sending in his resignation. He thought it a pity C.-B. would not go to the Lords, and said there was no inconsistency in his doing so with his House of Lords policy. I told him I was sure C.-B. would never do it. He said he thought C.-B. very useful so long as he was equal to the job, as making things smooth and keeping people together. But it was evident that he was breaking up, and we must provide for the future: what were my plans? I told him I should do as little as possible—probably nothing —to alter the composition of the Cabinet or shift the men, at any rate until after the Session was over, and that in the meantime at any rate I should keep the Exchequer. He didn't know that this had ever been done, but I reminded him that Mr. G. combined the Offices twice, not to mention Pitt and others. He said it would be far the best arrangement. He talked a little all over the place, smoking a cigar, about Roosevelt, Macedonia, Congo, etc. He said that if a change became necessary he hoped I would at once come out to him at Biarritz. He was very agreeable, and ended by asking after you. Altogether it was quite a satisfactory interview.

(b) King Edward VII to H. H. Asquith, 4 April 1908

The King has received a letter from the Prime Minister tendering his resignation of the important post he occupies, owing to the very precarious state of his health and also by the advice of the medical men who are attending him. Under these circumstances the King regrets that he has no other alternative but to accept the resignation, and has answered Sir Henry Campbell-Bannerman to that effect.

The King now calls on the Chancellor of the Exchequer to form a government, and will be glad to see him here at any time that he can conveniently come in order to hear from him what proposals he has to make.

Spender and Asquith, Asquith, I, 195–6

C THE CABINET AND THE MINISTRY

The character of the Cabinet and of the ministry as a whole depended very largely on the Prime Minister (79). What every Cabinet had in common was that it included the heads of the major departments—the Chancellor of the Exchequer, the Secretaries of State for the Home, Foreign, Colonial, India and War Offices, and the First Lord of the Admiralty—along with the

Lord Chancellor, the Lord President of the Council and the Lord Privy Seal. Most Cabinets also included the Chancellor of the Duchy of Lancaster, the President of the Board of Trade and, (after 1859) the Chief Secretary for Ireland. In addition, there were a number of offices whose holders occasionally sat in the Cabinet. The usual size of the Cabinet was twelve to fifteen until 1885; thereafter the number gradually crept up to about twenty.[1] Asquith thought this was too big, and in retrospect thought that it might be reduced by doing away with all but one of the great sinecure offices. But because the increase in size was really dictated by the creation of new offices (Secretary for Scotland, President of the Board of Education, and President of the Board of Agriculture) and the need to find places for elder statesmen and young handymen in the Cabinet, not much could be done in practice to reduce the size of the Cabinet.

The main constitutional characteristic of the Cabinet was that it was charged collectively with responsibility for the work of the government as a whole. On some issues Cabinets could afford to differ, and did differ in public, although never so vehemently as members of the Liverpool government differed on Catholic emancipation. But the doctrine of collective responsibility was already well established by 1815, and ministers recognised that they must resign when they were out of sympathy with their colleagues. The chief problem here was that nineteenth-century Cabinets were often excessively vague about what their policy was. After 1839 no proper minutes were kept. The rule that discussions in Cabinet should be absolutely secret, that formal votes should be avoided and that no one but the Prime Minister should take notes,[2] made it hard for ministers to know just what had been decided. The only record formally kept was a report from the Prime Minister to the Sovereign after each meeting of the Cabinet. These reports, specimens of which are printed as numbers **65**, **68** and **69** below, often gave a good account of what had happened. But even the Prime Minister rarely kept duplicates of his Cabinet reports. And disconcertingly often ministers went away with quite erroneous ideas about what had actually happened (**67, 70**). Nor could anything be done to remedy this state of affairs, until after a Cabinet Secretariat was established in 1916.

The members of the Cabinet were chosen from among the relatively small group of people with official experience or a great public position, either as landed magnates or as popular leaders. Liverpool, Peel and Gladstone tried to ensure that the busy offices should so far as possible be held by those who had worked their way up the official ladder from an under-secretaryship or some similar office. They were very conscious that the reputation of the

[1] Lord Liverpool's Cabinet numbered 14 in 1812, Lord Grey's 13 in 1830, Peel's 14 in 1841, Gladstone's 15 in 1868, Disraeli's 12 in 1874, Salisbury's 19 in 1895, and Asquith's 20 in 1908.
[2] Morley, *Gladstone*, III, 114.

government depended in the last resort not on the number of dukes in the government (Disraeli started his career as Prime Minister with three) but on the way in which it handled everyday business. The working members of the government tended to be less aristocratic than their colleagues, and more likely to hold office for long periods. W. H. Smith, the newsagent, who was the most bourgeois of all nineteenth-century Tory ministers, actually ended up as Leader of the House of Commons under Lord Salisbury, and many Lord Chancellors had risen from very plebeian surroundings. However, every Cabinet also included quite a number of hereditary peers (96). The very few men who rose by their oratorical or political gifts alone (Disraeli, Bright, Lloyd George) were bad administrators whose chief value was their ability to get other people to do things and a certain shrewdness in general Cabinet discussions.

Because Cabinets were teams of like-minded men, it was usually possible to do most Cabinet business at meetings of the full Cabinet. But inevitably many topics had to be delegated to committees. For the most part, these committees were organised on an ad hoc basis to draft particular bills (usually with the assistance of the law officers). But committees were also set up to supervise particular military compaigns, and the Boer War was largely conducted by the newly formed Defence Committee of the Salisbury Cabinet (83–5). The Campbell-Bannerman and Asquith Cabinets were particularly prolific in Cabinet committees because of the large number of proposals for reform which were discussed, with the result that by 1907 there was a marked tendency for the Cabinet to divide into groups, and for members of the government to feel that it was not functioning satisfactorily as a team (81–2).

The amount of work a minister was expected to get through differed greatly from department to department, and so did the amount of control the cabinet exercised over his policies. Chancellors of the Exchequer, unless they were of a reforming turn of mind like Gladstone, or unless they were professional financiers like Goschen, would select the work they were interested in and leave the rest to the Financial Secretary of the Treasury, who managed the government's financial business in both the Treasury and the House of Commons. The annual budget, the highlight of the Chancellor's year, was prepared with very little reference to the Cabinet, unless the spending departments were demanding substantially increased allocations. Palmerston as Prime Minister actually let it be known that he disapproved of the major feature of Gladstone's 1861 budget, the repeal of the paper duties, but there was little he could do to control his headstrong Chancellor (157). Nonetheless, when the estimates on which the budget was based were debated in the Cabinet, Chancellors were often defeated, and Lord Randolph Churchill resigned in 1887 rather than accept increases in military expenditure.

The Foreign Secretary enjoyed a very real measure of independence in the making of policy, provided that he could carry the Prime Minister and the monarch along with him. The Cabinet was shown important foreign despatches, but few ministers had the knowledge to make useful comments upon them. Canning and Palmerston had very much their own way as Foreign Secretary, and so had Lord Clarendon, Lord Rosebery, Sir Edward Grey, and even the nimble but idle Lord Granville, who as a matter of principle referred all decisions to the Cabinet (**87**). It was very unusual for a Cabinet to become passionately concerned about foreign policy, as happened before and after the Crimean War, during the Near Eastern crisis of 1876, and at the time of the Agadir crisis in 1911. Lord Rosebery, indeed, worked for a bipartisan foreign policy outside the ordinary range of party politics (**88**). Elder statesmen argued that the Cabinet should be fully informed of foreign developments, and Gladstone disapproved of Lord Salisbury holding the premiership and the foreign secretaryship simultaneously, because it put him beyond the possibility of effective control by the Cabinet. But in fact the power of the Cabinet was on the decline at the end of the nineteenth century in both colonial and foreign affairs, because international negotiations were so complex that only a few ministers had the time to follow them in detail. Lord Rosebery and Joseph Chamberlain were able to pursue policies of their own with seeming impunity, and the negotiations which constituted the backbone of the twentieth-century *Entente* with France were carried on with little reference to the Cabinet (**86, 89**).

The relative independence of the Chancellor of the Exchequer and the Foreign Secretary was shared to a large extent by the other ministers, because the doctrine of the individual responsibility of ministers to parliament made all but the service ministers look as much to parliament as to the Cabinet. In law and in theory the minister was, in effect, the same as the department: he was responsible for everything that went on in his office, whether he had cognisance of it or not, and might be forced to resign if parliament disapproved his actions. In the heyday of the private member such forced resignations were sufficiently common to be a real threat to errant ministers. There were no full-scale impeachments after the attack on Lord Melville in 1806, but the House of Commons could easily secure its object by a simple motion of censure. Such motions were not common, and were rarely successful.[1] But during the period of uncertain parliamentary majorities in the 1850s and 1860s, a number of resolutions did bring down ministers. In 1855 Lord John Russell resigned the office of Colonial Secretary before a vote could be taken on the motion 'That the conduct of our Minister in the recent negotiations at Vienna has, in the opinion of this House, shaken the con-

---

[1] There is a useful list in Todd, *Parliamentary Government*, II, 471–84, and in Finer, *Public administration*, XXXIV, 377–96.

fidence of this country in those to whom its affairs are entrusted'[1]. In 1864 Robert Lowe, Vice-President of the Committee of Council on Education, resigned after a fierce attack on the work of the Education Department. And in 1865 Lord Westbury resigned after the House of Commons had passed a resolution condemning him for 'laxity of practice and a want of caution with regard to the public interests...in sanctioning the grant of retiring pensions to public officers against whom grave charges were pending'. Normally, however, a formal motion was not required. Most ministers were only too glad to get themselves out of a difficult position as soon as possible.

Ministers were normally expected to speak and vote on the same side of a question and to avoid public controversy with their colleagues (71–81). But the degree of cohesion enforced was a variable one. Some ministries formed a tightly-knit team that readily shed dissenters. Others resembled a loose coalition of uneasy allies. All ministries were forced to regard some subjects as 'open questions' because the government was incurably divided on them (women's suffrage was an important example of such an open question). And individual ministers working away in their departments were often conscious of playing little part in the formulation of the general policy of the government.

Happily, there was only a tiny number of cases of misuse of public office. Augustus Stafford-O'Brien-Stafford, Secretary of the Admiralty, would have been turned out in 1852 for misusing his position at the Admiralty to fix the result of elections in the dockyard towns, had not the government as a whole been defeated. A. J. Mundella, Gladstone's President of the Board of Trade, was forced to resign in 1894 because he was involved in the unsavoury affairs of a company which as President of the Board he was supposed to be investigating. And in 1911 there was the famous Marconi scandal, the rights and wrongs of which are very obscure: certainly a number of senior members of the government behaved very foolishly when they exposed themselves to the charge that they had used inside knowledge to make big financial gains on the stock exchange. Unfortunately the government chose to make the case a party issue and the rights and wrongs of the matter were never finally elucidated. The case left a nasty taste behind and supplied the anti-parliamentarians with welcome ammunition.[2]

The functions of posts outside the Cabinet changed from time to time. The great officers of the royal household (the Lord Chamberlain, Lord Steward, and Master of the Horse) gradually ceased to be active counsellors of the sovereign under Queen Victoria, though Lord Sydney, as Lord Chamberlain, was occasionally used as a link between the Cabinet and the court. The great officers still changed with the government, but their main qualification was now knowledge of court ceremonial, and the Duke of Bedford actually refused to become Master of the Horse in 1895 solely

---

[1] *Annual Register*, 1855, Pt. 1, p. 154.   [2] For details see Donaldson, *The Marconi Scandal*.

because he was not interested in horses. The junior officers of the royal household, by contrast, gradually became more political. Those in the House of Commons became government Whips and those in the Lords became spokesmen of individual departments or government Whips, carrying out these functions in addition to their turn of duty at court. Indeed, during the agricultural depression at the end of the nineteenth century many peers became very anxious to hold these offices on any terms, because their incomes were declining. Another significant change was the transfer of the Postmaster Generalship to the Commons in 1866. Before then it was not tenable with a seat in the Commons and was usually held by a peer. But as the Post Office grew in size and took on all the characteristics of a great commercial organisation, it was deemed expedient to make it answerable to the public through a minister in the Commons.

The functions of junior ministers were never clearly defined, nor their degree of independence (80). Secretaries of State and other busy ministers claimed the right to suggest a parliamentary under-secretary to the Prime Minister on the ground that the under-secretary was essentially the minister's personal assistant. On this ground Peel in 1822 wanted his brother as his under-secretary at the Home Office (90*a*) and Joseph Chamberlain insisted in 1886 on having his Birmingham crony, Jesse Collings, as his parliamentary secretary at the Local Government Board. But few active ministers, in fact, made efficient use of their parliamentary under-secretaries, unless the minister was in the Lords and the under-secretary in the Commons, where he was responsible for answering questions and presenting the departmental estimates. Peel found that his under-secretary at the Home Office had little to do (90*b*) and the same was true of Jesse Collings at the Local Government Board. As a consequence there was a hierarchy of junior ministers. The under-secretaries representing important departments with a Cabinet minister in the Lords, along with the secretaries of the Treasury, who had well-defined functions, constituted an elite on the verge of the Cabinet, which they hoped to enter in due course. Other junior ministers hoped to win promotion to an important under-secretaryship, but were just as likely to be fobbed off with a privy councillorship or a colonial governorship.

THE RECORDING OF CABINET PROCEEDINGS

65. A Cabinet letter, 1839[1]

[Viscount Melbourne to Queen Victoria, 10 February 1839]

Lord Melbourne presents his humble duty to your Majesty, and thinks it right and necessary to acquaint your Majesty that the Cabinet

---

[1] For a formal cabinet minute of the 1830s see (151).

yesterday was very stormy and unpleasant. Lord John Russell brought on the question of the Civil Government of the Army, in a temperate and judicious manner, but Lord Howick made a most violent speech, strongly condemning the whole of the present system and arraigning the conduct of the Treasury and other Departments, saying that he should not throw up his office because no measure was brought forward, but that, when questioned upon the subject by Mr. Hume in the House of Commons, as it was certain that he would be, he should say that Government would do nothing upon the subject, until he (Mr. Hume) compelled them, and that he should express his entire disapprobation of the present system, and his reasons in detail for that disapprobation. Your Majesty will perceive that nothing could be more violent than this course. It was borne with great patience by the rest of the Cabinet, although Mr. Rice [Chancellor of the Exchequer], against whom the greater part of Lord Howick's speech was directed, felt himself most deeply hurt, and so expressed himself in private afterwards to Lord Melbourne. Upon the whole, Lord Melbourne cannot but consider that affairs are in a most precarious state, and that whilst there is so much discontent fermenting within the Cabinet itself, there must be great doubt of Lord Melbourne's being much longer able to hold the Administration together.   *LQV*, 1st ser. I, 184–5

66. An unofficial Cabinet report on the Prusso-Danish War crisis, 1864
[Sir Charles Wood to General Grey, 24 June 1864]

We have had a long and not a conclusive Cabinet.
Decision:
1. Against war single-handed.
2. Against war [in conjunction] with France.
Then came the question:
3. Whether we should be quiet, reserving to ourselves to act or not if the existence of Denmark was threatened?
4. Or should intimate to Austria that her fleet should not enter the Baltic; and as a variety of this should send our fleet to the Cattegat.

This last was very much disliked as leading to complications in all probability which might end in war; and the opinion against sending the fleet gained ground during the discussion.

I think the Cabinet is very evenly divided; Gladstone, Granville, and I took the decided peace line. My position was that we were quite free in consequence of the refusal of both sides to agree to arbitration; that we stood, as we did in January, on the original proposal to act alone, or, with the European neutral Powers, for an European object; that as regarded the integrity of Denmark that was given up, and that, if its existence was threatened, it would be a new state of things to be dealt with by the other Powers of Europe as well as ourselves.

Granville took the same line, as did Gladstone, and Milner Gibson.

I think that the peace side is the heaviest. We meet again to-morrow at three, and I am in hopes that something will occur at the Conference to-morrow, which will strengthen us. The Emperor has backed out of all that Drouyn de Lhuys said. *LQV, 2nd ser. I, 228–9*

67. Hartington's secretary tries to find out what happened at Cabinet, 1882

[R. B. Brett to E. W. Hamilton, 6 July 1882]

Harcourt and Chamberlain have both been here this morning and *at* my Chief about yesterday's Cabinet proceedings. They cannot agree about what occurred. There must have been some decision, as Bright's resignation shows. My Chief has told me to ask you [Gladstone's Private Secretary] what the devil *was* decided, for he be damned if he knows. Will you ask Mr. G. in more conventional and less pungent terms? *Hankey, Diplomacy by Conference, pp. 66–7*

68. The Prime Minister's Cabinet report conveyed by telegraph, 1886

[Marquess of Salisbury to Queen Victoria, 17 January 1886]

Humble duty. Great differences in Cabinet to-day. Sir M. Beach, Lord R. Churchill, Lord G. Hamilton, and Viceroy were against measures for suppressing National League: the other twelve in favour. Discussion adjourned to Monday. *LQV, 3rd ser. I, 10*

69. A Gladstonian Cabinet letter, 1886

[W. E. Gladstone to Queen Victoria, 25 February 1886]

Mr. Gladstone reports to Your Majesty with his humble duty that the Cabinet today further considered the Crofters' Bill and the very peculiar circumstances with which it has to deal. They agreed upon the leading proposals of the Bill, which may lead to a good deal of debate.

The Cabinet were of opinion that it would be desirable to treat the question of the Woman's Suffrage Bill, which is expected to come on next week, as what is termed an open question. The Ministers generally however are as individuals disinclined to the Bill, & disposed to vote accordingly.

The question of Sir D. Wolff's mission to the East, which stands for early decision on the vote for the expences, was also considered by the Cabinet. The Government will support this vote, but will reserve their judgment on the policy and effect of the mission, until they are in possession of fuller information. They do not desire to disturb it if this can be avoided.

The Chancellor of the Exchequer informed the Cabinet that although the demands of the Military and Naval Departments had by careful effort been much reduced, there still remained an increase of a million more or less. This increase the Cabinet had no option but to accept, as unavoidable under the circumstances, although sensible that the great and frequent augmentations of these Estimates has now brought them to a point highly inconvenient in many points of view.

Cabinet Papers. Cab. 41/20/8

70. Confusion over Cabinet decisions: retrospect by Lord Curzon, 19 July 1918

There was no agenda, there was no order of business. Any Minister requiring to bring up a matter either of Departmental or of public importance had to seek the permission of the Prime Minister to do so. No one else, broadly speaking, was warned in advance. It was difficult for any Minister to secure an interstice in the discussion in which he could place his own case. No record whatever was kept of our proceedings, except the private and personal letter written by the Prime Minister to the Sovereign, the contents of which, of course, are never seen by anybody else. The Cabinet often had the very haziest notion as to what its decisions were; and I appeal not only to my own experience but to the experience of every Cabinet Minister who sits in this House, and to the records contained in the memoirs of half-a-dozen Prime Ministers in the past, that cases frequently arose when the matter was left so much in doubt that a Minister went away and acted upon what he thought was a decision which subsequently turned out to be no decision at all, or was repudiated by his colleagues. No one will deny that a system, however embedded in the traditions of the past and consecrated by constitutional custom, which was attended by these defects was a system which was destined, immediately it came into contact with the hard realities of war, to crumble into dust at once.

5 Hansard (Lords) xxx, 265

THE UNITY OF THE ADMINISTRATION

71. Canning endeavours to construct a ministry in which Roman Catholic emancipation is an open question, 1827

[George Canning to the Marquess of Lansdowne, 23 April 1827]

1. The Catholic question is to remain, as in Lord Liverpool's Government, an open question, upon which each member of the Cabinet is at perfect liberty to exercise his own judgment in supporting that question if brought forward by others, or in propounding it either in the Cabinet or to Parliament. But if any member of the Cabinet should deem it an indispensable duty to bring forward individually the Catholic question in Parliament, he is distinctly to state that he does so in his individual capacity.

2. The inconvenience (now unavoidable) of having *one* open question in the Cabinet, makes it the more necessary to agree that there should be no other. All the existing members of the Cabinet are united in opposing the question of Parliamentary Reform, and could not acquiesce in its being brought forward or supported by any member of the Cabinet.

3. The present members of the Cabinet are also united in opposition to the motion for the repeal of the Test Act, of which notice stands on the books of the House of Commons. They see great inexpediency in now stirring a question which has slept for upwards of 30 years, and they could not consent to a divided vote by the members of the Cabinet upon it. Aspinall, Formation of Canning's Ministry, p. 158

72. The Cabinet in disorder, 1828

[Viscount Palmerston's journal, 22 May 1828]

The Cabinet has gone on for some time past as it had done before, differing upon almost every question of any importance that has been brought under consideration:—meeting to debate and dispute, and separating without deciding. Bulwer, Palmerston, I, 250

73. A minister turned out for not voting for the government, 1832

[Earl Grey to King William IV, 29 January 1832]

...there is another office of much greater importance [Secretary-at-War], in which Earl Grey has now to inform your Majesty of a vacancy. Amongst those who left the House of Commons before the division on Mr. Herries's motion [with regard to the Russian-Dutch loan] was Sir H. Parnell. The strongest representations were made to him upon the nature of the question; the consequence of which, if it had been carried, must have been that your Majesty's servants could not have continued in office under a recorded censure of the House of Commons. Sir H. Parnell, notwithstanding, refused to vote; and upon Earl Grey's bringing this matter under the consideration of the Cabinet this morning, it has been unanimously agreed that a communication should be made, without loss of time, to Sir H Parnell, that, after such an occurrence, he cannot continue to hold his present office. Of this determination Earl Grey trusts that your Majesty will be pleased to approve.

[Sir J. C. Hobhouse was appointed to the vacancy.]

Grey, *Reform Act, 1832*, II, 164

74. Macaulay on 'open questions' in the Cabinet, 18 June 1839

Nothing was more common than to hear it said, that the first time a great question was left open was when Lord Liverpool's Administration left the Catholic question open. Now, there could not be a grosser error. Within the memory of many persons living, the general rule was this, that all questions whatever were open questions in a cabinet, except those which came under two classes—namely, first, measures brought forward by the Government as a Government, which all the members of it were, of course, expected to support; and, second, motions brought forward with the purpose of casting a censure, express or implied, on the Government, or any department of it, which all its members were, of course, expected to oppose.   3 *Hansard* XLVIII, 464

75. A disunited government, 1846

[Memorandum by Prince Albert, 6 July 1846]

The Government is not a united one, however, by any means. Mr. Wood and Lord Clarendon take the greatest credit in having induced Lord Grey to join the Government, and are responsible to Lord John to keep him quiet, which they think they will be able to do, as he had been convinced of the folly of his former line of conduct. Still, they say Lord Lansdowne will have the lead only nominally, that Lord Grey is to take it really in the House of Lords. There is the *Grey Party*, consisting of Lord Grey, Lord Clarendon, Sir George Grey, and Mr. Wood; they are against Lord Lansdowne, Lord Minto, Lord Auckland, and Sir John Hobhouse, stigmatising them as old women. Lord John leans entirely to the last-named gentlemen. There is no cordiality between Lord John and Lord Palmerston, who, if he had to make a choice, would even forget what passed in December last, and join the Grey Party in preference to Lord John personally. The curious part of all this is that they cannot keep a secret, and speak of all their differences. They got the *Times* over by giving it exclusive information, and the leading articles are sent in and praise the new Cabinet, but the wicked paper added immediately a furious attack upon Sir John Hobhouse, which alarmed them so much that they sent to Sir John, sounding him, whether he would be hereafter prepared to relinquish the Board of Control.

LQV, 1st ser. II, 101-2

76. Ministers complain that they are too busy to think about policy, 1850

Lord John Russell to the Select Committee on Official Salaries

I think that...it is rather a defect in the Government of this country, that while persons who are out of office, and who are in the House of Lords and in the House of Commons, can give their attention to great subjects, the time of the Ministers is so very much absorbed with the duties of their offices, that there are very few of them who can give their attention to a great subject, and look at the consequences to the country of the measures which are adopted.

SCOS, H.C. 611, pp. 128-9 (1850), XV, 227-8

Earl of Minto to the same

...at the time when I was First Lord of the Admiralty, it would have been quite impossible for me to give my attention to any other subject out of my own department. I was employed from breakfast time till a late hour in the evening, exclusively occupied in the business of the department; and I felt when I went into the Cabinet, that I was quite unable to give, or to form an opinion that was worth having, upon the great majority of questions that were there to be considered.

Ibid. pp. 147–8

77. Palmerston on the freedom of action of ministers, 1864

[Viscount Palmerston to W. E. Gladstone, 16 June 1864]

...a Member of the Government when he takes office necessarily divests himself of that perfect Freedom of individual action which belongs to a private and independent Member of Parliament and the Reason is this, that what a Member of the Government does and says upon public Matters must to a certain Degree commit his colleagues, and the Body to which he belongs if they by their Silence appear to acquiesce: and if any of them follow his Example and express as publicly, opposite opinions, which in particular Cases they might feel obliged to do, Differences of opinion between Members of the same Government are unnecessarily brought out into Prominence and the Strength of the Government is thereby impaired.

Upon a similar Principle it is undesirable that a Member of the Government should advise the House of Commons to object to, or try to reduce Estimates which the Government have proposed; or that he should Endeavour to excite Agitation out of Doors for the Purpose of forcing upon the Government, Measures which the Parliament may not be disposed to adopt, & which the Government upon a Review of the State of Things, may not think it advisable to propose.

Guedalla, *The Palmerston Papers*, p. 288

78. Three ministers abstain from supporting the Franchise Bill, 1884

[Cabinet Memorandum by W. E. Gladstone, 13 June 1884]

It has probably come to the notice of my colleagues that, in a division early this morning, which was known to be vital to the Franchise Bill and to the Government, three of its members abstained from voting.

Preliminary intimations had been given to this effect, and some effort had been made to bring about a different intention. This change of mind was hoped for, but no question of surprise can be raised.

It is however an elementary rule, necessary for the cohesion and character of Administrations, that on certain questions, and notably on questions vital to their existence their members should vote together.

In the event of their not doing so, their intention to quit the Government is presumed, and in all ordinary circumstances ought to take effect.

At the present moment, however, besides the charge of a great legislative measure, and an ever increasing mass of other business, the Ministry is rapidly approaching a crisis on a question of Foreign affairs which involves principles of the deepest importance not only to the welfare of Egypt but to the character and honour of the country, and to the law, the concord, and possibly even the peace of Europe.

It would be most unfortunate, were the minds of men at such a juncture to be disturbed by the resignation of a Cabinet Minister, and of two other gentlemen holding offices of great importance, on a question which important as it is relates mainly to the internal discipline & management of the official corps.

I therefore propose to my colleagues that I be authorised to request the President of the Local Government Board, the Postmaster General, and the Secretary to the Treasury, that they will do us the favour to retain their respective offices. Cabinet Papers. Cab. 37/12/31

79. John Morley on the structure of the Cabinet, 1889

The principal features of our system of Cabinet government to-day are four. The first is the doctrine of collective responsibility. Each Cabinet minister carries on the work of a particular department, and for that department he is individually answerable....In addition to this individual responsibility, each minister largely shares a collective responsibility with all other members of the government, for anything of high importance that is done in every other branch of the public business besides his own. The question whether the mistakes or misdeeds of one minister involves all the rest, is of course not quite independent of the position of the minister, or of the particular action. The censure and impeachment of Lord Melville, for example, was so purely personal in its bearings that it did not break up the government of Mr. Pitt. But as a general rule every important piece of departmental policy is taken to commit the entire Cabinet, and its members stand or fall together. The Chancellor of the Exchequer may be driven from office by a bad dispatch from the Foreign office, and an excellent Home Secretary may suffer for the blunders of a stupid Minister of War. The Cabinet is a unit—a unit as regards the sovereign, and a unit as regards the legislature. Its views are laid before the sovereign and before Parliament, as if they were the views of one man. It gives its advice as a single whole, both in the royal closet, and in the hereditary or the representative chamber. If that advice be not taken, provided the matter of it appear to be of proper importance, then the Cabinet, before or after an appeal to the electors, dissolves itself and disappears. The first mark of the Cabinet, as that institution is now understood, is united and indivisible responsibility.

The second mark is that the Cabinet is answerable immediately to the majority of the House of Commons, and ultimately to the electors whose will creates that majority. Responsibility to the Crown is slowly ceasing to be more than a constitutional fiction, though even as a fiction it possesses many practical conveniences. William IV, it is true, dismissed the Melbourne Government in 1834 of his own motion, and Sir Robert Peel stuck to the helm for his hundred days in spite of a hostile majority. But though such experiments may by bare possibility recur, they will hardly recur often, and they will never last long. The only real responsibility is to the House of Commons. Responsibility to the House of Lords means no more than that that House may temporarily resist bills of which it disapproves, until the sense of the electors of the House of Commons has been taken upon them. Even in Walpole's time, when the House of Lords passed a motion of censure upon the Spanish Convention in 1739, the minister paid no attention to it.

Third, the Cabinet is, except under uncommon, peculiar, and transitory circumstances, selected exclusively from one party. There have been coalitions of men of opposite parties, but in most cases, down to the present time, coalition has been only the preliminary of fusion. There have been conjunctions, again, of men openly holding directly opposite opinions on subjects going to the very foundations of government, and turning on the very principles that mark party difference. Lord Liverpool's Ministry, for instance, lasted for fourteen years, with so important an issue as Catholic emancipation left an open question. But notwithstanding both coalitions and open questions, it remains generally true that Cabinets are made from one party.

Fourth, the Prime Minister is the keystone of the Cabinet arch. Although in Cabinet all its members stand on an equal footing, speak with equal voice, and, on the rare occasions when a division is taken, are counted on the fraternal principle of one man, one vote, yet the head of the Cabinet is *primus inter pares*, and occupies a position which, so long as it lasts, is one of exceptional and peculiar authority. It is true that he is in form chosen by the Crown, but in practice the choice of the Crown is pretty strictly confined to the man who is designated by the acclamation of a party majority. If a party should chance to be divided or uncertain as to its leader, then undoubtedly, the favour of the Crown might suffice to turn the balance. There might be some exaggeration in saying that the veto of the Crown on a First Minister is virtually as dead as its veto on a bill; still the Crown could hardly exercise any real power either of selection or exclusion against the marked wishes of the constituencies.

The Prime Minister, once appointed, chooses his own colleagues, and assigns to them their respective offices. It sometimes happens that, in the case of very important colleagues, they are almost as effectually designated to him by public opinion and parliamentary position, as he is himself designated to the sovereign for his own high office. Still, there is more than a margin for his free exercise of choice in the persons admitted to his Cabinet, and in all cases it is for him alone to settle the distribution of posts. Constitutional respect for the Crown would inspire a natural regard for the personal wishes of the sovereign in recommendations to office, but royal predilections or prejudices will undoubtedly be less and less able to stand against the Prime Minister's strong view of the requirements of the public service.

The flexibility of the Cabinet system allows the Prime Minister in an emergency to take upon himself a power not inferior to that of a dictator, provided always that the House of Commons will stand by him. In ordinary circumstances he leaves the heads of departments to do their work in their own way. It is their duty freely and voluntarily to call him into council, on business of a certain order of importance. With the Foreign Secretary alone he is in close and continuous communication as to the business of his office. Foreign affairs must always be the matter of continuous thought in the mind of the Prime Minister. They are not continuously before the Cabinet; it has not therefore the same fulness of information as the Prime Minister; and consequently in this important department of public action, the Cabinet must for the most part, unless there be some special cause of excitement, depend upon the prudence and watchfulness of its head.

In case of differences arising between departments, it is to the Prime Minister that the appeal lies, and the regular course for a minister who is dissatisfied with his chief's decision is to retire. Where the Prime

Minister is displeased with the language or the action of a colleague, he possesses, indeed, no direct prerogative to call for his resignation, without going first to the sovereign and procuring her assent. But that assent could practically never be refused to a Prime Minister with a parliamentary majority, unless the sovereign were prepared to take new advisers and face a dissolution. Though it is just conceivable that the sovereign might remonstrate successfully against the minister's request for a colleague's dismissal, yet it is not likely that a minister would make a request of such moment without intending to abide by it and to press it to the end.

An important qualification of the Prime Minister's power exists in the case of the Crown. Here it is well understood that the sovereign has a right to demand the opinion of the Cabinet as a court of appeal against the Prime Minister or any other minister. It is now publicly known, for instance, that in the difficult foreign crisis of 1859–61 dispatches were frequently referred back by the sovereign from the Foreign Secretary and the Prime Minister to the Cabinet as a whole, and were there constantly modified in the sense desired. This is clearly a practical power left to the Crown, and if there chanced to be a strong Cabinet, the use of such a power might result in a considerable reduction of the Prime Minister's normal authority, and its transfer to the general body of his colleagues.

In filling up the highest posts within a department, such as the headship of the permanent staff, the nomination of an ambassador, or the appointment to the governorship of an important colony or the great dependency of India, the Prime Minister, though not taking the initiative, would still usually expect to be consulted by the minister more directly concerned. Even the Lord Chancellor is believed sometimes to go through the form of consulting him in filling vacancies on the judicial bench. Finally, just as the Cabinet has been described as being the regulator of relations between Queen, Lords, and Commons, so is the Prime Minister the regulator of relations between the queen and her servants. 'As the Cabinet stands between the sovereign and Parliament, so the Prime Minister stands between the sovereign and the Cabinet.' This does not mean that any minister is out of immediate communication with the Crown, in matters strictly affecting his own department as to which the Crown may desire to be informed; but only that outside of these matters it is the Prime Minister only who conveys to the sovereign the views of his colleagues. Such attempts to intrigue with the sovereign against a colleague as were common with Sunderland, Stanhope, Townshend, and Carteret, and as were long afterwards repeated with particular baseness by Lord Loughborough, when he secretly warned George III of Pitt's Catholic policy and advised him against it, are, we may be very confident, never likely to recur. Morley, *Walpole*, pp. 154–60

80. Salisbury on the importance of a reputation for loyalty in ministers, 1891

Marquess of Salisbury to Sir John Gorst, 7 September 1891

[Gorst, Under-Secretary for India, had on several occasions embarrassed the government by seeming to dissociate himself from his colleagues' actions.]

You claim a much wider freedom in the expression of your independent opinions than is customary among members of a government under our system: and you have in consequence embarrassed us considerably more than once during the past year. No serious evil resulted from it ultimately; but it gave rise to a good deal of angry comment in the party at the time; and I should not be surprised, if there were many who viewed your candidature [for promotion to Postmaster General] with apprehension as doubting how far you could be relied upon in difficulties....

I entertain—as everybody must do—the very highest estimate of your abilities, & I have seen with great sorrow the impediments you have thrown in your own way. I do not attempt to lay down any rule as to the amount of independence in his public action that a member of Government or a supporter of a Government may reasonably claim, without acting incompatibly with those designations. It is a mere question of prudence. You complain that you have not got on to the extent your abilities justified you in expecting. In order to secure the general support & confidence of a political party, something is more necessary than ability—& that is the general confidence that the party can rely upon you to stand by them at a pinch. No one can lay down by what acts, or by what abstinence from action, this confidence is to be won. I only express the fear, which what I heard in the Session suggested to me—& what you now tell me confirms—that your action on two or three occasions has seriously qualified the confidence which your great powers should otherwise inspire. Salisbury Papers

81. The ministry fails to work as a team, 1907–9

[The Diary of Sir Almeric FitzRoy.]

August 14th [1907]....Ministers are so overwhelmed with work, administrative and parliamentary, that departmental legislation falls more and more into the hands of the Minister in charge. Cabinet Committees are ineffective instruments for the preparation or criticism of Bills, and when circulated to the whole Cabinet, if seen at all, they obtain nothing but the most perfunctory attention. It thus happens that the Government is often deeply pledged to a scheme of reform wholly unsuited to the objects it has in view, and their *amour-propre* irretrievably involved in its promotion, before it is discovered that no one whose opinion is of any weight cares for it, and that the best course is to drop it outright....

November 12th [1908]. I had a somewhat confidential talk with the Lord President [Lord Wolverhampton] this morning which threw some light on the problems of Cabinet government at the present time. He reminded me that he and Asquith were the only two members of the Ministry who had ever held Cabinet office before, a fact which very much weakened the sense of collective responsibility affecting the whole body.

Lord Wolverhampton quoted Mr. Gladstone, who in sonorous phrase had declared the Cabinet to be 'one and indivisible', whereas, in the happy-go-lucky system which prevails to-day, there is constant risk of this or that member of it finding himself isolated, if not repudiated....

December 14th [1909]. I saw Hopwood [Permanent Under Secretary at the Colonial Office] this morning....

We had some talk about the personal idiosyncrasies of Ministers and the disposition to shirk trouble most of them display. With the exception of Haldane and Crewe, and perhaps Lord Morley and the Chancellor, there is not a hard worker among them, and their disinclination to read Cabinet papers, an incurable malady, has resulted in a departmental independence not far from ministerial anarchy. He told me that his practice at the Board of Trade, when he found Lloyd George would not read anything, was to put before him in a personal interview the salient points of the case, which he absorbed with a quickness and power of assimilation wholly remarkable. At the Treasury the practice has always been to enlighten Ministers by written minutes, and from this practice there has been no departure, so that the Chancellor of the Exchequer has had very little assistance from the permanent Heads of the Office, Chalmers of the Inland Revenue and his own private secretary having been his only official support. Of Crewe he had nothing to say but in the highest praise; his power of work and readiness to listen to and weigh all the evidence in a case contributed to make his judgments of permanent value in the evolution of colonial government. His prudence and tact in Council are no less remarkable: Lord Morley thinks his influence in the Cabinet of the highest value; John Burns attributes to his address the compromise which saved the Town Planning Bill.... FitzRoy, *Memoirs*, I, 329, 365–6, 390–1

CABINET COMMITTEES

82. Some Cabinet committees of the Asquith government, 1908–13

[H. H. Asquith to the King]

[29 April 1908] A Committee of the Cabinet was appointed to consider what changes are necessary in the status of the Board of Trade & some other public departments. Cabinet Papers. Cab. 41/31/53

[23 June 1910] Lord Crewe brought under notice the proposals which are being mooted in the Dominions to divide the Colonial Office, leaving to the Colonial Secretary the administration of the Crown Colonies, and transferring the affairs of the Dominions to the Prime Minister. This scheme is not viewed with favour by many members of the Cabinet, but a Committee on Colonial Office re-organisation was appointed, consisting of Lord Crewe, Lord Beauchamp, Mr. Haldane, Mr. Buxton, & Mr. Samuel. *Ibid.* Cab. 41/32/63

[30 July 1910] The question of continuing the temporary annual grant of £50,000 (which has now been made for three years) to Cyprus was referred to a Committee of the Cabinet, consisting of the Prime Minister, the Chancellor of the Exchequer, Lord Crewe & Mr. Churchill. Later in the day the Committee met, and after a careful investigation of the financial position of Cyprus agreed to make the temporary grant of £50,000 permanent. *Ibid.* Cab. 41/32/68

[9 November 1910] Questions connected with the renewal of the West Indian Mail Contract, and with the site of the Science Museum at South Kensington, were referred to Cabinet Committees.

Ibid. Cab. 41/32/70

[23 February 1911] Sir E. Grey reported that the Cabinet Committee which is considering the form of the memorandum to be submitted by Sir E. Goschen to the Imperial Chancellor has not yet completed its task, but the draft, as finally approved by the Committee, will be circulated to the Cabinet next week....

The Estimates Committee of the Cabinet which is still sitting will bring up its report at the ordinary meeting of the Cabinet next Wednesday.

Ibid. Cab. 41/33/3

[1 March 1911] The Estimates Committee reported that they had examined & approved without substantial alteration the Estimates of the Education Office and the Post Office, which are the two principal spending departments of the Civil Service.

The Army Estimates show a small nominal deduction, but are practically stationary....

The Navy Estimates, which will be the object of a vigorous attack from the party of economy in the House of Commons, have been carefully & anxiously reviewed by the Cabinet Committee. Ultimately an arrangement was come to between the Chancellor of the Exchequer and Mr. McKenna....

The position was discussed at length by the Cabinet, and divergent opinions were developed....

Ibid. Cab. 41/33/4

[9 March 1911] ...yesterday's meeting of the Cabinet was occupied by a careful examination & revision of the Memorandum, drawn up by the Foreign Affairs Committee, which is to be communicated by Sir E. Goschen to the Imperial Chancellor at Berlin.... *Ibid.* Cab. 41/33/5

[30 March 1911] Mr. Churchill presented a Bill which has been drawn by a Committee of the Cabinet to deal with the 'Osborne' Judgment.

Ibid. Cab. 41/33/8

[3 July 1913] At the suggestion of the Prime Minister a Cabinet Committee was appointed to consider the question of decorations, and how far a case is made out either for the enlargement of existing, or the creation of new, marks of distinction. *Ibid.* Cab. 41/34/24

THE CABINET AND MILITARY POLICY[1]

83. A Cabinet Defence Committee created, 1895

[The Marquess of Salisbury to the Duke of Devonshire, 25 June 1895]

I quite think it ought to be announced that you have joined the Government. But I think a communiqué might be sent to the Times, to the effect that it was contemplated that you should undertake as President of the Council, the conduct of a Committee of Council in which the principal officers of the defensive departments should sit, and whose duty it would be to secure greater efficiency and unity in the action of those departments. Devonshire Papers, 340.2619

84. The Defence Committee acts without consulting the Commander-in-Chief, 1899

[Viscount Wolseley, Commander-in-Chief, to Sir Arthur Bigge, 17 December 1899]

I have just returned from seeing Lord Lansdowne, who told me that the Defence Committee of the Cabinet which sat yesterday decided to send out Lord Roberts as C.-in-C. to the Cape of Good Hope, with Lord Kitchener as his Chief of the Staff.

In justice to myself I think the Queen should know that this decision has been arrived at without any reference to me or any previous knowledge on my part that it was in contemplation. I can only add that, whilst I deeply regret the supersession of Buller, whom I consider by far the most fitted of our Generals to deal with the present military situation in South Africa, I realise that the Government must recommend to her Majesty what in their judgment is best.

And whilst I feel strongly the fact that such an important military step has been taken without any consultation with me as Commander-in-Chief, the Queen may rest assured that at the present crisis I shall allow no personal considerations to interfere with my endeavour to serve her and the nation as best I may. *LQV*, 3rd ser. III, 437

[1] See also pp. 356–72 below.

85. The Cabinet and generals in the field, 1900

(a) *Queen Victoria to the Marquess of Salisbury, 7 April 1900 (telegram)*

I cannot refrain from expressing my regret that the Cabinet should have decided to urge upon Lord Roberts the supersession of General Gatacre and Colonel Broadwood.

The Government selected Lord Roberts as Commander-in-Chief [in South Africa]. Having thus proved their complete confidence in him, they surely cannot now so far interfere as to advise him to supersede Colonel Broadwood, when he has placed on record that, even after that officer's misfortune, his opinion of him was greater than before. As to General Gatacre, it does not appear that he was responsible for the loss of the detachment, but if Lord Roberts considers him to blame, no doubt he will take what steps he feels are necessary.

(b) *Marquess of Salisbury to Queen Victoria, 9 April 1900*

The telegram to Lord Roberts on which your Majesty comments was sent by Lord Lansdowne [Secretary of State for War] under the instructions of the Cabinet; and was not even proposed by him. He has therefore no more responsibility in respect to it than was shared by all the Ministers who were present.

In your Majesty's telegram to Lord Lansdowne you say, 'Lord Roberts is the only judge of what is necessary, and must really not be interfered with by civilians at a distance who cannot judge the exact state of the case.'

With the deepest respect Lord Salisbury would submit to your Majesty that, under our present constitution, the doctrine that the Cabinet have *no* control over a General in the field is not practicable. If they have no control, of course they have no responsibility. In the case, which is, of course, possible, that some grave evil were to result from the policy of the General, the Cabinet could not accept the responsibility of what had been done, or be under any obligation to defend him in Parliament; and in case Parliament took an adverse view, a condition of great embarrassment would result.

Of course, the Cabinet should not interpose without serious cause. In the present instance they think there *is* serious cause. The successive loss of so many bodies of men in consequence of the officers taking no precautions against ambush amounts to a scandal. These repeated exhibitions of negligence are most injurious to the service, and require severer notice than they have received. But if Lord Roberts does not agree with the Cabinet, he will no doubt reply; and his reply will be very carefully considered before the Cabinet submits any further step for the consideration of your Majesty. *LQV*, 3rd ser. III, 524–6

86. The Cabinet and military affairs, 1911

[H. H. Asquith to King George V, 2 November 1911]

Lord Morley raised the question of the inexpediency of communications being held or allowed between the General Staff of the War Office & the General Staff of foreign States, such as France, in regard to possible military co-operation, without the previous knowledge & directions of the Cabinet. Lord Haldane explained what had actually been done, the communications in question having been initiated as far back as 1906 with Sir H. Campbell Bannerman's sanction, & resumed in more detail during the spring & summer of the present year. The Prime Minister pointed out that all questions of policy have been & must be reserved for the decision of the Cabinet, and that it is quite outside the function of military or naval officers to prejudge such questions. He added that he believed (& Sir E. Grey concurred) that this was fully recognised by the French Government. Considerable discussion ensued, and no conclusion was come to, the matter being adjourned for further deliberation later on. Cabinet Papers. Cab. 41/33/28

THE CABINET AND FOREIGN POLICY

87. The Duke of Argyll on Lord Granville at the Foreign Office

His foreign policy was the foreign policy of the Cabinet. The administration of the Foreign Office ought never to be, and certainly never was in his hands, as personal, or even as predominantly departmental, as the administration of the other great departments often is, and may safely be. The Home Office, the Colonial Office, and the India Office may all be worked with only occasional references to the Cabinet. But in a department where, sometimes at least, a single imprudent act...may light the flames of war, or commit the country to courses of action leading inevitably to the same result, it is the duty of the Minister to reflect faithfully the deliberate opinions of his chief and of the Government as a whole. We all know that this has not always been kept in view. The powerful personality of one Minister, or the generous impulsiveness of another, has often forced the hands of Governments. But no colleague of Lord Granville's could ever make this complaint. He had an unequalled aptitude for gathering and reflecting that general and combined opinion, which might be largely determined, indeed, by his own advice, but of which all his colleagues were bound—not formally alone, or in a mere official sense, but really and in conscience—to bear the full responsibility.

Fitzmaurice, Granville, II, 506-7

88. Rosebery on a bi-partisan foreign policy, 1895
[Speech at the Albert Hall, 5 July 1895]

There is one point in which I hope to be able to give my support to the new Government, and that is on questions of foreign policy. If there is one thing in my life I should wish to live after me, it is that, when I first went to the Foreign Office as Secretary for Foreign Affairs, I argued for, and maintained the principle of a policy of continuity in foreign administration. My view was this, that whatever our domestic differences may be at home, we should preserve a united front abroad; and that foreign statesmen and foreign courts should feel that they are dealing, not with a Ministry, possibly fleeting and possibly transient, but with a great, powerful, and united nation. Rosebery, *Speeches*, p. 337

89. Lloyd George complains that there was no Cabinet consideration of foreign policy, 1906–14

During the eight years that preceded the war, the Cabinet devoted a ridiculously small percentage of its time to a consideration of foreign affairs....

Of course, certain aspects of foreign policy were familiar to those Ministers who attended the Committee of Imperial Defence, but apart from that the Cabinet as a whole were never called into genuine consultation upon the fundamental aspects of the foreign situation. There was a reticence and a secrecy which practically ruled out three-fourths of the Cabinet from the chance of making any genuine contribution to the momentous questions then fermenting on the Continent of Europe, which ultimately ended in an explosion that almost shattered the civilisation of the world. During the whole of those eight years, when I was a member of the Cabinet, I can recall no such review of the European situation being given to us as that which Sir Edward Grey delivered to the Colonial Conference in 1907, or to the Prime Ministers of the Dominions at the Committee of Imperial Defence in 1911. Even there the information that was withheld was more important than that which was imparted. For instance, nothing was said about our military commitments. There was in the Cabinet an air of 'hush hush' about every allusion to our relations with France, Russia and Germany. Direct questions were always answered with civility, but were not encouraged. We were made to feel that, in these matters, we were reaching our hands towards the mysteries, and that we were too young in the priesthood to presume to enter into the sanctuary reserved for the elect. So we confined our inquisitiveness and our counsel to the more mundane affairs in which we had taken part in Opposition during the whole of our political careers. Discussions, if they could be called discussions, on foreign affairs, were confined to the elder statesmen who had seen service in some previous ministerial existence. Apart from the Prime Minister and the Foreign Secretary there were only two or three men such as Lord Loreburn, the Lord Chancellor, Lord Morley, Lord Crewe, and, for a short time, Lord Ripon, who were expected to make any contribution on the infrequent occasions when the Continental situation was brought to our awed attention. As a matter of fact, we were hardly qualified to express any opinion on so important a matter, for we were not privileged to know any more of the essential facts than those which the ordinary newspaper reader could gather from the perusal of his morning journal.

Lloyd George, *War Memoirs*, I, 46–7

THE SELECTION OF MINISTERS

90. Peel anxious to make his brother Parliamentary Under-Secretary at the Home Office, 1822

(a) Robert Peel to Sir Robert Peel, January 1822

I spoke to William on the subject of the office after evening service on a Sunday. I told him it was vacant, and that I had not said a word to any person respecting the appointment. I said the mere official duties were light; that the parliamentary duties would be by far the heaviest, and also of the greatest importance to me. I dare say I said what I feel, that the Parliamentary Under Secretary would be like my right hand to me. I said these parliamentary duties consisted in the attendance on committees, there might be one on Criminal Law, one on Pensions, one on Education.

The Secretary of State could not attend all these, and must devolve on his Under Secretary the charge of attending such as he could not, and watching the progress of the business there. If at any time the Secretary of State were unavoidably absent from the House, the Under Secretary would have to conduct such business there as belonged to the office, for it would be a mortification to him to see that business in the hands of another. I said the performance of these duties must be difficult at first, that nothing but experience could render them less so, but that experience would. I declared my readiness to do anything in my power to make them easier, adding that there was a material difference between the situation of an Under Secretary who represented the office in the House of Commons, his principal being in the House of Lords, and that of one whose principal was in the House of Commons.

(b) Robert Peel to the Earl of Liverpool, 24 December 1825

...I am desirous that some official promotion should be given to Dawson (my brother-in-law) when a fair opportunity shall offer. He is capable of greater exertion than any which is now called for from him. He is most anxious to exert himself, but I find it very difficult to transfer to anyone any portion of the business of my office which is to be transacted in the House of Commons. I prefer doing the whole of it myself. A vacancy in the office of Under Secretary of State would enable me to appoint my brother William to it.... Parker, *Peel*, I, 304, 388–9

91. An M.P. seeks office, 1857
[From the diary of Chichester Fortescue]

1857 *Apr. 30.* Arr. London. Went to No. 7. A great deal of talk about office, whether I should *ask*, Henry Grenfell urging me to apply for the Under-Secretaryship of the Colonies.

May 4. Strawberry Hill. Took Lord Stanley of A[lderley] into the 'Star Chamber' after breakfast & consulted him about applying for the Colonial Office. He evidently had thought of it or heard it mentioned, and advised me by all means to apply to Ld. Palmerston; said he thought he would be ready to give it to me, that it would suit me etc., and was very civil about it. Wrote to Ld. Palmerston.

May 5. Called on Lord Palmerston, he was not at home, but met

Lady P. at the door. She advised me to come again just before dinner. I found him then, & he was very civil, but made no promise.

May 6. Called on Labouchere [Colonial Secretary] at the Colonial Office. He received me far more favourably & decidedly than I expected; said that Lord Stanley of A. had told him that I should like the Colonial Office, that he would 'rather have me than anyone else', & had written to Lord Palmerston to say he should like it. Lord P. had asked him to take Sir R. Peel, which he did not like at all; would see Lord P. & settle it, but could not refuse Peel, if Ld. P. insisted & R. Peel would take it. To Pembroke Lodge. Dined & slept there. Read aloud some of The Princess & of Matt. Arnold's Poems.

May 7. Pembroke Lodge. The Queen's speech came from Lord P. to Lord John [Russell]. 'Very civil of Palmerston' said he. Talked it over, & then a good deal about China. Did not tell him of my affair. Found a note from Labouchere at St. James's Place. I am Under-Secretary, if John Ball does not get a seat very soon.

May 8. Went to Ld. Palmerston, he was complimentary, 'we could not have a better man. I'm glad to put you into harness.'

May 13. Called on Lord Grey [ex Colonial Secretary], by Lady W[aldegrave]'s advice. He was shy & I was shy, but he was civil & kind. He *objected* of course to things done by the Colonial Office, thought a Reform Bill inevitable but dangerous; called Gladstone 'a thorough Jesuit'.

May 15. To House, talked to Labouchere. He warned me that there was hard work, & nearly all the year round. Many Irish members congratulated me very much. O'Flaherty said it gave general satisfaction among them, but they wished I had been Chief Secretary. They thought me the most likely man for it, & I was the man they most wished for. He hoped I might still have it. Milnes made light of the Under Sectship.

May 16. To Lady Palmerston's. A great many congratulations. Met Lord Carlisle, who was very affectionate, he whispered 'I haven't caught my Secretary yet, I wish I had you'. Hewett,...*and Mr. Fortescue,* pp. 105–6

92. Gladstone contemplates a government reshuffle, 1869

[W. E. Gladstone to Earl Granville, 18 August 1869]

The *personnel* of the Government generally has been proved by the experience of the Session to be good. But I think from my own observation and still more from the judgments & experience of others that one or two improvements might be made.

Ayrton has great talent and is a most pertinacious worker, with a good deal of experience and widely dispersed knowledge of public affairs. But he seems to be somewhat angular and better adapted for doing business within a defined province of his own, than in common stock or partnership with others, as his present office would require his business to be shared with Lowe and Stansfeld. It appears also that they are strong enough to undertake the whole business of the Treasury by themselves, so that one place might be spared, which is much wanted for the War Department.

Again Layard, though he has great talents, remarkable powers of speech, and some special qualifications for his Department, has not succeeded in it with the House of Commons and does not seem very thoroughly to understand pecuniary responsibility and the management of Estimates. And there is no doubt whatever that in his department the present House of Commons will be vigilant and exacting: while the rapid growth of its expenditure certainly shows that it should be filled by some one capable of exercising controul.

At the same time it appears that Layard desires a diplomatic appointment: and the mission at Madrid for which he would be extremely well qualified is vacant. To this as I understand Clarendon would agree to appoint him.

GG1, I, 45

93. The government Chief Whip recommends M.P.s for appointment as ministers, 1874

[The Hon. Gerard Noel to Benjamin Disraeli, 12 February 1874]

...I am most anxious to see four *new men* brought prominently to the front because I am sure they would add greatly to its strength not only in the House of Commons but in the country. These are W. H. Smith, Cross, Beach and Sandon, all good speakers and men of ability and sound judgment....

[W. H. Smith became Financial Secretary to the Treasury, R. A. Cross became Home Secretary, Sir Michael Hicks Beach became Chief Secretary for Ireland, and Lord Sandon became Vice President of the Committee of Council for Education.] Disraeli Papers

94. Gladstone holds that the Cabinet has no say in the appointment of ministers, 1882

I can affirm with confidence that the notion of a title in the cabinet to be consulted on the succession to a cabinet office is absurd. It is a title which cabinet ministers do not possess. During thirty-eight years since I first entered the cabinet, I have never known more than a friendly announcement before publicity, and very partial consultation perhaps with one or two, especially the leaders in the second House.

Morley, *Gladstone*, III, 101 n

95. Harcourt on the power of the Prime Minister to dismiss other ministers, 1884

[Sir W. V. Harcourt to W. E. Gladstone, 22 September 1884]

... I confess I have never doubted that Cabinet offices were held *durante bene placato* of the Prime Minister. No doubt when it comes to an open breach as between Pitt and Thurlow the direct interposition of the Crown may have to be invoked, and the removal would be at the Sovereign's command. But in the ordinary working of a Cabinet I have always supposed that the Prime Minister had the same authority to modify it as he has to construct it....

In my opinion it is no more open to the head of a department in the Cabinet to say to the potter that he will be an *urceus* or an *amphora* than it is to a Commander of a Division to say to the Commander-in-Chief that he will not be superseded in the command by another officer. The interests at stake are far too serious to admit of the doctrine of fixity of tenure.

That this must be so is obvious because the first Minister can always say to any other member of the Administration, 'if you don't go I will'. But it is incredible that things should ever be pushed to such a point as that. Good feeling as well as good sense forbids it. And a man must be pachydermatous indeed who is incapable of accepting the first hint that his room is wanted whether he is on a visit or in a Cabinet. I am sure much less than you have said would have made me pack up my traps....

Gardiner, *Harcourt*, I, 508–9

96. Harcourt on the balance of the Cabinet between Lords and Commons, 1892

[Sir W. V. Harcourt to W. E. Gladstone, 14 August 1892]

I think it necessary to place on record the opinion which I expressed this afternoon that the proposed distribution of the principal offices in the Cabinet as between the House of Lords and the House of Commons is one which will not meet with the approval or support of the Liberal Party. More than half of what are considered the places of greatest emolument and dignity are assigned to the Peers. The significance of this constitution of the Cabinet is emphasized by the fact that one of the greatest spending departments is placed in the Lords. Tory Governments in the last forty years have set a much better example in this matter than recent Liberal Administrations. I entertain a profound conviction that this arrangement will give rise to great discontent in the House of Commons, and will probably prove fatal to the Government. Campbell-Bannerman, who came in at the end of the discussion, expressed strongly the same view which John Morley and I had placed before you, and I know it is shared by Arnold Morley and by Edward Marjoribanks, who in this matter, I doubt not, reflect the general opinion of the Liberal Members of the House of Commons....

No former precedents can be of any avail in the presence of the increased and increasing strength of democratic sentiment in the Liberal Party and their indisposition to acquiesce in the paramount claims of the Peers. I feel that besides all the tremendous difficulties which you have to face and the powerful opposition you will have to encounter you will add the greatest of all discouragements, that of a dissatisfied party.

Gardiner, *Harcourt*, II, 182–3

CHAPTER 3

PARLIAMENT

A GOVERNMENT AND PARLIAMENT

It was the almost invariable practice of contemporaries to laud parliament as the central feature of the British constitution. 'Parliament', said that grand old Whig, the eighth Duke of Devonshire, in 1893, 'does actually and practically, in every way, directly govern England, Scotland and Ireland (11). In speaking thus the Duke was merely echoing a long line of Whig lawyers, going back to Coke, who maintained that 'The power and jurisdiction of Parliament is so transcendant and absolute, that it cannot be confined, either for causes or persons, within any bounds'.[1] And he was fortified by the best legal authorities of his own day, headed by Dicey, who reaffirmed and restated Coke's doctrine in modern language (10).

Yet for most of the nineteenth century the sovereignty of parliament was more a matter of legal theory than of substance. The effective direction of the affairs of the country was in the hands of a government backed by a party majority in the House of Commons. The effective limits of a government's freedom of action were set by the views and prejudices of its own supporters, rather than by those of parliament as a whole. Only when there was no clear party majority in the House of Commons was parliament in any real sense in control of events. Only then, during what has come to be spoken of as the heyday of the private member, from 1832 to 1842 and again from 1846 to 1868, was it possible for the individual members of parliament to exercise a decisive control over government, and to bring down a ministry when they so chose.

The story of parliament during the nineteenth century is one of a rapid decline in the traditional influence of the crown and its ministers, as a consequence of a reduction in the number of placemen in the Commons and of pensions and other payments which might be bestowed upon supporters of the government, followed by the gradual reassertion of governmental control by way of party management, with a period of some uncertainty in between.

The decline of the traditional influence of the crown had already begun in the eighteenth century with a series of Place Bills which restricted the number of placemen. These were popular with the independent country gentlemen and difficult for any ministry to resist. As a result Lord Liverpool and his colleagues found it increasingly difficult to satisfy the expectations

[1] Coke, 4 *Inst.* 36.

of their supporters and were forced to rely on less tangible means to hold their followers together. But the capacity of the ministry to satisfy its supporters was soon to be limited further. Joseph Hume and other advocates of 'peace, retrenchment and reform' began to attack the whole governmental apparatus as simply a means of featherbedding the aristocracy. With the aid of the *Extraordinary Black Book*, which attempted to list every government post in church and state and every pension, under the name of the recipient, this campaign was strikingly effective. The Civil List was dramatically pruned and government patronage correspondingly reduced. Moreover, the success of the campaign inspired a group of businessmen calling themselves the Financial Reform Association to set up a permanent organisation, which published an annual *Almanack* of facts and figures and aimed at an even more drastic limitation of government expenditure.

Parallel with the reduction in government patronage came a reduction in the number of seats in the House of Commons over which the government could exercise some control, either directly, as in the case of Treasury and Admiralty boroughs, or indirectly, through patrons. With the House of Commons divided into small groups, as it was in the ten years before 1832, this mattered less than might be supposed since the very fact that the supporters of the administration acted as a bloc gave them disproportionate influence. Certainly, the Whigs grumbled mightily in 1831 that they had not got the advantage of nominating a new parliament. The real difficulty came after 1832. The number of nomination boroughs was now so reduced that it was natural for patrons to wish to keep them for their own family, even if it meant turning out a minister. And public opinion quickly turned against government boroughs, particularly after the blatant use made of government influence in the dockyards by the first Derby ministry which led to a committee of enquiry.[1] Knowledgeable men began to complain that parliamentary reform had made it unduly difficult to bring ministers and bright young men into the House, and had made ministers unduly sensitive to the demands of the electorate (**105**). Hard-working ministers had always avoided popular constituencies because of the burden of work which they involved and the risk of perpetual strife. But few ministers could now avoid a perpetual round of elections. Not only had they to fight general elections; whenever they took office, and sometimes when they changed office, ministers had to seek re-election. And it became a matter of honour to oppose prominent ministers wherever possible. As a result, men like Peel, Russell, Palmerston, Gladstone, Harcourt, Balfour and Churchill were forced to move from one constituency to another as each place became too hot for them. And in a great many ministries before 1880 individual ministers were for quite long periods out of the House of Commons. The law officers, in

---

[1] *Report from the Select Committee on Dockyard Appointments*, H.C. 511 (1852–53), xxv, 1.

particular, became very hard to provide with seats, and those for Scotland and Ireland were inconveniently often out of parliament.

Because government could no longer command a solid block of members in either house *qua* government it had to find an alternative source of support. This was discovered in the rapidly growing number of good party men, who could be relied upon to vote the right way for fear lest they disappoint their constituents. But for many years the weakness of government in the House of Commons was a source of anxiety to students of the constitution (**105**). The number of relatively independent men on the back benches continued large until the 1860s, and the tempo of public business was apt to be dictated by the whims of individual members and the extent to which members could be persuaded to forgo social occasions or the hunting field. Even the new party clubs formed in the 1830s and a bevy of political hostesses often failed to keep the main phalanx of the two major parties together.

Sir Robert Peel, between 1842 and 1845, showed that it was possible to restore much of the parliamentary predominance of government by relying on a combination of ministerial expertise and party management. The work of parliament was directly geared to the ministerial initiatives of a team of men of quite unusual administrative abilities, headed by Peel himself and Sir James Graham, who dominated the House of Commons in a way in which none of their predecessors since Pitt had done. But Peel's work was largely undone by the Corn Law repeal crisis, and it was only when the party situation had again been stabilised after 1868 that ministers were able to reassert a Peel-like dominance over the House of Commons. In between, everything depended on the personality of individual ministers. Palmerston for the most part got his own way (**104**), but Russell and Disraeli were less fortunate.

With party discipline restored at Westminster after 1868, the proportion of parliamentary time controlled by ministers quickly increased. When frondeurs on the opposition benches in the House of Commons responded by adopting obstructive tactics, governments slowly and reluctantly moved to take responsibility for the business out of the hands of the House and into their own hands. The 'closure', first used in 1882 and made permanent in 1887 (**138**), was merely the most bitterly contested of a series of changes which culminated in a new code of procedure for the Commons. The struggle for government control over parliament was then transferred to the Lords, where party discipline was weak because the peers had no constituents, and because the overwhelming majority of the peers were on the Unionist side of the Irish question. Until the debates over the Reform Bill of 1884, the House of Lords, though periodically obstructive, had been largely quiescent since it had accepted the 1832 Reform Bill rather than be swamped by an influx of new peers. Now the Lords emerged as a willing tool of any Conservative Opposition in the House of Commons, and sometimes as an obstructive force which even Conservative governments found difficult to control. The Reform Bill of 1884 was carried in the end, but Home Rule was thrown out in 1893, and there was constant friction between the Lords and the Liberal governments in office after 1905, which culminated in the rejection of the budget of 1909. This amounted to a declaration of war on the government and the government responded by bringing in what was to become the Parliament Act of 1911, which enabled a government in certain circumstances to use its majority in the House of Commons to override the objections of the Lords to a Commons bill (**174**). But the very fact that the Lords gave way in 1911 to a threat to create enough peers to override the hostile majority very largely destroyed the will of the Lords to resist, and after 1911 the Lords were never again to be regarded as a serious threat to the supremacy of a government with a majority in the Commons.

Governments entrusted relations between themselves and parliament to a Leader and a team of Whips in each house. The Prime Minister was almost invariably the Leader in one house, while the Leader in the other house was inevitably one of his closest colleagues. When the Prime Minister was in the Lords, this could sometimes lead to tension, since the Leader in the Commons was frequently driven by the necessities of debate to make pronouncements on matters of policy without full consultation with his colleagues (**57–60**). But even over a wayward Commons Leader like Disraeli, a Prime Minister in the Lords could exercise a considerable measure of control so long as he retained the backing of his colleagues. The relationship was a difficult one, but given some sort of understanding, such as Gladstone secured from Russell in 1865 (**57**), it could be made a tolerable one. Day-to-day details of parliamentary management were left to the Whips, who also suggested the names of M.P.s for appointment as ministers (**93**).

The extent of government control over the Commons, even after 1868, should not be exaggerated. The statistics of divisions, it is true, show that on most issues there was a straightforward confrontation between government and Opposition.[1] But the statistics do not tell everything. They fail to indicate the extraordinary way in which the strength of governments fell away during the life of most parliaments. By 1873 the first Gladstone ministry had been all but abandoned by considerable numbers of its supporters. By 1885 the same thing had happened to the second Gladstone ministry. The life of the 1886–92 Salisbury administration was precarious from beginning to end because it was dependent on Liberal Unionist support. The Rosebery ministry was defeated in the Commons in 1895. And the Balfour ministry, with a big Commons majority, had lost control of its followers by 1905 (**149**).

---

[1] Lowell, 'The Influence of Party upon Legislation', *Annual Report of the American Historical Association for 1901.*

Nonetheless, the government gradually assumed almost complete control over the legislative timetable. Government bills had always enjoyed some sort of priority over private members' bills. By 1907 they were liable to choke out private members' bills entirely, unless the government found time for them (**141**). Provided that it remained on good terms with its followers, a government after 1887 could by the use of the closure usually get three or four major bills through the House of Commons in a session, and a good many minor bills as well.

Responsibility for bringing governments to book and for scrutinising the action of ministers inevitably rested on those who sat on the front benches in the House of Commons opposite ministers, who after 1826, when John Cam Hobhouse invented the phrase, were wont to be referred to as 'His Majesty's Opposition' (**97–108**). The first modern leader of the Opposition was George Tierney, who led the Whigs in the House of Commons from 1817 to 1821, and to whom Derby attributed the well-known *mot* that the duty of the opposition is to oppose everything and propose nothing.[1] The doctrine that opposition should always be responsible was largely the creation of Sir Robert Peel, who in the 1830s refused to be a party to merely factious attacks on the government (**101**). Peel also laid down what came to be the accepted view of how minority governments should react to opposition in the Commons (**115**). By the 1860s Alpheus Todd and other commentators were writing of the Opposition as one of the essential features of Cabinet government, and were endeavouring with the aid of quotations from Peel to lay down rules of etiquette which Oppositions should follow (**107**). By the 1870s, it had become usual for the leader of the Opposition party to hold occasional meetings of what came to be known as the 'shadow cabinet', consisting of those ex-ministers who would be expected to take a leading part in a new government.

The rituals of the confrontation of government and Opposition in the Commons were slowly built up over the years. The ultimate Opposition sanction, a vote of no confidence in the government, such as was carried in 1841, was rarely resorted to because it tended to polarise opinion and to rally support to the government. The Opposition usually preferred to attack individual items of government policy. If the government then made the resultant division a 'test of confidence', the same effect would be achieved as by a vote of no confidence, with less risk of dissident government supporters rallying to the support of the government. For a long time governments had a pretty free hand in deciding which measures should be regarded as tests of confidence, and even items of the budget might be successfully attacked by groups of back benchers without bringing the government down. Gradually, however, it came to be recognised that an attack on the budget,

---

[1] 3 *Hansard* LVIII, 1188.

the principal items in the annual estimates, or major legislation, involved a vote of no confidence in the government.

Governments defeated in the House of Commons on an issue which they regarded as a test of confidence had a choice between resignation and the dissolution of parliament. Usually they chose resignation. Indeed, the government of Lord Rosebery in 1895 went so far as to resign when defeated not on an orthodox test of confidence but in a 'snap vote' on the estimates, and the Balfour government resigned in 1905 with what many regarded as indecently little excuse.

The dissolution of parliament was regarded as a dangerous weapon, only to be used in emergency or at the end of the life of a parliament (**109–14**). In theory the monarch could refuse to grant a dissolution, and Prime Ministers were always a little uneasy lest one should actually be refused them. Dissolution was indeed a very powerful weapon, since it cost M.P.s a great deal of money and threatened the loss of their seats, as Palmerston demonstrated when he routed his critics in 1857. Moreover, it was a weapon capable of unexpected uses, as Disraeli demonstrated in 1868 when he taunted the opposition to move a vote of no confidence against his government and face a general election before the registers of the new electors enfranchised in 1867 were ready. Hence, all statesmen tried to hedge round the power of dissolution as much as possible. Peel in 1846 argued that the dissolution of parliament merely to strengthen the party in office was inadmissible (**110**). And Gladstone in 1868 restated Peel's view.[1] But Gladstone did not hesitate to dissolve parliament in 1886 when the Home Rule Bill was defeated in the Commons, and one cannot help feeling that there was something unreal about the Peel–Gladstone doctrine.

Parallel with the endeavour to develop rules for the conduct of Opposition and for the dissolution of parliament, there developed a species of folk-lore concerned with the circumstances in which the Opposition must take office while in a minority in parliament. Peel felt strongly the discomfort of being in a minority in the House of Commons in 1835, and persuaded his colleagues to resign (**115**). But it was left unsettled whether when a government was defeated in the Commons the Opposition was bound to take office. Peel in 1839 saw that there were some advantages in being prevented from taking office while in a decided minority as a result of the refusal of the Queen to change the ladies of her household. Russell refused to take office in 1845, largely because he wished Peel to bear the responsibility of the repeal of the Corn Laws. And Derby refused office in 1855 because he felt that he had no prospect of forming a lasting ministry (**116**). When Disraeli refused to take office in 1873 after the defeat of the ministry on the Irish University question, Gladstone maintained that his behaviour was contrary to the

---

[1] 3 *Hansard* CXCI, 1710–13.

accepted norms of constitutional behaviour, and after 1873 no Opposition refused to take office when given the opportunity.

As time went on the business of the House of Commons was increasingly arranged by agreement between the government and Opposition Whips. As early as 1832 this collaboration was firmly established (**100, 143**). At the beginning of the session the time available was mapped out, 'supply days' being chiefly allocated to the Opposition. Changes in the timetable were then negotiated on the basis of an exchange of facilities, and major divisions were planned well in advance so that both government and Opposition could bring up as many as possible of their followers. As a result the Opposition became part of the parliamentary establishment, with its own offices, and it was clearly only a matter of time before the Leader of the Opposition would be accorded some sort of official recognition akin to that given the Prime Minister in 1905.

A major innovation in the relations between government and parliament resulted from the creation of new machinery for watching over government expenditure. In 1845 a Treasury committee on Ordnance expenditure strongly urged the creation of a proper system of audit followed by a scrutiny of the audited accounts by a committee of the House of Commons. In 1860 a resolution was carried in the Commons against the government 'that it would be desirable to appoint, every year, a select committee to enquire into the miscellaneous civil service expenditure of the preceding year; into the payments made out of the Consolidated Fund; and into those on account of the woods, forests, and land revenues'. And at last on 19 April 1861 'The Committee of Public Accounts' was established, consisting of nine members (increased in 1870 to eleven) with suitable qualifications for the task (**136**). With the aid of the newly established audit machinery and with a senior ex-minister in the chair, the Public Accounts Committee speedily established a detailed control over expenditure parallel to that of the Treasury and the Comptroller and Auditor General. The House of Commons finally recognised that it could no longer control the details of public expenditure when in 1912 it delegated yet further powers of financial review to the Select Committee on Estimates (**142**).

Another major innovation was the development of question time in the House of Commons. Questions were a relatively unimportant feature of parliamentary life before the 1850s. In 1830 the Speaker of the House ruled that 'there is nothing in the orders of this House to preclude any member from putting a question, and receiving an answer to it' and added that the practice 'though not strictly regular, affords great convenience to individuals.' A question first appeared upon the notice paper in 1835. Questions were incorporated in the Commons standing orders in 1854 and were gradually developed by members for a variety of purposes. To some they seemed a waste of time (**124**), but after 1869 a section of the notice paper was regularly given to questions, and until 1882 a debate might take place on any question. In 1886 it was agreed that questions might be asked by the member simply rising in his place in the House and calling out the number of his question, and in 1902 provision was made for written answers. By then the number of questions in the Commons had risen from 129 in 1847 to 6,448 in 1901.

The rapid growth in the number of questions and in the amount of other business to be transacted inevitably placed great strains on the parliamentary timetable. Private members and the public alike complained (**127**) and the Scots and Welsh became increasingly restive at the way Scottish and Welsh business was neglected. After Gladstone's conversion to Home Rule in 1886 there was therefore a good deal of pressure to grant Scotland and Wales a degree of legislative autonomy, to match that offered to Ireland, and to follow up the administrative change made by the creation of the Scottish Office in 1885. Welsh pressure was strong for a time during the 1890s, in the heyday of Cymru Fydd. But the Scottish home rule movement was much more persevering, backed as it was by the overwhelming majority of Scottish Liberal and Labour M.P.s, including Keir Hardie. In the House of Commons the Scots for a long time made little headway, but in 1912 they finally won over the Liberal government. Asquith announced himself in favour of a general measure of legislative devolution (**119**). And the Secretary for Scotland, McKinnon Wood, backed a series of home rule bills put forward by private members in 1912, 1913 and 1914. The Scottish Liberals did their best to make home rule all round palatable to their English colleagues (who supported them by substantial majorities) but the difficulties were very considerable. As Winston Churchill pointed out to the Cabinet in 1911, devolution raised almost insuperable difficulties in the case of England, because 'It seems to me absolutely impossible that an English Parliament, and still more an English Executive, could exist side by side with an Imperial Parliament and an Imperial Executive'. His solution was a form of regional devolution in England (**118**). But, fortunately for the Cabinet, this very explosive issue could be put on one side when war broke out, and no government bill was called for.

GOVERNMENT AND OPPOSITION

97. His Majesty's Opposition gets its title, 10 April 1826

[On a proposal to separate the offices of Treasurer of the Navy and President of the Board of Trade]

Mr. *Hobhouse* said, he would take that opportunity...to enter his protest against this proceeding, and to express his astonishment, that his majesty's ministers should have chosen that very peculiar time for ...making an unnecessary addition to the burthens of the country, and to the number of placemen and pensioners now sitting in the House of Commons.... It was said to be very hard on his majesty's ministers to raise objections to this proposition. For his own part, he thought it was more hard on his majesty's opposition....

Mr. Secretary *Canning* said.... that the opportunity was not selected by his majesty's government, neither did the suggestion emanate from them. It originated, not with his majesty's government, but with those whom the hon. gentleman had designated his majesty's opposition....

Mr. *Tierney* [in course of a long speech, said] An hon. friend near him had called the opposition the 'king's opposition'. The propriety of this appellation had been recognized by gentlemen on the other side; and indeed it could not be disputed. From his personal experience, he could bear testimony to the truth of the designation... For years he had opposed the measures of government, because he disapproved of their principles; but when they changed their tone, he had not been backward in giving them his feeble support. My hon. friend...could not have invented a better phrase to designate us than that which he has adopted, for we are certainly to all intents and purposes, a branch of his majesty's government. Its proceedings for some time past have proved, that though the gentlemen opposite are in office, we are in power. The measures are ours, but all the emoluments are theirs....

Mr. *Tierney* [at the end of the debate, after the government had abandoned the proposal] rose...to assure his majesty's Government that they had, by this act, justly earned the approbation of 'his majesty's Opposition'.

2 Hansard xv, 133-7, 145, 149

98. The effective opposition on the government side, 1826

[Viscount Palmerston to the Hon. William Temple, 17 July 1826]

...As to the commonplace balance between Opposition and Government, the election will have little effect upon it. The Government are as strong as any Government can wish to be, as far as regards those who sit facing them; but in truth the real opposition of the present day sit behind the Treasury Bench; and it is by the stupid old Tory party, who bawl out the memory and praises of Pitt while they are opposing all the measures and principles which he held most important; it is by these that the progress of the Government in every improvement which they are attempting is thwarted and impeded. On the Catholic question; on the principles of commerce; on the corn laws; on the settlement of the currency; on the laws regulating the trade in money; on colonial slavery; on the game laws, which are intimately connected with the moral habits of the people: on all these questions, and everything like them, the Government find support from the Whigs and resistance from their self-denominated friends. However, the young squires are more liberal than the old ones, and we must hope that Heaven will protect us from our friends, as it has done from our enemies....

Bulwer, *Palmerston*, I, 171–2

99. The government's supporters meet, 1832

(a) *From the diary of E. J. Littleton, M.P., 8 March 1832*

A great meeting of the English members supporting Government was held by invitation from Lord Althorp in the dining room at the Foreign Office this morning at 12. About 200 attended. The Irish members had been there yesterday. The object was to beg support for the Government plan with respect to the gradual extinction of tithes in Ireland. The Irish members, especially the Catholics, were many of them disposed to be refractory, and nothing but a sacrifice of opinion on minute points of difference on the part of the English members would keep the helm of the vessel straight amidst the conflict of interests and opinions. Althorp opened the business. Surely never was there such a figure for an orator—especially to my eye—who had there seen on similar occasions Castlereagh, with his elegant and well-dressed figure and high bred carriage, and Canning, with his air of quickness and intelligence greater than ever distinguished man. There stood Althorp at the top of the room, with his stout, honest face, and farmer-like figure, habited in ill-made black clothes, his trousers rucked up in a heap round his legs, one coat flap turned round, and exposing his posterior, and the pocket of the other crammed full of papers—his hat held awkwardly in one hand and his large snuff box in the other, with which he kept playing the Devil's tattoo on his thigh—while he briefly and bluntly told his plain, unsophisticated tale with his usual correct feeling and stout sense, and was warmly responded to by the whole party.... Hume expressed his individual dissent.... This meeting had, as such meetings always have had (with the single exception of one called several years ago [13 April 1818] by Lord Liverpool to coax the country gentlemen to agree to a large increase of the Royal Princes' annuities, when we all rebelled after we got into the House....) the very best effect. We acted in a body....

(b) 9 May 1832

About 180 of the friends of the expiring Administration met at Brookes's Club this evening to consider the form of an Address to the King to be moved tomorrow in the House of Commons. After a good deal of discussion...we agreed to a form.   Aspinall, *Three Diaries*, 205–6, 245

100. Government and Opposition communicate, 1833

[The Leader of the House of Commons, Lord Althorp, to the Leader of the Opposition, Sir Robert Peel, 28 April 1833]

As Mr. Holmes [the Conservative Whip] gave Ellice [the Government Whip] a message from you, very handsomely offering to support us if we proposed to rescind the resolution of Friday, I take the liberty of letting you know that we have determined that I should to-morrow give notice, that on Sir John Key's motion on Tuesday I shall move as an amendment, 'That the deficiency in the revenue which would be occasioned by a reduction of the duty on malt to ten shillings the quarter, and by the repeal of the taxes on houses and windows, could only be supplied by the substitution of a general tax on property and income, and an extensive change in our whole financial system, which would at present be inexpedient.'

As I shall not communicate this intention further than to say that we have not resigned, I shall be obliged to you to consider it confidential.

Parker, *Peel*, II, 216

101. Peel on responsible Opposition, 1834

[Sir Robert Peel to Charles Arbuthnot, 27 May 1834]

I have long felt that the best chance—and that probably a very fair one—for the establishment of a Conservative Government would be the failure of the present Government from its own weakness, or dissensions, the Conservatives having manifested no anxiety for power, having adhered to principle, above all having eschewed all the finesse and petty manœuvring, which might perhaps in former times be useful elements of party tactics, when there were but two parties in the State, and those pretty equally balanced.

The only hope can be that the country, wearied by successive and frequent changes of Government, will at length determine that there shall be a Government, and will give it confidence, until there be cause shown for withdrawing it.

Many people think that the whole art of conducting a party consists in eternal fussy manœuvring, and little cunning schemes for putting a Government in a minority.

I believe, on the contrary, that the present strength of the Conservative party and the present condition of the Government have mainly resulted from our having taken exactly the opposite course—from our having kept aloof from Radical union, and from our having honestly supported the Government whenever we thought the Government right. Parker, *Peel*, II, 247

102. The Commons forced to rescind a vote, 1844

[Viscount Melbourne to Queen Victoria, 19 June 1844]

Lord Melbourne will not make any observation upon what is known and understood to have passed, further than to say that, as far as he is acquainted with the history of public affairs in this country, it is an entire novelty, quite new and unprecedented. Many a Minister has said to the Crown, 'My advice must be taken, and my measures must be adopted,' but no Minister has ever yet held this language or advanced this pretension to either House of Parliament. However, it seems to be successful at present, and success will justify much. *LQV*, 1st ser. II, 21

103. Opposition party organisation: Lord Derby writes to his Chief Whip about the meeting of the House of Commons, 1854

[Earl of Derby to Sir William Jolliffe, 6 January 1854]

When Disraeli was down here, he had of course some conversation on the mode of carrying on the business of the party; and I told him that I entirely approved of the suggestion of appointing frequent meetings of the members of the H. of Commons at his house; and also of appointing fixed times at which the principal members of our party might have an opportunity of conferring with him. I have often urged upon him before the necessity of more frequent intercourse of this kind between himself and our friends; and also of his occasionally seeing the whole party at *his* house; for though I am very willing to interfere where I can do so usefully, there is much that must be managed by the Leader of the House of Commons; and I cannot but think that much of the disorganisation which has prevailed has been owing to the want of unrestricted intercourse of this kind. I hope and believe that Disraeli is himself convinced of this; and also of the necessity for the maintenance of his position, of taking a really Conservative tone in and out of the House. I am quite ready to have a meeting, as usual, at my House on the first day of the Session, and you had better summon it for an early hour, 12 o'clock, or even 11, so as to give some time between its termination and the meeting of the Houses. It may perhaps be convenient to you to see the Circular which I am sending out to the Peers, and I therefore enclose you an unsigned copy. You should send out something of the same kind, avoiding of course an announcement of 'Certain Division' which people do not like to have for nothing; and I should certainly discourage, under almost any circumstances, an Amendment on the Address. You can add to your request of attendance in the House, an invitation to attend at my House, for the purpose of considering the course to be pursued during the Session. What that course may be must depend in some measure on the line to be taken by the Government.... I should wish you also to make me out, with Disraeli's aid, if he will take the trouble, lists for two H. of Commons dinners, which I will fix for Saturday the 4th and Wednesday the 8th. They should be invited simultaneously; and you must remember that my dining room will not hold more than 32, and even that rather doubtfully. I shall have a dinner of the Peers on Monday the 30th and it would not be amiss if Disraeli would do the same with the Commons at his house. You might perhaps suggest this to him.   Hylton Papers

104. Palmerston on the power of the government to make war without consulting parliament, 16 July 1857

Sir, I cannot approve either the constitutional doctrine or the constitutional conduct of the hon. and learned Gentleman who has moved these Resolutions [Mr. Roebuck]. If I understand the doctrine which he has endeavoured to lay down, it is this—that the Crown has no right either to make war or to make peace without previous communication with, and without the previous concurrence of, Parliament. Now, Sir, I deny that that doctrine is any part of the British constitution. I contend, on the contrary, that our constitution wisely and properly vests in the Crown the prerogative and the discretion of declaring war and of making peace, with this reserve, however, which I readily admit, that when the advisers of the Sovereign have deemed it their duty to counsel the Crown either to engage in or to put an end to war, it is incumbent on them to lay before Parliament, if it is sitting, the grounds upon which the one course or the other has been adopted; or, if Parliament is not sitting, when the interests of the country are deemed to be such as to require recourse to be had to war, I frankly and freely admit it to be their duty to take the earliest opportunity of calling Parliament together in order to submit to it their reasons for resorting to hostilities. I should be the last man to deny that general proposition. I maintain, however, that in the case to which the Motion alludes [the initiation of a war in Persia], there were circumstances which rendered it a special case, and excepted it for the moment from the application of that general rule.... If the war had been one with a European Power, involving great and serious consequences, and likely to require the immediate co-operation of this House, I admit that even ...[a] brief delay ought to have been avoided. But, considering the remoteness of the scene of action—considering that no immediate requisition was necessary to be made to Parliament for the purposes of the war, we thought it would be attaching more importance to the matter than it intrinsically deserved to anticipate the period for which Parliament stood convoked, and to issue a proclamation calling it together a fortnight sooner for the purpose of announcing to it that operations were going on in Persia. *3 Hansard* CXLVI, 1638–40

105. The third Earl Grey concerned by the weakness of ministers, 1858

On considering the whole scheme of the Parliamentary Reform of 1832...I am inclined to think that its greatest fault was, that it failed to provide adequately against the danger that the removal of abuses might incidentally diminish too much the power of the Government in Parliament. It has often been said, and with truth, that, under our present Constitution, the worst Administration we can have is a weak one. A weak Ministry has not the power of acting rightly; it must bring forward in Parliament, not the measures it knows to be best for the interests of the Country, but those it can hope to carry; it cannot venture to conduct the Executive Government according to the dictates of its own judgment; and in the exercise of the authority and patronage of the Crown, it is compelled to yield to every popular cry and to the unreasonable claims of its adherents; it is under a constant temptation unduly to court popularity, and to exaggerate the faults of party Government, by striving, in all its measures, to promote the interests of its Party rather than those of the Nation. Such a Government has a tendency to become more than usually corrupt, because an evenly-measured contest of Parties affords to unscrupulous men, desirous of using their votes or political interest for their own selfish advantage, peculiar facilities for driving hard bargains with the Administration.

Nor is this all; our whole system of Parliamentary Government rests ...upon the Ministers of the Crown possessing such authority in Parliament as to enable them generally to direct its proceedings, and especially those of the House of Commons.... Should such a state of things arise, with parties in the country so divided as to afford no prospect of a House of a different character being obtained by a dissolution of Parliament, it would be inevitable that new rules of political conduct, and a new mode of carrying on the public business, should be introduced. Hitherto it has been considered to be the duty of the Ministers of the Crown to resign, if they find themselves without adequate support in the House of Commons. Their doing so would be useless in the case supposed; and there would be no resource but to tolerate the existence of an Administration unable to guide the proceedings of Parliament.

...What particularly distinguishes our present system of government, and constitutes...one of its main advantages, is the responsibility which it imposes, both on Parliament and on the Servants of the Crown. Every Member of the House of Commons feels, or ought to feel, that it is a serious step to give a vote which may compel the existing Government to retire, without a reasonable prospect that another better able to conduct the affairs of the Country can be formed. The Ministers, on the other hand, know that they are not held to be absolved from responsibility for unwise measures, because they have been forced upon them by the House of Commons; but that, if they continue to ad-minister the affairs of the Country when powers they think necessary have been refused, or a course they disapprove has, in spite of their advice, been adopted by the House, they are justly held answerable for the policy of which they consent to be the instruments. But if it should ever come to be regarded as not being wrong, that Ministers should retain office though they were no longer able to guide the proceedings of the House of Commons, there would cease to be in any quarter an effective responsibility for the prudence and judgment with which the affairs of the Nation are conducted in Parliament. Ministers could not be held answerable for the conduct of a Parliament they had no power to direct, and the only responsibility left would be that of the House collectively.   Grey, *Parliamentary Government*, pp. 88–93

106. Palmerston as Leader of the Commons, 1861

[Viscount Palmerston to Queen Victoria, 26 July 1861]

Viscount Palmerston sits in that House [the Commons] four days in every week during the Session of Parliament, from half-past four in the afternoon to any hour however late after midnight at which the House may adjourn. It is his duty carefully to watch the proceedings of the House, and to observe and measure the fluctuating bearings of Party and of sectional associations on the present position of the Government, and on its chances for the future; and he is thus led to form conclusions as to persons and parties which may not equally strike, or with equal force, those who from without and from higher regions may see general results without being eye- and ear-witnesses of the many small and successive details out of which those results are built up.   *LQV*, 1st ser. III, 570

107. Alpheus Todd on government and opposition

The opposition exercise a wholesome influence upon parliamentary debate, and upon the conduct of the business of the crown in Parliament, for they are the constitutional critics of all public affairs; and whatever course the government may pursue, they naturally endeavour to find some ground for attack. It is the function of an opposition to state the case against the administration; to say everything which may plausibly be said against every measure, act, or word of every member of the ministry; in short, to constitute a standing censorship of the government, subjecting all its acts and measures to a close and jealous scrutiny.

But on questions of foreign policy, while they would naturally criticise freely the action of government, especially in the preliminary stages of such questions, it has been customary of late years for the opposition to refrain from any party warfare, and to extend the utmost forbearance, and, so far as may be possible, a generous assistance, to ministers, in maintaining the honour of the crown and the just influence of the British government in foreign affairs....

A leader of opposition should not lend himself to any attempts to thwart unnecessarily the progress of legislation in the hands of ministers; but should rather endeavour 'to secure as far as he could for both sides of the House a fair and free discussion; and when that discussion has been obtained, to facilitate the progress of public business, even if he disapproved of the measures of the government'. In proof of the amenities which grace the proceedings of the British Parliament, notwithstanding the keenness and severity of party strife, it is regarded in both Houses as the appropriate duty of the leader of the opposition to second any motion proposed by the leader of the government, for the adoption of addresses of sympathy or of congratulation to the sovereign, or for giving the thanks of the House to particular individuals for meritorious conduct. Furthermore, it is customary for members of the opposition who formerly held office to co-operate with ministers in endeavouring to prevent the passing of any measures prejudicial to the crown or to the public service, by affording to the House the benefit of their advice and official experience on the subject....

Moreover, it is usual, with a view to the furtherance of business in Parliament, for the leader of the House, or other prominent ministers, to communicate freely with the heads of the opposition, in order to arrive at an understanding in regard to the conduct of public business or of debate—which will tend to the convenience of members,—or to facilitate the settlement of delicate questions,—affecting the privileges of Parliament, the interests of the throne, the royal family, or otherwise, —which are not necessarily of a party character.

Todd, *Parliamentary Government*, II, 415–16, 418–19

108. Gladstone on the resignation of ministers before a vote against them, 20 May 1880

I wish to draw the attention of the House for one moment to the fact that on the last three occasions of a change of Administration the method pursued by the outgoing Government has been peculiar. From my quoting the last three changes which have occurred, it will be obvious that I do not refer to anything that belongs exclusively to one side of the House or to the other. In December, 1868, in February, 1874, and again in May, 1880, a change of Administration was made. Usually, in this country, changes of Administration are connected with the Votes of Parliament. It is when they are connected with the Votes of Parliament that we regard them as thoroughly normal and regular. I wish to bear testimony in favour of the regular and normal method of procedure. The method pursued in 1841, when the Government of Lord Melbourne found itself in a minority at the Elections, the method pursued in 1859, when in like manner the Government of Lord Derby was in a minority at the Elections, and when in each case they met the Parliament and allowed a Vote to be taken on their conduct, undoubtedly was that which most thoroughly satisfies the spirit of our Constitution. In these three cases it has unfortunately happened, or it has been thought, that the immediate and urgent exigencies of the public interest made it necessary to adopt a summary method of proceeding, and to resign on the result of the Elections as popularly known, without taking the more strictly Constitutional course of abiding a judgment of the House of Commons. Now, I have thought it was desirable, on behalf of the old and better system, to place upon record these few words of comment. I myself, of course, am fully responsible for one of these cases—namely, the case of 1874. If we had not retired as we did, we should have seriously abridged the Session of that year; and everyone who knows what are the duties of Parliament, what are the calls of this vast and diversified Empire, and how unequal this

House is, even with its unparalleled exertions, to meet the whole of these calls, must at once perceive that the saving of its time is, under certain circumstances, invaluable. Whenever that motive does not operate with the same commanding force with which it operated in 1874, and with which, as I am fully prepared to assert, it has operated more stringently now, I hope the old method of the Constitution will not be forgotten, and that the Party in power which has submitted its claims to the judgment of the country will be content to ascertain that judgment in the most regular manner—namely, by awaiting the issue of discussion and a Vote in that Parliament itself when the House of Commons re-assembles.   3 *Hansard* CCLII, 147–8

THE DISSOLUTION OF PARLIAMENT

109. The end of the Melbourne government, 1841

[Journal of Queen Victoria, 15 May 1841]

Lord Melbourne came to me at twenty minutes past one, and we talked about this question of dissolution. 'We shall have a long debate upon it this morning at the Cabinet,' Lord Melbourne said. 'The worst thing is, that if we carry the Sugar duties, we must dissolve. If we were to dissolve,' he continued, 'and were to have the parties equal as they are now, it would be very bad; if we *were* to have a *majority*, it would be a great thing; *but* if we were to have a minority it would be still worse.... We know that Charles I. and Charles II., and even Cromwell, appealed to the country, and had a Parliament returned into their very teeth' (so strong an Opposition), 'and that produced deposition, and convulsion, and bloodshed and death; but since then the Crown has always had a majority returned in favour of it. Even Queen Anne,' he continued, 'who removed Marlborough in the midst of his most glorious victories and dissolved Parliament, had an immense majority, though her measures were miserable; William IV.,' he said, 'even though he had a majority against him which prevented him from keeping his Ministers, had a much stronger feeling for him in that Parliament, than he ever had before. But I am afraid', he added, 'that for the first time the Crown would have an Opposition returned smack against it; and that would be an affront to which I am very unwilling to expose the Crown.'[1]   *LQV*, 1st ser. I, 347–8

[1] None the less, Melbourne did dissolve parliament and the ministers were beaten at the general election.

110. Peel argues that a dissolution may not be used for party advantage, 29 June 1846

I do not think a dissolution justifiable for the purpose merely of strengthening a party. The power of dissolution is a great instrument in the hands of the Crown; and it would have a tendency to blunt the instrument if it were employed without grave necessity. If the purpose were to enable the country to decide whether Ministers had been justified in proposing the measures of commercial policy brought forward at the beginning of the Session, those measures having passed into a law, I do not think such a purpose alone would be a sufficient ground for a dissolution. There ought also to be a strong presumption that, after a new election there would be returned to this House a party with strength sufficient to enable the Government, by their support, to carry on that system of public policy of which it approved. I do not mean a support founded upon mere temporary sympathy, or a support founded upon concurrence in one great question of domestic policy, however important. We ought not, in my opinion, to dissolve without a full assurance that we should have the support of a powerful party united with us by accordance in general views and principles of government. In the present state and divisions of party, and after all that has occurred, I do not entertain a confident hope that a dissolution would give us that support. I think, too, that after the excitement that has taken place—after the stagnation of trade that has necessarily followed our protracted discussion on the Corn Laws and the Tariff, it is not an advantageous period for a dissolution, but that the country should be allowed an interval of tranquillity and repose. We have, therefore, on these several grounds preferred instant resignation to the alternative of dissolution. *3 Hansard* LXXXVII, 1043

111. Queen Victoria supports Peel's view, 1846

[Queen Victoria to Lord John Russell, 16 July 1846]

As Lord John touches in his letter on the possibility of a Dissolution, the Queen thinks it right to put Lord John in possession of her views upon this subject *generally*. She considers the power of dissolving Parliament a most valuable and powerful instrument in the hands of the Crown, but which ought not be to used except in extreme cases and with a certainty of success. To use this instrument and be defeated is a thing most lowering to the Crown and hurtful to the country. The Queen strongly feels that she made a mistake in allowing the Dissolution in 1841; the result has been a majority returned against her of nearly one hundred votes; but suppose the result to have been nearly an equality of votes between the two contending parties, the Queen would have thrown away her last remedy, and it would have been impossible for her to get any Government which could have carried on public business with a chance of success.   *LQV*, 1st ser. II, 108

112. Russell asks for a dissolution, 1847

[Lord John Russell to Queen Victoria, 19 March 1847]

Lord John Russell presents his humble duty to your Majesty. Lord John Russell thinks it right to state to your Majesty that the prevailing opinion in the Cabinet is that when the necessary business in the House of Commons has been finished, a Dissolution of Parliament should take place.

This course would be conformable to the usage from the passing of the Septennial Act till 1830. From 1830 to the present year no House of Commons has been allowed to continue six years. The Dissolutions of Lord Grey in 1831 and 1832, of Sir Robert Peel in 1834, the death of William the Fourth in 1837, Lord Melbourne's Dissolution in 1841, have all interrupted the natural life of Parliaments. But all Governments since the accession of the House of Hanover have been of opinion (with one or two exceptions) that it is hazardous to allow a Parliament to continue seven years, as circumstances may arise making a Dissolution very detrimental to the public welfare.

These being general considerations, Lord John Russell would reserve any decision on the subject till the moment shall arrive when a Dissolution may appear to your Majesty's advisers to be the course most likely to secure moderate and fair elections.   *LQV*, 1st ser. II, 142

113. Aberdeen advises Queen Victoria not to refuse Derby a dissolution, 1858

[Memorandum by Sir Charles Phipps, *c.* 15 May 1858]

Upon being admitted to Lord Aberdeen, I informed him...that I had been...directed to call upon him, with a view of obtaining his opinion and advice upon certain important points.

The first was the question of a Dissolution of Parliament in the event of the Government being defeated upon the question which was at present pending. I told him that I was permitted to communicate to him in the strictest confidence, that in a late Audience which Lord Derby had with the Queen, he had asked her permission to be allowed to announce that, in the event of an adverse majority, he had Her Majesty's sanction to a Dissolution of Parliament.

That the Queen had declined to give such sanction, or even such a pledge, and equally guarding herself against being supposed to have made up her mind to refuse her sanction to a Dissolution, had told Lord Derby that she could not then make any prospective decision upon the subject. I told him that in point of fact Her Majesty was disinclined to grant to Lord Derby her authority for a Dissolution, but that the Queen had at once refused to grant to Lord Derby her sanction for making the announcement he wished, as she considered that it would be a very unconstitutional threat for him to hold over the head of the Parliament, with her authority, by way of biassing their decision.

Lord Aberdeen interrupted me by saying that the Queen had done quite right—that he never heard of such a request being made, or authority for such an announcement being sought—and he could not at all understand Lord Derby making such an application. He knew that the Government had threatened a Dissolution, that he thought that they had a perfect right to do so, but that they would have been quite wrong in joining the Queen's name with it.

He said that he had never entertained the slightest doubt that if the Minister advised the Queen to dissolve, she would, as a matter of course, do so. The Minister who advised the Dissolution took upon himself the heavy responsibility of doing so, but that the Sovereign was bound to suppose that the person whom she had appointed as a Minister was a gentleman and an honest man, and that he would not advise Her Majesty to take such a step unless he thought that it was for the good of the country. There was no doubt of the power and prerogative of the Sovereign to refuse a Dissolution—it was one of the very few acts which the Queen of England could do without responsible advice at the moment; but even in this case whoever was sent for to succeed, must, with his appointment, assume the responsibility of this act, and be prepared to defend it in Parliament.

He could not remember a single instance in which the undoubted power of the Sovereign had been exercised upon this point, and the advice of the Minister to dissolve Parliament had been rejected—for it was to be remembered that Lord Derby would be still at this time her Minister—and that the result of such refusal would be that the Queen would take upon herself the act of dismissing Lord Derby from office, instead of his resigning from being unable longer to carry on the Government.   *LQV*, 1st ser. III, 363–5

114. Salisbury offers reasons for the dissolution of parliament, 1900

[Marquess of Salisbury to Queen Victoria, 5 September 1900]

Reasons for submitting that Parliament should be dissolved this month:

1. The Parliament is in its sixth year; and precedents are in favour of a dissolution in the sixth year.

2. It would be almost useless to continue the Parliament during another Session; for with the strong expectation which prevails of a dissolution, members spend all their time in canvassing their constituents, and cannot be got together for the work of the House; whereas, if there is a dissolution this autumn, they can devote themselves without reserve to their Parliamentary duties next year.

3. A critical period has been reached in the South African War; and also in the Chinese campaign; and your Majesty's Government, to whomsoever it may be entrusted, will act with much more confidence and effect if they are fully acquainted with the views of the electors, and are assured of their support. Europe is in an uneasy condition; and, if there should be any disturbance within the next few months, it will be highly inconvenient [if] your Majesty should be compelled, by the efflux of time, to hold a general election in the middle of it.

LQV, 3rd ser. III, 586

MINORITY GOVERNMENTS

115. Peel advises his colleagues to resign, 1835

[Cabinet Paper by Sir Robert Peel, 25 March 1835]

Sir Robert Peel feels it to be his duty to call, previously to the meeting of the next Cabinet, the serious attention of his colleagues to the position of the Government in the House of Commons, and to this grave question, whether it is consistent either with the credit and character of public men or the interests of the King's service to continue the attempt to conduct a Government with a minority in the House of Commons.

Let us calmly review what has taken place. The Government has been beaten since the meeting of Parliament on the choice of a Speaker, and on the amendment to the Address I was obliged to name Mr. Bernal for the Chair of the Committee of Ways and Means, from inability to secure the election of any one in the confidence of the Goverment. The first diplomatic appointment which we made could not have been persisted in, and was resigned in consequence of the interference of the House of Commons by the person designated for it. We have made no progress whatever with public business, have only yet passed through three or four votes on Navy estimates in the Committee of Supply, have been obstructed every night by frivolous debates....

Nothing can, in my opinion, justify the Administration in persevering against a majority, but a rational and well-founded hope of acquiring additional support, and converting a minority into a majority. I see no ground for entertaining that hope. But I foresee the greatest prejudice to the cause of good government, to the character of an Administration, and of the public men who compose it, and to the prerogatives of the Crown, in a long-continued course either of acquiescing in what you believe to be wrong, for fear of being in a minority, or of exhibiting the Executive Government without control over the House of Commons, and attempting—after sufficient proof of their failure—to govern with a minority. Parker, *Peel*, II, 292–3

116. Derby justifies his refusal to form a minority government, 8 February 1855

My Lords, I can conceive no object of higher or nobler ambition, none more worthy of the anxiety of a true patriot and lover of his country, than to stand in the high and honourable position of the Chief Minister of the Crown and leader of the councils of this great Empire, assisted and supported by colleagues combined with him by unity of sentiment and mutual and personal respect, and with the knowledge that this and the other House of Parliament would give to such a Minister the assurance that, except on most extraordinary and unusual occasions, he would be enabled with life and energy to carry out his plans and to mature and accomplish his objects and, practically as well as nominally, control and govern the legislation and internal economy of this great country. On the other hand, to hold that high and responsible situation dependent for support from day to day upon precarious and uncertain majorities, compelled to cut down this measure, and to pare off that—to consider with regard to each measure not what was for the real welfare of the country, but what would conciliate some half-dozen men here, or obviate the objections of some half-dozen there—to regard as a great triumph of Parliamentary skill and Ministerial strength to scramble through the Session of Parliament, and to boast of having met with few and insignificant defeats—I say this is a state of things which cannot be satisfactory to any Minister, and which cannot be of advantage to the Crown, or to the People of this country. But, my Lords, to enter on the duties of office, not with a precarious majority, but with a sure minority of the other House of Parliament— to be aware that from day to day you were liable to defeats at any moment by the combination of parties, amounting to a sure majority, and only waiting for the moment when it would be most convenient to introduce Motions for the attainment of such an end; to be a Minister on sufferance; to hold such a position without any security for enforcing your own views; with the fear of exposing your own friends and the country—your friends to perpetual mortification, and the country to constant disappointment—to undertake the responsibilities and the duties of office under such circumstances, and in such a state of things, would be such an intolerable and galling servitude as no man of honour or character would voluntarily expose himself to, and such as no man willingly would submit to, except from motives of the purest patriotism, and on proof of the absolute necessity of such self-sacrifice.   3 *Hansard* CXXXVI, 1336–7

117. The Salisbury government decides to seek a quick defeat, 1885
[Marquess of Salisbury to Queen Victoria, 14 December 1885]

...at the Cabinet held to-day it was, after much discussion, resolved that it was the duty of Ministers to meet Parliament [after the narrow defeat in general election]; but that, in order to avoid the humiliations which would be inflicted on them if they remained as a Ministry on sufferance, controlled by an adverse majority, they should take an early opportunity of compelling the House of Commons to declare whether it is prepared to repose confidence in them or not. *LQV*, 2nd ser. III, 710–11

PROPOSALS FOR PARLIAMENTARY DEVOLUTION

118. Winston Churchill on devolution, 1911

Cabinet Paper of 24 February 1911

It seems to me absolutely impossible that an English Parliament, and still more an English Executive, could exist side by side with an Imperial Parliament and an Imperial Executive, whether based on separate or identical election. Imperial affairs could not in practice be separated from English party politics, which consist principally of domestic questions. The persons who are prominent in British party politics will be so mainly because of their following in England on internal questions; and it is not conceivable that such persons, having acquired mastery in the decisive field of home politics, would be willing, or would be able, to surrender the control of foreign, colonial, military, and naval affairs to another class of Ministers or politicians. The external sphere touches the internal at almost every point. The fortunes of the country abroad and at home are interdependent and indissoluble. Persons are trusted by the nation to manage the external affairs of the country because of the confidence and support accorded to their political action on great social, economic, and political issues at home; and the principles which are affirmed by the nation in domestic politics have always governed, and will always govern, the character and conduct of external affairs. No separation of the issues is possible in practice, and none is desirable. The strong positions of a British Foreign Minister, Chancellor of the Exchequer, or Ministers of Defence are based upon the support of vast organised party followings which come together for all purposes, but primarily for domestic purposes, and would be incompetent for action in either sphere alone.

Cabinet Papers. Cab. 37/105/16

Cabinet Paper of 1 March 1911

I put the following outline forward as a basis for discussion:—

1. The Imperial Parliament to remain unaltered, except by a strict numerical redistribution between countries.
2. The United Kingdom to be divided into ten areas, having regard to geographical, racial, and historical considerations.
3. A legislative and administrative body, separately elected, to be created for each area.

4. In Ireland, Scotland, and Wales these bodies to be clothed with Parliamentary form so far as may be desirable in each case.

5. Women to vote and serve on all these bodies [except in Ireland, where the National Parliament will decide].

6. These bodies to assume—

(a) All the powers now exercised by County Councils;

(b) Certain powers now exercised by municipal bodies;

(c) Certain powers to be devolved upon them by the Imperial Parliament, including—

(1) Education.

(2) Licensing.

(3) Land. (All provision for compensation shall be on principles to be laid down by Imperial Parliament, and officials settling amount of compensation in individual cases shall be appointed and removed by Imperial authority.)

(4) Housing.

(5) Police.

(6) All local Judges and Magistrates. (After an interval of, say, five years, during which period all Judges shall be appointed as at present. These Judges to be removable on address by either local or Imperial Parliament.)

(7) Poor Law.

(8) Agriculture:

Technical instruction.

Experimental farms.

Credit banks.

Co-operation.

Afforestation.

(9) Fisheries.

(10) Private Bill legislation.

(11) Roads.

(12) Boundary questions between counties, towns, and urban and rural areas.

(d) Such further powers as Parliament shall from time to time devolve to any or all of them.

7. The Imperial Parliament to retain all powers not specifically devolved.

8. The policy to be put forward in two separate Bills simultaneously announced but independently justified, one to deal with Ireland and

the other with Great Britain. As the Bill dealing with Great Britain must involve a complete recasting of the methods of local taxation, the Irish Bill to be proceeded with in the first year, and the Bill affecting the larger island in the second year. *Cabinet Papers.* Cab. 37/105/18

119. Asquith on parliamentary devolution, 1912

[Speech on the Government of Ireland Bill, 11 April 1912]

I myself, while recognising to the full the priority and paramount urgency of the Irish claim have always presented the case for Irish Home Rule as the first step, and only the first step in a larger and more comprehensive policy. I said so with the utmost distinctness in a speech which I made on the Second Reading of the Bill of 1893, and in the twenty years which have since elapsed there is not one year which has not illustrated and emphasised with ever-growing cogency and clearness the imperative need, in the interests of the United Kingdom and of the Empire as a whole, for the emancipation from local cares and local burdens of the Imperial Parliament. Look, first of all, at the effect of our present system upon purely domestic legislation and administration. It inflicts every year a double injury upon each of the component parts of the United Kingdom.... In the first place there is no time or room to deal with their separate needs. It is hardly an exaggeration to say that when the season annually comes round for compiling the King's Speech, the practical question for those concerned with its composition is what is the least instalment of that which is admittedly overdue by which England, Scotland, and Wales can respectively for the Session be bought off. That is what it comes to, and further, not only is our local legislation hopelessly in arrear but under our existing arrangements it is constantly coloured and twisted and warped by the voices and votes of those who have no direct concern in the matter. Local experience, local sentiment, and local interest are over-ridden and set at nought. You will never get...the separate concerns of the different parts of this United Kingdom treated either with adequate time or with adequate knowledge and sympathy until you have the wisdom and the courage to hand them over to the representatives whom alone they immediately affect. 5 *Hansard (Commons),* XXXVI, 1403–4

B THE HOUSE OF COMMONS

The House of Commons enjoyed an astonishing measure of prestige down to 1914. Occasionally there were demonstrations against the House and for a time in the 1830s there was a widespread feeling that electoral reform would lead to some sort of popular domination of the House (211). But as Disraeli pointed out in 1835, the reformed electorate was only a small section of the people of England (122), and its backing served simply to increase the prestige of the House of Commons. To be a member of parliament was to be a notable, mixing with the great and enjoying the facilities of a rather old-fashioned club. Young men were often bored by Commons life and old men sometimes found it uncomfortable, but there was always a long string of barristers, retired businessmen and manufacturers looking for a seat. Indeed, the mystique of the House was sometimes almost oppressive, and some of the radicals and the early working-class M.P.s set themselves resolutely to resist it. But in spite of Keir Hardie's picturesque headgear, the mystique almost invariably won in the end. The House continued to have a marked collective ethos which new members soon assimilated, and it was long before even the traditional adjournment on Derby Day was abandoned.

The House normally met in the afternoon, which allowed busy men time to earn a living or to sit on committees. The first hour of business usually attracted a good attendance, because it was concerned with petitions, questions and the business of the House. A conscientious member might devote twelve hours a day or more to the business of the House (129), but many members rarely appeared in the House until after dinner, and divisions were usually delayed until late in the evening for their benefit. A member might be regarded as a good attender by the party managers, and still be able to carry on a business in the provinces (132) or be an active chairman of Quarter Sessions. Only great parliamentary occasions were normally staged early in the day, in order to give plenty of time for debate and to attract a really full attendance. Most of the time the House was a convenient size for the members who used it, the tone was relaxed, and members were in close touch with the life of the country. All-night sittings were rare before the 1880s, and became infrequent again in the 1890s.

The qualifications for membership of the Commons changed substantially in character in the course of the century. In 1815 the law excluded members of certain suspect religious groups (Roman Catholics, Jews, and those who would not take the parliamentary oath, chiefly Quakers), the clergy, most government officials and pensioners, government contractors, certain convicted malefactors, and all those not possessing the substantial property qualifications laid down in Queen Anne's reign. The laws which excluded persons on account of religion were abandoned after a series of struggles, those against Roman Catholics in 1829 and those against Jews in 1858, and the oaths were frequently modified, first to enable the Quaker Joseph Pease to sit, and subsequently to allow members to make an affirmation instead of an oath. The position was not finally clarified until the Oaths Act (1888) which made it possible for a member of any religious denomination or none to make an appropriate declaration. The range of government pensioners excluded from membership was likewise modified from time to time, notably by the removal of the disqualification for those in receipt of Civil Service and diplomatic pensions. The property qualification was finally abandoned in 1858, when it was already something of an anachronism, since members were only rarely unseated because they lacked it.

After the passage of the 1867 Reform Act membership of the House began to be regarded not so much as a privilege, hedged about by disqualifications, but as something which every citizen might aspire to. The problem now was how to enable poor men to enter the House. A few were financed by trade union or party funds, but others, just as desirable as members, were excluded by lack of an independent income. There was much talk of the danger of the Commons becoming a rich man's club (**130**), and of the need for a parliamentary salary (**133**). But the case for a positive measure of assistance for poor members was not fully met until 1911. From the beginning of the financial year 1911–12 all M.P.s were entitled to £400 a year, paid quarterly, and subject to income tax, provided that they were not receiving an official salary.

Controversies over the right of the House of Commons to prescribe qualifications for its membership on several occasions brought about a head-on confrontation between the Commons and the electorate of particular constituencies. The Commons had always claimed that its privileges included the exclusive right to regulate its membership where there was no statutory bar to doing so, but the controversy over John Wilkes in the eighteenth century had pointed to the danger of carrying privilege too far, so that nineteenth-century governments avoided another Wilkes case. Yet there were crises enough over the membership of the Commons. In 1828 the election of Daniel O'Connell, a Roman Catholic, for County Clare, gave the government a severe jolt. Rather than provoke a rebellion in Ireland and a defeat in the Commons the government decided to give way and to agree to Catholic emancipation. O'Connell himself was, however, refused permission to take his seat, and he had to go through the form of re-election. The election of Baron Lionel de Rothschild for the City of London in 1847 led to a protracted dispute. The House would not allow him to take the oath, because he was a Jew, the City of London continued to re-elect him, and it was 1858 before Disraeli and other champions of Jewish emancipation secured his admission. In 1875 the election of the Irish nationalist John

Mitchel for County Tipperary was followed by his exclusion from the House on the ground that he had been convicted of treason felony in 1848 and had escaped before he had served the whole of his sentence. Tipperary promptly re-elected him, but on this occasion the matter was referred to the courts on petition, and the courts, by holding that Mitchel was disqualified, cut short a potentially dangerous dispute. Finally in 1880 there was the protracted Bradlaugh case. Charles Bradlaugh, elected for Northampton, was a well-known atheist propagandist whose opinions were anathema to the great majority of members of the Commons. The House, disregarding the advice of the government, would permit him neither to affirm nor to take the oath, on the ground that his principles were such as to make either alternative inappropriate. The courts on the whole agreed with the House, but the electors of Northampton did not. Unseated by the House, he was re-elected in 1881; ejected from the House by force, he was expelled in 1882; twice re-elected, he was again excluded in 1883 and 1885. Finally in 1885, after yet another election, a new Speaker, Arthur Peel, ruled that he had no power to prevent a member from taking the oath and refused to permit members to question the decision.[1] Meanwhile the unseemly controversy had done much to damage the prestige of the Gladstone government.

The Bradlaugh controversy was also the last of a notable series which affected the privileges of the House in general. The privilege of members to speak their minds in parliament without fear of retaliation in the courts, challenged in Stockdale v. Hansard, 1839, was put on a statutory basis by the Parliamentary Papers Act, 1840. Newspaper reports of parliamentary proceedings were accorded qualified privilege by the courts in Wason v. Walter, 1868. The privilege of the House to expel members was reaffirmed not only in the Bradlaugh case but in other cases as well. The privilege of the House to draw up its own rules of procedure and to interpret them freely was explicitly confirmed in Bradlaugh v. Gosset, 1884. The courts, after showing much reluctance in the early stages of Stockdale v. Hansard, thus accepted the traditional privileges of the Commons as well-founded in law, provided that they did not conflict with the statutory rights of individuals.

On two points the House was prepared to abandon its privileges. In 1868 it agreed to a bill transferring responsibility for the trial of election petitions to special election courts, over which the House exercised no control whatever. This was an important change, because it put an end to the old charge that the House was partisan in its hearing of petitions and that it was half-hearted about putting down corruption. In Ireland the new system was for a time scarcely less partisan than the old, because of the character of some Irish judges, and there were still occasional complaints about particular judges in England, but the new system generally worked well after a number of

---

[1] For the Bradlaugh case see Arnstein, *The Bradlaugh Case*.

changes in 1872. More dramatic was the failure of the House to demand the immunity of members from arrest in the case of the Irish nationalists in the 1880s and 1890s. Arthur Balfour—'Bloody Balfour'—actually succeeded at one point in imprisoning no fewer than twenty-nine Irish members within a short space of time. Nor were English members immune from arrest if they went to Ireland. The Irish police were constantly on the look-out for suspicious characters, and incautious English Liberal M.P.s were liable to find their Irish expeditions singularly uncomfortable.

The Speaker of the House in 1815 was Charles Abbot, a keen politician, who was succeeded in 1816 by Charles Manners-Sutton, an even keener politician, who was considered a possible Prime Minister in 1832. Both were accustomed to take part in debates, both expressed strong opposition to Catholic emancipation, and both were in constant communication with the Tory leaders. At a time of intense party feeling such actions were injudicious to say the least, and in the parliament of 1832–5 Manners-Sutton finally lost the confidence both of the Whig government and of its supporters. When parliament met in 1835 his re-election was opposed and in an unusually large division James Abercromby was selected to succeed him by 316 votes to 306. During the debate members endeavoured to establish the doctrine of the political impartiality of the Speaker and this was eventually secured during the long rule of Speakers Shaw-Lefevre and Denison. On the occasion of the next two vacancies the Liberal ministries of the day perhaps injudiciously nominated two ex-Chief Whips, Brand and Peel, but both men proved to be impartial Speakers. By 1911, so firmly established was the doctrine of the impartiality of the Speaker that the Parliament Act of that year imposed upon the Speaker the key responsibility of deciding which bills were money bills, and therefore did not require the assent of the Lords.

The staff of the House was steadily increased in the course of the century. The most important development was undoubtedly the growing professionalisation of the Clerk's office and of the private bill office. As a result of the labours of Thomas Erskine May, the rules of the House were successfully codified, and May and Speaker Denison established a new type of working relationship between Clerk and Speaker which was very similar to that which existed in a government department between a permanent secretary and a minister. The Clerk of the House became a notable figure in his own right, was frequently consulted, and did his best to build up the House's own civil service. A parallel development within the House itself gave the Speaker some assistance in debate. The Chairman of Ways and Means was in 1855 empowered by statute to act as Deputy Speaker in the absence of the Speaker and to exercise all the powers of the Speaker. The Deputy Speaker in turn found it necessary to have the assistance of a Deputy Chairman of Ways and Means, who in 1902 was also empowered to act as a deputy speaker.

The major changes in procedure, the introduction of the closure and the creation of standing committees, along with the growing emphasis on parliamentary questions, made surprisingly little difference to the way in which business was conducted. All major matters were still taken on the floor of the House, and question time at the beginning of the day tended to emphasise the corporate character of the House rather than to point the way to a further delegation to committees. Such changes as there were in the tone of business owed far more to the growing earnestness of members, their increased expectation of governmental action for the benefit of their constituents, and the increasing volume of legislation, than to matters of procedure. Indeed, there was a growing tendency for groups of members to try to get as much business as possible settled outside the House, so that it would not be delayed by controversy on the floor of the House itself. This had long been the practice of the Scottish members, who held unofficial meetings to discuss Scottish legislation. And the Scottish example was followed not only by the Welsh members but by groups of members interested in such topics as labour legislation, land reform, and local government.

The introduction of the closure was the most dramatic of a long series of changes in procedure designed to give more sense of purpose to the reformed House of Commons. Obstruction and time-wasting of various sorts were a recurrent feature of parliamentary life, as Sir Thomas Erskine May pointed out (137), and a variety of methods had been adopted in order to deal with them. Successive Speakers did their best to keep up with each new form of obstruction, and came to rely heavily on the party Whips to help them arrange the course of debate (134). But not until 1881 was there a complete breakdown of the House's machinery. Outside opinion had been growing increasingly critical of the failure of the House to do its business in an orderly way (124), but it took Irish obstruction to make the House act. A small number of Irish members deliberately kept the House in session for $41\frac{1}{2}$ hours between 31 January and 2 February 1881, until the Speaker, after consulting the Leader of the House and the Leader of the Opposition, brought the debate to a sudden close. In the following year the Speaker was formally given power to close a debate, and in 1887 the closure became an integral part of Commons procedure (138). Any member might now move the closure, but the consent of the Speaker was necessary before a closure motion might be put. During the period 1887 to 1899 the closure was claimed on an average 62 times a session and was allowed 36 times. For the period 1900 to 1913 the corresponding figures rose to 75 and 56. Governments could at last draw up a timetable for legislation with a reasonable expectation of its being followed.

The introduction of standing committees was also designed to assist the government to carry through a programme of legislation. Until 1882 public bills were normally referred to a committee of the whole House, which could easily be obstructed by a minority of members. In 1883 two experimental standing committees (on law and on trade) were established, but abandoned almost at once. Revived again in 1888, they dealt only with minor matters until in 1907 a new system of standing committees was established. All bills were now referred automatically to a standing committee, unless they dealt with finance, major items of legislation, or provisional orders (**140**). One of the new standing committees was a specialised one—the Scottish Grand Committee—but the other four provided for by the 1907 standing orders were intended to be simply replicas in miniature of the House, reflecting its party composition, and styled Standing Committee A, B, C and D.

These changes in procedure reflected the growing professionalisation of the House. The 1880–5 House was the last in which the country gentlemen served in great numbers (**131**). With their departure there was no longer any sizeable group of members whose interests were unconnected with money making and who were free to disregard the whims of their constituents. After 1885 M.P.s were hard pressed by their constituents to watch over their interests at Westminster and to come down frequently among them to be seen and to be talked to. The M.P. who could not speak gradually became a thing of the past, and so did the man who looked on the House of Commons as little more than a club. Members began to take themselves more seriously, and by the 1890s had begun to demand better working conditions (**127**).

There was also a growing tendency for members to grow restive about the activities of the party Whips (**143–9**). The 'Whippers-in' as they were called were already hard at work in 1815, but their activities attracted little attention until the 1860s, probably because the late nineteenth-century practice which gave the government nearly 85 per cent of parliamentary time had not yet come to be recognised for what it was, a permanent feature of Commons life.[1] Thereafter, M.P.s became increasingly aware of the extent to which their own comfort depended on the quality of the government and Opposition Whips. It was they who arranged the timetable of the House, gave members permission to go home or go on holiday, and arranged the order of speakers in debate. Memoirs of parliament in the 1890s are full of comments on the Whips of the day, and by 1910 they had come to be among the best-known parliamentary figures. Critics of parliament were prone to suggest that the Whips exercised a sort of tyranny over private members, and that they had destroyed the independence of the Commons. The truth was less picturesque. Before 1832 it had been not uncommon for the government to be very weak in the Commons or for the members on the government benches to be very

---

[1] Lowell, *Government of England*, I, 312.

much divided (**98**). During the 1840s the balance tilted heavily in favour of the government, and Lord Stanley actually left the Commons for the Lords because he had not enough work to do, so dominant were his colleagues.[1] Thereafter, the balance tilted again against the government until Lord Palmerston took over the leadership of the House. Thereafter the government was almost always in the ascendant, so much so indeed that Belloc and Chesterton scented a conspiracy (**180**). The influence of the Whips merely reflected the moral dominance of the government and Opposition front benches. As Asquith pointed out (**147**), the methods of individual Whips varied from the mailed fist to the velvet glove, but their effectiveness depended entirely on the willingness of members to do as the Whips suggested. And this in turn reflected the growing professionalisation of parliament. M.P.s by the 1890s expected to be put to work for the public good, and the only source of guidance to them was provided by the Whips' office. When a party became divided on a major issue and members were no longer able to rely on the Whips for guidance, the morale of the party rapidly deteriorated. Indeed, by 1905 the supporters of the Balfour government, far from following the Whips, had become a demoralised rabble (**149**).

In ordinary times there were three ways in which members could find worthwhile parliamentary duties. First, by specialising in a particular topic and working hard behind the scenes in conjunction with interested parties they could build up an independent reputation which would ensure their being consulted by government and listened to by the House of Commons. Members like William Rathbone, W. R. Cremer of the Peace Society, and Sir John Henniker Heaton the postal reformer, in this way became national figures. Secondly, there were opportunities for detailed work in parliamentary committees, notably in the Public Accounts Committee and private bill committees. Men who chose this path were highly respected in the House and were in much demand (**135**). Finally, but less satisfying, there was the opportunity to establish a reputation as a cogent critic of government at question time.

THE CHARACTER OF THE HOUSE

120. Sir Robert Inglis defends the unreformed House of Commons, 1 March 1831

This House is not a collection of Deputies... We are not sent here day by day to represent the opinions of our constituents. Their local rights, their municipal privileges, we are bound to protect; their general

---

[1] Parker, *Peel*, III, 155.

interests we are bound to consult at all times; but not their will, unless it shall coincide with our own deliberate sense of right.... We are sent here to legislate, not for the wishes of any set of men, but for the wants and the rights of all....If in our conduct there be error, our constituents have their remedy at a dissolution....

Our Constitution is not the work of a code-maker; it is the growth of time and events beyond the design or the calculation of man: it is not a building, but a tree....there is, so far as I know, no evidence that our House was ever selected upon any principle of a Representation of population, or upon any fixed principle of Representation whatever. ...It has adapted itself, almost like another work of nature, to our growth. How different is the county representation of England now from what it once was; how little are the country gentlemen now in this House like those a century ago; how have they grown with the growth of the country; how completely do they now reflect, in their own intelligence, the mind of their constituents, as well as advocate their local wants! Such, generally speaking, as the House of Commons is now, such it has been for a long succession of years: it is the most complete representation of the interests of the people, which was ever assembled in any age or country. It is the only constituent body that ever existed, which comprehends within itself, those who can urge the wants and defend the claims of the landed, the commercial, the professional classes of the country; those who are bound to uphold the prerogatives of the Crown, the privileges of the nobility, the interests of the lower classes, the rights and liberties of the whole people. It is the very absence of symmetry in our elective franchises which admits of the introduction to this House of classes so various. The *concordia discors* opens the door to the admission here of all talents, and of all classes, and of all interests. How far, under any other than the present circumstances, the rights of the distant dependencies, of the East Indies, of the West Indies, of the Colonies, of the great Corporations, of the commercial interests generally...could find their just support in this House, I know not.   3 *Hansard* II, 1095–7, 1108–9

121. J. A. Roebuck on the reformed House of Commons, 1833

If the public could nightly see all that passes within our walls, I fear the reverence now so rife towards our respected selves would be wo-fully diminished. But the useful press, that immaculate instrument of rule or misrule, puts a fair gloss over everything that occurs, and preserves an appearance of decorum and common sense, to which, I regret to say, the reality can lay no claim. . . .

A small, ill-conditioned room, with a high backed chair and green table on the floor, with benches rising on each side, is the House of Commons. The Speaker, with his full-blown wig and flowing gown, occupies the chair, three clerks in wigs sit at his feet; and around and about, overhead in the galleries, on the floor, lying at full length on the benches, talking, laughing, hooting, coughing, sleeping, are to be seen the members; the *élite* of this great nation in the character of legislators; and *one* unfortunate wight is, amidst this strange and uncouth assembly, endeavouring, in the slang phrase, to obtain the attention of the House —in other words, is making a speech. Why, amidst such an uproar, does he continue, is the first question of every stranger? He is talking, not to the House but the newspapers,—to the country. The din and turmoil around him is the ordinary condition of our House. Were he to wait till they were attentive, he would be dumb for ever.

As this is my first appearance in Honourable House, I often ask old members, whether the reformed Parliament is worse or better in point of behaviour than its predecessors. From all I can gather it is evidently worse; and the reason assigned is satisfactory. It is not, as the Conservatives would assert, that the more enlarged constituency, has made the representatives more vulgar; for, on my knowledge, I can assert that the most rude and boisterous portion of the House are the young fry of TORY nominees. I could name one or two Lords of that set, who can and do emulate the gods of Drury. But in former Houses there were two distinct and organized parties: these parties had well-known leaders, upon whom devolved the business of advocating and opposing the measures before the House. Everybody knew this; and no one interfered with the part assigned to a given individual. The debate then went on quietly; and the House generally listened with something like attention and patience. But now there is no organization. Everybody is at sea: no guides, no rulers, no leaders are acknowledged. Every one sets up for himself, speaks for himself, thinks and acts for himself. The consequence is, that fifty speakers will rise at once, all impatient to be heard; while two or three hundred are around them, impatient to be away, to parties, to the opera, &c. So, confusion, riot, calls of 'question, question,' 'bar, bar,' which is uniformly pronounced ba, ba, with emphasis,—groans, and braying, are the order of the day. One member possesses the faculty of hooting like an owl, to the great disturbance of the gravity of the assembly, and evident annoyance of the Speaker....

Nothing is permitted to be *discussed*: the opinion of the majority may be reiterated till attention tire, and all common patience be worn out, but wo unto the unlucky wight who should attempt to *argue* in the popular sense. One or two broad assertions of opposition will be permitted; but the moment any argument is attempted—any endeavour made to illustrate and prove, then come yells and all the many means of silencing an opponent practised in Honourable House. I may make one exception to this. Mr. Grote was, as if by miracle, allowed to argue the ballot.... But there are many men who have actually been scared into silence. Of these I remark Mr. Clay—a man of instructed taste; a thinking, studious, accomplished, right-minded, and peculiarly courteous gentleman; often, with all these qualities, have I seen him shrink from the ordeal of the House, and after a vain attempt to bear up against the storm, be content to be silent. Poor Mr. Buckingham, too, has been silenced.... If, on the other hand, a silly nobleman, like poor Lord Ebrington, who cannot put two sentences together without difficulty to himself and pain to all who hear him,—if he get up and talk nonsense by the hour in favour of the notions popular in the House, he is listened to with patience. J A. Roebuck, *Tait's Edinburgh Magazine*, III, 413–14

122. Disraeli on the House of Commons, 1835

What do they [the Radicals] mean by their favourite phrase, THE PEOPLE'S HOUSE? The available constituency of England amounts to three hundred thousand. Are these three hundred thousand men the people of England? No, these three hundred thousand men are the Commons, not the people of England; and these Commons form a class in the State, privileged, irresponsible, and hereditary, like the Peers. Hutcheon, *Whigs and Whiggism*, p. 96

123. The third Earl Grey argues that the character of the Commons derives from the inequalities of the electoral system, 1858

This superiority of the House of Commons is, I think, to be ascribed in a great measure to the circumstance of its Members not all owing their seats to the choice of large bodies of constituents. Had they all been thus returned, experience justifies the inference, that they would have consisted almost exclusively of men ready to adopt, and make themselves the organs of, the popular feeling of the day, whatever it may be. The men of enlightened views and independent character, but unfitted for encountering the storms of a popular election, who have hitherto been found in the House of Commons, would have been almost, if not altogether, excluded from it. But it is the mixture of men of this sort with others sympathizing more closely with the People, and expressing their passions and feelings,—the great variety, in short, of different elements entering into its composition,—which has given to the House of Commons its very peculiar character. To this we owe, more especially, its having answered so admirably the purpose of a public instructor. If there had not existed facilities for the entrance into the House of Commons of able men holding unpopular opinions, as well as of Members expressing the conflicting views of the various classes of society, and of the many different interests which exist in the Nation, its debates would have lost much of their interest, and still more of their value, as the means of enlightening the minds of the People, and gradually dispelling prevailing errors. I must add, that an examination of our Parliamentary records will prove, that a large majority of the chief ornaments of the House of Commons, from the Revolution to the present time, have been indebted for their first entrance within its walls to the existence of those irregularities in our system of Representation which have been so much complained of.

Grey, Parliamentary Government, pp. 64–5

124. Frederic Harrison on the impotent despotism of the Commons, 1881

In the course of centuries everything in the working of the complex machinery of this nation has become concentrated in, or absorbed into, the House of Commons. The House has, in fact, become the most gigantic and heterogeneous Bureau that the world ever saw. Our miscellaneous Empire and our complicated society demand the most elaborate executive organization. Now the House of Commons has no traditional forms but those adapted to consultative, not to executive, bodies. The traditional House of Commons came from a single social class trained in the same ideas, and having the *esprit de corps* of a governing order.... The House of Commons is no longer, and never again will be, an aristocratic council, where honourable members, however much they contended for office, had been at the same schools, had common family connexions, and belonged to the same small class.

Upon this chamber, with no personal traditions but those of wealth and good society, with no machinery but that fitted to the deliberating council of a trained political order, there has been thrown within this century the entire control of the most complicated executive in the world. Things have grown up, under cover of the dogmas of popular freedom, until the result is a despotism centred in the House of Commons, more absolute and absorbing than that of any Tsar or Sultan. Everything has to be done in, or by the sanction of, or subject to control by, the House of Commons. And yet this House is, of any body in the range of all political history, the least equipped with the precision and authority required for executive action. The so-called Ministers are really becoming clerks (not at all permanent) who, during the recess, elaborate ingenious and complicated drafts for the House to consider: drafts usually too technical for the body of the House to understand, and which can only be spoiled by ignorant or self-interested meddling. These drafts accumulate into incredible mountains of printed matter, encrusted with fresh mountains of inconsistent and impossible amendments. A few experts alone understand the effect of this pile of projects and counter-projects. But the House goes, as it is called, 'working on', as a blindfolded horse turning a mill-wheel goes working on. And in the end, after six months of this toil, it is found that the material has choked up the machine: but few of the drafts, or not a twentieth part of them, can get turned into Acts; and the exhausted senators go off to shoot or to fish....

The old theory was that before the faithful Commons granted the King his subsidies, they had a right to lay before him any grievance that they had against any of his officers. And in order to inform the House, any member had the right to bring to its notice any act of the administration of which he might complain. Such is the old theory. The modern practice, as we know too well, is this. During the session of Parliament it is the right of every member to arrest the whole of the ordinary business, in order to question the Ministers or to make a speech about any single incident, however trivial, however technical, however incapable of being treated as a grievance, in any part of Her Majesty's dominions, or indeed in any part of the habitable world.... The interminable flow of 'questions' has often of late occupied a fifth, a fourth, or even more of an entire sitting. Beside this, half-nights, quarter-nights, sometimes even whole nights, are consumed about anything under the sun, from the Colorado beetle to the whipping of a small thief, about a scuffle amongst the Turkoman Tartars of the Steppe, or the cattle plague in Russia or the fisheries in Hudson Bay. Everything in fact which may reasonably serve for a paragraph or a letter in *The Times* newspaper, is the fitting material for a question or a debate.... We all wish to see the due investigation of abuses by Parliament. But there are limits to the omniscience and omnipotence even of Parliament; and if its myriad-faceted eye is to be turned sleeplessly on every act of the entire human and animal race, if every fact recorded in the daily newspapers is the fit subject of a night's debate, we need a thousand Parliaments all sitting simultaneously and in permanence to get through the work....

The consequences of this interminable chatter are obvious. Serious politicians avoid the whole business. It is the favourite preserve of the busybodies, the bores, and the mischief-makers. No valuable information is ever extracted. It is a point of honour with a Minister to give such an answer as a well-bred man gives to an inquisitive stranger.... The real interrogation of officials is impossible without cross-examination, the power of following up questions and driving the witness to a final definite issue. All cross-examination being forbidden by the rules of the House, the question system is now a method by which the Ministers can state half the case, and actually mislead those who question them....

...If Committees of the House existed like the Foreign Affairs Committee of the United States Senate, if Ministers could be publicly or privately summoned to explain their acts and their plans, with full power of cross-examination, and all the facilities of a strict official inquiry, something like a real control over the home and foreign policy of a Government would be established in Parliament. But then these committees must sit, or have the power of sitting, continuously, and be ready to act at a week's notice, whether the House be in session or not. It is ludicrous to ask in Parliament questions about foreign and home affairs, as to which it is often the bounden duty of an honest Minister to refuse premature information. But there is no reason why real and important questions should not be privately pressed to the satisfaction of a properly constituted committee of ex-Ministers and Privy Councillors.   F. Harrison, *Nineteenth Century*, x, 318–20, 336–9

125. Hartington on the limited powers of parliament vis-à-vis the constituencies, 9 April 1886

...I am perfectly aware that there exists in our Constitution no principle of the mandate. I know that the mandate of the constituencies is as unknown to our Constitution as the distinction between fundamental laws and laws which are of an inferior sanction. But, although no principle of a mandate may exist, I maintain that there are certain limits which Parliament is morally bound to observe, and beyond which Parliament has morally not the right to go in its relations with the constituents. The constituencies of Great Britain are the source of the power, at all events, of this branch of Parliament; and I maintain that, in the presence of an emergency which could not have been foreseen, the House of Commons has no more right to initiate legislation, especially immediately upon its first meeting, of which the constituencies were not informed, and of which the constituencies might have been informed, and as to which, if they had been so informed, there is, at all events, the very greatest doubt as to what their decision might be.   3 *Hansard* CCCIV, 1244

126. Robert Wallace, M.P., on the powerlessness of the Commons, 1895

The House has no voice in the selection of the Government, only the invidious and practically useless option of objecting. Once in, the party heads, not elected, but co-opted by predecessors similarly co-opted, are masters of the situation. On any signs of independent action in their party, they can put the pistol of Dissolution to their heads and say, 'Your vote or your life; if you do not come to heel, we will blow your Parliamentary brains out,' and so bring mutineers to their senses. Looking at facts rather than phrases, the actual Government of this country is properly neither a Monarchy nor a Democracy, but mainly an alternation of two traditional Oligarchies, each composed of an aristocratic nucleus, continually drawing recruits that suit it into its 'ring,' getting into power and place through the efficacious manipulation of party resources, and then sticking to them as long as it can, by managing the members of its Parliamentary following through a dexterous blending of menace, cajolery, and reward.

R. Wallace *Nineteenth Century*, XXXVII, 192–3

127. Augustine Birrell on the frustrations of private members, 27 February 1896

Private Members had to live in the House under conditions which were well nigh intolerable. He had no sympathy with Ministers, and did not care at all about them. They were bold, bad men, and, if they were not, they would not be Ministers. And they became Ministers only by elbowing others—nice, quiet, private Members—on one side. Ministers had large salaries, paid quarterly, and he was told there was great consolation in a salary so certain to be paid. But they had something he should value more than salary. They had private rooms to which they could retire when they were bored by the ceaseless chatter of this House, where they could sit in silence, blissful silence, in solitude,... from which they could be summoned to their places in this House should any ill-advised Member move the reduction of their salary by £100 in order to increase the Estimates by £100,000. But they had something more precious than salaries and private rooms; they had occupation, something to do, interesting departmental work, which any man might be proud to do, and that saved their minds from feeding upon themselves—a scanty herbage, he dare say, and none the less disagreeable and bitter in the mouth. Nor did he care at all for his Friends on the Front Opposition Bench; they, too, had occupation; they had great oratorical reputations to maintain; they had repartees to reduce into writing; they had the right—of which they freely availed themselves, and he was glad they did—of intervention in Debate just at the time those repartees were most naturally effective in argument. The private Member had none of these things; he had no salary, he had no room, he had no business to occupy his mind, and he had no reputation to maintain; and if he had repartees to make, they must be made on the spur of the moment—something quite out of character with the nature of the repartee. He was not now speaking of the labour in Committee-rooms Upstairs, recorded in so many Blue-books, which occupied the private Member, and gave him information of which he stood sorely in need; but on the floor of that House, unless the private Member was a bore of the first magnitude, what could he find to occupy his mind? There was in the building a magnificent library, full of books of historical interest and philosophical value; but he had been a Member for six years and had not read a single book in the library. The reason was he had no mind to bring to bear upon a book in the asphyxiating atmosphere of the House, and the distress which came of being condemned to spend so much time in doing nothing. At one time the private Member had an opportunity of making some reputation by legislative effort, but now he had hardly any chance. His occupation was well nigh gone, and there was nothing for him to do but to stroll listlessly about the Lobbies, and to come in and out when a Division was threatened. Of course, he could spend time in the Smoking-room or other places. In these circumstances private Members ought to guard jealously the conditions of Parliamentary life. It might be, as an hon. Member said, that the House had fallen in public repute; but he could not agree with the suggested remedy that they should talk twice as much as they did. If they had fallen it was because, in the opinion of the country, they talked too much; and it was not by talking more their reputation would be regained.   4 *Hansard* XXXVII, 1277–8

128. The Commons losing ground, 1901

March 23rd. The political dulness of the week has been broken by the hysterics of the House of Commons. In making a communication to the House of Lords that the crisis over the siding at Tientsin was at an end, the Secretary of State omitted to see that a similar intimation was made in the Commons, though many members of that House were present in the other Chamber, and the Exchange Telegraph Company's slips placed the House at large in possession of what had been said a few minutes later. The House of Commons has, however, to compensate itself for the loss of dignity involved in almost daily displays of violence and bad manners, by occasional fits of self-importance, and such an opportunity could not be lost. Members of Parliament are slow to realise how rapidly the credit of the House of Commons as an institution is declining. The public at large care not a jot how information reaches them, and it would seem to any reasonable mind that either branch of the Legislature was a fitting channel for ministerial communications to the Empire. Relations between Parliament and the country have become radically altered. The power of the Press, and the creation, partly thereby and partly by the operation of other agencies, of a public opinion independent of and indifferent to the claims of the popular Chamber, have relegated Parliament, as a political mouthpiece, to a subordinate position, where, if it so wills, it can still play a useful though less authoritative part.   FitzRoy, *Memoirs*, I, 49

MEMBERS OF PARLIAMENT

129. A hard-working M.P. in the 1850s: Charles Cowan

The duties of a representative for a city like Edinburgh were often unceasing and laborious...[and]...the daily correspondence was oppressive. I made it my endeavour to answer every letter which appeared to require a reply, and the work was largely augmented by the frequent necessity of corresponding with one or more of the departments of Government....I considered myself fortunate if the two pockets in the skirts of my coat contained all the letters required to be answered. The House meets usually at 4 p.m., and is generally full till 5.30, the time being occupied in the presentation of petitions, thereafter by questions of members to the different departments of Government, and notices of motion. From 5.30 to 7 I almost invariably devoted to answering letters, either in the library or one of the division lobbies, until a loud voice was heard at 6.55, 'Five minutes for post,' and thereafter, 'The man is come,' made it imperative to stop writing for that mail. I remember on one occasion counting the number of letters which I had written, addressed, and despatched during these one and a half hours, and it was eighteen....

A vast proportion of the letters I received were from persons begging for situations, particularly for that of letter-carrier, as it was, in ignorance, considered to be a ' canny post'.... I made it a rule never to recommend any one for office who was not likely to do me credit....

On one occasion I went down on a Friday to Torquay, where my family were resident, and returned on the Tuesday following. I had desired the porter of my club to retain all my letters till my return, and when I went to the club, after but three days' absence, he put into my hand 197....

I often thought that members of the House of Commons, members of committees, had a particularly strong claim for the limitation of the hours of labour. I was in some sessions a member of three different committees, sitting generally on two of the days of the week. The committees generally met at twelve, sometimes so early as eleven. We sat till 3.45 P.M., when 'Mr. Speaker is at prayers' was announced in a stentorian voice. The House generally sat till midnight, occasionally an hour or two later, so that it was not very unusual for me to be twelve hours, or even longer, continuously within the House or its precincts.   Cowan, *Reminiscences*, pp. 235–8

130. Gladstone argues that the quality of M.P.s has dangerously declined, 1877

It seems to me that, as a whole, our level of public principle and public action was at its zenith in the twenty years or thereabouts which succeeded the Reform Act of 1832, and that it has since perceptibly gone down. I agree with Mr. Lowe that we are in danger of engendering both a gerontocracy and a ploutocracy....[1]

The two circumstances which strike me most forcibly, and most painfully, are, first, the rapid and constant advance of the money power; secondly, the reduction, almost to zero, of the chances of entrance into Parliament for men who have nothing to rely upon but their talent and their character; nothing, that is to say, but the two qualities, which certainly stand before all others in the capacity of rendering service to the country. These, again, are chiefly the young; for such men have usually, by the time they reach middle life, attained, without great difficulty, to wealth or to competence. But they have then passed the proper period for beginning an effective Parliamentary education. There have been honourable and distinguished exceptions; but, as a rule, it would be as rational to begin training for the ballet at forty-five or fifty, as for the real, testing work of the Cabinet. That union of suppleness and strength which is absolutely requisite for the higher labours of the administrator and the statesman is a gift the development of which, unless it be commenced betimes, nature soon places beyond reach.... The only education for the highest work in the House of Commons is, as a rule, that given in the House of Commons. Happily, we have still a supply, in cases where high birth and family influence can be brought to bear. But we cannot afford the confinement of the admission to these cases: first, because they are not enough; secondly, because our being confined to that class for the statesmen of the future is a limitation highly adverse to the free action of popular principles, and tending to add enormously to the weight cast into the other scale. If I must hold the language of party, I say it is the Liberal party that is the great sufferer by the exclusion of this class; for its members have had a large, if not the largest, share in the promotion of Liberal measures.

Their place has been taken mainly by men who have been recommended to their constituents by the possession of money.... The loss

[1] *Fortnightly Review*, n.s. XXII, 437–52.

has been among those who had the very best capacity to serve the country. The gain has accrued to those whose main object is to serve themselves. I do not mean in a corrupt sense. It is to serve themselves by social advancement. The total exclusion of such men is probably not to be desired; but their swollen and swelling numbers are a national calamity. It is a calamity with a double edge. For what becomes of the excluded? Where do they now obtain their education? They are mainly driven to the Press. The services of the Press to the community, and most of all to public men, are invaluable; but the value of the education it affords to the young is a very different question. It gives them a laborious training in irresponsible, anonymous, and pungent criticism, in lieu of the manly and noble discipline which a youth spent in Parliament imparts. In the light of day, under the eye and judgment of the best, at once stimulated and restrained, at once encouraged and abashed, our youth had everything to sustain a high sense of political warfare, to develop the better parts of a knightly nature, and to rebuke the sordid and the base. Invert all these expressions, and we obtain a tolerably accurate description of the kind of education which our modern arrangements have provided for the most ready, brilliant, and serviceable of the young men of England, in lieu of a seat in Parliament. These are not pleasant things to say; but it is perhaps time they should be said.   Gladstone, *Gleanings*, I, 160–3

131. The country gentlemen begin to desert the Commons in the 1880s

(a) *From the autobiography of Sir J. C. Astley, Bt., M.P. for North Lincolnshire, 1874–80*

Well, the precincts of St. Stephen's held few charms for me, and I was always glad when I could get out of that political atmosphere; had it not been for the good old Serjeant-at-Arms (Gossett), who had a snug room up-stairs where most of the cheeriest members used to congregate, and over a drop of Scotch and a cigar discuss the leading topics of the day, capping each other's good stories whilst waiting for the division bell to ring, I don't know what I should have done. I can well understand a man who wants to extend his acquaintance, or is desirous of obtaining some remunerative appointment in or under the Government of the day, sacrificing the pleasures of home and other congenial pursuits for the sake of a seat in Parliament; but to a country gentleman who already knows pretty well all the best men in the House, and has no hankering after office, or, if he has, feels that he don't possess the brains or qualifications requisite to lift him out of the ordinary herd—that man, I say, I cannot understand taking much trouble to become an M.P.; for even when the House is up, and you retire to the bosom of your family, you are allowed no rest, you are constantly called upon to attend meetings all over the constituency, and are considered fair game for silly questions and childish interrogatories, in some cases put to you by creatures who have not education enough to write them down. No! it isn't good enough in my humble opinion.   Astley, *Fifty Years of My Life*, pp. 262–3

(b) W. St. J. Brodrick, M.P. for West Surrey, 1883

The House of Commons has lost much of its old attractiveness. The duties of a member become yearly more engrossing. It is not only that the hours of work are longer than they were and attendance more trying, but constituencies are much more exacting. The recess is far from being a holiday. A borough likes to see its member at local functions; a county calls its representative to half-a-dozen agricultural meetings, each of which is more important than the others, and quite distinct. Beyond this, political associations have been largely formed on either side and need stimulant in the shape of 'extra-Parliamentary utterances'.... All this makes Parliamentary life something else than the goal of social ambition, or the reward of hereditary connection. It has lately been whispered that the general disposition to pass the Corrupt Practices Bill is not unconnected with the inability of party managers to find candidates ready to spend enormous sums to enter Parliament under such conditions. Certainly the supply of available young men is not so large as it was, and whether this be due to landed depression, or to whatever cause, it is a force which touches the Conservatives first. A party which has from time immemorial included a large section of men in whose lives politics are only an incident must feel the loss when a Parliamentary career becomes too irksome for any but a devotee. Such is the tendency of the day. Men are wanted who will work up constituencies so rigorously as to ensure success, and they are not to be found.   *Nineteenth Century*, XIII, 159

(c) From the autobiography of Walter Long

The House of Commons of 1880 was the last to contain the 'Country Gentleman Party,' as it had existed for many decades. Although the character and general tone of this ancient and splendid assembly have not altered materially, in many respects it is a very different body from that which I first joined over forty years ago. The average country gentleman entered the House of Commons in much the same way that I did, performing what he regarded as his duty, without any particular ambition to do more than serve his county and his country and the agriculturist interests to the best of his ability. As a rule he made few speeches and did not desire to take part in debate. He was content to be present in the afternoon, and, when required, after dinner; to record his vote if there was a division, but otherwise to take no active part in the proceedings, except as a member of the various committees which did then, and still do, a great deal of the work of Parliament. The consequence was that any of the younger men who were prepared to devote themselves to the daily work of the House and were able to take part in its debates, found themselves given opportunities which are not enjoyed by their successors. Long, *Memories*, p. 80

132. The attendance required of a Liberal M.P., 1891
[F. Schnadhorst to Thomas Morris, 21 February 1891]

With regard to the time necessary to attend the House of Commons. It is not possible to say 2 or 3 or 4 months. The attendance must be necessarily spread over the time the House is sitting. This in ordinary times may be said to extend from February to July—the beginning and end of the period being of little importance.

During that period a member to attend *well* can come to town on Monday evening (say by 9 p.m.), return on Wednesday morning (say 12 midnight train to Warrington), come again for Thursday evening (leave Warrington say 3 o'clock) & return as a rule on Friday evening. Saturday, Sunday of course, Monday and Wednesday would be practically quite clear. Many men do this. But besides there are periods when a man need not come up at all. Although the House has been sitting a month some have not yet arrived. Absences can always be arranged by the Whips and pairs secured. Henry Roberts MSS

133. Campbell-Bannerman on the need to provide a salary for M.P.s, 7 March 1906

What, after all, is the object of our whole system of registration and of voting from one end to the other?

It is to obtain a genuine and straightforward representation of the people. And do we obtain that object now when the first question applied to a candidate, not openly, but behind the scenes, no doubt, is not 'are you a man of sufficient character, ability, and sound sense to represent this constituency?' but 'have you money enough either of your own, or derived from some other source, to meet the public expense of maintaining yourself in the discharge of your duties in attendance upon the House?' I believe that that is a most mischievous state of things. I conceive that the giving of a small allowance to a member of Parliament, sufficient for his subsistence—and the difference, of course, between this and other assemblies, such as boards of guardians ...where excellent public work is done, is [that] there is no expense involved in their membership—it does not take [him] away from his home and interrupt his daily life.

But the question is, what would be the advantage if this impediment in the way of a candidate were removed? In the first place there would be a free choice open to the constituency, which surely comes to something. Secondly, I maintain that under the present system—whether due to that system or not I cannot wholly say—but too often, I believe, the relations between constituents and members are perverted. The idea pervading men's minds is that a constituency is doing the member a favour by returning him to Parliament. It ought to be exactly the reverse. The candidate is doing the constituents a favour by undertaking arduous, difficult, and often tiresome work for them; and until you get that balance readjusted I believe you will not remedy many of those evils from which we are suffering. Why is it that members are so overwhelmed in some places by demands for subscriptions? It is because the constituencies look upon him as a man who has received a great benefit from them, and they hold that he ought to give a return. The whole of that conception of the relations between a member and his constituents is entirely wrong. Then I hold that, if every member of this House had this small sum to cover the extra expenses he is put to by living in London, it would, so far from debasing, exalt his feeling of independence. He would no longer feel that he had to look to any one to maintain him in the position in which he stood. The burden of proof in this case rests upon those who would refuse a moderate payment to members. We hear of the professional politician. What do you mean by a professional politician? If you take a man who devotes himself to his work, to the study of public affairs, in order to qualify himself here, and contrast with him a man who comes here as a pastime or a means of social advancement, which of the two is the better man? Have there not been in past Parliaments men who, quite independently of money, have had some purpose—a trade purpose or some other purpose peculiar to themselves, perhaps, or shared by others—to serve by their presence and action here?   Campbell-Bannerman, *Speeches*, 195–6

COMMONS PROCEDURE
134. Alpheus Todd on the order of speaking in debates

It is customary, in debates of the House, to allow priority to members of the administration who wish to speak; and to permit the prime minister, or leader of the House, to have the last word. In all important debates, it is usual for the Speaker to give preference, alternately, to the known supporters and opponents of the question; and it would be considered irregular to interfere with the Speaker's call in favour of any other member. When many members desire to address the House, an arrangement is sometimes made in the Commons, between the government and the opposition 'whippers-in'...as to the order in which the Speaker shall name those who are to take part in the debate. ...But the speaker is not bound to any list of intending debaters...

Since 1830, the number of members who take an active part in debate has steadily increased. Thus, before the Reform Bill, the speaking and business of the House were in the hands of about 150 members. In 1841 there were 231 members who took part in the proceedings. In 1861 the number had gone up to 300; and in 1876 to 385 members.

Todd, *Parliamentary Government*, II, 400–1

135. The number of committees and petitions increasing, 1848
[Benjamin Disraeli in the House of Commons, 30 August 1848]

...I should state what, independent of our debates, this House of Commons, which it is the fashion to blame at present, has really done; and, in doing so, I will refer to a short paragraph in the report of the

Committee on Public Business.... It appears from that report that there have been this year forty-five public Committees, some of more than usual importance, with an average number of fifteen Members serving on each Committee. Then there have been twenty-eight Election Committees, with five Members serving on each Committee; fourteen groups on Railway Bills, with five Members on each group; seventeen groups on private Bills, with five Members on each group; and there have been also one hundred and eleven other Committees on private business. Of the public Committees, that on commercial distress sat thirty-nine days; that on sugar and coffee planting, thirty-nine days; that on the Navy, Army, and Ordnance expenditure, forty days; and that on the miscellaneous expenditure, thirty-seven days. There have, besides, been presented this year upwards of 18,500 petitions, showing an increase of 25 per cent above the greatest number presented in any former year, except 1843.   3 *Hansard* CI, 672–3

136. The Public Accounts Committee created, 1861

The CHANCELLOR of the EXCHEQUER [W. E. Gladstone], in moving [on 9 April 1861] for the appointment of a Select Committee on Public Accounts, said that the object of the Committee would be to revise the accounts of the public expenditure after they had gone through the regular process of examination in the hands of the executive Government. That was obviously the true completion of the duty of that House with regard to the public money. The Committee on Public Monies which sat two or three years ago had made this recommendation, and made it unanimously. He should, therefore, move that a Select Committee be appointed for the examination from year to year of the audited accounts of the public expenditure; and if that Motion was adopted, he would on a future day move that a Committee of that nature be appointed at the commencement of every Session; and, likewise, that the order for the appointment of that Committee be made a standing order of the House.

Motion *agreed to.*   3 *Hansard* CLXII, 318

The CHANCELLOR of the EXCHEQUER [on 19 April 1861 recommended on behalf of the government the names of nine members to serve on the committee]. These names had been chosen with a view to give satisfaction to both sides of the House, and fairly to represent all parties, while bringing as much talent, knowledge, and experience as possible to discharge these important functions. [When asked why no Scottish nor Irish members had been nominated Gladstone replied that he] could not sanction the notion that on a question of public accounts, which had no imaginable bearing on any separation of interests between one part of the kingdom and another, these national distinctions should be imported into the appointment of a Committee of that House. The Government had sought to ascertain what hon. Members were best qualified to undertake these duties, which were of a dry and repulsive kind, and he believed their choice was correct.

[The government's names were then accepted.]   3 *Hansard* CLXII, 773-4

137. Erskine May on the losing battle against obstruction, 1832–81

The period of political excitement while the Reform Bills were being passed (1830–32) first disclosed the difficulties of Parliamentary government, which continued, with little abatement, in the Reformed Parliament.

It was a new political era. Public opinion had been awakened; larger classes had been enfranchised; powerful constituencies had been created; important interests were represented in Parliament, and free discussion was everywhere developed to a degree unknown before the Reform agitation. Prodigious energy was directed to legislation, and the redress of grievances; and it was soon found that the irresponsible eagerness of Members to press forward their own views, and the interests of their constituents, on every practicable occasion, was a serious obstacle to the regular and orderly dispatch of public business.

The old Parliamentary forms offered numerous opportunities for debate, which had never been designed for that purpose. A multitude of formal questions were put from the Chair, which were superfluous and unnecessary for the effective discharge of Parliamentary functions. They had grown up in the course of time, and as attempts were rarely made to take advantage of them, for discussion or delay, they were suffered to continue. But every question put from the Chair, being debatable, formal questions now offered opportunities for debate and seriously disturbed the regular course of public business.

The first trouble arose from the presentation of petitions. The number of petitions had suddenly increased; they related to every conceivable subject of public or private interest, and they were exposed to unlimited discussion. Under the old rules four separate questions were open to debate:

1st. 'That the petition be brought up.'
2nd. 'That it be read.'
3rd. 'That it do lie upon the table.'
4th. 'That it be printed.'

Early in the session of 1833 (6th February), the House resolved that two of these Questions should be discontinued, but imposed no other restriction upon debate. It need scarcely be said that so trifling a change was of little avail; and debates became so frequent and prolonged that it was found necessary, during that and the succeeding Session, to appoint morning sittings from 12 to 3, for the presentation of petitions. But even these additional hours proved wholly insufficient for the purpose. Members assembled in crowds to ballot for precedence; but the whole sitting was occupied with a few petitions early on the list, and even adjourned debates were not infrequent.

In 1835, and succeeding years, Mr. Speaker Abercromby contrived gradually to enforce a greater measure of strictness in these debates. He endeavoured to confine Members to a general statement of the material objects of the petitions....

...It was the boldest change of procedure ever yet introduced affecting not only the accustomed privileges of Members, but the rights of the people, as petitioners....

While these restrictions were being introduced, in one direction, another irregular practice had arisen, scarcely less obstructive to business. On arriving at the Orders of the Day, a separate Question was put, that each successive Order 'be now read'; and to this purely formal Question, irrelevant Amendments were moved, and debates forced on, to the interruption of the business appointed for the day. In 1837, the Select Committee on Public and Private Business reported that on more than a third of the Government nights, during that Session, the Orders of the Day had been so interfered with.... It was not until 1849 that the reasonable practice was introduced of reading the Orders of the Day *seriatim*, without any Question being put.... Henceforth, none but Amendments relevant to the subject matter of a particular Order of the Day could be moved. Committees of Supply and Ways and Means, however, continued to be an exception to this rule; and amendments, on going into those Committees, were accordingly multiplied beyond all previous experience.

At this period, another change in the same direction was also adopted. Although none but relevant Amendments could be moved to the Order of the Day, an Order for a Committee of the whole House was exposed to this ordeal on every day on which it stood upon the Order Book. In 1848, the Select Committee on Public Business recommended that when any Bill or other matter (except Supply or Ways and Means) had been partly considered in Committee, the Speaker should afterwards leave the Chair without putting any Question. This was subsequently adopted by the House and confirmed by Standing Order, in 1853.

It was difficult to overrate the importance of this 'Rule of progress', as it has since been called....

In later years, many Bills as, for example, the Irish Church Bill, the Education Bill, the Ballot Bill and the Irish Land Bill, could scarcely have been passed, if exposed to interruptions on each successive day appointed for Committee....

In 1853, the Wednesday sittings from 12 till 6, and morning sittings from 12 till 4 on other days, were introduced. The latter hours have been changed since 1867 to 2 and 7, and have certainly afforded great facilities to the dispatch of business.

It has been seen that the Committees of Supply and Ways and Means were excepted from all the rules applicable to Amendments to Orders of the Day, and such Amendments naturally increased to a most inconvenient extent. In 1861, Mr. Speaker Denison vainly endeavoured to persuade the Select Committee on the business of the House to enforce, for Supply and Ways and Means, some restrictions equivalent to the Rule of Progress in other Committees. The evil, however, continued unchecked for several years, and for a considerable part of the Session, nearly every Government Supply night was, more or less, appropriated for notices wholly unconnected with the Estimates....

At length, Mr. Lowe's Committee, in 1872, offered a recommendation which was substantially adopted by the House in 1873....

The principle of 'Progress' was now partially applied to the Committee of Supply. But this moderate rule was relaxed in 1876, when Members were permitted to move relevant Amendments, not only on *first* going into Committee upon any class of Estimates, but on every occasion. Nor was this attenuated Resolution allowed to be made a Standing Order....

Some of these changes of procedure may appear trifling in themselves, but it is certain that unless they had been made, the legislation of the last fifty years could not have been accomplished, even with far greater toil and sacrifices than Statesmen and Members of Parliament have endured during that period.

At the same time, it is an embarrassing reflection that notwithstanding these necessary changes, difficulties in the dispatch of business continue to be as rife as ever, and obstacles, in new forms, have since arisen. The removal of one abuse has generally aggravated another. When the discussion of petitions was restrained, Amendments to Orders of the Day were multiplied. When these were restricted, Amendments on going into Committee of Supply increased in number. And, again, when these were partially limited, Motions for Adjournment became more frequent. In 1831–32, during the Reform crisis, there were only 21 dilatory Motions for Adjournment and Reporting Progress, etc., while in 1881 there were no less than 122.

Quoted by E. Hughes, Public Administration, XXXIV, 419–23

138. The closure adopted, 18 March 1887
[Standing Orders of the House of Commons 1887]

CLOSURE OF DEBATE

XIV A. That, after a Question has been proposed, a Member rising in his place may claim to move, 'That the Question be now put,' and, unless it shall appear to the Chair that such Motion is an abuse of the Rules of the House, or an infringement of the rights of the minority, the Question, 'That the Question be now put,' shall be put forthwith and decided without Amendment or Debate....

Provided always, that Questions for the Closure of Debate shall not be decided in the affirmative, if a Division be taken, unless it shall appear by the numbers declared from the Chair, that such Motion was supported by more than Two Hundred Members, or was opposed by less than Forty Members, and supported by more than One Hundred Members:

Provided always, that this Rule shall be put in force only when the Speaker or the Chairman of Ways and Means is in the Chair.

H.C. 294, p. 5. (1887). LXVI, 125

139. Parliamentary obstruction, 1887

[W. H. Smith (Leader of the House of Commons) to Queen Victoria, 11 May 1887]

Mr. Smith with his humble duty to your Majesty has to repeat the same story again. Unblushing obstruction has prevailed the whole afternoon; and, after disposing of a series of amendments, the five hours and a half sitting advanced the Bill by six words ! and then only by the use of the closure with a majority for Government of 100.   *LQV*, 3rd ser. I, 307

140. Standing committees become a normal feature of Commons procedure, 1907

[Standing Orders of the House of Commons, 1907]

46.—(1) When a bill has been read a second time it shall stand committed to one of the standing committees, unless the house, on motion to be decided without amendment or debate, otherwise order.... But this order shall not apply to—

(*a*) Bills for imposing taxes, or Consolidated Fund, or Appropriation Bills; or

(*b*) Bills for confirming Provisional Orders....

47.—(1) Four standing committees shall be appointed for the consideration of all bills committed to them....

(2) One of the standing committees shall be appointed for the consideration of all public bills relating exclusively to Scotland and committed to a standing committee, and shall consist of all the members representing Scottish constituencies, together with not more than fifteen other members to be nominated in respect of any bill by the committee of selection, who shall have regard in such nomination to the approximation of the balance of parties in the committee to that in the whole house....

(3) Subject as aforesaid the bills committed to a standing committee shall be distributed among the committees by Mr. Speaker.

(4) In all but one of the standing committees government bills shall have precedence....

48.—Each of the said standing committees shall consist of not less than sixty nor more than eighty members, to be nominated by the committee of selection, who shall have regard to the classes of bills committed to such committees, to the composition of the house, and to the qualifications of the members selected.... Provided that, for the consideration of all public bills relating exclusively to Wales and Monmouthshire, the committee shall be so constituted as to comprise all members sitting for constituencies in Wales and Monmouthshire....

H.C. 113, pp. 11–12. (1907), LXVI, 160–1

141. The Cabinet and private members' bills, 1907

[Sir H. Campbell-Bannerman to King Edward VII, 7 August 1907]

The usual practice of the Government, in addition to its own Bills, giving facilities for the progress of private members' Bills, which, though generally supported and desirable, are, through all the time of the House of Commons being taken by the Government, stranded and lost unless assistance is given them, has now to be considered. It was resolved to confine this Assistance to the following:—

(1) Deceased Wife's Sister Bill, which has been carried by overwhelming majorities, and has passed all its stages except Report (& this completed except a few lines) and 3rd Reading;

(2) Limited Partnerships
(3) Advertisement Regulations
} which have passed both Houses and have only a few formal amendments to be considered;

(4) Notification of Births
(5) Lights on Vehicles
} if agreed on by both sides of the House.

Cabinet Papers. Cab. 41/31/31

142. A Select Committee on Estimates established, 17 April 1912

The CHANCELLOR of the EXCHEQUER (Mr. Lloyd George).... The House of Commons is supposed to exercise very strict supervision over the spending of money. With all respect, I say the House of Commons does nothing of the kind.

During the whole twenty years or more that I have been a Member of this House they have not done it.... I remember very well in 1901 £67,000,000 were passed without a word of discussion, and, on the Report stage, £86,000,000 were passed. I think last year £62,000,000 were passed without discussion.... The House of Commons has not within living memory exercised any control over expenditure in the sense of directors exercising control over expenditure in their business. Discussions in Supply...are confined to two points. First of all, there is the very important one of redress of grievances before Supply.... The second is criticism of the administration.... Most of the time is directed to pressing the Executive to spend money.... I have heard vague phrases about extravagance and how much better things ought to be done, but I never heard practical, concrete suggestions for reducing expenditure in any Department....you have no real check upon recurring expenditure but the check of the Treasury.... The Public Accounts Committee can investigate only past expenditure....what we propose now [is] that a Committee...should be appointed...to examine each of the Estimates one after another, including recurring expenditure. It should not be confined to questions of irregularities in the Accounts. It should examine them exactly as a Finance Committee of a municipal corporation examines its accounts, taking its directions as to policy from the House of Commons....

[Motion as follows agreed to:] 'That a Select Committee be appointed to examine such of the Estimates presented to this House as may seem fit to the Committee, and to report what, if any, economies consistent with the policy implied in those Estimates should be effected therein.' 5 *Hansard* (*Commons*) XXXVII, 363–5, 371–3, 434

PARTY ORGANISATION IN THE COMMONS

143. The Whips work together, 1832

[From the diary of E. J. Littleton, M.P., 24 February 1833]

Ellice amused us much with stories of his interviews with Billy Holmes, when during the last Session they acted as Whippers-in respectively to the two Parties. He said they had certain conventional points of honour between them. For instance if one wanted to go home to dinner, the other agreed to send word to him if there was a prospect of a division. Billy Holmes [the Opposition Whip] frequently used to send a note to Charles Grant, the President of the Board of Control, to tell him to come to his place. One day when Ellice and Holmes were going through the list of the House of Lords previous to the division on Lord Lyndhurst's motion on the Reform Bill, they found they agreed as to every vote except one, which both claimed eagerly. Holmes said, 'I give you my word of honour he will vote with us. I *know* it.' To which Ellice replied, 'I know too by the same means that he will vote with us,' to which Holmes immediately replied, 'Then, by G—, you have paid him 430 pounds,' meaning Holmes's party had promised him 400 guineas. I can hardly credit the story, but Ellice vouched for it. Aspinall, *Three Diaries*, p. 307

144. Party recognition withdrawn from an M.P.: Disraeli, 1844

(a) Benjamin Disraeli to Sir Robert Peel, 4 February 1844

I was quite unaware until Friday night, when I was generally apprised of it, that the circumstance of my not having received the usual circular from yourself to attend Parliament was intentional.

The procedure, of course, admits of only one inference.

As a mere fact, the circumstance must be unimportant both to you and to myself. For you, in the present state of parties, which will probably last our generation, a solitary vote must be a matter of indifference; and for me, our relations, never much cultivated, had for some time merged in the mere not displeasing consciousness of a political connection with an individual eminent for his abilities, his virtues, and his station.

As a matter of feeling, however, I think it right that a public tie, formed in the hour of political adversity, which has endured many years, and which has been sustained on my side by some exertions, should not terminate without this clear understanding of the circumstances under which it has closed.

I am informed that I am to seek the reason of its disruption in my parliamentary conduct during the last Session.

On looking over the books, I perceive that there were four occasions on which I ventured to take a principal part in debate.

On the first I vindicated your commercial policy....

In the second instance I spoke on a Treaty of a difficult and delicate nature, against which the Opposition urged no insignificant charges....

At the very end of the Session there were two other occasions on which I spoke, and against isolated points of the existing policy; I mean with respect to Ireland and the Turkish Empire....

Under these circumstances, stated without passion, and viewed, I am sure, without acrimony, I am bound to say that I look upon the fact of not having received your summons, coupled with the ostentatious manner in which it has been bruited about, as a painful personal procedure which the past by no means authorised.

(b) Sir Robert Peel to Benjamin Disraeli, 6 February 1844

Although the omission on my part to request your attendance at the meeting of Parliament was not an accidental or inadvertent omission, it certainly was not the result of any feeling of personal irritation or ill-will on account of observations made by you in the House of Commons....

My reason for not sending you the usual circular was an honest doubt whether I was entitled to send it—whether towards the close of the last Session of Parliament you had not expressed opinions as to the conduct of the Government in respect to more than one important branch of public policy, foreign and domestic, which precluded me, in justice both to you and to myself, from preferring personally an earnest request for your attendance.

If you will refer to the debate on the Irish Arms Bill, and to that on Servia, and recall to your recollection the general tenor of your observations on the conduct of the Government, you will I think admit that my doubt was not an unreasonable one.... Parker, *Peel*, III, 144–6

145. The pledge required of parliamentary candidates by the Irish party, 1885

I...pledge myself that in the event of my election to parliament I will sit, act and vote with the Irish parliamentary party and if at a meeting of the party convened upon due notice specially to consider the question, it be decided by a resolution supported by a majority of the entire parliamentary party that I have not fulfilled the above pledge I hereby undertake forthwith to resign my seat. O'Brien, *Parnell and his Party*, p. 143

146. The Opposition Whips at work in 1890

The arrangements governing the Whips' rooms and messengers were curious. The rooms were in the Inner Lobby, that of the Government Whip being on the right and that of the Opposition on the left (as you looked from the entrance to the House) of the passage leading from the Inner to the Central Lobby. The Government messengers were Civil Servants, whilst those of the Opposition were paid for out of party funds and thus had to look for their subsistence to Conservatives and Liberals alternately. They were a fine set of men, hard working, most obliging and very intelligent; but I found that they worked under very severe conditions. The House then sat from 2.30 up to any hour of the night or early morning, except on Wednesdays when the hours were from 12 to 6. They had to be on duty whenever the House was sitting. When it rose, however late the hour, the Chief Whip wrote out the 'whip' (or summons to M.P.s) for the following day, with a varying number of lines beneath the words according to the importance of the business of the day. This practice was, to my mind, carried to absurd lengths, as 'whips' of four or even five lines were not uncommon. These 'whips' had then to be lithographed and taken round by hand by the various messengers and delivered at Members' residences not later than 9.30 a.m. I wonder how, on late nights, the poor fellows got any sleep at all.   Leveson-Gower, *Years of Endeavour*, pp. 33–4

147. Asquith on some Liberal Whips, 1892–1912

No one could have been found better fitted to deal with such a precarious situation than Marjoribanks [Edward Marjoribanks, government chief Whip 1892–4]. A fine upstanding man, he enjoyed unfailing health and an inexhaustible flow of high spirits. He was rich and fond of pleasure, but worked at his job like a galley-slave. He was geniality incarnate to the good party man who did his duty by listening and not replying to other people's speeches, and voting consistently in the Government lobby. Withal, he had at his command all the resources of a fiery temper and a copious vocabulary of vituperation, which were drawn upon without scruple or reserve for the punishment of slackness or 'independence'. The member who was detected, by one of his underlings or scouts, slinking away unpaired by some devious route at the dinner-hour, was infallibly marked down for one of these bouts of exemplary castigation. Majoribanks, it must be added, harboured no malice, and would be 'hail fellow well met' the next time he encountered one of his victims. He was very popular with the rank and file, and his removal by the death of his father to the House of Lords, just about the time of Mr. Gladstone's resignation in March, 1894, was an irreparable loss to the party. His successor, Tom Ellis, a charming and gifted man, and one of my greatest personal friends, was more at home among the children of light than with the children of this world, with whom a Chief Whip is in daily and even hourly converse.

A marked contrast in every way to Edward Marjoribanks was another Scotsman, Alexander Murray, the Master of Elibank....

'The Master,' as he was always called, has probably had no superior among the incumbents of his responsible office in the art of parliamentary management. I have never seen him out of temper. His method of dealing with defaulters or cranks was the very reverse of that pursued by Marjoribanks. His round, slightly rubicund face, wreathed with its habitual smile, and his soft and almost caressing voice, were brought into play more, it would seem, in mild surprise or even in subdued sympathy than in anger, and the transgressor was lured rather than driven back to the straight path. His scouting was, as a rule, admirably organized, and the daily report which he made to me as Chief of the Staff was almost always a trustworthy reflection of the passing moods and tenses of the House of Commons.

Asquith, Memories and Reflections, I, 190–1

148. Party membership dependent on the receipt of the Whip, 1903

January 19th [1904] . . . I had an interesting conversation with Sandars. . . . Whips will not be sent to Winston Churchill and Sir J. Poynder, but no others will for the present be drummed out of the party.

FitzRoy, Memoirs, I, 180

149. The Whips fail to prevent the disintegration of the Conservative party in the Commons, 1905

March 3rd. [1905]—Yesterday evening showed an alarming declension in the Government majorities. The disintegrating effects of the last fortnight's debates began to tell decisively on the cohesion of the Ministerialists; in five successive divisions the majority never rose above 31, and was twice as low as 24. Nor, as I hear, was this the worst feature of the situation: the spirit displayed in the lobbies among those who might have voted, and refused to do so, was most ominous. Though there were five hundred members in the House during the afternoon, it was found impossible to keep a sufficient number to render a division safe before the dinner interval. The character of the defection made it all the more remarkable. Old-fashioned Tories, who, in the whole course of their parliamentary lives, had never entertained the thought of voting against their party, now left the House swearing that nothing would induce them to stay and vote. They swept past the Whips at the doors, ignoring their presence or rudely repelling their efforts to detain them, till the Whips themselves deserted their posts in despair, and defeat was only averted by putting up stalwarts to talk against time. A spirit of aggressive violence towards the Ministerial bench displayed itself in the House. Tommy Bowles, fresh from his correspondence with Stanley and Ailwyn Fellowes, and the easy triumph they had given him, told Bromley-Davenport he got all his information from under the gallery, and Winston Churchill surpassed himself in offence. It is true he made one legitimate score that amused the House hugely: the only occupants of the Treasury bench happened to be Arnold-Forster and, at a great interval, St. John Brodrick. Failing to get a reply to some query from the first-named, he turned to the other, and invited him with pointed satire to come to the assistance of his hardly pressed and much-loved colleague. The question is now being asked whether the Government can possibly hold out to the Budget; Chamberlain's impatience at the situation is growing visibly, and when it becomes known that the Prime Minister has had to go outside the ranks of active politicians to find a successor to Selborne the public will realise how exhausted are his ordinary resources. Not that the choice he has made in offering the place to Cawdor is other than an admirable one, but it is a curious comment on the refusal a year and a half ago to make him a Privy Councillor at the suggestion of the Duke of Devonshire.

July 21st.—The Government were beaten last night on a motion to reduce the Chief Secretary's salary after he had expounded the ministerial plans for removing the block in Irish land purchase under the Act of 1903. The division was not a surprise, as it took place at the expected hour and full warning had been given to the supporters of the Government; yet seventy of them were away unpaired two days after the rafters of the Foreign Office had rung with the acclamations of the faithful in response to the Prime Minister's appeal to their loyalty. The Government will not, however, resign.

FitzRoy, *Memoirs*, I, 240–1, 260

C THE HOUSE OF LORDS

The House of Lords of the United Kingdom, established in 1800, numbered about 372 members in 1820. Already informed opinion thought it too large, and was inclined to blame Pitt the Younger for having created too many peers. But the House continued to grow—to 439 in 1837, to 591 in 1901, and to 623 in 1910. Membership was by now essentially a mark of wealth or of social status, since Prime Ministers rarely nominated men for peerages unless they had a settled income of at least £5,000 a year. Until the 1880s it was usual to look askance at any applicant for a peerage who did not possess broad acres, but thereafter peerages were readily given to those whose money came from industry or commerce. As a result, the House of Lords came to be regarded as a rich man's club, totally unrepresentative of the country at large.

Peerages were normally given either as a reward for party services, whether in the House of Commons or in the country, or as a mark of distinction to leading public servants—diplomats, generals, admirals, colonial governors, and civil servants. But at the very end of the nineteenth century the range of recipients was widened to include poets (Tennyson), artists (Leighton) and scientists (Kelvin). Acceptance of the offer of a peerage usually carried with it an implicit or explicit agreement not to side with the opponents of the Prime Minister making the nomination. In the case of wealthy men, the offer of a peerage often reflected the size of their contributions to party funds, but the outright purchase of peerages was strongly disapproved of when it was revived in the 1890s, with the result that the sale of political honours became an important political issue in the years 1895–1922 (**209**).

Relatively few peers attended regularly in the Lords, although there was often a good showing when passions were roused. Usually the business was left to the handful of leaders on each side, ministers, the Whips, and a score or two of regular attenders. Indeed, one reason why ministers insisted on retaining a considerable number of office-holders in the Lords was to make sure that routine business could be transacted. As it was, the Household Officers were often dilatory in attendance and had from time to time to be reprimanded, and the Lords Whips found it hard to ensure that even Conservative governments got their bills through. The judicial business of the House also led to considerable difficulties until the 1870s, because there were simply not enough qualified members to hear appeals. Lord Palmerston tried to meet the difficulty by the creation of life peers, but the nomination of Sir James Parke, a baron of the exchequer, to be a life peer as Lord Wensleydale, led in 1856 to a major constitutional dispute between the government and the Lords, who were led by the aged Lord Lyndhurst, and the government was defeated. The need to strengthen the judicial resources of the Lords was not satisfactorily met until 1876, when the Appellate Jurisdiction Act provided for the creation of four Lords of Appeal in Ordinary (increased to six in 1913). Until 1887 these Lords of Appeal were deprived of their seats in the House of Lords on demitting office, but thereafter they were permitted to retain their seats for life.

The great strength of the Lords during most of the nineteenth century was the high quality of its leading members. Not only did a number of extremely able men inherit peerages—including Liverpool, Melbourne, Aberdeen, Derby, Salisbury and Rosebery, who became Prime Minister—but there was a steady influx of newly created peers from the Commons. This was partly a result of the law which provided that only a limited number of

offices could be held by members of the Commons, but chiefly a reflection
of the prestige which membership of the Lords conferred and of the un-
demanding character of Lords procedure. Cabinet ministers getting on in
years often preferred to take a peerage in order to secure a little more rest
out of office hours. And there was a widespread feeling that the Foreign
Secretary, whose diplomatic work was very time-consuming, should, whenever possible, be a peer, so that he would be free to concentrate on his work.
After the Home Rule split in 1886, however, it became increasingly un-
realistic to expect Liberal governments to recruit many senior ministers from
the Lords, because the Liberal ranks were so thin there. Instead, every new
Liberal government was forced to create a number of new peers simply to
make sure that it could comply with statutes and get through day-to-day
business in the Lords.

Before 1832 the connection between Lords and Commons was close; the
leading peers had for the most part served an apprenticeship in the Commons;
peers controlled a large number of Commons seats; and both Lords and
Commons were recruited from much the same class of people, and included
spokesmen of almost every shade of Whig and Tory opinion. Indeed, Lord
Liverpool avoided substantial creations of peers, on the ground that the lavish
distributions of the younger Pitt had already put too high a proportion of
country gentlemen into the Lords, with the result that the pool of recruitment for the Commons had been narrowed and the danger of a clash between
the Houses had increased (**150**). However the House of Lords was never
easy to manage, even before 1832. Many of the leading peers, including the
royal dukes, were self-centred and irresponsible. Lords' procedure favoured
frondeurs, since the Lord Chancellor had no power to control debate. And
on a number of key issues, including Catholic emancipation, Lords and
Commons differed profoundly. Ministers, as a consequence, paid a good deal
of attention to the problem of handling the Lords, and able debaters, both
before and after 1832, were elevated from the Commons to the Lords to
strengthen the government there.

The general election of 1831 and the reform crisis which followed isolated
the Lords alike from the monarch, the ministry, the Commons and public
opinion. The Lords became impossible to manage and, led by a bevy of
resisters to reform, deliberately challenged the country to a fight. Lord
Grey's ministry, itself essentially aristocratic, was extremely reluctant to take
up the challenge, and so was the king. But in the end the king agreed that
enough peers should be created to allow the Reform Bill to be carried (**151**).
Whether the threat to create peers would actually have been carried out is
uncertain, but sufficient peers were influenced by the threat to follow the
lead of the Duke of Wellington and to absent themselves from the key
division, so permitting the Reform Bill to pass.

The reform crisis for a time seriously weakened the political standing of the Lords. The very fact that the king had agreed to a creation of peers, which many still held to be unconstitutional because it offended against the declarations of the Commons made in 1715 after the Treaty of Utrecht, made future creations possible. Many of the Conservative peers felt that they had been twice betrayed by their leaders—over Catholic emancipation and over Reform—and refused to follow the lead of Wellington and Peel. Headed by Lyndhurst, they commenced a factious war against the Whigs, of which the Conservative leaders strongly disapproved, and provoked a series of disputes between Lords and Commons in which Peel and the Whigs were liable to find themselves uncomfortably allied.

The Whig government of Lord Melbourne set in motion a general debate about the position of the Lords, from which resulted a set of principles which were to guide the actions of governments down to the 1880s. It was agreed 1. that there was no alternative to a steady creation of peers if a Whig government could not get through its work in the Lords without them (**154**), 2. that a government defeat in the Lords on an issue of confidence could be counteracted by a vote of confidence in the Commons (**155**), 3. that major bills defeated in the Lords should eventually be allowed to pass only if they were backed by repeated Commons assertions of the desirability of the measures proposed (**158**). These principles meant a weakening of the authority of the Lords, but it was not possible for the Lords in practice to resist them. On one point, however, the Lords won a belated victory. In 1856 they put a stop to the proposal to create life peers on the ground that it could lead readily to a swamping of the Lords by newly created life peers. For the most part, however, the Lords accepted the role which Bagehot attributed to them in 1867:

> Since the Reform Act the House of Lords has become a revising and suspending House. It can alter Bills; it can reject Bills on which the House of Commons is not thoroughly in earnest—upon which the nation is not yet determined. Their veto is a sort of hypothetical veto. They say, 'We reject your Bill for this once, or these twice, or even these thrice; but if you keep on sending it up, at last we won't reject it'.[1]

The Lords accepted this essentially Whig doctrine, not from choice but from necessity: in the Lords itself the parties were fairly evenly balanced in terms of day-to-day attendance—Lord Derby complained in 1852 that he lacked a majority in the Lords as well as in the Commons[2]—but in the country the Whigs and Radicals could always, except in 1841, command a comfortable majority, so that the Lords had small incentive to challenge Whig governments, because if they did so they might be beaten.

---

[1] Bagehot, *English Constitution*, p. 88.   [2] *LQV*, 1st ser. II, 447.

Apart from the Wensleydale case, there was only one major conflict between the government and the Lords between 1842 and 1869. In 1860, encouraged no doubt by the fact that the government was divided on the matter and the House of Commons unenthusiastic, the Lords threw out Gladstone's Paper Duties Bill. Gladstone regarded this as a grave blow at the Commons supremacy in matters of finance and promptly re-arranged the financial business of the government so that in future all money bills should be consolidated into a single Finance Bill (157). Palmerston, the Prime Minister, who hated the Paper Duties Bill, also moved a Commons resolution laying down that the Lords should not amend money bills though they might still reject them (156). In 1869 there was a further crisis, because it seemed likely that the Lords would prevent the disestablishment of the Irish Church, but a compromise was at length arranged at the instance of the Queen. By 1869, however, the Liberal ministers had become uneasily aware that their position in the Lords was a difficult one, and Gladstone and other Liberal leaders began to contemplate a measure of Lords reform designed partly to strengthen the Liberal party in the Lords and partly to redress the preponderance of landowners (159–60). Meanwhile, the Gladstone government accepted a surprisingly large number of Lords' amendments to its Bills (161), and Disraeli did his best to suggest that the maintenance of the Lords was a major aim of the Conservative party.

The Lords, however, did not begin to assert themselves positively until the 1880s. By 1881 Gladstone's leadership of the Liberal party had so speeded up the normal steady erosion of Liberal strength in the Lords that it was hard for Lord Granville to know just whom he could count on in a crisis, and when heads were counted after the great schism of 1886 it was found that the great majority of Liberal peers were now Liberal Unionists. There had also been a change on the Conservative side. The fact that from 1874 to 1880 the Conservatives had a secure majority in the Commons, suggested to the Conservative peers that a Conservative majority would be re-established as a matter of course if Gladstone could only be driven from office. Conservatives now talked boldly of the Lords forcing the government to go to the country on issues in dispute between the government and the Lords. Such language alarmed the Queen, who laboured hard to prevent the Lords from damaging their position by obstructing legislation (162), and it became clear that a new crisis was impending.

The growing assertiveness of the peers was a major problem for all Liberal ministers, because it suggested that, except at the beginning of a new parliament, a Liberal government's legislative timetable would be entirely at the mercy of the Lords. Moreover, as Gladstone pointed out, the Lords' inclination to force a dissolution on a Liberal government before passing its measures amounted to a claim by the Lords to overrule the Commons and to give to the Lords the right to overthrow a government (163). While the votes of no confidence in the Lords might have no effect, the defeat of a major government measure had very nearly the same consequences as a vote of no confidence. During the prolonged crisis over the 1884 Reform Bill, which the Lords successfully insisted should be accompanied by a Redistribution Bill, there was inevitably a good deal of discussion not merely of ways in which government business might be speeded, but of the future role of the Lords. Joseph Chamberlain denounced the Lords in no uncertain terms, and the position of the Lords became one of the issues at the 1885 election. Queen Victoria was seriously alarmed (164), and literary men began to argue the case for a new second chamber to replace the Lords.

By 1885 the role of the Lords and that of the Commons were manifestly quite different, as they had not been before 1832. The Lords represented property and the Commons the popular will. The struggle between Lords and Commons was, therefore, generally represented in the radical press as a struggle between property and privilege on the one hand and the people on the other. Thinking peers like Lord Salisbury and Lord Rosebery were anxious to avoid so clear-cut a dichotomy, by introducing a representative element into the Lords. Without it, they argued, the Lords must always be beaten in a struggle with the Commons, especially as young peers had become reluctant to play an active part in the work of the Lords. But the mass of the Lords were reluctant to move, and a number of motions in the Lords advocating reform were pushed to one side, as was a Commons move, sponsored by a group of eldest sons of peers, to avoid their being translated from Commons to Lords. Lord Rosebery in 1894-5 tried hard to persuade his Cabinet that Lords reform should have first priority in the Liberal programme, but he was overruled by his colleagues (165), and licensing reform was put in its place, with disastrous results at the 1895 election when Sir William Harcourt and John Morley, the two leading Liberals in the Commons, lost their seats.

The failure to achieve a measure of Lords' reform left the Lords in a very isolated position in the 1906 parliament, when the Conservatives were in a small minority in the House of Commons. Yet the Conservative leaders persisted in behaving as though the Conservative peers in the Lords were a substitute for the lost Conservative majority in the Commons. Conservative strategy was concerted between the leaders of the two houses (166), and a long series of Liberal measures was deliberately mutilated. No Liberal government could allow such an assertion of the arbitrary power of the Lords over Liberal legislation, and Campbell-Bannerman began to plan a comprehensive measure of Lords' reform incorporating changes in both the composition and powers of the Lords. The main government proposal, adopted by the House of Commons by 432 votes to 147 in 1907, was that the Lords' powers of veto 'should be so restricted by law as to secure that within the limits of a single Parliament the final decision of the Commons shall prevail' (167). The Lords would still retain at the end of a parliament the right to hold up legislation until after a general election, but during the earlier years of a parliament the will of the Commons was to be absolute. Far from accepting Campbell-Bannerman's scheme, the Lords prepared to fight, even though in the propaganda war that had been going on since 1884 the Radical reformers had had much the best of the argument.

The battle between Lords and Commons came to a climax when the Lords decided to reject the controversial 1909 budget, on the ground that it contained material not appropriate to a budget (168–74). The Lords' action went far beyond anything seriously contemplated since 1832. When the Commons resolved to censure the Lords for committing a breach of the constitution (169), they were, therefore, relying on what seemed to be an established rule of the constitution. The Lords' action gave the government the opportunity to fight an election on the issue of the Lords versus the People, which revived the flagging fortunes of the Liberal party. In the first parliament of 1910 the government reverted to Campbell-Bannerman's 1906 proposals, with additions to cover money bills and a reduction of the life of future parliaments from seven to five years. After a good deal of delay, caused by the death of Edward VII, and an abortive 'constitutional conference' at which government and Opposition considered a variety of ways of dealing with disagreements between Lords and Commons (171), King George V agreed that, if necessary, enough peers would be created to secure the passage of the necessary legislation, and the Parliament Bill duly passed into law in 1911 (174).

The Parliament Act, which destroyed the Lords' absolute veto over legislation, was accompanied by a drive for a reconsideration of the composition and functions of the House as a second chamber. The preamble to the Parliament Act explicitly promised legislation on the subject, and the Lords themselves agreed in 1910 that further change was required and that peers should cease to sit in the Lords as of right (170). The attention of parliament was, however, distracted from the matter before anything could be done, and when the question was again taken up by the Bryce Conference in 1918 all sense of urgency had passed. The Lords, after a last fling on Welsh disestablishment and Irish Home Rule, lapsed into another period of quiescence, which was to last a generation.

150. Lord Liverpool on the need for caution in the creation of peers, 1814

[Earl of Liverpool to E. Wilbraham Bootle, 5 November 1814]

...I cannot avoid observing that a considerable creation of peers is a great evil to the Constitution. The character of the House of Lords as a legislative and judicial body is essentially altered by the number of peers Mr. Pitt created during his Administration; and it is likewise a greater evil to withdraw any considerable number of the natural landed aristocracy of the country from the House of Commons. For it is this body [the natural landed aristocracy] that makes the House of Commons what it is in the British Constitution, and it is the want of such a body that is the principal reason why the British constitution is inapplicable to every other country in Europe.   *EHD*, XI, 206

151. The Grey Cabinet requests a creation of peers, May 1832

(a) *Cabinet Minute of 8 May 1832*

PRESENT

The Lord Chancellor,	The Viscount Palmerston,
The Lord President,	The Lord Holland,
The Lord Privy Seal,	The Lord John Russell,
The Duke of Richmond,	The Viscount Althorp,
The Earl Grey,	Sir James Graham,
The Viscount Melbourne,	The Rt. Hon. E. G. Stanley,
The Viscount Goderich,	The Rt. Hon. C. Grant.

Your Majesty's servants having been assembled to consider the situation in which they are placed by the vote of the Committee of the House of Lords last night, beg leave humbly to represent to your Majesty, that they find themselves deprived of all hope of being able to carry the Reform Bill through its further stages in a manner that would be for the advantage of your Majesty's Government, or satisfactory to the public.

So circumstanced, your Majesty's servants would naturally be led at once to tender to your Majesty, with every sentiment of respect and gratitude, the resignation of the offices which they hold from your Majesty's favour, if they did not feel it to be a paramount duty, not to withdraw themselves from your Majesty's service in a moment of so much difficulty, so long as they can contemplate the possibility of remaining in it with advantage to your Majesty and to the public interests, and without dishonour to themselves.

They, therefore, feel themselves bound humbly to suggest to your Majesty the expediency of advancing to the honour of the Peerage such a number of persons as might insure the success of the Bill in all its essential principles, and as might give to your Majesty's servants the strength which is necessary for conducting with effect the business of the country.

In the opinion thus humbly submitted to your Majesty the Duke of Richmond alone of your Majesty's servants does not coincide.

(b) King William IV to Earl Grey, 9 May 1832

It is not without the truest concern that the King acquaints his confidential servants that, after giving due consideration to the Minute of Cabinet which was brought to him yesterday afternoon by Earl Grey and the Lord Chancellor, and to the consequences of the alternative which it offers for his decision, of being deprived of the benefit of their further services, or of sanctioning the advancement to the Peerage of a sufficient number of persons to insure the success of the Reform Bill in all the principles which they consider essential, His Majesty has come to the painful resolution of accepting their resignations.

The King assures Earl Grey and his colleagues, that his sense of the value of their services, and of the zeal, ability, and integrity with which they have discharged their duties at a period and under circumstances of extreme difficulty, is unimpaired and undiminished; but His Majesty cannot reconcile it to what he considers to be his duty, and to be the principles which should govern him in the exercise of the prerogative which the constitution of this country has entrusted to him, to consent to so large an addition to the Peerage as that which has been mentioned to him by Earl Grey and the Chancellor to be necessary towards insuring the success of the Reform Bill in the House of Lords.

His Majesty has received too many proofs of the attachment and devotion of his confidential servants not to rely with confidence upon their readiness to comply with his request, that they will respectively continue in the discharge of their official functions until he shall be enabled to make due arrangement for the public service, and that they will thus relieve him from the immediate difficulty in which he is placed, by an event for which he was altogether unprepared.

(c) *Extract from Cabinet Minute of 18 May 1832, after the Tories had failed to form a government*

The first security...proposed in the Cabinet Minute of the 16th instant having failed, your Majesty's servants see no other possible except the second, which was submitted in the same Minute, viz. 'such a creation of Peers as would afford your Majesty's servants sufficient power to overcome the opposition to the Bill.' An assurance of your Majesty's consent to such a creation, in the event of any fresh obstacle arising, which should, in the humble judgment of your Majesty's servants, render it necessary for the success of the Bill, would afford to your Majesty's servants the security which, for the public safety, they feel themselves compelled to require as a condition of their continuance in office.

(d) *King William IV to Earl Grey, 18 May 1832*

The King's mind has been too deeply engaged in the consideration of the circumstances in which this country is placed, and of his own position, to require that His Majesty should hesitate to say, in reply to the Minute of Cabinet left with him this afternoon by Earl Grey and the Lord Chancellor, that it continues to be, as stated in his recent communications to his confidential servants, His Majesty's wish and desire that they remain in his councils.

His Majesty is, therefore, prepared to afford to them the security they require for passing the Reform Bill unimpaired in its principles and in its essential provisions, and as nearly as possible in its present form; and with this view His Majesty authorises Earl Grey, if any obstacle should arise during the further progress of the Bill, to submit to him a creation of Peers to such extent as shall be necessary to enable him to carry the Bill, always bearing in mind that it has been and still is His Majesty's object to avoid any permanent increase to the Peerage, and therefore that this addition to the House of Peers, if unfortunately it should become necessary, shall comprehend as large a proportion of the eldest sons of Peers and collateral heirs of childless Peers as can possibly be brought forward. In short (to quote the Lord Chancellor's own words used in the interview between His Majesty, his Lordship, and Earl Grey), that the lists of eldest sons and collaterals who can be brought forward shall be completely exhausted before any list be resorted to which can entail a permanent addition to the Peerage.

Subject to these conditions, which have been already stated verbally, and admitted by Earl Grey and the Lord Chancellor, His Majesty assents to the proposal conveyed in the Minute of Cabinet of this day; and this main point being so disposed of, it is unnecessary that His Majesty should notice any other part of the Minute.

Grey. Reform Act, 1832, II, 394–6, 432–5

152. Grey explains the Cabinet's request in the Lords, 17 May 1832

We were under the necessity of offering the advice to create as many new Peers as would carry the measure of Reform through this House [the House of Lords] unmutilated in any of its essential provisions, or resign our offices. Now I say that, under these circumstances, the advice to create new Peers was required. The noble and learned Lord [Lord Lyndhurst] says, that it was not constitutional; but I say that it was constitutional, and I can refer him to books of authority on that subject, in which it is distinctly asserted, that one of the uses of vesting the prerogative of creating new Peers in the Crown is, to prevent the possibility of the recurrence of those evils which must otherwise result from a permanent collision between the two Houses of Parliament; and this danger was rendered imminent by the opposition made to the Reform Bill by the noble Lords on the other side of the House. And, I ask, what would be the consequences if we were to suppose that such a prerogative did not exist, or could not be constitutionally exercised? The Commons have a control over the power of the Crown by the privilege, in extreme cases, of refusing the Supplies; and the Crown has, by means of its power to dissolve the House of Commons, a control upon any violent and rash proceedings on the part of the Commons; but if a majority of this House is to have the power, whenever they please, of opposing the declared and decided wishes both of the Crown and the people, without any means of modifying that power, then this country is placed entirely under the influence of an uncontrollable oligarchy. I say that, if a majority of this House should have the power of acting adversely to the Crown and the Commons, and was determined to exercise that power without being liable to check or control, the Constitution is completely altered, and the government of this country is not a limited monarchy: it is no longer, my Lords, the Crown, the Lords, and Commons, but a House of Lords—a separate oligarchy—governing absolutely the others.   3 <i>Hansard</i> XII, 1005–6

153. The Whig peers reluctant to attend, 1835

[From the diary of Lord Hatherton, 20 July 1835]

Went to Lord Melbourne's Private Secretary's Office with Stanley [Secretary to the Treasury] to look at the list of Peers, opposing and supporting: minors, lunatics, those in town and absent, and proxies, a very disgraceful account. The total of our available numbers out of the whole House of Lords is only 87—and of those not half are now in town —and very few of the others will be induced by any entreaty to come. But the unintelligible thing to me, who am used to the whipping-in of the House of Commons, is the squeamishness that exists about asking Peers to stay in town and attend the Committees. Who shall make such a request to such august persons as the Dukes of Devonshire and Sutherland? The list is put into the hands of Lord Strafford (the late Sir John Byng) who is a perfect old woman, totally devoid of the address and tact requisite for the task. The Postmaster-General has usually kept the list—but neither he nor anyone else would now undertake it. Accordingly the state in which things are even in our own party in the House of Lords is enough to break one's heart.

Aspinall, *Parliamentary Affairs*, XVII, 255

154. Russell suggests a steady creation of peers to support the Liberal government in the Lords, 5 June 1836

I beg to call the attention of the Cabinet to the position in which the present conduct of the House of Lords may place the Ministry and the country. It is evident that a majority of that House are combined, not to stop or alter a particular measure, but to stop or alter all measures which may not be agreeable to the most powerful, or, in other words, the most violent, among their own body. Both the Tories and the Radicals have the advantage of a definite course with respect to this state of things. The Tories praise the wisdom of the Lords, and wish to maintain their power undiminished. The Radicals complain of a mischievous obstacle to good government, and propose an elective House of Lords. The Ministers stand in the position of confessing the evil and not consenting to the remedy. The influence of public opinion is, indeed, to be looked to as some check to the House of Lords; but, on Irish questions, it is a very imperfect one. It is certainly possible to wait till the beginning of next session before any definite course is taken. But I own it appears to me better to take every opportunity of increasing the strength of the Liberal party in the House of Lords, than to begin a struggle against a majority such as that which the Tory Peers now possess. It is possible, nay probable, that, if the Tories could see a steady and gradual creation of peers to meet this obstinate resistance, they would be disposed to yield. Before the passing of the Reform Bill they were coerced by [the threat of] a large creation and by that alone. It appears to me, therefore, that this opportunity should be taken for the creation of eight, ten, or twelve peers, and that the Ministry be prepared to advise a similar creation whenever it is *provoked*.

Walpole, Lord John Russell, I, 266–7

155. The Melbourne government responds to a defeat in the Lords, 1839

[Viscount Melbourne to Queen Victoria, 22 March 1839]

Lord Melbourne presents his humble duty to your Majesty, and begs to acquaint your Majesty that the Cabinet have decided—

1. That it is impossible to acquiesce in the vote of last night in the House of Lords. [Lord Roden had carried a motion for a Select Committee to enquire into the state of Ireland.]

2. That it would not be justifiable to resign in the face of the declaration which I made in the year 1836, in the House of Lords, that I would maintain my post as long as I possessed the confidence of the Crown and of the House of Commons, particularly as there is no reason to suppose that we have lost the confidence of the House.

3. That the course to be pursued is to give notice in the House of Commons to-night, that the sense of that House will be taken immediately after the Easter Holidays, upon a vote of approbation of the principles of Lord Normanby's government of Ireland.

If we lose that question, or carry it by a small majority, we must resign. If we carry it, we may go on.

[The motion was carried by 318 to 296 on 19 April.]

LQV, 1st ser. I, 188–9

156. The House of Commons limits the Lords' control over money bills, 6 July 1860

Resolved, That the right of granting Aids and Supplies to the Crown is in the Commons alone, as an essential part of their constitution; and the limitation of all such Grants, as to matter, manner, measure, and time, is only in them....

Resolved, That although the Lords have exercised the power of rejecting Bills of several descriptions relating to Taxation by negativing the whole, yet the exercise of that power by them has not been frequent, and is justly regarded by this House with peculiar jealousy, as affecting the right of the Commons to grant the Supplies and to provide the Ways and Means for the Service of the year....

Resolved, That, to guard for the future against an undue exercise of that power by the Lords, and to secure to the Commons their rightful control over Taxation and Supply, this House has in its own hands the power so to impose and remit Taxes, and to frame Bills of Supply, that the right of the Commons as to the matter, manner, measure, and time may be maintained inviolate. *CJ*, cxv, 360

157. Gladstone on the Lords' rejection of the Paper Duties Bill, 1860

...During a long course of years there had grown up in the House of Commons a practice of finally disposing of the several parts of the budget each by itself. And the House of Lords had shown so much self-control in confining itself to criticism on matters of finance, that the freedom of the House of Commons was in no degree impaired. But there was the opportunity of mischief; and round the carcass the vultures now gathered in overwhelming force. It at once became clear that the Lords would avail themselves of the opportunity afforded them by the single presentation of financial bills, and would prolong, and virtually re-enact a tax, which the representatives of the people had repealed.

★ ★ ★

I...proposed a budget reducing the income tax by one penny, and repealing the paper duties from October 10, 1861. With this was combined what was more essential than either—the adoption of a new practice with respect to finance, which would combine all the financial measures of the year in a single bill. We had separate discussions in the cabinet on the constitutional proposal [the single bill]. It was not extensively resisted there, though quietly a good deal misliked. I rather think the chancellor, Campbell, took strong objection to it; and I well remember that the Duke of Newcastle gave valuable and telling aid. So it was adopted. The budget was the subject of a fierce discussion, in which Lord Palmerston appeared to me to lose his temper for the first and only time. The plan, however, to my great delight, was adopted. It was followed by a strange and painful incident. I received with astonishment from Lord Palmerston, immediately after the adoption of the budget, a distinct notice that he should not consider it a cabinet question in the House of Commons, where it was known that the opposition and the paper makers would use every effort to destroy the plan. I wrote an uncontroversial reply (with some self-repression) and showed it to Granville, who warmly approved, and was silent on the letter of Lord Palmerston. The battle in parliament was hard, but was as nothing to the internal fighting: and we won it. We likewise succeeded in the plan of uniting the financial proposals in one bill. To this Spencer Walpole gave honourable support; and it became a standing rule. The House of Lords, for its misconduct, was deservedly extinguished, in effect, as to all matters of finance.

Morley, Gladstone, II, 31, 39

158. Salisbury on the Lords and the Irish Church, 17 June 1869

It has been represented that, in admitting it to be the duty of this House to sustain the deliberate, the sustained, the well-ascertained opinion of the nation, we thereby express our subordination to the House of Commons, and make ourselves merely an echo of the decisions of that House. In my belief no conclusion could be more absolutely inconsequential. If we do merely echo the House of Commons, the sooner we disappear the better. The object of the existence of a second House of Parliament is to supply the omissions and correct the defects which occur in the proceedings of the first. But it is perfectly true that there may be occasions in our history in which the decision of the House of Commons and the decision of the nation must be taken as practically the same. In ninety-nine cases out of 100 the House of Commons is theoretically the representative of the nation, but is only so in theory. The constitutional theory has no corresponding basis in fact; because in ninety-nine cases out of 100 the nation, as a whole, takes no interest in our politics, but amuses itself and pursues its usual avocations, allowing the political storm to rage without taking any interest in it. In all these cases I make no distinction—absolutely none—between the prerogative of the House of Commons and the House of Lords. Again, there is a class of cases small in number, and varying in kind, in which the nation must be called into council and must decide the policy of the Government. It may be that the House of Commons in determining the opinion of the nation is wrong; and if there are grounds for entertaining that belief, it is always open to this House, and indeed it is the duty of this House, to insist that the nation shall be consulted, and that one House without the support of the nation shall not be allowed to domineer over the other. In each case it is a matter of feeling and of judgment. We must decide by all we see around us and by events that are passing. We must decide—each for himself, upon our consciences and to the best of our judgment, in the exercise of that tremendous responsibility which at such a time each Member of this House bears—whether the House of Commons does or does not represent the full, the deliberate, the sustained convictions of the body of the nation. But when once we have come to the conclusion from all the circumstances of the case that the House of Commons is at one with the nation, it appears to me that—save in some very exceptional cases, save in the highest cases of morality—in those cases in which a man would not set his hand to a certain proposition, though a revolution should follow from his refusal—it appears to me that the vocation of this House has passed away, that it must devolve the responsibility upon the nation, and may fairly accept the conclusion at which the nation has arrived.

. . . I have tried to guard my words against any interpretation which should seem to imply that, in the ordinary course of legislation, there is any inferiority between one House of Parliament and the other. But one of the rare occasions to which I have referred has now occurred [in the case of the disestablishment of the Irish church which had been endorsed by the electors in the general election of 1868]. The opinion of Scotland and Ireland, and I may add, of Wales is passionately in favour of this measure of disestablishment. England, though more doubtfully and languidly, is also in favour of the same measure. And looking at these facts, and at the general current of opinion; looking at all quarters of the political horizon, and seeing succour in none; seeing that the opinion of literary men is against you; seeing that the mass of religious opinion among Dissenters and Catholics is against you; seeing that what the Foreign Secretary laid so much stress on last year—the opinion of foreigners—is also against you, though I take this opinion not as worth much as a guide to our conduct, but as worth a good deal as indicating the tide of opinion—seeing that nowhere is there any appearance of any movement that can reverse the decision of the nation, save in assemblages of which the power has been tried and has been so often found wanting—on all these grounds, my Lords, I can conscientiously come to no other conclusion than that the nation has decided against Protestant ascendancy in Ireland, and that this House would not be doing its duty if it opposed itself further against the will of the nation.   3 *Hansard* CXCVII, 83–5

159. Granville on the position of the Liberals in the Lords, 1869
[Earl Granville to Queen Victoria, 23 August 1869]

The position of Your Majesty's Government in the Lords is almost intolerable. The majority were wise enough at the last moment to pass the Irish Church Bill, supported as it was by the Commons and the country,—but it is absolute in all ordinary matters of Legislation, on which the credit and utility of a Government so much depend. It does not scruple to exercise that power, a course ultimately sure to create great dissatisfaction.

Lord Bessborough has lost from his list of 1850, of those whom he used to summon, 45 Peers whose Peerages have become extinct, who are incapacitated, or who in their own persons or in that of their sons have become Conservatives.

The majority is between 60 and 70 without counting Bishops or Liberals who vote oftener for the Opposition than for the Government. No one would pretend that a dozen Peers could swamp such a majority; but Her Majesty's Government requires moral support in the House. They are not cordially supported by even the small minority, of whom the most eminent are ex-place men, who many of them are not friends of Mr. Gladstone, and prefer the failure to the success of his colleagues. If only 3 or 4 Peers are created, they get awed by the atmosphere in which they find themselves.

Guedalla, *Queen and Mr. Gladstone*, I, 199

160. Gladstone on the size and future of the House of Lords, 1869

[Memorandum by W. E. Gladstone for Queen Victoria, 14 September 1869]

1. Within the last ten years, the House of Lords appears to have declined in numbers by about 25, although 45 Peers or thereabouts, have been made. These figures seem to show a natural waste in the Peerage approaching 7 cases annually, or in other words to indicate that less than 7 creations in each year might not suffice to keep the Peerage up to its present No.

2. In the present year four seats in the House of Lords have been destroyed by the Irish Church Act.

3. The actual number of the House of Lords, after deducting Irish Bishops is 429. It may be difficult to say at what precise figure it would become inconveniently large for its purposes as a deliberative assembly. But certainly not until it was well past 500.

4. At present the House of Lords may be said to be inconveniently small. The greater part of its business is transacted, & the greater part of its Divisions are taken with numbers so very limited as to stand in marked contrast with those of the House of Commons, and somewhat to shock public opinion; and it can hardly be doubted that within just limits, numbers are an element of weight.

5. While the real numbers of the House of Lords are small, the effective numbers of the House of Lords fall short of the real numbers; owing to the fact that its members sit for life, and therefore that it contains an unusual proportion of members incapacitated by old age and infirmity. Employments at a distance, & in the case of Bishops their episcopal duties, further diminish the effective attendance. And the rules recently adopted with regard to proxies reduces the numbers available for voting on the greatest and most critical occasions. The second reading of the Irish Church Bill in 1869 was decided on by a smaller number of Peers than the second reading of the reform Bill of Lord Grey in October 1831.

6. For many years passed [*sic*], the House of Commons has tended to outweigh the House of Lords in an inconvenient degree. There can be no doubt that the adoption of Household Suffrage has considerably added to the relative strength of the House of Commons; which more and more speaks for the nation, and not for any class or portion of it only. The crisis of this year was impatiently borne by the House: and

there was an appearance of combustible temper which might easily have burst into flame. The greatest security of the House of Lords lies in its own prudence: but it is far from having any strength to spare. Its constitution after the reform Act of 1867, might readily be brought into controversy. But without doubt it is a cardinal object of good sense and good policy, to keep this, if possible, out of the category of debateable and debated questions. Now it is true that no great or signal measure can be adopted for giving greater relative strength to the House of Lords. The appointment of some Peers for Life may be desirable: but it is not easy to arrange, and it could not effect much. Reasonable and moderate addition to the present numbers of the House, though it cannot effect any great results, appears to me to be desirable rather than otherwise. For if, with reference to any given end, the means of action are but moderate, it is the more important that they should not be overlooked.

7. A very large portion of the influence of the House of Peers depends upon, & indeed in one way represents the aggregate of the influence of its members individually. Every well conducted, nay even every not flagrantly illconducted Peer, is a distinct centre of influence on behalf of the House to which he belongs: of moral and social influence, over and above the mere weight of his property. In this view all such creations of Peers as do not degrade the order by excessive intrusion are real additions to the power of the House of Lords. And, besides their direct action, they tell in an important manner through elections to the House of Commons.

8. It may be said that Lord A. as a Peer fills the place which he formerly filled, under the name of Mr. A., as a commoner. But this is not the whole truth. For in this country, attached as it is to hereditary distinctions, more regard is paid, more influence accorded in the long run, and in the greater number of instances to an ennobled, than to an untitled family. And not only so, but beyond all doubt, as a general rule, the family itself by a natural & unblameable process, becomes when itself ennobled more attached to aristocracy by the habits of mind which the situation imperceptibly creates. This tendency, indeed, sometimes is developed to an inconvenient degree.

9. Is there, then, any fear, that the dignity of the House of Lords is likely, in present or in any probable circumstances to suffer through undue multiplication of its numbers? This could hardly happen, unless the number of Peers relatively to that of the Population were carried

sensibly beyond the proportion which it has borne in former days. But if we compare these numbers (taken roughly) we find that there are in the United Kingdom. In 1869 about 14 peers for each million of the population. But in 1840 there were about 17 Peers for each million. Therefore we are not beyond, but within the proportion of former times and the country does not seem to be near the point at which any danger on this score is to be apprehended: while it has already been pointed out that for the simple purpose of transacting business the House of Lords needs not fewer but more members than heretofore.

10. It will be borne in mind that the whole of these topics are distinct from, and are over and above, the arguments which have been urged with much force by Lord Granville with reference to the position of the Liberal party in the House of Lords. They refer simply to the public interest involved in maintaining the power of that House as a great limb of the Constitution: although at one point the two lines of argument coincide, that namely, at which it may be urged that it cannot be for the interest of the House of Lords or for the interest which the country has in the House of Lords, that this assembly should stand in marked contrast with the steady and permanent judgment of the country which on every occasion since 1830 except one has returned a Liberal majority. *GG1, 1, 56–7*

161. Lords' amendments accepted by the Commons, 1870

[W. E. Gladstone to Earl Granville, government leader in the Lords, 22 July 1870]

We had to cram dishes of the Lords amendments down the throats of our men today; two points we altered. 1. We put in the £15 *valuation* according to the rule promised all through the Bill: secondly we restored 'or character' with Balls full and distinct approval and according to our resolution in Downing Street.

We have strained ourselves as well as our friends a good deal for the sake of peace: I hope the Lords will not tempt us any further.

I am unable to join in the compliments paid to their moderation, but I have kept silence thus far. They would have acted more wisely for the order as well as for the country, had they acted more liberally.

I hope the Bill will not come back: if it does our debates will I fear be of a different colour. *GG1, 1, 113*

162. The Queen labours to prevent a clash between Lords and Commons, 1882

[Queen Victoria to the Marquess of Salisbury (in opposition), 4 August 1882]

When the Queen took leave of Lord Salisbury two years ago—he said to her that he would always be glad to do anything to serve her if she would only tell him or let him know.

In *strictest confidence*, the Queen writes to Lord S. to say that now is a moment when he can be of great use to her. It is, if he would NOT insist on pressing his amendment on the Arrears Bill in the House of Lords. The Queen does not wish to enter into any argument for or against the Bill, but merely appeals to him if possible to try and adopt the Duke of Abercorn's amendment, as a collision between the two Houses is at all times very serious, and *now* any crisis brought on by the House of Lords would, the Queen fears, be very dangerous, and might do harm to the very cause which Lord S. wishes always to uphold and defend.

No one knows of this letter and she asks that Lord S. may consider it quite confidential.
LQV, 2nd ser. III, 320

163. Gladstone objects to the doctrine that the Lords may force a dissolution of the Commons, 1884

[W. E. Gladstone to Queen Victoria, 14 July 1884]

With respect to the suggestion, fully considered by the Cabinet, that the Parliament might have been dissolved on the occasion of the recent vote [on the Franchise Bill], your Majesty has not perhaps been fully informed as to the depth and strength of the objections that are felt to such a plan. Mr. Gladstone will not trouble your Majesty with details, beyond observing that at no period of our history, known to him, has the House of Commons been dissolved at the call of the House of Lords, given through an adverse vote; that in his opinion the establishment of such a principle would place the House of Commons in a position of inferiority, as a Legislative Chamber, to the House of Lords; and that the attempt to establish it would certainly end in organic changes, detrimental to the dignity and authority of the House of Lords.
LQV, 2nd ser. III, 517–18

164. Queen Victoria on the advantages of the House of Lords, 1886

[Queen Victoria to W. E. Gladstone, 7 March 1886]

The Queen...cannot but think that he [Mr. Gladstone] might with advantage have dwelt on the following points:—

1. The *benefit* derived by the Nation, in possessing a Chamber of the *independent* nature of the House of Lords;—independent especially, because *unlike* the House of Commons, its Members have *not* to *solicit* their *Seats* at the *hands* of the *people* by holding out promises which are frequently regretted afterwards by those who made them.—

2. The fact that any attack *directed against* the *House of Lords* as *an integral part of the Constitution* cannot fail to affect the *stability* of the *other two*, viz: the *Sovereign* & the *House of Commons*—a consideration wh it strikes the Queen does not seem to have been present to Mr. Gladstone's mind at the time he spoke.

3. The *great* importance (w^h the Queen is *sure* Mr. Gladstone *must* himself *fully* appreciate) of maintaining a power like the House of Lords in order that it may exercise a legitimate & wholesome check upon the greatly increasing radicalism of the present day.

Guedalla, *Queen and Mr. Gladstone*, II, 396–7

165. Rosebery urges Lords reform, 1894

[Earl of Rosebery to Queen Victoria, 1 November 1894]

Lord Rosebery's own view of the situation is this, that it is from the broadest point of view important to take advantage of the present opportunity. He believes that the system by which the House of Lords —now, unfortunately, owing to causes on which he will not dwell, a party organisation—controls a Liberal but not a Conservative Government is obnoxious to the conscience of the country as well as to its best interests. But he also believes that this is a moment of calm, and therefore favourable to revision. What he has always dreaded, as he has stated in public, is that the question of the House of Lords should come for decision at a crisis of passion and storm. Then the Constitution would be hurriedly cast into the crucible with lamentable and incalculable results.

The policy of the Government practically comes to this, that the Constitution cannot long stand the strain of a permanent control exercised by a Conservative branch of the legislature on all Liberal Governments; that it is well that this question should be decided at a peaceful juncture; and that in the issue between the House of Lords and the House of Commons the Government takes the side of the House of Commons.

LQV, 3rd ser. II, 439

166. Lord Lansdowne expects the House of Lords to play an active part in politics, 1906

Marquess of Lansdowne to A. J. Balfour, 5 April 1906

It seems to me very desirable that after the Easter holidays an endeavour should be made to set up some machinery for establishing closer contact between the Opposition Front Benches in the two Houses of Parliament.

The Opposition is lamentably weak in the House of Commons, and enormously powerful in the House of Lords. It is essential that the two wings of the army should work together, and that neither House should take up a line of its own without carefully considering the effects which the adoption of such a line might have upon the other House. In dealing with such Bills as the Trade Disputes Bill or the Robartes Bill, I cannot help thinking that the leaders in the House of Commons should have before them at the very outset a definite idea of the treatment which the question might receive in the event of either of those Bills coming before the House of Lords later in the session. Similarly, there are many important questions which will from time to time be debated in the House of Lords and which should be discussed with an eye to the effect of the discussion upon the temper of the House of Commons. At this moment no such machinery as I have suggested is in existence.

Mr. Balfour might like to call a few of us together after the holidays in order to consider the procedure which might be adopted.

I should myself be inclined to propose that he should institute a not too numerous Committee, including, say, four or five members of each House, who might meet in his room at the House of Commons, once a week at least, for an exchange of ideas. Such a Committee might appoint other Committees *ad hoc* to deal with any particular subject, and on these any prominent members of the Opposition might be invited to serve.

As a House of Lords' delegation I would suggest Lord Halsbury, Lord Cawdor, Lord Salisbury, and myself.

A. J. Balfour to Lansdowne, 13 April 1906

I have to-day emerged from my three weeks' hibernation, and have ready your memo. on the advisability of a weekly conference.

There is not the least doubt that your idea must, in some shape or other, be carried out; but if we are to have, as you suggest, a Committee consisting of members selected from the Front Bench in both Houses, I think it would be very difficult to exclude any member of the late Cabinet who had a seat in the present Parliament, and, if that be so, what we should really have would be a shadow Cabinet once a week. This, however, is all a question of detail. The real point is, as you truly say, to secure that the party in the two Houses shall not work as two separate armies, but shall co-operate in a common plan of campaign. This is all-important. There has certainly never been a period in our history in which the House of Lords will be called upon to play a part at once so important, so delicate, and so difficult. From what I hear of the events of the three weeks in which I have been lying *perdu*, I conjecture that the Government methods of carrying on their legislative work will be this: They will bring in Bills in a much more extreme form than the moderate members of their Cabinet probably approve: the moderate members will trust to the House of Lords cutting out or modifying the most outrageous provisions: the Left Wing of the Cabinet, on the other hand, while looking forward to the same result, will be consoled for the anticipated mutilation of their measures by the reflection that they will be gradually accumulating a case against the Upper House, and that they will be able to appeal at the next election for a mandate to modify its constitution.

This scheme is an ingenious one, and it will be our business to defeat it, as far as we can.

I do not think the House of Lords will be able to escape the duty of making serious modifications in important Government measures, but, if this be done with caution and tact, I do not believe that they will do themselves any harm. On the contrary, as the rejection of the Home Rule Bill undoubtedly strengthened their position, I think it quite possible that your House may come out of the ordeal strengthened rather than weakened by the inevitable difficulties of the next few years.

It is, of course, impossible to foresee how each particular case is to be dealt with, but I incline to advise that we should fight all points of importance very stiffly in the Commons, and should make the House of Lords the theatre of compromise. It is evident that *you* can never fight for a position which *we* have surrendered; while, on the other hand, the fact that we have strenuously fought for the position and been severely beaten may afford adequate ground for your making a graceful concession to the Representative Chamber.

Newton, Lansdowne, pp. 353–5

167. The House of Commons claims legislative supremacy over the Lords, 26 June 1907

Resolved, That, in order to give effect to the will of the people as expressed by their elected representatives, it is necessary that the power of the other House to alter or reject Bills passed by this House should be so restricted by Law as to secure that within the limits of a single Parliament the final decision of the Commons shall prevail.

CJ, CLXII, 283

168. Lord Curzon challenges the Commons' supremacy, 30 November 1909

What is the real character of the issue before this House and the country? The Government are fighting for the principle that the House of Commons may send up any measure, however dangerous, Socialistic, and subversive in our view it may be, and provided it can be cramped within the four quarters of the Finance Bill of the year we are to have no alternative but to pass it. That is a novel, a revolutionary, and an intolerable claim. It is one which your Lordships have never acknowledged, and which you have no right to acknowledge now. You have no right to acknowledge it in the interests of this House, because it is clear that this House would be reduced to legislative impotence if it were possible to take particular Bills out of the ordinary course of legislative procedure and tie them up under the cover and label of a Finance Bill, and in that way circumvent your Lordships and pass them through your Lordships' House. You have no right to give away without a struggle the rights and privileges which you have enjoyed and which have been vindicated by many of your greatest Statesmen and orators for 250 years.   5 Hansard (Lords) IV, 1258–9

169. The Commons censure the Lords for refusing to pass the budget, 2 December 1909

A Motion was made, and the Question being put, That the action of the House of Lords in refusing to pass into Law the financial provision made by this House for the Service of the year is a breach of the Constitution, and a usurpation of the rights of the Commons—(The Prime Minister);

The House divided.... Yeas...349...Noes...134.
So it was resolved in the Affirmative.   *CJ*, CLXIV, 546

170. The House of Lords clears the way for constitutional reform, 1910

The House being resumed [17 November 1910]:

The Earl of Onslow [Lord Chairman of Committees] reported, 'That the Committee had agreed to the following resolutions, vizt:
Resolved—

1. That a strong and efficient Second Chamber is not merely an integral part of the British Constitution, but is necessary to the well-being of the State and to the balance of Parliament;
2. That such a chamber can best be obtained by the reform and re-constitution of the House of Lords;
3. That a necessary preliminary of such reform and reconstitution is the acceptance of the principle that the possession of a Peerage should no longer of itself give the right to sit and vote in the House of Lords;
4. That in future the House of Lords shall consist of Lords of Parliament—
   A. Chosen by the whole body of hereditary peers from among themselves and by nomination by the Crown;
   B. Sitting by virtue of offices and of qualifications held by them;
   C. Chosen from outside.'   *Journals of the House of Lords*, CXLII, 295

171. A report on the Constitutional Conference of 1910 by Sir Robert Finlay

Legislation was to be divided into ordinary, financial, and constitutional legislation.

1. *Ordinary Legislation.*

If a difference arose on two occasions in two sessions, in two years, between the Houses of Parliament, it was to be settled by a joint sitting of the two Houses. The joint sitting was to consist of the whole of the House of Commons and 100 peers, 20 of them members of the Government and 80 to be selected on a system of proportional representation.

2. *Financial Legislation.*

The Budget not to be rejected by the Lords unless in case of tacking.

Legal tacking presents no difficulties; but in the event of 'equitable' tacking, the Government proposed that such a Bill should be treated like ordinary legislation.

3. *Constitutional Legislation.*

The Prime Minister stated that no differentiation was possible between that and ordinary legislation.

But the Government were willing that Bills affecting the Crown or the Protestant Succession or the Act which is to embody this agreement should be subject to special safeguards. If the two Houses differed, the Bill would drop; if they agreed, there should be a plebiscite.

On October 16, the Conference broke off on the difficulty of Home Rule. Mr. Balfour proposed that if a Home Rule Bill was twice rejected by the House of Lords, it should go to a plebiscite. Mr. Lloyd George, while admitting the reasonableness of this, said it was impossible for the Government to assent.

Subsequently the Government proposed a compromise, viz. that a general election should intervene on the next occasion on which a Home Rule Bill, having passed the House of Commons, was rejected by the House of Lords—but only on this one occasion; and that Home Rule Bills if introduced afterwards should be treated like ordinary Bills.

Newton, *Lansdowne*, pp. 402–3

172. Asquith on the power to create peers, 1910

[Memorandum by H. H. Asquith of a conversation with King George V, 11 November 1910]

Mr. Asquith pointed out that this would be [the] second time in the course of twelve months that the question of the relations between the two Houses had been submitted to the electorate. It was necessary, therefore, that in the event of the Government obtaining an adequate majority in the New House of Commons, the matter should be put in train for final settlement. This could only be brought about (if the Lords were not ready to give way) by the willingness of the Crown to exercise its prerogative to give effect to the will of the nation. The House of Lords cannot be dissolved and the only legal way in which it can be brought into harmony with the other House is by either curtailing or adding to its members. In theory, the Crown might conceivably adopt the former course by withholding writs of summons. But this has not been done for many centuries; it would be most invidious in practice; and it is at least doubtful whether it can be said to be constitutional. On the other hand the prerogative of creation is undoubted; it has never been recognised as having any constitutional limit; it was used for this very purpose in the 18th century, and agreed to be used on a large scale by King William IV in 1832. There could, in Mr. Asquith's opinion, be no doubt that the knowledge that the Crown was ready to use the prerogative would be sufficient to bring about an agreement without any necessity for its actual exercise.

Spender and Asquith, *Asquith*, 1, 296

173. Asquith advises the Leaders of the Opposition of the decision to force through the Parliament Bill, 1911

[H. H. Asquith to A. J. Balfour and the Marquess of Lansdowne, 20 July 1911]

I think it is courteous and right, before any public decisions are announced, to let you know how we regard the political situation.

When the Parliament Bill in the form which it has now assumed returns to the House of Commons, we shall be compelled to ask that House to disagree with the Lords' Amendments.

In the circumstances, should the necessity arise, the Government will advise the King to exercise his Prerogative to secure the passing into law of the Bill in substantially the same form in which it left the House of Commons; and His Majesty has been pleased to signify that he will consider it his duty to accept, and act on, that advice.

Spender and Asquith, Asquith, I, 312–13

174. The Parliament Act, 1911

An Act to make provision with respect to the powers of the House of Lords in relation to those of the House of Commons, and to limit the duration of Parliament [18th August 1911]

Whereas it is expedient that provision should be made for regulating the relations between the two Houses of Parliament:

And whereas it is intended to substitute for the House of Lords as it at present exists a Second Chamber constituted on a popular instead of hereditary basis, but such substitution cannot be immediately brought into operation:

And whereas provision will require hereafter to be made by Parliament in a measure effecting such substitution for limiting and defining the powers of the new Second Chamber, but it is expedient to make such provision as in this Act appears for restricting the existing powers of the House of Lords:

Be it therefore enacted...

1.—(1) If a Money Bill, having been passed by the House of Commons, and sent up to the House of Lords at least one month before the end of the session, is not passed by the House of Lords without amendment within one month after it is so sent up to that House, the Bill shall, unless the House of Commons direct to the contrary, be presented to His Majesty and become an Act of Parliament on the Royal Assent being signified, notwithstanding that the House of Lords have not consented to the Bill.

(2) A Money Bill means a Public Bill which in the opinion of the Speaker of the House of Commons contains only provisions dealing with all or any of the following subjects, namely, the imposition, repeal, remission, alteration, or regulation of taxation; the imposition for the payment of debt or other financial purposes of charges on the Consolidated Fund, or on money provided by Parliament, or the variation or repeal of any such charges; supply; the appropriation, receipt, custody, issue or audit of accounts of public money; the raising or guarantee of

any loan or the repayment thereof; or subordinate matters incidental to those subjects or any of them. In this subsection the expressions 'taxation,' 'public money,' and 'loan' respectively do not include any taxation, money, or loan raised by local authorities or bodies for local purposes.

(3) There shall be endorsed on every Money Bill when it is sent up to the House of Lords and when it is presented to His Majesty for assent the certificate of the Speaker of the House of Commons signed by him that it is a Money Bill. Before giving his certificate, the Speaker shall consult, if practicable, two members to be appointed from the Chairmen's Panel at the beginning of each Session by the Committee of Selection.

2.—(1) If any Public Bill (other than a Money Bill or a Bill containing any provision to extend the maximum duration of Parliament beyond five years) is passed by the House of Commons in three successive sessions (whether of the same Parliament or not), and, having been sent up to the House of Lords at least one month before the end of the session, is rejected by the House of Lords in each of those sessions, that Bill shall, on its rejection for the third time by the House of Lords, unless the House of Commons direct to the contrary, be presented to His Majesty and become an Act of Parliament on the Royal Assent being signified thereto, notwithstanding that the House of Lords have not consented to the Bill: Provided that this provision shall not take effect unless two years have elapsed between the date of the second reading in the first of those sessions of the Bill in the House of Commons and the date on which it passes the House of Commons in the third of those sessions.

(2) When a Bill is presented to His Majesty for assent in pursuance of the provisions of this section, there shall be endorsed on the Bill the certificate of the Speaker of the House of Commons signed by him that the provisions of this section have been duly complied with.

(3) A Bill shall be deemed to be rejected by the House of Lords if it is not passed by the House of Lords either without amendment or with such amendments only as may be agreed to by both Houses.

(4) A Bill shall be deemed to be the same Bill as a former Bill sent up to the House of Lords in the preceding session if, when it is sent up to the House of Lords, it is identical with the former Bill or contains only such alterations as are certified by the Speaker of the House of Commons to be necessary owing to the time which has elapsed since

the date of the former Bill, or to represent any amendments which have been made by the House of Lords in the former Bill in the preceding session, and any amendments which are certified by the Speaker to have been made by the House of Lords in the third session and agreed to by the House of Commons shall be inserted in the Bill as presented for Royal Assent in pursuance of this section:

Provided that the House of Commons may, if they think fit, on the passage of such a Bill through the House in the second or third session, suggest any further amendments without inserting the amendments in the Bill, and any such suggested amendments shall be considered by the House of Lords, and, if agreed to by that House, shall be treated as amendments made by the House of Lords and agreed to by the House of Commons; but the exercise of this power by the House of Commons shall not affect the operation of this section in the event of the Bill being rejected by the House of Lords.

3. Any certificate of the Speaker of the House of Commons given under this Act shall be conclusive for all purposes, and shall not be questioned in any court of law.

4.—(1) In every Bill presented to His Majesty under the preceding provisions of this Act, the words of enactment shall be as follows, that is to say:—

'Be it enacted by the King's most Excellent Majesty, by and with the advice and consent of the Commons in this present Parliament assembled, in accordance with the provisions of the Parliament Act, 1911, and by authority of the same, as follows.'

(2) Any alteration of a Bill necessary to give effect to this section shall not be deemed to be an amendment of the Bill.

5. In this Act the expression 'Public Bill' does not include any Bill for confirming a Provisional Order.

6. Nothing in this Act shall diminish or qualify the existing rights and privileges of the House of Commons.

7. Five years shall be substituted for seven years as the time fixed for the maximum duration of Parliament under the Septennial Act, 1715.

PGS, 1 & 2 Geo. V, c. 13

CHAPTER 4

PARTIES AND ELECTIONS

A THE PARTY SYSTEM

That parliamentary government meant party government was generally accepted throughout the nineteenth century, though there were few serious studies of party before the publication of Ostrogorski's *Democracy and the Organization of Political Parties* in 1902. Contemporary opinion was chiefly concerned with what in retrospect seems a rather limited problem—how far the actions of party leaders should be determined by party considerations rather than by considerations of public policy. The *voltes-face* which enabled Wellington and Peel to adopt Catholic emancipation in 1829, Peel to repeal the Corn Laws in 1846, Derby and Disraeli to carry household suffrage in 1867, Gladstone to adopt Home Rule for Ireland in 1886, and Joseph Chamberlain to take up protection in 1903, were a source of wonder and dismay. Gladstone, ruminating on his own change of opinion about the Irish Church, argued in 1868 that since the 1820s the whole character of politics had changed in such a way that consistency of policy had become exceptionally difficult for party leaders (**193**). Disraeli, who in his attacks on Peel maintained that party leaders owed it to their followers not to abandon the key points of party policy, found himself in 1867 championing a measure of parliamentary reform hateful to most of his followers. It was not until the crisis over Irish Home Rule in 1885–6 that leading party figures—Salisbury, who had condemned Peel (**191**), on the Conservative side and Hartington on the Liberal—began to argue that they could not adopt the policy of Home Rule because their supporters were already committed against it. By then a new factor was at work which made them cautious: the new party organisations created since 1867 had not yet become habituated to sudden changes of policy and might well have broken up under pressure. As it was, the Home Rule issue disrupted the Liberal party in the 1880s and Tariff Reform disrupted the Conservatives between 1902 and 1905.

Party leaders for the most part guarded themselves against charges of inconsistency before 1867 by avoiding clear statements of party policy. They spoke of the principles of their party and of its election platform rather than of a party programme. Peel's Tamworth Manifesto of 1835, which set the fashion for publishing statements of policy in the form of an election address, was the most forthcoming of early party statements, since it was designed to set the tone of Conservatism after the Reform Act (**181**). But, like Disraeli's speeches in the seventies, it was not much concerned with details.

The object was to create the right atmosphere, not to spell out a detailed programme.

Disraeli's Manchester and Crystal Palace speeches in 1872, which stressed the relevance of traditional Conservatism to the problems of the 1870s, were characteristic of their period in laying emphasis on the continuity of political traditions (182). Politicians were very conscious that though the names Conservative and Liberal were a product of the 1820s and 1830s, the Tory and Whig parties dated back to the seventeenth century and beyond. Few workaday politicians would have carried the history of the Liberal party as far back as Freeman the historian (8), but the Reformation Settlement and the Glorious Revolution of 1688 were very much in their minds, and the continuing problem of how best to govern Ireland served as a reminder of the unchanging character of some political problems. The Conservatives remained the party of church and King, aristocratic paternalism, the Protestant ascendancy in Ireland and the landed interest, while becoming also under Disraeli the party of imperialism and the new suburban middle classes. The Liberals claimed credit for the achievements of the Whigs in 1688 and 1832, and adopted the Whig policy of concessions to Protestant dissenters and Roman Catholics, while attempting to break away from the ascendancy of the great Whig houses and to take up the doctrines of the Radicals. The attempt to link past and present inevitably created tensions in both parties, with the result that there was a long history of breakaways: the Canningites, the Peelites, the Liberal Unionists, and the Unionist Free Traders were only the most important of a number of breakaway groups which for a time enjoyed an independent existence with their own party organisation. But these tensions were often fruitful, and Gladstone's long political career, which led from eighteenth-century Toryism to late nineteenth-century Radicalism, was made up of a wonderful mosaic of old traditions and new ideas.

After 1867 the election speeches of the Liberal party leaders and their election addresses began to contain many more specific proposals for reform than hitherto. As a result, a Liberal government could claim that it had a mandate for certain reforms, such as the disestablishment of the Irish Church in 1868, and have its claim to a mandate recognised by the Opposition (158), even though the doctrine of the mandate was generally denounced by political leaders (125). The number of measures which might be held to fall within a government's mandate was, however, a small one. Gladstone's 1880 election address promised very little, partly because he was not the party's official leader. And in 1885 we find Gladstone arguing that a new Liberal government required little more than a few agreed issues to get it started, rather than a general agreement on the direction of Liberal policy (183).

Wide-ranging programmes were first developed by the Radical wing of the Liberal party, notably in the *Radical Programme* of 1885, and were urged by the Radicals on the National Liberal Federation. In 1891 the various Radical groups within the Liberal party agreed at the Newcastle conference of the Federation to adopt a common programme—the Newcastle programme (**184**). Backed by Gladstone the Newcastle programme became the policy of the Liberal party in the 1892 general election, and as such the first British party programme. Reactions to the Newcastle programme were not, however, what the Liberal leaders had hoped they would be. The range covered was too wide and the number of interests threatened was too great to make it a popular programme with the electors. After the disastrous results of the 1895 general election the party managers accordingly did their best to drop it (**185**). Emphasis was now chiefly placed on the mass of semi-official and official party publications issued by the party offices after 1885—speeches by the party leaders, compendia of facts and argument like the Conservative *Campaign Guide*, leaflets from a variety of sources, and periodicals like the *Liberal Magazine*. The National Liberal Federation tacitly abandoned its claim to dictate Liberal policy, and by 1905 the Liberal programme was simply that put forward by Sir Henry Campbell-Bannerman.

Except in times of crisis, as in 1831, there was normally a substantial measure of agreement as to the way in which the country should be run. Those like Cobbett (**211**) and the Chartists (**214**) who challenged the political system were long uncomfortably isolated on the periphery of politics, and were liable to prosecution for expressing seditious views.[1] But John Bright and most of the Radicals were gradually drawn into the party system, and became active members of the Liberal party. From the 1880s, however, the party system was challenged from a number of quarters. There was an intellectual revulsion from the party system (**177**) and talk of class politics replacing party politics (**178**). The Irish Home Rulers in the House of Commons disrupted the balance of parties, backed by the fundamentally anti-parliamentary Land League. And in Great Britain the Fabian Society (**186**), the Independent Labour party (**187**), and the Labour party (**208**) began to talk in terms of an alternative socialist system, while the Labour members of parliament began to bring a new style to politics. The Labour party itself was not a direct threat to the system, but the fact that sober trade unionists thought a new party to be necessary underlined the failure of the party system to keep pace with the expectations of some sections of the electorate. Cries from the left that the party system was a fraud were echoed from the Radical right by Belloc and Chesterton (**180**). Within the trade unions a syndicalist movement emerged, and there was uneasiness even in the government. Lloyd George began to talk in 1910 about a new party to be formed by a mixed bag

[1] For the legal status of extra-parliamentary movements see Hamburger, *James Mill and the Art of Revolution*, ch.1.

of Liberals and Conservatives to renovate the party system. And in the tense years immediately before the war of 1914–18 there was a ground-swell of discontent with the system.

THE PARTY STRUGGLE

175. The Whigs and Tories distinct, 1828

[From the diary of J. W. Croker]

January 6th [1828]—The Duke of Clarence...is for a Government founded on a union of parties. He says the names Whigs and Tories meant something a hundred years ago, but are mere nonsense nowadays. I agreed with His Royal Highness that Whigs in power soon assimilated themselves to Tories, and that Tories in opposition would soon become Whigs, but that I still thought that there were two marked and distinct parties in the country, which might for brevity be fairly called Whig and Tory.   Jennings, *Croker Papers*, I, 401

176. Gladstone on the essentially Liberal character of the nation, 1884

How is it with regard to the solid and permanent opinion of the nation? We have had twelve parliaments since the Reform Act,—I have a right to say so, as I have sat in every one of them,—and the opinion, the national opinion, has been exhibited in the following manner. Ten of those parliaments have had a liberal majority. The eleventh parliament was the one that sat from 1841 to 1847. It was elected as a tory parliament; but in 1846 it put out the conservative government of Sir Robert Peel, and put in and supported till its dissolution, the liberal government of Lord John Russell. That is the eleventh parliament. But then there is the twelfth parliament, and that is one that you and I know a good deal about [Lord Beaconsfield's parliament], for we talked largely on the subject of its merits and demerits, whichever they may be, at the time of the last election. That parliament was, I admit, a tory parliament from the beginning to the end. But I want to know, looking back for a period of more than fifty years, which represented the solid permanent conviction of the nation?—the ten parliaments that were elected upon ten out of the twelve dissolutions, or the one parliament that chanced to be elected from the disorganized state of the liberal party in the early part of the year 1874? Well, here are ten parliaments on the one side; here is one parliament on the other side....

Morley, Gladstone, III, 128

177. Maine on party, 1885

No force acting on mankind has been less carefully examined than Party, and yet none better deserves examination. The difficulty which Englishmen in particular feel about it is very like that which men once experienced when they were told that the air had weight. It enveloped them so evenly and pressed on them so equally, that the assertion seemed incredible. Nevertheless it is not hard to show that Party and Party Government are very extraordinary things.....let us imagine some modern writer, with the unflinching perspicacity of a Machiavelli, analysing the great Party Hero—leader or agitator—as the famous Italian analysed the personage equally interesting and important in his day, the Tyrant or Prince. Like Machiavelli, he would not stop to praise or condemn on ethical grounds: 'he would follow the real truth of things rather than an imaginary view of them.' 'Many Party Heroes,' he would say, 'have been imagined, who were never seen or known to exist in reality.' But he would describe them as they really were. Allowing them every sort of private virtue, he would deny that their virtues had any effect on their public conduct, except so far as they helped to make men believe their public conduct virtuous. But this public conduct he would find to be not so much immoral as non-moral. He would infer, from actual observation, that the party Hero was debarred by his position from the full practice of the great virtues of veracity, justice, and moral intrepidity. He could seldom tell the full truth; he could never be fair to persons other than his followers and associates; he could rarely be bold except in the interests of his faction. The picture drawn by him would be one which few living men would deny to be correct, though they might excuse its occurrence in nature on the score of moral necessity. And then, a century or two later, when Democracies were as much forgotten as the Italian Princedoms, our modern Machiavelli would perhaps be infamous and his work a proverb of immorality.

Party has many strong affinities with Religion. Its devotees, like those of a religious creed, are apt to substitute the fiction that they have adopted it upon mature deliberation for the fact that they were born into it or stumbled into it. But they are in the highest degree reluctant to come to an open breach with it; they count it shame to speak of its weak points, except to co-religionists; and, whenever it is in serious difficulty, they return to its assistance or rescue. Their relation to those outside the pale—the relation of Whig to Tory, of Conservative to Liberal—is on the whole exceedingly like that of Jew to Samaritan. But the closest resemblances are between party discipline and military discipline; and indeed, historically speaking, Party is probably nothing more than a survival and a consequence of the primitive combativeness of mankind. It is war without the city transmuted into war within the city, but mitigated in the process. The best historical justification which can be offered for it is that it has often enabled portions of the nation, who would otherwise be armed enemies, to be only factions. Party strife, like strife in arms, develops many high but imperfect and one-sided virtues; it is fruitful of self-denial and self-sacrifice. But wherever it prevails, a great part of ordinary morality is unquestionably suspended; a number of maxims are received, which are not those of religion or ethics; and men do acts which, except as between enemies, and except as between political opponents, would be very generally classed as either immoralities or sins.   Maine, *Popular Government*, pp. 98–101

178. Gladstone on the classes and the masses, 1886
[Speech at Liverpool, 28 June 1886]

...you are opposed throughout the country by a compact army, and that army is the case of the classes against the masses. I am thankful to say that there are among the classes many happy exceptions. I am thankful to say that there are men wearing coronets on their heads who are as good, as sound, as genuine Liberals as any working man who hears me at this moment. Still, as a general rule, it cannot be pretended that we are supported by the dukes, or by the squires, or by the established clergy, or by the officers of the Army, or by any other body of very respectable persons. And what I observe is this, whenever a profession is highly privileged, whenever a profession is publicly endowed, it is in these cases you will find that almost the whole of the class and the profession are against us. But if I go to more open professions, if I take the Bar...if I take the medical profession...in these open professions I am thankful to say that we make a very good and respectable muster indeed.... Still...I am sorry to say, there is class against the mass, classes against the nation.   *The Times*, 29 June 1886

179. Ostrogorski on the party system, 1902

Introduced with the intention of making the government of the historic parties more democratic, the Caucus has succeeded in this to a certain extent, especially in the destructive portion of its work. Falling upon the leadership, which it regarded as oligarchical, it dismantled it and dealt a heavy blow at the old parties which were grouped around it; it powerfully contributed to overthrow Whiggism; it pressed the last life-breath out of expiring classic Radicalism, and helped to drive back old-fashioned Toryism. But it has been less successful in the constructive part of the task which it undertook. It has not been able to provide the parties with a really democratic government; it has created the forms of it, but not the essence....

The ex-ruling class, the middle class, confronted on the one hand by its official dethronement, and on the other by the political incapacity of the masses, wished, both from ambition and duty...to reconcile this contradiction by dint of adroitness, by preserving in the management of parties the reality of power, of which it had been legally divested by the establishment of the Caucus. And this English middle class, which had played a glorious part in the conquest of public liberties and in the development of political spirit and civic dignity, now appeared in a new rôle, of an anything but lofty character; pretending to bow down before the masses, it let them say what they liked, allowed them the satisfaction of holding forth and of voting extravagant resolutions in the caucuses, provided that it was permitted to manage everything; and to cover its designs it developed the practice of wire-pulling. Being powerless, however, without the small ward leaders, created by the democratic party organization, it undertook to corrupt them systematically, to win them by acting on their 'social tendencies.' Invitations to 'at homes,' to garden-parties, to dinners with the big men of the party, free admission to gentlemen's clubs, methodically demoralized the leaders of the lower middle class and of the working class, by developing and fostering in them the abject snobbishness which infects social relations in England. Having given a democratic form to party government, in order to liberate it from 'social influences,' the Caucus managed by the middle-class men itself appealed to those influences and borrowed from them the most disreputable part of their methods and conduct. The middle class often had good sense on its side and understood what was fitting in politics, but it was too faint-hearted to face the masses and it preferred to circumvent them by devices of management. Withholding from them the plain truth and offering them only the bait of gratification of self-love and vanity, it enervated and disgusted a good many of the best set to such an extent as to fling them into the sectarian but honest fanaticism of the Independent Labour parties, into the wild ideas of Utopia-mongers and collectivist agitators....

Having gone to war with party leadership, held by the representatives of the old ruling classes, the Caucus has not annihilated it—far from it; but it has subdivided it, broken it into fragments, or, if the expression is preferred, decentralized it; the leaders belonging to the upper middle class, the men of means and social position, have had to share their power with the crowd of small local leaders created by the autonomist organization of the Caucus. But, by working out autonomy and decentralization in too formal a way, with a multiplicity of subdivisions, in accordance with the strict logic of the democratic principle, the Caucus has succeeded mainly in bringing forward local mediocrity, and then installing it in the counsels of the party. The local man with limited views, who, left to his own resources, would never have been able to thrust himself on his fellow-citizens, has been hoisted up by the mere play of the machinery of the Caucus, automatically, so to speak. While these small leaders were rising to the surface, the old leaders, who were theoretically overthrown, but in reality still standing, saw their prestige decline, their influence diminish, and this twofold action produced a general levelling, which tended to shorten the average stature of public men, to make the type a poorer one.

...Unqualified adhesion to the official creed of the party having become the supreme political virtue which singled a man out for the confidence of his fellow-citizens in the discharge of every public duty, and his claims being made clear to them by the machinery of the Organization, which aimed especially at the imagination, the personal worth of the individual became of less importance....

The deterioration of the men in charge of public affairs can be clearly discerned already; we have seen it break out more strongly in municipal life since the Caucus introduced party orthodoxy into it and placed its machinery at its disposal. Parliament has not been spared either; the choice of the Caucus, contrary to the promises of its founders, does not always fall on men of a class superior to that from which the national representation was recruited before the advent of the Caucus; the average of its nominees bears the stamp rather of mediocrity. The Caucus has by no means ousted the plutocratic element from Parliament nor from the counsels of the party. It needs it itself to provide for the upkeep of its machinery. Even the influence of social rank proved to be indispensable to the Caucus.

True, the type of these political zealots created by the Caucus in England has not the objectionable features of the 'professional politician' of other countries; he is not a parasite, who lives on society and makes politics a trade, often a low trade. The number of persons who live exclusively by 'politics,' although increased by the Caucus, is not yet a large one. They are (I am still speaking of the extra-constitutional sphere) the secretaries of Associations, the employés of the central and provincial Organization, the 'missionaries,' and the lecturers or other political agents. Even at a liberal computation they would hardly reach the figure of 2000 for the whole of England, with Scotland and Wales. Still they are becoming a marked body in the midst of society; the Caucus has given them a permanent status, and the 'political agents' are beginning to form, if not exactly a separate class, at all events a guild. They already have a collective consciousness of themselves; they possess their professional societies, their benefit clubs. The best foretaste, however, of the professional politician is given rather by the small local leaders created by the organization of the Caucus. These men seldom make money out of their political situation, but most of them always expect some advantage from it, if not in cash, at all events in some other form. . . .

The first, the most tangible, result produced by this autocracy of the Caucus was to put an end to the free competition of candidates in the party; there are now only candidatures of one kind, the orthodox ones, stamped with the Caucus trademark; the others are doomed. The loss of this freedom inevitably diminishes that of the electorate. A party which lives under such a régime is already half enslaved, and it will have, perhaps, to use very vigorous efforts to recover its liberty. The compulsion implied by the approved candidature is completed in the case of the individual voter by the behests of party piety, which the Caucus is watching over and which consists in voting obediently and blindly. The voter who is not refractory but simply thoughtful is regarded as an obstacle. And with perfect good faith, from simple devotion to professional interest, a tendency arises, even in the governing circles of the Organization, to look with envy on neighbours whose voters do not exhibit this vicious propensity to argue. In fact, military discipline is the secret aspiration of the 'organizers,' when they do not proclaim it....

Moreover, a phenomenon is arising which is at once the effect and the stimulant of those which have just been described,—the political apathy which is creeping over society. 'Politics is no longer popular' is the unanimous impression of people in the business.... The middle class is retiring from the political arena, deliberately, so to speak, obeying alike its feelings of selfishness and its *amour propre* wounded by the political advent of the lower social strata. It looks as if this class had exhausted its ardour in the great battles which it fought one after another in the first half of the century. It has no longer any grievances to urge or claims to keep alive in the political and social sphere.... While the cultivated classes tend to turn aside from politics, the new strata of political society show no eagerness to fill the vacant space; public spirit is not developing sufficiently among the masses, to a great extent through the fault of the Caucus. At the same time that it assists the selfishness of the middle classes in discouraging their efforts by the democratic pretensions of which it has assumed the championship, it withholds from the masses the real political education calculated to broaden and stimulate the mind; it keeps it back, offering them in its place a wretched substitute, which has the property of delivering them more easily into its hands. Thus is witnessed alike an abatement of interest in politics in the community, and a diminution of the moral and material facilities for the rise and the popularity of the best men and for rallying the masses around them, side by side with a decline in the readiness of the educated and well-to-do classes to come forward and put their shoulders to the wheel.

While these combined tendencies reveal the dawn of a separation of society as a whole from the small minority given up to politics, under a constitution which now denies hardly any one the power of exerting his influence on public affairs, in the narrower sphere of politics an important phenomenon is appearing: the political parties are more and more losing their distinctive characteristics.... No longer representing clearly defined opposing principles, no longer having a monopoly, the one of progress, the other of reaction, the one of solicitude for the masses, the other of aristocratic or capitalist privilege, the parties as such tend to become simple aggregates, drawn together, by the attractive force of a leader, for the conquest or the preservation of power.

In a word, parallel with the separation of society from politics, are seen indications of the divorce of politics from principles. When these last have disappeared, the only vital system of the parties will be a mechanical organization, all the more powerful the more it will be spread over the country, the more widely it will cover the constituencies with its network. In other words, the parties will live only by and thanks to a machine like the Caucus. The latter will not only have helped to drive back the living forces of the political community, to make a vacuum in it, but will also install itself in the empty citadel, and almost as a matter of right. Ostrogorski, *Political Parties*, I, 580–2, 591–4, 603–4, 622–3

180. Belloc and Chesterton argue that the party system is a sham, 1911

The theory of the Constitution is that Ministers are nominated by the Crown. Everyone knows that this has ceased to be the fact. Many people would tell you that now Ministers are in effect nominated by Parliament. But this is equally far from the truth. The plain truth is that Ministers nominate themselves. They form a self-elected body, filling up its vacancies by co-option.

The two Front Benches are close oligarchical corporations; or, to speak more accurately, one close oligarchical corporation, admission to which is only to be gained by the consent of those who have already secured places therein. The price which has to be paid for admission is, of course, a complete surrender of independence, and absolute submission to the will of the body as a whole.

The greater number of the members of this close corporation enter by right of their relationship, whether of blood or marriage, to other members of the group, no matter of what social rank. They may be called the Relations. This family arrangement must not be confused with what once was the old aristocratic privileges of the Great Houses.

There are still indeed certain wealthy political families whose members are regarded as having a prescriptive right to share in the government of the country. Their wealth is more and more important, their lineage less and less.

The traditions of the English political system having been aristocratic in character, render the presence of the members of such families (in lessening degree) antecedently probable; but while the public realises this, it is not aware of the degree in which mere relationship, high or low born, enters into the making of Ministries, still less of the way in which family ties enter into the formation of the two closely connected Front Benches, where there is no question of aristocratic descent.

It is neither novel nor astonishing to discover a Duke of Norfolk acting as Postmaster-General under a Conservative Administration. As the Duke of Devonshire was a member of former governments, so one would imagine that the present Duke, his nephew, would naturally hold office in any future Unionist Administration. The public even expects Mr Austen Chamberlain should inherit, as it were, Cabinet rank from his father; nor is it much scandalised to see the Prime Minister's brother-in-law, Mr Tennant, sitting by his side on the Treasury bench. Mr Churchill, of course, as a member of the family whose name he bears, and as heir to his father's career, has a double right.

But the list begins to grow long when we see Lord Selborne, the son-in-law of a former Prime Minister, Lord Salisbury, governing South Africa at a moment when his first cousin, Mr Arthur Balfour, is the Prime Minister of the day (being retained there subsequently by Mr Balfour's 'opponents'), while that Prime Minister's brother, Mr Gerald Balfour, not only enjoys long years of office through his family connection, but a considerable public pension into the bargain when office is no longer open to him. That Lord Gladstone should inherit from his father may seem normal enough, though his name does swell this extended category. But to find Lord Portsmouth Under Secretary for War, while a cousin of his wife's, Sir John Pease, has yet another post under the present Government, and his cousin again, Mr Pike Pease, the reversion of a 'Conservative' post; and to have to add to this that the Liberal Whip, Sir John Fuller, is actually the brother-in-law of the Parliamentary Secretary to the Treasury, Mr Hobhouse, both being grandchildren by blood or marriage of a Conservative Chancellor, Lord St Aldwyn (Sir Michael Hicks-Beach), touches upon the comic when we remember how large a proportion of the paid offices available this list represents. Nor do the names here jotted down almost at random present more than a very small sample of the whole system.

It must be noted that these family ties are not confined to the separate sides of the House. They unite the Ministerial with the Opposition Front Bench as closely as they unite Ministers and ex-Ministers to each other....

Points of this kind are of importance, for they show to how restricted a group of men the functions of government have come to be entrusted. They are effects, not causes, of its narrowness. None can deny that the phenomena are peculiar to a political condition exceedingly abnormal. Groups of this sort could not possibly arise in a genuinely democratic society; and, what is more, are more closely and intricately bound together even than they were in the days when the government of this country was avowedly that of an oligarchy. The tendency to govern by clique is not decreasing; it is increasing.

Belloc and Chesterton, *The Party System*, pp. 37–41

PARTY POLICIES

181. Peel's Tamworth Manifesto, 1835

...I will not accept power on the condition of declaring myself an apostate from the principles on which I have heretofore acted. At the same time, I never will admit that I have been, either before or after the Reform Bill, the defender of abuses, or the enemy of judicious reforms. I appeal with confidence, in denial of the charge, to the active part I took in the great question of the Currency—in the consolidation and amendment of the Criminal Law—in the revisal of the whole system of Trial by Jury—to the opinions I have professed, and uniformly acted on, with regard to other branches of the jurisprudence of the country—I appeal to this as a proof that I have not been disposed to acquiesce in acknowledged evils, either from the mere superstitious reverence for ancient usages, or from the dread of labour or responsibility in the application of a remedy.

But the Reform Bill, it is said, constitutes a new era, and it is the duty of a Minister to declare explicitly—first, whether he will maintain the Bill itself, and, secondly, whether he will act upon the spirit in which it was conceived.

With respect to the Reform Bill itself, I will repeat now the declaration which I made when I entered the House of Commons as a Member of the Reformed Parliament, that I consider the Reform Bill a final and irrevocable settlement of a great Constitutional question—a settlement which no friend to the peace and welfare of this country would attempt to distrub, either by direct or by insidious means.

Then, as to the spirit of the Reform Bill, and the willingness to adopt and enforce it as a rule of government: if, by adopting the spirit of the

Reform Bill, it be meant that we are to live in a perpetual vortex of agitation; that public men can only support themselves in public estimation by adopting every popular impression of the day,—by promising the instant redress of anything which anybody may call an abuse,—by abandoning altogether that great aid of government—more powerful than either law or reason—the respect for ancient rights, and the deference to prescriptive authority; if this be the spirit of the Reform Bill, I will not undertake to adopt it. But if the spirit of the Reform Bill implies merely a careful review of institutions, civil and ecclesiastical, undertaken in a friendly temper, combining, with the firm maintenance of established rights, the correction of proved abuses and the redress of real grievances,—in that case, I can for myself and colleagues undertake to act in such a spirit and with such intentions.

Such declarations of general principle are, I am aware, necessarily vague; but, in order to be more explicit, I will endeavour to apply them practically to some of those questions which have of late attracted the greater share of public interest and attention.

I take, first, the inquiry into Municipal Corporations:

It is not my intention to advise the Crown to interrupt the progress of that inquiry, nor to transfer the conduct of it from those to whom it was committed by the late Government. For myself, I gave the best proof that I was not unfriendly to the principle of inquiry, by consenting to be a member of that Committee of the House of Commons on which it was originally devolved. No report has yet been made by the Commissioners to whom the inquiry was afterwards referred; and, until that report be made, I cannot be expected to give, on the part of the Government, any other pledge than that they will bestow on the suggestions it may contain, and the evidence on which they may be founded, a full and unprejudiced consideration.

I will, in the next place, address myself to the questions in which those of our fellow-countrymen who dissent from the doctrines of the Established Church take an especial interest.

Instead of making new professions, I will refer to the course which I took upon those subjects when out of power.

In the first place, I supported the measure brought forward by Lord Althorp, the object of which was to exempt all classes from the payment of Church-rates, applying in lieu thereof, out of a branch of the revenue, a certain sum for the building and repair of churches. I never expressed, nor did I entertain, the slightest objection to the principle of a bill of which Lord John Russell was the author, intended to relieve the conscientious scruples of Dissenters in respect to the ceremony of marriage. I give no opinion now on the particular measures themselves: they were proposed by Ministers in whom the Dissenters had confidence; they were intended to give relief; and it is sufficient for my present purpose to state that I supported the principle of them.

I opposed—and I am bound to state that my opinions in that respect have undergone no change—the admission of Dissenters, as a claim of right, into the Universities; but I expressly declared that if regulations, enforced by public authorities superintending the professions of law and medicine, and the studies connected with them, had the effect of conferring advantages of the nature of civil privileges on one class of the King's subjects from which another was excluded—those regulations ought to undergo modification, with the view of placing all the King's subjects, whatever their religious creeds, upon a footing of perfect equality with respect to any civil privilege.

I appeal to the course which I pursued on those several questions, when office must have been out of contemplation; and I ask, with confidence, does that course imply that I was actuated by any illiberal or intolerant spirit towards the Dissenting body, or by an unwillingness to consider fairly the redress of any real grievances?

In the examination of other questions which excited public feeling, I will not omit the Pension List. I resisted—and, with the opinions I entertain, I should again resist—a retrospective inquiry into pensions granted by the Crown at a time when the discretion of the Crown was neither fettered by law nor by the expression of any opinion on the part of the House of Commons; but I voted for the Resolution, moved by Lord Althorp, that pensions on the Civil List ought, for the future, to be confined to such persons only as have just claims to the Royal beneficence, or are entitled to consideration on account either of their personal services to the Crown, or of the performance of duties to the public, or of their scientific or literary eminence. On the Resolution which I thus supported as a private Member of Parliament, I shall scrupulously act as a Minister of the Crown, and shall advise the grant of no pension which is not in conformity with the spirit and intention of the vote to which I was a party.

Then, as to the great question of Church Reform. On that head I have no new professions to make. I cannot give my consent to the alienating of Church property, in any part of the United Kingdom, from strictly Ecclesiastical purposes. But I repeat now the opinions that I have already expressed in Parliament in regard to the Church Establishment in Ireland—that if, by an improved distribution of the revenues of the Church, its just influence can be extended, and the true interests of the Established religion promoted, all other considerations should be made subordinate to the advancement of objects of such paramount importance.

As to Church property in this country, no person has expressed a more earnest wish than I have done that the question of tithe, complicated and difficult as I acknowledge it to be, should, if possible, be satisfactorily settled by the means of a commutation, founded upon just principles, and proposed after mature consideration.

With regard to alterations in the laws which govern our Ecclesiastical Establishment, I have had no recent opportunity of giving that grave consideration to a subject of the deepest interest, which could alone justify me in making any public declaration of opinion. It is a subject which must undergo the fullest deliberation, and into that deliberation the Government will enter, with the sincerest desire to remove every abuse that can impair the efficiency of the Establishment, to extend the sphere of its usefulness, and to strengthen and confirm its just claims upon the respect and affections of the people.

It is unnecessary for my purpose to enter into further details. I have said enough, with respect to general principles and their practical application to public measures, to indicate the spirit in which the King's Government is prepared to act. Our object will be—the maintenance of peace—the scrupulous and honourable fulfilment, without reference to their original policy, of all existing engagements with Foreign Powers—the support of public credit—the enforcement of strict economy—and the just and impartial consideration of what is due to all interests—agricultural, manufacturing, and commercial....

Peel, *Memoirs*, II, 61–6

182. Disraeli on Conservative principles, 1872

(a) *Speech at Manchester, 3 April 1872*

... Our opponents assure us that the Conservative party have no political programme.... If by a programme is meant a plan to despoil churches and plunder landlords, I admit we have no programme. If by a programme is meant a policy which assails or menaces every institution and every interest, every class and every calling in the country, I admit we have no programme. But if to have a policy with distinct ends, and these such as most deeply interest the great body of the nation, be a becoming programme for a political party, then, I contend, we have an adequate programme, and one which, here or elsewhere, I shall always be prepared to assert and to vindicate.

Gentlemen, the programme of the Conservative party is to maintain the Constitution of the country....

(b) Speech at the Crystal Palace, 24 June 1872

Now, I have always been of opinion that the Tory party has three great objects. The first is to maintain the institutions of the country—not from any sentiment of political superstition, but because we believe that they embody the principles upon which a community like England can alone safely rest. The principles of liberty, of order, of law, and of religion ought not to be entrusted to individual opinion or to the caprice and passion of multitudes, but should be embodied in a form of permanence and power. We associate with the Monarchy the ideas which it represents—the majesty of law, the administration of justice, the fountain of mercy and of honour. We know that in the Estates of the Realm and the privileges they enjoy, is the best security for public liberty and good government. We believe that a national profession of faith can only be maintained by an Established Church, and that no society is safe unless there is a public recognition of the Providential government of the world, and of the future responsibility of man....

Gentlemen, there is another and second great object of the Tory party. If the first is to maintain the institutions of the country, the second is, in my opinion, to uphold the Empire of England....

Gentlemen, another great object of the Tory party, and one not inferior to the maintenance of the Empire, or the upholding of our institutions, is the elevation of the condition of the people.... It is, gentlemen, a large subject. It has many branches. It involves the state of the dwellings of the people, the moral consequences of which are not less considerable than the physical. It involves their enjoyment of some of the chief elements of nature—air, light, and water. It involves the regulation of their industry, the inspection of their toil. It involves the purity of their provisions, and it touches upon all the means by which you may wean them from habits of excess and of brutality.

Kebbel, II, 491, 525, 529–32

183. Gladstone suggests a limited Liberal programme, 1885

[W. E. Gladstone to Earl Granville, 5 October 1885]

It seems to be felt that the ground has now been sufficiently laid for going to the Election with an united front: that ground being the common profession of a limited creed or programme in the Liberal sense, with an entire freedom, for those so inclined to travel beyond it but not to impose their own sense upon all other people....

... If the party and its leaders are agreed as to the immediate measures on the three subjects of Local Government, Land, & Registration (so-called), are not these enough to find a Liberal Administration plenty of work, as principal subjects, especially with Procedure, for several years; and, if so, do they not supply a ground broad enough to start a Government, which would hold over, until the proper time should come, all the questions on which its members might not be agreed, just as the Government of Lord Grey held over, from 1830 to 1834, the question whether Irish Church property might or might not be applied to secular uses?

I would suggest for consideration, whether you might not, at some time before the Dissolution, promote a small meeting of leading men of the late Cabinet, to weigh this subject. It seems to me that even after all that has been said there exist rational and sufficient grounds for common action, probably reaching over a considerable time.

GG2, II, 401-2

184. The Newcastle programme, 1891

[Resolutions at the Newcastle-upon-Tyne Council meeting of the National Liberal Federation, 1-2 October 1891]

IRELAND

Moved by Sir EDWARD GREY, Bart., M.P.; seconded by Mr. J. ROWNTREE, M.P.:—

'That this Council holds that the case for Home Rule in Ireland has been still further confirmed by the steadfastness, sound judgment, and moderation with which the great body of the Irish people have, during the last year, successfully faced one of the sharpest ordeals in political history;

And it looks with unshaken confidence to Mr. Gladstone, upon his return to power, to frame and—in spite of idle menaces from the House of Lords—to pass a Measure which shall fully satisfy the just demands of Ireland, and leave the Imperial Parliament free to attend to the pressing claims of Great Britain for its own reforms.'

WELSH DISESTABLISHMENT

Moved by Mr. T. E. ELLIS, M.P.; seconded by MAJOR EVAN JONES (Cardiff):—

'That this Council re-affirms its belief that the time has come for the disestablishment and disendowment of the Church of England in Wales, and for the application of the tithes to the public purposes of the Principality, and declares that this question should be dealt with in the next Parliament, as soon as Irish Home Rule is attained.'

LONDON

Moved by Mr. JAMES BRYCE, M.P.; seconded by Mr. JAMES STUART, M.P.:—

'That this Council declares that the interests of good Government urgently demand that the London County Council should without delay be put in possession of full municipal powers, including the control of its own gas and water supplies, markets and police, and should, by taxation of ground values and by other financial reforms, be enabled to govern and improve the Metropolis without undue pressure upon the occupying ratepayers, and that such powers should be enjoyed by all other municipalities.'

FREE EDUCATION

Moved by Mr. SYDNEY BUXTON, M.P.; seconded by Mr. CHARLES FENWICK, M.P.:—

'That this Council expresses its satisfaction that the principle of Free Education, which for five years has been a prominent feature in the resolutions of the Federation, has been embodied in Legislation, but regards the Act now in operation as partial and defective since it fails to recognise the right of public control, and does not secure that the increased grant shall be devoted to greater educational efficiency; and by omitting, at the instance of the House of Lords, the provision that free accommodation shall be suitable as well as sufficient, disregards, the conscientious convictions of many parents;

The Council again declares "that no system of public elementary Education can be regarded as satisfactory or final unless it secures that every family shall have, within reasonable reach, a Free School, and that all schools supported by public money shall be subject to public representative control".'...

REGISTRATIONS AND ELECTORAL REFORM

Moved by the Right Hon. Sir G. O. TREVELYAN, Bart., M.P.; seconded by Mr. JAMES CRAIG, M.P.:—

'That this Council condemns the action of the Government in resisting, with the full support of the Dissentient Liberals, Mr. Stansfeld's motion for the amendment of the Registration Laws; regarding the present state of these Laws as a public scandal and injustice; and trusts that one of the first efforts of a Liberal Government will be to amend them, by the appointment of responsible Registration Officers, the reduction of the qualifying period to three months, and the abolition of the disqualifications now attaching to removals. The Council believes that only by such Amendments, and by basing the Franchise solely on the principle of "one man one vote", can a full and fair expression of the national will be secured;

The Council also declares that the duration of Parliaments should be shortened, Returning Officers' expenses at Parliamentary Elections be placed upon the rates, all Elections be held on one and the same day, and that the principle of payment of Members of Parliament by the State should be recognised, as the only means of securing an adequate representation of Labour in the House of Commons.'

THE CONDITION OF THE RURAL POPULATION

Moved by the Most Hon. the Marquis of RIPON, K.G.; seconded by Sir WALTER FOSTER, M.P....:—

'That in the opinion of this Council the well-being of the nation, no less than that of the districts immediately concerned, requires that the condition of the rural population should receive the immediate attention of Parliament;

The Council regards with satisfaction the action taken by the General Purposes Committee of the Federation, and, while approving generally of the suggestions it has formulated, affirms, as of primary importance—

(a) The establishment of District and Parish Councils popularly elected;

(b) The concession of compulsory powers to local authorities to acquire and hold land for Allotments, Small Holdings, Village Halls, Places of Worship, Labourers' Dwellings, and other public purposes;

(*c*) The reform of existing Allotment Acts by the removal of restrictions, by giving security of tenure and the power to erect buildings, and the right of full compensation for all improvements.'

'OMNIBUS' RESOLUTION

Moved by Sir WILFRID LAWSON, Bart., M.P.; seconded by the Right Hon. H. H. FOWLER, M.P.:—

'That this Council again affirms its declaration in favour of—
A thorough Reform of the Land Laws, such as will secure—

(*a*) The Repeal of the Laws of Primogeniture and Entail;
(*b*) Freedom of Sale and Transfer;
(*c*) The just taxation of Land values and ground rents;
(*d*) Compensation, to town and country tenants, for both disturbance and improvement, together with a simplified process for obtaining such compensation;
(*e*) The Enfranchisement of Leaseholds;
The direct and popular veto on the Liquor traffic;
The Disestablishment and Disendowment of the Established Church in Scotland;
The Equalisation of the Death Duties upon real and personal property;
The just division of rates between owner and occupier;
The taxation of Mining Royalties;
A "Free Breakfast Table";
The extension of the Factory Acts; and
The "mending or ending" of the House of Lords.'

National Liberal Federation, *Proceedings*, 1891, pp. 6–8

185. The National Liberal Federation disavows the Newcastle programme, 1898

[Report of the Committee of the Federation, 1898]

From the first days of its existence to the present time the Federation has steadily refused to formulate a political programme. Liberalism when rightly understood is too vast and too progressive to permit of the hard and fast formalism of a specific creed. How then did the Newcastle Programme come into existence? No Newcastle Programme was ever framed by the Federation or by anyone connected with it; no programme whatever was presented at the Annual Council Meeting at Newcastle or elsewhere or at any other meeting of the Federation.... The Council of the Federation meets once a year.... It is customary at these gatherings to pass certain resolutions which are believed to express the wishes of the vast majority of the Liberal party upon the leading questions of the day. These resolutions are prepared by the Executive Committee after consultation with all the Federated Associations, and after taking into full consideration any resolutions which may have been passed by the General Committee of the Federation, or at local conferences held under its auspices. These resolutions are intended to inform the party leaders of the subjects in dealing with which they may rely upon the support of the party as a whole. The Federation does not interfere with the time or order in which questions should be taken up. That is the province of the leaders of the party.... A considerable number of subjects were brought forward at the Newcastle Meeting, but no new subject was introduced. All the reforms which were embodied in resolutions had been demanded at previous meetings. Some had been advocated by Liberals for many years.... But the resolutions of this particular meeting received a special significance from the fact that without reference to any person connected with the Federation, and to the surprise of everyone, our great leader, Mr. Gladstone, instead of, as was anticipated devoting his speech at the great Public Meeting to the subject of Ireland, took up *seriatim* the resolutions which had been passed at the Council Meetings and gave them the weight of his direct approval. The newspapers at once spoke of 'the Newcastle Programme'. For a time the members of the Executive Committee protested, but the name stuck and entered into common use....

National Liberal Federation, *Proceedings*, 1898, 40–2

186. The programme of the Fabian Society, 1896

BASIS OF THE FABIAN SOCIETY

The Fabian Society consists of Socialists.

It therefore aims at the re-organization of society by the emancipation of Land and Industrial Capital from individual and class ownership, and the vesting of them in the community for the general benefit. In this way only can the natural and acquired advantages of the country be equitably shared by the whole people.

The Society accordingly works for the extinction of private property in Land and of the consequent individual appropriation, in the form of

Rent, of the price paid for permission to use the earth, as well as for the advantages of superior soils and sites.

The Society, further, works for the transfer to the community of the administration of such Industrial Capital as can conveniently be managed socially. For, owing to the monopoly of the means of production in the past, industrial inventions and the transformation of surplus income into Capital have mainly enriched the proprietary class, the worker being now dependent on that class for leave to earn a living.

If these measures be carried out, without compensation (though not without such relief to expropriated individuals as may seem fit to the community), Rent and Interest will be added to the reward of labor, the idle class now living on the labor of others will necessarily disappear, and practical equality of opportunity will be maintained by the spontaneous action of economic forces with much less interference with personal liberty than the present system entails.

For the attainment of these ends the Fabian Society looks to the spread of Socialist opinions, and the social and political changes consequent thereon. It seeks to promote these by the general dissemination of knowledge as to the relation between the individual and Society in its economic, ethical and political aspects. *Fabian Tract* No. 70

187. The programme of the Independent Labour party, 1906-7

NAME

'The Independent Labour Party.'

MEMBERSHIP

Open to all Socialists who endorse the principles and policy of the Party, are not members of either the Liberal or Conservative Party, and whose application for membership is accepted by a Branch.

Any member expelled from membership of a Branch of the I.L.P. shall not be eligible for membership of any other Branch without having first submitted his or her case for adjudication of the N.A.C.

OBJECT

The object of the Party is to establish the Socialist State, when land and capital will be held by the community and used for the well-being of the community, and when the exchange of commodities will be organized also by the community, so as to secure the highest possible standard of life for the individual. In giving effect to this object it shall work as part of the International Socialist movement.

METHOD

The Party, to secure its objects, adopts—

1. *Educational Methods*, including the publication of Socialist literature, the holding of meetings, etc.
2. *Political Methods*, including the election of its members to local and national administrative and legislative bodies.

PROGRAMME

The true object of industry being the production of the requirements of life, the responsibility should rest with the community collectively, therefore—

The land, being the storehouse of all the necessaries of life, should be declared and treated as public property.

The capital necessary for industrial operations should be owned and used collectively.

Work, and wealth resulting therefrom, should be equitably distributed over the population.

As a means to this end, we demand the enactment of the following measures:—

1. A maximum forty-eight hours' working-week, with the retention of all existing holidays, and Labour Day, May 1, secured by law.

2. The provision of work to all capable adult applicants at recognized trade-union rates, with a statutory minimum of sixpence per hour.

In order to remuneratively employ the applicants, parish, district, borough, and county councils to be invested with power to—

(a) Organize and undertake such industries as they may consider desirable.

(b) Compulsorily acquire land; purchase, erect, or manufacture, buildings, stock, or other articles for carrying on such industries.

(c) Levy rates on the rental values of the district, and borrow money on the security of such rates for any of the above purposes.

3. State pensions for every person over fifty years of age, and adequate provision for all widows, orphans, sick and disabled workers.

4. Free, secular, moral, primary, secondary and university education, with free maintenance while at school or university.

5. The raising of the age of child labour, with a view of its ultimate extinction.

6. Municipalization and public control of the drink traffic.

7. Municipalization and public control of all hospitals and infirmaries.

8. Abolition of indirect taxation, and the gradual transference of all public burdens on to unearned incomes, with a view to their ultimate extinction.

The Independent Labour Party is in favour of adult suffrage, with full political rights and privileges for women, and the immediate extension of the franchise to women on the same terms as granted to men; also triennial parliaments and second ballot.

Ensor, Modern Socialism, 3rd ed, pp. 356–8

B PARTY ORGANISATION

The concept of party leadership was very ill-defined before the 1870s. Lord Liverpool and most of his immediate successors as Prime Minister thought of themselves as the King's or Queen's chief minister rather than as a party chieftain. Even Peel, who might have been expected to be a keen party leader, was uncomfortable about his obligations to his followers, and reluctant to give them the sort of encouragement from which party fervour develops. For most Prime Ministers before 1867, party was useful in keeping men together and for arranging elections (many of which were uncontested anyway), but it was essentially a tool of management, not an end in itself. Whether the party leader in the Commons or the Lords was acknowledged as leader of the party as a whole depended on the personality of the men concerned and their efficiency as ministers, rather than on their popular appeal. Lord Liverpool was never a popular Prime Minister, nor were Melbourne, Russell or Aberdeen: they were respected and admired, but that was all. Peel was the first Prime Minister since Pitt deliberately to rest his claims on popular rather than parliamentary support, but he did so reluctantly, and the numerous Peel statues up and down the country are a tribute to his courage as a man rather than to his skill as a party leader. Indeed, as a party leader Palmerston was infinitely more successful than Peel; so successful in fact that he came to transcend the party system, by appealing to all sections of middle-of-the-road opinion, Whig, Tory and Radical. Derby and Disraeli were the first men whose position depended on their skill in creating and leading a party, but even they had very restricted views of what party leadership involved. Disraeli made few speeches outside the House of Commons, most of them to meetings of agriculturalists, and never much cared for large popular audiences, though he was a good speaker. Gladstone was the first major statesman to take it for granted that a party leader with a policy to expound must go amongst the people to expound it.

His speeches in South Lancashire in 1865 and 1868 offered an entirely new type of party leadership. Thereafter, every party leader was in great demand for oratorical forays, the pace being set by the untiring Gladstone. But party leaders could still be relatively inert if they so chose, and could even avoid attending the party conferences. Indeed, Rosebery and Balfour tried to keep their party obligations down to a minimum and relied on their colleagues to cope with most of the party problems that required attention.

There was no formal machinery for electing a party leader. When a party was in Opposition it was usual to fill a vacancy in the party leadership in Lords or Commons by holding an election. The early elections such as the choice of Tierney and Althorp to lead the Whigs in the Commons, were made in an informal and casual manner, but by the 1870s it was agreed that an election must take place in two stages. First, the party Whips must take an informal poll of party members and report the result to the candidates and the leader in the other house: then, all the candidates except the one with the largest number of votes were expected to withdraw, leaving the victor to be acclaimed leader at a party meeting. This was the procedure adopted by the Liberals in the House of Commons in 1876 and by the Conservatives in 1911 (**198**). It satisfied those who believed that party leaders should emerge by general agreement rather than by election and reduced the danger of a rift in the party to a minimum.

Whether the leader of the party in the Lords or the leader of the party in the Commons was recognised as overall leader of the party, or whether there was no overall party leader, depended very much on the standing of the individuals concerned. A Prime Minister or ex-Prime Minister was automatically the overall leader of his party until he resigned. But where there was no ex-Prime Minister available there was sometimes uncertainty. Gladstone was lucky in 1868 that when Russell resigned the Liberal leadership no peer challenged his claim to lead, for it rested on no formal decision. After Gladstone had in his turn resigned in 1875, neither Lord Granville in the Lords nor Lord Hartington in the Commons enjoyed an ascendancy, so that they became in effect joint leaders. Much the same happened in the Conservative party when Disraeli, by then Earl of Beaconsfield, died in 1881. The Queen might prefer Sir Stafford Northcote in the Commons to Lord Salisbury,[1] but by 1885 Salisbury was the only possible Conservative Prime Minister. And, of course, the pattern was repeated in the Conservative party after 1911, when Bonar Law the Conservative leader in the Commons had no claim to pre-eminence over the much more experienced Lansdowne in the Lords.

The character of a party depended on the interplay between leaders who were anxious to lead and party members who were willing to be led only

[1] *LQV*, 2nd ser. III, 218–19.

so long as they approved of the direction in which the leadership was moving. All parties included some men like John Bright who found it morally repugnant to surrender their freedom of action (195). Yet equally all parties included a considerable body of men who regarded loyalty to the party leaders as a virtue. The problem of how to strike the right balance was most acute in the case of the Liberal party, which was not a unitary party but a loose confederation of peers, M.P.s, local councillors, members of reformist organisations, and trades unionists. In his later years Gladstone guided this confederation with too loose a rein, with the result that indiscipline in parliament became endemic and the reformist organisations in the country got into the habit of acting without very much regard for the rest of the party (196). The first victim was Lord Rosebery, who in 1896 abandoned the party leadership in disgust.[1] Sir William Harcourt in his turn resigned the leadership in a very short time and left to Sir Henry Campbell-Bannerman the task of pulling together a thoroughly demoralised party. Campbell-Bannerman had no illusions as to the difficulty of his task, which was made more complicated by the reluctance of the Liberal imperialists to accept his leadership. But in the end he pulled the party through and as Prime Minister was able to restore the control of the leadership over the rank and file. Not that the Liberals were alone in finding it hard to hold their party together in the period 1895–1905; Joseph Chamberlain's campaign for tariff reform so split the Conservatives and Liberal Unionists that between 1902 and 1905 they quickly fell apart (149).

The day-to-day management of each party was normally vested in the chief party Whip in the House of Commons, who controlled the party funds and the party offices. But most parties also possessed acknowledged experts on party business to whom the party leader could turn for help and advice, among them paid agents, who could be consulted about such questions as whether it was better for a government to resign or to dissolve parliament (206) as well as on more technical matters, and experienced politicians, including ex-Whips like Gladstone's friend Lord Wolverton, who made a hobby of electioneering. Until the opening of the Carlton and Reform Clubs in 1832 and 1836 respectively there were no formal party headquarters from which the party managers could operate, although temporary offices were taken from time to time. After that there was a long period of 'club government', during which much of the technical business of the registration of electors and negotiations with the local party leaders was entrusted by the party managers in the Carlton and the Reform Clubs to one of the partners in a firm of attorneys, usually with the title of Principal Agent. Party offices as such were only necessary after the business of the managers had been extended by the Reform Act

---

[1] Rosebery, *Speeches*, pp. 460–6.

of 1867. The Conservative Central Office was established in 1870, and for a time had at its head two very notable Principal Agents, J. E. Gorst and R. W. E. Middleton, both men of higher status than attorneys. Its Liberal counterpart, the Liberal Central Association (1877), originally founded in 1860 as the Liberal Registration Association, shared its offices with those of the National Liberal Federation after 1886, when Frank Schnadhorst came down from Birmingham to reorganise the party after the Liberal Unionist secession.

In the country the basic units of organisation after 1832 were the polling district, the borough, and the parliamentary constituency. Down to 1867 most of these were managed by a knot of local party magnates on each side, often calling themselves a Registration Society because they paid for the supervision of the registration of electors (though there were more popular organisations in a few places, notably in Rochdale). Contested elections were expensive and were avoided as often as possible, and the forming of party associations was sometimes deprecated because they led to local strife (200). The management of elections was largely in the hands of the local attorneys who attended to the registration of electors. Indeed, attorneys were the real controlling body in a great many of the smaller boroughs which existed in some numbers down to 1885. There were also down to 1885 a good many boroughs and county divisions where seats were in the gift of a great landed magnate.[1]

After 1867 the character of local organisation began to change, because the extended constituencies created by the Reform Act could no longer be managed in the old way. The party headquarters strongly advised the local party leaders to adopt a more popular form of organisation, the model on the Liberal side being either the pioneer Rochdale Reform Association (201) or Joseph Chamberlain's Birmingham Liberal Association (204). However, neither Liberal nor Conservative associations with a wide membership were by any means universal until after 1885 when, along with the Liberal and Conservative clubs which became their social centres, they became an almost invariable feature of the political scene.

The new associations had two chief characteristics. They involved a measure of popular initiative, and they threw up a new type of local leader, firmly rooted in the control of his local association. The best known of the new associations was the Birmingham Liberal Association, nicknamed the 'Birmingham caucus', but there were plenty of comparable bodies, each of them with its own leaders, usually of the middle classes. These new local leaders presented something of a problem for the parties, because they naturally felt that they should have some place in the national party hierarchy. The Conservatives managed to fit them into the National Union of Con-

[1] For lists see Gash, *Politics in the Age of Peel*, and Hanham, *Elections and Party Management.*

servative and Constitutional Associations,[1] a body formed in 1867 primarily to bring together Conservative working men (**203**). The annual conference of the National Union gradually became a general assembly of the local party leaders, and for a time in the 1880s caused a stir by backing the efforts of Lord Randolph Churchill to overthrow the Conservative party leadership (**205**). Its main function thereafter was to express the hopes, aspirations, and prejudices of the party workers in the country, sometimes in harmony with the party leadership, at others in a spirit of resentment or hostility. In addition, there were a number of Conservative party auxiliaries, the most important of which were the Primrose League—for a time in the 1890s the most effective electioneering body in the country—and the Association of Conservative Clubs.

The Liberal Associations, not having a ready-made organisation to turn to, were first supplied with one by the Birmingham Radicals, who created the National Liberal Federation in 1877 (**204**). This was a curious combination of a Radical ginger group and a federation of Liberal Associations. During the 1880s it made itself very unpopular with many Liberals by more or less openly sanctioning the hostility of radically minded local associations towards old-fashioned Liberal M.P.s. But after Joseph Chamberlain had failed to carry the Federation into the Liberal Unionist camp in 1886 and its headquarters had been moved to London, the Federation gradually settled down into a livelier counterpart of the National Union, its main gathering being an annual conference.

The creation of the new local associations and the militancy of the non-conformist Radicals whose organ the National Liberal Federation was, caused a great deal of uneasiness among political commentators and among those politicians who thought of party organisations as fetters upon the liberty of M.P.s. The journals carried articles for and against the 'Birmingham caucus', and the Polish writer Moisei Ostrogorski worked much of this material into his book *Democracy and the Organization of Political Parties*, first published in English in 1902. Ostrogorski took the line that the 'caucus', whether Liberal or Conservative, was a real danger to democracy, since it could develop into a political machine capable of dominating parliament and forcing minority views on the country as a whole (**179**). But clearly this was to exaggerate. Power never really rested with the local associations or the National Liberal Federation. The party leaders and the members of parliament were always masters of the party because they alone were popularly elected and enjoyed a wide following in the country. The National Liberal Federation needed the backing of Gladstone or Campbell-Bannerman far more than the latter needed the Federation's backing.

The minor parties were organised on the model of the major ones, until

[1] Later the National Union of Conservative and Unionist Associations.

the creation of the Labour party. The major difference was that their strength was confined to a number of localities. The Peelites had little strength except where their leaders had local influence; the Liberal Unionists were strong only in Birmingham, Cornwall, and parts of Scotland; and the Irish nationalists had little influence except among the Irish communities of Liverpool (where the Scotland Division was held by an Irish Nationalist M.P., T. P. O'Connor, after 1885), Manchester, Newcastle, the West of Scotland, and London. The Labour party, essentially a federation of trades unions, socialist societies and the I.L.P. (208), was different from the other minor parties, because its chief strength lay in the country rather than in parliament. Its parliamentary representatives, some of whom in 1906 owed their seats largely to an agreement with the Liberal party (207), normally acted as one wing of the Liberal party rather than as an independent force, except on trade union questions.

The creation of new forms of party organisation had less effect on the selection of candidates than might have been expected. Candidates had always been selected by the local magnates or local leaders and continued to be so selected. Where there were no outstanding local candidates the local leaders were free to seek the advice of the party managers, who from time to time discreetly advertised the fact that they were in business to supply candidates (202). A candidate vouched for by the party managers was more likely to be a satisfactory one than an adventurer who thrust himself on a constituency, but for the most part the local leaders were perfectly capable of finding a suitable candidate without much outside help. In rural constituencies the leading country gentlemen on each side usually nominated one of their own number, and it was rare for their choice to be challenged. In the towns the situation was more complex, since the Liberal party was often divided into more or less hostile factions, each of which was liable to nominate its own candidates without reference to the others. Here one of the chief merits of the 'Birmingham caucus' was that it provided a means for settling differences: the choice of candidates was made by a selection committee in the first instance, but its decision required the endorsement of a general meeting of the local association. At this general meeting the merits and defects of the candidates could be ventilated and an unpopular selection could be overturned. The consequence was a considerable increase in party unity, since candidates now knew that they must appeal to all sections of the party if they were to be selected, and that they must play down issues that might tend to split the party. Men with strong views which could not readily be played down were driven to seek Radical constituencies with a strong tradition of independence (such as Northampton), or amorphous constituencies which were glad to get a strong (and often wealthy) candidate and lacked the makings of an effective opposition to him.

The party managers were ambivalent in their attitude to working-class candidates. For propaganda purposes working-class candidates had obvious merits, and the early working-class M.P.s were welcomed by their fellow members. But both the Liberals and the Conservatives felt unhappy about the prospect of pushing working-class candidates, except where they were the choice of local associations and where suitable arrangements could be made to finance them. Many Liberals and Conservatives shared Bright's objections to class representation in any form,[1] and the Conservatives were further handicapped by a shortage of suitable candidates. However, the party managers on both sides did their best to seek out suitable men. The Conservatives made little headway except at the local level,[2] but on the Liberal side Herbert Gladstone hit upon an ingenious plan by which he was able to enlist the infant Labour party on the Liberal side (207).

PARTY LEADERSHIP

188. Creevey on the election of George Tierney as Whig leader in the Commons, 1818

[Thomas Creevey to the Hon. H. G. Bennet, M.P., 30 December 1818]

...I think you deceive yourselves by supposing the leader of the Whigs of England to be an article that can be created by election, or merely by giving it that name. A man must make himself such leader by his talents, by his courage, and above all by the excellence and consistency of his publick principles. It was by such means that Fox was our leader without election and that Romilly was becoming so, and believe me, there is no other process by which a leader can be made.

Maxwell, *Creevey Papers*, I, 290

189. Peel deprecates party preoccupations in a Prime Minister, 1841

[Sir Robert Peel to J. W. Croker, 20 September 1841]

I wish you could...point out the difference between a Prime Minister in these days and in former times, when Newcastles and Pelhams were ministers.

That now (particularly if the minister is in the House of Commons, and if he is fit to be minister), his life is one of toil and care and drudgery. His reward is not patronage, which imposes nothing but a curse, which enables him to do little more than make *dix mécontents et un ingrat*; not ribbons or hopes of peerage, or such trumpery distinctions,—but

---

[1] Bright, *Public Letters*, p. 234.   [2] Chilston, *Chief Whip*, pp. 175–7.

the means of rendering service to his country, and the hope of honourable fame.

But the man who looks to such objects and such rewards will not condescend to humiliating submissions for mere party purposes; will have neither time nor inclination to be considering how many men will support this public measure, or fly off to gratify some spite or resentment; he will do his best for the great principles that his party supported and for the public welfare, and, if obstructed, he will retire from office, but not from power; for the country will do justice to his motives and will give him the strength which his party had denied to him.

Jennings, *Croker Papers*, II, 409–10

190. Peel justifies his change of front on the Corn Laws, 1846

[Sir Robert Peel to the Lord Justice Clerk, John Hope, 3 August 1846]

I am much gratified by your letter, though it does not surprise me that the course which I have pursued for the purpose of averting serious danger from the aristocracy, of adjusting in the time of tranquillity, when they could be adjusted, questions that brook no delay, and of recommending to the confidence and attachment of the People the institutions by which they are governed—should have met with your cordial approbation.

This is the true Conservative policy—but gentlemen who call themselves Conservatives will be content with nothing but that their own passions and sordid interests should be the rule of a Minister's conduct.

George Peel, *Private Letters of Sir Robert Peel*, pp. 280–1

191. Salisbury (as Lord Robert Cecil) disagrees with Peel's concept of party leadership, 1865

Sir Robert Peel never seems rightly to have understood the obligations which the exertions of a party impose upon a party chief. Party has been cynically defined to be the madness of the many for the profit of the few. There is this amount of truth in the description that the labour and the reward are very unequally distributed. The gratification to pride or pocket, whatever its amount may be, which is conferred by office, can only be the lot of a small fraction in the party. The rest labour, in the main, for their opinions alone. That these may triumph, they take part in an expensive and laborious organisation; spend health and time to little profit and less pleasure in the labours of Parliament; and, often at enormous cost both of money and of ease, fight for the cause they love in their own constituencies. The leaders, on the other hand, spend laborious lives within the walls of Parliament; but it is labour of which every step carries its own reward to those who are actuated by ambition. The result of these conjoint labours is that the leaders obtain place, and what is called in this country power; while the followers obtain the pleasure of seeing their own opinions prevail in the Government and legislation of the country. But the leaders obtain these distinctions, which are evidently of great value inasmuch as men struggle so hardly to secure them, entirely by the help of their followers; and these offer their help at so much cost to themselves distinctly on the understanding that their own opinions are to prevail. The leaders, therefore, in consenting to accept office by the aid of followers who offer it with this aim, pledge themselves that they will use the power so confided to them to promote these opinions. A party struggle is a campaign fought in the main by volunteers, who ask for no pay except the triumph of their cause. The leader, who gathers more substantial spoils, and who in reputation at least receives a disproportionate reward, is bound in honour to the scrupulous payment of the solitary recompense demanded by the followers to whom his victory is due. He is bound to it both as a fair return for effective aid, and as the fulfilment of an implied pledge. He would never have been their leader, if they had not believed him true to their principles. It is a belief which every leader diligently encourages; they trust him with power precisely because he has encouraged it with success, and induced them to entertain it undoubtingly. The power of a Prime Minister in Parliament is something very different from that which his own abilities would by themselves have attained. The position gives him an influence far beyond what could be commanded by any personal qualities. He has accepted that position, and the influence which attaches to it from his party for the purpose of giving effect to their political opinions. If he does not use it for that purpose, but on the contrary employs it in promoting the opinions to which they are opposed, he commits a clear breach of the understanding upon which it was received. To accept an agency or representative position of any kind upon the understanding that you will use it to promote the views of the person from whom you accept it, and then to use it against him, is in every other sphere of action treated as the gravest crime. In law it is punished as dishonesty. In society it is scouted as dishonour. We are well aware, and gladly concede, that neither of those terms could receive any application, in the slightest degree just, to the upright motives and noble disinterestedness of Sir Robert Peel. But it is no slight calamity that he should have himself devised, and have handed down for the misguidance of others, a perverted conception of duty, which not only relaxes, but reverses, the rule of ordinary morality, and holds up as the ideal of a politician's patriotism, acts that in private life would, by common consent, be shunned as fraud.

...He had been invested with power that he might uphold Protection. No change of opinion could justify him in retaining power that he might destroy it.... He was bound to have remembered that the influence of [the] Government was not merely his own creation. It had been built up for him laboriously by the co-operation of thousands of men on the faith of an understanding which he was scattering to the winds....

Sir Robert Peel's best defence is, that he never appears to have admitted the existence of any reciprocal duty between a Minister and his party. He was a strict disciplinarian, and looked with official horror upon independent members. But the obligation in his mind was all upon the side of the followers....　　　*Quarterly Review*, CXVII, 554-5, 557, 559

192. The Duke of Newcastle argues that party leaders should not be elected, 1851

[Duke of Newcastle to Sidney Herbert, 27 October 1851]

...That Lord Aberdeen is, all things considered, our [the Peelites'] natural leader and the *only* man who could properly assume that position, I think there can be no doubt. If he would *place himself* in that post, we should all recognise the claim. It has always appeared to me that the idea of *electing* a leader is a mistake, and an inversion of the proper constitutional view of party mechanism. A leader should become such, either because he is generally recognised as *facile princeps* in position, popularity, talent, discretion, debating power, or other qualifications necessary to balance the differences of opinion to be found in all parties, or by being selected by the Sovereign as her adviser when her Ministers have resigned. In the first case, public opinion and Parliament have pointed out to the Queen the man fitted to be consulted by her in an emergency; in the second, she either, having no such guide or repudiating it, selects him whom, if Parliament will support, she thinks fittest to be her Minister. If, however, a leader is *elected* by his party without the claims of superiority and obvious reasons which others beside his party must recognise, it appears to me that he must be placed in a false position, and be subject to suspicions of cabal which will be alike injurious to his friends and himself.   Stanmore, *Sidney Herbert*, I, 145

193. Gladstone on the changing opinions of political leaders, 1868

It can hardly escape even cursory observation, that the present century has seen a great increase in the instances of what is called political inconsistency. It is needless, and it would be invidious, to refer to names. Among the living, however, who have occupied leading positions, and among the dead of the last twenty years, numerous instances will at once occur to the mind, of men who have been constrained to abandon in middle and mature, or even in advanced life, convictions which they had cherished through long years of conflict and vicissitude: and of men, too, who have not been so fortunate as to close or continue their career in the same political connexion as that in which they commenced it. If we go a little farther back, to the day of Mr. Pitt and Mr. Fox, or even to the day of Mr. Canning, Lord Londonderry, or Lord Liverpool, we must be struck with the difference. A great political and social convulsion, like the French Revolution, of necessity deranged the ranks of party; yet not even then did any man of great name, or of a high order of mind, permanently change his side.

If we have witnessed in the last forty years, beginning with the epoch of Roman Catholic Emancipation, a great increase in the changes of party, or of opinion, among prominent men, we are not at once to leap to the conclusion that public character, as a rule, has been either less upright, or even less vigorous. The explanation is rather to be found in this, that the movement of the public mind has been of a nature entirely transcending former experience; and that it has likewise been more promptly and more effectively represented, than at any earlier period, in the action of the Government and the Legislature.

If it is the office of law and of institutions to reflect the wants and wishes of the country (and its wishes must ever be a considerable element in its wants), then, as the nation passes from a stationary into a progressive period, it will justly require that the changes in its own condition and views should be represented in the professions and actions of its leading men. For they exist for its sake, not it for theirs. It remains indeed their business, now and ever, to take honour and duty for their guides, and not the mere demand or purpose of the passing hour; but honour and duty themselves require their loyal servant to take account of the state of facts in which he is to work, and, while ever labouring to elevate the standard of opinion and action around him, to remember that his business is not to construct, with self-chosen materials, an Utopia or a Republic of Plato, but to conduct the affairs of a living and working community of men, who have self-government recognised as in the last resort the moving spring of their political life, and of the institutions which are its outward vesture.

The gradual transfer of political power from groups and limited classes to the community, and the constant seething of the public mind, in fermentation upon a vast mass of moral and social, as well as merely political, interests, offer conditions of action, in which it is evident that the statesman, in order to preserve the same amount of consistency as his antecessors in other times, must be gifted with a far larger range of foresight. But Nature has endowed him with no such superiority. It may be true that Sir Robert Peel showed this relative deficiency in foresight, with reference to Roman Catholic Emancipation, to Reform, and to the Corn Law. It does not follow, with respect to many who have escaped the reproach, that they could have stood the trial. For them the barometer was less unsteady; the future less exacting in its demands. But let us suppose that we could secure in our statesmen this enlargement of onward view, this faculty of measuring and ascertaining to-day the wants of a remote hereafter; we should not even then be at the end of our difficulties. For the public mind is to a great degree unconscious of its own progression; and it would resent and repudiate, if offered to its immature judgment, the very policy, which after a while it will gravely consider, and after another while enthusiastically embrace.

Gladstone, Gleanings, VII, 100–3

194. Salisbury refuses to countenance a Conservative Home Rule Bill, 1885

[Marquess of Salisbury to the Marquess of Bath, 27 December 1885]

I never admired the political transformation scenes of 1829, 1846, 1867; and I certainly do not wish to be the chief agent in adding a fourth to the history of the Tory party.

Cecil, Salisbury, III, 281

195. Bright on the limits of loyalty to a party leader, 1888
[John Bright to an unnamed correspondent, 13 February 1888]

You evidently think parties are everything, and that to keep the Liberal party together it is necessary to follow your leader. There are great questions on which leaders and parties may go wrong. I did not go with the Liberal party in 1854 when they plunged into the war with Russia. I was then attacked and blamed more than I am now. I was, it is said, burned in effigy in Manchester, and soon after lost my seat for that great constituency, but who now condemns me for the course I then took? I left Mr. Gladstone's Government when they bombarded Alexandria and entered into war with the Soudan. Who blames me now for my desertion of the Liberal leader at the time for that cause? The Russian war cost more than half a million of human lives. The bombardment of Alexandria and what followed cost most probably more than 50,000 lives, most of which were of men of whom I think Mr. Gladstone said they were rightly struggling to be free. Am I to prostrate myself before a leader in whose great career there are blunders so enormous as those to which I now refer?... Are you willing to go on blind-fold—happy to follow and in total ignorance as to where you are going? If Mr. Gladstone has made so grievous a blunder less than two years ago in measures which are now universally condemned, how dare you trust him further in that which he studiously conceals from Parliament and the country? I am, and always have been, against having two Parliaments in the United Kingdom; and so long as the Liberal and Gladstone policy is in favour of two Parliaments I must follow my own judgment and conscience, and not the voice of any party leader. Bright, *Public Letters*, pp. 163–4

196. A Liberal minister on the weakness of the Liberal leadership, 1895
[Sir Ughtred Kay-Shuttleworth to Earl Spencer, 23 July 1895]

The fact seems to me to be that our party needs much firmer leadership, & guiding, & even controlling, than it has had for a long time. During the later period of Mr. Gladstone, when he was getting old, and since, I think that the Federation (or Caucus), the screaming sections of our party, & the whips (who are not statesmen, with a due sense of proportion, but often trimming opportunists) have had too much say in shaping our policy & programme.

I think the yielding to the cry against excluding the Irish Members of H. of C., the inclusion of so many items in the Newcastle Programme, & the pushing of some of them in a crude form, (as of equal importance, or almost equal importance, with Home Rule) have been *consequences* of this abdication of true leadership & statesmanship, & *causes* of our tremendous reverse.

I have written to a great many of our defeated friends. The answers from them, & what I see in the papers, point to Harcourt's Local Veto Bill, & to want of confidence in him, as among the more active causes of the disaster.... The men who together constitute the leadership must be men loyal to each other, & capable of putting enthusiasm into the party, inspiring it with confidence, & getting it into sufficient control. The Rosebery–Harcourt arrangement has broken down.

Stansky, *Ambitions and Strategies*, p. 179

197. Ostrogorski on the character of party leadership, 1902

Parliamentary government reposes on a division of labour and an apportionment of powers between public opinion and the leaders, the rulers,—an apportionment prescribed by the very nature of both. While public opinion by a sort of volcanic process upheaves and hurls forth one problem after another, the party leaders who alternately come into office, the rulers, fasten on those problems the solution of which appears to them necessary and possible; they are not to meddle with the others, and it is a crime on their part to play with them. Taking up the questions which await solution on their own responsibility, they must not shirk it or let their hand be forced, no more than they may arrest or dam the current of opinion which fertilizes the soil of every free political community. It is this which constitutes the real separation of power on which parliamentary government rests, rather than that mechanical separation which Montesquieu fancied he had discovered in English constitutionalism, and which has since been naïvely copied in various countries. Ostrogorski, *Political Parties*, I, 304–5

198. The selection of a Conservative leader in the House of Commons, 1911

Austen Chamberlain to Mrs Joseph Chamberlain, 8 November 1911

There were, I understood, four men whose names were before the Party [Austen Chamberlain, Walter Long, Sir Edward Carson, and Bonar Law]. It was unfortunate that there was no one whose qualifications were so pre-eminent as to make him the obvious and necessary choice, but, that being so, the Party must make their election between them. It might be that between then and Monday [13 November], Balcarres [the Conservative Chief Whip], in whom all streams of feeling in the Party would naturally centre, would be in a position to tell us that there was a clear majority of the Party for A, B, C or D, or even for Z whom none of us had yet thought of. In that case I thought that all of us who were not the one indicated ought to go to the Party meeting to support the one so selected. If Bal., on the other hand, could not gather a sufficient consensus of opinion before Monday, then our names must go before the meeting and we ourselves must remain away. I did not consider that either of us (i.e. Long or myself) was bound, or indeed in the circumstances ought, to withdraw his name. Even if Long were willing to withdraw, his friends would not allow it, and similarly, if I were, my friends would refuse their assent....

In discussing the question of date I had already said [to Long]:— 'You know I think it is very likely that the result of an early meeting will be that neither you nor I will be chosen. I do not believe that if either *you or I were out of the way*, Law would be chosen. But since we are both in the field, I think that Bonar Law with his admittedly great qualities may be their choice. If we divide the Party too equally, I think that very possibly it will be felt that your friends and mine will more easily unite in support of some third person than accept either of us by a narrow majority of votes....'.

Austen Chamberlain to Mrs Joseph Chamberlain, 10 November 1911

Bal. came again at 11 o'clock in the morning. He said that Carson would not allow his name to go forward. Bonar Law was determined that his should be submitted.... By Monday, therefore, he could not say what the position would be. We should each [Chamberlain and Walter Long] poll something over 100 votes and then the votes cast for Law would have to be distributed between us. What the result would be he couldn't say. Either of us might be chosen with a majority of between 10 and 20.

I replied that that was very much what I had expected to hear; I was therefore prepared for it and had made up my mind what I ought to do:

Of course I had had my ambitions, but the acceptance of the position in my private circumstances would have involved heavy personal sacrifices to which I did not now feel called upon to submit. If a clear majority of the Party had desired me to take the position, or if I could have expected loyal support from the minority, I should have felt bound to make these private sacrifices and should have undertaken the task as a duty. But neither condition was fulfilled. There was no clear call from the Party and it was evident that if chosen I should not be heartily accepted by Long or his friends.

On the other hand, I had no confidence in Long's judgment and shared the opinion which he and so many of the men in the councils of the Party had expressed to me that Long's leadership would be a brief but disastrous fiasco.

Bal. suggested that for this very reason I should retire in Long's favour now, let him have it and expose his incapacity. Before six months were over, he would be done for and the leadership would fall to me.

I replied that the same thought had occurred to me the day before, no doubt at Satan's suggestion. But I definitely and at once rejected it. The Party was on the eve of a really critical year. Our fortunes for years to come depended on the fight we made next session. To choose a leader whom we all thought would be so mauled and mishandled that he couldn't retain the post for six months would be disastrous to the Party and to our cause and I could have nothing to do with it.

'I therefore ask you,' I concluded, 'to go now to Long and to say to him from me that I understand from you that we divide the Party very evenly and that the result of a vote on Monday is uncertain but that whichever of us won would win by a very small majority. Tell him that I think that such a result would be bad for the Party, that it would accentuate differences and make it difficult for the friends of the one who was not chosen to give the full and cordial support which is necessary to the one who is chosen. That I therefore propose that he and I should both withdraw our names and that he as the senior Privy Councillor should propose and I should second the election of Law.'...

A little later he telephoned that Long 'very cordially accepted my proposal' and would like the decision known at once. I said that so should I. Chamberlain, *Politics from Inside*, pp. 385, 388–9

PARTY MANAGEMENT

199. The Tories form election committees to fight the 1832 election
[From Lord Ellenborough's diary, 20 May 1832]

Charles Street [the party office] at 2. We formed an English Committee of Elections: C. Ross, Holmes, Ld. Lowther, Peach, Praed, Herries, Bonham.

The Scotch will be Clerk, Cumming Bruce, Ld. Rosslyn, Ld. Maitland, Stormont.

The Irish: Hardinge, Roden, Farnham, Dawson, Ld. Fitzgerald.

They will obtain information as to all the new boroughs.

Aspinall, *Three Diaries*, p. 266

200. Lord Stanley objects to the formation of party associations, 1835
[Lord Stanley to Sir T. D. Hesketh, 8 June 1835]

I have this morning received a copy of *The Preston Pilot*, containing an account of a meeting which was held in that town on Thursday last, for the purpose of forming a Conservative Association for North Lancashire.... I avail myself of the occasion...for the purpose...of explaining why I deprecate the formation of such an association....

...where, let me ask, is the cogent necessity which calls for the formation of such a society? Are your objects general, or local? If local—if this be indeed a meeting of the constituency of North Lancashire, for the purpose of impressing or enforcing upon those who are the legitimate organs by which their sentiments are made known to, and effectual with, the Legislature—namely, their county members, the views which are set forth in your first resolution, I ask to which of us...is this hint addressed?...

But you assure me, I will suppose, that I deceive myself; and that your Association is directed neither against my colleague nor myself; and with no purpose but the dissemination, within the sphere of your respective influence, of the principles which you possess in common.... I cannot divest my mind of the conviction that your means are injudicious. Against what are you defending yourselves? Are you united for the purpose of protecting your principles, and the representatives of your principles, against some dangerous counter organization...? If such general organization there be in North Lancashire, I have lived in an ignorance of it which I do not wish disturbed. But if there be none such...could the ingenuity of man suggest a source more certain to send forth such bitter waters, than the spirit which will be engendered by the establishment of your association? All the arguments of self-defence...pass at once to the side of your opponents. ...beware how you organize the whole country in such a manner that every man must be a partisan.... Beware, above all things, how you array the landed gentry and their dependants, in our mixed population, against the inhabitants of the mercantile and manufacturing towns. You ask no change in your county representatives, but you fear the democratic influence in the manufacturing boroughs. If you wish to create, to foster, to envenom it, interfere in their elections by your Conservative associations....

But if, extending your views beyond local objects, you seek to form part of a general organization throughout the empire, of county clubs, and local clubs, and district associations, acting in concert, usurping, in fact, the powers of a government, and combining to carry on the affairs of the country through their instrumentality—I can conceive nothing more dangerous to public liberty, nothing more injurious to a stable or a rational Administration than such a state of things. Power vested in clubs acting in concert for national objects was one of the most dangerous symptoms of the early stages of the French Revolution. Thank God! I see no cause here to anticipate such scenes as then occurred; but if there be a course calculated first to control the House of Commons, next to call in question and put in jeopardy the privileges of the House of Lords, the Church, and the Throne, and in the progress of the operation to destroy public peace, private happiness, and national confidence, it would be a system which should establish throughout the country, for political objects, and for permanent and systematic exertions, two rival sets of political associations engaged in a deadly struggle with each other for the maintenance of extreme principles—throwing over by joint consent, at the first onset, the incumbrance of all those who would lend themselves neither to the one nor to the other, and then entering upon a protracted (and the more protracted the more embittered and irreconcilable) warfare of opinion.

Morning Chronicle, 18 June 1835

201. The Rochdale Reform Association, 1841
[John Bright to George Crosfield, 20 June 1841]

We have a very zealous & active Secretary—a young man who is a shopkeeper, & who for several years has done the work without any regular salary—We now give him about £25 per year, & for that sum he keeps the Books & superintends the registration of the Voters. His Book is much like a regular counting House *Bill Book*—in it he has arranged in sheets the name of every Elector, & in the several columns he has their color or party, as, Red, Blue, doubtful, neuter, removed, in the Borough still, or out of the Boro', dead, & a column for 're-marks'. He has also a communication with a few good men & true living in different parts of the Town from whom he receives informa-tion of any change in the above or views or circumstance of any Elector & he makes it his business to walk thro' different streets to see if any change in the signs of shops or public houses have occurred &c. He has also a great number of very small Books or Cards, on which the Electors names (say 8 or 10 on each) are written (often those in a particular street) to whom he appoints a Captain, & whose business it is to see after them on the morning of Election & previously as may be needed. Our Borough is in three Townships & consequently we divide it into three districts. We have a committee of 6 or 8 or 10 as may be in each district, & from these district Committees, a general & *select* Committee is chosen, to whom all important matters are re-ferred. When the time comes to see about the payment of rates, the Secretary goes to the Overseers' Books, (as a ratepayer he can do this, & in the Townships in which he is not he gets some one else to do it if the Overseer be a Tory & refuse, but which is not our case) and copies the names of such of our friends as have not paid—he then calls upon the defaulters, persuades them to pay up—if too poor, he lends them money, but *always is repaid by them*—he also sees that the Registration Shilling is paid, and examines the rate Book to discover if any of our friends can be placed upon the register who have heretofore been omit-ted. When the time comes for watching the Lists, the district Com-mittees are called together to go thro' the Lists, & to see to whom objections can properly be made—again before the Barrister comes round—they meet to give & to obtain information, in order that the Secretary may have matter for the Briefs for the Solicitor's defence of our friends, & for his attacks upon our antagonists. At an election we have a small committee, say of two or three, without whose order no expense whatsoever is to be incurred—and also another small Committee, on whom devolves the superintendence of all printing for which the Election Committee will pay. After all, these arrangements will do little for you unless you have a *very active and zealous Secretary*, who knows the town well & almost every body in it—for Committees are not often very well attended, & one *good secretary* is worth a host of lounging, idle enquirers for news, & for the state of the Borough. Get a Secretary as good as ours, & you will find every year that your List of Voters stands better for you—We do this, & have now nearly disabled the Tories from doing us any mischief—and don't forget to choose a good honest Candidate—No *mere* Whig will enable you to fight a Tory—You must have a man who can really *offer something* in his opinions, rather than be content to be the supporter of either of the two great parties.   Hanham, *Political Studies*, IX, 188–9

202. The Conservative Chief Whip offers to find candidates, 1859
[Private and Confidential Circular from Sir W. J. Hylton Jolliffe to Conservative agents and others, 10 March 1859]

A General Election appears likely to take place in the course of a few weeks. I earnestly trust this event, upon which the future of the Country depends, will not fail to call forth the energy of the Conservative Electors, and that you will to the utmost encourage their active co-operation.—

It is most desirable that in every Borough and District local candidates should be found, who are ready and willing to oppose the attempts now making to revolutionize the Country, and who are prepared to stand by Conservative principles.

Should there be any difficulty, however, in finding men who are disposed to take this task upon themselves, I shall be most desirous, and I hope I may be able, to suggest such a candidate to your Notice, as may commend the respect, and deserve the support of the Constituency.

Hylton Papers

243

203. The National Union of Conservative and Constitutional Associations, 1872

The National Union was established for the purpose of effecting a systematic organisation of Conservative feeling and influence throughout the country, by helping in the formation and work of the Constitutional Associations which have so rapidly increased in numbers. It is notorious that the Constitutional cause has suffered much from the want of organisation amongst its supporters. Through this want the great Conservative strength, which has existed in all parts of the country and in every class of the people, has been deprived of its just influence upon public affairs. It is now obvious that the measure of Reform achieved for the nation by the late Lord Derby and Mr. Disraeli, widening the basis and deepening the foundations of the Constitution, has greatly strengthened the hold of Constitutional principles upon the important constituencies. In all directions—and especially among working men—old Associations have been enlarged and new ones sprung into vigorous life. All that is needed to make them a source of great and abiding strength to the Constitutional cause is that there shall be some National organisation ready at all times to give information and advice; to strengthen each Association by combining the influence of all; and to supply a means of bringing to bear upon any public question the united weight of the Constitutional party.

That organisation is found in the *National Union*.

It was founded in the Autumn of 1867, and its rules were framed at a Conference, in November of that year, at which many Conservative and Constitutional Associations, in every part of the country, were represented.

The Council, with its various special Committees, has since been meeting constantly, and its work is of a threefold nature.

In the first place, it keeps a register of all existing Conservative and Constitutional Associations, with the number of their members, their rules of action, the names and addresses of their officers, and all other particulars which may enable the National Union to act promptly and effectively as their London agency. In the second place, it is always ready to assist with advice, or the personal co-operation of its members, in the service of the existing Associations or the formation of new ones. It will from time to time offer suggestions, where they are required, as to the direction of local effort—suggestions which the Associations will, of course, be perfectly free to accept or reject. And when any Association wishes to have a speaker to take part in its meetings and address it upon political matters, the Council will endeavour to send an efficient representative. Its third class of work is the publication from time to time of short pamphlets on important political questions, and the re-printing of speeches and lectures which may be of enduring and universal interest. It is confidently hoped that these publications, suppled to the affiliated Associations at a merely nominal price, and circulating far and wide amongst working men, will aid in the spread of sound political education, and therefore in the extension of Constitutional principles. It also hopes to be able to afford gratuitous Lectures to such Associations as may desire such aid. In carrying out its work, the Council carefully avoids any unsought interference with local action, and strives simply by every means at its disposal to gather up the whole strength of the Constitutional party throughout the kingdom into one compact organisation.

The aid of the National Union has been cordially welcomed by the local associations, and it has secured both from them and from individual members of the party, support so large and influential, that its permanence and usefulness may be now considered as certain.

The Vice-Presidents now number 367, amongst whom are 66 noblemen and 143 past and present members of the House of Commons, in whose names an ample guarantee is afforded of the value attached to the Union by leading members of the Party. The Honorary Members number 219.

The Council has printed 120,000 pamphlets, over 90,000 of which have been distributed gratuitously. Besides these, nearly 160,000 circulars, handbills, and broadsides have been printed and distributed with good effect, principally during the general election of 1868, in every place contested throughout the kingdom.

During the debate on Mr. Gladstone's Irish Church Resolutions in 1868, upwards of 37,000 letters and circulars were issued from the office, and 864 petitions, bearing 61,792 signatures, were presented through the Union, a considerably larger number being forwarded direct to Members of Parliament; and during the recent debates on the Ballot Bill, in the House of Lords, 150 petitions praying the Peers to abide by their amendments, with upwards of 21,500 signatures, were prepared and forwarded to the Hon. Secretaries for presentation in little more than six days, thus affording a gratifying proof of the energy and organisation existing among the Associations.

Many lectures and addresses have been delivered in different towns by Members of the Council and others, and there is abundant proof of the good effect thereby produced.

National Union, *Principles and Objects*, pp. 5–8

204. Statement of the proposed constitution and objects of the National Federation of Liberal Associations, 1877

[This document was circulated to Liberal Associations throughout the country]

The Birmingham Liberal Association has brought to the test of practical experience the principles upon which a thoroughly represent-ative organisation can be formed to promote progressive Liberal prin-ciples, and its success is the justification of an appeal to Liberals generally to establish in other towns and districts of the country corresponding methods of political action.

The Birmingham Liberal Association consists of all Liberals who are elected to serve on any of its committees, or who signify their adherence to its objects and organisation. The *objects* of the Association are the return of Liberal members to Parliament and to local governing bodies, and the general promotion of Liberal principles. Its *organisation* is entirely representative in character. The central body, having charge of the whole direction of its affairs, is termed the 'Committee of Six Hundred', and is composed of members freely chosen at public meetings of Liberals, held annually in each municipal ward of the borough. The constituency of the 'General Committee' is, therefore, the whole Liberal party publicly called together in the various districts of the borough. Every Liberal who chooses can attend in his own ward, and take part in the election of ward representatives.

The General Committee discusses political subjects, selects School Board and Parliamentary candidates, and decides the general policy of the Association. It is an established rule, that if any person consent to be nominated as a candidate of the Association, in case he is not selected he must submit to the decision of the Committee.

Each ward elects a certain number of members to constitute an Executive Committee. The Executive Committee, which is thus also a directly representative body, calls a meeting of the General Committee upon all important occasions, takes its opinion, and carries out its decisions.

In each ward a Ward Committee, appointed at a public meeting, watches over its special Liberal interests; the Chairman and Secretary of each Ward Committee being, by virtue of their offices, members of the General Committee and of the Executive Committee. Candidates at municipal elections are selected for each ward by the Ward Committee.

The principles upon which the Association is based are, therefore, the following:—

(1) The whole body of Liberals in the borough is recognised as the constituency of the Association; and every Liberal has a vote in the election of its committees.

(2) Political responsibility, and the ultimate power of control, belong to the largest representative body, and the policy of the Association is loyally guided by its decision.

(3) The decision of the majority, in the selection of candidates and other matters of practical business, is regarded as binding upon those who consent to be nominated, as well as upon the general body of members.

(4) A broad and generous meaning is given to Liberalism, and no subject of public or political importance is excluded from its deliberations.

The width of the base on which the Association rests prevents the divisions so often caused by sectional interests; and its representative character is so thoroughly sustained that combined action is rendered not only possible, but vigorous, determined, and enthusiastic.

It is proposed that all Liberal Associations, established on a similar popular basis, should enter into a Federal Union.

While local circumstances will, of course, cause variations in points of detail, yet a popular basis is essential in order that a Liberal Association may obtain the hearty co-operation of its members, and occupy its just position in the Liberal party.

No interference with the local independence of the Federated Associations is proposed or contemplated. Each one of the Associations will arrange the detail of its own organisation and administer its own affairs; but from time to time, and on all occasions of emergency, the representatives of all the Associations in union will be convened to consider the course of action which may be recommended to their respective organisations. No formal political programme will be submitted for general acceptance.

The Federation is designed to assist the formation of Liberal Associations, on a popular representative basis, throughout the country; to bring such organisations into union, so that by this means the opinions of Liberals, on measures to be supported or resisted, may be readily and authoritatively ascertained; and to aid in concentrating upon the promotion of reforms found to be generally desired the whole force, strength, and resources of the Liberal party.

The essential feature of the proposed Federation is the principle which must henceforth govern the action of Liberals as a political party—namely, the direct participation of all members of the party in the direction of its policy, and in the selection of those particular measures of reform and of progress to which priority shall be given. This object can be secured only by the organisation of the party upon a representative basis: that is, by popularly elected committees of local associations, and by the union of such local associations, by means of their freely chosen representatives, in a general federation.

National Liberal Federation, *Proceedings attending the Formation*, pp. 5–7

205. Lord Randolph Churchill demands that the National Union shall be given the same status as the National Liberal Federation, 1884

[Churchill to the Marquess of Salisbury, 3 April 1884]

The resolution of the Conference at Birmingham in October—a Conference attended by upwards of 450 delegates from all parts of the country—directed the Council of the National Union to take steps to secure for that body its legitimate share in the management of the party organisation. This was an expression of dissatisfaction with the condition of the organisation of the party, and of a determination on the part of the National Union that it should no longer continue to be a sham, useless, and hardly even an ornamental portion of that organisation.

The resolution signified that the old methods of party organisation—namely, the control of Parliamentary elections by the leader, the Whip, the paid agent, drawing their resources from secret funds—which were suitable to the manipulation of the 10*l.* householder, were utterly obsolete, and would not secure the confidence of the masses of the people who were enfranchised by Mr. Disraeli's Reform Bill, and that the time had arrived when the centre of organising energy should be an elected, representative, and responsible body. The delegates at the Conference were evidently of opinion that, if the principles of the Conservative party were to obtain popular support, the organisation of the party would have to become an imitation, thoroughly real and *bona fide* in its nature, of that popular form of representative organisation which had contributed so greatly to the triumph of the Liberal party in 1880, and which was best known to the public by the name of the Birmingham Caucus. The Caucus may be, perhaps, a name of evil sound and omen in the ears of the aristocratic or privileged classes, but it is undeniably the only form of political organisation which can collect, guide, and control for common objects large masses of electors; and there is nothing in this particular form of political combination which is in the least repugnant to the working classes in this country.

Gorst, Fourth Party, 276–8

206. Robert Hudson opposes the resignation of the government, 1895

[Robert Hudson (Secretary of the National Liberal Federation) to T. E. Ellis (Chief Government Whip), June 1895]

By hook or by crook, *we ought if we can to go on*. We want the autumn & winter for campaigning, & we want a new Register on which to fight. We want 50 more candidates fixed with time to make themselves known to their constituencies. We want some good clear issues before the country such as the country can understand.

If the Government can go on & we can get these things, there is no reason why we should fear an appeal to the country.

But to go at a moment's notice on an issue which people don't understand & abt wh. they don't care—to go unprepared, with work half performed, with some of our chief measures untouched, with no cry, no campaign—seems to be suicidal. Of course it may be that we *have* to perform the happy despatch.... Try and set things up again in the House on Monday. You will have some good staunch, straight voting from our men after this, & it might be made the means of getting well thro' the rest of the session.

Give us the autumn & winter—& then we'll make a show.

Stansky, Ambitions and Strategies, pp. 170–1

**207. The Liberal party managers agree to let labour candidates have
first priority in 42 constituencies, 1903**

[Memorandum by Herbert Gladstone (Chief Liberal Whip), 13 March
1903]

1. No compact alliance agreement or bargain.
2. There being no material points of difference in the main lines of
Liberal [and Labour] policy we are ready to ascertain from qualified
and responsible Labour leaders how far Labour candidates can be given
an open field against a common enemy.
3. We are ready to do this as an act of friendship and without any
stipulation of any kind, because we realize that an accession of strength
to Labour representation in the House of Commons is not only required
by the country in the interests of Labour but that it would increase
progressive forces generally and the Liberal party as the best available
instrument of progress.
4. The question then arises how and when can this open field be
secured?
  The Liberal Council is bound to act for and with recognized local
Liberal Associations and this principle cannot be departed from *under
any circumstances*. On the other hand, the Liberal Council can use its
influence with the local associations to abstain from nominating a
Liberal candidate, and to unite in support of any recognized and competent Labour candidate who supports the general objects of the Liberal
party.
5. It is understood that the Labour Representation Committee propose
to run about 30 candidates. This does not include (*a*) Scotland, (*b*)
Miners' Federation, (*c*) Socialist bodies. It is not proposed to consider
as a material question any action bodies like the S.D.F. and the N.S.F.
may take. The Miners propose to run 15 or 18 candidates themselves.
6. [A list of possible Labour seats.]
7. [A list of seats occupied or claimed by miners.]
  In all at present 55.
8. At a friendly conference it is quite possible to arrange that Labour
candidates should have an open field in 30 seats desired by the L.R.C.;
that Miners' candidates should have 12.
9. It must however be distinctly understood that if in any agreed
constituency the Liberal local association breaks away and runs a Liberal
candidate, the Liberal Council must support that candidate.

10. But the Liberal Council will use every legitimate effort to secure this open field and to maintain it for authorized and responsible Labour candidates.

Bealey, Bull. Inst. Hist. Res. xxix, 269–70

208. The constitution of the Labour party, 1906

ORGANIZATION

I.—*Affiliation*

1. The Labour Party is a Federation consisting of Trade-Unions, Trades-Councils, Socialist Societies, and Local Labour Parties.

2. A Local Labour Party in any constituency is eligible for affiliation, provided it accepts the constitution and policy of the Party, and that there is no affiliated Trades Council covering the constituency, or that, if there be such a council, it has been consulted in the first instance.

3. Co-operative Societies are also eligible.

4. A National Organization of Women, accepting the basis of this Constitution and the policy of the Party, and formed for the purpose of assisting the Party, shall be eligible for affiliation as though it were a Trades Council without having the right to vote in the election of the Executive.

II.—*Object*

To secure the election of Candidates to Parliament and organize and maintain a Parliamentary Labour Party, with its own whips and policy.

III.—*Candidates and Members*

1. Candidates and members must accept this constitution; agree to abide by the decisions of the Parliamentary Party in carrying out the aims of this constitution; appear before their constituencies under the title of Labour candidates only; abstain strictly from identifying themselves with or promoting the interests of any Parliamentary Party not affiliated, or its candidates; and they must not oppose any candidate recognized by the Executive Committee of the party.

2. Candidates must undertake to join the Parliamentary Labour Party, if elected.

IV.—*The National Executive*

The National executive shall consist of fifteen members, eleven representing the Trade-Unions, one the Trades-Councils and Local

Labour Parties, and three the Socialist Societies, and shall be elected by ballot at the annual conference by their respective sections.

v.—*Duties of the National Executive*

The national Executive Committee shall—

1. Appoint a chairman, vice-chairman, and treasurer, and shall transact the general business of the party;

2. Issue a list of its candidates from time to time, and recommend them for the support of the electors;

3. Report to the affiliated organization concerned any Labour member, candidate, or chief official who opposes a candidate of the party, or who acts contrary to the spirit of this constitution;

4. And its members shall strictly abstain from identifying themselves with or promoting the interests of any Parliamentary party not affiliated, or its candidates.

vi.—*The Secretary*

The Secretary shall be elected by the annual conference, and shall be under the direction of the National Executive.

vii.—*Affiliation Fees and Delegates*

1. Trade-Unions and Socialist Societies shall pay 15s. per annum for every 1000 members or fraction thereof, and may send to the annual conference one delegate for each thousand members.

2. Trades-Councils and Local Labour Parties with 5000 members or under shall be affiliated on annual payment of 15s.; similar organizations with a membership of over 5000 shall pay £1 10s., the former Councils to be entitled to send one delegate with one vote to the annual conference, the latter to be entitled to send two delegates and have two votes.

3. In addition to these payments a delegate's fee to the annual conference may be charged.

viii.—*Annual Conference*

The National Executive shall convene a conference of its affiliated societies in the month of January each year.

Notice of resolutions for the conference and all amendments to the constitution shall be sent to the secretary by November 1st, and shall be forthwith forwarded to all affiliated organizations.

Notice of amendments and nominations for secretary and National Executive shall be sent to the secretary by December 15th, and shall be printed on the agenda.

IX.—*Voting at Annual Conference*

There shall be issued to affiliated societies represented at the annual conference voting cards as follows:—

1. Trade-Unions and Socialist Societies shall receive one voting card for each thousand members, or fraction thereof paid for.

2. Trades-Councils and Local Labour Parties shall receive one card for each delegate they are entitled to send.

Any delegate may claim to have a vote taken by card.

PARLIAMENTARY FUND

I.—*Object*

To assist in paying the election expenses of candidates adopted in accordance with this constitution, and in maintaining them when elected, and to provide the salary and expenses of a national party agent.

II.—*Amount of Contribution*

Affiliated societies, except Trades-Councils and Local Labour Parties, shall pay a contribution to this fund at the rate of 2*d*. per member per annum, not later than the last day of each financial year.

On all matters affecting the financial side of the Parliamentary Fund only contributing societies shall be allowed to vote at the annual conference.

III.—*Trustees*

The National Executive of the Party shall, from its number, select three to act as trustees, any two of whom, with the secretary, shall sign cheques.

IV.—*Expenditure*

1. *Maintenance.*—All members elected under the auspices of the Labour Party shall be paid from the fund equal sums not to exceed £200 per annum, provided that this payment shall only be made to members whose candidatures have been promoted by societies which have contributed to this fund: provided further that no payment from this fund shall be made to a member or candidate of any society which has not

253

contributed to this fund for one year, and that any society over three months in arrears shall forfeit all claim to the fund on behalf of its members or candidates, for twelve months from the date of payment.

2. *Returning Officers' Expenses.*—Twenty-five per cent. of the returning officers' net expenses shall be paid to the candidates, subject to the provisions of the preceding clause, so long as the total sum so expended does not exceed twenty-five per cent. of the fund.

3. *Administration.*—Five per cent. of the annual income of the fund shall be transferred to the general funds of the party to pay for adminitrative expenses of the fund.   Ensor, *Modern Socialism*, 3rd ed, pp. 364–8

209. The Earl of Selborne on the sale of honours, 1914

[Speech in the House of Lords, 23 February 1914]

There is a prevalent belief—I do not think that I should be guilty of exaggeration if I said a very widely prevalent belief—that persons are often recommended for [political] honours whom no one would have thought of so recommending if they had not contributed largely to Party funds. That prevalent belief takes three forms, as I know, not only from the Press, but from a voluminous correspondence on this subject. It is believed that persons who have social ambition, or whose wives have social ambition, and who have really no claim at all to receive an honour, can purchase it if they go to the right place. Again, the belief takes this form, that there have been cases where social ambition has never entered into the soul of the innocent rich man, but where he has been tempted and where an honour has been actually hawked to him on condition that he would make this contribution. The third case is rather of a different kind, but still, I maintain, a great evil. It is the case of men who have really done public service, whom public opinion would be very content to see honoured, and who have had pressure—I would almost say brutal pressure—put upon them to make a contribution to Party funds which they did not wish, and in some cases could not afford, to make. If it were necessary, I could quote sheaves of cuttings from the public Press.... And further, every playgoer knows that this matter of the sale of honours is now openly scoffed at in the theatre, and it has also even been thrown across the floor of the House of Commons as a taunt from one member to another.

I say at once that this prevalent belief applies to both political Parties, to both those great political Parties that have held office, and that the evil is a growth of our Party system and that both political Parties are responsible for it....

Why do the Parties want money? And they want more and more every year as time goes on. It is because a very large proportion of the Democracy take no interest in politics, know nothing about politics, and would not take the trouble to vote unless a refusal to do so became more irksome than acquiescence in going to the poll. It is the necessity of endeavouring to educate this large part of the Democracy, however superficially, and above all of having such a machinery as will bring the last man to the poll, however unwilling he may be, which is forcing both political Parties to cry out more and more for money. And think, my Lords, of the incongruity of the position. Just at the very moment when those who pay most taxes have least political power, and when there is a real danger lest certain forms of property should be the subject of unjust legislation—just at that very moment wealth, as mere wealth, and without responsibility, has the most opportunity of illicit and secret influence....

Now the whole of this controversy centres round the Whips and the Whips' Office. Whips are not more depraved than other people. That would be a complete misapprehension. How is it that they have got into this position? They have a very weary and thankless life, and they are being subjected ever more and more to claims from sections of their Party for money. Because the Party machinery is ever becoming more and more elaborate, the Whip is ever being asked for more and more money, and he becomes obsessed with the idea that the only thing that matters in this world and probably in the next is that his Party should remain in office. He begins to think that money is an essential condition to his Party remaining in office, and in the end—well, the end justifies the means, and, however scrupulous he may have been when he begins, he ends by thinking that the Party must have funds at all costs. He is very loyal to his chiefs. He tells them everything about the Party except about the Party funds, and his loyalty there is shown by telling them as little as possible. The Party chiefs are busy men, and they are careful students of the Book of Genesis, and they avoid the tree of knowledge of good and evil. My Lords, the position is really perfectly intolerable both for Whips and chiefs. I do not believe there are any men in England who would be more delighted if they could be freed from this curse of the Party system than would the Whips and their chiefs. But I very much doubt if they can free themselves. I doubt if this servitude imposed upon them by the Party system is one from which they can escape of their own action and their own desire. I believe it is public opinion and public opinion alone which can rescue them.   5 *Hansard (Lords)* xv, 252–3, 258–9

C THE FRANCHISE AND THE ELECTORAL SYSTEM

The old electoral system, which lasted down to 1832, was based on the enfranchisement of particular communities—the counties and the parliamentary boroughs—and as Sir Robert Inglis pointed out (**120**), it was never intended to be uniform. Except in the English counties, where there was a common forty-shilling franchise which made for some quite large electorates, the franchise was based on local customs or special enactments (**210**). In some boroughs practically every adult man could vote, in others the franchise was confined to a small corporation, and there were a few utterly rotten boroughs, notably Old Sarum and Gatton, which had only one elector each, and were almost completely depopulated. A very high proportion of the English borough seats, and most of the Scottish, Irish and Welsh seats were in the gift of patrons, or else were open to influence by bribery and other forms of 'management'.[1]

The reforms of 1832 had three main effects: they for the first time created a series of uniform qualifications for the borough franchise, of which the most important in England, Wales, and Scotland was the occupation of a house worth £10 a year; they provided for the creation of registers of electors and for the more efficient holding of elections; and they redistributed a considerable number of seats from the smaller boroughs to the counties and the towns (**212–13**). The franchise was still a narrow one, and in many places the pattern of political life was little affected, but in several respects the change made in 1832 had dramatic consequences. Scotland was liberated from the control of the government's Scottish manager and was given a new electorate intended to parallel the English one.[2] The big manufacturing towns were at last effectively represented in the House of Commons. And the number of patrons was greatly reduced. By contrast, landlord influence was, if anything, increased. The counties and many of the boroughs became more than ever the preserves of the great landowners who could command the votes of their tenants (**227**). County politics continued down to 1885 to be largely the politics of landlord influence because the law made the tenant dependent on his landlord (**228**). Nor was corruption diminished. If anything, corruption was on the increase after 1832 and it was probably more

---

[1] There is a useful summary of the extent of patronage in *EHD* xi, 217–41.

[2] The Scottish electoral law was, however, so badly drafted that much confusion resulted and there was a great multiplication of faggot votes. See Ferguson, *Scot. Hist. Rev.* xlv, 105–14.

widespread in 1880, eight years after the passage of the Ballot Act, than at any other time (229). Parliament tried to restrict landlord influence and corruption by Act of Parliament and, after the report of the Hartington Committee in 1870 had pointed out the evils of the existing system (227), adopted vote by secret ballot in 1872 (220). But until the 1883 Corrupt Practices Act effectually limited electoral expenditure for the first time, the machinery was quite ineffective. Those who had hoped that the 1832 Reform Act would make a big difference to the conduct of elections were disappointed. The 1832 Act tilted the balance of power, giving the industrial towns some of what in equity they deserved. But it was in no sense a revolutionary measure.

The operation of the 1832 Act, and of successive franchise acts down to 1918, depended very largely on the way in which the electoral registers were kept (224–6). Before 1832 there were no registers of electors: thereafter the duty of compiling them was added to the responsibilities of the overseers of the poor, who were directed to compile once a year a list of those with sufficient property to qualify them for the vote, and to publish it in time to allow for claims and objections to be made before a new part-time official, the revising barrister.[1] All would, perhaps, have been well if the task of compiling the registers had been entrusted to the county clerk or the town clerk, but the overseers were quite unfitted for the task. Most of them were farmers or shopkeepers, many of them were illiterate or very near so, and all of them were unwilling conscripts, finding it hard to fit their work as overseers into a busy life. As a result they neglected the registers, which would have become hopelessly corrupt and unusable had not the local leaders of the political parties clubbed together to try to make sure that the dead and the disqualified were removed from the register and the qualified put on it. The annual sessions at the revising barrister's court became a struggle between rival attorneys paid by the local parliamentary candidates, M.P.s, or party magnates, and on the outcome of these struggles depended the results of elections. So important was the business of registration that both the Liberals and the Conservatives established special registration offices in London in the 1860s to deal with the problems of non-resident voters, and in big constituencies it became increasingly common to employ full-time registration agents. Indeed, all over the country the main function of the local party organisations down to 1914 was the supervision of the registration (226). Useful as this might be as a spur to party organisation, it had the inevitable effect of excluding from the register a considerable number of people, and of making inclusion on the register essentially a matter for the local party organisation.

Between 1832 and 1872 parliamentary elections were conducted in two

---

[1] In Scotland the revision was allocated to the sheriffs.

stages. First there was a public nomination at the hustings, which in a good many cases led at once to an unopposed return. Then, if there were more nominations than seats, there was an election a few days later, conducted in the open, each elector being required to say for whom he wished to vote. Both at the hustings and at the subsequent election, there was often a good deal of rowdiness, and sometimes there was a riot. In old towns, where bad habits were endemic, it was, indeed, the custom to pay a small army of 'watchers' to watch the voters, carry placards and generally make a noise, in between bouts of drinking. Beer was sometimes issued free on election day, and there were usually bands and processions for several days or even weeks beforehand. County elections were usually more dignified, and right down to 1868 some candidates continued to ride to the nomination at the head of their tenants, accompanied by their neighbours. In 1872 the conduct of elections was greatly simplified by the Ballot Act. Hustings were no longer required and voting now consisted simply of marking a voting paper with a cross, folding it, and depositing it in a locked box (**220**).

Parliamentary reform, which had raised such unreasonable hopes before 1832 (**211**), continued to be one of the central issues of politics down to 1885. From 1832 onwards the Chartists and extreme Radicals demanded manhood suffrage, the secret ballot, and more frequent elections (**214**). And after some initial hesitations both Whigs and Tories announced that they were willing to contemplate a further measure of reform, provided that only citizens of proved responsibility were enfranchised. From 1851 onwards a number of proposals were put forward which would have involved a small lowering of the qualification for the vote in the boroughs (usually from £10 to £6) a readjustment of the county franchise, which was more restrictive than that in the boroughs, and a minor redistribution of seats, possibly by grouping a number of small boroughs together to form a number of 'districts'. In addition there was a good deal of talk about 'fancy franchises'—extra votes for university graduates, post office savings bank depositors and so on—and about securing the more equitable representation of minorities in large constituencies. This was also the period when Thomas Hare and John Stuart Mill advocated a drastic modification of the existing electoral system and the creation of 'voluntary constituencies' (**216**).

The 1867 Reform Act went far beyond what most people had expected: it granted household suffrage outright in the boroughs and it led to a considerable redistribution of seats, the smallest boroughs being sacrificed to find seats for the counties and the big towns (**217**). Judged purely in party terms, the 1867 Act helped the Conservatives, by giving them a number of extra county seats and a few more seats in the towns. But it also made further reform inevitable because it emphasised the anomalies of the post-1832 system. A large proportion of the new electors were liable to be influenced by their landlords or employers or to be bribed, and the Ballot Act of 1872 which introduced secret voting was not sufficient to destroy old habits of behaviour (229–30). The discrepancy between household suffrage in the boroughs and the old forty-shilling freehold franchise in the counties was too great to be tolerable for long. And not nearly enough had been done to recast the pattern of representation to bring it into line with the shifts of population which had taken place since the Industrial Revolution. Wiltshire and other rural counties were still grossly over-represented whereas Lancashire, Yorkshire and London were under-represented.

The complete remodelling of the electoral system, which was so badly needed, took place between 1883 and 1885, and was for the first time undertaken on a United Kingdom basis, so that the electoral laws became uniform for England and Wales, Scotland, and Ireland. In 1883 a new Corrupt Practices Prevention Act severely restricted the amount candidates could spend at elections and greatly tightened up the law relating to the employment of paid staff at elections (230). In 1884 the county and borough franchises were assimilated, with the result that male householders could now vote whether they lived in town or country (222). And in 1885 most of the small boroughs were disfranchised and most of the old county divisions and the bigger boroughs were broken up into a series of single-member constituencies (233). For the first time London had a reasonably fair share of the representation, and so had Yorkshire and Lancashire. Some anomalies still remained, and both the Balfour and the Asquith governments contemplated a further Reform Act. But the main features of the twentieth-century electoral system had been created.

Attention shifted in the twentieth century to the case for women's suffrage, first put forward in the late 1860s. Attitudes had for the most part been formed by the early 1880s (221), so that there was very little new to say on the subject. As with so many earlier Reform Bills the problem was essentially one of getting parliament to agree that action was necessary and then of creating the sort of tension necessary to drive parliament to act. The parties were divided on the issue: Balfour favoured giving women the vote, but his party was in general against the change, whereas Asquith was against giving women the vote and most of his party were for it. The case for reform was taken up by a number of women's organisations, several of which showed an extraordinary militancy. Mrs Pankhurst and the Suffragettes became national figures. The country was convulsed, and there was so much ill feeling on both sides that the speedy enfranchisement of women became more difficult. As a result women's suffrage made no progress until the middle of the war, when the Lloyd George government began to yield.

Local elections were conducted on a different basis from parliamentary elections. There were, broadly speaking, three different types of electoral system. In the municipal boroughs there was a ratepayer franchise, created in 1835, and voting was until 1872 by open voting paper, each voter having as many votes as there were vacancies to fill. In practice most resident householders who paid their rates regularly for three years were entitled to vote. A similar franchise was created in the counties in 1888, with additional provision for a £10 occupation franchise. Secondly, in the elections for local boards of health and poor law guardians, there was a franchise based not on the occupation of property and the payment of rates but on property values. For instance, in poor law elections owners up to £50 assessed value had one vote, and those over £50 had one extra vote for every additional £25 assessed value, up to a total of six votes, and in addition ratepayers under £200 had a single vote, those between £200 and £400 had two votes, and those over £400 had three votes. Thirdly, there was the cumulative vote, used in school board elections after 1870. Here every elector had as many votes as there were places to be filled, and might give them all to one candidate, or give them in blocks to a small number of candidates, or distribute them one each to a larger number of candidates. This was avowedly an experiment aimed to prevent the swamping of denominational minorities. Nor were these the only experiments. Women were allowed to vote in municipal elections after 1869 (a privilege which single women had nominally enjoyed in most parish and poor law elections since 1739). The first women to hold local offices appear to have been members of the school boards elected after 1870, a woman poor law guardian elected in 1875, and two women elected to the first London County Council in 1889. But their status was uncertain, and the two women county councillors were disqualified by the courts. Women were not formally qualified to sit on county and borough councils until 1907, under the Qualification of Women (County and Borough Councils) Act, 1907.

THE FRANCHISE
210. Qualifications for voting in 1816

The members for the fifty-two counties are all elected by one uniform right. Except in certain cities and towns having peculiar jurisdictions, every man, throughout England and Wales, possessed of forty shillings per annum freehold, is entitled to vote for the county in which such freehold is situated.

With respect to the different cities, towns, and boroughs, they exercise a variety of separate and distinct privileges, scarcely capable of being classed in any methodical order, and still less of being ascertained by the application of any fixed principle. In the greater part of them, indeed, the right of voting appears to be vested in the *freemen of bodies corporate*; but under this general term, an infinite diversity of peculiar customs is to be found. In some places, the number of votes is limited to a select body not exceeding *ten*; in others, it is extended to *eight* or *ten thousand*. In some places, the freeman must be a resident inhabitant to entitle him to vote; in others, his presence is required only at an election. The right to the freedom is also different in different boroughs, and may, according to peculiar usage, be obtained by birth, servitude, marriage, redemption, &c., &c.

The remaining rights of voting are of a still more complicated description. Burgageholds, leaseholds, and freeholds, scot and lot inhabitants, householders, inhabitants at large, potwallopers, and commonalty, each in different boroughs prevail, and create endless misunderstandings and litigation. This arises from the difficulty which is daily found in defining and settling the legal import of those numerous distinctions which, in some places, commit the choice of two members to as many inhabitants as every house can contain; in others, to the possessor of a spot of ground, where neither houses nor inhabitants have been seen for years; and which, in many instances, have even baffled the wisdom of parliament to determine who are entitled to vote, or what constitutes their right.

In the city of London, and many other cities and towns having peculiar jurisdiction, a man possessed of an income of one thousand pounds, or any greater sum, arising from copyhold, leasehold for ninety-nine years, trade, property in the national funds, or even freeholds, is not thereby entitled to vote.

Religious opinions create an incapacity to exercise the elective franchise. All catholics are excluded generally; and by the operation of the test laws, protestant dissenters are deprived of a voice in the election of representatives in all those boroughs, where the right of voting is confined to the corporate officers alone.

A man paying taxes to any amount, however great, for his domestic establishment, does not obtain a right to vote, unless his residence be in some borough where that right is vested in the inhabitants.

Oldfield, *Representative History*, II, 1–3

211. Excessive hopes placed on electoral reform: William Cobbett, 1 April 1831

It may be asked, Will a reform of the Parliament give the labouring man a cow or a pig; will it put bread and cheese into his satchell instead of infernal cold potatoes; will it give him a bottle of beer to carry to the field instead of making him lie down upon his belly to drink out of the brook; will it put upon his back a Sunday coat and send him to church, instead of leaving him to stand lounging about shivering with an unshaven face and a carcass half covered with a ragged smock-frock, with a filthy cotton shirt beneath it as yellow as a kite's foot? Will parliamentary reform put an end to the harnessing of men and women by a hired overseer to draw carts like beasts of burden; will it put an end to the practice of putting up labourers to auction like negroes in Carolina or Jamaica; will it put an end to the system which caused the honest labourer to be fed worse than the felons in the jails; will it put an end to the system which caused almost the whole of the young women to incur the indelible disgrace of being on the point of being mothers before they were married, owing to that degrading poverty which prevented the fathers themselves from obtaining the means of paying the parson and the clerk: will parliamentary reform put an end to the foul, the beastly, the nasty practice of separating men from their wives by force, and committing to the hired overseer the bestial super-intendence of their persons day and night; will parliamentary reform put an end to this which was amongst the basest acts which the Roman tyrants committed towards their slaves? The enemies of reform jeeringly ask us, whether reform would do these things for us; and I answer distinctly that IT WOULD DO THEM ALL!

Cobbett's Weekly Political Register, LXXII, 4–5

212. Representation of the People Act, 1832

An Act to amend the Representation of the People in *England* and *Wales*. [7th June 1832]

'Whereas it is expedient to take effectual Measures for correcting divers Abuses that have long prevailed in the Choice of Members to serve in the Commons House of Parliament, to deprive many in-considerable Places of the Right of returning Members, to grant such Privilege to large, populous, and wealthy Towns, to increase the

Number of Knights of the Shire, to extend the Elective Franchise to many of His Majesty's Subjects who have not heretofore enjoyed the same, and to diminish the Expence of Elections;' be it therefore enacted...

[Fifty-six boroughs to be disfranchised: Aldborough, Aldeburgh, Amersham, Appleby, Beeralston, Bishops Castle, Bletchingley, Boroughbridge, Bossiney, Brackley, Bramber, Callington, Camelford, Castle Rising, Corfe Castle, Downton, Dunwich, East Grinstead, East Looe, Fowey, Gatton, Great Bedwin, Haslemere, Hedon, Heytesbury, Higham Ferrers, Hindon, Ilchester, Lostwithiel, Ludgershall, Milborne Port, Minehead, Newport, New Romney, Newton, Newtown, Okehampton, Old Sarum, Orford, Plympton, Queenborough, St Germans, St Mawes, St Michael's, Saltash, Seaford, Steyning, Stockbridge, Tregony, Wendover, Weobley, West Looe, Whitchurch, Winchelsea, Wootton Bassett, Yarmouth.]

[II. Thirty boroughs to lose one member: Arundel, Ashburton, Calne, Christchurch, Clitheroe, Dartmouth, Droitwich, Eye, Great Grimsby, Helston, Horsham, Hythe, Launceston, Liskeard, Lyme Regis, Malmesbury, Midhurst, Morpeth, Northallerton, Petersfield, Reigate, Rye, St Ives, Shaftesbury, Thirsk, Wallingford, Wareham, Westbury, Wilton, Woodstock.]

[III. Twenty-two new boroughs created with two members each: Birmingham, Blackburn, Bolton, Bradford, Brighton, Devonport, Finsbury, Greenwich, Halifax, Lambeth, Leeds, Macclesfield, Manchester, Marylebone, Oldham, Sheffield, Stockport, Stoke-upon-Trent, Stroud, Sunderland, Tower Hamlets, Wolverhampton.]

[IV. Twenty new boroughs created with one member each: Ashton-under-Lyne, Bury, Chatham, Cheltenham, Dudley, Frome, Gateshead, Huddersfield, Kendal, Kidderminster, Rochdale, Salford, South Shields, Tynemouth, Wakefield, Walsall, Warrington, Whitby, Whitehaven in England; Merthyr Tydfil in Wales.]

[V. The boroughs of New Shoreham, Cricklade, Aylesbury, and East Retford to be extended over a considerable area.]

[VI. Weymouth and Melcombe Regis to return only two members; Penryn to include Falmouth; Sandwich to include Deal and Walmer.]

[X. Swansea, Loughor, Neath, Aberavon and Kenfig to form a single borough.]

[XII. Yorkshire to have six members, two for each Riding.]

[XIII. Lincolnshire to have four members, two for Parts of Lindsey, two for Kesteven and Holland.]

[XIV. Twenty-five counties to be divided, each division returning two members: Cheshire, Cornwall, Cumberland, Derbyshire, Devonshire, Durham, Essex, Gloucestershire, Hampshire, Kent, Lancashire, Leicestershire, Norfolk, Northamptonshire, Northumberland, Nottinghamshire, Shropshire, Somerset, Staffordshire, Suffolk, Surrey, Sussex, Warwickshire, Wiltshire, Worcestershire.]

[XV. Seven counties to be given a third member: Berkshire, Buckinghamshire, Cambridgeshire, Dorset, Herefordshire, Hertfordshire, Oxfordshire. Three Welsh counties to have a second member: Carmarthen, Denbigh, Glamorgan.]

[XVI. The Isle of Wight, severed from Hampshire, to return one member.]

[Additional qualifications for the county franchise]

XIX.... That every Male Person of full Age, and not subject to any legal Incapacity, who shall be seised at Law or in Equity of any Lands or Tenements of Copyhold or any other Tenure whatever except Freehold, for his own Life, or for the Life of another, or for any Lives whatsoever, or for any larger Estate, of the clear yearly Value of not less than Ten Pounds over and above all Rents and Charges payable out of or in respect of the same, shall be entitled to vote in the Election of a Knight or Knights of the Shire to serve in any future Parliament for the County, or for the Riding, Parts, or Division of the County, in which such Lands or Tenements shall be respectively situate.

XX.... That every Male Person of full Age, and not subject to any legal Incapacity, who shall be entitled, either as Lessee or Assignee, to any Lands or Tenements, whether of Freehold or of any other Tenure whatever, for the unexpired Residue...of any Term originally created for a Period of not less than Sixty Years...of the clear yearly Value of not less than Ten Pounds over and above all Rents and Charges...or for the unexpired Residue...of any Term originally created for... Twenty Years...of the clear yearly Value of not less than Fifty Pounds... or who shall occupy as Tenant any Lands or Tenements for which he shall be *bonâ fide* liable to a yearly Rent of not less than Fifty Pounds, shall be entitled to vote...

[provided that sub-lessees or assignees of underleases shall not be qualified.]

[XXI. No public taxes or rates to be deemed Charges.]

[xxii. Lands need not be assessed to the Land Tax.]

[xxiii. Only trustees and mortgagees in actual possession may vote.]

[xxiv–xxv. The occupation of a freehold house, warehouse, counting-house, shop or other building or land entitling a man to a borough vote shall not carry with it a county vote.]

[xxvi. County voters to be registered and have been in possession of qualification for six calendar months in the case of freeholders &c., and twelve calendar months in the case of lessees, occupiers, tenants &c, save that in certain circumstances the period may be shorter.]

[*Qualifications for the borough franchise*]

xxvii. ...That in every City or Borough which shall return a Member or Members to serve in any future Parliament, every Male Person of full Age, and not subject to any legal Incapacity, who shall occupy, within such City or Borough, or within any Place sharing in the Election for such City or Borough, as Owner or Tenant, any House, Warehouse, Counting-house, Shop, or other Building, being either separately, or jointly with any Land within such City, Borough, or Place occupied therewith by him as Owner, or occupied therewith by him as Tenant under the same Landlord, of the clear yearly Value of not less than Ten Pounds, shall, if duly registered according to the Provisions herein-after contained, be entitled to vote in the Election of a Member or Members to serve in any future Parliament for such City or Borough:

Provided always, that no such Person shall be so registered in any Year unless he shall have occupied such Premises as aforesaid for Twelve Calendar Months next previous to the last Day of *July* in such year,

nor unless such Person, where such Premises are situate in any Parish or Township in which there shall be a Rate for the Relief of the Poor, shall have been rated in respect of such Premises to all Rates for the Relief of the Poor in such Parish or Township made during the time of such his Occupation so required as aforesaid,

nor unless such Person shall have paid, on or before the Twentieth Day of *July* in such year, all the Poor's Rates and Assessed Taxes which shall have become payable from him in respect of such premises previously to the Sixth Day of *April* then next preceding:

Provided also, that no such Person shall be so registered in any Year unless he shall have resided for Six Calendar Months next previous to the last Day of *July* in such Year within the City or Borough, or within the Place sharing in the Election for the City or Borough, in respect of which City, Borough, or Place respectively he shall be entitled to vote, or within Seven Statute Miles thereof or of any Part thereof.

[XXVIII. A qualification may be preserved in spite of a move from place to place in a borough.]

[XXIX. Joint-occupiers to be entitled to separate votes if the value of the property allows each a £10 qualification.]

[XXXI. Existing freeholders or burgage tenants in counties of cities or towns to retain the right to vote if in actual possession.]

[XXXII. Freemen not to vote in boroughs unless resident. Freemen created since 1 March 1831 not to be qualified.]

XXXVI. ...That no Person shall be entitled to be registered in any Year as a Voter in the Election of a Member or Members to serve in any future Parliament for any City or Borough who shall within Twelve Calendar Months next previous to the last Day of *July* in such Year have received Parochial Relief or other Alms which by the Law of Parliament now disqualify from voting in the Election of Members to serve in Parliament.

[Registration]

XXXVII. And whereas it is expedient to form a Register of all Persons entitled to vote in the Election of a Knight or Knights of the Shire...and that for the Purpose of forming such Register the Overseers of every Parish or Township shall annually make out lists....

[Overseers on 20 June each year to put up a notice asking for claims to vote to be made by 20 July.]

Provided always, that after the Formation of the Register to be made in each Year...no Person whose Name shall be upon such Register... shall be required thereafter to make any such Claim, as long as he shall retain the same Qualification, and continue in the same Place of Abode described in such Register.

[XXXVIII. The Overseers to make up by 31 July lists of persons on the Register and of persons claiming.]

XXXIX.... That every Person who shall be upon the [county] Register ...or who shall have claimed to be inserted in any List for the then current Year of Voters...may object to any Person as not having been entitled...to have his Name inserted in any List of Voters....

[XLI. Judges of assize to name barristers to revise the borough registers.]

[XLIV. Borough overseers also to draw up lists.]

[XLVI. Town clerks to prepare lists of freemen.]

[XLIX. Judges of assize also to name barristers to revise the borough registers.]

LXII. ... That at every contested Election of a Knight or Knights to serve in any future Parliament for any County, or for any Riding, Parts, or Division of a County, the Polling shall commence at Nine o'Clock in the Forenoon of the next Day but Two after the Day fixed for the Election, unless such next Day but Two shall be *Saturday* or *Sunday*, and then on the *Monday* following, at the principal Place of Election, and also at the several Places to be appointed as hereinafter directed for taking Polls; and such polling shall continue for Two Days only, such Two Days being successive Days; (that is to say,) for Seven Hours on the first Day of polling, and for Eight Hours on the Second Day of polling; and no Poll shall be kept open later than Four o'Clock in the Afternoon of the Second Day; any Statute to the contrary notwithstanding.

[LXIII. The counties to be divided into districts for polling.]

LXVII. ... That at every contested Election of a Member or Members to serve in any future Parliament for any City or Borough in *England*, except the Borough of *Monmouth*, the Poll shall commence on the Day fixed for the Election, or on the Day next following, or at the latest on the Third Day, unless any of the said Days shall be *Saturday* or *Sunday*, and then on the *Monday* following, the particular Day for the Commencement of the Poll to be fixed by the Returning Officer; and such polling shall continue for Two Days only, such Two Days being successive Days, (that is to say), for Seven Hours on the First Day of polling, and for Eight Hours on the Second Day of polling; and that the Poll shall on no Account be kept open later than Four o'Clock in the Afternoon of such Second Day; any statute to the contrary notwithstanding.

[LXVIII. Polling for boroughs in England to be at booths, not more than 600 voters voting at one compartment in a booth: records of the voting to be kept in poll books.]

[LXX. The returning officer to have power to adjourn the poll if the elections shall be interrupted or obstructed by any Riot or open Violence.]

PGS, 2 Will. IV, c. 45

213. Representation of the People (Scotland) Act, 1832

An Act to amend the Representation of the People in *Scotland*. [17th July 1832]

'Whereas the Laws which regulate the Election of Members to serve in the Commons House of Parliament for *Scotland* are defective.... And...that those Defects should be remedied, and especially that Members should be provided for Places hitherto unrepresented, and the Right of Election extended to Persons of Property and Intelligence....'

[Scotland to be represented by 53 members, 30 from the shires and stewartries, 23 from the cities, burghs and towns.]

[III. The county members to be chosen one from each county, except that Elgin and Nairn, Ross and Cromarty, and Clackmannan and Kinross to be combined to return one member for each of the three groups.]

[IV. The burgh members to be chosen, two each from Edinburgh and Glasgow, one each from Aberdeen, Paisley, Dundee, Greenock, and Perth, and the remaining fourteen from fourteen sets or districts of burghs, viz. Wick District (Kirkwall, Wick, Dornoch, Dingwall, Tain, Cromarty), Inverness District (Fortrose, Inverness, Nairn, Forres), Elgin District (Elgin, Cullen, Banff, Inverurie, Kintore, Peterhead), Montrose District (Inverbervie, Montrose, Aberbrothwick, Brechin, Forfar), St Andrews District (Cupar, St Andrews, Anstruther Easter, Anstruther Wester, Crail, Kilrenny, Pittenweem), Kirkcaldy District (Dysart, Kirkcaldy, Kinghorn, Burntisland), Stirling District (Inverkeithing, Dunfermline, Queensferry, Culross, Stirling), Kilmarnock District (Renfrew, Rutherglen, Dumbarton, Kilmarnock, Port Glasgow), Haddington District (Haddington, Dunbar, North Berwick, Lauder, Jedburgh), Leith District (Leith, Portobello, Musselburgh), Falkirk District (Linlithgow, Lanark, Falkirk, Airdrie, Hamilton), Ayr District (Ayr, Irvine, Campbeltown, Inveraray, Oban), Dumfries District (Dumfries, Sanquhar, Annan, Lochmaben, Kirkcudbright), Wigtown District (Wigtown, New Galloway, Stranraer, Whithorn).]

[VI. Possessors of existing freehold franchise to have the right to vote for their lives, but no new votes to be created except under new franchises.]

[*Qualifications for the county vote*]

VII. And it be enacted, That from and after the passing of this Act every Person, not subject to any legal Incapacity, shall be entitled to be registered as herein-after directed, and thereafter to vote at any Election for a Shire in *Scotland*, who, when the Sheriff proceeds to consider his Claim for Registration in the present or in any future Year, shall have been, for a Period of not less than Six Calendar Months next previous to the last Day of *August* in the present or the last Day of *July* in any future Year, the Owner (whether he has made up his Titles, or is infeft, or not,) of any Lands, Houses, Feu Duties, or other Heritable Subjects (except Debts heritably secured) within the said Shire, provided the Subject or Subjects on which he so claims shall be of the yearly Value of Ten Pounds, and shall actually yield, or be capable of yielding, that Value to the Claimant, after deducting any Feu Duty, Ground Annual, or other Consideration...provided he be, by himself, his Tenants, Vassals, or others, in possession of the said Subjects, and be either himself in the actual Occupation or in receipt of the Profits and Issues thereof....

[VIII. Where two or more persons are interested in property the vote to be in the liferenter, not the fiar, and in as many joint owners as the value of the property will permit. Husbands to be entitled to vote in right of their wives.]

[IX. Leaseholders for 57 years or life where clear yearly value of the tenant's interest after paying rent &c. is £10. Leaseholders for 19 years where value is £50. Leaseholders who have paid £300 for their lease.]

[*Qualifications for the Burgh Vote*]

X. ...Members...for any single City, Town, or Burgh...shall no longer be elected by the Town Councils...but directly by the several Individuals on whom the Right of electing such Members...is by this Act conferred; and where the Election is by Districts or Sets of Cities, Burghs, or Towns conjoined, the Right of electing shall no longer be in the Town Councils or Corporations...or in Delegates appointed by them, but in the individual Voters....

XI. ...every Person, not subject to any legal Incapacity, shall be entitled to be registered...and to vote...who...shall have been, for a Period of not less than Twelve Calendar Months next previous to the last Day of *August* in the present or the last Day of *July* in any future Year, in the Occupancy, either as Proprietor, Tenant, or Life-renter, of any House, Warehouse, Counting-house, Shop, or other Building ...which either separately or jointly with any other House, Warehouse, Counting-house, Shop, or other Building..., or with any Land owned and occupied by him, or occupied under the same Landlord... shall be of the yearly Value of Ten Pounds...[provided that Assessed Taxes have been paid and no parochial relief has been received, and that the elector was resident for 6 months before 1 July within 7 miles. Owners not in occupation to vote provided they live within 7 miles].

[XIII. Claims to Vote in Counties to be given in to Parish Schoolmasters.]

[XIV. Sheriffs to hold Courts to decide on claims.]

[XV. Claims to Vote in burghs to be given in to the town clerk.]

PGS, 2 Will. IV, c. 65

214. The Chartist demands, 1837

THE SIX POINTS OF THE PEOPLE'S CHARTER

1. A vote for every man twenty one years of age, of sound mind, and not undergoing punishment for crime.

2. THE BALLOT.—To protect the elector in the exercise of his vote.

3. NO PROPERTY QUALIFICATION for members of Parliament—thus enabling the constituencies to return the man of their choice, be he rich or poor.

4. PAYMENT OF MEMBERS, thus enabling an honest tradesman, working man, or other person, to serve a constituency, when taken from his business to attend to the interests of the country.

5. EQUAL CONSTITUENCIES, securing the same amount of representation for the same number of electors,—instead of allowing small constituencies to swamp the votes of larger ones.

6. ANNUAL PARLIAMENTS, thus presenting the most effectual check to bribery and intimidation, since though a constituency might be bought once in seven years (even with the ballot), no purse could buy a constituency (under a system of universal suffrage) in each ensuing twelvemonth; and since members when elected for a year only, would not be able to defy and betray their constituents as now.

Cole and Filson, *British Working Class Movements*, p. 352

215. The third Earl Grey on the case for a new type of Reform Bill, 1858

...a new Reform Bill ought not, like the former one, to aim at the transfer of a large amount of political power from one class of society to another, since this is no longer necessary, in order to protect the general interests of the community from being sacrificed to those of a minority of its Members. It is not however to be inferred, that no reform of our Representation is required, because there is no occasion for altering the existing distribution of political power among different classes of society. A reform is wanted, though not for the same reasons as formerly. In the present state of things, the objects that ought to be aimed at by such a measure are, to interest a larger proportion of the people in the Constitution, by investing them with political rights, without disturbing the existing balance of power; to discourage bribery at elections, without giving more influence to the arts of demagogues; to strengthen the legitimate authority of the Executive Government, and at the same time to guard against its being abused; and to render the distribution of the Parliamentary franchise less unequal and less anomalous, but yet carefully to preserve that character which has hitherto belonged to the House of Commons, from its including among its Members men representing all the different classes of society, and all the different interests and opinions to be found in the Nation.

Grey, *Parliamentary Government*, pp. 128–9

216. Thomas Hare advocates voluntary constituencies, 1859

In considering the process...of interesting greater numbers in the constitution by investing them with political rights, we meet with the fact that the proportionate interest felt by the constituency appears to diminish as the numbers of the constituency increase. Upon a careful deduction, it is found that in the larger constituencies about fifty-five per cent., and in the smaller ones about ninety-two per cent., of the electors recorded their votes on the occasion of contests at the same general election.[1] This is not an argument against adding to the numbers of the voters, for the effect still is to extend the interest of the people, inasmuch as fifty-five per cent. of a constituency of 5,000 amounts to more than ninety-two per cent. of a constituency of 500; but it proves the existence of other moral forces or laws which power-

[1] *Edinburgh Review*, xcv, 279–80.

fully operate to disturb and divert the course of political progress from the point of true representation towards some other end. This divergence from representation is still more apparent when the active elements,—the fifty-five per cent.,—are further reduced by taking from them the minority,—the voice of which is extinguished, and which consists of about two-thirds,—leaving the numbers actually represented in the larger constituency as about thirty-three per cent. The unrepresented portion is not only great in numbers, but there is no doubt that in many populous boroughs it also contains the largest portion of the educated classes, of those to which, in every view of representative institutions, it is desirable that full weight should be given. It is therefore of paramount importance to discover, and if possible remove, the causes which tend practically to exclude from representation so extensive and valuable a part of the electoral element. . . .

Nothing is more remarkable in the early history of this country, than the disposition to form guilds and associations. . . . It was the same spirit which led the larger communities, the cities and boroughs, to solicit and obtain incorporation, and its attendant powers. It has been always active amongst us, from that time to the present. . . .

It is to this voluntary and natural disposition to associate, to which full scope should be given in forming our electoral divisions. It is thus, that, when we amend, we build in the old style. If this be permitted, the huge agglomerations of voters combined in some modern boroughs, the wide expanse of acres added to some ancient ones, and the legal bonds by which many boroughs, having otherwise no connexion with each other, are tied together, will be gradually dissolved; and the communities will assume, without any legislative interference, their natural and convenient form. . . . The electoral amendment which would be most in accordance with the historical forms of social progress in this country, would be that which would enable every locality, every community, and every great or ancient association having a distinct corporate existence, and the ordinary conditions of permanency, to form a constituency, or electoral nucleus.   Hare, *Treatise*, X–XI, 53–5

217. Representation of the People Act, 1867

An Act further to amend the Laws relating to the Representation of the People in *England* and *Wales* [15th *August*, 1867].

3. Every Man shall, in and after the Year [1868], be entitled to be registered as a Voter, and, when registered, to vote for a Member or Members to serve in Parliament for a Borough, who...

   1. Is of full Age, and not subject to any legal Incapacity; and

   2. Is on the last Day of *July* in any Year, and has during the whole of the preceding Twelve Calendar Months been, an Inhabitant Occupier, as Owner or Tenant, of any Dwelling House within the Borough; and

   3. Has during the Time of such Occupation been rated as an ordinary Occupier in respect of the Premises so occupied by him within the Borough to all Rates (if any) made for the Relief of the Poor in respect of such Premises; and

   4. Has on or before the Twentieth Day of *July* in the same Year *bonâ fide* paid an equal Amount in the Pound to that payable by other ordinary Occupiers in respect of all Poor Rates that have become payable by him in respect of the said Premises up to the preceding Fifth Day of *January*:

Provided that no Man shall under this Section be entitled to be registered as a Voter by reason of his being a joint Occupier of any Dwelling House.

4. [1 & 2. A borough qualification established for lodgers in lodgings] of a clear yearly Value, if let unfurnished, of Ten Pounds or upwards; and [provided that the lodger]

3. Has resided in such Lodgings during the Twelve Months immediately preceding the last Day of *July*, and has claimed to be registered as a Voter at the next ensuing Registration of Voters.

[5. A county franchise established for those with lands or tenements of a clear yearly value of five pounds a year owned by them or leased on a 60-year or longer lease.]

[6. A county franchise established for occupiers of lands or tenements of a rateable value of twelve pounds a year or more who have paid the relevant poor rates.]

[7. All borough occupiers to be rated.]

9. At a contested Election for any County or Borough represented by Three Members no Person shall vote for more than Two Candidates.

10. At a contested Election for the City of *London* no Person shall vote for more than Three Candidates.

[12. The boroughs of Lancaster, Reigate, Totnes, and Yarmouth disfranchised for corruption.]

[17. The following 38 boroughs in future to return only one member: Andover, Bodmin, Bridgnorth, Bridport, Buckingham, Chichester, Chippenham, Chipping Wycombe, Cirencester, Cockermouth, Devizes, Dorchester, Evesham, Great Marlow, Guildford, Harwich, Hertford, Honiton, Huntingdon, Knaresborough, Leominster, Lewes, Lichfield, Ludlow, Lyminton, Maldon, Marlborough, New Malton, Newport (Isle of Wight), Poole, Richmond, Ripon, Stamford, Tavistock, Tewkesbury, Thetford, Wells, Windsor.]

18. ...the City of *Manchester*, and the Boroughs of *Liverpool, Birmingham*, and *Leeds*, shall each respectively return Three Members....

[19. Ten new boroughs created: Chelsea with two members, and Burnley, Darlington, Dewsbury, Gravesend, the Hartlepools, Middlesbrough, Stalybridge, Stockton, Wednesbury with one member.]

[21. Merthyr Tydfil and Salford to receive a second member: the Tower Hamlets to be divided into two, the boroughs of Hackney and Tower Hamlets, each with two members.]

[23. Thirteen new county divisions created, each with two members, for Cheshire, Derbyshire, Devonshire, Essex, West Kent, North Lancashire, South Lancashire, Lincolnshire, Norfolk, Somerset, Staffordshire, East Surrey, West Riding of Yorkshire.]

24. ...the University of *London* shall return One Member....

PGS, 30 & 31 Vict., c. 102

218. Representation of the People (Scotland) Act, 1868

An Act for the Amendment of the Representation of the People in *Scotland* [13th July 1868].

3. Every Man shall...be entitled to be registered as a voter...who...
    1. Is of full Age, and not subject to any legal Incapacity; and
    2. Is, and has been for a Period of not less than Twelve Calendar Months next preceding the last day of *July*, an Inhabitant Occupier

as Owner or Tenant of any Dwelling House within the Burgh: [and has paid the appropriate rates.]

[4. A lodger franchise as in England.]

[5. An ownership franchise for counties as in England.]

[6. An occupation franchise for counties, but at fourteen pounds annual value, instead of twelve pounds as in England.]

[7. Electors in Glasgow to have two votes in the election of three members.]

[9. New seats created: Universities of Edinburgh and St. Andrews 1, Universities of Glasgow and Aberdeen 1. One further seat given to Dundee, Glasgow, Aberdeenshire, Ayrshire, and Lanarkshire.]

[10. Counties of Peebles and Selkirk united; one new district created (Hawick District) consisting of Hawick, Galashiels and Selkirk; each constituency to return one member.]

[11. Counties of Aberdeenshire, Ayrshire, and Lanarkshire to be divided into two single-member constituencies.]

43. Whereas, in order to provide for the Seats herein-before distributed, it is expedient that certain Boroughs in *England* having small Populations should cease to return Members... *Arundel, Ashburton, Dartmouth, Honiton, Lyme Regis, Thetford,* and *Wells* shall respectively cease to return any Member to serve in Parliament.   *PGS*, 31 & 32 Vict., c. 48

219. Russell opposes the Ballot Bill, 8 July 1872

No doubt, open voting gives opportunity for intimidation; but, in my opinion, the system embodied in the present measure will increase personation, will increase bribery, will increase fraud and falsehood of every kind—indeed, in whatever light secret voting is viewed, it seems a bad system; it is nothing but an increased power of corruption in every direction. It will encourage falsehood, for it is quite possible under the Ballot that a voter may be intimidated by his landlord into promising his vote; but having the power to vote, will secretly vote against his promise. He would then go to his landlord and say, 'I voted as you asked me; I quite agree in your opinions, and have voted with you.'....

It seems, however, to me that though the intimidation may fail as to the actual vote, the Ballot will introduce a new form of fraud and distrust which will not be much preferable to the old-fashioned intimidation. The Englishman's privilege of public voting should be as sacredly respected; he should have the same right of voting openly as he has by the existing law; and at least there is no reason why the electors of Old England should be deprived of a privilege of open voting which is enjoyed by the voters of New England. It seems to me a great argument in support of open voting that a man who is desirous of promoting some great public question; of something that would improve the condition of his fellow-creatures—is more likely than any other man to give his vote publicly, and will be proud of proclaiming his support of a candidate who holds large and liberal views. When Sir Samuel Romilly was engaged in his endeavours to mitigate the severity of our criminal code, and was a candidate for Westminster, an elector, sympathising with his efforts, was proud to say, 'I vote for Samuel Romilly!' Why should not a voter be allowed to proclaim his sympathy with a man whose life is devoted to mitigating the sufferings of his fellow-men? Or again, when Wilberforce stood before the great constituency of Yorkshire, the champion of the abolition of slavery throughout the world—a great and noble aspiration—surely the electors should not be prohibited from proclaiming openly, in the face of all men, 'I vote for Mr. Wilberforce and the Emancipation of the human race!' This Bill will make the revelation of his vote an offence and a crime on the part of the official persons who are in the polling-booth at the time. It is provided by this Bill that the voter, having secretly marked his vote on the ballot-paper, and folded it up so as to conceal his vote, shall place it in a closed box. There is, indeed, no penalty imposed on the voter for telling his vote, but every officer, clerk, and agent in attendance at a polling-station who shall communicate at any time, to any person, any information obtained in a polling-station, as to the candidate for whom any voter in such station is about to vote, or has voted, will be liable, on summary conviction before two Justices of the Peace, to imprisonment for any term not exceeding six months, with or without hard labour. . . .

. . . I must, in addition, point out that our whole progress for the last century and a half has been in favour of publicity. There was a time when the proceedings of Parliament were published under the disguise of 'Debates in the Senate of Lilliput,' and notes of the speeches were prefixed by fictitious names. I remember, in my own time, seeing the Serjeant-at-Arms bring before the House a man whom he found making notes in the Gallery. Since that time we have gone on introducing more and more publicity in the transaction of public affairs. The debates in Parliament are reported day by day, under the real names of the speakers, and are openly discussed the next morning in the journals throughout the kingdom. The proceedings of the Courts of Law are public, and the man who is called upon to give evidence in a Court of Law is not allowed the shelter of secrecy even where—as is too often the case in Ireland—his evidence may be attended with risk to his life....

The people of England have for hundreds of years been free to go to the poll and say, 'I vote for such and such a man, because I look upon him as the most fit.' But this is no longer to be allowed,—secrecy, not freedom of voting, is henceforth to be the rule.

Wagner, Modern Political Orations, pp. 159–62

220. The Ballot Act, 1872

An Act to Amend the Law relating to Procedure at Parliamentary and Municipal Elections [18th July, 1872].

PARLIAMENTARY ELECTIONS
Procedure at Election

1. A candidate for election to serve in Parliament for a county or borough shall be nominated in writing. The writing shall be subscribed by two registered electors of such county or borough as proposer and seconder, and by eight other registered electors of the same county or borough as assenting to the nomination, and shall be delivered during the time appointed for the election to the returning officer by the candidate himself, or his proposer or seconder...

2. In the case of a poll at an election the votes shall be given by ballot. The ballot of each voter shall consist of a paper (in this Act called a ballot paper) showing the names and description of the candidates. Each ballot paper shall have a number printed on the back, and shall have attached a counterfoil with the same number printed on the face. At the time of voting, the ballot paper shall be marked on both sides with an official mark, and delivered to the voter within the polling station, and the number of such voter on the register of voters

shall be marked on the counterfoil, and the voter having secretly marked his vote on the paper, and folded it up so as to conceal his vote, shall place it in a closed box in the presence of the officer presiding at the polling station (in this Act called the 'presiding officer') after having shown to him the official mark at the back.

Any ballot paper which has not on its back the official mark, or on which votes are given to more candidates than the voter is entitled to vote for, or on which anything, except the said number on the back, is written or marked by which the voter can be identified, shall be void and not counted.

After the close of the poll the ballot boxes shall be sealed up, so as to prevent the introduction of additional ballot papers, and shall be taken charge of by the returning officer, and that officer shall, in the presence of such agents, if any, of the candidates as may be in attendance, open the ballot boxes, and ascertain the result of the poll by counting the votes given to each candidate, and shall forthwith declare to be elected the candidates or candidate to whom the majority of votes have been given, and return their names to the Clerk of the Crown in chancery. The decision of the returning officer as to any question arising in respect of any ballot paper shall be final, subject to reversal on petition questioning the election or return.

Where an equality of votes is found to exist between any candidates at an election for a county or borough, and the addition of a vote would entitle any of such candidates to be declared elected, the returning officer, if a registered elector of such county or borough, may give such additional vote, but shall not in any other case be entitled to vote at an election for which he is returning officer....

Form of Directions for the Guidance of the Voter in voting, which shall be printed in conspicuous Characters, and placarded outside every Polling Station and in every Compartment of every Polling Station.

The voter may vote for   candidate .

The voter will go into one of the compartments, and, with the pencil provided in the compartment, place a cross on the right-hand side opposite the name of each candidate for whom he votes, thus X.

The voter will then fold up the ballot paper so as to show the official mark on the back, and leaving the compartment will, without showing the front of the paper to any person, show the official mark on the back to the presiding officer, and then, in the presence of the presiding officer, put the paper into the ballot box, and forthwith quit the polling station.

If the voter inadvertently spoils a ballot paper, he can return it to the officer, who will, if satisfied of such inadvertence, give him another paper.

If the voter votes for more than   candidate , or places any mark on the paper by which he may be afterwards identified, his ballot paper will be void, and will not be counted.

If the voter takes a ballot paper out of the polling station, or deposits in the ballot box any other paper than the one given him by the officer, he will be guilty of a misdemeanour, and be subject to imprisonment for any term not exceeding six months, with or without hard labour.
Note.—These directions shall be illustrated by examples of the ballot paper.

Form of Ballot Paper

Form of Front of Ballot Paper

Counterfoil No. Note: *The counterfoil is to have a number to correspond with that on the back of the Ballot Paper.*		
	1	BROWN (John Brown, of 52 George St., Bristol, merchant.)
	2	JONES (William David Jones, of High Elms, Wilts, Esq.)
	3	MERTON (Hon. George Travis, commonly called Viscount Merton, of Swanworth, Berks.)
	4	SMITH (Henry Sydney Smith, of 72 High Street, Bath, attorney.)

Form of Back of Ballot Paper

No.

Election for   county [*or* borough, *or* ward].

18 .

Note.—The number on the ballot paper is to correspond with that in the counterfoil.

PGS, 35 & 36 Vict., c. 33

221. Bright opposes women's suffrage, 1882

[J. Bright to T. Stanton, 21 October 1882]

...I act from a belief that to introduce women into the strife of political life would be a great evil to them, and that to our sex no possible good could arrive. If women are not safe under the charge and care of fathers, husbands, brothers, and sons, it is the fault of our non-civilization and not of our laws. As civilization founded upon Christian principle advances, women will gain all that is right for them, although they are not seen contending in the strife of political parties. In my experience I have observed evil results to many women who have entered hotly into political conflict and discussion. I would save them from it. If all the men in a nation do not and cannot adequately express its will and defend its interests, to add all the women will not better the result, and the representative system is a mistake....

Bright, *Public Letters*, p. 235

222. Representation of the People Act, 1884

An Act to amend the Law relating to the Representation of the People of the United Kingdom [6th December, 1884].

Extension of the Household and Lodger Franchise

2. A uniform household franchise and a uniform lodger franchise at elections shall be established in all counties and boroughs throughout the United Kingdom, and every man possessed of a household qualification or a lodger qualification shall, if the qualifying premises be situate in a county in England or Scotland, be entitled to be registered as a voter, and when registered to vote at an election for such county, and if the qualifying premises be situate in a county or borough in Ireland, be entitled to be registered as a voter, and when registered to vote at an election for such county or borough....

Assimilation of Occupation Qualification

5. Every man occupying any land or tenement in a county or borough in the United Kingdom of a clear yearly value of not less than ten pounds shall be entitled to be registered as a voter...

Supplementary Provisions

6. A man shall not by virtue of this Act be entitled to be registered as a voter or to vote at any election for a county in respect of the occupa-

tion of any dwelling-house, lodgings, land, or tenement, situate in a borough.

[7. The household qualification and the lodger qualification to be as defined in the 1867 and 1868 Acts and their amendments.]   PGS, 48 & 49 Vict., c. 3

223. Redistribution of Seats Act, 1885

An Act for the Redistribution of Seats at Parliamentary Elections, and for other Purposes [25th June 1885].

[2. The following English and Welsh boroughs to cease to return members: Abingdon, Andover, Aylesbury, Banbury, Barnstaple, Beaumaris district, Berwick-upon-Tweed, Bewdley, Bodmin, Brecon, Bridgnorth, Bridport, Buckingham, Calne, Cardigan dist., Chichester, Chippenham, Chipping Wycombe, Cirencester, Clitheroe, Cockermouth, Cricklade, Devizes, Dorchester, Droitwich, East Retford, Evesham, Eye, Frome, Great Marlow, Guildford, Harwich, Haverfordwest district, Helston, Hertford, Horsham, Huntingdon, Kendal, Knaresborough, Launceston, Leominster, Lewes, Lichfield, Liskeard, Ludlow, Lymington, Maldon, Malmesbury, Malton, Marlborough, Midhurst, Newark, Newport, New Shoreham, Northallerton, Petersfield, Poole, Radnor district, Richmond, Ripon, Rye, St. Ives, Shaftesbury, Stamford, Stroud, Tamworth, Tavistock, Tewkesbury, Thirsk, Tiverton, Truro, Wallingford, Wareham, Wenlock, Westbury, Weymouth and Melcombe Regis, Whitby, Wilton, Woodstock.

The following Scottish Districts of Burghs to cease to return members: Haddington, Wigtown.

The following Irish boroughs to cease to return members: Armagh, Athlone, Bandon, Carlow, Carrickfergus, Clonmel, Coleraine, Downpatrick, Drogheda, Dundalk, Dungannon, Dungarvan, Ennis, Enniskillen, Kinsale, Lisburn, Mallow, New Ross, Portarlington, Tralee, Wexford, Youghal.]

[3. The following English boroughs to be disfranchised for corruption: Macclesfield, Sandwich.]

4. From and after the end of this present Parliament, the City of London shall return two members, and no more, and each of the Parliamentary boroughs named...shall return one member, and no more.

[The following boroughs to lose one member: Bedford, Boston, Bury St. Edmunds, Cambridge, Canterbury, Carlisle, Chester, Colchester, Coventry, Dover, Durham, Exeter, Gloucester, Grantham, Hastings, Hereford, King's Lynn, Lincoln, Maidstone, Newcastle-under-Lyme, Oxford, Penryn and Falmouth, Peterborough, Pontefract, Reading, Rochester, Salisbury, Scarborough, Shrewsbury, Stafford, Stoke-upon-Trent, Taunton, Warwick, Wigan, Winchester, Worcester—Galway, Limerick, Waterford.]

5. From and after the end of this present Parliament, each of the Parliamentary boroughs named...shall return the number of members named opposite to such borough

[viz. Birmingham 7, Bradford 3, Bristol 4, Hull 3, Leeds 5, Liverpool 9, Manchester 6, Nottingham 3, Salford 3, Sheffield 5, Southwark 3, Swansea 2, Tower Hamlets 7, Wolverhampton 3—Aberdeen 2, Edinburgh 4, Glasgow 7—Belfast 4, Dublin 4.]

[6. New boroughs created with the members specified: Aston Manor 1, Barrow-in-Furness 1, Battersea and Clapham 2, Bethnal Green 2, Camberwell 3, Chelsea 1, Croydon 1, Deptford 1, Finsbury 3, Fulham 1, Great Yarmouth 1, Greenwich 1, Hackney 3, Hammersmith 1, Hampstead 1, Hanley 1, Islington 4, Kensington 2, Lambeth 4, Lewisham 1, Marylebone 2, Newington 2, Paddington 2, St George, Hanover Square 1, St Helen's 1, St Pancras 4, Shoreditch 2, Strand 1, Wandsworth 1, West Bromwich 1, West Ham 2, Westminster 1, Woolwich 1.]

8. (1) From and after the end of this present Parliament, each of the Parliamentary Boroughs mentioned in the Sixth Schedule of this Act[1] shall, for the purpose of returning members to serve for such borough in Parliament, be divided into divisions....

9. (1) From and after the end of this present Parliament, each of the counties at large named in the Seventh Schedule to this Act shall return the number of members in that behalf named in the said schedule; and for the purpose of returning such members, if more than one, shall be divided into the same number of divisions as the number of members; and each division shall return one member....

[Seventh Schedule lists county representation as follows.
England: Counties of Bedford 2, Berkshire 3, Buckinghamshire 3, Cambridge 3, Chester 8, Cornwall 6, Cumberland 4, Derby 7, Devon 8, Dorset 4, Durham 8, Essex 8, Gloucester 5, Hants 5, Hereford 2, Hertford 4, Huntingdon 2, Kent 8, Lancaster 23, Leicester 4, Lincoln 7, Middlesex 7, Norfolk 6, Northampton 4, Northumberland 4, Nottingham 4, Oxford 3, Rutland 1,

[1] All multi-member boroughs except for the following two-member boroughs which were not divided: City of London, Bath, Blackburn, Bolton, Brighton, Derby, Devonport, Halifax, Ipswich, Leicester, Newcastle-on-Tyne, Northampton, Norwich, Oldham, Plymouth, Portsmouth, Preston, Southampton, Stockport, Sunderland, York—Merthyr Tydfil—Dundee—Cork.

Salop 4, Somerset 7, Stafford 7, Suffolk 5, Surrey 6, Sussex 6, Warwick 4, Westmorland 2, Wilts 5, Worcester 5, Yorkshire 26.
Wales: Carmarthen 2, Carnarvon 2, Denbigh 2, Glamorgan 5, Monmouth 3.
Scotland: Fife 2, Lanark 6, Perth 2, Renfrew 2.
Ireland: Antrim 4, Armagh 3, Carlow 1, Cavan 2, Clare 2, Cork 7, Donegal 4, Down 4, Dublin 2, Fermanagh 2, Galway 4, Kerry 4, Kildare 2, Kilkenny 2, King's 2, Leitrim 2, Limerick 2, Londonderry 2, Longford 2, Louth 2, Mayo 4, Meath 2, Monaghan 2, Queen's 2, Roscommon 2, Sligo 2, Tipperary 4, Tyrone 4, Waterford 2, Westmeath 2, Wexford 2, Wicklow 2.]

PGS, 48 & 49 Vict., c. 23

REGISTRATION

224. Peel on the importance of electoral registration, 1838

[Sir R. Peel to Charles Arbuthnot, 8 November 1838]

The Reform Bill has made a change in the position of parties, and in the practical working of public affairs, which the author of it did not anticipate.

There is a perfectly new element of political power—namely, the registration of voters, a more powerful one than either the Sovereign or the House of Commons.

That party is the strongest in point of fact which has the existing registration in its favour. It is a dormant instrument, but a most powerful one, in its tacit and preventive operation.

What a check it is at this moment upon the efficiency and influence of the existing Government, backed as it is by all the favour and private goodwill of the Crown, and by a small majority of the House of Commons. It meets them every day, and at every hour. Of what use is the prerogative of dissolution to the Crown, with an unfavourable registry, and the fact of its being unfavourable known to all the world? The menace of dissolution is only laughed at.

Then it is almost impossible to make any promotion, or vacate any office, for fear of sustaining a defeat.

The registration will govern the disposal of offices, and determine the policy of party attacks; and the power of this new element will go on increasing, as its secret strength becomes better known, and is more fully developed. We shall soon have, I have no doubt, a regular systematic organisation of it. Where this is to end I know not, but substantial power will be in the Registry Courts, and there the contest will be determined.

Parker, *Peel*, II, 368

225. James McComb on registration in Liverpool, 1883

The subject of Registration has occupied the attention of our Association (Liverpool) for many years, and considerable sums have been spent from time to time to secure its efficiency. With a constituency numbering from 62,000 to 63,000 voters, this is not a very inexpensive work. Our method of procedure is, a month or so before the Register is published, to make a house to house survey of the whole city, to make out street registers of all persons on our side of politics who are not on the present list and ought to be on the new list, and correct errors in the present Register by giving to the Overseers information obtained in our survey, so that such errors shall not reappear. As a rule, they receive such information, check it, and if correct, insert the names. On an average we send 14,000 to 15,000 names of persons entitled to be placed on the list, and the later our survey is made so much the better, for we can then send information to correct the Register almost up to the time it is in the printer's hands.

Our city is divided into four townships and one parish, and persons who have removed from one township to the other are enrolled for the new township on producing from the old one a note stating in effect that all rates have been paid. In this way a great amount of useful work is done, and certainly more than three-fourths of our friends are placed upon the Register without any trouble or loss of time to them. After publication it has been our practice to make the usual claims for persons omitted, and also objections, and from time to time it has been my duty to object to from between 4,000 and 5,000 voters. Liberal Secretaries' and Agents' Association, *Report*, 1883, p. 28

226. Registration still the main concern of the Manchester Liberal Union, 1896

...The registration of voters had occupied a large share of the attention of the divisional associations and of this Committee; it, indeed, demanded not only much time and attention, but involved an expenditure of about two-thirds of the entire cost of organisation. ...

Manchester Liberal Union, Annual Report, 1896

227. Lord Hartington's Committee on the pathology of elections, 1870

THE SELECT COMMITTEE appointed to inquire into the present modes of conducting PARLIAMENTARY and MUNICIPAL ELECTIONS, in order to provide further guarantees for their tranquillity, purity, and freedom;—HAVE considered the matters to them referred, and have agreed to the following REPORT:—

CONDUCT OF ELECTIONS

It has been proved to your Committee that in many boroughs great corruption prevails at Municipal Elections. In some boroughs it appears that a considerable class of voters will not vote unless they are paid; and the fact that the power at the election is mainly in the hands of such persons, prevents respectable persons from becoming candidates, or taking part in the voting. Treating is also practised at municipal elections to a great extent. In some instances the bribery takes the form of payment by drink tickets instead of money; and more frequently the election is accompanied by an amount of drinking which is described as demoralising to the town.

Other corrupt practices prevail, but apparently to a minor extent. Serious rioting frequently takes place on the polling day, and there is evidence to show that intimidation of individual voters is practised. In some cases the corrupt influences which are at work in a Municipal Election are made use of with a view of influencing the Parliamentary Elections, which, in the case of the last General Election, followed the former almost immediately. In most cases, however, party spirit or local questions appear sufficient to cause an extensive use of corrupt practices.

Although the educated and respectable inhabitants would gladly see measures adopted which would put a stop to these practices, they take no active steps for this purpose....

With regard to Parliamentary Elections in Boroughs your Committee have examined many witnesses, but the evidence does no more than confirm what has been frequently established before Committees of the House, Royal Commissions, and the Judges who have been engaged in the trial of Election Petitions. The returns in the Appendix to the Report of the Select Committee on Parliamentary and Municipal Elections in the last Session of Parliament show that both in former and in the last Elections various corrupt practices, of which bribery and treating were the chief, have prevailed, and to such an extent as to invalidate many Elections; and it cannot be supposed that either now or formerly have the whole of such practices been brought to light. It has been proved that in some instances rioting and violence to person and property have occurred on the nomination and polling days so as to interfere with the freedom of the Election, while in a much larger class of case Elections are accompanied by drunkenness and disorder.

It is difficult to arrive at the truth of the allegations of intimidation of workmen by masters, of tenants by landlords, of tradesmen by customers, and of working men by each other. This also applies to intimidation by ministers of religion. That intimidation in these forms is not extensively practised in a mode capable of legal proof, is evident from the rarity of cases in which a return has been set aside on this ground. But that it is practised, though in a manner difficult of proof before a legal tribunal, cannot be doubted. We have examined many witnesses who have alleged the existence of intimidation of each kind above described. As soon as this evidence has become known in the locality, applications have been received that witnesses on the other side should be examined, who have denied the charges brought against themselves, but have usually attributed similar practices to their opponents. It is certain, at least, that whether intimidation is extensively practised or not, the fear of it widely prevails among that class of voters who are liable to its influence. There exists during the canvass in most boroughs a system of working upon voters through private considerations, whether of interest, hope, or fear, for political purposes, and this system enables undue influence in a modified form to be constantly practised.

Your Committee have had much less evidence relating to County Elections. The returns above referred to show that, as compared with Borough Elections, a very small number have been called in question before Committees or the Judges. This fact proves, in our opinion, that they have been in the main free from bribery.

It is, however, alleged that intimidation and undue influence are very largely practised in county elections, and evidence from Wales and Scotland, to the effect that tenants have been actually turned out of their farms on account of their votes, has been brought before us to substantiate the allegation. It is difficult for a Committee examining witnesses, not upon oath, and without the services of any persons who act in the character of counsel for the prosecution or defence, to form an opinion worth much, on disputed matters of fact; and contradictions more or less specific, have generally been advanced against the charges which have been made. In some instances the allegations have not been contradicted. We have endeavoured to investigate some of these cases, but found ourselves involved in inquiries which unduly protracted our proceedings, and, for the reasons mentioned above, were not altogether satisfactory. It is certain, however, that an influence, exceeding in a greater or less degree the legitimate influence which a popular and respected landlord must always exercise in his neighbourhood, is often brought to bear on tenant farmers, and other voters in agricultural districts. The agent frequently holds language which the landlord would shrink from using, but which the latter does not think it necessary to disown. An instance was given where tenants who had signed the requisition to a candidate, all voted with their landlord against that candidate; another, where no tenant on the estate would promise the same candidate a vote until they had received an assurance from their landlord that they might vote as they pleased, on receiving which they all both promised and voted for the candidate opposed to the landlord's politics. The inducement to vote with the landlord may frequently proceed rather from the hope of future advantages to be conferred than from the fear of injury to be inflicted; but of whichever character the inducement may be, we think that the influence so exercised comes under the description of undue influence, and, as such, ought, if possible, to be checked.

The different political and social conditions existing in England, Scotland, and Ireland, produce some differences in the character of their elections, and of the influences at work in them, which ought to be noticed. In England and Ireland the Borough Elections are often extremely corrupt. In Scotland, it is stated, without contradiction, that bribery is almost unknown. This is attributed in a great measure to the superior education of the Scotch people; and partly to the fact that the constituencies being comparatively new, there exists no corrupt class, long familiar with the traditions of bribery, similar to that which in many English and Irish boroughs has not only retained in itself but spread through the constituency the desire for a corrupt expenditure.

In each of the three countries it is alleged that intimidation by land-lords prevails in County Elections. In England tenants generally vote in accordance with the wishes or known opinions of their landlords. In Scotland they have in some recent instances voted almost in a body against their landlords. This has been attributed partly to the nature of the relations between landlord and tenant in Scotland, which are usually of a more strictly commercial character than in England, partly to the fact that the Scotch tenant farmers take a very warm interest in certain public questions in which they consider that their own and their landlord's interests are not identical.

In Ireland, again, the influence of the landlord is often opposed by that of the Roman Catholic clergy. Organized mobs also appear to be an almost generally recognised part of the system of conducting an Irish election. The object of their employment is either to intimidate an unwilling voter, or one who is supposed to be under coercion, so as to force him to vote on the side of the popular party, or to prevent, by physical force, the voters of the opposite side from reaching the poll. To so great an extent is this system carried, that the employment of troops in aid of the police, is the ordinary rule at an Irish election. The military force in the country is distributed before a general election with a view to that event, and not only are the troops employed to preserve order at the polling-places, but escorts are frequently given on the requisition of candidates or their agents, for the purpose of protecting voters coming from a distance. It is alleged that in some cases the voters go under the charge of these escorts against their will, and consider themselves under coercion. Notwithstanding these precautions, scenes of violence, including loss of life, are not unfrequent. Mr. Justice Keogh, in his judgment on the Drogheda Election Petition, has given a vivid description of the events which took place on the polling-day, and of the absence of freedom of election in that case.

As might have been expected, the views of this state of things taken by Irish witnesses whom we have examined, were extremely divergent.

On the one hand it is contended that Roman Catholic tenants would frequently, from conviction, or from feelings of attachment to a good landlord, desire to record their votes on his side; that in so doing they are exposed to spiritual intimidation from the clergy, and to the risk of violence from the mobs assembled by the influence of the priests, and directed by them; that these influences entirely destroy the freedom of action of the voter, and give an excuse for some amount of pressure on the part of the landlord. On the other hand it is maintained that the influence of the priests is used only for the purpose of strengthening the determination of the voters to vote according to their convictions, notwithstanding the pressure which may be brought to bear on them;

that Roman Catholic voters would never willingly oppose the cause espoused by the great majority of their countrymen and by their clergy; and that often the mob intimidation—the existence of which is admitted—is desired and invited by the supposed victims as an excuse for escaping from coercion of another character.

We cannot doubt that there is some truth in the assertions made by both parties; and we are convinced that, under the present system of conducting elections, there exists in many boroughs and counties of Ireland no real freedom of election. We consider that some change is urgently required. *HC 115, pp. 3–6 (1870) VI, 133–6*

228. Pollock on the legal basis of landlord influence

Except as regards the special legislation for agricultural tenancies... there is no difference in law between urban and agricultural leaseholds. But in practice and custom the difference is very great. Farm holdings are always or almost always taken by the tenant direct from the freeholder, and there is generally something of a personal relation between them (even where the landlord is a college or other corporate body) beyond the mere receipt and payment of rent. The farmer is legally bound to pay the full amount of his agreed rent, without regard to the goodness or badness of the season; but in bad years it is the constant practice for the landlord to remit such a percentage of the rent as to leave the tenant answerable only for so much as the farm seems fairly capable of paying under the circumstances. A great landlord who refused to follow this practice would be entirely within his legal rights, but would certainly be thought the worse of in the country. In many counties, unfortunately, reductions of 15 or 20 per cent have now been rather the rule than the exception for some years past. The landlord in return expects a certain amount of deference and compliance in various matters from his tenant. Not only does the farmer meet him half-way on questions of shooting rights, and allow free passage to the hunt, but his political support of the landlord is not unfrequently reckoned on with as much confidence as the performance of the covenants and conditions of the tenancy itself. In the case of holdings from year to year it may be not unfairly said that being of the landlord's political party is often a tacit condition of the tenancy.

Pollock, *The Land Laws*, 2nd ed, pp. 152–3

229. Corrupt practices at Sandwich, 1880

[From the Report of the Royal Commission of Enquiry]

We felt ourselves...precluded...from inquiry into the election of 1874 or earlier elections. But observing the nature and manner of the bribery committed at the contest between Mr. Crompton Roberts and Sir Julian Goldsmid [in May 1880], the general expectation that money would be distributed in bribery, the almost universal willingness and even avidity to accept bribes, the great proportion of the population implicated, the ease with which the most extensive bribery was carried out, the organization for the purpose of bribery, which was far too facile and complete to be inexperienced, the readiness on the part of many to accept bribes from both sides, and the total absence of a voice to warn, condemn, or denounce, we cannot doubt that electoral corruption had long and extensively prevailed in the borough of Sandwich.

We do not think it within the scope of our duties to offer any recommendations on the subject of the means by which corruption may be better prevented; but we may be permitted to say that evidence given before us appears to establish some conclusions of practical importance.

(1.) It did not appear that the mode of taking votes by ballot had the slightest effect in checking bribery. On the contrary, while it enabled more voters to take bribes on both sides, it did not, as far as we could ascertain, render a single person unwilling to bribe for fear of bribing in vain.

(2.) The law as to the return of election expenses in its present form appears to us practically useless for any purpose. It would seem that the provisions intended to compel the real expenses to be returned, are in effect disregarded, and do not even ensure any return at all. There is nothing to compel or even enable the election expenses agent to exercise any effective control over the return. If the law had compelled a strict audit of election expenses, and provided that the candidates should disclose the amount and manner of their real expenditure at the election, bribery could not probably have been committed at the election at Sandwich, certainly not in the way by which or by means of the resources out of which it was accomplished.

(3.) The engagement of committee-rooms at public-houses afforded a method by which the keeper of the public-house and his clientèle were very easily bribed.

(4.) The payment of the expenses to out-voters appeared to us to degenerate very readily into over-payment amounting to a bribe.

(5.) The employment of canvassers, clerks, and messengers, to an extent not measured by any real requirement, and the extravagant display of party emblems offered abundant opportunities for corruption.

[C. 2796], pp. xv–xvi. H.C. (1881) XLV, 15–16

230. Gorst on the Corrupt and Illegal Practices Prevention Act, 1883

The necessity for the Act arose from the fact that in English counties and boroughs election expenses had, during recent years, increased to a scandalous amount. The cause of this was not to be sought in expenditure upon the grosser forms of bribery and treating. The direct violation of law is believed to prevail extensively only in a few constituencies, whose bad character is well known to election managers. Nor is even wholesale bribery and treating of itself a costly operation. The amount actually distributed to electors is never very large, and though it is enhanced by the liability which the greater part of the sum of money provided for the purpose has to stick in the hands of intermediate agents, the enormous cost of an election contest cannot be accounted for by an item of this kind. But the practice had become almost universal for candidates to lavish immense sums of money upon purposes not in themselves corrupt, but quite useless for the attainment of any legitimate object. The true aim of such expenditure was to distribute money amongst the greatest possible number of electors, and a candidate who refused to conform to this universal custom had, or was believed to have, no chance of being returned. Indeed, the candidate had frequently no choice in the matter; the money was often advanced and spent for him without his knowledge by zealous friends, and the only part he took was to repay the sums so provided after the election was over. The accounts of the expenses of candidates delivered to the returning officer in pursuance of the law, though these frequently exceeded £1 for every voter polled, revealed a part only of the real expenditure. These accounts were almost invariably cooked, and few elections took place, at least in English boroughs, in which there was not a very large amount of secret expenditure, not of a directly corrupt character, over and above that which was returned and published.

Every article purchased, every service rendered, was paid for at more than double its market value. It was not enough to advertise the election address at special rates in every newspaper circulating in the constituency, to placard it on every blank wall, to display it in the shop windows or bar-parlour of every supporter, and to send it by post to each elector. To insure that everybody should be aware of the existence of the candidate it was usual to have his name posted in gigantic characters all over the neighbourhood, thus affording lucrative employment to printers and bill-stickers, and an excuse for payments to the owners of premises on which the posters were displayed. Each side was accustomed to engage in a merry warfare by posting their own bills over those of their opponents, thus causing the initial expenditure to be repeated again and again, and giving occasion to a fresh employment of electors as watchmen to prevent the bills being torn down. Every elector who could write a few doggerel verses, or compose a political catechism, or sketch a caricature of Mr. Disraeli or Mr. Gladstone, was entitled to have the same printed, published, and circulated at the candidate's expense. Both sides concurred in a complete distrust of the post-office, and employed an army of messengers to deliver their communications to the electors, with not half the certainty but with ten times the expense. Canvassers were engaged to go round and ask the electors how they intended to vote, in some cases in such excessive numbers that they could find nothing to do but meet in public-houses and canvass one another. Committee-rooms were hired in every part of the constituency, in few of which was there the slightest pretence made of transacting business. The ingenuity of the election managers was taxed to invent the greatest possible amount of clerical work in the few real committee-rooms, and twice as many clerks were engaged as were necessary to perform it. Watchers to stop or detect bribery on the other side, 'lambs' to create disorder at the opponent's meeting or to protect the candidate and his friends, 'sandwich-men' to exhibit in the streets the placards which the electors were weary of looking at on the walls, carriers of banners, performers on all sorts of musical instruments, boys and girls old enough to display the party colours and shout out praise or abuse in doggerel verse to popular melodies, all found congenial employment in the election contest at wages more than double the amount that could be earned in any regular and useful branch of industry. Finally on the day of polling there was a grand field-day of all the cabdrivers, messengers, canvassers, clerks, agents, and watchers employed in bringing the independent electors to the poll, all entitled not only to special pay by reason of the arduous and peculiar character of their services, but to 'reasonable refreshment,' supplied to them with unstinted liberality by the publicans of their party.

This is the expenditure which the new Corrupt Practices Act is intended to stop. In every constituency the maximum amount which a candidate may spend upon an election contest is fixed by the Act, and any expenditure in excess of this will render his return, if he is elected, void. The number of committee-rooms, agents, clerks, and messengers is in each case specified, and no person may be employed in any other capacity. The most accurate account of the candidate's expenditure has to be rendered to and published by the returning officer, which is verified by a solemn declaration both of the candidate himself and his election agent, that they know of no other payments being made; and the former further pledges himself that except so far as he may be permitted by law he will make no further payment. These provisions appear to limit effectually the election expenditure of the candidate himself. No zealous partisan could provide further sums without running a great personal risk. Any outsider who independently of the candidate spends money upon the election other than any small expense legally incurred by himself is guilty of an illegal practice, and is liable to a fine of £100 and the loss for five years of electoral rights.

Fortnightly Review, new ser. XXXIV, 690–2

CHAPTER 5

CENTRAL AND
LOCAL ADMINISTRATION

A THE ROLE OF GOVERNMENT RESTRICTED

The British have always lacked a clear concept of the state, such as has long existed on the continent of Europe. Whereas on the Continent the state has been regarded as an entity set apart from the community, responsible for the welfare of the community and attracting its loyalty in return, in Britain the powers of the state were dissipated during the nineteenth century between a monarchy serving a largely symbolic function, a parliament claiming to represent the people and to be able to deal with all their problems, ministers primarily concerned with external relations, who also administered certain laws laid down by parliament, and local authorities responsible for public order and public welfare, which claimed to have their own mandate from the people. Moreover, modern officialdom is in Britain largely a twentieth-century creation. During the nineteenth century there were no bodies of officials such as existed in France and Prussia capable by themselves of running the country and of getting on without ministers. Whereas in Prussia manhood suffrage and social welfare schemes could be thrust on a grateful people from above, it was unusual in Britain for anything to be done except in response to popular or parliamentary pressure. The centre of initiative was parliament, not the government. And as a consequence there was perpetual discussion as to just how far parliament was justified in intervening in the lives of the people and in the operations of business and industry.

The orthodox view of the 1830s and 1840s was that parliament was entitled to intervene when there was a demand from a particular locality for legislation, or when there was a widespread difficulty to be dealt with, which could not readily be met by purely local enactments. Legislation was, therefore, largely attuned to local demand. Towns were governed under acts of their own, and much general legislation was of an adoptive character—the local authorities, that is to say, were free to apply the provisions of an act or not, as they chose. Some local acts, such as those of Liverpool and Manchester, were extremely comprehensive in scope: but towns which chose to do without local acts were free to do so. Parliament was expected to be cautious about intervening, except to provide against a general scourge, such as cholera. Even the legislation relating to protective duties was often framed on a local basis, because it was aimed to give protection to particular industries with a local base.

The most important feature of the orthodox view of the eighteen thirties and forties was that it was not doctrinaire. Everything turned on whether parliament could be persuaded to cease to regard a problem as best dealt with on a local basis and to agree instead to general legislation. Parliament was willing to be persuaded that particular industries needed to be regulated, but it was uneasy about general laws restricting the hours of labour or prescribing standards of safety. It was prepared to appoint inspectors to watch over emigration, factories, chemicals, railways and the like, but it expected them to use considerable discretion in the application of their powers to particular localities. It was prepared to enact a general Poor Law in 1834, but it was insistent that the relief of the poor should be managed by local committees—the boards of guardians. It was prepared to repeal some protective duties, but it was uneasy about repealing them all. Yet in the last resort, parliament, as Macaulay pointed out so persuasively, was always ready to act, even contrary to its general principles, if action could be shown to be necessary (235).

Interest must therefore centre on how general changes in the law were made. The main structural changes of the 1830s and 1840s were a direct result of the interests and preoccupations of Lord Grey's ministers and of Peel's interest in modernising the establishment in church and state. But the Whig ministers soon lost interest in reform and Peel was long out of power, so that initiatives for change had to come from elsewhere. Many were made as a result of persistent agitation by a handful of members of parliament, of whom much the most notable was the philanthropic Lord Ashley (later Earl of Shaftesbury). Some were made as a result of pressure from the interests concerned, who in some cases retained a full-time lobbyist (231). Some were made as a result of pressure from officials—inspectors who found the existing laws inadequate, like the emigration inspectors,[1] and civil servants in Westminster who were troubled by the confusion of the existing jumble of statutes which they were trying to administer. But many of the most important changes were those which resulted from a combination of pressures—parliamentary agitation backed by some degree of ministerial and official approval and popular support. This was the key to the success of the Anti-Slavery Movement, the Penny Post movement, and the Anti-Corn Law League. In each case the support of some ministers and officials was crucial: the Colonial Office was notorious for its support of the Anti-Slavery movement; without Rowland Hill the penny post would not have been carried; the Anti-Corn-Law League was immensely strengthened by the backing of free-trade officials in the Board of Trade. And at the end of the day a minister had to carry the necessary bill through parliament. But much of the impetus came from popular support, pressed home at elections.

[1] On them see MacDonagh, *A Pattern of Government Growth*.

The Anti-Slavery agitation was here the pioneer, and the Anti-Corn-Law League (the only such organisation whose activities can be recorded in this book at any length) the examplar for future generations, with its gradual extension from a small base in the Manchester Chamber of Commerce (233).

Two minorities stood outside the general acceptance of state intervention: those who argued that nearly all state activity was mischievous, notably Joseph Hume, John Bright, and Herbert Spencer, and those who sympathised with the views of Jeremy Bentham's circle and wanted to create a comprehensive state apparatus comparable with, but superior to, that created by Napoleon in France. The opponents of state intervention had a good deal of backing both in parliament and in the country, where there was a groundswell of hostility to government as merely an expression of aristocratic parasitism. The Benthamites were chiefly influential in literary and official circles and had very little parliamentary or popular backing. When Sir Henry Taylor called for positive government in *The Statesman* his appeal fell on hostile ears (232). The Benthamite view of administration also suffered from its association with Edwin Chadwick who, as virtual creator of the new Poor Law administration, provoked intense hostility, partly on personal grounds and partly by his dogmatic championing of centralisation as against local self-government (272). So strong indeed was the opposition to Chadwick that much of the rudimentary framework of central control over local administration was for a time abandoned (268).

During the 1850s and 1860s new champions of central intervention emerged in the medical profession. Like Chadwick, they seem to have had little knowledge of human nature or of the conventions of British politics and they championed causes which were bound to be unpopular, and whose scientific basis was sometimes uncertain: compulsory powers to enter private houses to examine their sanitary condition, compulsory vaccination, vivisection, state-regulated prostitution in garrison towns (with the power to examine women against their will to see whether they were suffering from contagious diseases). The consequence was once more a strong reaction, with the campaigns against state-regulated prostitution and compulsory vaccination soon building up into formidable and in the end irresistible movements. As with the earlier campaign against the Poor Law, much of the opposition arose from mistakes by those charged with the administration of the law, and in the case of vaccination, the fact that some children died from the effects of being vaccinated. But the result was clear: Sir John Simon, the leading medical man in government service, retired prematurely in 1876[1], and by 1883 we find one of the most politically conscious medical men of

---

[1] For Simon's career see Lambert, *Sir John Simon*. For the anti-vaccination campaign see MacLeod, *Public Law* (1967), 107–28, 189–211.

the day, Balthazar Walter Foster, later Lord Ilkeston, publishing a pamphlet entitled *The Political Powerlessness of the Medical Profession*.

Already at the end of the 1860s, however, public attitudes towards government had begun to change. Few M.P.s were quite so anxious to see the state assume a positive role as was Edward Denison (**236**), but many important interests had begun to expect more of the state. Employers expected a higher standard of education in their workers, and looked to the state to supply it. Agriculturalists, hard hit by cattle diseases and fearful of parliamentary neglect, combined to establish a Central Chamber of Agriculture in 1866; an Association of Chambers of Commerce was established in 1860; and the Trades Union Congress in 1868. The onset of the 'great depression' during the late 1870s found both agriculture and industry prepared to look to the state for help. Royal Commissions were appointed to look into their problems and the House of Commons in 1881 actually passed a resolution, backed by the Central Chamber of Agriculture and the Association of Chambers of Commerce, calling for a Department of Commerce and Agriculture with a minister in the cabinet to watch over commercial and agricultural matters. A further royal commission, on the housing of the poor, which included the Prince of Wales, Lord Salisbury, Cardinal Manning, and many leading politicians, appointed in 1884, was a symptom of a growing readiness to contemplate social reform by state action. A Board of Agriculture was established in 1889, although long with few significant duties. Joseph Chamberlain continued to champion social reform even when he had become a Liberal Unionist. And people actually began to complain that the veteran Gladstone was not sufficiently prepared to move with the times, though John Morley defended him from the charge.

The era of royal commissions during the last twenty years of the nineteenth century was fertile in ideas, but deficient in achievement. The party leaders were willing to act, but only if they could establish a consensus within their party as to what should be done. And a consensus was very difficult to find. The Liberal party was prone to champion policies acceptable to Nonconformist opinion rather than to offer a coherent programme of social reform, with the result that the Newcastle Programme became a ragbag of proposals designed to win support rather than to make political sense (**184–5**). The Conservative leaders were afraid of the right wing of the party, which made the carrying of such measures as the 1888 Local Government Act and the 1903 Irish Land Act so difficult, and failed to hold the party together when Joseph Chamberlain did put forward a constructive policy of tariff reform. The ethos of the country was still essentially a free-enterprise one, with socialists in a tiny minority. (A departmental committee on the Board of Trade and the Local Government Board remarked in 1904 'that it is not the province of the Board of Trade to create or to control commerce. That must be left to private enterprise and to individual effort and initiative'.[1]) It was not until the Liberals had been in office for some years after 1905 that they began to contemplate carrying into effect some of the more positive policies advocated by Joseph Chamberlain and leading reformers since the 1880s: the introduction of old age pensions, the creation of a system of labour exchanges to help tackle the problem of unemployment, the introduction of national health insurance, and the appointment of a development commission. Little was done, however, to encourage the modernisation of an economy based on obsolescent industries, to foster the decayed sections of agriculture, or to stem rural depopulation, because the Liberal government was committed to laissez-faire economic doctrines. The only person to point out most of the real problems of the British economy and to offer a comprehensive solution was Joseph Chamberlain. And he, like earlier doctrinaire reformers, asked for too much. His vision of a protectionist Britain kept buoyant in an increasingly hostile world by its imperial links was too ambitious. Yet an end of free trade there had to be, for which, alas, the war 1914–18 provided the necessary opportunity.

Behind the fumbling reassessment of the role of government after 1880 lay a growing awareness that Britain was no longer the pacemaker in the world. Imperial expansion meant rivalry in all parts of the world with France, Germany, Russia, and even the United States. German military efficiency, German technological innovations, and German social welfare schemes, were all seen to be superior to those of Britain. German competition, even in British markets, became a matter of serious concern to British manufacturing industry. And increasingly Britain's fate was felt to be more bound up with that of Europe than at any time since 1815. The Entente Cordiale with France led to negotiations between the British and French general staffs. The trade unions and socialist organisations began to feel that they formed part of a European-wide movement and that they might emulate the successes of their French and German opposite numbers. British officials were despatched to study German social welfare. And a few British politicians, notably Haldane, even began to talk in terms which meant a rapprochement between British and German ideas of the state. But this process had not gone far by 1914, and when war broke out Britain was still the champion of international free trade and the seat of a world-wide empire, rather than a primarily European power.

[1] [Cd. 2121], p. iv. H.C. (1904), LXXVIII, 443.

231. A lobbyist in 1830

[Evidence before the Select Committee on the Affairs of the East India Company, 25 March 1830]

John Crawfurd, Esq. called in; and Examined.

3650. You are residing here at present as agent to certain parties at Calcutta?

I was appointed agent to the inhabitants of Calcutta without solicitation. I am now fulfilling my duty as their parliamentary agent.

3651. Is there a salary attached to it?

There is a very handsome one.

3652. To what amount?

£1,500 a year, besides extra expenses, which I do not draw. I think the salary too much, and I have proposed to my constituents that it should be reduced.

3653. Had they previously a parliamentary agent in this country?

They never had. I am the first.

3654. Is that appointment exclusive to the question now depending before the House of Commons?

It has no view to the mercantile pursuits of my constituents; it is for political questions only.. . .

3660. Were your instructions transmitted to you, or did you receive them at Calcutta?

They were transmitted to me long after I left Calcutta. . . .

3661. You have resided in different parts of the East?

I resided in various parts of the East for about 19 years.

HC 644, pp. 295–6 (1830) v, 295–6

232. Sir Henry Taylor on reform of the executive, 1836

Till the government of the country shall become a nucleus at which the best wisdom in the country contained shall be perpetually forming itself in deposit, it will be, except as regards the shuffling of power from hand to hand and class to class, little better than a government of fetches, shifts, and hand-to-mouth expedients. Till a wise and constant instrumentality at work upon administrative measures (distinguished as they might be from measures of political parties) shall be understood to be essential to the government of a country, that country can be considered to enjoy nothing more than the embryo of a government,—a means towards producing, through changes in its own structure and constitution and in the political elements acting upon it, something worthy to be called a government at some future time. For governing a country is a very different thing from upholding a government.

Taylor, *The Statesman*, p. 83

233. The creation of the Anti-Corn-Law League, 1838–43

(a) *Petition of the Chamber of Commerce and Manufactures of Manchester, 20 December 1838*

Humbly showeth,

That your petitioners deem it their imperative duty to call the immediate attention of your honourable house to the consideration of the existing laws affecting the free importation of food.

That your petitioners would premise that you are already acquainted with the nature and extent of the cotton trade; combining, as it does, a larger amount of capital, with greater enterprise and skill, and giving more extensive and better regulated employment than any other branch of manufacturing industry. This source of increasing population and wealth, which is now become essential to our well-being as a nation, owes no sort of allegiance to the soil of England; and if it has grown up with a rapidity unparalleled in the annals of trade, history affords us many examples to show how speedily it may, by misgovernment, be banished to other shores.

That your petitioners view, with great alarm, the rapid extension of foreign manufactures, and they have in particular to deplore the consequent diminution of a profitable trade with the continent of Europe; to which, notwithstanding the great increase of population since the termination of the war, the exports have actually been less in value during the last five years after the peace; and whilst the demand for all those articles in which the greatest amount of the labour of our artisans is comprised has been constantly diminishing, the exportation of the raw materials has been as rapidly increasing.

That several nations of the continent not only produce sufficient manufactures for their own consumption, but they successfully compete with us in neutral foreign markets. Amongst other instances that might be given to show the formidable growth of the cotton hosiery of Saxony, of which, owing to its superior cheapness, nearly four times as much is exported as from this country, the Saxons exported annually to the United States of America alone, a quantity equal to the exports from England to all parts of the world; whilst the still more important fact remains to be adduced, that Saxon hose, manufactured from Engligh yarn, after paying a duty of twenty per cent., are beginning to be introduced into this country, and sold for home consumption at lower prices than they can be produced for by our own manufacturers.

That further proof of the rapid progress in manufacturing industry going on upon the continent is afforded in the fact that establishments for the making of all kinds of machinery for spinning and weaving cotton, flax, and wool, have lately been formed in nearly all the large towns of Europe, in which skilled English artisans are at the present moment diligently employed in teaching the native mechanics to make machines copied from models of the newest inventions of this country; and not a week passes in which individuals of the same class do not quit the workshops of Manchester, Leeds, and Birmingham, to enter upon similar engagements abroad.

That the superiority we have hitherto possessed in our unrivalled roads and canals is no longer peculiar to this country; railroads to a great extent, and at a less cost than in England, are proceeding in all parts of Europe and the United States of America; whilst, from the want of profitable investments at home, capital is constantly seeking employment in foreign countries, and thus supplying the greatest deficiency under which our rivals previously laboured.

That, whilst calling the attention of your honourable house to facts calculated to excite the utmost alarm for the well-being of our manufacturing prosperity, your petitioners cannot too earnestly make known that the evils are occasioned by our impolitic and unjust legislation, which, by preventing the British manufacturer from exchanging the produce of his labour for the corn of other countries, enables our foreign rivals to purchase their food at one-half the price at which it is sold in this market; and your petitioners declare it to be their solemn conviction that this is the commencement only of a state of things, which, unless arrested by a timely repeal of all protective duties upon the importation of corn and all foreign articles of subsistence, must eventually transfer our manufacturing industry into other and rival countries.

That, deeply impressed with such apprehensions, your petitioners cannot look with indifference upon, nor conceal from your honourable house, the perilous condition of those surrounding multitudes whose subsistence from day to day depends upon the prosperity of the cotton trade. Already the million have raised the cry for food. Reason, compassion, and sound policy demand that the excited passions be allayed, otherwise evil consequences may ensue. The continuance of the loyal attachment of the people to the established institutions of the country can never be permanently secured on any other grounds than those of commercial justice. Holding one of those external principles to be— the inalienable right of every man freely to exchange the results of his labour for the productions of other people; and maintaining the practice of protecting one part of the community at the expense of all other classes to be unsound and unjustifiable, your petitioners earnestly implore your honourable house to repeal all laws relating to the importation of foreign corn and other foreign articles of subsistence; and to carry out to the fullest extent, both as affects agriculture and manufactures, the true and peaceful principles of *free trade*, by removing all existing obstacles to the unrestricted employment of industry and capital.—And your petitioners, &c.

(b) *The constitution of the Manchester Anti-Corn-Law Association, 28 January 1839*

1. That the association be called 'The Manchester Anti-Corn-Law Association,' and its object is hereby declared to be, to obtain by all legal and constitutional means, such as the formation of local Anti-Corn-Law Associations, the delivery of lectures, the distribution of tracts, the insertion of articles in the public papers, and forwarding petitions to Parliament, the total and immediate repeal of the corn and provision laws.

2. No party political discussions shall, on any account be allowed at any of the general or committee meetings of the association; nor shall any resolution be proposed, or subject entertained which shall be at variance with the declared object of the association.

3. Every person who shall pay in advance an annual subscription shall be a member of the association.

4. Every person on paying a subscription of five shillings or upwards, per annum, shall receive from the secretary a ticket, which shall entitle the subscriber to attend all general meetings of the association, and to take part in the proceedings of the same.

5. The management of the officers of the association shall be vested in a council, to consist of a president, vice president, treasurer, and not

less than one hundred members, to be chosen by the members out of their own body.

6. The council shall elect out of its own body an 'Executive Committee,' consisting of twelve members, three to be a quorum, and other committees if necessary, whose duty shall be to conduct the business of the association.

7. The council shall also select out of its own body, a 'Finance Committee,' consisting of eight members, three to be a quorum, whose duty shall be to receive all moneys on account of the association, and to pay the same to the treasurer, to examine all accounts and to direct payment by the treasurer.

8. The president, vice-president, and treasurer of the association shall be, *ex-officio*, members of every committee.

9. Every committee, at its first meeting, shall appoint out of its own body a chairman and deputy-chairman.

10. The council shall meet at least once a fortnight, to receive the reports of the sub-committees, and for the transaction of the general business of the association.

11. No alteration shall be made in the rules of the association, except at a general meeting of the members, convened for that purpose, of which a week's notice shall be given by public advertisement, in at least two of the Manchester newspapers.

(c) *The constitution of a National Anti-Corn-Law League agreed upon, 20 March 1839*

The formation of a permanent union, to be called the Anti-Corn-Law League, composed of all the towns and districts represented in the delegation, and as many others as might be induced to form Anti-Corn-Law Associations and to join the League.

Delegates from the different local associations to meet for business, from time to time, at the principal towns represented.

With the view to secure the unity of action, the central office of the League shall be established in Manchester, to which body shall be entrusted, among other duties, that of engaging and recommending competent lecturers, the obtaining the co-operation of the public press, and the establishing and conducting of a stamped circular, for the purpose of keeping a constant correspondence with the local associations.

That, in addition to the funds subscribed for local purposes by the several associations, at least £5,000 should be raised to defray the expenses of the general League for the ensuing year, and that every sum of £50 entitle the individual, or association subscribing it, to one vote in the appropriation of the funds of the League, and that on all other questions the votes of the persons present be equal.

That this meeting adjourn, subject to the call of the Manchester Anti-Corn-Law Association; that it be left to their discretion at what time to bring forward the substantive question for the total abolition of the Corn Laws before Parliament, and to adopt any other measures to secure the great object of the association which they may think fit.

(d) *The League Council sets out a programme of agitation, September 1843*

1. Copies will be obtained of the registration lists of all boroughs and counties throughout the kingdom, and the collection lodged at the Metropolitan Office of the League, as a central place of deposit, to be consulted as occasion may require.

2. An extensive correspondence, by means of the post, and of stamped publications, will be kept up with electors, in all districts, upon matters connected with the progress and success of our cause.

3. It is intended that every borough in the kingdom shall be visited by deputations of the League, and meetings held, which the electors will be specially invited to attend.

4. Prompt measures will be taken to ascertain the opinions of each elector in every borough, with the view of obtaining an obvious and decided majority in favour of the total and immediate repeal of the Corn Laws.

5. Every constituency, whose representatives have not hitherto supported Mr. Villiers's motion for the repeal of the Corn Laws, will be invited to memorialise its members to vote for such motion when next brought forward.

6. Whenever a vacancy occurs in the representation of any borough, the electors will be recommended to put a free-trade candidate in nomination; and the League pledges itself to give such candidate every possible support, by deputations, lectures, and the distribution of publications.

7. In the event of any borough being unable to procure a suitable candidate, the League pledges itself to bring forward candidates, so as to afford every elector an opportunity of recording his vote in favour of free trade, until the question be decided.

Prentice, History of the League, I, 85–7, 104–5, 124–5; II, 118–19

234. Peel contemplates a comprehensive scheme of economic and social reform to be undertaken by government, 1845

[Memorandum by Prince Albert, 25 December 1845]

Sir Robert has *an immense scheme in view*; he thinks he shall be able to remove the contest entirely from the dangerous ground upon which it has got—that of a war between the manufacturers, the hungry and the poor against the landed proprietors, the aristocracy, which can only end in the ruin of the latter; he will not bring forward a measure upon the Corn Laws, but a much more comprehensive one. He will deal with the whole commercial system of the country. He will adopt the principle of the League, *that of removing all protection and abolishing all monopoly*, but not in favour of one class and as a triumph over another, but to the benefit of the nation, farmers as well as manufacturers. He would begin with cotton, and take in all the necessaries of life and corn amongst them. The experiments he had made in 1842 and 1845 with boldness but with caution had borne out the correctness of the principle; the wool duty was taken off, and wool sold higher than ever before; foreign cattle were let in, and the cattle of England stood better in the market than ever. He would not ask for compensation to the land, but wherever he could give it, and at the same time promote the social development, there he would do it, but on that ground. For instance, one of the greatest benefits to the country would be the establishment of a rural police on the same principle as the metropolitan police. By taking this on the Consolidated Fund, the landowners would be immensely relieved in all those counties which kept a police. One of the heaviest charges on the land was the present administration of law and the carrying on of prosecutions. Sir Robert could fancy this to be very much improved by the appointment of a *public* prosecutor by the State, which would give the State a power to prevent vexatious, illegal, and immoral prosecutions, and reduce the expenses in an extraordinary degree. Part of the maintenance of the poor, according to the Poor Law, might be undertaken by the State. A great calamity must be foreseen, when the innumerable rail-roads now in progress shall have been terminated, which will be the case in a few years. This will throw an enormous labouring population suddenly out of employment. There might be a law passed which would provide employment for them, and improve the agriculture and production of the country, by enabling the State to advance money to the great proprietors for the improvements of their estates, which they could not obtain otherwise without charging their estates beyond what they already have to bear.

Sir Robert means to go with Mr. Gladstone into all these details.

LQV, 1st ser. II, 78–9

235. Macaulay on the Ten Hours Bill, 22 May 1846

The details of the bill, Sir, will be more conveniently and more regularly discussed when we consider it in Committee. Our business at present is with the principle: and the principle, we are told by many gentlemen of great authority, is unsound. In their opinion, neither this bill, nor any other bill regulating the hours of labour, can be defended. This, they say, is one of those matters about which we ought not to legislate at all: one of those matters which settle themselves far better than any government can settle them. Now it is most important that this point should be fully cleared up. We certainly ought not to usurp functions which do not properly belong to us: but, on the other hand, we ought not to abdicate functions which do properly belong to us. I hardly know which is the greater pest to society, a paternal government, that is to say a prying, meddlesome government, which intrudes itself into every part of human life, and which thinks that it can do everything for everybody better than anybody can do anything for himself; or a careless, lounging government, which suffers grievances, such as it could at once remove, to grow and multiply, and which to all complaint and remonstrance has only one answer: 'We must let things alone: we must let things take their course: we must let things find their level.' There is no more important problem in politics than to ascertain the just mean between these two most pernicious extremes, to draw correctly the line which divides those cases in which it is the duty of the State to interfere from those cases in which it is the duty of the State to abstain from interference. In old times the besetting sin of rulers was undoubtedly an inordinate disposition to meddle. The lawgiver was always telling people how to keep their shops, how to till their fields, how to educate their children, how many dishes to have on their tables, how much a yard to give for the cloth which made their coats. He was always trying to remedy some evil which did not properly fall within his province.... Some eminent political philosophers of the last century exposed with great ability the folly of such legislation, and, by doing so, rendered a great service to mankind. There has been a reaction, a reaction which has doubtless produced much good, but which, like most reactions, has not been without evils and dangers. Our statesmen cannot now be accused of being busy bodies. But I am afraid that there is, even in some of the ablest and most upright among them, a tendency to the opposite fault. I will give an instance of what I mean. Fifteen years ago it became evident that railroads would soon, in every part of the kingdom, supersede to a great extent the old highways. The tracing of the new routes which were to join all the chief cities, ports, and naval arsenals of the island was a matter of the highest national importance. But unfortunately, those who should have acted for the nation refused to interfere. Consequently, numerous questions which were really public, questions which concerned the public convenience, the public prosperity, the public security were treated as private questions. That the whole society was interested in having a good system of internal communication seemed to be forgotten. The speculator who wanted a large dividend on his shares, the landowner who wanted a large price for his acres, obtained a full hearing. But nobody applied to be heard on behalf of the community. The effects of that great error we feel, and we shall not soon cease to feel. Unless I am greatly mistaken, we are in danger of committing to-night an error of the same kind. The honorable Member for Montrose [Joseph Hume] and my honorable friend the Member for Sheffield [John Parker] think that the question before us is merely a question between the old and the new theories of commerce. They cannot understand how any friend of free trade can wish the Legislature to interfere between the capitalist and the labourer. ...I cannot see this matter in the light in which it appears to them. ...I am, I believe, as strongly attached as any member of this House to the principle of free trade, rightly understood. Trade, considered merely as trade, considered merely with reference to the pecuniary interest of the contracting parties, can hardly be too free. But there is a great deal of trade which cannot be considered merely as trade, and which affects higher than pecuniary interests. And to say that Government never ought to regulate such trade is a monstrous proposition, a proposition at which Adam Smith would have stood aghast. We impose some restrictions on trade for purposes of police. Thus, we do not suffer everybody who has a cab and a horse to ply for passengers in the streets of London. We do not leave the fare to be determined by the supply and the demand. We do not permit a driver to extort a guinea for going half a mile on a rainy day when there is no other vehicle on the stand. We impose some restrictions on trade for the sake of revenue. Thus, we forbid a farmer to cultivate tobacco on his own ground. We impose some restrictions on trade for the sake of national defence. Thus, we compel a man who would rather be ploughing or weaving to go into the militia; and we fix the amount of pay which he shall receive without asking his consent. Nor is there in all this anything inconsistent with the soundest political economy. For the science of political economy teaches us only that we ought not on commercial grounds to interfere with the liberty of commerce; and we, in the cases which I have put, interfere with the liberty of commerce on higher than commercial grounds.

And now, Sir, to come closer to the case with which we have to deal, I say, first, that where the health of the community is concerned, it may be the duty of the State to interfere with the contracts of individuals; and to this proposition I am quite sure that Her Majesty's Government will cordially assent. I have just read a very interesting report signed by two members of that Government, the Duke of Buccleuch, and the noble earl who was lately Chief Commissioner of the Woods and Forests, and who is now Secretary for Ireland [the Earl of Lincoln]; and, since that report was laid before the House, the noble earl himself has, with the sanction of the Cabinet, brought in a bill for the protection of the public health. By this bill it is provided that no man shall be permitted to build a house on his own land in any great town without giving notice to certain Commissioners. No man is to sink a cellar without the consent of these Commissioners. The house must not be of less than a prescribed width. No new house must be built without a drain. If an old house has no drain, the Commissioners may order the owner to make a drain. If he refuses, they make a drain for him, and send him in the bill. They may order him to whitewash his house. If he refuses, they may send people with pails and brushes to whitewash it for him, at his charge. Now, suppose that some proprietor of houses at Leeds or Manchester were to expostulate with the Government in the language in which the Government has expostulated with the supporters of this bill for the regulation of factories. Suppose that he were to say to the noble earl, 'Your lordship professes to be a friend to free trade. Your lordship's doctrine is that everybody ought to be at liberty to buy cheap and to sell dear. Why then may not I run up a house as cheap as I can, and let my rooms as dear as I can? Your lordship does not like houses without drains. Do not take one of mine then. You think my bedrooms filthy. Nobody forces you to sleep in them. Use your own liberty: but do not restrain that of your neighbours. I can find many a family willing to pay a shilling a week for leave to live in what you call a hovel. And why am not I to take the shilling which they are willing to give me? And why are not they to have such shelter as, for that shilling, I can afford them? Why did you send a man without my consent to clean my house, and then force me to pay for what I never ordered? My tenants thought the house clean enough for them; or they would not have been my tenants: and, if they and I were satisfied, why did you, in direct defiance of all the principles of free trade, interfere between us?' This reasoning, Sir, is exactly of a piece with the reasoning of the honorable Member for Montrose, and of my honorable friend the Member for Sheffield. If the noble earl will allow me to make a defence for him, I believe that he would answer the objection thus: 'I hold,' he would say, 'the sound doctrine of free trade. But your doctrine of free trade is an exaggeration, a caricature of the sound doctrine; and by exhibiting such a caricature you bring discredit on the sound doctrine. We should have nothing to do with the contracts between you and your tenants, if those contracts affected only pecuniary interests. But higher than pecuniary interests are at stake. It concerns the commonwealth that the great body of the people should not live in a way which makes life wretched and short, which enfeebles the body and pollutes the mind. If, by living in houses which resemble hogstyes, great numbers of our countrymen have contracted the tastes of hogs, if they have become so familiar with filth and stench and contagion, that they burrow without reluctance in holes which would turn the stomach of any man of cleanly habits, that is only an additional proof that we have too long neglected our duties, and an additional reason for our now performing them.'

Secondly, I say that where the public morality is concerned it may be the duty of the State to interfere with the contracts of individuals. Take the traffic in licentious books and pictures. Will anybody deny that the State may, with propriety, interdict that traffic? Or take the case of lotteries. I have, we will suppose, an estate for which I wish to get twenty thousand pounds. I announce my intention to issue a thousand tickets at twenty pounds each. The holder of the number which is first drawn is to have the estate. But the magistrate interferes; the contract between me and the purchasers of my tickets is annulled; and I am forced to pay a heavy penalty for having made such a contract.

I appeal to the principle of free trade, as expounded by the honorable gentlemen the Members for Montrose and Sheffield. I say to you, the legislators who have restricted my liberty, 'What business have you to interfere between a buyer and a seller? If you think the speculation a bad one, do not take tickets. But do not interdict other people from judging for themselves.' Surely you would answer, 'You would be right if this were a mere question of trade: but it is a question of morality. We prohibit you from disposing of your property in this particular mode, because it is a mode which tends to encourage a most pernicious habit of mind, a habit of mind incompatible with all the qualities on which the wellbeing of individuals and of nations depends.'

It must then, I think, be admitted that where health is concerned, and where morality is concerned, the State is justified in interfering with the contracts of individuals. And, if this be admitted, it follows that the case with which we now have to do is a case for interference.

Will it be denied that the health of a large part of the rising generation may be seriously affected by the contracts which this bill is intended to regulate? Can any man who has read the evidence which is before us, can any man who has ever observed young people, can any man who remembers his own sensations when he was young, doubt that twelve hours a day of labour in a factory is too much for a lad of thirteen?

Or will it be denied that this is a question in which public morality is concerned? Can any one doubt,—none, I am sure, of my friends around me doubts,—that education is a matter of the highest importance to the virtue and happiness of a people? Now we know that there can be no education without leisure. It is evident that, after deducting from the day twelve hours for labour in a factory, and the additional hours necessary for exercise, refreshment, and repose, there will not remain time enough for education.

I have now, I think, shown that this bill is not in principle objectionable; and yet I have not touched the strongest part of our case. I hold that, where public health is concerned, and where public morality is concerned, the State may be justified in regulating even the contracts of adults. But we propose to regulate only the contracts of infants. Now was there ever a civilised society in which the contracts of infants were not under some regulation? Is there a single member of this House who will say that a wealthy minor of thirteen ought to be at perfect liberty to execute a conveyance of his estate, or to give a bond for fifty thousand pounds? If anybody were so absurd as to say, 'What has the Legislature to do with the matter? Why cannot you leave trade free? Why do you pretend to understand the boy's interest better than he understands it?'—you would answer; 'When he grows up, he may squander his fortune away if he likes: but at present the State is his guardian; and he shall not ruin himself till he is old enough to know what he is about.' The minors whom we wish to protect have not indeed large property to throw away: but they are not the less our wards. Their only inheritance, the only fund to which they must look for their subsistence through life, is the sound mind in the sound body. And is it not our duty to prevent them from wasting that most precious wealth before they know its value?

But, it is said, this bill, though it directly limits only the labour of infants, will, by an indirect operation, limit also the labour of adults. Now, Sir, though I am not prepared to vote for a bill directly limiting the labour of adults, I will plainly say that I do not think that the limitation of the labour of adults would necessarily produce all those frightful consequences which we have heard predicted. You cheer me in very triumphant tones, as if I had uttered some monstrous paradox. Pray, does it not occur to any of you that the labour of adults is now limited in this country? Are you not aware that you are living in a society in which the labour of adults is limited to six days in seven? It is you, not I, who maintain a paradox opposed to the opinions and the practices of all nations and ages. Did you ever hear of a single civilised State since the beginning of the world in which a certain portion of time was not set apart for the rest and recreation of adults by public authority? In general, this arrangement has been sanctioned by religion. The Egyptians, the Jews, the Greeks, the Romans, had their holidays: the Hindoo has his holidays: the Mussulman has his holidays: there are holidays in the Greek Church, holidays in the Church of Rome, holidays in the Church of England. Is it not amusing to hear a gentleman pronounce with confidence that any legislation which limits the labour of adults must produce consequences fatal to society, without once reflecting that in the society in which he lives, and in every other society that exists, or ever has existed, there has been such legislation without any evil consequence? It is true that a Puritan Government in England, and an Atheistical Government in France, abolished the old holidays as superstitious. But those governments felt it to be absolutely necessary to institute new holidays. Civil festivals were substituted for religious festivals.   Macaulay, *Works*, VIII, 361–7

236. Edward Denison, M.P., calls for more government, 1868–9

From an election speech at Newark, 1868

You have got to reform the whole administrative organization of this country, and if you don't do it we shall fall into a state of confusion in this nineteenth century which will make us the laughing-stock of the civilized world. You have to give much greater power to your agents—the public officers of the Crown. You must sweep away Boards, and you must substitute individual men, and men invested with large power, with wide discretion, and weighted with heavy responsibility— men accountable directly to Parliament, and acting under the even pressure of an enlightened, powerful, vigilant public opinion. You must, I say, give that additional power to your agents, if you are to exact greater efficiency. But you cannot safely give that power, unless it is to be exercised under the pressure of that public opinion.

Letter to an unnamed correspondent, 8 January 1869

It is quite clear to every one blessed with eyes that during the last fifty years we have been slipping out of an oligarchical habit of administration into a popular habit of administration; the theory of government remaining all the while so unchanged, that too many people ignore the change of practice. Is it utopian to hope that the sincere recognition of the change by the people at large will bring a vast accession of strength to government as government? I want Government to come out clearly and boldly as the great mediator, to draw to itself the hearts of the people as the one power capable of saving them from themselves....

I believe that a Cabinet which would put away for the nonce all the old prejudices about interfering with the liberty of the subject, and would quietly bring in bills for such regulation of our internal economy as every reasonable man in private conversation admits to be called for, would not only occupy an unassailable position within the walls of Parliament, but would command the allegiance of the nation in a way no Government has ever yet done.

Leighton, *Letters of Edward Denison*, pp. 72–3, 82–3

237. Bright still hostile to state intervention, 1879
[John Bright to Frederick Blood, 26 June 1879]

Mr. Chaplin is about to move for an inquiry by Royal Commission into the existing agricultural distress, and I do not see how or why such an inquiry should be granted without including in it a more general inquiry as to the present depression in other branches of industry. Some people still have faith in Parliamentary Committees and Royal Commissions on matters of this kind; I confess that I have none.

A few years ago we had a panic about the scarcity and price of coal, and a Parliamentary Committee sat upon it and about it. The Committee led to nothing. More recently we had a Committee on the Fall in the Value of Silver, and the inquiry led to nothing. Just now we have a Committee on Co-operative Stores, and it will lead to nothing, except to show generally the uselessness of such inquiries. If Mr. Chaplin gets his Committee or Commission it will lead to nothing, except to prove that, with free imports of corn, bad harvests are bad for farmers, and that the omnipotence of Parliament fails when it seeks to control the seasons; and that, therefore, Parliament cannot step in by legislation materially to mitigate the admitted sufferings of the farmers.

As to the present depression of trade, we owe some of it to the bad harvests, which have impoverished many farmers, who are not an inconsiderable portion of our home-trade customers; we owe much of it to famines in India and China, and to the commercial and manufacturing distress which has prevailed in almost every country, and not least in those countries which have sought to secure themselves by high protective duties. If our harvest this year is unfavourable, I fear the recovery we all hope for will be delayed; if it is abundant, which seems not probable, we shall soon see, not symptoms only, but proofs of a revival.

In the United States, with a great harvest last year, trade is reviving. We followed them in their depression, but not to so deep a depth, and we shall follow them in their recovery. These great changes are not in the power of Congresses or Parliaments; they are in the ordering of nature, and we must accept them, always endeavouring not to aggravate them by our own follies.

There is one great consolation in our present condition; the food of our people is cheap. But for the free imports the price of bread would be more than double, the price of sugar would be three times its present price, the price of cheese and bacon would be double, or nearly so, and of the price of labour it may be said that it would be much lessened by a greater prostration of every industry in the country not immediately connected with the growth of food. The freedom of our imports will enable us to pass through the present time of depression with less suffering than at any former period of disastrous seasons.

As to Parliament and its inquiries, I have seen much of it and of them. If Parliament would keep out of foreign broils; if it would conduct the government of the country at an expenditure of sixty millions instead of eighty millions in the year; if it would devote its time and labours to questions of home interest rather than to those which involve the sacrifice of the blood and treasure of our people in remote lands, we might have hope and faith that Parliament could serve the nation in times of depression, and we should find that such times of suffering would visit us more rarely.

If an inquiry, such as you refer to, is granted, I hope it may do some good, if it only shows once more how useless such inquiries are.

Bright, *Public Letters*, pp. 44–5

B THE CIVIL SERVICE

The idea that public appointments should be filled by men of ability and that public offices should cease to be nests of parasites upon the establishment had always appealed to men of sense. But in the eighteenth century the all-pervading demand for political patronage to oil the parliamentary machine made all but the mildest reforms practically impossible. Burke succeeded in destroying a few sinecures, but it was not until the French wars that parliamentary opinion began to take seriously the case for administrative reform. During the wars a series of committees recommended sweeping changes in the conduct of government offices, including the total abandonment of sinecures, and both during the wars and once the wars were over a number of major reforms were undertaken with the encouragement of Lord Liverpool. In 1816 the salaries of officials in public offices were made a parliamentary rather than a departmental responsibility—the first step towards a unified civil service; in 1817 a mass of sinecures was swept away, leaving very few in the civil offices, and a number of departments were reorganised; and in 1821 Lord Liverpool abandoned the First Lord of the Treasury's patronage in the Customs service to the heads of the department in order to secure that promotion should go to the efficient, not to the well-connected. By the time of Liverpool's death in 1827 the first steps had already been taken towards the creation of a career service based on merit rather than patronage, while the distinction between ministers who changed with the government and permanent officials became more clear cut in 1830 (**238**).

Liverpool's reforms were not generally understood by his colleagues and were resented by the party managers. Some of them were undone by his Whig successors, and further reform was bitterly opposed by the party managers. The young Gladstone was firmly put in his place when he tried to secure posts for those without political influence (**239**), and all civil service reforms down to the 1890s were obstructed by the party managers. Even Gladstone's close friend and patronage secretary, George Glyn, complained bitterly about the reforms of 1870: 'I lose, without notice, and at once, the great advantage of the daily correspondence and communication with members of the party which the ordinary dispensing of the Treasury patronage gave me, to say nothing of the power which it placed in my hands.'[1] Nor was much sympathy to be expected from the civil service itself, where few men recruited by the method which enabled Anthony Trollope to enter the Post Office[2] cared for reform. Bentham and the philosophical radicals alone supported administrative reform, and their support was far from welcome to administrative reformers like Peel and Graham, because the Benthamites wished to put an end to the old system and to start again afresh, which was just what Peel and Graham wanted to avoid. The latter were anxious to retain the aristocratic character of the administration, but to change the emphasis from patronage for the unworthy to the careful selection of the best-qualified gentlemen for the government service. The social and political system they regarded as essentially aristocratic, and to match it they felt that there must be an aristocratic administration. As Sir Charles Trevelyan made clear, aristocratic Oxford and Cambridge were to be allowed to fill up the civil service with their ablest graduates by a system of open competition which kept all but a very few non-gentlemen out of the service (**243**).

The creation of a career civil service chosen by open competition was the goal of Sir Charles Trevelyan, assistant secretary (i.e. permanent head) of the Treasury, 1840–59. A series of official enquiries into the work of a number of major departments was staged to provide background information. Then a general committee of enquiry, composed of Sir Stafford Northcote and Trevelyan himself, pulled together this background information into the short and rather carelessly worded Northcote–Trevelyan Report of 23 November 1853 (**242**), which is generally regarded as the charter of the modern civil service. Its main proposals, that candidates for admission to the civil service should be selected by open competitive examination, that the civil service should be regarded as a single service embracing all departments,

---

[1] Hughes, *Public Administration*, XXXIII (1955), 305–6.
[2] Trollope, *Autobiography*, ch. III.

and that a distinction should be drawn between the higher class of administrative work and mere routine, became the programme of reformers for the rest of the nineteenth century. Trevelyan's immediate object, backed by Gladstone and the Peelite members of the Aberdeen Cabinet, was to make open competitive examinations *at once* the sole means of entry to the public service, and to form a single unified public service with civil servants moving from department to department as required.

Trevelyan's reforming zeal aroused such an extraordinary amount of hostility, both within and without the civil service, that prompt implementation of the Northcote–Trevelyan Report was not possible. Efficient officials bitterly resented Trevelyan's denunciations of the existing civil service, and argued strongly for a departmental as against a unified civil service (244). Old-guard politicians were not reconciled to the loss of patronage which the new scheme implied. Nor were they convinced by the argument that the proposed system was essentially aristocratic in character. They (rightly) had no faith whatever in written examinations as a predictor of administrative ability. And they doubted whether the new examination system pioneered by Balliol tutors at Oxford was educationally sound. The literary world was divided. John Stuart Mill and Dickens, among others, supported Trevelyan; Disraeli, Trollope and a host of others were on the other side; and Thomas Carlyle thundered from the sidelines calling for 'a new State Architecture' and 'Industrial Regiments of the New Era';[1] Anthony Trollope, himself a civil servant recruited in the old way, actually devoted a whole novel, *The Three Clerks*, to the reforms.

The storm was so great that Trevelyan might well have saved nothing from the wreck of his plans had it not been for the public outcry against the administrative inefficiency which marred the conduct of the Crimean War. The government very narrowly escaped having a radical scheme of reform thrust upon it by a hostile House of Commons, and the very least it could do was to introduce a preliminary examination designed to exclude the unfit from serious consideration for the civil service. A Civil Service Commission was accordingly established to conduct a new qualifying examination for civil servants[2] and unrestricted patronage, in principle at least, came to an end. In practice, the change was very limited in character, as contemporary guides to the service made clear (245). In the major departments there was an element of competition, since nominees were required to compete with one another for a limited number of places. But as 'the proportion of competitors to vacancies is less than three to one', most of those nominated actually secured a place. If they were well-connected, candidates could, indeed, still be jobbed in, even where there was a limited competition. The

---

[1] Thomas Carlyle's 'Downing Street' and 'The New Downing Street' in the *Latter-Day Pamphlets* were published in 1850.   [2] *London Gazette*, 22 May 1855.

civil service was still a gentlemanly profession, attractive to those lacking the energy or self-confidence to make an independent career, and enjoying sufficient political influence to get a start on the official ladder (246).

Reformers now for the most part concentrated on the creation within the civil service of an élite of the very best university graduates to man the higher reaches of the service, which was to be achieved by the introduction of the open competition advocated by Sir Charles Trevelyan. A further measure of civil service reform was finally approved by a Cabinet committee appointed by the first Gladstone government (247) and open competition came into effect under an Order in Council of 4 June 1870 (248). Although the Treasury was given considerable powers by the 1870 and subsequent Orders in Council, it was still left to each department to decide just how open competition was to be implemented and the measure of administrative reform required. The Foreign Office opted out of the new system; so did most of the Scottish and Irish offices; and even the Home departments were often extremely loath to change. It was to take more than forty years and three enquiries by royal commission, before the Home Civil Service began to look like a single career service, providing uniform conditions of service and a single method of entry by open competitive examination. In the meantime, four systems existed side by side. In the high-grade government departments there was an administrative élite, chiefly recruited from the universities, reinforced by a less highly educated group of middle-range officials, plus a mass of low-grade clerical workers, porters and the like. The main groups of officials were recruited by open competition, the remainder by a mixture of systems. Secondly, there was the Foreign Office and its adjuncts abroad, each of them separately recruited, and each with its own peculiar methods of selection. Thirdly, there were the survivals of the old era of undiluted patronage, notably in the legal offices, where nepotism had long been a public scandal,[1] and of the post-1855 system of nomination and limited competition, notably in Scotland, Ireland, the Customs Waterguard Service and in some of the smaller offices.[2] Finally, there were the very big opportunities for a career in the colonies (where posts were in the gift of the Colonial Secretary) or in India (where recruitment was by open competitive examination).

The reformed civil service, although still largely departmental in character (251), had by 1914 come to assume all the characteristics of a settled system. Royal commissions might propose detailed reforms, but the main structure was settled, and the type of man recruited had become stabilised. Dominated by Oxford and Cambridge graduates of the highest distinction, the higher

---

[1] One Lord Chancellor, Westbury, was forced to resign in 1865 after being censured by the House of Commons for nepotism, and another, Halsbury, was constantly under attack for the use of his patronage.   [2] Hanham, *Historical Journal*, III, 75–84.

Civil Service now formed a sort of mandarin caste to which ministers were bound to accord the greatest respect. Such great respect, indeed, that it became in the 1880s the custom to elevate the most distinguished civil servants to the peerage on retirement. The problem was now how to secure administrative innovations without disturbing the system. This could be done in two ways. The most common method was to promote able younger men, such as ministerial private secretaries, out of turn, which gave men like John Arthur Godley (Lord Kilbracken) and Robert Morant the chance to head major departments. The civil service lobby protested, but to no avail. A second method involved the creation of an entirely new administrative structure such as Lloyd George created for National Insurance and Winston Churchill created for the Labour Exchanges (250). A new structure could be staffed by a mixture of career civil servants and outsiders brought in specially for the purpose, in order to provide greater drive and flexibility. This too produced civil service complaints, but on the whole the new organisations justified themselves in action.

Over the century the size of the civil service changed quite markedly. For a long time the main objective was to cut down the swollen numbers in the bigger offices, recruited during the Napoleonic Wars, then to make further retrenchment in offices like the Army departments, to counteract the tendency towards increases elsewhere. But after a great economy drive in the 1870s, for which the initiative came from Gladstone, the trend was all towards increased numbers as the state took on new functions. There are no fully reliable figures, but the following represent the overall changes in the size of the service.[1]

1797	16,267	1871	53,874
1815	24,598	1881	50,859
1821	27,000	1891	79,241
1832	21,305	1901	116,413
1841	16,750	1911	172,352
1851	39,147	1914	280,900
1861	31,943		

During the nineteenth century most of these officials were in the revenue departments—the Post Office, the Inland Revenue, the Customs and Excise—or in the dockyards, but increasingly at the beginning of the twentieth century they were in the new social service departments.

The size of the civil service created a number of political problems. In the eighteenth century it had been possible to argue that civil servants should not have the vote because if they did vote they would have to vote for their employers, the government of the day, and so increase government control

---

[1] Figures from Mackenzie and Grove, *Central Administration in Britain*, p. 7.

over the limited pre-reform constituencies. This was the principle behind Crewe's Act of 1782 which disfranchised revenue officers (including officials of the Post Office). Subsequently other legislation was passed, which prevented policemen from voting. And in 1860 a royal commission recommended that workers in government dockyards should likewise be disfranchised, because they exercised a bad influence on dockyard elections and dockyard M.P.s. This proposal was incorporated in Gladstone's 1866 Reform Bill, avowedly in order to protect dockyard M.P.s from their constituents, but was dropped from subsequent bills. Indeed, so far had parliamentary opinion changed by 1868 that the self-appointed spokesman of the revenue officers, C. J. Monk, M.P. for Gloucester,[1] actually succeeded in getting the revenue officers re-enfranchised, in spite of the hostility of the government and Opposition front benches in the Commons, and of the official spokesmen of the Revenue Boards. About the same time the service departments and the Treasury began to be alarmed about the extent to which political influence was exerted on behalf of particular officials. A number of official minutes were issued admonishing both civil servants and service officers, and the first steps were taken to formulate clear rules about the candidacy of civil servants for parliament, which were eventually formalised in 1884 (249).

The main concern of the government soon became not the political activities of government officials, though these were much debated,[2] but the growth of civil service trade unions. Here the pioneers were the Post Office unions. After 1869, when the Post Office took over the telegraph services, the postal staffs were in an almost constant state of discontent. They were told that they must not lobby M.P.s, but the Post Office trade unions continued to do so, and to demand a parliamentary enquiry into the management of the Post Office. They stuck to the letter of the Post Office rules that:

> No postmaster, or other servant of the Department, shall serve on a committee having for its object to promote or prevent the return of a particular candidate to Parliament. He shall not support or oppose any particular candidate or party, either by public speaking or writing.[3]

But they constantly departed from its spirit. The Post Office at first refused to recognise trade unions among its employees: then repented under trade union pressure, but tried to apply the Post Office policy of political neutrality to postal trade unions as well as to individual Post Office employees, and in the 1890s actually dismissed two of the Post Office trade union officials from the service. One of the men, W. E. Clery, had rashly stated in a speech in August 1892 that:

[1] Monk, *Reminiscences*, pp. 35–62.
[2] There is a useful account of political activities in the dockyards in Lowell, *Government of England*, I, 149–53.   [3] 4 *Hansard* LIII, 1131.

They must approach the House on its weak side; they must influence Members through their susceptibilities as opportunity presents itself when candidates appeal to their respective constituencies.[1]

This brought down upon him a fierce attack in 1898 from the then Financial Secretary of the Treasury, R. W. Hanbury:

What private employee is able to say, 'I am the permanent servant of my employer; I have a share in deciding who that employer shall be; I will attack him on his weak side when he comes up for re-election, and then I will use my power. I will bring organised pressure to bear throughout the constituencies, and I will make this bargain: that if he will not vote for an increase in my pay, or diminish my duties, then I will not give him my vote.' We have done away with personal and individual bribery, but there is a still worse form of bribery, and that is when a man asks a candidate to buy his vote out of the public purse.[2]

But this soon proved to be only one incident in a bigger battle to work out a satisfactory relationship between the government and its army of employees. And between 1898 and 1914 there was an almost continuous battle over the position of civil service trade unions and the civil rights of public officials.

238. The Secretaryship of the Admiralty becomes a political office, 1830

[J. W. Croker to Sir James Graham, 20 November 1830]

As there never has been an instance of the Secretary of the Admiralty being removed on a change of Ministry, it cannot be improper, though it may be superfluous, to acquaint you, who, I understand, are to be at the head of the new Board, that it is my intention to resign that office.

Permit me, however, to add that if there is any information or assistance which twenty-two years' experience may enable me to afford you in the outset of your arduous duties, I shall feel it my duty to do so, readily and frankly.   Jennings, *Croker Papers*, II, 74–5

[1] 4 *Hansard* LIII, 1137–8.   [2] *Ibid.* 1138.

239. The Patronage Secretary emphasises the political character of Treasury patronage, 1843
[Sir Thomas Fremantle to W. E. Gladstone, 27 December 1843]

I hear that your application in favor of young Mr. Walker is not founded on strong political claims. It is more a case of kindness and charity—such as I should more readily consider than any others if I were at liberty to do so—but at the Treasury we must look first to the claims of our political supporters & our patronage is, as you know, quite inadequate to meet the applications of members of the H of C in favor of their constituents who naturally consider all our patronage as theirs.

The son of a good voter at Newark would stand a better chance under your recommendation than the son of a poor clergyman who probably made it a point of duty not to interfere with politics.

If, however, I have misunderstood the case, let me know and I will note the name & pray excuse me for my frankness in explaining to you how these things are viewed within the corrupt walls of a Sec[retary of the] Treasury's room.   Hughes, *English Historical Review*, LXIV, 67

240. The decline of patronage in the Revenue departments, 1820–54
[George Arbuthnot's Comments, 6 March 1854]

It was my fortune to enter the Public Service about the period (1820) when Lord Liverpool, with a patriotism for which he never received due credit, voluntarily surrendered the influence obtained by the power of making direct appointments to the superior offices in the Customs department, for the purpose of improving the efficiency of that service. From that period, all collectorships and other offices of importance were filled by the advancement of officers already in the Service, instead of by the appointment of strangers to it on political recommendations; and in the year 1827 the principle was organized by the establishment of a graduated system of promotion throughout the Service, proceeding partly according to seniority, but, as respects the superior offices, entirely by selection. I have watched the commencement and development of this system. It has been found to work well; and in the late investigations into the department, conducted with critical severity, no imputations were raised, amidst all the outcry in regard to forms of procedure, against the general efficiency of the establishment. Proofs of the estimation in which this extended system of promotion is held by the public has been afforded by a clause in the recent Customs Act, by which two-fifths of vacant landing-waiterships are required to be filled by the promotion of officers of an inferior grade, thus further enlarging the area of promotion, and opening to officers of the lowest rank the opportunity for eventual advancement to the highest offices in the Service—a measure which, it may be observed, is in a contrary direction from the recommendations contained in this Report.

The department of Inland Revenue is regulated on the same principle, and successful efforts have been made recently to improve the general character of the Service, by requiring a higher standard of qualification for admission, and by the education of the most promising young officers of Excise in those branches of chemistry the knowledge of which is useful in the business of the Service.

In both these departments, the secretaryships have been filled, in successive appointments for many years past, by the advancement of officers who had acquired experience in the routine work of the Service; and I believe every one will admit that they are ably filled.

Papers &c, [1870] pp. 406–7. H.C. (1854–5) xx, 406–7

241. Lord Palmerston on ministers and officials in Britain and on the continent, 1838

[Viscount Palmerston to Queen Victoria, 25 February 1838]

...in the Governments of the Continent, and more especially in those which have no representative Assemblies, the second class of persons in the public offices possess and exercise much more power and influence than the corresponding class of persons do in this country. In England the Ministers who are at the head of the several departments of the State, are liable any day and every day to defend themselves in Parliament; in order to do this, they must be minutely acquainted with all the details of the business of their offices, and the only way of being constantly armed with such information is to conduct and direct those details themselves.

On the Continent, where Ministers of State are not liable so to be called to account for their conduct, the Ministers are tempted to leave the details of their business much more to their Under-Secretaries and to their chief clerks. Thus it happens that all the routine of business is

generally managed by these subordinate agents; and to such an extent is this carried, that Viscount Palmerston believes that the Ministers for Foreign Affairs, in France, Austria, Prussia, and Russia, seldom take the trouble of writing their own despatches, except, perhaps, upon some very particular and important occasion.

Your Majesty will easily see how greatly such a system must place in the hands of the subordinate members of the public departments the power of directing the policy and the measures of the Government; because the value and tendency, and the consequences of a measure, frequently depend as much upon the manner in which that measure is worked out, as upon the intention and spirit with which it was planned.

Another circumstance tends also to give great power to these second-class men, and that is their permanence in office.

In England when, in consequence of some great political change, the Heads of Departments go out, the greater part of the Under-Secretaries go out also; thus the Under-Secretary (with two or three exceptions) having come in with his Chief, has probably no more experience than his Chief, and can seldom set up his own knowledge to overrule the opinion, or to guide the judgment, of his superior.

But on the Continent, changes of Ministers are oftener changes of individual men from personal causes, than changes of parties from political convulsions; and therefore when the Chief retires, the Under-Secretary remains. There are consequently in all the public offices abroad a number of men who have spent the greater part of their lives in their respective departments, and who by their long experience are full of knowledge of what has been done in former times, and of the most convenient and easy manner of doing what may be required in the time present. This affords to the Chiefs an additional motive for leaning upon their subordinates, and gives to those subordinates still more real influence.   *LQV*, 1st ser. I, 136–7

242. The Northcote-Trevelyan report on the civil service, 23 November 1853

That the Permanent Civil Service, with all its defects, essentially contributes to the proper discharge of the functions of Government, has been repeatedly admitted by those who have successively been responsible for the conduct of our affairs. All, however, who have had occasion to examine its constitution with care, have felt that its organisation is far from perfect, and that its amendment is deserving of the most careful attention.

It would be natural to expect that so important a profession would attract into its ranks the ablest and the most ambitious of the youth of the country; that the keenest emulation would prevail among those who had entered it; and that such as were endowed with superior qualifications would rapidly rise to distinction and public eminence. Such, however, is by no means the case. Admission into the Civil Service is indeed eagerly sought after, but it is for the unambitious, and the indolent or incapable, that it is chiefly desired. Those whose abilities do not warrant an expectation that they will succeed in the open professions, where they must encounter the competition of their contemporaries, and those whom indolence of temperament or physical infirmities unfit for active exertions, are placed in the Civil Service, where they may obtain an honourable livelihood with little labour, and with no risk; where their success depends upon their simply avoiding any flagrant misconduct, and attending with moderate regularity to routine duties; and in which they are secured against the ordinary consequences of old age, or failing health, by an arrangement which provides them with the means of supporting themselves after they have become incapacitated....

One more peculiarity in the Civil Service remains to be noticed. It is what may be called its fragmentary character.

Unlike the Military and Naval, the Medical, and the Commissariat Services, and even unlike the Indian Civil Service, the public establishments of this country, though comprising a body of not less than 16,000 persons, are regulated upon the principle of merely departmental promotion. Each man's experience, interests, hopes, and fears are limited to the special branch of service in which he is himself engaged. The effect naturally is, to cramp the energies of the whole body, to encourage the growth of narrow views and departmental prejudices, to limit the acquisition of experience, and to repress and almost extinguish the spirit of emulation and competition; besides which, considerable inconvenience results from the want of facilities for transferring strength from an office where the work is becoming slack to one in which it is increasing, and from the consequent necessity of sometimes keeping up particular departments on a scale beyond their actual requirements....

The general principle...which we advocate is, that the public service should be carried on by the admission into its lower ranks of a carefully selected body of young men, who should be employed from the first upon work suited to their capacities and their education, and should be made constantly to feel that their promotion and future prospects depend entirely on the industry and ability with which they discharge their duties, that with average abilities and reasonable application they may look forward confidently to a certain provision for their lives, that with superior powers they may rationally hope to attain to the highest prizes in the Service, while if they prove decidedly incompetent, or incurably indolent, they must expect to be removed from it.

The first step towards carrying this principle into effect should be, the establishment of a proper system of examination before appointment, which should be followed, as at present, by a short period of probation....

We accordingly recommend that a central Board should be constituted for conducting the examination of all candidates for the public service whom it may be thought right to subject to such a test. Such board should be composed of men holding an independent position, and capable of commanding general confidence; it should have at its head an officer of the rank of Privy Councillor; and should either include, or have the means of obtaining the assistance of, persons experienced in the education of the youth of the upper and middle classes, and persons who are familiar with the conduct of official business. It should be made imperative upon candidates for admission to any appointment, (except in certain special cases which will presently be noticed), to pass a proper examination before the Board, and obtain from them a certificate of having done so.

We are of opinion that this examination should be in all cases a competing literary examination. This ought not to exclude careful previous inquiry into the age, health, and moral fitness of the candidates....

For the superior situations endeavours should be made to secure the services of the most promising young men of the day, by a competing examination on a level with the highest description of education in this country. In this class of situations there is no limit to the demands which may ultimately be made upon the abilities of those who, entering them simply as junior clerks, gradually rise to the highest posts in them. To obtain first-rate men, it is obvious that recourse should be had to competition....

Another point to which the attention of the chiefs of offices should be called is, the importance of transferring the clerks from one department of the office to another, so that each may have an opportunity of making himself master of the whole of the business before he is called upon, in due course of time, to take a leading position. A proper system of transfers according to fixed rules in each office, and insured by periodical reports to the chief, must exercise a beneficial influence both upon the clerks themselves, and upon the general efficiency of the establishment. Periodical reports upon the manner in which each clerk has been employed, should be made to the chief of the office. . . .

Upon a review of the recommendations contained in this paper it will be seen that the objects which we have principally in view are these:—

1. To provide, by a proper system of examination, for the supply of the public service with a thoroughly efficient class of men.
2. To encourage industry and foster merit, by teaching all public servants to look forward to promotion according to their deserts, and to expect the highest prizes in the service if they can qualify themselves for them.
3. To mitigate the evils which result from the fragmentary character of the Service, and to introduce into it some elements of unity, by placing the first appointments upon a uniform footing, opening the way to the promotion of public officers to staff appointments in other departments than their own, and introducing into the lower ranks a body of men (the supplementary clerks) whose services may be made available at any time in any office whatever. . . . [1713] pp. 3–23. H.C. (1854) xxvii, 3–23

243. Sir Charles Trevelyan argues that open competition would favour the sons of gentlemen, 1854

[Memorandum by Sir C. E. Trevelyan, 18 January 1854]

The effect of a system of open competition will be to secure for the public offices generally and especially for the principal offices the best portion of the best educated of our youth.

Who are so successful in carrying off the prizes at competing scholarships, fellowships, &c. as the most expensively educated young men? Almost invariably, the sons of gentlemen, or those who by force of cultivation, good training and good society have acquired the feelings and habits of gentlemen. The tendency of the measure will, I am confident, be decidedly *aristocratic*, but it will be so in a good sense by securing for the public service those who are, in a true sense, οἱ ἄριστοι. At present a mixed multitude is sent up, a large proportion of whom, owing to the operation of political and personal patronage, are of an inferior rank of society...*and they are, in general, the least eligible of their respective ranks.* The idle and useless, the fool of the family, the consumptive, the hypochondriac, those who have a tendency to insanity, are the sort of young men commonly '*provided for*', as the term is, in a public office. I could mention off-hand scores of instances, some of which are of so wholesale a character as must command conviction. All this will be remedied by the proposed arrangement....

Hughes, *English Historical Review*, LXIV, 72

244. George Arbuthnot attacks the basic assumptions of the North-cote–Trevelyan report, 6 March 1854

Our Constitution vests the legislation in Members of Parliament, and the Ministers of the Crown are necessarily selected from that order. The officers of our Civil Service cannot in ordinary cases aspire to become statesmen, and to carry out systems of policy. Their humble but useful duty is, by becoming depositaries of departmental traditions, and by their practical acquaintance with the working of those laws, by which constitutional jealousy has guarded the Civil administration, as they affect their own departments, to keep the current business in its due course; to warn Ministers of the consequences of irregular proceedings into which they might inadvertently fall; to aid in preparing subjects for legislation; and possibly to assist by their suggestions the development of a course of reform. To fulfil these duties with efficiency, it is necessary that, as a general rule, each man's experience should be confined to the special branch of the Service in which he is himself engaged. Such is the complicated character of our institutions, that, without such division of labour, no man could obtain that intimate acquaintance with details, and the bearing of those details upon general principles, which constitute the distinction between the permanent executive officers and the members of Government who are charged with the duty of administration.

Occasionally the transfer of officers from one department to another of a cognate character, may be attended with advantage, and infuse new life into a waning office; but, as a general rule, promotion within each department is preferable, and forms an essential feature in the system of organization which has been attended with so much success in the establishments to which I have above referred. A good Treasury officer would make a very inefficient head of a department in the Foreign Office, and *vice versâ*.

The effect of this 'fragmental' division is not, I believe, 'to encourage the growth of narrow views and departmental prejudices,' or 'to limit the acquisition of experience,' to an extent injurious to the Service. If such prejudices are sometimes engendered, the reproach is not peculiar to the Civil Service. Learned and scientific bodies, the Law, the Church, the Legislature, are all open to a similar charge. Prejudice is, in fact, but the exaggeration of that safeguard against rash innovation which is afforded by peculiar knowledge or experience.

The proposal for the separation of the intellectual from mechanical labour is to some extent mixed up with the views stated in the Report condemnatory of the departmental system. It is true that in most offices there is a large amount of mere copying work, which when not of a confidential character may be entrusted with advantage to an inferior class of clerks. It is a matter of discretion to what extent recourse ought to be had to this description of assistance. In some few departments, also, the duties of the administrative or directing functionaries are so distinct from those of the clerks who carry into effect the routine duties, that the line of demarcation is easily drawn. But in the great mass of the Revenue departments a thorough acquaintance with forms is so essential to a full comprehension of the business to be carried on, that to fulfil the superior offices satisfactorily a previous apprenticeship in the inferior classes is essential. In order to direct details effectively, an officer ought to know how to do them himself. In order to become acquainted with technical or legal phraseology, the young clerk must begin by copying documents. As in professional pursuits, the efficient Civil Servant is formed by making him in the first instance a good workman. The most distinguished officers of this class commenced early in life at the drudgery of the desk. It is upon this principle that the system of promotion which has worked so well in the Customs has been established, and the value of the theory which would disturb that system has yet to be tested.

I have avoided all reference to the plan proposed for recruiting the Civil Service by the system of a competing literary examination, but

I cannot refrain from impressing upon your Lordships the fact, upon which I apprehend there can be little dispute, that the real practical education of an official man must be within the office; and that there will be danger lest, in case a supplementary class of clerks are introduced, as proposed, into the lower ranks—those men, by acquiring a superior mastery of the details of an office, may become its most efficient servants, and be really more eligible for promotion (from which they will yet be debarred) than the class who are to be admitted with the recommendation of superior mental cultivation.

In all the public departments there is a vast amount of mere routine work, which yet requires attention, ability, and, above all, integrity. A very large majority of the Public Servants must be engaged in such occupation, and few can emerge from it to superior situations. The few prizes may be a great stimulus to the mass, when all are contending for them; but it cannot be pretended that the immediate work requires a high order of intellectual attainment. There will be, on the one hand, danger lest persons having high claims on the ground of intellectual attainment, and stimulated by the expectation of a prize, find themselves condemned among the mass to a life of hopeless drudgery. On the other hand, if to avoid this result the best appointments are reserved for an intellectual class, the general body of the Civil Servants will be disheartened and degraded in character.

Papers &c, [1870] pp. 411–13. H.C. (1854–55) xx, 411–13

245. Limited competition at home, open competition in India, 1860

An idea has been hastily propagated, and extensively circulated, that public employment is now given, without distinction or selection from any privileged class, to all who will prove their claim to it, and that young men of fair character and ability, subjects of the Queen, within the prescribed limits of age, and possessed of the stipulated amount of book-learning, have only to enter their names and appear at the lists to contend for the prizes of junior situations at the disposal of the Ministers and heads of departments. This is altogether an error. As yet entrance into the public offices of the United Kingdom is obtained only in the old-fashioned way, by the favour, friendship, or discretion of the authorities for the time being, and no one can be admitted to any situation, or be allowed to adduce evidence of his fitness to fill one, who is not first named by the patron as a person *prima facie* eligible.

The step gained is, that, whereas in the good old times the Treasury or patron appointed absolutely their first favourites to vacant offices—and often appointed the ignorant, the incompetent, and the good-for-nothing—they now nominate two, three, four, or more, at their discretion, for each post, and send them to compete before the examination tables of the Civil Service Commissioners, on the principle of *detur digniori*. In a good many cases only one person is still named for each vacant office, the effect of which is that the patron maintains his ancient privilege in substance untouched, except that he must nominate one who comes up to the standard intellectually, physically, and morally fitted for the office, and cannot plant on the country the lame, the halt, the blind, and the idiotic.

Those who advocate the principle of popularising the Public Service in the full sense, are making unceasing efforts, and strong influences are constantly in operation with the object of compelling a closer approach to the system of open competition. Recently the plan has been urged, and partly acted upon, of setting up several situations at the same time, instead of each singly, and allowing all who are nominated to compete in a group. By this mode, should there be ten places to fill and thirty or more candidates, the ten best answerers at the examination would obtain the places; whereas, had each place been put up singly, some of the least informed of the whole number might have obtained admission to the service, provided that they barely reached the prescribed standard of qualification. . . .

But for the great victory already gained over the old place monopolists, and the substantial conquest secured for the people, we must look to India itself. That vast field for distinction and wealth, heretofore held as a preserve for the Directors, their relatives and friends, is now, by Act of Parliament, opened to all who have the enterprise and intelligence to seek their fortunes in it. As yet this important acquisition is not fully understood or appreciated by the community, but when it is, doubtless public employment in India will be sought with eagerness by classes that hitherto felt themselves excluded from all hope of obtaining it, and the youths of the United Kingdom will learn to regard our glorious empire of Hindostan as the most promising and profitable sphere under the Crown for the exercise of superior talent and administrative ability.

Entrance into the Civil Service of India is now free to all natural-born British subjects, within the prescribed age, 18 to 22, whose education

and moral character will bear the test of investigation, and who are
not disqualified for a residence in India by physical or constitutional
defects. There are two competitive examinations ordained for the candidates preparatory to their proceeding to their destination. Forty or
more appointments are set up periodically for distribution, and after the
first examination the successful competitors are permitted to choose,
in the order in which they stand on the prize list, the presidency in
which they desire to serve, in Bengal, Madras, or Bombay. A year's
residence in England is then prescribed to the selected candidates, to
prepare for their second examination, which is to test their proficiency
in Oriental languages, in the history and geography of India, in the
principles of jurisprudence, the elements of Hindoo and Mahommedan
law, and in political economy. Towards the expense of this, a sum of
£100 is allowed to each successful competitor, who is then commis-
sioned to proceed to India, and to take rank according to the date of
his second certificate of examination, as a civil servant of India.

When it is borne in mind what a writership in India is, and what it
leads to; what splendid immediate salary and large allowances, ranging
from £500 to £8,000 a year; what rapid promotion, what distinguished
positions, and what liberal and early retiring pensions are attached to it,
the East India Civil Service will be readily acknowledged to be a
career full of promise, and presenting the certainty of great advancement and wealth beyond any other employment.

Boulger, *Master-Key to Public Offices*, pp. 1–4

246. The advantages of becoming a civil servant, 1866

The Civil Service is quiet, secure, not laborious; it has advantages in
sickness and old age, for holidays, for freedom from anxiety, and the
advantage of a net instead of a gross income. The social position of a
Government clerk is superior to that of a clerk at the same salary in a
commercial undertaking. The average pay is higher than the average
pay in the Army or in the Church. On the whole, the young man or
his friends who first understand the service and then distinctly select it,
make, I should suppose, a very wise selection. The Civil Servant can
have many physical and mental pleasures after his work is done, and
the monotony of daily routine, and the slow increase of salary need
not fall heavily upon him. But a man who is ambitious of money or a
career will commonly be disappointed, though in a few instances he

may win his way. The great danger of the Civil Service to a few candidates, and to more parents, is the commencing salary. The difference is great between the receipt and the disbursement of 100 *l.* or more annually for some years, and the enticing bait cannot be rejected prudently by average men. On the other hand, those who are confident in their strength, or who love some other work for its own sake, should try for a higher place. To such, if they have the means, the reward is worth the risk; and whether they would acquire excellence in art or distinguish themselves in the Army or the Navy, at the Bar or in Commercial Pursuits, energetic industry is never lost, and often leads them to their end. So much for the few; and now let me point out to intending candidates that the variety of choice between different offices is very considerable....Promotion is regulated mainly by seniority, and a candidate can form an opinion as to his prospects, by observing the sums attainable and the number of clerks in each class. The number of situations in the nature of clerkships to which candidates were nominated in the year 1864 is stated in the 10th Report of the Civil Service Commissioners to have been 768,[1] a number nearly equal to the number of gentlemen who entered the Army and Navy, or the ranks of Law, Medicine, or the Church.[2]

Handbook to Government Situations, pp. x–xi

247. Civil service reform recommended by a Cabinet committee, 29 June 1869

1. The body of the Civil Service to consist of four divisions, viz.:
    (*a*) First class, permanent.
    (*b*) Second class, permanent.
    (*c*) Writers, non-permanent.
    (*d*) Attendants, etc., non-permanent.

[1] The corresponding number of inferior situations, such as out-door officer in Her Majesty's Customs, letter carrier, warder, matron, &c., was 1,931.
[2] Average annual entries in the United Kingdom.

Barristers, attorneys, &c.	750
Physicians, surgeons, &c.	650
Church of England	1000
Army and Navy	800
Total	3200
Average of four professions	800

These numbers are intended as an approximate estimate only; information sufficient for a precise statement being not readily (if at all) obtainable.

2. The principle of open competition to be applied to the first and second classes.

3. Members of the second class to rise by promotion within that class, but not to be promoted into the first class.

4. First class. The number to be limited. A high standard of examination on first appointment and an increase to be made to the present minimum of salary.

5. Second class. Commercial education examination, not to include special subjects which should be acquired, when necessary, after admission.

6. Periodical examinations to be held by the Civil Service Commissioners to whom application will be made by the heads of departments on the occurrence of vacancies.

7. Writers. Not to be exclusively confined to copying, but may be employed on work of confidence, if requiring nothing more than care and attention.

No arbitrary limit of age; examination in handwriting, writing from dictation and elementary arithmetic, to be conducted under the directions of the department. Payment at the rate of 6s. 6d. a day for six days during the first year, rising afterwards by threepence a day each year to a maximum of 9s. 6d. a day.

Advancement to higher rates of pay to be dependent on efficiency and good conduct.

Writers may be discharged at a month's notice if service has been less than a year; if more than a year's service, three months' notice.

Writers not entitled to superannuation, but after five years' service to receive, on retirement, one month's pay for each whole year's service, but not to exceed on the whole a 12 months' pay.

8. Attendants. This class to be taken from retired soldiers, sailors or policemen of good character and health, certified by the War Office, Admiralty or Chief Commissioner as the case may be; to be examined by the department in reading, writing and the first two rules of arithmetic; not to be entitled to pension and may be dismissed on short notice. Registers of eligible men to be kept at the War Office, Admiralty, etc.

9. No present alteration to be made in the constitution of the Civil Service Commission. Hughes, *Public Administration*, XXXIII, 304–5

248. Order in Council of 4 June 1870 introducing open competition

Whereas it is expedient to continue, with certain amendments, the existing provision for testing, according to fixed rules, the qualifications of persons who may, from time to time, be proposed to be appointed, either permanently or temporarily, to any situation or employment in any of Her Majesty's Civil Establishments, except as hereinafter mentioned....

III. No person shall be appointed to any office or employment in any of Her Majesty's Civil Establishments until he shall be reported by the...Commissioners to have satisfied them—

1st. That he is within the limits of age prescribed for the situation or employment to which he desires to be admitted;

2nd. That he is free from any physical defect or disease which would be likely to interfere with the proper discharge of his duties;

3rd. That his character is such as to qualify him for such situation or employment; and

4th. That he possesses the requisite knowledge and ability to enter on the discharge of his official duties.

IV. The rules applicable to each Department, under each of the above heads, shall be settled, subject to the approval of the Commissioners of Her Majesty's Treasury, by the said Civil Service Commissioners and the chief Authorities of the Department.

V. Except as hereinafter is excepted, all appointments which it may be necessary to make, after the 31st day of August next, to any of the situations included, or to be included, in Schedule A to this Order annexed, shall be made by means of competitive examinations, according to regulations to be from time to time framed by the said Civil Service Commissioners, and approved by the Commissioners of Her Majesty's Treasury, open to all persons (of the requisite age, health, character, and other qualifications prescribed in the said regulations) who may be desirous of attending the same, subject to the payment of such fees as the said Civil Service Commissioners, with the consent of the said Commissioners of Her Majesty's Treasury, may from time to time require; such examinations to be held at such periods, and for such situations, or groups of situations, in the same or different Departments, as the said Civil Service Commissioners, with the approval of the said Commissioners of Her Majesty's Treasury, shall from time to time determine, and to have reference either to the vacancies existing at the time of the examinations respectively, or to the number which may be estimated to occur within any period, not exceeding six months after the commencement of the examinations, as the said Civil Service Commissioners, after consultation with the chief authorities of the various Departments, and with the approval of the said Commissioners of Her Majesty's Treasury, may deem expedient.

VI. After the candidate, reported as aforesaid by the Commissioners, has been appointed to an office or employment, he shall enter on a period of probation. . . . *London Gazette*, 7 June 1870

249. Treasury minute of 12 November 1884 on civil servants as parliamentary candidates

My Lords find that, as a matter of fact, the usage of the Public Deparments has been for a Civil Servant, seeking a seat in the House of Commons, to resign his office as soon as he issues his address to the electors, or in any other manner announces himself as a candidate.

My Lords consider that this usage should be binding, and They declare it to be so in the Treasury, and in all other Departments which depend upon the Treasury for the regulation of their discipline.

[C. 4229] H.C. (1884–85) XLV, 171–3

250. The recruitment of staffs for labour exchanges, 1909–11

[From the Majority Report of the MacDonnell Commission, 1914]

In recent years several important Acts of Parliament, (the Old Age Pension Act, the Labour Exchanges Act, and the National Health Insurance Act) have been passed requiring the creation of new, or the extension of existing official establishments.

These Acts called for the immediate services of large staffs of officials often with qualifications and experience somewhat differing from those commonly required in officers of the Civil Service, and tested by the Civil Service entrance examinations.

In the case of the Labour Exchanges, a system of selection was adopted which marks a new departure in Civil Service procedure. This new system may, perhaps, be most conveniently described by the following quotations from the 55th and 56th Reports of the Civil Service Commissioners:—

'At the end of 1909 and the beginning of 1910 the First Commissioner, by the invitation of the President of the Board of Trade, acted as Chairman of two Committees. The first Committee's. . .duties were to recommend to the President of the Board of Trade persons suitable to be Managers of Labour Exchanges. An immense number of applications were received, which were examined in the first instance by the officers of the Board of Trade under instructions from the Committee. The Committee themselves examined the credentials of some 800 candidates, and selected more than 200 as apparently possessing the requisite experience and qualifications. These candidates were interviewed and examined by the Committee. On the results of these interviews which occupied nine whole days, the Committee recommended rather more than 100 to the President of the Board of Trade as best fitted for the posts in question.

'The second Committee's duties were to recommend suitable women candidates for superior posts under the Labour Exchanges. A large number of applications were received; procedure similar to that of the other Committee was adopted; more than 30 candidates were interviewed; and 12 were recommended to the President as most fit for the duties of the posts.

'All these posts are at present temporary and unpensionable, and are included in Schedule B of the Order in Council of 10th January 1910. They are not, therefore, under the jurisdiction of our Board, but should any of the candidates recommended by either of the Committees come up hereafter before us for certificates of qualification for the posts for which they were recommended, we shall have no difficulty, after learning that they have discharged their duties to the satisfaction of the Board of Trade, in certifying from personal knowledge that they are qualified in point of experience and ability for these posts. This procedure constitutes a new precedent; and in view of the number of posts that are being created, for which special experience and capacity in dealing with practical affairs are of more importance than attainments such as can be tested by open or limited competition, we regard with satisfaction the apparent success of this novel method of selection. It is, in fact, a new kind of open competition, in which tests are applied such as men of business use in the choice of their employees.'

'During the year [1911] the Civil Service Commissioners, at the request of the Board of Trade, appointed representatives to preside at a series of interviews held by Selection Committees in various districts for the purpose of choosing the necessary subordinate staff in view of the immediate demands for the increase in the number of Exchanges. These Committees consisted of the representative of the Commissioners, as chairman, assisted by two more representatives of the Labour Exchange Department of the Board of Trade acting as assessors. Each applicant recommended by the Board of Trade, or whose credentials appeared promising to the Commissioners, was personally interviewed, and, whilst the assessors advised on matters of technical knowledge and local conditions, the Commissioners accept the sole responsibility for the selection of the most suitable applicants from amongst those who appear before their representatives. The credentials of some 847 applicants were submitted for preliminary scrutiny, and from these the Commissioners selected about 347 for interview. The interviews were held during September, November and December in the East Midlands, West Midlands, Yorkshire and Wales, and occupied altogether 15 days, two Committees occasionally sitting simultaneously. On the results of these interviews the Commissioners recommended about 114 applicants for immediate appointment, whilst a further 82 were reported as qualified.'

This system of appointment has recently been adopted to some extent for the purpose of recruiting officials under the National Health Insurance Act. It claims—and herein lies its essential character—to determine the comparative fitness of candidates by an appraisement, through personal interview, supplemented by testimonials, of their qualities of character and intelligence. Examination is often dispensed with, or, if used at all, is used only as a qualifying test. Substantially the system of appointment is selection by patronage, the abuses of patronage being, it is claimed, precluded by the substitution of a Board or Committee of Selection for the 'Patron.' It makes a new departure in recruitment for the Civil Service, which calls for the most careful examination.

[Cd. 7338], pp. 22–3. H.C. (1914) xvi, 28–9

251. The civil service still organised on departmental lines, 1914
[From the Minority Report of the MacDonnell Commission]

The Civil Service differs in matter of organisation from the two other great branches of the Public Service [the army and navy] in one very important particular—it is much less homogeneous than either.... The several units of which it is composed, the Public Departments, are separate and distinct from each other, with very different duties to perform, with, in consequence, great varieties of internal organisation and classification, and, as a further consequence, with great differences of prospect for those employed in them.

Before the middle of last century the several civil departments had little or nothing in common except the regulations governing the grant of superannuation. In 1855 a first step was made towards a general regulation of the conditions of *entry* into the service, and this movement was powerfully accelerated by the introduction, in 1870, of Open Competition, which of necessity entailed material modifications in the system of separate recruitment of each department. As a necessary consequence, the area of uniform law for the whole service was gradually extended to other conditions of employment—hours of attendance, holidays, sick leave, and, most important of all, to rates of pay for the rank and file of the service. In this way the detached units gradually acquired much of the appearance, and something of the character, of a unified service. But there continued to remain, and still remains, outside the region of uniform regulation, much of what most intimately affects the interests of persons in the permanent employ of the State. Differences of function in the several Departments of necessity entail differences in the proportion and in the value of situations carrying higher responsibilities and higher remuneration; and as promotion runs in the Department, and not in the Service, the organisation is in this highly important region based on the particularist and not on the unified principle. [Cd. 7338] p. 124. H.C. (1914) XVI, 130

C THE CENTRAL DEPARTMENTS

The central administration which the eighteenth century bequeathed to the nineteenth was essentially departmental in character. Each office was a law unto itself, with its own methods of recruitment, its own accounting system, and its own office routine. The role of each office was determined by tradition rather than function: the Treasury and the revenue offices formed a rabbit-warren of overlapping jurisdictions and quasi-autonomous administrative units: and the administration of military affairs was divided among a jungle of offices, three of them with cabinet ministers at their head (the Secretary of State for War and the Colonies, the Secretary at War, and the Master-General of the Ordnance), and the remainder more or less under the jurisdiction of the Commander-in-Chief. Reform began during the French wars, but generations passed before it became fully effective. Indeed, in the case of some branches of the administration, reform always lagged far behind the need for change: the War Office and the army departments continued to give trouble right up to the First World War, even though their administrative inadequacies caused a major public outcry during the Crimean and the Boer Wars; and the Irish administration throughout the century was notorious for its slackness.

Down to the 1850s the reform of old offices and the proliferation of new ones were largely unregulated by general principles of administration, beyond those of economy and common sense. The Northcote–Trevelyan report, the growth of an administrative reform lobby in the House of Commons, and Sir Charles Trevelyan's ambitious schemes of reform, all alike suggested during the fifties the need for a coherent policy of administrative reform, but little was done until the sixties. Ministers and the public were much more interested in economy and in restraining the excesses of Edwin Chadwick than in new ideas. As a consequence it was largely left to Gladstone to formulate general principles of sound administration while he was Chancellor of the Exchequer. Gladstone's main aim was to secure effective and unified control over departmental expenditure by a three-pronged attack: 1. Parliament was encouraged to vet all departmental expenditure in advance on the basis of detailed annual estimates, 2. the Treasury was constituted a watchdog over departmental staffing and expenditure, and 3. an efficient system of audit was created to enable both parliament and the Treasury to make sure that the money allocated to departments was spent only for the purposes authorised.

All the tools needed to make this policy effective were readily to hand. Thanks to Joseph Hume and other reformers, the House of Commons had become accustomed to the idea of maintaining a close scrutiny of the estimates, and the large-scale transfer of items from the sovereign's civil list to the estimates, notably in 1830, had closed the largest of the traditional loopholes. Thanks to Sir James Graham's work at the Admiralty, a model system of financial administration was available for adoption by other departments. The Treasury, regarded by Sir Charles Trevelyan as a sort of Whitehall overlord staffed by the ablest men in the service, was well on the way to becoming what he called 'a *supervising* Office, possessed of a firm hold of all the branches of business which it had to deal with' and acting as 'a powerful principle of unity' in the public service.[1] And after 1861, when the Public Accounts Committee of the House of Commons was established, there was in being an effective support for the public auditors, who were in 1866 combined in a single office under the control of the Comptroller and Auditor General. Under the new system there were now two main sets of accounts made available for parliamentary scrutiny: the departmental estimates and the appropriation accounts which showed just how the money authorised had been spent.

These developments towards uniformity of financial control were accom-

[1] Hughes, *English Historical Review*, LXIV, 55.

panied by a measure of departmental reorganisation. In 1815 there were five main types of government offices. First, there were the 'first-class offices', the Treasury, the Foreign Office, the Home Office, and the office of the Secretary of State for War and the Colonies, with the Admiralty a rung below on the official ladder. All these offices were invariably headed by a Cabinet minister and possessed a fairly similar administrative structure. Secondly, there were the lesser offices, of which the most important were the Board of Trade, the Board of Control and the Board of Ordnance, all nominally managed by boards, but in practice controlled by their minister. Thirdly, there were the revenue offices, including not only the Commissioners of Customs, the Commissioners of Excise, the Commissioners of Stamps, the Commissioners of Taxes, the Commissioners of Inland Revenue, the Mint, the various offices of the Exchequer, and what was to become the Paymaster General's office, but also the Post Office, the Commissioners of Woods, Forests and Land Revenues, and the Office of Works. These offices were managed in a great variety of ways. The Mint was headed by a minister, the Post Office by two ministers, neither of whom could sit in the Commons, and the other offices by officials or by a junior minister, the exact arrangement depending largely on chance. Fourthly, there were the offices of the Lord President of the Council, the Lord Privy Seal, the Chancellor of the Duchy of Lancaster, all of them small and unimportant. Fifthly there were the offices nominally supervised by a committee of the Privy Council, which were answerable to the Lord President. Finally there were the various military and naval departments, some headed by serving officers, others by civilians.

The process of weeding out sinecures and amalgamating offices of no great size, which had begun in the eighteenth century, gradually introduced some order into the chaos of lesser offices. The revenue offices, in particular, were severely pruned until by 1849 only the Board of Customs and Excise, the Board of Inland Revenue, the Office of Woods, the Office of Works, and the Post Office remained. But the drive to create new small offices continued and most of these took the form of official Boards or Commissions—the Poor Law Commission, the Tithe Commission, the Ecclesiastical Commission, the Emigration Commission, the Lunacy Commission, the Inclosure Commission, the Railway Commission and the General Board of Health, to name only those founded between 1832 and 1850. And because the work of the new offices was often controversial, notably in the case of Edwin Chadwick's Poor Law Commission, M.P.s began to feel dissatisfied with a form of administration which omitted to provide for what they regarded as acceptable ministerial representation in the Commons. The Treasury ministers were responsible for those offices directly dependent upon the Treasury, like the Boards of Customs and Inland Revenue, and could speak for them in the House of Commons. But the parliamentary spokesmen of other offices, such as the Poor Law Commissioners', were not directly responsible for them. Matters came to a head over the Poor Law Commissioners—'the three kings of Somerset House'—who were replaced in 1847 by a new type of Poor Law Board (252) headed by a minister who usually sat in the Cabinet. This did not prevent Parliament from agreeing to create another commission with the First Commissioner of Works as nominal head, but of which Edwin Chadwick was again the leading member, called the General Board of Health, but already the practice was obsolescent. In 1850 the Select Committee on Official Salaries gave a good deal of attention to the 'increasing necessity to have for the control even of the details in all the public departments, persons acquainted with the views and practice of the House of Commons'.[1] And gradually the principle of ministerial control was extended to cover all the major offices (254). The Board of Health was given a President like the President of the Poor Law Board in 1854, who acted as minister of health until the Board was allowed to die in 1858. Departments with anomalous constitutions like the Board of Trade (255) were remodelled, and even the Post Office had several changes of constitution, with the result that after 1866 the single Postmaster General could sit in the Commons.

There were now three acceptable forms of departmental organisation outside the Treasury and its subordinate departments: 1. an office headed by a secretary of state with a seat in the Cabinet; 2. an office headed by a working board acting under the direction of a Cabinet minister, of which the only example was long the Board of the Admiralty, and 3. an office nominally headed by a phantom board, or a Committee of the Privy Council like the Board of Trade, the reconstituted Poor Law Board, and the Committee of Council for Education, but in fact directed by a minister with the title of President or Vice-President. And within each office there was intended to be a good deal of organisational similarity, as the reorganisation of the Board of Trade in 1867 indicated (255). New offices, provided that they were too important to be attached to the Privy Council office or another department, were now fitted into one of these categories. Scotland was given a second-class secretary of state, the Secretary for Scotland, in 1885. The India Office was given a structure similar to that of the Admiralty (though not so well conceived and with a secretary of state at its head) in 1858 (253), and the War Office in 1904 (265). And phantom boards were created for the Local Government Board, which replaced the Poor Law Board in 1871, for the Board of Agriculture in 1889 and the Board of Education in 1899 (257). All these new offices were from the first subjected by statute to Treasury control of a far-reaching character, and all of them were given fairly precise terms of reference. The remaining independent official boards were gradually attached

[1] SCOS, H.C. 611, p. 7. (1850) xv, 206.

to other offices, one of the last group of them to survive being the Scottish boards in Edinburgh (258).

In all departments it was now intended that a minister answerable to parliament should be unquestioned master. But he was of course expected to rely heavily on officials. The day was past, except perhaps in the Foreign Office, when Palmerston's distinction between continental bureaucracy and British methods held good (241). Gladstone still tried to insist that junior ministers should take their share of the routine office work and be trained in official habits before being promoted to the Cabinet. But the importance of political under-secretaries was clearly on the decline in Whitehall, because ministers preferred to rely on their permanent advisers.

Within the departmental system there was relatively little room to experiment. One of the few permitted innovations was the creation of consultative committees. Such committees were rare until the very end of the nineteenth century, when a consultative committee was instituted by the statute which created the Board of Education (257). But thereafter they became increasingly common, and were specifically recommended to the Scottish Office by the MacDonnell Commission in 1914 (258). Administrative experiments were again entrusted, as in the first half of the nineteenth century, to ad hoc boards like the National Health Insurance Commissioners and the Development Commission (whose staff were not even civil servants).

252. The Poor Law Commission to be replaced by a government department, 1847

[Sir George Grey explains the government's scheme to the House of Commons, 3 May 1847]

In the year 1834, when an extensive change was made in the [poor] law, it was thought that the persons who were to be invested with the discretionary powers to be exercised by a central authority ought not to form any part of the Executive Government; that they should remain free from that popular influence which must necessarily operate in a greater or less degree upon all public men—upon all who take part in carrying on the government of the country. It was at that time thought better, also, that no political changes should be allowed to affect those who were to be entrusted with these powers. Upon these grounds, the Poor Law Commission was separated from the Executive Government.... Looking to the results of that arrangement...I think I may assert that it has not been as successful as was anticipated. The responsibility of the Poor Law Commissioners to Parliament was indirect and imperfect. The power they exercised was free from that check which is imposed upon those public functionaries who are obliged to listen in this House to charges made against them, either by Members of Parliament, or suggested by other parties; and, on the other hand, they were not enabled to explain their official conduct in this House— they were not enabled to answer their accusers face to face, and their vindication has been for this reason necessarily incomplete. They have laboured under a manifest disadvantage in this respect. When complaints as to any of the ordinary departments of the Government are made, the representative of that department is familiar with the details of the subject to which the complaint relates: he has followed them, step by step; he knows the correspondence relating to it, and remembers the reasons which led to the course that has been pursued; and, therefore, he is able to state fully the grounds of his vindication, and to offer, if not a satisfactory, at least a full and complete explanation of the conduct of the department which he represents. But, under the existing Poor Law Commission, what really happens? Complaints are made, and questions asked of the Home Secretary respecting some matter connected with the administration of the Poor Law. The Home Secretary is expected to give an answer; and his first answer almost necessarily is, that he is entirely ignorant of the matter, but that he will inquire into the facts of the case, and come down on a future day and give a reply: and, consequently, either by personal conversation, or written communication, he obtains an explanation from the Commissioners; but still without a knowledge of all the circumstances which led to the act in question; and in this state he is expected to give full information to the House on the subject. This, unquestionably, leads to great inconvenience; and the administration of the law has been, to a certain degree, prejudiced by it. The principle, therefore, of the Bill which I have to propose is...that there shall be a general superintending authority immediately responsible to Parliament. My general proposition is, that the existing powers shall be transferred to a new Board, which in its constitution will be similar to the Board of Control. The chief member of the Board will be called the President, and he will be responsible for the ordinary administration of the law. But associated with the President of the Board there will be certain Members of the Cabinet, *ex-officio* members of the Board, namely, the President of the Council, the Lord Privy Seal, one of the Secretaries of State, and the Chancellor of the Exchequer. There will also be two

Secretaries to the Board, and it is proposed that the President and one of the Secretaries shall be allowed to have seats in Parliament. I do not say that they both shall have seats in the House; but it is essential that the Board shall be directly represented in this House either by the President or Secretary.   *3 Hansard* XCII, 342–3

253. The Government of India Act, 1858

An Act for the better Government of *India* [2d *August* 1858]

Transfer of the Government of India to Her Majesty

I. The Government of the Territories now in the Possession or under the Government of the *East India* Company, and all Powers in relation to Government vested in or exercised by the said Company...shall become vested in Her Majesty, and be exercised in Her Name....

II. ...all the Territorial and other Revenues of or arising in *India*, and all Tributes and other Payments...shall be applied and disposed of for the Purposes of the Government of *India* alone, subject to the Provisions of this Act.

III. Save as herein otherwise provided, One of Her Majesty's Principal Secretaries of State shall have and perform all such or the like Powers and Duties in anywise relating to the Government or Revenues of *India*, and all such or the like Powers over all Officers appointed or continued under this Act, as might or should have been exercised or performed by the *East India* Company, or by the Court of Directors or Court of Proprietors of the said Company, either alone or by the Direction or with the Sanction or Approbation of the Commissioners for the Affairs of *India*...and also all such Powers as might have been exercised by the said Commissioners alone; and any Warrant or Writing under Her Majesty's Royal Sign Manual, which by [17 & 18 Vict. c. 77] or otherwise, is required to be countersigned by the President of the Commissioners for the Affairs of *India*, shall in lieu of being so countersigned be countersigned by One of Her Majesty's Principal Secretaries of State.

[IV. The number of Secretaries of State and Under-Secretaries capable of sitting in the House of Commons increased to four of each.] ...

VI. In case Her Majesty be pleased to appoint a Fifth Principal Secretary of State, there shall be paid out of the Revenues of *India* to such Principal Secretary of State and to his Under Secretaries respectively the like yearly Salaries as may for the Time being be paid to any other of such Secretaries of State and his Under Secretaries respectively.

Council of India

VII. For the Purposes of this Act a Council shall be established, to consist of Fifteen Members, and to be styled the Council of *India*; and henceforth the Council in *India* now bearing that Name shall be styled the Council of the Governor General of *India*.

[VIII. The East India Directors to nominate seven members of the Council and the Crown eight members, unless the Directors fail to nominate, when the Crown shall nominate all of the Councillors.]

[IX. Vacancies among Crown nominees to be filled by the Crown, other vacancies to be filled by the Council itself, by election.]

X. The major Part of the Persons to be elected by the Court of Directors, and the major Part of the Persons to be first appointed by Her Majesty after the passing of this Act to be Members of the Council, shall be Persons who shall have served or resided in *India* for Ten Years at the least, and...shall not have last left *India* more than Ten Years next preceding the Date of their Appointment; and no Person other than a Person so qualified shall be appointed or elected to fill any Vacancy in the Council unless at the Time of the Appointment or Election Nine at the least of the continuing Members of the Council be Persons qualified as aforesaid.

XI. Every Member of the Council appointed or elected under this Act shall hold his Office during good Behaviour; provided that it shall be lawful for Her Majesty to remove any such Member from his Office upon an Address of both Houses of Parliament.

XII. No Member of the Council appointed or elected under this Act shall be capable of sitting or voting in Parliament.

XIII. There shall be paid to each Member of the Council the yearly Salary of One thousand two hundred Pounds, out of the Revenues of *India*.

[XIV. Members of the Council to be entitled to retirement pensions.]...

[XVII. Present staffs to be compensated for loss of office.]...

Duties and Procedure of the Council

XIX. The Council shall, under the Direction of the Secretary of State, and subject to the Provisions of this Act, conduct the Business transacted in the United Kingdom in relation to the Government of *India* and the Correspondence with *India*, but every Order or Communication sent to *India* shall be signed by One of the Principal Secretaries of State; and, save as expressly provided by this Act, every Order in the United Kingdom in relation to the Government of *India* under this Act shall be signed by such Secretary of State; and all Despatches from Governments and Presidencies in *India*, and other Despatches from *India*, which if this Act had not been passed should have been addressed to the Court of Directors or to their Secret Committee, shall be addressed to such Secretary of State.

XX. It shall be lawful for the Secretary of State to divide the Council into Committees for the more convenient Transaction of Business, and from Time to Time to re-arrange such Committees, and to direct what Departments of the Business in relation to the Government of *India* under this Act shall be under such Committees respectively, and generally to direct the Manner in which all such Business shall be transacted.

XXI. The Secretary of State shall be the President of the Council, with Power to vote, and it shall be lawful for such Secretary of State in Council to appoint from Time to Time any Member of such Council to be Vice-President thereof, and any such Vice-President may at any Time be removed by the Secretary of State.

XXII. [The quorum at Council meetings to be five: the Secretary of State or Vice-President normally to preside:] Meetings of the Council shall be convened and held when and as the Secretary of State shall from Time to Time direct; provided that One such Meeting at least be held in every Week.

XXIII. At any Meeting of the Council at which the Secretary of State is present, if there be a Difference of Opinion on any Question other than the Question of the Election of a Member of Council, or other than any Question with regard to which a Majority of the Votes at a Meeting is herein-after declared to be necessary, the Determination of the Secretary of State shall be final; and in case of an Equality of Votes at any Meeting of the Council, the Secretary of State, if present, and in his Absence the Vice-President, or presiding Member, shall have a Casting Vote; and all Acts done at any Meeting of the Council in the Absence of the Secretary of State, except the Election of a Member of the Council, shall require the Sanction or Approval in Writing of the Secretary of State; and in case of Difference of Opinion on any Question decided at any Meeting, the Secretary of State may require that his Opinion, and the Reasons for the same, be entered in the Minutes of the Proceedings, and any Member of the Council who may have been present at the Meeting may require that his Opinion, and any Reasons for the same that he may have stated at the Meeting, be entered in like Manner.

[XXIV. Orders or communications to India not submitted to Council shall be available in Council Room for seven days before dispatch and Council Members to have the right to record dissents.]

XXV. If a Majority of the Council record...their Opinions against any Act proposed to be done, the Secretary of State shall, if he do not defer to the Opinions of the Majority, record his Reasons for acting in Opposition thereto.

[XXVI. Special provision for emergencies.]

[XXVII–XXVIII. Secret despatches and orders need not be shown to Council.]

PGS, 21 & 22 Vict., c. 106

254. The department headed by a minister regarded as the administrative norm, 1864

[Speech of Sir John Pakington, 12 May 1864]

Under our Parliamentary system, it is the object and desire of the country that at the head of each Department there should be a man whose time, attention, and mind are concentrated on it, and who has full control over it, subject only to the general check of the Cabinet and of the responsibility which he owes to Parliament. That is the system under which the great Departments of State are administered....

3 *Hansard* CLXXV, 373–4

255. The structure of the Board of Trade to be brought into line with that of other departments, 1866

[Report of a Treasury Committee of Enquiry, 27 November 1866]

The difficulties usually experienced in recommending changes in the organization of an office have, in this instance, been increased by the twofold nature of the functions performed by the Board of Trade, namely, consultative and executive, and by the double Secretariat designed to keep the working of those functions distinct, but which has led to a want of cohesion in the staff of the establishment.

Within these distinct branches we found the office broken up into separate fragmentary sub-divisions, the subjects under the control of each crossing and recrossing each other in a manner which could only have been the result of temporary arrangement....

The Board of Trade has, indeed, been for a considerable time in a transition state. Originally a Committee of the Privy Council meeting occasionally for consultative purposes, with the President and Vice-President at either end of the Board, it has gradually become a Department with mixed consultative and executive functions, the latter of which have grown to by far the larger dimensions....

Whatever may have been the original position of the Vice-President, he has now fallen into the unsatisfactory state of an irresponsible officer, of almost equal rank with the President in the Office. In the absence of the President he is paramount. When the President is present he has no duties whatever, except such as he may undertake by arrangement with the President. He may refuse to do anything, or the President may refuse to allow him to do anything; and for these reasons, perhaps, he has also to fill another office which bears no relation to the Board of Trade, namely, that of Paymaster-General without salary.

It would seem better that a Parliamentary Secretary should be substituted for the Vice-President. He would have definite duties to perform in connection with office work, and his position with regard to the President would be, as we think it should, a subordinate one. If this plan were adopted...we think that one permanent Secretary would be sufficient, and that, in the event of a vacancy occurring in the post of one of the Joint Secretaries, it had better not be filled up.

We have already pointed out that the work of the Executive Departments has so largely increased that it has outgrown the present Staff; and especially that an unfair amount of the details of business is thrown upon some of the principal officers, for which their subordinates ought to be responsible. We think, therefore, that the time has come for again subdividing the main work of the Office into distinct departments, each having at its head an officer upon whom much of the responsibility would devolve. We propose that there should be six such departments, namely:—

1. The Commercial and Miscellaneous.
2. That relating to Railways and Telegraphs.
3. That relating to Harbours, &c.
4. That relating to the subjects now comprised under the two branches of Mercantile Marine and Wreck.
5. The Statistical.
6. The Financial.

Over each of the first four of these should be placed an Assistant Secretary, having a Senior Clerk as next in rank below him.... In the case of the two remaining Departments, no change will...be required.... *HC* 47, pp. 4, 7–8. (1867) xxxix, 217, 220–1

256. Sir Reginald Welby on the Treasury, 21 November 1879

The Treasury superintends the financial administration of the United Kingdom. Two of the leading ministers of the Crown preside over it. The first is now always the Prime Minister; the second is the Chancellor of the Exchequer, who is the real Finance Minister.

The Treasury itself is rather an office of superintendence and appeal than an office of administration. It requires, therefore, a smaller staff than might be expected. The staff is composed of seven parliamentary officers, who change with a change of ministry—of twenty-five or twenty-six permanent officers who prepare business for and execute the orders of the Finance Minister—of three accountants—and of a small staff of subordinate clerks and copyists. Under the Treasury, but separate from it, are the great Departments which collect the revenues, viz., the Customs, the Inland Revenue, the Post Office, the Woods and Forests, and also various offices of expenditure, such as the Mint, the Office for the Reduction of the National Debt, the Office of the Commissioners who lend Imperial moneys for the purpose of executing public works, etc.

Most of the above-named Departments have no representative in Parliament, and the Finance Minister defends their acts and explains their measures before the House of Commons. They are in fact subordinate branches of the Treasury, and though the Treasury does not interfere in the ordinary course of their business, it receives from them on reference and decides all questions of organization and all important questions of administration for which existing regulations do not provide. Further, the Treasury is the office to which individuals of the public appeal in the event of disputes between themselves and the Departments which have been named.

It will thus be seen that the Treasury is the chief and superintendent of a body of Departments which collect the revenues and generally conduct the financial operations of the State.

The functions of the Finance Minister are fourfold:

1. He on behalf of the Executive Government, but under Parliament, is responsible for the regulation of taxation. He therefore proposes the imposition, modification, and reduction of duties.

2. He sees that the money required to meet the necessities of the State from day to day is duly provided, and for that purpose Parliament gives large powers of making temporary loans. He superintends the movement of the funds required for Imperial expenditure throughout the Empire.

3. He initiates and carries out measures affecting the Public Debt, and he is also responsible for measures affecting banking in the United Kingdom and currency throughout the Empire.

4. He controls the public expenditure.

The first three of these duties are common to him with all Finance Ministers, but the fourth, at all events in its present development, is, we believe, peculiar to the United Kingdom, and care must therefore be taken in explaining the nature of the control over expenditure which the Finance Minister exercises. The English Government appear to have learned very early the important fact that, if the Finance Minister is to establish sound finance, he must know what he is doing, and that expenditure must not be incurred behind his back. He is expected to keep a certain depth of water in the reservoir, and to do that he must have command over the sluices of outflow.

Instances of the exercise of this power of control by the Treasury may be found more than 200 years ago, and from precedent to precedent the broad principle has been built up—that no Department of the State may adopt any measure increasing or tending to increase the public expenditure, without the previous assent of the Treasury thereto.

It may be added that this principle is accepted in its logical completeness. The Military and Naval Departments cannot undertake and execute a new work, however small, without Treasury assent; a new clerk cannot be added to an establishment without Treasury assent; a gratuity cannot be given for services rendered without Treasury assent; and this rule applies in its minuteness to all the numerous Departments of the State which are charged with an expenditure now exceeding in its sum total £80,000,000 sterling a year.

If a Minister fails to comply with the rule and incurs new expenditure without Treasury assent, the Auditor-General, a parliamentary officer altogether independent of the Executive Government, would detect the irregularity, and would report such expenditure to Parliament for disallowance. Thus the supreme financial control of the Treasury over the other Departments of the State is indisputably established, and contravention of that control is inevitably detected and reported to Parliament. Of course, in practice, the Treasury allows to Departments discretion within certain limits, but usually accompanied with an obligation to report the manner in which such discretion has been exercised. The grant, however, of a discretionary power is matter of arrangement between the Treasury and the Department concerned, and can be revoked at pleasure by the former. It does not, therefore, conflict with the principle which is described as established.

It may be objected that the complete control thus reserved to the Treasury must lead to the assumption by that Department of administrative duties for which it is not qualified. In other words the Treasury must be led to encroach on the proper functions of other Departments. That, however, is not the case. It is well understood that the Treasury control is purely financial, that it is given to enable the Finance Minister to measure his outgoings against his incomings, and to cut his coat according to his cloth. He is justified in requiring his colleagues to show the reasons which lead them to propose increase of expenditure, and if not satisfied he may refuse his sanction, leaving them to appeal to the Cabinet if they cannot acquiesce. He can exercise a judgement as to which of the Departmental demands before him is most pressing, and can give it a preference; and, if the demands made upon him are too heavy for the revenue or calculated to impede the general financial policy of the country, he can force a re-consideration of them on the Minister immediately interested and on his colleagues, but he would not be sustained if he used his power of control in order to interfere in Departmental business of which the Treasury has no knowledge.

On the other hand, if the control of the Treasury be properly exercised, the Government ought always to know beforehand the cost of the policy on which it is entering, while a complete knowledge of his liabilities can alone enable the Finance Minister to show the duly balanced account which is essential to sound finance.

Bridges, *The Treasury*, pp. 222–4

257. The Board of Education Act, 1899

An Act to provide for the Establishment of a Board of Education for England and Wales, and for matters connected therewith. [9th August 1899]

Be it enacted...

1.—(1.) There shall be established a Board of Education charged with the superintendence of matters relating to education in England and Wales.

(2.) The Board shall consist of a President, and of the Lord President of the Council (unless he is appointed President of the Board), Her Majesty's Principal Secretaries of State, the First Commissioner of Her Majesty's Treasury, and the Chancellor of Her Majesty's Exchequer.

(3.) The existing Vice-President of the Committee of the Privy Council on Education shall also be a member of the Board, but on the next vacancy in his office the office shall be abolished, and the enactments mentioned in the schedule to this Act shall be repealed.

(4.) The President of the Board shall be appointed by Her Majesty, and shall hold office during Her Majesty's pleasure.

(5.) The Board shall be deemed to be established on the appointment of the President thereof.

2.—(1.) The Board of Education shall take the place of the Education Department (including the Department of Science and Art), and all enactments and documents shall be construed accordingly.

(2.) It shall be lawful for Her Majesty in Council, from time to time, by Order, to transfer to, or make exerciseable by, the Board of Education any of the powers of the Charity Commissioners or of the Board of Agriculture in matters appearing to Her Majesty to relate to education, and the Order may make such provision as appears necessary for applying to the exercise of those powers by the Board of Education the enactments relating to the Charity Commissioners or to the Board of Agriculture.

Provided that any question as to whether an endowment or any part of an endowment is held for or ought to be applied to educational purposes shall be determined by the Charity Commissioners.

3.—(1.) The Board of Education may by their officers, or, after taking the advice of the Consultative Committee herein-after mentioned, by any University or other organisation, inspect any school supplying secondary education and desiring to be so inspected, for the purpose of ascertaining the character of the teaching in the school and the nature of the provisions made for the teaching and health of the scholars, and may so inspect the school on such terms as may be fixed by the Board of Education with the consent of the Treasury: Provided that the inspection of schools established by scheme under the Welsh Inter-mediate Education Act, 1889, shall, subject to regulations made by the Treasury under section nine of that Act, be conducted as heretofore by the Central Welsh Board for Intermediate Education, and that the said Board shall be recognised as the proper organisation for the inspec-tion of any such schools as may be desirous of inspection under this section.

(2.) The council of any county or county borough may out of any money applicable for the purposes of technical education pay or contribute to the expenses of inspecting under this section any school within their county or borough.

4. It shall be lawful for Her Majesty in Council, by Order, to establish a Consultative Committee consisting, as to not less than two-thirds, of persons qualified to represent the views of Universities and other bodies interested in education, for the purpose of—

(a) framing, with the approval of the Board of Education, regulations for a register of teachers, which shall be formed and kept in manner to be provided by Order in Council: Provided that the register so formed shall contain the names of the registered teachers arranged in alphabetical order, with an entry in respect to each teacher showing the date of his registration, and giving a brief record of his qualifications and experience; and

(b) advising the Board of Education on any matter referred to the committee by the Board.

5. The draft of any Order proposed to be made under this Act shall be laid before each House of Parliament for not less than four weeks during which that House is sitting, before it is submitted to Her Majesty in Council.

6.—(1.) The Board of Education may appoint such secretaries, officers and servants as the Board may, with the sanction of the Treasury, determine.

(2.) There shall be paid, out of moneys provided by Parliament, to the President of the Board, unless he holds another salaried office, such annual salary not exceeding two thousand pounds, and to the secretaries, officers and servants of the Board such salaries or remuneration, as the Treasury may determine. . . .

8.—(1.) The office of President of the Board of Education shall not render the person holding it incapable of being elected to, or of voting in, the Commons House of Parliament. . . .

(2.) After the abolition of the office of the Vice-President of the Committee of the Privy Council on Education, one of the secretaries of the Board of Education shall not by reason of his office be incapable of being elected to or of voting in the Commons House of Parliament.

9.—(1.) This Act shall not extend to Scotland or Ireland.

(2.) This Act shall come into operation on the first day of April one thousand nine hundred. . . .   *PGS*, 62 & 63 Vict., c. 33

258. The attack on boards continues: the MacDonnell Commission on the Scottish departments, 1914

67. The Office of the Secretary for Scotland, which is situated in London, is organised and staffed on the plan of a Secretary of State's Department. . . .

68. A different system of organisation, however, prevails in several of the more important Scottish Departments. In the Scottish Departments of Agriculture, Fishery, and Local Government, as well as in those of Lunacy and Prisons, we find Boards whose members share administrative work and responsibility, a system the explanation of which is to be sought in historical circumstances.

69. We believe that the time has now come when this system of Boards should be reconsidered, for the following reasons:—

In the first place the evidence which we have received indicates that the Board system is less effective in securing responsibility for official action and advice than the system followed in the office of the Secretary for Scotland.

The Vice-President, for instance, of the Scottish Local Government Board (who is himself a member of such an administrative Board) told us that he thought it 'a great advantage to have one man responsible, because you can then fix the responsibility,' and the Secretary of the Scottish Education Department spoke of 'a thorough-going responsibility which I think a Board weakens.'

In the next place, the Board system, as it exists in Scotland, must tend to weaken in some degree the important distinction between the qualities, and the methods of selection, which are suitable for political, and those which are suitable for permanent, appointments. The Under Secretary for Scotland told us:—'Of course, the Boards are mainly patronage appointments'; and again:—

'I think that any Minister who has had a large exercise of patronage, as it exists in my own Department, would not be sorry if, at least in some of the smaller matters, his powers were taken away. He finds it a great burden upon his time, and for every person he pleases, of course, he offends others.'

Our third reason for reconsidering the Board system is that the higher business of administration is apparently sometimes performed by men who bring to it no special knowledge of the work. Members of Scottish Boards are usually appointed by patronage from outside the Civil Service; and in the early years of their service they are learning their duties. The system affords no room for that type of selected and trained permanent administrative official which is represented by the Administrative Class. 'The Edinburgh Boards,' we were told, 'take the place of the Higher Division in London offices.' In our belief, however, this arrangement is not satisfactory; and we recommend that the Scottish Departments be no longer deprived of the advantages which would come from employing officers of the Administrative Class....

70. We therefore recommend that Your Majesty's Government should take such steps as may be necessary to substitute the organisation which prevails in the Scottish Office for the Board system as the normal form of organisation in the Edinburgh Departments....

The local sympathy and knowledge which it may be contended is provided by the existing system might, we believe, continue to be secured, partly by the natural tendency of Scottish officials to seek service in Scottish offices and partly by the creation in suitable cases of such unpaid advisory Boards as that which exists in connection with the English Board of Education.   [Cd. 7338] pp. 77–9. H.C. (1914) XVI, 83–5

D THE MANAGEMENT OF THE ARMED FORCES

The principle of civilian control of the armed forces is one of the most difficult of all administrative principles to apply. It cannot be satisfactorily applied to the conduct of operations in the field; nor can it be easily applied to the recruitment and management of soldiers and sailors either in peace or war. There is therefore in all states an area in which misunderstanding, or even conflict, is endemic between, on the one hand, the civilian ministers and officials exercising overall control over the size and disposition of the armed forces, and on the other hand the higher command of the armed forces. As a result, there is a tendency for both sides to withdraw to their tents in peacetime, and to emerge ready for combat as soon as war breaks out. Then it is discovered that the financial and logistic arrangements made by the civilian side of the higher command are incomplete, and that the organisation, equipment, strategy and tactics of the military are equally out of date and inadequate. There is then in Britain an outcry in parliament and the press and distress at court; new ministers are drafted in, and commissions of enquiry are set up. Then public interest wanes and the whole cycle begins again.

Public interest in the armed forces has never been at a lower ebb than during the forty years after the great victory of Waterloo. The army was run down and neglected, its men despised (**259**), its generals old and ineffective. The navy was in process of changing reluctantly from sail to steam. There were few substantial colonial wars to serve as training exercises. Even worse, the higher command of the army was still singularly unco-ordinated. Responsibility was shared uneasily between the Secretary of State for War and the Colonies, the Commander-in-Chief, the Master-General of the Ordnance, the Secretary at War, and the Treasury. The chaos which marked the logistic arrangements for the Crimean War led to a public outcry and the demand for major administrative reforms, with the result that the Board of Ordnance and the office of Secretary at War were abolished and their functions transferred to the new Secretary of State for War. But Parliament still cared more for economy than for efficiency, so that little attention was given to the future role of the army or to clarifying the relative status of the Secretary of State and the Commander-in-Chief.

The great difficulty in the way of reform was that, except during occasional short-lived invasion scares, public opinion could not believe that Britain would ever be again engaged in a major European war. War was thought

356

to be primarily a matter of the defence of India and the Colonies, and could safely be left to the Indian army (once it had repressed the Mutiny) and to small colonial garrisons. For most purposes the effective war-makers were the India and Colonial Offices and the government of India: the War Office and the Horse Guards (the office of the Commander-in-Chief) were chiefly concerned with problems of supply and recruitment rather than with the conduct of military operations. As a result wars managed by the War Office were rarely as efficiently conducted as those (like the 1868 Abyssinian campaign) conducted by the Indian army, or even those conducted by colonial governors.

The essentially secondary role of the War Office and the Commander-in-Chief tended to lead to a fossilisation of the structure of the military high command. This tendency was confirmed by the unfortunate decision to treat the office of Commander-in-Chief as a permanent one, which did not change hands regularly like other military commands. As a result the Duke of Cambridge was entrenched in the Horse Guards for nearly forty years. Reforming Secretaries of State for War, concerned about the inefficiency of the home forces, tried vainly to change the bureaucratic routine which was the Duke of Cambridge's delight. But they made little progress. Edward Cardwell was able to make many useful reforms in the army (including the abolition of the purchase of commissions) but the structure of the high command was unchanged, and military planning was at a discount.

The mishandling of the arrangements for the relief of Gordon in Khartoum, the growing threat of Russian imperialism in the Middle East and on the frontiers of India, the partitioning of Africa, and the growing assertiveness of the self-governing colonies, combined in the mid 1880s to force upon the Salisbury government a reassessment of the whole pattern of military administration. As usual the defence of the colonies was the first preoccupation. A Colonial Defence Committee consisting of permanent officials and military experts was established in 1885, and provided the technical advice required by the various colonial conferences, the first of which met in 1887. But the government was also prepared to contemplate a substantial reform of the whole structure of the armed forces, and created in 1888 a royal commission of enquiry under Lord Hartington to make recommendations. The Hartington Commission considered the possibility of creating a ministry of defence, but decided instead to rely on army reform (262). The office of Commander-in-Chief was to be abolished and the structure of military administration modified to resemble that of the navy, which had a minister in complete control, advised by a professional board. To link the army and navy the Hartington Commission recommended the creation of an informal army and navy council.

Many of these proposals were not accepted by Campbell-Bannerman, a member of the commission, on the ground that they would amount to a concession to militarism in an essentially pacific state, so that when in 1895 as Secretary of State for War he finally succeeded in persuading the Duke of Cambridge to retire little change was made. The office of Commander-in-Chief was retained, with Lord Wolseley as its holder, and the confused command structure was little clarified by a new Order in Council setting out the Commander-in-Chief's functions. Authority continued to be divided and planning neglected. When General Buller was sent out to take command in South Africa at the beginning of the Boer War he was given no guidance by anybody (263). The Commander-in-Chief was little consulted by the government (84), and the Cabinet made it clear that it retained the right even to dismiss generals in the field (85).

The disasters which marked the early stages of the Boer War, Lord Salisbury's blunt comment that Britain was not willing to pay the price of an adequate defence system (264), and the crop of committees of enquiry after the war, all helped to create a new public attitude towards the problems of defence. Comparisons between the British and German armies, to the disadvantage of the British, became more common. The defence committee of Cabinet was reorganised in December 1902 as a mixed committee consisting of the Prime Minister, the Service Ministers, at least two soldiers and two sailors, a varying supplementary membership, and the Duke of Devonshire as chairman. It began at once a general review of defence policy and in February 1903 resolved to call itself the Committee of Imperial Defence. Two existing committees, the Colonial Defence Committee and the Joint Military and Naval Committee, became sub-committees of the new Defence Committee. But this was only a preliminary move. In 1903–4 the Balfour government sponsored a systematic review of military organisation under Lord Esher. Esher was offered the Secretaryship of State for War in 1903, but refused because he was less interested in politics and army affairs than in the general direction of defence policy. He argued that he would be far more useful as head of a small committee devoted to thinking out a new structure for the War Office.[1] He was thereupon made chairman of the War Office (Reconstruction) Committee. The Committee moved fast and in 1904 recommended a strengthening of the Defence Committee, the remodelling of the War Office on Admiralty lines, and the abolition of the office of Commander-in-Chief (265). Although there was some disposition to question the status of the Esher Committee, its proposals were accepted. The Committee of Imperial Defence was given a full-time secretary, the War Office was reorganised, and the first steps were taken towards creating a general staff. There were some who thought that the Committee of Imperial Defence would usurp the functions of the Service Ministers, and both Campbell-Bannerman and Asquith had doubts about a committee

[1] Esher, *Journals*, pp. 22–3.

whose function it was to plan for war. But the Liberal Government found it useful, and gave it a non-partisan character by inviting both A. J. Balfour and Esher to attend. As a result, the C.I.D., though ineffective in military terms, became the sole overall military planning organisation, occasionally eyed a little uneasily by the more pacific members of the Cabinet (86).

Meanwhile, under Haldane, much was being done to professionalise the army in order to make it capable of fighting a European war. As a result by 1914 there was at last in existence an efficient, though small, professional army, guided by a general staff equipped with suitable plans. Paradoxically, the naval command was not given the comprehensive overall reshaping which the army received. Fisher obtained new ships and instituted new training methods, but he was averse to the creation of a naval staff. The Board of the Admiralty, long held up to the army as a model, continued to be recruited on traditional lines from among the old-style sea-dogs, rather than from among the new young specialists who were so badly needed when war broke out. A naval war staff was, indeed, created in 1912, but its creation was little more than a political gesture. As a result, the navy, though it had good ships, entered the war less prepared for modern war than were the Germans.

259. The army unknown to the constitution, 1829

[Memorandum by the Duke of Wellington, 22 April 1829]

Let us now consider what the British army is. It is an exotic in England, unknown to the old Constitution of the country; required, or supposed to be required, only for the defence of its foreign possessions; disliked by the inhabitants, particularly by the higher orders, some of whom never allow one of their family to serve in it. Even the common people will make an exertion to find means to purchase the discharge of a relation who may have enlisted, notwithstanding the advantages of pay, &c., which a soldier enjoys, compared with the common labourer.

In the moments of the greatest distress in the country, recruits cannot be obtained for the army. Service in the army is an advantage to none. The officers and soldiers of the army are an object of dislike and suspicion to the inhabitants while serving with their regiments, and of jealousy afterwards, and they are always ill-treated.

It was the object of Mr. Windham's Act to make the army a popular service in England, by rendering service therein profitable as well as honourable, but his measures totally failed.

Then the man who enlists into the British army is, in general, the most drunken and probably the worst man of the trade or profession to which he belongs, or of the village or town in which he lives. There is not one in a hundred of them who, when enlisted, ought not to be put in the second or degraded class of any society or body into which they may be introduced; and they can be brought to be fit for what is to be called the first class only by discipline, and the precept and example of the old soldiers of the company, who, if not themselves in that same second or degraded class, deserve to be placed there for some action or other twenty times in every week.   Wellington, *Despatches*, v, 592–3

260. The constitution of the Board of the Admiralty: Order in Council, 14 January 1869

Whereas we have had under our consideration the present recognised constitution of the Board of Admiralty, the position occupied by the Controller of the Navy in regard to the Board, and the general transaction of business at the Admiralty offices.

The Board of Admiralty, as hitherto, consisted of—

The First Lord, receiving four thousand five hundred a year (4,500*l.*);

Four Naval Lords, at a salary of one thousand (1,000*l.*) a year each, with allowances and a house, or twelve hundred a year without a house; and

The Civil Lord, who receives one thousand (1,000*l.*) a year only;

The First or Parliamentary Secretary receives two thousand (2,000*l.*) a year, with allowances and a house.

The Second or Permanent Secretary receives fifteen hundred (1,500*l.*) a year, with allowances and a house.

The Secretaries have jointly charge of the Secretariat, and the First Secretary has important duties in Parliament in connexion with the Department.

We most humbly beg leave to propose to your Majesty that, with a view of simplifying and facilitating the transaction of the business of the Department, and more effectually controlling naval expenditure, the office of Controller of your Majesty's Navy should be merged into that of the Third Lord, the office of Fourth Naval Lord being dispensed with.

The Board will then be constituted as follows:—

The First Lord of the Admiralty,
The First Naval Lord,
The Third Lord and Controller,
The Junior Naval Lord, and
The Civil Lord,
with the Parliamentary Secretary and the Permanent Secretary.

The First Lord being responsible to your Majesty and to Parliament for all the business of the Admiralty, the other members of the Board should act as his assistants in the transaction of the duties, which we propose should be divided into three principal branches:—

(a.) The First Naval Lord to be responsible to the First Lord of the Admiralty for the administration of so much of the business as relates to the 'Personnel' of the Navy, and for the movement and condition of your Majesty's Fleet.

The Junior Naval Lord to assist the First Naval Lord in this division of the business.

(b.) The Controller of the Navy being, as we have proposed, the Third Lord, to be responsible to the First Lord of the Admiralty for the administration of so much of the business as relates to the 'Matériel' of your Majesty's Navy, i.e., to the building and repairing of ships, to guns, and to naval stores.

(c.) The Parliamentary Secretary to be responsible to the First Lord of the Admiralty for the 'Finance' of the Department, and the Civil Lord to act as an Assistant to the Secretary.

The Permanent Secretary should have the exclusive charge of the Secretariat, under the directions of the First Lord of the Admiralty.

The merging of the Controllership of the Navy in the office of the Third Lord, and the reduction of one of the Naval Lords, will effect a saving of two thousand five hundred pounds (2,500l.) a year; but to mark the special responsibilities of the First Naval Lord and the Third Lord, we humbly propose that their salaries should be increased by five hundred (500l.) a year each, with official residences, the other allowances to the members of the Board ceasing.

We are further of opinion that the Parliamentary Secretary should have the salary as hitherto apportioned to that appointment, but without a house or allowances.

And we beg leave most humbly to acquaint your Majesty that the Lords of the Treasury have signified their concurrence in the financial part of these arrangements. [C. 5979] pp. 24–5. H.C. (1890) XIX, 62–3

261. A Little Englander's view of the army, 1871

[Earl of Derby to Sir T. D. Acland, 2 January 1871]

The problem to solve appears to me to be the creation of a force which shall be effective for defence, and not capable of being used for other purposes. The love of fighting without object or necessity seems to be as strong as ever, in a large section of the community, and I really believe that if we had had, during the last six months, a powerful force to send abroad, the pressure on the Government to interfere on one side or the other [in the Franco-Prussian War] would have been serious.

Acland, Memoir of Sir T. D. Acland, pp. 282–3

262. The Hartington Commission on the co-ordination of defence policy, 1889

7. The first point which strikes us in the consideration of the organisation of these two great departments [the War Office and the Admiralty] is, that while in action they must be to a large extent dependent on each other, and while in some of the arrangements necessary as a preparation for war, they are absolutely dependent on the assistance of each other, little or no attempt has ever been made to establish settled and regular inter-communication or relations between them, or to secure that the establishments of one service should be determined with any reference to the requirements of the other....

10. It has been stated in evidence before us that no combined plan of operations for the defence of the Empire in any given contingency has ever been worked out or decided upon by the two Departments; that some of the questions connected with the defence of military ports abroad, and even of those at home, are still, after much departmental correspondence, in an unsettled condition; and that the best mode of garrisoning some of the distant coaling stations is also undecided....

13. To remedy this unsatisfactory and dangerous condition of affairs it has been proposed by some of the authorities whom we have consulted, that the Admiralty and the War Office should be placed in closer relation to each other. This might be effected, in the opinion of some witnesses, by the creation of a Minister of Defence who would be the supreme and responsible head of both services, the immediate control of each service being entrusted to a professional officer. Another suggestion, which has been made by one of our colleagues..., is that each

Department should be entrusted to the supreme and responsible control of a professional head, the necessary link between the two services being provided by the appointment of a civilian Minister of high rank, whose principal duty would be to settle with the heads of each service the amount of annual expenditure required, to audit their accounts, and to form a channel of communication between them on all subjects of mutual importance.

14. There appear, however, to be grave objections to each of these proposals.

15. With reference to the first, we desire to point out that neither the Admiralty nor the War Office could under this arrangement be individually and constantly represented in the Cabinet, and the interests of both services would, in our opinion, suffer by the change. Although the position of a Minister of Defence would be necessarily a very powerful one, his opinion could not be final, as it might be overruled either by the Cabinet or the Prime Minister. Under the existing system, it lies with the Cabinet or with a Cabinet Committee to maintain a just balance between the demands of the First Lord of the Admiralty and of the Secretary of State for War, and financial exigencies as represented by the Chancellor of the Exchequer. The centralization of the two departments under a single Minister, who must still be subject to Cabinet control in larger matters of policy, would merely introduce a new link in the chain of a responsibility already difficult to define. The Ministers who now undertake the duties of First Lord or Secretary of State for War rarely possess professional knowledge of the services which they are called upon to administer. The difficulty which they must find at present in mastering the details of one of these departments would be doubled in the case of a Minister of Defence made responsible for both. Moreover, the existing tendency towards centralization would be greatly aggravated, and in the result, the Minister of Defence would be involved in a complex mass of work with which no one man could adequately deal. No European power has adopted the principle of the administration of the Navy and Army under a single Minister, and in the United States, where the experiment was tried in the last century, it was definitely abandoned. The opinion of the Naval officers whom we have consulted is unanimously opposed to the proposal. Rightly or wrongly, there appears to be a conviction on the part of Naval officers that in a department where the affairs of the Army and Navy should be jointly administered, the influence of the Army would be

so much greater than that of the Navy that the interests of the latter service would be certain to suffer. On all these grounds we consider that it would be inexpedient to adopt this proposal.

16. We have very carefully considered the second proposal, which appears to us to be a bold attempt to introduce into the system the principle of placing direct responsibility upon those who are qualified by professional training and experience to bear it. But while it is possible that Parliament might be disposed to accept in principle a system intended to place such responsibility on professional Ministers who would not necessarily have seats in Parliament at all, and would certainly not be members of the House of Commons, we doubt whether this result could be practically attained. The Minister who would be in direct contact with the House of Commons would be the civilian Minister responsible for proposing the annual expenditure on the two services, and we believe that there would be a constant and inevitable tendency to hold him responsible as well for the administration of the services as for the supplies which he would demand from Parliament. We think that the position of such a Minister, in respect to the administration of the services, would gradually become more powerful than that intended by this proposal, and would ultimately approach closely to that of the Minister of Defence, which we have already discussed.

17. Under these circumstances, we consider that a remedy for the undoubted evils which have been brought under our notice must be sought in other directions, and that the proposals to combine the services under a single head or by the connecting link of a third department cannot be entertained....

19. We think, however, that means might be devised for bringing about more regular and constant communications between the Admiralty and the War Office. These might be found to some extent in departmental changes...which might provide for very constant communication and consultation between two highly placed responsible Naval and Military officers on all questions where common action and preparation on the part of the two departments is required.

20. There might be some advantage in the formation of a Naval and Military Council, which should probably be presided over by the Prime Minister, and consist of the Parliamentary Heads of the two services, and their principal professional advisers. In this Council also possibly might be included one or two officers of great reputation or experience who might not happen to hold any official appointment in

the Admiralty or War Office at the time. This Council might meet in all cases before the Estimates of the year are decided upon by the Cabinet, so that the establishments proposed for each service should be discussed from the point of view of the other, and the relative importance of any proposed expenditure might be fully considered. It might also be summoned from time to time, to consider and authoritatively decide upon unsettled questions between the two departments, or any matters of joint Naval and Military policy, which in the opinion of the heads of the two services required discussion and decision. It would be essential to the usefulness of such a Council and to the interests of the country that the proceedings and decisions should be duly recorded, instances having occurred in which Cabinet decisions have been differently understood by the two departments, and have become practically a dead letter.   [C. 5979] pp. vi–viii. H.C. (1890) xix, 6–8

263. The War Office sends a general to South Africa, 1899

[Lord Esher to King Edward VII on the proceedings of the War Commission, 18 February 1903]

Lord Esher presents his humble duty and begs to say that Sir Redvers Buller's evidence was given to-day, from the appointment of that officer to the command in S. Africa until the day previous to the attack on Colenso.

The most noticeable points elicited were, first, the disregard of their chosen commander's request to prepare for war by the Government, and secondly, the remarkable absence of all confidential communication between Sir Redvers and the Ministers before he left England.

No business firm, or indeed any private person, would be likely to send an agent abroad, upon a mission fraught with difficulty, without holding conferences upon the subject-matter of the mission. Yet General Buller attended no meeting of the Cabinet; nor any meeting of the Defence Committee. He never attended an 'Army Board' at the War Office. He had no interview with the Prime Minister nor with the Colonial Secretary; and only saw Lord Lansdowne infrequently.

Esher, *Journals*, I, 378

264. Salisbury on the imperfections of the British Constitution as an instrument of war, 30 January 1900[1]

I do not believe in the perfection of the British Constitution as an instrument of war. As an instrument of peace it has not yet met its match, but for purposes of war there is more to be said. If you look back over the present century you will see there have been four occasions on which the British Government has engaged in war. On each occasion the opening of these wars was not prosperous, and on each occasion the Government of the day and the officers in command were assailed with the utmost virulence of popular abuse. These were the Walcheren expedition, the Peninsular War, the Crimean War, and now the South African War. In all those cases at first—in the case of Walcheren not only at first—there were lamentable losses. In all those cases there was the fiercest denunciation of the Government of the day and of the generals who had charge of the operations. Did I hear the noble Earl deny that?

The EARL of KIMBERLEY: No, I said there was a great deal of truth in it.

The MARQUESS of SALISBURY: I do not know whether the noble Earl has read the life of the Duke of Wellington, recently published, written by Sir Herbert Maxwell—a most admirable book.

The EARL of KIMBERLEY: Yes.

The MARQUESS of SALISBURY: Then the noble Earl will have noticed that even so dignified, sedate, sober, and far-seeing a body as the Common Council of the City of London denounced the rashness and inexperience of the Duke of Wellington, and exhorted the Government to recall him. In the case of Walcheren the miscarriage was too great to allow for any mistake that was made, and nobody interfered on behalf of Lord Chatham and Sir Richard Strachan. In the Crimean war, as the noble earl will himself remember, a fierce attack was made on the unfortunate Duke of Newcastle, who was a very able and conscientious man, and not in the least degree guilty of the things laid to his charge, but the fury of popular indignation was so great that he made way before it. I think he made a great mistake in doing so, because before a couple of years had passed away a complete reaction set in. But the moral I wish to draw from this uniformity of experience is that it is not the extraordinary folly or feebleness of particular Ministers

---

[1] Salisbury expressed similar views to Queen Victoria in 1886: see *LQV*, 3rd ser. I, 193–5.

or generals with which you have to deal, which is the sole cause of your reverses. There must be something else. We cannot have been so unlucky as to have fought four times and to have lighted upon the most incompetent and worthless Ministers that the world has ever produced. It is evident there is something in your machinery that is wrong, and that leads me to accept with a very doubting mind the glowing eulogism which the noble Earl passed upon the fighting qualities of the British Constitution. I am inclined to doubt these qualities, and I will recommend to the meditation of the noble Lord these considerations.

The art of war has been studied on the continent of Europe with a thoroughness and self-devotion that no other science has commanded, and at the end we find ourselves surrounded by five great military Powers, and yet on matters of vital importance we pursue a policy wholly different from those military Powers. Do not understand for a moment that I am guilty of such profanity as to blame the British Constitution. I am not. I am pointing out that in this matter we enjoy splendid isolation. Of course, first and foremost stands conscription, and no one imagines, even among the youngest of us, that he will ever live to see conscription adopted in this country. Then comes the employment as experts of persons sitting in Parliament exercising power over the military administration, who are named by the Government, but who have not to obtain the approval of the electors and the constituencies. It is an important and very difficult question. Then there is the big question of promotion by seniority, a delicate subject; but I doubt if you will find that promotion by seniority prevails in any of the great armies of Europe to the extent it prevails here. Then there is that matter of secret service.... There is no other country which is content to protect itself with so slight a supply of funds as our own; and last of all I feel I am laying my hand on the sacred feature of the Constitution when I say there is the Treasury. At the present time I feel assured that the powers of the Treasury have been administered with the greatest judgment, and the greatest consideration, and do not imagine for a moment that I support the idiotic attacks which have been made on the present Chancellor of the Exchequer. He is a Minister who has filled the office with the greatest consideration to the powers of the Treasury; but I say that the exercise of its powers in governing every department of the Government is not for the public benefit. The Treasury has obtained a position in regard to the rest of the departments of the Government that the House of Commons obtained in the time of the Stuart dynasty. It has the power of the purse, and by exercising the power of the purse it claims a voice in all decisions of administrative authority and policy. I think that much delay and many doubtful resolutions have been the result of the peculiar position which, through many generations, the Treasury has occupied.

4 *Hansard* LXXVIII, 30–2

265. The Esher Committee on War Office reorganisation, 1904

[*Defence Committee*]

To the Defence Committee, acting as the co-ordinating head of all the departments concerned in the conduct of, and in the preparations for war, we look to fulfil the main functions of a General Staff, as they are now understood all over the civilised world by Statesmen who have considered the necessities and conditions of Empire.

The scientific study of Imperial resources, the co-ordination of the ever-varying facts upon which Imperial rule rests, the calculation of forces required, and the broad plans necessary to sustain the burden of Empire, have, until quite recently, found no place in our system of government.

Although the Defence Committee of the Cabinet germinated a few years back, work has only recently become a reality. While fully appreciating the incalculable value of this achievement, we cannot conceal from ourselves that the guarantees for, first, the permanent and continuous labours of the Committee, and, second, their adequate discharge, are not at present secured.

In considering the constitution of the Defence Committee itself, we are fully alive to the vital necessity for having as its invariable President the Prime Minister of the day. Under our political institutions, based on the authority of a Parliament with traditions like ours, no body of experts, however highly trained and qualified, would carry sufficient weight and authority to give practical effect to their conclusions, unless the Prime Minister, in whom governing power is vested, were present at their deliberations, and personally committed to their policy.

If, therefore, and we assume this to be an essential condition, the Prime Minister is to preside over the Defence Committee, we fully realise the importance of leaving to him absolute discretion in the selection and variation of its Members; but we would venture to suggest the vital importance of giving to that institution, yet in its infancy, as powerful a sanction for continuity and permanence as may be consistent with the retention, by the Prime Minister, of perfect freedom of action in regard to its component parts....

We should...fail in our duty, were we not clearly to define the urgent and vital importance of providing, in some shape or form, a permanent Institution, charged with the duties and responsibilities of calling the attention of the Prime Minister of the day to strategic problems of defence, which are never constant, to the actual condition of our armaments, and to the relation which the latter should bear to the former if the King's Dominions are to remain secure.

For this reason we have suggested the creation of a 'Department,' to use a well-understood term, for the Defence Committee, containing elements of a permanent character, following the well-tried and established precedents of British administration, located in close proximity to the residence of the Prime Minister, and under his exclusive control. We have not proposed that this Department shall be organised on a lavish scale. At present the material of which to compose it is scanty, but while we believe that the growth of all permanently useful institutions must necessarily be slow, we confidently look forward to a time, if our proposal is adopted, when Great Britain shall possess a scientific body of expert opinion, highly trained to deal with all the problems of war, suitable to her Imperial requirements, and necessary for her safety....

The permanent nucleus of the Defence Committee should consist of:—

I. A Permanent Secretary who should be appointed for five years renewable at pleasure.

II. Under this official, two naval officers, selected by the Admiralty, two military officers chosen by the War Office, and two Indian officers, nominated by the Viceroy, with, if possible, one or more representatives of the Colonies. These officers should not be of high rank, and the duration of their appointment should be limited to two years.

The duties of the permanent nucleus of the Defence Committee would be:—

A. To consider all questions of Imperial Defence from the point of view of the Navy, the Military Forces, India and the Colonies.

B. To obtain and collate information from the Admiralty, War Office, India Office, Colonial Office, and other departments of State.

C. To prepare any documents required by the Prime Minister and the Defence Committee, anticipating their needs as far as possible.

D. To furnish such advice as the Committee may ask for in regard to Defence questions involving more than one Department of State.

E. To keep adequate records for the use of the Cabinet of the day and of its successors.

We consider that the functions now vested in the Joint Naval and Military Committee for Defence, and in the Colonial Defence Committee, should be transferred to the Defence Committee. These two Committees should, therefore, be dissolved, as soon as the permanent office which it is proposed to attach to the Defence Committee can be formed. [Cd. 1932] pp. 1–2, 4–5, H.C. (1904) VIII, 103–4, 106–7

[*War Office Reorganisation*]

We have been directed to make recommendations for the reconstitution of the War Office. Our task, as we understand it, is specially difficult from the fact that for many years this Department of State has been administered from the point of view of peace. It is necessary to make a complete breach with the past, and to endeavour to reconstitute the War Office with a single eye to the effective training and preparation of the Military Forces of the Crown for war.... The object should be to secure for the British Empire, with the least possible derangement of existing machinery, the immense advantages which the General Staff has conferred upon Germany....

We are directed, by the terms of our Reference, to take the Admiralty system of higher administration as the basis of our action, and we are convinced that, while there may be imperfections in the working of that system, it is absolutely sound in principle. It has been handed down without material change from the period of great naval wars. It may be said to have been founded on the proved requirements of war, and although it has not in recent times been put to the supreme test, it has smoothly and successfully met new demands as they have arisen, including an enormous increase of *personnel* and *matériel*. It conforms closely to the arrangements under which the largest private industries are conducted. Finally, it has retained the confidence of the Navy and of the nation.

This cannot be said of the War Office, where great changes have been frequent, and stability of administration has never been attained. ...no public department has been so frequently examined or so scathingly criticized by Commissions and Committees as the War Office....

We consider that, as a first step in the reconstruction of the War

Office, the position of the Secretary of State should be placed on precisely the same footing as that of the First Lord of the Admiralty, and that all submissions to the Crown in regard to military questions should be made by him alone.

The next step is the constitution of a Board, or as we prefer to call it, an 'Army Council,' following the general principles which obtain at the Admiralty.

The Council should consist of seven members—four military and three civil—with the Permanent Under-Secretary as Secretary....

Speaking broadly, the distribution of duties must be as follows:—

A. *Secretary of State.*

B. *1st Military Member.*[1]—Military Policy in all its branches. War Staff duties, Intelligence, Mobilization, Plans of Operations, Training, Military History, Higher Education, War Regulations.

C. *2nd Military Member.*—Recruiting, Pay, Discipline, Rewards, Peace Regulations.

D. *3rd Military Member.*—Supply, Clothing, Remounts, Transport.

E. *4th Military Member.*—Armaments and Fortifications.

F. *Civil Member.*—The Parliamentary Under-Secretary of State.—Civil Business other than Finance.

G. *Civil Member.*—The Financial Secretary.—Finance, Audit, Accounting, Estimates.

Or, summarizing, the grouping would be:—

A.—Minister responsible to the Crown and to Parliament.

B.—Operations of War.

C.—Personnel.

D.—Supply.

E.—Armament.

F.—Civil Business.

G.—Finance....

For the exercise of effective action, the sphere of the Commander-in-Chief, as at present understood, is far too wide; while for administrative purposes, he may be sometimes not the most efficient, and sometimes too fine an instrument. In order to secure effective control, a Commander should be in constant touch with the units of his command. Owing to the wide extent of the King's Dominions, this necessary condition cannot be fulfilled by a Commander-in-Chief, and even in Germany—a homogeneous empire—executive command, in time of

---

[1] Renamed Chief of the Imperial General Staff by Order in Council, 22 November 1909.

peace, has been completely decentralized. We, therefore, consider that it is imperative to abolish the Office of Commander-in-Chief, which was only revived as late as 1887, and we urge the divorce of administration from executive command, and the decentralization of the latter.

[Cd. 1932] pp. 3, 7–10. H.C. (1904) VIII, 105, 109–13

E LOCAL SELF-GOVERNMENT

The virtues of local self-government had become part of the orthodox Liberal creed by the 1850s. Originating in the Radical campaigns for the displacement of the unreformed borough corporations by popularly elected municipalities and of Colonial Office rule by locally elected legislatures in Canada, Australia, and New Zealand, it was nourished by the researches of antiquarians interested in the 'free' Teutonic communities of the remote past, and given a widespread popularity by the campaign against Edwin Chadwick's centralising Poor Law Commission and General Board of Health. In the works of the lawyer-antiquarian Joshua Toulmin Smith, belief in local self-government was worked up into a system (267). And by John Stuart Mill it was incorporated into the Millite creed expounded in the *Principles of Political Economy*, *On Liberty* and *Representative Government* (269). Liberal ministers did their best to prevent their officials from interfering in local affairs (271). But it was 1894 before the Liberals at last extended the benefits of local self-government to every community in England under the astonishingly far-reaching Local Government Act of that year, which provided elected local authorities for every village of over 300 people and for some villages of even smaller size (276).

Liberal enthusiasm for local self-government was fed from a variety of non-intellectual sources. First there was the desire to give the ratepayers a greater say in the management of local affairs and in the levying of the rates, which were the only major source of local revenue. This was clearly the main factor in fixing the complicated property franchise for Poor Law elections under the Poor Law Amendment Act of 1834, and in the allocation to local authorities of the chief responsibility for public works of all sorts. Secondly, there was the desire to give the Liberals a predominant say in the municipalities, which they for the most part secured by way of the Municipal Corporations Act of 1835. Thirdly, there was the rapid growth of local patriotism, particularly in the north of England, where the great town halls of the nineteenth century bear witness to a widespread desire to create a new corporate life of an almost Venetian splendour. Fourthly, there was the realisation that in party terms it was dangerous to offend either those who shared Herbert Spencer's fear of over-legislation[1] or those who endorsed

[1] Spencer, *Over-Legislation* (1854).

David Urquhart's cloudy rhetoric (266), since public opinion was decisively against the creation of what was generally thought of as a French-style centralising bureaucracy. Indeed, the Liberals deliberately lay low when the Conservative C.B. Adderley decided to abolish the General Board of Health in 1858, with the result that there was virtually no parliamentary opposition to its abolition (268).

In retrospect the extent of local self-government during the nineteenth century appears stupefying. As a matter of principle Whitehall thrust every type of administration on to elected local bodies. The poor law, public health, education, river management, and a whole host of other matters were delegated to specially elected ad hoc authorities. And slowly—too slowly for the Radicals—a comprehensive system of general-purpose authorities was established, which in the twentieth century gradually displaced the ad hoc authorities, beginning with the school boards which were wound up in 1902. The boroughs were given a new lease of life in 1835, but self-government in the rural districts was not a reality until the creation of county councils in 1888 and of parish and district councils in 1894. Until then the justices of the peace meeting at Petty and Quarter Sessions and acting as ex officio members of the boards of guardians for poor law unions managed the general business of the counties as they had done for centuries.

At county level even the coming of the county councils made little difference in many parts of Britain to the way in which county business was done. The new county councils attracted much the same type of people— resident country gentlemen, clergymen, professional men, and a sprinkling of farmers and independent businessmen—as the old quarter sessions. Brought up to a tradition of local service such men became J.P.s or councillors almost as of right, and bore the brunt of the increasing demands on local voluntary service both in the magistrates' courts and in the county committees, which looked after the highways and bridges, the police, and finance. Individual country gentlemen were able throughout the century to win a reputation for themselves as local administrators and reformers, and to carry with them into parliament a reputation for first-hand knowledge of local problems. Though the aristocracy was under constant fire from radical propagandists the country gentlemen encountered surprisingly little opposition outside Wales and parts of East Anglia. There were sporadic agitations for change but they came chiefly from aggrieved ratepayers whose views were shared by the country gentlemen themselves. The creation of the county councils involved surprisingly little controversy—it was carried by a Conservative government with Radical backing largely to please Joseph Chamberlain. The constitution of the new councils was copied from the boroughs—down to the institution of county aldermen, though there was to be a chairman and not a mayor. And the main innovation, the creation of the London County

Council, which at once became the leading local authority in the country, had little connection with rural problems. Indeed, it was largely envisaged as a democratic and more powerful alternative to the discredited Metropolitan Board of Works created in 1855, to which London owes the Thames Embankment.

The worst feature of the Local Government Act of 1888 was the failure to cut down the number of the counties (instead, several counties were divided) and to keep to a minimum the number of boroughs allowed to opt out of the counties altogether. As a result the new system was very unbalanced, with big counties like London and Lancashire at one end of the scale and little counties and county boroughs like Rutland, the Isle of Ely and Canterbury at the other. Ritchie, the minister responsible for the Bill, had not intended this to happen, but like so many other local government reformers he was defeated by the local government lobby in parliament.

Below the level of the counties there was still a gap after 1888. The boroughs had been reconstructed by the Municipal Corporations Act of 1835, on the basis of a highly biased set of reports produced by commissions of enquiry, or by the Municipal Corporations Act of 1882 which dealt with all the remaining unreformed corporations except the City of London. New boroughs had also been created by charter in considerable numbers after 1835, using the 1835 Act as a constitutional framework. Under the 1835 Act all boroughs had a common structure consisting of a mayor, aldermen elected by the council for six years, and councillors elected by the ratepaying householders for three years. But there still remained many small towns governed by commissioners or sanitary authorities. These were for the most part replaced in 1894 by urban district councils and rural district councils, and at the same time democracy was carried down to village level by the abolition of the ancient civil powers of the churchwardens and vestries. Finally in 1900 a set of metropolitan boroughs was created to provide a second administrative tier within the county of London. The City of London remained unreformed throughout.

The pioneers in local government were inevitably the big boroughs and the London County Council, because they had big problems to deal with and correspondingly big resources. Relying largely on local acts, towns such as Liverpool, Manchester, and Birmingham could afford to experiment and to pay skilled and highly paid officers. Each town had its own special interests, but inevitably the one town which developed a municipal programme, Birmingham under Joseph Chamberlain (270), attracted most of the public attention until the creation of the L.C.C. led to a spate of municipal programmes for the metropolis (273). By the end of the nineteenth century a big authority was expected to have its own gasworks, its own waterworks, its own tramways, its own housing estates, its own electricity supply plant, and other public utilities. And working-class councillors had come to look to the local authorities to set standards as employers which would serve as yard-sticks to private enterprise.

Until the Local Government Act of 1894 established a simple electoral system for boards of guardians, parish councils and district councils, local government was a field for electoral experiments (see p. 260). It was also one of the focuses of party political activity. The unreformed corporations, partly because many of them had the right to choose M.P.s, were actively involved in party politics. And in the first elections for the reformed councils after 1835 contests on party lines were usual. Thereafter, the councils reflected the dominant political climate of their town, being solidly Liberal in most of the towns in the north, solidly Conservative in some of the older boroughs, and hotly contested where the balance of power was fairly evenly divided. Occasionally a Ratepayers' Association broke the calm of the 'one-party' councils, but for the most part they were quiescent until municipal reform became fashionable in the 1870s. By then the party managers had begun to argue that municipal elections and elections for boards of guardians should always be fought on party lines in order to keep the local party machine in good working order. And the same argument was extended to the new county councils, this time backed by the party leaders. The L.C.C., in parti-cular, was too important for any party to neglect, and the two London municipal parties (Progressive = Liberal, and Municipal = Conservative) quickly obtained official party backing. Lord Salisbury called for Conser-vative participation in L.C.C. elections and, by implication, in other elections as well. And the party zealots did their best to fight even parish councils on party lines. But, in fact, though the boroughs continued to be fought on party lines, most county council, district council, and parish council elec-tions were not so fought. A large proportion of candidates preferred to be called Independents, especially where their seats were uncontested as they were in most of the rural districts, so that party gains and losses were re-ported in terms of Unionist, Liberal, Labour or Independent victories.

Scottish local government went through much the same process of reform as its English counterpart. The Scottish burghs were reformed in 1833, two years before the English boroughs. The Scots were given an English-style Poor Law in 1845, school boards in 1872, county councils in 1889, and parish councils (but no district councils) in 1894. But the Scottish system retained peculiarities of its own. The Convention of Royal Burghs continued after 1833 to be the dominant force in municipal affairs. The Scots burghs retained their provosts and bailies—councillors who acted as police court magistrates and the licensing authority—and were not required to have mayors and aldermen. Municipal regulation of building and social life was stricter in the royal burghs than in England. The Commissioners of Supply in the counties (persons with landed property worth £100 a year) occupied the place of quarter sessions in England until 1889, when they were replaced by county councils, again without aldermen. But in spite of these differences and the fact that Scottish local government law was quite different from that of England, Scottish local government by 1900 was markedly more similar to English local government than it had been in 1832.

LOCAL SELF-GOVERNMENT VERSUS CENTRALISATION

266. David Urquhart on centralisation, 1848

[Speech on the Public Health Bill, 5 May 1848]

It was because past Parliaments had given enormous power to the Government, that he, as a Member of a new Parliament, had determined to use every means in his power, not merely to prevent any increase to that power, but to reduce the amount of it which the Government at present enjoyed. The last election had brought out the feeling of the people of this country strongly against the principle of centralisation.... Centralisation dissolved the bonds of society...centralisation was usurpation. It was a usurpation by the Government of the powers of local bodies, and a destruction by the general Executive of local rights. The people of England loved and possessed municipal government, and they would not suffer themselves to be jockeyed out of it...centralisation...was undisguised corruption; and as a proof that it was so, he would adduce as an instance the late Government of France, the fate of which should be a warning to the would-be centralisers in this country.... He resisted this Bill because it was un-English and unconstitutional—corrupt in its tendency—it was an avowal of a determination to destroy local self-government, and, if carried, its effect would be to pass a roller over England, destroying every vestige of local pre-eminence, and reducing all to one dull and level monotony. It would place in the hands of the Government an immense amount of personal patronage, and add to the burdens of the country an enormous load of new taxation.   3 Hansard xcviii, 712–13

267. Toulmin Smith on local self-government and centralisation, 1851

Freedom and free Institutions and good government do not consist only in protection to person and property.... Person and property may be protected, and yet the nation be a nation of slaves....

True Freedom consists in the continual active consciousness of the position and responsibilities of a Free Man, a Member of the State, and a positive Item in it. The Free Man will feel that he has something to live for beyond the attainment of mere personal ease and comfort; that he has, as a member of the State, certain important and active Rights, and Duties and Responsibilities....

There are two elements to which every form of Government may be reduced. These are, LOCAL SELF-GOVERNMENT on the one hand, and CENTRALIZATION on the other. According as the former or the latter of these exists more or less predominant, will the state of any nation be the more or less free, happy, progressive, truly prosperous and safe.... The common divisions of forms of Government into monarchical, aristocratic, democratic, and mixed, convey none but superficial ideas; they have no reality as illustrative of the inner and actual condition of any nation....

LOCAL SELF-GOVERNMENT *is that system of Government under which the greatest number of minds, knowing the most, and having the fullest opportunities of knowing it, about the special matter in hand, and having the greatest interest in its well-working, have the management of it, or control over it.*

CENTRALIZATION *is that system of Government under which the smallest number of minds, and those knowing the least, and having the fewest opportunities of knowing it, about the special matter in hand, and having the smallest interest in its well-working, have the management of it, or control over it....*

LOCAL SELF-GOVERNMENT....

The life and spirit of free Institutions must depend wholly upon the consciousness of their reality. That consciousness, can only spring from constant personal experience.... The wholesome adjustment of practical arrangements suited to the exigencies of the times, and the satisfactory management of administrative functions, must depend upon the vital activity of Institutions which give to every freeman the full opportunity of discussing, and hearing discussed, all the questions which, directly or indirectly, concern him....

'Local jobbing', and the influence of 'local interests', are often held up as bugbears. But each of these, wherever it be found, exists, and only ever can exist, because true Local Self-Government is not there found; because the discussion and management of matters is practically left in the hands of a Local clique or oligarchy....

Local self-government can nowhere exist and be called into constant and regular activity, and so be a reality and not a name, without in itself producing men able and willing to originate new and valuable enterprises. It is when men are thus assured that full scope will be given for fairly discussing any proposition which may be brought forward for the common good, that each man is encouraged to exert himself to the best of his power.... He may thus best attain the approbation of his neighbours, as well as a just reward for his own efforts.

True patriotism finds in Local Self-Government its constant nurse.... But it will not be the patriotism of narrow prejudice; but the patriotism which hails every freeman of every free land with gladness, and seeks to impart the same solid blessings to others which are enjoyed at home....

Local Self-Government does not serve to stir up class against class, and interest against interest.... It draws all classes nearer in kindliness and in daily life to one another.... It will not let the festering places of society lie hidden and unknown....

Local Self-Government affords the only true Education.... the school of the active exercise of all the faculties in the earnest work of real life....

Men cannot discuss without having first paid some attention to the subject matter of discussion. As long as everything is done *for* them they have no occasion to think at all, and will soon become incapable of thinking. But the moment they are thrown on their own resources ...they wake from their torpor, put forth their energies, and rouse their faculties....

CENTRALIZATION

The fundamental idea of Centralization is, *distrust*.... Local Self-Government leads necessarily on, by its own inherent force, to steady Progress...Under Centralization the forces always acting to this end are crushed out.... Centralization is only Communism in another form. Its object is, to take away the free action of every man over his own property; to stay the free use, by every man, of his own resources, his own ingenuity, and his own free action and enterprise....an espionage is kept up over all society. Instead of all in a neighbourhood being drawn together by common interests, there are always some.... whose interests are made, as functionaries, to centre elsewhere....

Servility, sycophancy, selfishness, and apathy, are the moral qualities which it is the necessary effect of Centralization to engender.... Centralization always tends to induce the bowing down in worship to the *material* part of man's nature, to the degradation of his moral and spiritual part. It sets up material well-being, ease, and convenience, as paramount to every other consideration.... Men are taught that the best method is for the mass of mankind to remain in ignoble moral and mental unexertion, while bands of functionaries take care, for them, that these material conveniences shall be provided....

A system which destroys self-reliance, deadens self-respect, and anni-hilates forethought, can have but one character in its influences on the intellect. A system which dictates and controls, instead of stimulating every individual energy, can have but the effect of dwarfing and be-numbing every faculty, intellectual as well as moral.

Smith, *Local Self-Government and Centralization*, pp. 7–8, 11–12, 27–8, 32, 46–7, 50, 54, 56, 62–4, 66

268. The General Board of Health abolished, 1858

(a) *Speech of C. B. Adderley, President of the Board of Health, 22 April 1858*

The Public Health Act of 1848 constituted...a General Board of Health for five years. That General Board, exercising the powers con-ferred upon them by the Act, called into existence local boards, in various towns throughout the country, and then became to those boards their referee in a multitude of cases; serving at the same time as a court of final appeal. [In 1854 the Board was continued with its own President and officers and was renewed from year to year, though failing to carry the major bills it proposed.] The general principle of the measure which he was about to ask the House for leave to introduce was one the object of which was to decentralize the whole system; to allow the General Board of Health to expire in September; and to enable all those towns which desired to possess the power of self-administration to constitute local boards through the medium of meetings of owners and rate payers, two-thirds of whom must consent to the adoption of such a course; it being open to town councils or commissioners, who fairly represented the inhabitants of large towns, to exercise similar powers.... He also proposed that the boards which might be constituted...as well as all the local boards now in existence, should have the amplest powers of self-administration extended to them, and should be no longer subjected to the necessity of referring to a central board in London [subject to a right of individuals to appeal to the Home Secretary]. 3 *Hansard* CXLIX, 1554–5

(b) Speech by Adderley, 30 April 1858

No doubt, if any hon. Members were in favour of the retention of that Board, that would be a ground for delaying the second reading; but he believed that no such persons would be found. ...He thought it was better to leave localities to settle their own affairs, than to transfer them to a central authority. [The second Reading was carried unopposed.]

3 *Hansard* CXLIX, 2095

269. John Stuart Mill and the classical view of local self-government, 1861

It is but a small portion of the public business of a country, which can be well done, or safely attempted, by the central authorities; and even in our own government, the least centralized in Europe, the legislative portion at least of the governing body busies itself far too much with local affairs, employing the supreme power of the State in cutting small knots....After subtracting from the functions performed by most European governments, those which ought not to be undertaken by public authorities at all, there still remains so great and various an aggregate of duties, that, if only on the principle of division of labour, it is indispensable to share them between central and local authorities. Not only are separate executive officers required for purely local duties... but the popular control over these officers can only be advantageously exerted through a separate organ. Their original appointment, the function of watching and checking them, the duty of providing, or the discretion of withholding, the supplies necessary for their operations, should rest, not with the national Parliament or the national executive, but with the people of the locality....

In considering these questions, two points require...our attention: how the local business itself can be best done: and how its transaction can be made most instrumental to the nourishment of public spirit and the development of intelligence. In an earlier part of this inquiry, I have dwelt...on the importance of that...which may be called the public education of the citizens. Now, of this operation the local administrative institutions are the chief instrument....in the case of local bodies, besides the function of electing, many citizens in turn have the chance of being elected, and many, either by selection or by rotation, fill one or other of the numerous local executive offices. In these positions they have to act, for public interests, as well as to think and to speak, and the thinking cannot all be done by proxy. It may be added, that these local functions, not being in general sought by the higher ranks, carry down the important political education which they are the means of conferring, to a much lower grade in society....

The proper constitution of local representative bodies does not present much difficulty. The principles which apply to it do not differ in any respect from those applicable to the national representation. The same obligation exists...for making the bodies elective; and...for giving them a widely democratic basis....

Besides the controlling Council, or local sub-Parliament, local business has its executive department....each executive officer should be single, and singly responsible for the whole of the duty committed to his charge...nominated, not elected.

Mill, Representative Government, pp. 363–6, 372

270. Joseph Chamberlain urges a municipal programme upon Birmingham, 1874

[Speech as Mayor of Birmingham on the proposal to purchase the gasworks, 13 January 1874]

In the first place, he would endeavour to carry the Council with him in two principles on which he thought these negotiations should proceed. He distinctly held that all monopolies which were sustained in any way by the State ought to be in the hands of the representatives of the people—by the representative authority should they be administered, and to them should their profits go, and not to private speculators. Moreover...he was always inclined to magnify his office; he was inclined to increase the duties and responsibilities of the local authority, in whom he had himself so great a confidence, and would do everything in his power to constitute these local authorities real local parliaments, supreme in their special jurisdiction. He was aware it had been said that these undertakings...should be left to private enterprise and energy; but he would say...that John Stuart Mill, the greatest political thinker of his age, always asserted...that such undertakings... should be excluded from the rule...and should be placed in the hands of the local authority.

He had been struck with the inadequate means of the Council for the responsible work placed upon them. If they proposed to recompense the faithful service of an officer of the Corporation, and if they proposed to increase their own duties and responsibilities, they were met with a chorus of opposition from the ratepayers...and this diffi- culty was continually increasing, because every day new duties were being imposed upon the Corporation. For instance, there was the great business of the sewage at Saltley.... Then very recently they were called upon to take advantage of the Sanitary Act. That again had already involved the Council in a very largely increased expenditure, and must involve it in a still larger expenditure in the future.... Birmingham had unfortunately fallen from its high position, and was no longer the healthiest town in the kingdom; it had become one of the most unhealthy of the large cities and boroughs in the country. Under these circumstances it was absolutely necessary that they should devote their attention to the sanitary condition of the town. He need not allude to other matters except to remind them that at the last meeting of the Council a new duty was thrown upon them of pro- tecting property from fire. All these duties involved a largely increased expenditure, and he believed that the pressure of the rates would be- come intolerable unless some compensation could be found by some new proposal, such as the one he now laid before them. That com- pensation was secured in the case of other large towns....In Manchester the Corporation possessed the gas and water works, and they secured from the profits of these undertakings an enormous capital. He was told that at present the amount was something like a million sterling, with which they were able to erect those corporate buildings which were the glory of the town.   *Birmingham Daily Post*, 14 January 1874

271. Harcourt on police inspections, 1883

[Memorandum by Sir W. Harcourt as Home Secretary, 25 January 1883]

...The view I have always taken on this matter is that if local self- government means anything at all it means that the Local Authority and not the Government Inspector is the proper judge of the number of police required by them. On this ground I stated to a deputation of the Corporation of Manchester in 1880 that I should certainly not compel them to keep on foot more police than they thought requisite, for that it was they who would suffer from the deficiency.

I have on two occasions seen the Inspectors of Constabulary on this subject collectively and explained to them that I considered it no part of their duty to increase the charge on the Exchequer by insisting on Boroughs and Counties keeping up a force according to the standard of the Inspectors and not according to their own view of their local wants. One of the great evils of centralised government is this tendency to apply an artificial standard to all cases regardless of local wants....

Hart, *Public Administration*, XXXIV, 411

272. Edwin Chadwick attacks local self-government, 1885

FALLACY OF THE PHRASE 'LOCAL SELF-GOVERNMENT'

The term, 'local self-government', signifying as it does the direct individual knowledge of the local affairs of the local unit of administration and the participation of the ratepayer in the expenditure of his own money, is in the majority of cases a mischievous fallacy. As the demands of attention to his own personal or private affairs increase, the citizen's power of attention to the public affairs of increasing magnitude diminishes, and he is obliged to let his local affairs go as they may to persons of whose fitness he has no knowledge, and with whom he has only an infinitesimal power of interfering....

Suppose, however, on the theory of local self-government, of the individual cognizance of the individual voter of his own affairs, what means were there of his knowing anything about them—although they really affected the purity of his water supplies, and his health and life, and his relief from the excessive burden of the sickness and other rates? If he could be made aware of them, by reading reports...what are his prospects of bringing that knowledge of his own affairs—with which the political theory of self-government credits him—by the application of his twenty thousandth share of the administration as a voter?

Besides science, chiefly sanitary science, to be applied, there is administrative science to be acquired. Besides the demand for such sciences, to effect large economies in local administration, there is required, moreover, business or administrative science to insure their application. In places where there are great displays of ability in arts, manufacturing, and commerce, as in Manchester, there is very little wisdom exhibited in local sanitary administration....

I may here meet the exclamation apt to be raised by certain classes of politicians, 'Then you are all for centralisation!' Even if it were so, it would be for you, the advocate of decentralisation and disunity, to say whether you prefer disease and premature mortality and waste with what is called local self-government, to health and strength, and economy with centralisation. But I answer, that I am, on principle, for extensive decentralisation—actually for decentralisation to the greatest extent by well-arranged local consolidation for superior self-government over that which now exists; and that is your real choice—a true representation of the best local intelligence under unity in the place of disunity and local ignorance....

EFFECT OF UNITY IN LEGISLATION

In regard to the effect of superior legislation produced by the attainment of unity, by doing everywhere the same thing in the same way, as closely as may be, choosing the best, I would point to...the Code Napoleon.... But we may advance beyond...to the practical working of our own Code for India.... The most experienced India administrators speak of it, so far as it has been carried, as a vast success, in producing order where there was chaos, and giving a strong binding force of unity to the administration....

The cheapest means of...getting the local administration under complete unity, and getting future legislation under unity...would be by a division of labour amongst highly qualified and well paid separate commissions, as by a commission for the assimilation of the administration of the laws for the protection of the public health; by a commission for the assimilation of the law and administration for the relief of destitution; by a commission for the assimilation of the penal law and the administration of constabulary and police forces; by a commission for the assimilation of the laws and administration of the law and the better application of rates for the maintenance of the roads and the means of transit; by a commission for the assimilation of the laws and the assimilation of the civil procedure for the administration of justice, as far as may be, throughout the empire.

Chadwick, *On the Evils of Disunity*, pp. 72, 76, 78–9, 90, 92

273. John Burns's programme for the London County Council, 1898

If elected, I will, as heretofore, devote my time to the Council's work, and am in favour of—

1. The extension of the powers of the Council, so that the City, with all its funds and endowments, be included in and used by a real Municipality for London.

2. That all monopolies, such as gas, water, tramways, omnibuses, markets, docks, river steamboats, and electric lighting, should be municipalized, and the profits, amounting to £4,000,000 annually, or three times the Council's revenue, devoted to public purposes.

3. Establishment of municipal hospitals in every district, and control by the Council of those which already exist.

4. Artisans' dwellings, as now, to be constructed and owned by the Council.

5. Enlargement of powers so as to enable the County Council to undertake the organization of industry and distribution, especially in those departments dealing with the necessaries of life.

6. Rigorous enforcement of Public Health Acts, and efficient sanitary and structural inspection of dwellings and workshops.

7. The organization of unemployed labour on useful work at trade-union wages.

8. The direct employment of all labour by the Council at eight hours per day at trade-union rates, women and men receiving equal pay for equal work. Nine years' experience has proved that contract work, however well supervised, does not produce such good buildings and workmanship as the Council has secured by its own workmen.

9. Direct control by the Council of the five millions of money now spent, and too often squandered, on useless officialism and feasting by charitable institutions and City companies.

10. The police of the City and Greater London to be controlled by the County Council.

11. Cumulative rating, the taxation of ground landlords for the relief of the occupier, and the provision of new sources of revenue. Sevenpence—half our present rate—now goes to pay the old debt left by our predecessors, thus depriving London of many necessary improvements.

Besides these measures, I will work and vote for any plan that will enable London to reduce its poverty and brighten the lives and increase the comfort of its people.   Ensor, *Modern Socialism*, 3rd ed, pp. 282–3

THE CREATION OF ALL-PURPOSE LOCAL AUTHORITIES

274. Burgesses and councils defined by the Municipal Corporations Act, 1835

IX. And be it enacted, That every Male Person of full Age who on the last Day of *August* in any Year shall have occupied any House, Warehouse, Counting-house, or Shop within any Borough during that Year and the whole of each of the Two preceding Years, and also during the Time of such Occupation shall have been an Inhabitant Householder within the said Borough, or within Seven Miles of the said Borough, shall, if duly enrolled in that Year according to the Provisions herein-after contained, be a Burgess of such Borough and Member of the Body Corporate of the Mayor, Aldermen, and Burgesses of such Borough: Provided always, that no such Person shall be so enrolled in any Year, unless he shall have been rated in respect of such Premises so occupied by him within the Borough to all Rates made for the Relief of the Poor of the Parish wherein such Premises are situated during the Time of his Occupation as aforesaid, and unless he shall have paid on or before the last Day of *August* as aforesaid all such Rates, including therein all Borough Rates, if any, directed to be paid under the Provisions of this Act, as shall have become payable by him in respect of the said Premises, except such as shall become payable within Six Calendar Months next before the said last Day of *August*: Provided also, that the Premises in respect of the Occupation of which any Person shall have been so rated need not be the same Premises or in the same Parish, but may be different Premises in the same Parish or in different Parishes: Provided also, that no Person being an Alien shall be so enrolled in any Year, and that no Person shall be so enrolled in any Year who within Twelve Calendar Months next before the said last Day of *August* shall have received Parochial Relief or other Alms, or any Pension or charitable Allowance from any Fund intrusted to the charitable Trustees of such Borough herein-after mentioned: Provided that in every Case provided in this Act the Distance of Seven Miles shall be computed by the nearest public Road or Way by Land or Water.

[x. Assistance from charitable trustees or endowed schools not to disqualify.]

[xi. Occupiers may claim to be rated.]

[xiii. No new burgesses to be enrolled except under this Act.]

[xv–xxiv. Burgess Rolls to be drawn up by the overseers and revised by the mayor and two assessors, except in the first year, when the revision to be done by revising barristers.]

xxv. And be it enacted, That in every Borough shall be elected, at the Time and in the Manner herein-after mentioned, One fit Person, who shall be and be called 'The Mayor' of such Borough; and a certain Number of fit Persons, who shall be and be called 'Aldermen' of such Borough; and a certain Number of other fit Persons, who shall be and be called 'The Councillors' of such Borough; and such Mayor, Aldermen, and Councillors for the Time being shall be and be called 'The Council' of such Borough; and the Number of Persons so to be elected Councillors of such Borough shall be the Number of Persons in that Behalf mentioned in conjunction with the Name of such Borough in the Schedules (A.) and (B.) to this Act annexed; and the Number of Persons so to be elected Aldermen shall be One Third of the Number of Persons so to be elected Councillors; and on the Ninth Day of *November* in this present Year the Councillors first to be elected under the Provisions of this Act, and on the Ninth Day of *November* in the Year One thousand eight hundred and Thirty-eight, and in every Third succeeding Year, the Council for the Time being of every Borough, shall elect from the Councillors, or from the Persons qualified to be Councillors, the Aldermen of such Borough, or so many as shall be needed to supply the Places of those who shall then go out of Office according to the Provisions herein-after contained; and that upon the Ninth Day of *November* in the Year One thousand eight hundred and thirty-eight, and in every Third succeeding Year, One Half of the Number appointed as aforesaid to be the whole Number of the Aldermen of every Borough shall go out of Office; and the Councillors immediately after the first Election of Aldermen shall appoint who shall be the Aldermen who shall go out of Office in the Year One thousand eight hundred and thirty-eight, and thereafter those who shall go out of Office shall always be those who have been Aldermen for the longest Time without Re-election: Provided always, that any Aldermen so going out of Office may be forthwith re-elected, if then qualified as herein provided; provided also, that the Aldermen so going out of Office shall not be entitled to vote in the Election of a new Alderman.

xxvi. And be it enacted, That the Mayor and Aldermen shall, during their respective Offices, continue to be Members of the Council of the Borough, notwithstanding any thing herein-after contained as to Councillors going out of Office at the End of Three Years.

XXVII. And be it enacted, That whenever any extraordinary Vacancy shall take place in the Office of Alderman of any Borough, the Council of such Borough shall, within Ten Days after such Vacancy shall occur, on a Day to be fixed by the Mayor for such Purpose, elect some other fit Person to fill such Vacancy, either from the Councillors or from the Persons qualified to be Councillors; and in case any Councillor shall be elected to fill the Office of Alderman, then the Vacancy which will thereby be occasioned in the Council shall be filled up at the Time and in the Manner herein-after directed; and every Person so elected an Alderman to fill an extraordinary Vacancy shall hold such Office until the Time when the Person in the Room of whom he was chosen would regularly have gone out of Office, and he shall then go out of Office, but may be re-elected if then qualified as herein provided.

XXVIII. And be it enacted, That no Person being in Holy Orders, or being the regular Minister of any Dissenting Congregation, shall be qualified to be elected or to be a Councillor of any such Borough or an Alderman of any such Borough, nor shall any Person be qualified to be elected or to be a Councillor or an Alderman of any such Borough who shall not be entitled to be on the Burgess List of such Borough, nor unless he shall be seised or possessed of Real or Personal Estate or both to the following Amount, that is to say, in all Boroughs directed by this Act to be divided into Four or more Wards to the Amount of One thousand Pounds, or be rated to the Relief of the Poor of such Borough upon the annual Value of not less than Thirty Pounds, and in all Boroughs directed to be divided into less than Four Wards, or which shall not be divided into Wards, to the Amount of Five hundred Pounds, or be rated to the Relief of the Poor in such Borough upon the annual Value of not less than Fifteen Pounds, or during such Time as he shall hold any Office or Place of Profit, other than that of Mayor, in the Gift or Disposal of the Council of such Borough, or during such Time as he shall have directly or indirectly, by himself or his Partner, any Share or Interest in any Contract or Employment with, by, or on behalf of such Council; provided that no Person shall be disqualified from being a Councillor or Alderman of any Borough as aforesaid by reason of his being a Proprietor or Shareholder of any Company which shall contract with the Council of such Borough for lighting or supplying with Water or insuring against Fire any Part of such Borough.

xxix. And be it enacted, That every Burgess of any Borough who shall be enrolled on the Burgess Roll for the Time being of such Borough shall be entitled to vote in the Election of Councillors and of the Auditors and Assessors herein-after mentioned for such Borough, and no Person who shall not be enrolled in such Burgess Roll for the Time being shall have any Voice or be entitled to vote in any such Election.

xxx. And be it enacted, That upon the First Day of *November* in every Year the Burgesses so enrolled in every Borough shall openly assemble and elect from the Persons qualified to be Councillors the Councillors of such Borough, or such Part of them as shall be needed to supply the Places of those who shall then go out of Office: Provided nevertheless, that whenever any Day by this Act appointed for any Purpose shall in any Year happen on a *Sunday*, in every such Case the Business so appointed to be done shall take place on the *Monday* following.

xxxi. And be it enacted, That upon the First Day of *November* One thousand eight hundred and thirty-six, and in every succeeding Year, One Third Part of the Number appointed as aforesaid to be the whole Number of the Councillors of every Borough shall go out of Office; and in the said Year One thousand eight hundred and thirty-six those who shall go out of Office shall be the Councillors who were elected under the Provisions of this Act by the smallest Number of Votes in this present Year, and in the Next Year, One thousand eight hundred and thirty-seven, those who so go out of Office shall be the Councillors who were elected under the Provisions of this Act by the next smallest Numbers of Votes in this present Year, the Majority of the whole Council always determining, when the Votes for any such Persons shall have been equal, who shall be the Persons so to go out of Office; and thereafter those who shall so go out of Office shall always be the Councillors who have been for the longest Time in Office without Re-election: Provided always, that any Councillor so going out of Office shall be capable of being forthwith re-elected, if then qualified, as herein provided.

xxxii. And be it enacted, That every Election of Councillors within any Borough according to the Provisions of this Act shall be held before the Mayor and Assessors for the Time being of such Borough, except as herein is excepted; and the voting at every such Election shall commence at Nine o'Clock in the Forenoon, and shall finally close at Four o'Clock in the Afternoon of the same Day, and shall be conducted in manner following; that is to say, every Burgess entitled to vote in the Election of Councillors may vote for any Number of Persons not exceeding the Number of Councillors then to be chosen, by delivering to the Mayor and Assessors or other presiding Officer as herein-after mentioned a Voting Paper, containing the Christian Names and Surnames of the Persons for whom he votes, with their respective Places of Abode and Descriptions, such Paper being previously signed with the Name of the Burgess voting, and with the Name of the Street, Lane, or other Place in which the Property for which he appears to be rated on the Burgess Roll is situated.

[xxxiii. Polling to be in booths or rooms used as booths, under the direction of the Mayor.]

[xxxv. Voting papers to be examined and counted by the Mayor and assessors. In the case of an equality of votes the Mayor and assessors or any two of them to choose the successful candidate.]

[xxxvi. An alderman to preside in the absence of the Mayor.]

[xxxvii. The burgesses to choose two auditors and two assessors.]

PGS, 5 & 6 Will. IV, c. 76

275. The Local Government Act, 1888

PART I: COUNTY COUNCILS
Constitution of County Council

1. A council shall be established in every administrative county as defined by this Act, and be entrusted with the management of the administrative and financial business of that county, and shall consist of the chairman, aldermen, and councillors.

2.—(1.) The council of a county and the members thereof shall be constituted and elected and conduct their proceedings in like manner, and be in the like position in all respects, as the council of a borough divided into wards, subject nevertheless to the provisions of this Act, and in particular to the following provisions, that is to say:—

(2.) As respects the aldermen or councillors—

(*a.*) clerks in holy orders and other ministers of religion shall not be disqualified for being elected and being aldermen or councillors;

(*b.*) a person shall be qualified to be an alderman or councillor who, though not qualified in manner provided by the Municipal Corporations Act, 1882, as applied by this Act, is a peer owning property in the county, or is registered as a parliamentary voter in respect of the ownership of property of whatsoever tenure situate in the county;

(*c.*) the aldermen shall be called county aldermen, and the councillors shall be called county councillors; and a county alderman shall not, as such, vote in the election of a county alderman;

(*d.*) the county councillors shall be elected for a term of three years, and shall then retire together, and their places shall be filled by a new election; and

(*e.*) the divisions of the county for the purpose of the election of county councillors, shall be called electoral divisions and not wards, and one county councillor only shall be elected for each electoral division.

[(3.) Electoral divisions and number of members of the county councils to be fixed by the Local Government Board in the first instance.]

(4.) As respects the electors of the county councillors—the persons entitled to vote at their election shall be, in a borough, the burgesses enrolled in pursuance of the Municipal Corporations Act, 1882, and the Acts amending the same, and elsewhere the persons registered as county electors under the County Electors Act, 1888.

(5.) As respects the chairman of the county council—

(*a.*) he shall be called chairman instead of mayor; and

(*b.*) he shall, by virtue of his office, be a justice of the peace for the county; but before acting as such justice he shall, if he has not already done so, take the oaths required by law to be taken by a justice of the peace other than the oath respecting the qualification by estate.

(6.) The county council may from time to time appoint a member of the council to be vice-chairman, to hold office during the term of office of the chairman, and, subject to any rules made from time to time by the county council, anything authorised or required to be done by, to, or before the chairman may be done by, to, or before such vice-chairman.

Powers of County Council

3. There shall be transferred to the council of each county on and after the appointed day, the administrative business of the justices of the county in quarter sessions assembled, that is to say, all business done by the quarter sessions or any committee appointed by the quarter sessions, in respect of the several matters following, namely,—

(i.) The making, assessing, and levying of county, police, hundred, and all rates, and the application and expenditure thereof, and the making of orders for the payment of sums payable out of any such rate or out of the county stock or county fund, and the preparation and revision of the basis or standard for the county rate;

(ii.) The borrowing of money;

(iii.) The passing of the accounts of and the discharge of the county treasurer;

(iv.) Shire halls, county halls, assize courts, judges lodgings, lock-up houses, court houses, justices rooms, police stations, and county buildings, works, and property, subject as to the use of buildings by the quarter sessions, and the justices to the provisions of this Act respecting the joint committee of quarter sessions and the county council;

(v.) The licensing under any general Act of houses and other places for music or for dancing, and the granting of licenses under the Racecourses Licensing Act, 1879;

(vi.) The provision, enlargement, maintenance, management and visitation of and other dealing with asylums for pauper lunatics;

(vii.) The establishment and maintenance of and the contribution to reformatory and industrial schools;

(viii.) Bridges and roads repairable with bridges, and any powers vested by the Highways and Locomotives (Amendment) Act, 1878, in the county authority;

(ix.) The tables of fees to be taken by and the costs to be allowed to any inspector, analyst, or person holding any office in the county other than the clerk of the peace and the clerks of the justices;

(x.) The appointment, removal, and determination of salaries, of the county treasurer, the county surveyor, the public analysts, any officer under the Explosives Act, 1875, and any officers whose remuneration is paid out of the county rate other than the clerk of the peace and the clerks of the justices;

(xi.) The salary of any coroner whose salary is payable out of the county rate, the fees, allowances, and disbursements allowed to be paid by any such coroner, and the division of the county into coroners' districts, and the assignment of such districts;

(xii.) The division of the county into polling districts for the purposes of parliamentary elections, the appointment of places of election, the places of holding courts for the revision of the lists of voters, and the costs of and other matters to be done for the registration of parliamentary voters;

(xiii.) The execution as local authority of the Acts relating to contagious diseases of animals, to destructive insects, to fish conservancy, to wild birds, to weights and measures, and to gas meters, and of the Local Stamp Act, 1869;

(xiv.) Any matters arising under the Riot (Damages) Act, 1886;

(xv.) The registration of rules of scientific societies...the registration of charitable gifts...the certifying and recording of places of religious worship...the confirmation and record of the rules of loan societies...and

(xvi.) Any other business transferred by this Act.

[4. Powers under local Acts may be transferred to the county council by the Local Government Board by way of Provisional Order.]

[5. County coroners no longer to be elected but to be chosen by the county councils, and county coroners to be ineligible to sit on county councils in their district.]

6. The county council shall have power to purchase, or take over on terms to be agreed on, existing bridges not being at present county bridges, and to erect new bridges, and to maintain, repair, and improve any bridges so purchased, taken over, or erected.

7. There shall be transferred to the county council on and after the appointed day the business of the justices of the county out of session—

    (a.) in respect of the licensing of houses or places for the public performance of stage plays, and (*b*). in respect of the execution as local authority of the Explosives Act, 1875.

8.—(1.) Nothing in this Act shall transfer to a county council any business of the quarter sessions or justices in relation to appeals by any overseers or persons against the basis or standard for the county rate or against that or any other rate.

(2.) All business of the quarter sessions or any committee thereof not transferred by or in pursuance of this Act to the county council shall be reserved to and transacted by the quarter sessions or committee thereof in the same manner, as far as circumstances admit, as if this Act had not passed.

9.—(1.) The powers, duties, and liabilities of quarter sessions and of justices out of session with respect to the county police shall, on and after the appointed day, vest in and attach to the quarter sessions and the county council jointly, and be exercised and discharged through the standing joint committee of the quarter sessions and county council appointed as herein-after mentioned:

(2.) Provided that the powers conferred by section seven of the County and Borough Police Act, 1856, which requires constables to perform, in addition to their ordinary duties, such duties connected with the police as the quarter sessions may direct or require, shall continue to be exercised by the quarter sessions as well as by the said standing joint committee, and may also be exercised by the county council; and the said section shall be construed as if the county council and the said standing joint committee were therein mentioned as well as the quarter sessions.

(3.) Nothing in this Act shall affect the powers, duties, and liabilities of justices of the peace as conservators of the peace, or the obligation of the chief constable or other constables to obey their lawful orders given in that behalf.

[10. The Local Government Board empowered to transfer, by Provisional Order, additional powers of the central government to the county councils.]

[16. The county councils to have power to make bye-laws.]

PART II: APPLICATION OF ACT TO BOROUGHS, THE METROPOLIS, AND CERTAIN SPECIAL COUNTIES

Application of Act to Boroughs

31. Each of the boroughs named in the Third Schedule[1] to this Act being a borough which on [1 June 1888], either had a population of not less than fifty thousand, or was a county of itself shall, from and after the appointed day, be for the purposes of this Act an administrative county of itself, and is in this Act referred to as a county borough.

Provided that for all other purposes a county borough shall continue to be part of the county (if any) in which it is situate at the passing of this Act....

Application of Act to Metropolis

40. In the application of this Act to the Metropolis, the following provisions shall have effect:—

(1.) The Metropolis shall, on and after the appointed day, be an administrative county for the purposes of this Act by the name of the administrative county of London.

(2.) Such portion of the administrative county of London as forms part of the counties of Middlesex, Surrey, and Kent, shall on and after the appointed day be severed from those counties, and form a separate county for all non-administrative purposes by the name of the county of London; and it shall be lawful for Her Majesty the Queen to appoint a sheriff of that county, and to grant a commission of the peace and court of quarter sessions to that county; and, subject to the provisions of this Act, all enactments, laws, and usages with respect to counties in England and Wales, and to sheriffs, justices, and quarter sessions shall, so far as circumstances admit, apply to the county of London:

(3.) Provided that, for the purpose of the jurisdiction of the justices under such commission, and of such court, as well as other non-administrative purposes, the county of the city of

---

[1] The Third Schedule lists the following sixty-one county boroughs: Barrow, Bath, Birkenhead, Birmingham, Blackburn, Bolton, Bootle cum Linacre, Bradford, Brighton, Bristol, Burnley, Bury, Canterbury, Cardiff, Chester, Coventry, Croydon, Derby, Devonport, Dudley, Exeter, Gateshead, Gloucester, Great Yarmouth, Halifax, Hanley, Hastings, Huddersfield, Ipswich, Kingston-upon-Hull, Leeds, Leicester, Lincoln, Liverpool, Manchester, Middlesbrough, Newcastle-upon-Tyne, Northampton, Norwich, Nottingham, Oldham, Plymouth, Portsmouth, Preston, Reading, Rochdale, Saint Helen's, Salford, Sheffield, Southampton, South Shields, Stockport, Sunderland, Swansea, Walsall, West Bromwich, West Ham, Wigan, Wolverhampton, Worcester, York.

London shall continue a separate county, but if and when the mayor, commonalty, and citizens of the city assent to jurisdiction being conferred therein on such justices and court may by commission under the Great Seal be made subject to the jurisdiction thereof.

(4.) The number of the county councillors for the administrative county of London, shall be double the number of members which at the passing of this Act, the parliamentary boroughs in the metropolis are authorised by law to return to serve in Parliament; and each such borough, or if it is divided into divisions, each division thereof, shall be an electoral division for the purposes of this Act, and the number of county councillors elected for each such electoral division, shall be double the number of members of Parliament which such borough or division is at the passing of this Act entitled to return to serve in Parliament.

(5.) Provided that the number of county aldermen in the administrative county of London, shall not exceed one-sixth of the whole number of county councillors.

(8.) There shall also be transferred to the London county council the powers, duties, and liabilities of the Metropolitan Board of Works, and after the appointed day that board shall cease to exist, and the property, debts, and liabilities thereof shall be transferred to the London county council, and that council shall be in law the successors of the Metropolitan Board of Works.

Application of Act to Special Counties and to Liberties

[46. (1.) The ridings of Yorkshire and the divisions of Lincolnshire, the eastern and western divisions of Suffolk and Sussex, the Isle of Ely, and the soke of Peterborough to be separate administrative counties.]

[(2.) Joint committees to be established to transact business of whole counties where they have been divided.]

[(6.) City of London no longer to choose the sheriff of Middlesex.]

PGS, 51 & 52 Vict., c. 41

276. The Local Government Act, 1894

PART I: PARISH MEETINGS AND PARISH COUNCILS

Constitution of Parish Meetings and Parish Councils

1. (1) There shall be a parish meeting for every rural parish, and there shall be a parish council for every rural parish which has a population of three hundred or upwards [and also a parish council for smaller parishes of 100 people or groups of parishes, if asked for by the parish meeting and approved by the county council].

   (2) For the purposes of this Act every parish in a rural sanitary district shall be a rural parish.

2. (1) The parish meeting for a rural parish shall consist of...the persons registered in such portion either of the local government register of electors or of the parliamentary register of electors as relates to the parish.

   (2) Each parochial elector may, at any parish meeting, or at any poll consequent thereon, give one vote and no more on any question, or, in the case of an election, for each of any number of persons not exceeding the number to be elected.

   (3) The parish meeting shall assemble at least once in every year, and...shall begin not earlier than six o'clock in the evening.

3. (1) The parish council for a rural parish shall be elected from among the parochial electors of that parish or persons who have during the whole of the twelve months preceding the election resided in the parish, or within three miles thereof, and shall consist of a chairman and councillors, and the number of councillors shall be such as may be fixed from time to time by the county council, not being less than five nor more than fifteen.

   (2) No person shall be disqualified by sex or marriage for being elected or being a member of a parish council.

   (3) The term of a parish councillor shall be one year.

   (4) [Members to go out of office on 15 April.]

   (5) The parish councillors shall be elected by the parochial electors of the parish.

[4. Parish councils and parish meetings to have the use of public elementary schools free of charge.]

Powers and Duties of Parish Councils and Parish Meetings

[5. Parish councils to choose parish overseers and the churchwardens to cease to be overseers.]

6. (1) Upon the parish council of a rural parish coming into office, there shall be transferred to that council:—

    (*a*) The powers, duties, and liabilities of the vestry of the parish except—

        (i) so far as relates to the affairs of the church or to ecclesiastical charities;

        (ii) [powers transferred to other authorities.]

    (*b*) The powers, duties, and liabilities of the churchwardens of the parish, except so far as they relate to the affairs of the church or to charities, or are powers and duties of overseers, but inclusive of the obligations...with respect to...closed churchyards....

    (*c*) The powers, duties, and liabilities of the overseers or of the churchwardens and overseers of the parish with respect to—

        (i) appeals or objections by them in respect of the valuation list, or appeals in respect of the poor rate, or county rate, or the basis of the county rate; and

        (ii) the provision of parish books and of a vestry room or parochial office, parish chest, fire engine, fire escape, or matters relating thereto; and

        (iii) the holding or management of parish property, not being property...of the church or held for an ecclesiastical charity, and the holding or management of village greens, or of allotments, whether for recreation grounds or for gardens or otherwise for the benefit of the inhabitants or any of them;

    (*d*) The powers exerciseable with the approval of the Local Government Board by the board of guardians...in respect of the sale, exchange, or letting of any parish property.

[(2) Parish councils as well as householders to be able to complain of unhealthy dwellings and obstructive buildings.]

[(3 and 4) Parish councils to have certain powers over allotments.]

[7. Certain adoptive powers under existing legislation extended to parish meetings.]

[8. Parish councils to have power to provide offices, land for offices, recreation grounds and public walks, to apply to the Board of Agriculture under Section 9 of the Commons Act, 1878, to exercise certain powers over open spaces under the Public Health Acts, to provide wells, to clean ponds, ditches etc., to acquire rights of way, to receive gifts, to maintain let or sell property.]

[10. Parish councils to have power to hire land for allotments.]

11. (1) A parish council shall not, without the consent of a parish meeting, incur expenses or liabilities which will involve a rate exceeding threepence in the pound for any local financial year, or which will involve a loan.

[(2) No loans to be incurred without the consent of the county council.]

(3) The sum raised...by a parish council for their expenses...shall not exceed a sum equal to a rate of sixpence in the pound....
(4) ...the expenses of a parish council and of a parish meeting...
...shall be paid out of the poor rate....

17. (1) A parish council may appoint one of their number to act as clerk of the council without remuneration.

[(2 & 3) Failing this an assistant overseer, a collector of poor rates, or some other fit person to act as clerk and be paid.]
[(6) Parish council also to appoint a treasurer (unpaid).]

[18. The county council to have power to divide a parish into wards.]

[19. Parish meetings of small parishes to meet not less than twice a year, appoint committees, and choose a chairman.]

PART II: GUARDIANS AND DISTRICT COUNCILS

20...(1) There shall be no ex-officio or nominated guardians:

[(2) Guardians to be parochial electors or residents for 12 months.]

(3) The parochial electors of a parish shall be the electors of the guardians for the parish....
(4) Each elector may give one vote and no more for each of any number of persons not exceeding the number to be elected....

[(5) Rules to be framed by the Local Government Board.]

(6) The term of office of a guardian shall be three years, and one

third, as nearly as may be, of every board of guardians shall go out of office on the fifteenth day of April in each year...

(7) A board of guardians may elect a chairman or vice-chairman or both, and not more than two other persons, from outside their own body...

21...(1) Urban sanitary authorities shall be called urban district councils, and their districts shall be called urban districts [unless they are boroughs].

(2) For every rural sanitary district there shall be a rural district council whose district shall be called a rural district.

[22. Chairmen but not chairwomen of district councils to be J.P.s.]

[23. Ex officio and nominated members of urban sanitary authorities abolished; councillors to be parochial electors or residents for 12 months; parochial electors to choose councillors; electors to have only one vote per vacancy; term of office to be three years, and one third of the council to retire annually.]

[25. Powers of sanitary and highway authorities transferred to district councils.]

[26. Certain powers over rights of way, commons and roadside wastes given to district councils.]

[27. Certain licensing powers transferred from J.P.s to district councils.]

PGS, 56 & 57 Vict. c. 73

CHAPTER 6

THE ADMINISTRATION
OF JUSTICE

By 1815 a reform of the administration of justice was long overdue. The criminal law was too harsh, the system of police was totally inadequate, commercial law was neglected, there were inordinate delays in some of the higher courts, and the state of the prisons was appalling. Had it not been for the local justices of the peace on whom more and more duties were imposed the system would clearly have broken down. But even the J.P.s, who by using their knowledge of local conditions made the law work, were not a body of men on whom much reliance could be placed. Small wonder that Bentham and his friends talked of a root-and-branch reform on scientific lines, though all they obtained was in fact a model system of legal codes for India.

Reform began with the criminal law which was clearly archaic. A Select Committee of the House of Commons in 1819 called for a substantial reduction in the number of offences punishable by death and Peel as Home Secretary began to reform the criminal law. The process was a piecemeal one but within a generation the criminal law had been transformed. Those who wanted a criminal code on Continental lines were disappointed, but many of their objects were achieved. The next step was the reform of the police, begun by Peel in 1829 with the creation of the Metropolitan Police, which became the model for the provincial police forces created during the next thirty years. Meanwhile much was done to reform the prison system. An act of Peel's in 1824 obliged each county to have a gaol and house of correction and to classify prisoners, and in 1835 a system of inspection for prisons was created. Many new prisons were built, and thereafter the cost of mantaining them rose so fast that in 1877 local prisons were transferred to the central government which had already set up a Prison Commission to administer them. The use of transportation, that great relief to the prisons, was gradually abandoned as a result of pressure both from the colonies and from reformers, and the last convict ship sailed to Australia in 1867.

The reform of the superior courts was a very gradual process. Brougham in 1828 set out a whole programme of reforms in a speech in the House of Commons,[1] and as Lord Chancellor after 1830 was able to carry through some of them. He disposed of many of the arrears of Chancery decisions himself, and in 1833 set up the Judicial Committee of the Privy Council

[1] 2 *Hansard* xviii, 127–248.

as a court of appeal for colonial and ecclesiastical cases and for any other classes of case referred to it (278). The Judicial Committee quickly became an important court and in 1872 was strengthened by the addition of up to four permanent judges to serve in addition to the ex officio judges prescribed in 1833. Attempts to create a system of local courts to settle petty disputes about debts and contracts and other commercial matters were slower in coming to fruition, but in 1846 a new system of County Courts was established. These soon became popular and were reorganised from time to time, notably by the County Courts Act, 1888. The superior courts continued, however, to baffle reformers until 1873. The House of Lords was manifestly weak in legal talent, but resisted an attempt to create life peers to serve as judges. The delays in the Court of Chancery were gradually reduced, but the rationale behind the existence of separate systems of law and equity was widely questioned. And the manner of doing business and the clumsiness of the appeal system in the common law courts was a constant affront to clients, as was amply demonstrated during the immensely long Tichborne case.

A root and branch reform of the superior courts was at last carried in 1873. The Supreme Court of Judicature Act provided for the merging of nearly all of the existing common law, Roman law and equity courts in a single Supreme Court of Judicature consisting of two tiers, a high court divided into divisions corresponding to the old courts, and a court of appeal (279). Lord Selborne, who was responsible for the Bill, intended this Supreme Court to decide all cases whatever, except ecclesiastical cases, and even wrote into the Bill a provision for Scottish participation. But the powers of the Judicial Committee of the Privy Council were restored in the course of the passage of the Bill, and the powers of the House of Lords as the final court of appeal were restored in 1876 before the new system had come into effect, partly as a result of Scottish and Irish pressure. Fortunately, the Appellate Jurisdiction Act of 1876, which restored the appellate jurisdiction of the Lords, did do something to strengthen the House of Lords to fit it for its judicial responsibilities by providing for the appointment of four salaried lords of appeal in ordinary and for the House of Lords in its judicial capacity to sit at any time, whether parliament was in session or not (280). There was still difficulty in staffing both the House of Lords and the Judicial Committee of the Privy Council when both were sitting, as became increasingly usual, but the framework of a new system had been established. As soon as the new system had settled down, the five divisions of the High Court created in 1873 were reduced in 1880 to three, the Chancery, Queen's Bench, and Probate, Divorce and Admiralty Divisions.

An inevitable concomitant of reform was the dissociation of the courts from party politics. Traditionally, promotion to the bench had been a reward for party services, although there had always been a number of plain lawyers on the bench as well as political lawyers. The difficulty was how to reduce the number of political appointments to the bench without discouraging able lawyers from going into the House of Commons to provide a supply of future law officers and Lord Chancellors. This difficulty led Prime Ministers and Lord Chancellors to adopt an ambivalent attitude towards judicial appointments. On the one hand they wanted good judges, but on the other hand they wanted to encourage House of Commons lawyers, so that they tried to strike a balance between legal skill and political claims. This balance became highly controversial during the Lord Chancellorship of Lord Halsbury, who was widely denounced for indulging in political jobbery, but it does not appear that his appointments differed much in character from those of his predecessors. What had happened was that political appointments, except for those of the law officers, had become generally unacceptable to the legal profession.

The appointment of J.P.s was also a subject of continual political controversy. The J.P.s enjoyed a certain social status in the community since their appointment to the bench was regarded as an indication that they were the most important men in their localities. Their appointment was therefore a matter of concern to every country gentleman and every local political leader. Until 1910 county J.P.s were nominated to the Lord Chancellor (except in Lancashire where the Chancellor of the Duchy made all judicial appointments) by the Lords-Lieutenant, who were in turn nominated by the Prime Minister on political grounds. Borough J.P.s were appointed by the Lord Chancellor or the Chancellor of the Duchy on the nomination of town councils, M.P.s, and persons of local influence. Inevitably, since Lords-Lieutenant and local worthies chiefly nominated members of their own party, any party long enough in power to nominate a large proportion of the Lords-Lieutenant had many more opportunities of making J.P.s than its opponents. To some extent this political bias could be overcome by a strong-minded Lord Chancellor, particularly in the boroughs, where a man's political record was his chief claim to sit on the bench. But the party out of office often felt it had cause to complain. Complaints were particularly strong after the Liberal Unionist secession from the Liberal party in 1886 had deprived the Liberals of most of their Lord-Lieutenancies. Sir William Harcourt was particularly bitter about the increasingly Tory complexion of the local benches and there was much talk of what the Liberals would do when they were back in office. Between 1892 and 1894 Liberal backbenchers and party workers demanded that Herschell, the Liberal Lord Chancellor, should override the Lords-Lieutenant and appoint great masses of Liberal magistrates, and a similar demand was made of Loreburn after 1905. Both Herschell and Loreburn did their best to resist the pressure put on them because the nominations of M.P.s and political partisans were often ill-considered. The result was a major crisis of confidence in the relations between Loreburn and the Liberal backbenchers in the House of Commons, as a consequence of which it was decided to appoint a royal commission on J.P.s to reduce the pressure on the Lord Chancellor. And in 1910 it was decided to take the first stage in the process of nomination for the bench out of the hands of the Lords-Lieutenant and to entrust it to advisory committees, one in each county and one in each borough.

The political complexion of the judicial bench inevitably had some effect on the type of decisions arrived at in 'political' cases. This was obvious enough in early nineteenth-century trials for seditious libel and in other cases in which men were accused of disturbing the balance of the constitution. But for a long time in the middle of the century there were few 'political' cases. Whether married women might vote at elections, the issue in Reg. *v.* Harrald (1868), the powers of a colonial governor to suppress a riot, the issue in Phillips *v.* Eyre (1870), and the rights of an atheist elected to the Commons, the issue in the various Bradlaugh cases, were all topics which might well have led to considerable dissatisfaction with the bench, but in fact they did not do so. Cases in which the rights of the poor were thought to be involved (notably the Tichborne case) did, however, provoke widespread suspicion that the bench was prejudiced in favour of the rich and well-born. And this suspicion grew in intensity as the number of trade union cases before the courts began to increase, since so many of them were decided against the unions concerned: in Hornby *v.* Close in 1867 it was held that a trade union had no redress against a defaulting official, in the Taff Vale Case in 1901 it was held that a trade union could be sued for damages as a result of the actions of its agents, and in the Osborne Case in 1909, it was held that the Amalgamated Society of Railway Servants might not contribute to the support of Labour members of parliament. All these decisions were in time reversed by statute, but they left a feeling of uncertainty in the mind of the public about the impartiality of the bench. Small wonder that Sir William Robson, the Liberal Attorney General, warned Asquith in 1910 that he must be careful to maintain a balance of views among the judges in the House of Lords (**284**).

The Scottish judicial system was by 1815 in as bad a state as the English. Cases before the Court of Session dragged on for years because there was no effective limit to the number of appeals, the House of Lords was beset by Scottish litigants, and the judicial process was regarded with intense disfavour by the commercial classes. For a time relief was sought by the adoption of jury trial, notably in civil cases. But the Jury Court created in 1815 failed to answer its purpose. By 1823 the government had become desperate and appointed a commission to look into the matter. But though the Judicature Act of 1825 established a clear division of the Court of Session into an Inner

House of eight and an Outer House of Lords Ordinary and gave the lords ordinary additional powers over the conduct of litigation (**277**), many of the main difficulties were not met. Nor did structural reform in 1830, which swept away the Jury and Admiralty Courts, made a first attack on the Court of Exchequer (abolished in 1856), and reorganised the business of the Court of Session, have any substantial effect. Petty cases continued to go to the House of Lords for no reason except the gratification of the Scottish love of litigation, as Lord Westbury sharply pointed out in 1872; some judges continued to have more work than others because other judges were boycotted, with the result that some of the judges were permanently in arrears with their work; the reputation of the Court of Session continued to be uncertain; and the number of new entrants to the Faculty of Advocates actually fell. Business which might have gone to the Court of Session increasingly went to the sheriff courts, and particularly to the sheriff court of Lanarkshire in Glasgow, which was specially strengthened and soon became the main centre of commercial litigation. As a result of this diversion of business a succession of acts was passed to regulate the sheriff courts, among other things requiring the sheriff-substitutes to be trained lawyers in 1825, and making them crown appointees in 1877. The sheriff courts, in addition to their criminal business, attracted even more civil business than was allocated in England to the county courts, and a great many administrative functions as well, including the supervision of parliamentary elections and the process of registration. By the middle of the nineteenth century the strength of the Scottish judicial system lay with the sheriff courts in the counties rather than with the central courts in Edinburgh.

THE CONSTITUTION OF THE SUPERIOR COURTS

277. The Court of Session divided, 1825

...Whereas it is expedient...that certain Regulations should be established for the expediting of Business before the Courts of Law in *Scotland*...be it enacted...That from [11 November 1825] the Seven junior Ordinary Judges of the Court of Session shall be relieved from Attendance in the Inner House, and shall not sit therein, unless in so far as is hereinafter provided, but shall act as Lords Ordinary in the Outer House, to perform the Business which by the subsisting Acts and Usages belong to the Office of Lords Ordinary in the Outer House; and the Lord President, and Three of the senior Ordinary Judges of the Court of Session, shall form the Inner House of the First Division, and the Lord Justice Clerk, with the remaining senior Ordinary Judges, shall form the Inner House of the Second Division. *PGS*, 6 Geo. IV, c. 120

278. Judicial Committee Act, 1833

An Act for the better Administration of Justice in His Majesty's Privy Council [14 *August* 1833].

'Whereas by [2 & 3 Will. IV, c. 92] intituled *An Act for transferring the Powers of the High Court of Delegates, both in Ecclesiastical and Maritime Causes, to His Majesty in Council*, it was enacted, that from [1 February 1833 certain cases should go to the Privy Council]: And whereas, by Letters Patent...certain Persons...have been from Time to Time appointed to be...Commissioners for receiving, hearing, and determining Appeals from His Majesty's Courts of Admiralty in Causes of Prize: And whereas, from the divisions of various Courts...in the *East Indies*, and in the Plantations, Colonies, and other Dominions of His Majesty Abroad, an Appeal lies to His Majesty in Council...And whereas it is expedient to make certain Provisions for the more effectual hearing and reporting on Appeals to His Majesty in Council...:' Be it therefore enacted... That the President for the Time being of His Majesty's Privy Council, the Lord High Chancellor of *Great Britain*..., and such of the Members of His Majesty's Privy Council as shall from Time to Time hold any of the Offices following, that is to say, ...Lord Keeper...Lord Chief Justice or Judge of the Court of King's Bench, Master of the Rolls, Vice Chancellor of *England*, Lord Chief Justice or Judge of the Court of Common Pleas, Lord Chief Baron or Baron of the Court of Exchequer, Judge of the Prerogative Court of the Lord Archbishop of *Canterbury*, Judge of the High Court of Admiralty, and Chief Judge of the Court in Bankruptcy, and also all Persons Members of His Majesty's Privy Council who shall have been President thereof or held the Office of Lord Chancellor of *Great Britain*, or shall have held any of the other Offices herein-before mentioned, shall form a Committee of His Majesty's said Privy Council, and shall be styled 'The Judicial Committee of the Privy Council': [except that the Crown is to have power to appoint two additional Privy Councillors to the Committee not qualified as above.]

[II. Appeals from Vice Admiralty Courts Abroad also to be made to the Privy Council.]

v. ...That no Matter shall be heard, nor shall any Order, Report, or Recommendation be made, by the said Judicial Committee,...unless in the Presence of at least Four Members of the said Committee; and that no Report or Recommendation shall be made to His Majesty unless a Majority of the Members of such Judicial Committee present at the Hearing shall concur in such Report or Recommendation....

PGS, 3 & 4 Will. IV, c. 41

279. Supreme Court of Judicature Act, 1873

An Act for the constitution of a Supreme Court, and for other purposes relating to the better Administration of Justice in England; and to authorise the transfer to the Appellate Division of such Supreme Court of the Jurisdiction of the Judicial Committee of Her Majesty's Privy Council [5th August 1873].

PART I: *Constitution and Judges of Supreme Court*

3. From and after the time appointed for the commencement of this Act...the High Court of Chancery of England, the Court of Queen's Bench, the Court of Common Pleas at Westminster, the Court of Exchequer, the High Court of Admiralty, the Court of Probate, the Court for Divorce and Matrimonial Causes, and the London Court of Bankruptcy, shall be united and consolidated together, and shall constitute, under and subject to the provisions of this Act, one Supreme Court of Judicature in England.

4. The said Supreme Court shall consist of two permanent Divisions, one of which, under the name of 'Her Majesty's High Court of Justice,' shall have and exercise original jurisdiction, with such appellate jurisdiction from inferior Courts as is herein-after mentioned, and the other of which, under the name of 'Her Majesty's Court of Appeal,' shall have and exercise appellate jurisdiction, with such original jurisdiction as herein-after mentioned as may be incident to the determination of any appeal.

5. Her Majesty's High Court of Justice shall be constituted as follows:—
The first Judges thereof shall be the Lord Chancellor, the Lord Chief Justice of England, the Master of the Rolls, the Lord Chief Justice of the Common Pleas, the Lord Chief Baron of the Exchequer, the several Vice-Chancellors of the High Court of Chancery, the Judge of the Court of Probate and of the Court for Divorce and Matrimonial Causes, the several Puisne Justices of the Courts of Queen's Bench and Common Pleas respectively, the several Junior Barons of the Court of

Exchequer, and the Judge of the High Court of Admiralty, except such, if any, of the aforesaid Judges as shall be appointed ordinary Judges of the Court of Appeal.... All persons to be hereafter appointed to fill the places of the Lord Chief Justice of England, the Master of the Rolls, the Lord Chief Justice of the Common Pleas, and the Lord Chief Baron, and their successors respectively, shall continue to be appointed to the same respective offices, with the same precedence, and by the same respective titles, and in the same manner, respectively, as heretofore. Every Judge who shall be appointed to fill the place of any other Judge of the said High Court of Justice shall be styled in his appointment 'Judge of Her Majesty's High Court of Justice,' and shall be appointed in the same manner in which the Puisne Justices and Junior Barons of the Superior Courts of Common Law have been heretofore appointed.... The Lord Chief Justice of England for the time being shall be President of the said High Court of Justice in the absence of the Lord Chancellor.

6. Her Majesty's Court of Appeal shall be constituted as follows:— There shall be five ex officio Judges thereof, and also so many ordinary Judges (not exceeding nine at any one time) as Her Majesty shall from time to time appoint. The ex officio Judges shall be the Lord Chancellor, the Lord Chief Justice of England, the Master of the Rolls, the Lord Chief Justice of the Common Pleas, and the Lord Chief Baron of the Exchequer. The first ordinary Judges of the said Court shall be the existing Lords Justices of Appeal in Chancery, the existing salaried Judges of the Judicial Committee of Her Majesty's Privy Council, appointed under the 'Judicial Committee Act, 1871,' and such three other persons as Her Majesty may be pleased to appoint....

Besides the said ex officio Judges and ordinary Judges, it shall be lawful for Her Majesty...from time to time to appoint...as additional Judges of the Court of Appeal, any persons who, having held in England the office of a Judge of the Superior Courts of Westminster hereby united and consolidated, or of Her Majesty's Supreme Court hereby constituted, or in Scotland the office of Lord Justice General or Lord Justice Clerk, or in Ireland the office of Lord Chancellor or Lord Justice of Appeal, or in India the office of Chief Justice of the High Court of Judicature at Fort William in Bengal, or Madras, or Bombay, shall respectively signify in writing their willingness to serve as such additional Judges in the Court of Appeal....

The ordinary and additional Judges of the Court of Appeal shall be styled Lords Justices of Appeal. All the Judges of the said Court shall have, in all respects, save as in this Act is otherwise expressly mentioned, equal power, authority, and jurisdiction.

The Lord Chancellor for the time being shall be President of the Court of Appeal.

[8. Judges not in future required to be Serjeants-at-Law but to be barristers of 10 years standing.]

PART II: *Jurisdiction and Law*

16. The High Court of Justice shall be a Superior Court of Record, and, subject as in this Act mentioned, there shall be transferred to and vested in the said High Court of Justice the jurisdiction which, at the commencement of this Act, was vested in, or capable of being exercised by, all or any of the Courts following; (that is to say,)

(1.) The High Court of Chancery, as a Common Law Court as well as a Court of Equity, including the jurisdiction of the Master of the Rolls, as a Judge or Master of the Court of Chancery, and any jurisdiction exercised by him in relation to the Court of Chancery as a Common Law Court;

(2.) The Court of Queen's Bench;

(3.) The Court of Common Pleas at Westminster;

(4.) The Court of Exchequer, as a Court of Revenue, as well as a Common Law Court;

(5.) The High Court of Admiralty;

(6.) The Court of Probate;

(7.) The Court for Divorce and Matrimonial Causes;

(8.) The London Court of Bankruptcy;

(9.) The Court of Common Pleas at Lancaster;

(10.) The Court of Pleas at Durham;

(11.) The Courts created by Commissions of Assize, of Oyer and Terminer, and of Gaol Delivery, or any of such Commissions:

The jurisdiction by this Act transferred to the High Court of Justice shall include (subject to the exceptions herein-after contained) the jurisdiction which, at the commencement of this Act, was vested in, or capable of being exercised by, all or any one or more of the Judges of the said Courts, respectively, sitting in Court or Chambers, or elsewhere, when acting as Judges or a Judge, in pursuance of any statute law, or custom, and all powers given to any such Court, or to any such Judges or Judge, by any statute; and also all ministerial powers, duties, and authorities, incident to any and every part of the jurisdictions so transferred...

18. The Court of Appeal established by this Act shall be a Superior Court of Record, and there shall be transferred to and vested in such Court all jurisdiction and powers of the Courts following; (that is to say,)

(1.) All jurisdiction and powers of the Lord Chancellor and of the Court of Appeal in Chancery, in the exercise of his and its appellate jurisdiction, and of the same Court as a Court of Appeal in Bankruptcy:

(2.) All jurisdiction and powers of the Court of Appeal in Chancery of the county palatine of Lancaster, and all jurisdiction and powers of the Chancellor of the duchy and county palatine of Lancaster when sitting alone or apart from the Lords Justices of Appeal in Chancery as a Judge of re-hearing or appeal from decrees or orders of the Court of Chancery of the county palatine of Lancaster:

(3.) All jurisdiction and powers of the Court of the Lord Warden of the Stannaries assisted by his assessors, including all jurisdiction and powers of the said Lord Warden when sitting in his capacity of Judge:

(4.) All jurisdiction and powers of the Court of Exchequer Chamber:

(5.) All jurisdiction vested in or capable of being exercised by Her Majesty in Council, or the Judicial Committee of Her Majesty's Privy Council, upon appeal from any judgment or order of the High Court of Admiralty, or from any order in lunacy made by the Lord Chancellor, or any other person having jurisdiction in lunacy....

20. No error or appeal shall be brought from any judgment or order of the High Court of Justice, or of the Court of Appeal, nor from any judgment or order, subsequent to the commencement of this Act, of the Court of Chancery of the county palatine of Lancaster, to the House of Lords or to the Judicial Committee of Her Majesty's Privy Council....

21. It shall be lawful for Her Majesty, if she shall think fit, at any time hereafter by Order in Council to direct that all Appeals and Petitions whatsoever to Her Majesty in Council which according to the laws now in force ought to be heard by or before the Judicial Committee of Her Majesty's Privy Council, shall, from and after a time to be fixed

by such Order, be referred for hearing to and be heard by Her Majesty's Court of Appeal....

The Court of Appeal, when hearing any appeals in Ecclesiastical Causes which may be referred to it in manner aforesaid, shall be constituted of such and so many of the Judges thereof, and shall be assisted by such assessors being Archbishops or Bishops of the Church of England, as Her Majesty, by any General Rules made with the advice of the Judges of the said Court, or any five of them (of whom the Lord Chancellor shall be one), and of the Archbishops and Bishops who are members of Her Majesty's Privy Council, or any two of them (and which General Rules shall be made by Order in Council), may think fit to direct... [provided that the rules are laid before Parliament].

24. In every civil cause or matter commenced in the High Court of Justice law and equity shall be administered by the High Court of Justice and the Court of Appeal....

26. The Division of the legal year into terms shall be abolished so far as relates to the administration of justice....

[29. Power to continue assize courts with High Court judges and Commissioners.]

[31. The High Court to be divided into five divisions.]

The said five Divisions shall be called respectively the Chancery Division, the Queen's Bench Division, the Common Pleas Division, the Exchequer Division, and the Probate, Divorce, and Admiralty Division.

[32. The number of divisions may be changed by Order in Council.]

PGS, 36 & 37 Vict., c 66

280. Appellate Jurisdiction Act, 1876

An Act for amending the Law in respect of the Appellate Jurisdiction of the House of Lords; and for other purposes [11 August 1876].

3. Subject as in this Act mentioned an appeal shall lie to the House of Lords from any order or judgment of any of the courts following; that is to say,

(1.) Of Her Majesty's Court of Appeal in England; and

(2.) Of any Court in Scotland from which error or an appeal at or immediately before the commencement of this Act lay to the House of Lords by common law or by statute; and

(3.) Of any Court in Ireland from which error or an appeal at or immediately before the commencement of this Act lay to the House of Lords by common law or by statute.

4. Every appeal shall be brought by way of petition to the House of Lords, praying that the matter of the order or judgment appealed against may be reviewed before Her Majesty the Queen in her Court of Parliament, in order that the said Court may determine what of right, and according to the law and custom of this realm, ought to be done in the subject-matter of such appeal.

5. An appeal shall not be heard and determined by the House of Lords unless there are present at such hearing and determination not less than three of the following persons, in this Act designated Lords of Appeal; that is to say,

(1.) The Lord Chancellor of Great Britain for the time being; and

(2.) The Lords of Appeal in Ordinary to be appointed as in this Act mentioned; and

(3.) Such Peers of Parliament as are for the time being holding or have held any of the offices in this Act described as high judicial offices.

6. For the purpose of aiding the House of Lords in the hearing and determination of appeals, Her Majesty may, at any time after the passing of this Act, by letters patent appoint two qualified persons to be Lords of Appeal in Ordinary, but such appointment shall not take effect until the commencement of this Act.

A person shall not be qualified to be appointed by Her Majesty a Lord of Appeal in Ordinary unless he has been at or before the time of his appointment the holder for a period of not less than two years of some one or more of the offices in this Act described as high judicial offices, or has been at or before such time as aforesaid, for not less than fifteen years, a practising barrister in England or Ireland, or a practising advocate in Scotland.

Every Lord of Appeal in Ordinary shall hold his office during good behaviour, and shall continue to hold the same notwithstanding the demise of the Crown, but he may be removed from such office on the address of both Houses of Parliament.

There shall be paid to every Lord of Appeal in Ordinary a salary of six thousand pounds a year.

Every Lord of Appeal in Ordinary, unless he is otherwise entitled to sit as a member of the House of Lords, shall by virtue and according to the date of his appointment be entitled during his life to rank as a Baron by such style as Her Majesty may be pleased to appoint, and shall during the time that he continues in his office as a Lord of Appeal in Ordinary, and no longer, be entitled to a writ of summons to attend, and to sit and vote in the House of Lords; his dignity as a Lord of Parliament shall not descend to his heirs. . . .

A Lord of Appeal in Ordinary shall, if a Privy Councillor, be a member of the Judicial Committee of the Privy Council, and, subject to the due performance by a Lord of Appeal in Ordinary of his duties as to the hearing and determining of appeals in the House of Lords, it shall be his duty, being a Privy Councillor, to sit and act as a member of the Judicial Committee of the Privy Council.

8. For preventing delay in the administration of justice, the House of Lords may sit and act for the purpose of hearing and determining appeals, and also for the purpose of Lords of Appeal in Ordinary taking their seats and the oaths, during any prorogation of Parliament, at such time and in such manner as may be appointed by order of the House of Lords made during the preceding session of Parliament; and all orders and proceedings of the said House in relation to appeals and matters connected therewith during such prorogation, shall be as valid as if Parliament had been then sitting, but no business other than the hearing and determination of appeals and the matters connected therewith, and Lords of Appeal in Ordinary taking their seats and the oaths as aforesaid, shall be transacted by such House during such prorogation. . . .

9. If on the occasion of a dissolution of Parliament Her Majesty is graciously pleased to think that it would be expedient, with a view to prevent delay in the administration of justice, to provide for the hearing and determination of appeals during such dissolution, it shall be lawful for Her Majesty, by writing under her Sign Manual, to authorise the Lords of Appeal in the name of the House of Lords, to hear and determine appeals during the dissolution of Parliament, and for that purpose to sit in the House of Lords at such times as may be thought expedient; and upon such authority as aforesaid being given by Her Majesty, the Lords of Appeal may, during such dissolution, hear and determine

appeals and act in all matters in relation thereto in the same manner in all respects as if their sittings were a continuation of the sittings of the House of Lords, and may in the name of the House of Lords exercise the jurisdiction of the House of Lords accordingly....

[14. The four paid judges of the Judicial Committee of the Privy Council to be replaced by two Lords of Appeal in Ordinary as vacancies occur.

An Order in Council to be made prescribing rules for the hearing of ecclesiastical cases.]

[15. Three judges of the High Court to be transferred to the Court of Appeal, making a total of six ordinary judges in the Court of Appeal.]

[17. So far as possible cases in the High Court to be heard by a single judge, and divisional courts to consist of two judges.]   *PGS*, 39 & 40 Vict., c. 59

LEGAL PATRONAGE

281. Goulburn on the importance of giving legal patronage to government supporters, 1835

(a) *Sir Robert Peel to Henry Goulburn, 13 January 1835*

I will say to you what I should say if my own brother were a candidate, that I think the judicial office ought always to be filled without reference to any personal considerations whatever.

I think if a man has embarked violently in party politics, he has no right to expect promotion from the Government to which he was opposed. But with that exception, in my opinion on all occasions, but especially on the first when a new Government is called on to make a judicial appointment, that appointment ought to be made which, considering the professional character of the person to be appointed, will do the most credit to the Government.

If by his station in the profession your brother has the best professional claim, I think it would be exceedingly unjust to disregard it on account of his connection with you, but I am bound to say to you with perfect frankness that I do not think the connection ought to weigh against a higher professional claim.

I would really, my dear Goulburn, do for a brother of yours what I would do for a brother of my own, which would be to request in the case of a judicial appointment a fair consideration of the professional claim, without any reference to personal or political connections.

(b) Henry Goulburn to Sir Robert Peel, 14 January 1835

When there are no superior qualifications evidently marking out a man for an office, it is I think impolitic to select for appointment those men who have been uniformly opposed to a Government, or only recently converted.

I may live in a peculiar society, but I can assure you that I find nothing more prejudicial to our interests than the impression which prevails that such is our course. It deadens the exertions of zealous friends, and it makes the large mass, namely those who act on interested motives, oppose us as a matter of profitable speculation. I believe that we have suffered more from making Abercromby Chief Baron than from any act of our last Administration. So much I have thought it right to say on public grounds.   Parker, *Peel*, II, 272–3

282. Lord Westbury's method of appointing J.P.s, 1863

[Lord Westbury to Lord Advocate Moncreiff]

In England I judge, first (in cities and boroughs), of the sufficiency of the existing number; secondly, in cities, I submit the proposed names to the Town Council; thirdly, I endeavour to keep an even hand between Conservatives and Liberals, giving *a little* preponderance to the latter.

But I never appoint attorneys, clergymen (if others can be found), vintners, brewers, owners of public-houses; for the latter three have a direct interest in the decisions of the magistrates.   Nash, *Westbury*, II, 49

283. Salisbury in difficulties with a colleague about an applicant for a Law Officership, 1885

[Marquess of Salisbury to the Duke of Richmond, 29 June 1885]

These law appointments are a great source of anxiety. I cannot consent to regard them either as questions of seniority—or as rewards for party services. In not naming Grantham [William Grantham, M.P.] either to be Attorney or Solicitor General I am following the advice of the Lord Chancellor, of Sir Henry Holland who has great experience of the work that goes on between the departments & the Law Officers— & of Sir Michael Beach. The truth is that Grantham though a very good party worker is a poor speaker, no lawyer, & a very inferior man. I think the Bar would resent his appointment very much.[1]

Goodwood MSS., 871

284. Sir William Robson on the need for a political balance among the Law Lords, 1910

[Sir William Robson (Attorney General) to H. H. Asquith, 30 August 1910]

The Lord Chancellor is no doubt anxious to exclude from his court any appointment he believes to be political, but the political complexion of the court cannot be altogether ignored, especially in view of future developments. The tribunal will have to play a great part in disputes that are legal in form but political in fact, and it would be idle to deny the resolute bias of many of the Judges—there and elsewhere. That bias will probably operate more than ever in cases that touch on labour, educational, constitutional, and, for the future, I may perhaps add revenue questions. Keeton, *A Liberal Attorney General*, pp. 220–1

---

[1] When Grantham was made a High Court Judge in 1886 by Lord Chancellor Halsbury there was in fact a considerable outcry, as Salisbury had expected.

CHAPTER 7

CHURCH AND STATE

Throughout the eighteenth century church and state were indissolubly linked, the church upholding the state and the state regarding the church as an arm of government. As a consequence abuses in church and state were attacked on much the same footing by reformers, who regarded the church as little more than a system of out-relief for the younger sons of the gentry and aristocracy. The church itself was slowly changing between 1800 and 1828: non-residence was under attack; evangelicals were slowly working their way up the ecclesiastical hierarchy (the first evangelical bishop was chosen in 1815); missionary societies had begun to flourish; there was a move to provide more churches in new centres of population, which led to a programme of state-financed church building under the Additional Churches Act of 1818; and ministers had begun to regard ecclesiastical patronage as too important to be used solely for political purposes (285). But everywhere there were abuses, and it required very little effort on the part of the reformers to demonstrate that reform was overdue. Indeed, even the Tories were divided as to whether civil disabilities based on religion were any longer justified. The Test and Corporation Acts were repealed without much opposition at the instance of Lord John Russell in 1828, and Catholic emancipation was carried by the Wellington government in response to the difficulty of governing Ireland in 1829 (287).[1]

After the Reform Act institutional reform became inevitable. The question was simply how far reforms were to be shaped by the Whigs and how far by the Tories. The Grey ministry set up commissions of enquiry into ecclesiastical courts and church revenues, and proposed a reduction in the episcopate and revenues of the Irish Church as a first step towards church reform, a modest proposal which led to John Keble's assize sermon on national apostasy and the first *Tract for the Times* in 1833.[2] Peel advocated a measure of reform in order to prepare the church better to face the reformers' challenge (289); during his short ministry of 1834–5 he established an ecclesiastical commission and he was also largely responsible for the creation of the Tithe Commission in 1836, which took much of the sting out of agrarian discontent against the church. The main institutional changes which came out of all this activity were a substantial reduction in the Irish ecclesiastical establishment, an equalisation of episcopal incomes, and a centralisation of church property in the hands of a permanent Ecclesiastical Commission, established by the Estab-

---

[1] For these Acts see *EHD* XI, 674–5, 687–9.   [2] *EHD* XII (1), 339–40.

lished Church Act of 1836. But there was also a change in the structure of cathedral chapters under the Dean and Chapters Act of 1840 and a further limitation of the tenure of benefices in plurality. And the first steps were taken to transfer family law from the ecclesiastical to the civil authorities when civil registration of births, deaths and marriages was introduced in 1837.

These administrative reforms were accompanied by a spiritual revival in the church, part evangelical, part high church, which transformed its morale (288). Reforming clergymen began to demand a new measure of independence of the church from the state in order to enable it to strengthen its spiritual claims (286), and the revival of convocation to give the church its own parliament. The Convocation of Canterbury, suspended since 1717, at last met in 1852, and was in time supplemented by a revived Convocation of York, a church congress founded in 1861 to discuss problems of interest to clergy and laity alike, and consultative Houses of Laymen, first created for the province of Canterbury in 1886. The bishops also began the uphill task of reorganising their dioceses, encouraging their clergy to give more attention to pastoral care, and disciplining or exhorting the growing numbers of liturgical experimenters who presented a real threat to church unity.

The revival of the church did not exempt it from further criticism. The existence of different schools of thought within the church—anglo-catholic, high church, broad church, erastian, evangelical—led to continued controversy and criticism. The drift to Rome associated with Manning and Newman alarmed churchmen and nonconformists alike. A series of prosecutions aimed at disciplining Romanising clergy demonstrated the powerlessness of the church to enforce uniformity without a change in the law which parliament was reluctant to give. Foolish bishops, by the exercise of their patronage and the arrogance of their speech, made it harder for the bishops to get even a modest measure of reform, such as the Public Worship Regulation Act, 1874, which strengthened the hands of the bishops and set up a new ecclesiastical court under Lord Penzance as dean of the arches.[1] The religious census of 1851 showed that the claim of the church to be truly national was no longer valid (294), and undermined the case for compulsory church rates, church control of graveyards, and the regulation of marriage, divorce and probate by the ecclesiastical courts (abolished in 1857). And increasingly there was a demand for a change in the system of patronage, especially the abolition of the sale of benefices, and for a democratisation of the church, which seemed to many Liberals the last and most corrupt of the unreformed corporations.

Inevitably a great deal of energy went into the discussion of the case for the establishment of religion. Posed first as a major problem during the attack on the Irish establishment in 1835, raised again in an acute form by the

---

[1] *EHD* XII (1), 396–8.

events which led to the disruption of the Church of Scotland, it was kept alive by the Liberation Society (the Society for the Liberation of Religion from State Patronage and Control), a militant nonconformist body founded by Edward Miall as the British Anti-State-Church Association in 1844 (**292**). The controversy took many forms. Gladstone long maintained that it was a function of the state to propagate religious truth (**290**). The Church of Scotland in the Claim of Right claimed entire autonomy in spiritual matters and regarded establishment as essentially a civil device.[1] The lawyers in both Scotland and England maintained that it was for the courts to lay down church doctrines on the basis of the 'constitutions' of the churches, and applied their doctrine alike to the Church of Scotland, the Church of England and the unestablished Free Church of Scotland, the latter in 1903–4. And the consequences of the attempt by lawyers to lay down church doctrine in the Gorham Case (1850) and the *Essays and Reviews* Case (1864) were to haunt religious thinkers with a vision of state control of religion for the rest of the century, though at the time it attracted a good deal of lay support, suggested by the mock epitaph for Lord Westbury attributed to Sir Philip Rose:

RICHARD BARON WESTBURY,
Lord High Chancellor of England.
He was an eminent Christian,
An energetic and merciful Statesman,
And a still more eminent and merciful Judge.
During his three years' tenure of office
He abolished the ancient method of conveying land,
The time-honoured institution of the Insolvents' Court,
And
The Eternity of Punishment.
Towards the close of his earthly career,
In the Judicial Committee of the Privy Council,
He dismissed Hell with costs,
And took away from orthodox members of the
Church of England
Their last hope of everlasting damnation.[2]

Nor were straightforward erastians uncommon; Sir William Harcourt devoted his closing years to attacks on the indiscipline of the Church of England.

During the 1860s there was an increasing readiness among churchmen to recognise the disadvantages of establishment. Gladstone publicly acknowledged in 1868 that he now regarded establishment as a political device arising from the will of the people and changeable at will, and launched a campaign for the disestablishment of the Irish Church as a gesture of goodwill

[1] *Ibid.* pp. 354–61.   [2] Nash, *Westbury*, II, 78.

towards Ireland. The Whigs, long distrustful of the church, rallied to him and at the general election of 1868 Irish disestablishment was the chief issue. After the Liberals had won an easy victory the Irish Church was duly disestablished in the following year.

The attack on the Irish church coincided with a revival of nonconformist fervour. Heartened by the 1851 census nonconformists felt that they were now the leading religious force in the country and that their strength would soon be reflected in a nonconformist-dominated Liberal party. The abolition of compulsory church rates was conceded to them without a fight by the Conservatives in 1868. And in the early seventies there was a general nonconformist expectation that they would be able to get the sort of education and licensing systems that they wanted. Thwarted, they turned increasingly to nonconformist-based associations like the National Education League, the United Kingdom Alliance, and the Liberation Society, which found a new form of political expression in the National Liberal Federation under Joseph Chamberlain. Chamberlain himself was committed to disestablishment, and between 1883 and 1886 gave his full backing to campaigns for Welsh and Scottish disestablishment. After 1885 both the Scottish and Welsh Liberals favoured disestablishment, and Gladstone was prepared to go along with them. Welsh and Scottish disestablishment were included in the Newcastle programme (**184**), and in 1893 the Liberal government announced that it was proposing to take the first steps towards both Welsh and Scottish disestablishment. A bill providing for Welsh disestablishment was introduced by both the Rosebery and Asquith governments and Welsh disestablishment was one of the measures awaiting ratification under the Parliament Act when war broke out in 1914. Scottish disestablishment, however, gradually ceased to be a political issue, because the Scottish churches developed an interest in reunion rather than disestablishment. English disestablishment also receded as a political issue after 1895. By 1905 when the Liberals returned to office the nonconformist movement in politics had spent much of its force, and the failure of the nonconformists to force the repeal of the Education Act of 1902 marked the beginning of the end of their importance as an independent political force. By 1914 the major issues in politics were social rather than sectarian.

The campaign for the disestablishment of the Irish Church in 1868 coincided with a marked strengthening of the administrative side of the Church of England by the appointment of Archibald Campbell Tait as Archbishop of Canterbury. He and his successors, Benson, Temple, and Davidson, were all primarily ecclesiastical statesmen concerned with problems of church order, the rebuilding of the diocesan and parochial systems and the reform of the ecclesiastical law. Thanks to them, and to Queen Victoria and her advisers (chiefly Dean Wellesley and Randall Davidson), the standard of ecclesiastical patronage became a high one. The Prime Minister was still responsible for all the higher appointments, but even Disraeli, who was anxious to use church patronage for party purposes, found it impossible to override the objections of Queen Victoria and her advisers, who could point to the fact that even Lord Palmerston had been scrupulous about ecclesiastical appointments (296). Queen Victoria had very strong views about the essentially Protestant character of the Church (298) and did her best to see that as few high churchmen as possible were appointed to key dioceses. She was prepared to fight hard for the men of her choice (Tait was her nominee, appointed in spite of Disraeli's hostility, but she opposed the appointment of Temple), and she was prepared to quarrel with the high-church Gladstone and Salisbury about the men they wished to nominate. Gladstone and Salisbury, however, were remarkably scrupulous in their use of ecclesiastical patronage, with the result that the late Victorian episcopate was probably the strongest in the history of the church, and a fitting sponsor for the Lambeth Conference which began to bring together the bishops of the whole of the world-wide Anglican communion.

285. Liverpool on Church patronage, 1819
[Earl of Liverpool to Earl Talbot, 19 September 1819]

I believe that as to the Church patronage in England no Minister has ever paid more attention to merit or so little to political objects, as myself. But it is impossible where pretensions are nearly equal, wholly to set aside all other considerations.

The aristocracy of the country will naturally expect to have some share in the patronage of the Church, and it is desirable even for the sake of the Church itself that this should be the case. The man of learning and talents who is made a bishop is of more consequence as such when he finds at his side a man of rank and family holding perhaps a bishopric inferior in rank and importance to his own. It is of great consequence, however, that the proportion of men of rank raised to the bench should not be too large. In England there is no ground for complaint on this head. I cannot quite say as much of the distribution of patronage heretofore in Ireland. If, however, individuals of rank and connection are to be promoted, it cannot be expected that friends should not be preferred to foes—but I quite agree that no person, whoever he may be, should be promoted in the Church unless he possesses decided claims from his clerical character. *EHD* xi, 650

286. Bishop Lloyd argues that the Church is worse off in spiritual terms than the Dissenters, 1828

[Bishop of Oxford to Robert Peel, 21 March 1828]

The Church of England as far as regards the exercise of spiritual power is infinitely inferior to the Dissenters: not that the Legislature has directly done anything to assist or encourage the spiritual power of that body, but that it has placed the Church of England under so severe a cognizance, has passed such severe laws in relation to her exertion of such power, has so impeded and controlled the action even of the Ecclesiastical Courts, that the spiritual power of the Church of England is not only virtually but positively taken away by direct acts of the Legislature. For how stands the law? The Church of England cannot meet now in any assembly for the purpose of discussing points of doctrine, of denouncing schism, of making rules of discipline, or for any other purpose of the same kind. You abolished all this when you did in fact abolish Convocation. Nor can her ministers expel a noxious member, excommunicate, or any thing of the same kind. You force them at the same time, without any reference to right or conscience, to baptize, bury, marry Dissenters. Now, in regard to Dissenters, they meet, with the full allowance of the Legislature, in annual conferences; they expel their members; they refuse them the Sacraments, and so keep up their discipline by means of which the use is not permitted to the Church of England. What therefore does the Church of England derive from being the established religion of the country, in this point of view? Nothing whatever; but she loses much; and, if it were not for *civil* privileges, it would be impossible for the Church to cope at all with Dissent, in consequence of the restrictions which the Legislature has imposed upon her discipline.

There was a trial the other day in the King's Bench. A woman is expelled from a Methodist meeting for some alleged moral offence. She brings an action against the expellers for libel; the Court would not hear of it; they said any society had a right to expel its own members, and would not interfere. Can the Church of England do this? If not, which has the superiority?

The Legislature, in fact, say to the Church of England, 'So long as we guarantee you your property, we will take to ourselves the right of controlling your discipline, and of preventing you from exercising any spiritual power over your own members.' It is a villainous argument, and as oppressive as it is mean.

Well then, all the spiritual power of the Church being taken away by law, where can her superiority, where can her establishment be found, if there be on all points a perfect equality of civil rights between her and the Dissenters? Surely nowhere. And if I take for my essential characteristics of the Church of England those which you point out— namely, the necessity of the King's conformity, the seats of the chief ministers in the Legislature, and the property—I see nothing here but certain civil privileges, which, according to this definition of the Establishment, are necessary to its existence. Take then away these civil privileges, and where will be the Establishment?   Peel, *Memoirs*, I, 83–5

287. Peel on Catholic emancipation, 1829

[Robert Peel to the Bishop of Limerick, 8 February 1829]

I am the last person to express surprise that you should apprehend danger from concession to the Roman Catholics; but I entreat you dispassionately to consider the facts I am about to recall to your notice, the prospect which there is of being enabled to maintain permanent resistance to concession, and the danger that concession may be forced upon us under circumstances much more unfavourable than the present.

In the first place there has been a division between the House of Lords and the House of Commons on this subject that has now endured sixteen years.

Secondly, It has been found necessary, in carrying on the Government of this country for the last twenty-five years, not to exclude from the councils of the King such men as Mr. Pitt, the late Lord Melville, Lord Castlereagh, and Mr. Canning. Their exclusion from the Government in times of pressing difficulty was impossible. Their admission into it produced disunion in the Cabinet, and tended to advance Roman Catholic interests. Their inability immediately to carry their views into effect made them probably more decided in their language as to the necessity of ultimately adopting those views.

Thirdly, The opinions of the young men who are now entering into public life, and who are likely to distinguish themselves, are, with scarcely an exception, if with one, in favour of an adjustment of the question.

Fourthly, In the course of the last six months, England, being at peace with the whole world, has had five-sixths of the infantry force of the United Kingdom occupied in maintaining the peace and in police duties in Ireland. I consider the state of things which requires such an application of military force much worse than open rebellion.

Fifthly, There has been established an intimate union between the Roman Catholic laity and the Roman Catholic priesthood: in consequence of that union the representation of the counties of Waterford, Monaghan, Clare, and Louth has been wrested from the hands of the natural aristocracy of those counties; and if the present state of things is to continue, if parties in Parliament are to remain so nicely balanced that each can paralyse the other, that one can prevent concession, the other can prevent restraint and control, we must make up our minds to see sixty or seventy Radicals sent from Ireland when a General Election shall take place.

Sixthly, The state of society in Ireland will soon become perfectly incompatible with trial by jury in any political cases. The Roman Catholics have discovered their strength in respect to the elective franchise. Let us beware that we do not teach them how easy it will be to paralyse the Government and the law, unless we are prepared to substitute some other system of criminal jurisprudence for the present system.

Peel, Memoirs, 1, 360–2

288. Gladstone on the transformation of the Church, 1831–40

[Before 1830] Our churches and our worship bore in general too conclusive testimony to a frozen indifference. No effort had been made either to overtake the religious destitution of the multitudes at home, or to follow the numerous children of the Church, migrating into distant lands, with any due provision for their spiritual wants. The richer benefices were very commonly regarded as a suitable provision for such members of the higher families, as were least fit to push their way in any profession requiring thought or labour. The abuses of plurality and non-residence were at a height, which, if not proved by statistical returns, it would now be scarcely possible to believe. At Eton, the greatest public school of the country (and I presume it may be taken as a sample of the rest), the actual teaching of Christianity was all but dead, though happily none of its forms had been surrendered. It is a retrospect full of gloom; and with all our Romanising, and all our Rationalising, what man of sense would wish to go back upon those dreary times:

'Domos Ditis vacuas, et inania regna'?[1]

[1] Aeneid, VI.

But between 1831 and 1840, the transformation, which had previously begun, made a progress altogether marvellous. Much was due, without doubt, to the earnest labour of individuals. Such men as Bishop Blomfield on the Bench, and Dr. Hook in the parish (and I name them only as illustrious examples), who had long been toiling with a patient but a dauntless energy, began as it were to get the upper hand. But causes of deep and general operation were also widely at work. As the French Revolution had done much to renovate Christian belief on the Continent, so the Church of England was less violently, but pretty sharply, roused by the political events which arrived in a quick and rattling succession. In 1828, the repeal of the Test Act. In 1829, the emancipation of the Roman Catholics. In 1831–2, the agony, and triumph, of Reform. In 1833, the Church Temporalities Act for Ireland. There was now a general uprising of religious energy in the Church throughout the land. It saved the Church. Her condition before 1830 could not possibly have borne the scrutinising eye, which for thirty years past has been turned upon our institutions. Her rank corruptions must have called down the avenging arm. But it was arrested just in time.

It would be difficult to give a just and full idea of the beneficial changes which were either accomplished or begun during this notable decade of years. They embraced alike formal, official movements, of a nature to strike the general eye, and those local improvements in detail, which, as single changes, are known only in each neighbourhood, but which unitedly transform the face of a country. Laws were passed to repress gross abuses; and the altering spirit of the clergy seconded, and even outstripped, the laws. The outward face of divine worship began to be renovated, and the shameful condition of the sacred fabrics was rapidly amended, with such a tide of public approval as overflowed all the barriers of party and of sect, and speedily found its manifestations even in the seceding communions. There is no reason to doubt that at that time at least, and before such changes had become too decidedly the fashion, the outward embellishment of churches, and the greater decency and order of services, answered to, and sprang from, a call within, and proved a less unworthy conception of the sublime idea of Christian worship.

The missionary arm of the Church began to exhibit a vigour wholly unknown to former years. Noble efforts were made, under the auspices of the chief bishops of the Church, to provide for the unsatisfied spiritual wants of the metropolis. The great scheme of the Colonial Episcopate was founded; and in its outset, led to such a development of apostolic zeal and self-denial, as could not but assist, by a powerful reaction, the domestic progress. The tone of public schools (on one of which Arnold was now spending his noble energies) and of universities, was steadily yet rapidly raised.

The greatest change of all was within the body of the clergy.[1] A devoted piety, and an unworldly life, which had been the rare exceptions, became visibly from year to year more and more the rule. The spectacle, as a whole, was like what we are told of a Russian spring: when, after long months of rigid cold, almost in a day the snow dissolves, the ice breaks up and is borne away, and the whole earth is covered with a rush of verdure. These were bright and happy days for the Church of England. She seemed, or seemed to seem, as a Church recalling the description of Holy Writ; to be 'beautiful as the sun which goeth forth in his might,'[2] 'and terrible as an army with banners.'[3]

Gladstone, *Gleanings*, VII, 138–40

289. Peel on the need for the Conservatives to take up Church reform, 1835

[Sir R. Peel to the Bishop of Durham, 23 February 1835]

The important question connected with the Church which was forced upon me, and which required immediate decision, was this:

Is it prudent and safe on the part of the Crown to decline all interference with the state of the Church, and to leave that question to be disposed of as may seem best to the House of Commons, trusting implicitly either to the forbearance and caution of that House, or to the power of the House of Lords to reject what may be injurious?

I cannot with a safe conscience answer that question in the affirmative.

I entreat you to look with me at the constitution of the present House of Commons. We have a decided majority of the representatives of both Ireland and Scotland hostile to the Church, and, I fear, no inconsiderable number of the representatives of England either unfriendly or indifferent to the interests of the Church.

---

[1] It was, I think, about the year 1835, that I first met the Rev. Sydney Smith, at the house of Mr. Hallam. In conversation after dinner he said to me, with the double charm of humour and of good-humour, 'The improvement of the clergy in my time has been astonishing. Whenever you meet a clergyman of my age, you may be quite sure that he is a bad clergyman.'
[2] Judges, v. 31.   [3] Canticles, vi. 4.

On the first discussion that takes place in the House of Commons after my appointment as Prime Minister, on the proposal to replace in the Chair the late Speaker, who has served the House for eighteen years and during seven successive Parliaments, I find myself in a minority of ten.

It is in vain for me to disguise from myself that very few of those who voted in that majority will prove themselves in the day of trial friends to the Church.

The minority is composed in great part of members professing the utmost attachment to the Church, but all, with few exceptions, requiring the correction of whatever can justly be called an abuse in the Establishment.

In that minority Lord Stanley and his friends voted, increasing of course, to the extent of their numbers, the force we could bring into the field. At his late election for Lancashire, Lord Stanley, a declared friend of the Church, who sacrificed his office in maintenance of the principle that Church property in Ireland should not be applicable to secular purposes, delivered these opinions on the subject of Church reform:—

'I know also that Ecclesiastical Reform must come, and that it is certain with regard to two great branches, namely, both as to the temporalities of the Church and also as to her internal discipline. I too, like my honourable friend, would not be a consenting party to abstracting one farthing from the revenues of the clergy, who, I believe in my conscience, are not overpaid, but as a body are hardly adequate to supply the religious wants of the people. But I do say that it is absolutely necessary to have a different distribution of the revenues of the Church, to afford a more equal distribution of the means of religious instruction; that the abuses of non-residence, the abuses of pluralities, and the abuses of the present appropriation of Chapter and Cathedral property should be got rid of, and that the revenues of the Church should be so disposed of as to give the people of England the greatest amount of benefit from the exertion of competently but not overpaid ministers.'

Now, looking at the majority and at the constitution of the minority, what course is it prudent for us to take? Shall we leave Church reform in the hands of the House of Commons, or shall we make an honest, *bonâ fide* attempt to reserve to the Crown and to advisers selected by the Crown the cautious and deliberate review of a question of such extreme delicacy and importance? Peel, *Memoirs*, II, 78–80

290. Gladstone on church and state, 1 June 1836

...a Church Establishment is maintained, either for the sake of its members or its doctrines: for those whom it teaches, or for that which it teaches. On the former ground, it is not in equity tenable for a moment. Why should any preference be given to me over another fellow-subject, or what claim have I personally to have my religion supported, whilst another is disavowed by the State? No claim whatever in respect to myself. I concur entirely with Gentlemen opposite, hostile to an Establishment, that no personal privilege ought, in such a matter, to be allowed. But if, on the contrary, I believe, as the great bulk of the British Legislature does believe, that the doctrine and system of the Establishment contain and exhibit truth in its purest and most effective form—and if we also believe truth to be good for the people universally—then we have a distinct and an immovable ground for the maintenance of an Establishment; but it follows, as a matter of course, from the principle, that it must be maintained, not on a scale exactly and strictly adjusted to the present number of its own members, but on such a scale that it may also have the means of offering to others the benefits which it habitually administers to them. Therefore, we wish to see the Establishment in Ireland upheld, not for the sake of the Protestants, but of the people at large, that her ministers may be enabled to use the influences of their station, of kindly offices and neighbourhood, of the various occasions which the daily intercourse and habits of social life present; aye, and I do not hesitate to add, of persuasion itself, applied by a zeal tempered with knowledge and discretion, in the propagation of that which is true, and which, being true, is good, as well for those who as yet have it not, as for those who have it. It is the proposition of the noble Lord [Lord Stanley] which is really open to the charge of bigotry, intolerance, and arbitrary selection; because, disavowing the maintenance and extension of truth, he continues, by way of personal privilege to the Protestants, the legal recognition of their Church, which he refuses to the Church of the Roman Catholics.

3 *Hansard* XXXIII, 1319–20

291. Macaulay on church and state, April 1839

We consider the primary end of government as a purely temporal end, the protection of the persons and property of men.

We think that government, like every other contrivance of human wisdom...is likely to answer its main end best when it is constructed with a single view to that end.... A blade which is designed both to shave and to carve will certainly not shave so well as a razor, or carve so well as a carving-knife.... On this principle, we think that government should be organised solely with a view to its main end: and that no part of its efficiency for that end should be sacrificed in order to promote any other end however excellent....

Government is not an institution for the propagation of religion, any more than St George's Hospital is an institution for the propagation of religion.... But a government which considers the religious instruction of the people as a secondary end, and follows out that principle faithfully, will, we think, be likely to do much good and little harm.

We will rapidly run over some of the consequences to which this principle leads....

All persecution directed against the persons or property of men is, on our principle, obviously indefensible. For, the protection of the persons and property of men being the primary end of government, and religious instruction only a secondary end, to secure the people from heresy by making their lives, their limbs, or their estates insecure, would be to sacrifice the primary end to the secondary end....

Again, on our principles, all civil disabilities on account of religious opinions are indefensible. For all such disabilities make government less efficient for its main end: they limit its choice of able men for the administration and defence of the state; they alienate from it the heart of the sufferers; they deprive it of a part of its effective strength in all contests with foreign nations....

Again, on our principles, no government ought to press on the people religious instruction, however sound, in such a manner as to excite among them discontents dangerous to public order.... In our opinion, that religious instruction which the ruler ought, in his public capacity, to patronise, is the instruction from which he, in his conscience, believes that the people will learn most good with the smallest mixture of evil. And thus it is not necessarily his own religion that he will select....

A statesman, judging on our principles, would pronounce without hesitation that a church, such as [the Irish Church which is hateful to four-fifths of the population] never ought to have been set up.

Macaulay, *Works*, VI, 372–3, 375–7, 380

292. The British Anti-State-Church Association (afterwards the Liberation Society) founded, 1844

I. That a Society be now formed to be intituled 'The British Anti-State-Church Association.'

II. That this Society be based upon the following principle:— That in matters of religion man is responsible to God alone; that all legislation by secular governments in affairs of religion is an encroachment upon the rights of man, and an invasion of the prerogatives of God; and that the application by law of the resources of the State to the maintenance of any form or forms of religious worship and instruction is contrary to reason, hostile to liberty, and directly opposed to the genius of Christianity.

III. That the object of the Society be, the liberation of religion from all governmental or legislative interference.

IV. That this object be sought by lawful, peaceful, and Christian means, and by such means only.

V. That every individual subscribing to the principle upon which this Society is based, and contributing not less than one shilling annually to its general fund, be admissible as a member.

VI. That the officers of this Society consist of a treasurer and three secretaries, three auditors, and a council of five hundred, and an executive committee of fifty members.

VII. That the whole of the officers be, in the first instance, elected by the [first] Conference.   Miall, *Edward Miall*, pp. 95–6

293. A clergyman turned Baptist attacks the clergy, 1849

But what are the pastors of the Anglican Churches in fact? I grieve to write it. There are men among them of great virtues to whom I gladly do homage. I know and love many faithful, energetic, and sincere servants of Christ; but when these exceptions are subtracted, what are the rest? I grieve to write it. Chosen by peers and squires, by colleges and church-corporations, by chancellors and State-made prelates, many are made pastors by corrupt favouritism, many are allured to an uncongenial employment by the income which it offers them, and many embrace the profession of a pastor because they are too dull, inert, or timid, for any other. They have scarcely any theological training, they are pledged to all the errors in the prayer-book, and all the abuses sanctioned by the Union [of church and state]. They dread reforms, they are servile to patrons, they are intolerant to dissenters; their zeal is crippled by State restrictions, and their indolence tempted by un-bounded liberty to indulge it. Severed from the body of the people by their birth, by their early education, by their college life, by their aristocratical association, by their zeal for their ecclesiastical prerogatives, they have little popular influence. Lawyers, men of science, and editors of newspapers, do not listen to them; Chartists and Socialists dislike and despise them; they scarcely touch the operative millions; they make few converts among the devotees of fashion; and under their leadership the Christian army is inert, timid, and unsuccessful.

Noel, *Essay on the Union of Church and State*, pp. 311–12

294. 1851 census of religious worship

ACCOMMODATION AND ATTENDANCE IN ENGLAND AND WALES
Population, 17,927,609

RELIGIOUS DENOMINATION	Number of places of worship			Number of sittings				Number of attendants at public worship on Sunday, 30 March 1851		
	Separate buildings	Not separate buildings	Total	Free	Appropriated	Not distinguished	TOTAL	Morning	Afternoon	Evening
Total	30,959	3,508	34,467	3,947,371	4,443,093	1,077,274	9,467,738	4,428,338	3,030,280	2,960,772
PROTESTANT CHURCHES										
BRITISH										
Church of England and Ireland	13,854	223	14,077	1,803,773	2,123,395	995,244	4,922,412	2,371,732	1,764,641	803,141
Scottish Presbyterians—										
Church of Scotland	17	1	18	2,422	9,492	1,000	12,914	6,949	960	3,849
United Presbyterian Church	64	2	66	5,275	19,856	5,270	30,401	17,188	4,931	8,551
Presbyterian Church in England	73	3	76	5,669	32,899	1,890	40,458	22,607	3,345	10,684
Reformed Irish Presbyterians	1	—	1	120	—	—	120			
Independents, or Congregationalists	2,960	284	3,244	402,905	578,823	20,779	1,002,507	515,071	228,660	448,847
Baptists—										
General	85	8	93	10,593	6,889	1,050	18,532	5,228	7,865	8,283
Particular	1,776	171	1,947	260,596	281,459	8,720	550,775	286,944	172,145	267,205
Seventh Day	2	—	2	390	16	—	390	27	40	16
Scotch	11	4	15	2,021	16	—	2,037	649	986	312
New Connexion General	170	12	182	24,125	26,268	766	51,159	23,688	15,545	24,381
Baptists (*not otherwise defined*)	441	109	550	49,900	30,415	2,355	82,770	36,525	22,826	37,417
Society of Friends	343	28	371	80,683	920	7,948	89,551	14,016	6,458	1,459
Unitarians	217	12	229	23,153	37,787	2,830	63,770	26,612	8,610	12,406
Moravians, or United Brethren	29	3	32	7,768	455	500	8,723	4,681	2,312	3,202

Wesleyan Methodists—									
Original Connexion	5,625	954	6,579	729,928	5,081	1,361,443	482,753	376,202	654,349
New Connexion	269	28	297	55,086	—	91,716	36,428	22,391	39,222
Primitive Methodists	2,039	832	2,871	165,057	2,174	369,216	98,001	172,684	229,646
Bible Christians	387	95	482	29,502	675	60,341	14,655	24,002	34,038
Wesleyan Methodist Association	340	79	419	45,894	310	90,789	31,922	20,888	40,170
Independent Methodists	15	5	20	451	—	2,144	571	1,245	1,148
Wesleyan Reformers	177	162	339	14,576	445	57,126	30,018	15,841	44,286
Calvinistic Methodists—									
Welsh Calvinistic Methodists	792	36	828	120,730	1,289	198,242	79,728	59,140	125,244
Countess of Huntingdon's Connexion	98	11	109	21,461	55	35,210	19,966	4,099	17,929
Sandemanians, or Glassites	5	1	6	28	—	638	439	256	61
New Church	42	8	50	7,833	300	11,865	4,652	2,308	2,978
Brethren	77	55	132	1,623	30	15,869	5,613	4,441	7,272
Isolated Congregations	372	167	539	21,549	3,637	90,048	34,706	22,726	49,835
FOREIGN:									
Lutherans	5	1	6	1,241	—	2,172	960	220	—
French Protestants	3	—	3	—	—	560	150	21	100
Reformed Church of the Netherlands	1	—	1	—	—	350	70	—	—
German Protestant Reformers	1	—	1	60	—	200	120	—	60
OTHER CHRISTIAN CHURCHES:									
Roman Catholics	506	64	570	73,210	14,254	164,664	240,792	51,406	73,232
Greek Church	3	—	3	—	—	291	240	—	—
German Catholics	—	1	1	200	—	300	500	—	200
Italian Reformers	—	1	1	—	—	150	—	20	—
Catholic and Apostolic Church	29	3	32	373	240	6,973	3,077	1,607	2,622
Latter Day Saints, or Mormons	88	134	222	264	432	22,951	7,212	11,016	15,954
Jews	42	11	53	5,353	—	7,961	2,848	1,043	1,673

294. 1851 census of religious worship (cont.)

ACCOMMODATION AND ATTENDANCE IN ENGLAND AND WALES

Population, 17,927,609

RELIGIOUS DENOMINATION	Places of worship			Sittings			Dates at which the buildings were erected or appropriated to religious purposes							
	Morning	Afternoon	Evening	Morning	Afternoon	Evening	Before 1801	1801 to 1811	1811 to 1821	1821 to 1831	1831 to 1841	1841 to 1851	Not stated	TOTAL
Total	23,669	21,371	18,055	8,028,595	5,846,120	5,488,617	13,094	1,224	2,002	3,141	4,866	5,594	4,546	34,467
PROTESTANT CHURCHES														
BRITISH:														
Church of England and Ireland	11,794	9,933	2,439	4,546,521	3,498,289	1,701,575	9,667	55	97	276	667	1,197	2,118	14,077
Scottish Presbyterians—														
Church of Scotland	17	4	12	12,914	2,180	9,196	8	1	—	2	3	3	1	18
United Presbyterian Church	57	19	40	29,914	7,908	18,823	26	2	10	9	9	5	5	66
Presbyterian Church in England	74	20	44	40,258	7,250	27,540	27	1	4	6	10	24	4	76
Reformed Irish Presbyterians	1	1	—	120	120	—	—	—	—	—	—	—	1	1
Independents, or Congregationalists	2,261	1,406	2,539	871,176	426,964	844,795	849	210	314	484	564	593	230	3,244
Baptists—														
General	39	64	70	9,456	12,569	15,027	30	7	8	15	8	16	9	93
Particular	1,554	1,090	1,532	490,479	294,449	468,538	419	149	205	295	365	380	134	1,947
Seventh Day	2	1	1	390	300	300	1	—	—	—	—	1	—	2
Scotch	13	14	4	1,611	1,787	1,000	3	2	1	1	7	—	1	15
New Connexion General	107	94	140	39,875	22,679	42,335	64	9	18	22	19	38	12	182
Baptists (not otherwise defined)	340	287	380	63,834	42,072	65,266	75	20	51	69	111	123	101	550
Society of Friends	362	213	21	88,799	60,889	5,781	265	17	14	25	20	17	13	371
Unitarians	183	85	114	56,755	20,392	36,872	147	8	14	12	15	18	15	229
Moravians, or United Brethren	28	16	22	8,543	4,563	6,751	18	3	2	4	2	3	—	32

Number of places open for worship at each period of the day, on Sunday, 30 March 1851, and number of sittings thus available

Wesleyan Methodists—														
Original Connexion	3,124	3,881	5,288	923,615	758,315	1,211,884	644	523	927	1,075	1,411	1,247	752	6,579
New Connexion	188	184	252	74,257	42,820	84,775	34	19	30	59	92	47	16	297
Primitive Methodists	1,088	2,010	2,358	178,937	269,998	336,074	198	30	65	332	779	940	527	2,871
Bible Christians	203	309	381	29,403	40,626	51,756	23	15	73	164	148	55	482	
Wesleyan Methodist Association	202	221	345	65,903	38,442	84,442	26	12	19	29	178	109	46	419
Independent Methodists	8	16	17	901	1,997	2,052	—	1	4	2	9	3	20	
Wesleyan Reformers	177	175	289	43,346	24,353	53,066	46	8	18	26	114	114	339	
Calvinistic Methodists—														
Welsh Calvinistic Methodists	498	381	690	130,803	77,350	177,530	174	77	109	177	162	103	26	828
Countess of Huntingdon's Connexion	78	38	86	31,449	8,330	31,470	31	10	12	18	20	14	4	109
Sandemanians, or Glassites	6			638	438	170		3		3			6	
New Church	44	23	30	11,223	4,813	7,818	5	4	12	15	8	50		
Brethren	101	61	103	12,653	8,050	14,170	12	2	3	17	54	41	132	
Isolated Congregations	338	245	388	67,196	42,963	70,861	88	13	34	55	74	149	126	539
FOREIGN:														
Lutherans	6	1	1	2,172	1,202	300	5				1		6	
French Protestants	2	1	2	530	30	530	2						3	
Reformed Church of the Netherlands	1			350			1			1		1		
German Protestant Reformers	1			200	200		1					1		
OTHER CHRISTIAN CHURCHES:														
Roman Catholics	542	339	210	160,865	94,878	85,804	156	28	29	52	92	151	62	570
Greek Church	3			291				1		1	2		3	
German Catholics	1	1		300	300		1	1				3		
Italian Reformers		1			150							1	1	
Catholic and Apostolic Church	29	17	24	6,313	4,253	5,043	3		2	2	16	5	4	32
Latter Day Saints, or Mormons	147	187	193	18,823	19,297	20,892	28	5	11	13	52	113	222	
Jews	50	31	37	7,782	5,404	5,771	16	3	1	6	7	16	4	53

[1690] p. clxxviii–clxxix H.C. (1852–53) lxxxxix, 178–9.

295. Welsh-speaking bishops needed for Wales, 1859

[Earl of Derby to J. Wilson Patten, 28 April 1859]

No one values more highly than I do the many good qualities of our friend the Bishop of Sodor and Man; but among his merits he has not that of being able to speak and preach in Welsh; which in my judgment is all but essential in a Diocese [Bangor] 7/10 of the Inhabitants of which can speak no other language. I am looking out for a good man, and think I have found one [James Colquhoun Campbell was appointed]; but it is not a very easy task, and it has taken up a good deal of my time when I have not had a great deal to spare.   Winmarleigh Papers

296. Palmerston on the selection of bishops, 1860

[Viscount Palmerston to Queen Victoria, 2 December 1860]

With respect to bishops, Viscount Palmerston would beg to submit that the bishops are in the Church what generals of districts are in the Army: their chief duties consist in watching over the clergy of their diocese, seeing that they perform properly their parochial duties, and preserving harmony between the clergy and the laity, and softening the asperities between the Established Church and the Dissenters. For these purposes it is desirable that a bishop should have practical knowledge of parochial functions, and should not be of an overbearing and intolerant temperament. His diocesan duties are enough to occupy all his time, and the less he engages in theological disputes the better. Much mischief has been done by theological bishops, and if the Bench were filled with men like the Bishops of Oxford and Exeter there would be no religious peace in the land. Nor have men chosen merely for their learning succeeded better; Thirlwall, Bishop of St. David's, and Blomfield, the late Bishop of London, were chosen on account of their learning; the former is acknowledged to be inefficient, the latter greatly mismanaged his diocese. The theological learning of the Bishop of Exeter [Phillpotts] has caused much mischief to the Established Church. Viscount Palmerston would also beg to submit that the intolerant maxims of the High Church bishops have exasperated the Dissenters who form a large portion of the nation, and have given offence to many good Churchmen. The Bishop of Exeter, the late Bishop of Carlisle, and the late Bishop of Rochester, the two latter individuals kind-hearted and good-natured men, refused to consecrate burial grounds unless a wall of separation divided the portion allotted to Churchmen from the portion allotted to Dissenters—a demand which gave offence to both communities. Viscount Palmerston would beg to submit that several of the bishops whom he has had the honour of recommending to your Majesty had distinguished themselves by their classical and academical attainments, and he may mention in this respect the names of Baring, Longley, Tait, Wigram, and Waldegrave. Viscount Palmerston can assure your Majesty that although his selection of bishops has been much found fault with by the High Church, Puseyite, and semi-Catholic Party, they have given great satisfaction to the nation at large, and Viscount Palmerston has received communications to that effect, verbal and written, from persons of all classes, and political parties in all parts of the country. The people of this country are essentially Protestant, they feel the deepest aversion to Catholicism, and they see that the High Church, Tractarian, and Puseyite doctrines lead men to the Church of Rome. The disgraceful scenes last year at St George's in the East were only an exaggerated outburst of a very general and deeply-rooted feeling. Viscount Palmerston believes that the clergy of the Established Church were never more exemplary in the performance of their duties, more respected by the Laity and, generally speaking, on better terms with the Nonconformist body than at the present time.   *LQV*, 1st ser. III, 530–1

297. Gladstone abandons establishment as a doctrine, 1869–85

[W. E. Gladstone to Matthew Arnold, 30 March 1869]

...I am one of those who think that, when we pass away from the present Church Establishments, they will be succeeded, not by a new fashion of the like species, but by what is termed the voluntary system. I can contemplate this result without great uneasiness; not because I think it absolutely good, but because it may be the best and safest of the alternatives before us, as the most likely to keep in a state of freshness the heart and conscience of man.

Lathbury, *Correspondence of W. E. Gladstone*, I, 167–8

[W. E. Gladstone to the Rev. Dr. Hutton, 28 July 1885]

The basis of my own position in relation to the Established Church of Scotland remains precisely that which was laid down by Lord

Hartington, I think, about seven years ago. It is a Scotch question, and ought to be decided by the people of Scotland—*i.e.*, Parliament ought to accept their sense.   Lathbury, *Correspondence of W. E. Gladstone*, I, 182

298. Queen Victoria emphasises the Protestant character of the church, 1873

[Queen Victoria to A. P. Stanley, Dean of Westminster, 13 November 1873]

...The Queen *now* turns with much anxiety to the *very* pressing question of the *state* of the *English* Church; its Romanising tendencies which she fears are on the increase, its relations with other Protestant Churches, and the *universal struggle*, which has begun between the Roman Catholic Church and Protestant Governments in general. She is sure that the Dean has heard and seen much in Italy which will throw light on this last. But as regards the English Church, which she perceives is being greatly threatened with disestablishment, action seems becoming necessary. This disestablishment the Queen would regret. She thinks a *complete Reformation* is what we want. But if *that* is *impossible*, the Archbishop should have the *power* given him, by *Parliament*, to *stop all* these Ritualistic practices, dressings, bowings, etc., and everything of that kind, and, *above all*, *all* attempts at *confession*. As the Ecclesiastical Courts can afford no *assistance* on this head, let the Bishops ask for power to put a stop to all these *new* and *very* dangerous as well as absurd practices, and at the same time, give permission to other Protestant Ministers to preach in our churches, and where there is no other church to perform their different services in the same, as is always *done* abroad.

The Queen states all these points very crudely to the Dean, as her mind is greatly occupied with the state of the Church in England, and with the terrible amount of *bigotry* and *self-sufficiency* and *contempt* of all *other Protestant Churches*, of which she had some *incredible* instances the other day. The English Church should bethink itself of its dangers from *Papacy*, instead of trying to widen the breach with *all* other Protestant Churches, and to magnify small differences of form. The English Church should stretch out its arms to other Protestant Churches. The Queen has the greatest confidence in the Dean's courage and energy and wishes he could inspire the Archbishop and others with the same. For the time is coming, if not come, when *something will have* to be done, or—the Church will *fall*.   *LQV*, 2nd ser. II, 290–1

299. Salisbury on the political implications of selecting an Archbishop of York, 1890

[Marquess of Salisbury to Queen Victoria, 30 December 1890]

Lord Salisbury with his humble duty craves your Majesty's pardon for not having written sooner concerning the Archbishopric of York; but he has been unwell and unable to work for two or three days.

He would not recommend Dr. Westcott[1] to your Majesty. There is not only the objection arising from his very recent promotion, but a much more serious one arising from the Socialist tendencies of the speeches he has made since he became a bishop. The Archbishopric is a great political as well as ecclesiastical position; and to confer it on Dr. Westcott at this time, when Socialism is so burning a question, would in Lord Salisbury's humble judgment be a grave mistake, and likely to do much harm.

The other men mentioned by your Majesty are men of lesser note. Lord Salisbury would submit that, if possible, a position of this kind should be conferred on a man possessing high eloquence and intellect; and who, on political as well as polemical questions, is of moderate and safe opinions. With this standard in view Lord Salisbury would respectfully submit the name of the Bishop of Peterborough [Magee] to your Majesty's consideration. He is far the most eloquent preacher and speaker on the episcopal bench. His intellect is fully recognised and respected by those who stand outside the circle of purely ecclesiastical interests. He has done good service to the Party which now enjoys your Majesty's confidence; and that service has been done in the most legitimate way, by the defence of his own Church. His ecclesiastical proclivities were at one time Evangelical; but they are so ill-defined that his elevation would give offence to no party in the Church. The fact that during twenty years no scandals have come from the diocese of Peterborough shows that he can keep the Church in peace. Lord Salisbury recommends him very confidently to your Majesty's favour.

LQV, 3rd ser. 1, 666–7

[1] In a letter on 29th December, the Queen had suggested, in a tentative fashion, the names first of Dr Westcott, Bishop of Durham, and then of the Bishops of Lichfield, Wakefield, and Manchester.

CHAPTER 8

IRELAND

Nineteenth-century governments were but ill-adapted to cope with the problem of how to govern Ireland. No longer convinced of the case for Protestant ascendancy, yet unable to accept that the Catholic Irish were fit to govern themselves unaided, ministers drifted from crisis to crisis. There was not even the possibility of administering Ireland efficiently. The Irish administration was a by-word for pettiness and inadequacy, and English officials sent over to sort things out (like Sir Charles Trevelyan during the Famine) usually made things worse. The Unionist policy of resolute government might have worked if Ireland had been governed by the Indian Civil Service, but because it was largely governed by Irishmen, it was doomed to a long series of unsatisfactory compromises.

The Union of 1800, which abolished the Irish parliament, created a political vacuum which was speedily filled by the Catholic clergy and O'Connell's Repeal Movement. Elections in 1826, like elections fifty years later, were dominated either by landlords backed by English troops or by the priests (**300**). Attempts by the English government to reform the Irish courts and the Irish administration were half-hearted and had little effect. For a time the extraordinary popular backing for O'Connell and his policies (**301**), made more substantial concessions to Irish opinion inevitable if revolution were to be averted. Wellington and Peel carried Catholic emancipation; the Whigs reformed the Irish corporations, appointed Catholics to the judicial bench, created a (very unsatisfactory) Irish poor law, and began a root and branch reform of the Irish Church. But although O'Connell became Lord Mayor of Dublin in 1841, both the Repeal Movement and the Whig government had by then already run out of steam. The major threat to the administration was now to be the Great Famine. While English ministers and officials fumbled, and attempted to devise means for dealing with an unprecedented disaster, the Irish were dying or emigrating, and the whole dimensions of the Irish problem were being changed. The Great Famine left Ireland exhausted, and there was no further popular movement on the scale of the Repeal movement until the 1870s. Young Ireland and the Irish movements of the 1850s were a pale reflection of the Repeal movement, and were almost certainly much less important than the underground revolutionary movements, which the English called Fenian.

Fenianism in the sixties gave the English a new view of Ireland, for Fenian bombs were used in England as well as in Ireland, and Irish processions in

English cities showed that there was an unpalatable degree of solidarity between the Irish living in England and the underground movements. Yet the main significance of Fenianism was that it secured the backing of the Irish in America and helped to alienate American opinion from England. A projected Fenian invasion of Canada failed, but the Fenians, and other Irish national movements, could now count on money and (if required) arms from America.

The turning-point in English relations with Ireland came in 1868, when Gladstone decided that what was required was a gesture of reconciliation towards the Catholic Irish. The disestablishment of the Irish Church was the first step, but the main feature of Gladstone's scheme was the Irish Land Act of 1870, which set up a system of state regulation of land prices (302). Neither measure, however, had much effect on Irish opinion. Disestablishment did nothing to help the Catholics and the Land Act did little to assuage the land-hunger of the small tenantry. Nor was Gladstone's next major Irish venture, the Land Act of 1881, notably more successful, although it caused consternation among English landowners by interfering with the sanctity of freehold.

Gladstone's gestures were met by a growing Irish demand for Home Rule and for a new Irish land system. The first spokesman for Home Rule, Isaac Butt, was careful not to press the claim for Home Rule too far because he wanted to bring as many Irish Liberals and Conservatives as possible into the Home Rule movement (303). But already a strong nationalist movement was at work, and under the leadership of Charles Stewart Parnell it speedily came to dominate the Irish representation at Westminster. The nationalists demanded Home Rule at once and made it clear that if they did not get it they would disrupt the House of Commons and countenance agrarian terrorism. The urgency of their message was underlined by the assassination of the Chief Secretary for Ireland, Lord Frederick Cavendish, and his Under-Secretary in 1882, the work of an underground organisation. The Gladstone government tried coercion as an answer to nationalism, but to no effect: Parnell's demand for Home Rule was clearly backed by the Irish people at the 1885 general election.

By then it was clear that unless something were done at once, the nationalists at Westminster would entirely disrupt the pattern of parliamentary life. The nationalists could command at least eighty-five seats in Ireland, and with the aid of their followers in England they were in a position to intervene decisively between Liberals and Conservatives in a number of English and Scottish seats. Gladstone, after giving Salisbury the chance to move first, decided to offer the Irish Home Rule, but made the mistake of not announcing the fact to the already divided Liberal party until many prominent Liberals had already committed themselves to coercion. As a result, the first Home Rule Bill of 1886 (305) was defeated in the House of Commons by dissentient

Liberals, including John Bright (306), and at the general election which followed the Liberals were defeated.

Gladstone's adoption of Home Rule made the Liberals and Irish nationalists allies, and Home Rule a central issue in British politics. But it also led in Ireland to nearly twenty years (1886–92, 1895–1905) of resolute Unionist government. More important, it contributed to the break-up of the nationalist party; for when in 1890 Parnell was named as co-respondent in a famous divorce case, Gladstone announced that he must give up the leadership of the nationalists or lose Liberal support (308). The nationalists thereupon broke up into Parnellite and anti-Parnellite groups, and lost most of their political effectiveness.

The great achievement of the Unionists was the passage of a Land Act in 1903, which provided for the extinction of Irish landlordism by purchase. The Unionists also did much to improve Irish administration, and introduced a modified local government system. But the long years of Unionist rule also witnessed the growth of a new nationalist cultural movement aiming at an Irish-speaking republic, the creation of Sinn Fein, and the revival of underground opposition to the parliamentarianism and gradualism of the nationalists.

The succession of Home Rule Bills introduced by Liberal governments between 1886 and 1914 all made some provision for retaining a link between Great Britain and Ireland. The 1886 Bill provided for the government of Ireland by an executive in Dublin, responsible to a Dublin parliament (305). But responsibility for all matters affecting the crown, defence, foreign relations and, to some extent, finance, was to remain with the Union government and parliament at Westminster. The Bill proposed to exclude the Irish members from Westminster, but Gladstone was driven to reconsider the matter and the issue was never finally settled. The Second Home Rule Bill of 1893, which passed the Commons and was defeated in the Lords, followed the main lines of the 1886 Bill, but included Irish representation at Westminster (309). The Third Home Rule Bill of 1912 contained few innovations (310). The Union remained intact, and the powers of the Dublin parliament and government were severely restricted—more so, indeed, than was now acceptable to most Irish opinion. But the government was by now much more concerned by the determination of the Ulster leaders to resist their subordination to Dublin than with the opposition in the south. Carson and his colleagues made it clear that they would resort to force if subjected to a Catholic government and joined in the ceremonial signing of 'Ulster's solemn league and covenant'. The House of Lords delayed the Bill's passage until 1914, and in the meantime Asquith sought ways of conciliating Ulster, including a temporary exclusion from the provisions of the Home Rule Bill. But all was ready for a trial of military strength when the First World War broke out in 1914. Home Rule was postponed for the duration of the war, and by the end of the war conditions in Ireland had entirely changed as a result of the 1916 Dublin Rising and its aftermath.

300. An Irish landlord on the Louth election, 1826
[Leslie Foster to Robert Peel, 8 July 1826]

I entered upon the contest with upwards of five-sixths of the votes promised to me, and my opponent was the person in the whole county the most unacceptable to the gentry, who were unanimous in support of me, except the few Catholic proprietors who supported him only because he was opposed to me.

The scene opened by resolutions from the Catholic Association, and by a circular from old Curteis to all his priests; but who set Curteis in activity, is what I would rather tell you than write.

A systematic organisation was immediately developed. A lay committee was formed in every parish to levy forced subscriptions, to collect the people, harangue them, and make them drunk. The priests preached in all their chapels the most violent sermons, and visited every Catholic who had a vote. The eternal salvation of the voter being at stake, was distinctly the proposition insisted on with the tenantry. This was put to them in every variety of form, and believed by them more firmly than the Gospel. I was stated to be the enemy of the Church— the enemy of Christ. It was a choice between the distress warrant and the Cross, Sheil's own expression on the occasion. The tenantry, if ruined, were to be blessed martyrs, while the legs were to burn eternally in hell fire which should carry any voter to the poll for me. Even purgatory was not to save him.

A personal fury almost demoniacal was thus raised against me, and soon became directed against all my supporters. Very many Protestants were forced to vote against me by the threats of assassination or having their houses burnt. My voters were waylaid by large mobs along every line of road, and severely beaten, not merely in coming but in returning. Lord Oriel's tenantry, who most of them proved steady, were attacked ten miles distant from the county town by a mob of above a thousand persons collected for the purpose, and the continued escort of military became at last indispensable.

When the poll commenced, all the priests of the county were collected and distributed through the different booths, where they stood with glaring eyes directly opposite to the voters of their respective flocks as they were severally brought up. In the county town the studied violence and intimidation were such that it was only by locking up my voters in inclosed yards that their lives were preserved.

The result of all these proceedings was a very general defection of the tenants from their landlords as to their first votes, and one almost universal as to their second. Dawson's legitimate force was less than 120 votes; he polled 862, and all the difference proceeded from piracy. Lord Roden's interest was about 250 votes, he gave it to me heartily. Out of it I obtained about ten, and Dawson all the rest. There are two cousins of mine, Mr. Fosters, each of whom has about 3,000 l. a year in this county. From one of their estates I obtained about six votes, and from the other literally but one.

At the close of the election the Catholics threw in their votes to the other Protestant candidate merely to get me out, but they were a little too late in the manoeuvre, and matters ended—Dawson 862, Foster 552, Fortescue 547.

Now that all is over I hardly know what is to be the consequence. The landlords are exasperated to the utmost, the priests swaggering in their triumph, the tenantry sullen and insolent. Men who a month ago were all civility and submission now hardly suppress their curses when a gentleman passes by. The text of every village orator is, 'Boys, you have put down three Lords. Stick to your priests, and you will carry all before you.'

Many persons suppose that Catholic Emancipation would abate the influence of the priests. My impressions to the contrary are only confirmed by what I have seen. If any candidate after the carrying of the measure should resist their notions of education, or their being provided with chapels or glebe houses, or even belong to a Bible Society, or resist any of their projects of aggrandisement, I am persuaded he would equally be denounced as an enemy of the Church, and that all the same consequences would ensue. Parker, *Peel*, I, 410–11

301. Daniel O'Connell denounces the Irish Union, 1843

[Speech at the Hill of Tara, 15 August 1843]

On this spot I have a most important duty to perform. I here protest, in the name of my country and in the name of my God, against the unfounded and unjust Union. My proposition to Ireland is that the

Union is not binding on her people. It is void in conscience and in principle, and as a matter of constitutional law I attest these facts. Yes, I attest by everything that is sacred, without being profane, the truth of my assertions. There is no real union between the two countries, and my proposition is that there was no authority given to anyone to pass the Act of Union. Neither the English nor the Irish Legislature was competent to pass that Act, and I arraign it on these grounds. One authority alone could make that Act binding, and that was the voice of the people of Ireland. The Irish Parliament was elected to make laws and not to make legislatures; and, therefore, it had no right to assume the authority to pass the Act of Union. The Irish Parliament was elected by the Irish people as their trustees; the people were their masters, and the members were their servants, and had no right to transfer the property to any other power on earth. If the Irish Parliament had transferred its power of legislation to the French Chamber, would any man assert that the Act was valid? Would any man be mad enough to assert it; would any man be insane enough to assert it, and would the insanity of the assertion be mitigated by sending any number of members to the French Chamber? Everybody must admit that it would not. What care I for France?—and I care as little for England as for France, for both countries are foreign to me. The very highest authority in England has proclaimed us to be aliens in blood, in religion, and in language. ... To show the invalidity of the Union I could quote the authority of Locke on 'Parliament.' I will, however, only detain you by quoting the declaration of Lord Plunket in the Irish Parliament, who told them that they had no authority to transfer the legislation of the country to other hands. As well, said he, might a maniac imagine that the blow by which he destroys his wretched body annihilates his immortal soul, as you to imagine that you can annihilate the soul of Ireland—her constitutional rights.

I need not detain you by quoting authorities to show the invalidity of the Union. I am here the representative of the Irish nation, and in the name of that moral, temperate, virtuous, and religious people, I proclaim the Union a nullity. Saurin, who had been the representative of the Tory party for twenty years, distinctly declared that the Act of Union was invalid. He said that the Irish House of Commons had no right, had no power to pass the Union, and that the people of Ireland would be justified, the first opportunity that presented itself, in effecting its repeal. So they are. The authorities of the country were charged with the enactment, the alteration, or the administration of its laws. These were their powers; but they had no authority to alter or over-throw the Constitution. I therefore proclaim the nullity of the Union.

Wagner, *Modern Political Orations*, pp. 42–3

302. Gladstone's description of the Irish Land Bill, 1870

[W. E. Gladstone to Queen Victoria, 26 January 1870]

The scope of the Irish Land Bill now in preparation is perfectly distinct, and is such as it is hoped your Majesty will approve.

The most crying evil, which has for some time afflicted that country, the only one of great gravity now remaining, is the prevailing sense of instability in the tenure of the soil by those who cultivate it, with the train of consequences following thereon in bad agriculture, low profits, popular suffering, discontent, and crime (of a special class), and recently in a real and spreading paralysis of proprietary rights, which are neutralised by intimidation.

As a remedy for these evils it has been proposed to expropriate the landlords by public purchase, or to reduce them to incumbrancers upon the land by rents either fixed or varying only within limits, and in a manner directed by law. To such plans your Majesty's Government can lend no countenance.

The object the Government have in view is to give, to the occupiers of the soil in Ireland, that sense of security which they require in order to pursue their calling with full advantage to the community and to themselves, and to do this in such a way as to create the smallest possible disturbance to existing arrangements, and to preserve, it might almost be said, to restore, the essential rights of property.

The most essential provisions of the Bill in this view will be:

1. To confirm by law the custom called the Ulster Custom.[1]

2. To provide for the occupier disturbed by the act of his landlord, where that custom does not prevail, a just compensation on losing his holding, either to be measured by other prevailing usages, or according to a scale set out in the Act, in consideration of the serious injury done to him, under the circumstances of that country, by the loss of his means of employment.

3. But to provide that by giving leases of an adequate length land-

---

[1] By the Ulster Custom, so long as the tenant paid his rent he could not be evicted; and on giving up his farm he could claim compensation for unexhausted improvements and sell the goodwill for what it would fetch in the market.

lords may relieve themselves from the obligation to give compensation on this basis.

4. To lay down the principle that improvements in agricultural holdings effected by the tenant are to be henceforward presumed to be his property.

5. To create a judicial authority in Ireland which is to apply the provisions of the new law.... LQV, 2nd. ser. II, 5-7

303. Isaac Butt moves an amendment to the Address, 20 March 1874

The proposal I desire to submit to the House is that the following passage be added to the Address—

> We also think it right humbly to represent to Your Majesty that dissatisfaction prevails very extensively in Ireland with the existing system of Government in that country, and that complaints are made that under that system the Irish people do not enjoy the full benefits of the Constitution and of the free principles of the law; and we humbly assure Your Majesty that we shall regard it as the duty of Parliament, on the earliest opportunity, to consider the origin of this dissatisfaction with a view to the removal of all just causes of discontent.

I think there is one result of this dissatisfaction in Ireland, as exhibited by the recent elections, to which no person can be indifferent, and which no wise statesman can disregard. For the first time since the Act of Union, a majority—I will call it a decisive majority—of Irish members has been returned pledged to seek such a modification of the arrangements of the Union as would give to Irishmen in Ireland the right of managing their own affairs. I refer to this fact as evidence of dissatisfaction with the existing state of things. The Irish members who have been returned as Home Rulers are a decisive majority of the Irish representatives, and these have not been pledged to any mere vague declaration in favour of Home Rule. Those who have thought it right to endeavour to excite the attention of the country to the question of Home Rule have deliberately prepared and put before the country the plan contained in the Resolution, which, I venture to say, is framed in terms as clear and distinct as possible. We ask that Ireland shall have the management of exclusively Irish affairs. Our plan would relieve the House of business which it has not the time, and, I may say, without disrespect, the capacity, to manage. Our plan would not in the slightest degree affect the prerogative of the Crown or the stability of the Empire. We see no reason why an Irish Parliament could not manage exclusively Irish affairs without endangering the stability of the Empire. Has the grant of Parliaments to Canada, Australia, and other Colonies endangered the stability of the Empire? I believe I speak for every member who has been returned for Ireland on the Home Rule principle, when I say that we repudiate, in the strongest terms, the slightest wish to break up the unity of the Empire, or to bring about a collision between England and Ireland. We make no secret that they have all been elected to put forward the claim of Ireland to Home Rule, and, whether rightly or wrongly, we have come to an agreement among ourselves that we will act separately and independently of all existing political combinations in this House.

I think I may base the first part of this Amendment upon the mere fact that a majority of the Irish members are returned expressly to endeavour to obtain for Ireland self-government. I know not what stronger proof can be given of the dissatisfaction existing in Ireland. This dissatisfaction has been constitutionally expressed. It has not been expressed by any disturbances, such as on former occasions have been noticed in the Queen's Speech. The Irish people have made this great political movement at a time when perfect tranquillity prevails throughout the country, and in all the agitation by which the result has been brought about there has been nothing unconstitutional or illegal. It has been expressed through that political franchise which has been given to them for the purpose of declaring their political opinion. Ireland at present is in a state of perfect tranquillity. The Assizes that have just closed have ended in every place with congratulations from the Judges upon the peaceableness of the different counties. In the last Summer Assizes in the city I have the honour to represent (Limerick), white gloves were given to the Judge, there not being a single prisoner to be tried. In the city of Cork, another great city in the south of Ireland, the very same thing occurred. I think the dissatisfaction in Ireland calls upon the House, I will not say to alter or reverse any policy that has been hitherto pursued with reference to Ireland, but certainly to review calmly and deliberately that policy, and ascertain the causes that have given rise to the dissatisfaction as to the management of Irish affairs by this House.

I think I need not go far to justify the second part of this Amendment, which affirms that the Irish people complain that they have not had the full benefits of the Constitution of England. I believe that at this moment Ireland is under a code of law which for severity has not its parallel in any European State. I will not speak for a moment of the law that prevails all over Ireland independently of the will of the Lord-Lieutenant. The Lord-Lieutenant has power, by proclamation, to make it illegal in any district to carry arms without a licence from a police magistrate; and any man having a gun, a pistol, or dagger is liable, unless he have a magistrate's licence, to imprisonment for two years. Of the thirty-two counties in Ireland, twenty-six have been proclaimed; the greater part of five others has been proclaimed; and there is just one county in Ireland, designated Tyrone, which is free from proclamation. Of the eight counties and cities, Carrickfergus only is free from proclamation. Now this, I think, is a very startling state of things in Ireland. But more than this—at any time of the night, in any district where this law prevails, any policeman holding a warrant may demand to be admitted into any house in a proclaimed district, and may break open the door if admittance be refused, to search the house for arms; and one hundred and nineteen of these general warrants are now in operation. Even this is not all. By proclamation the Lord-Lieutenant may make it a crime to be out of doors after dark; while by another proclamation he can empower the police to seize any stranger; and a large portion of Ireland is at present under this law. By another proclamation any magistrate or police officer may demand admittance to any man's house, and ransack his papers for the purpose of comparing the handwriting with the handwriting of a threatening letter. Let it not be insinuated that these powers are never used. On one occasion a number of young men, one of whom was the son of a respectable merchant, determined to play 'Hamlet.' A police inspector, hearing of this, went to the theatre, arrested the young gentleman, and kept him in prison from Saturday night till Monday morning...on a charge of having arms in his possession.

This, I think, amply justifies me in saying that Ireland does not enjoy the advantages of the British Constitution, nor the free principles of the English law.

Wagner, *Modern Political Orations*, pp. 164–8

304. Gladstone moves towards Home Rule, 1883

[W. E. Gladstone to Earl Granville, 22 January 1883]

Under the present highly centralised system of Government, every demand, which can be started on behalf of a poor and ill-organised country, comes directly on the British Government and Treasury; if refused it becomes at once a head of grievance, if granted not only a new drain but a certain source of political complication and embarrassment, the peasant proprietary—the winter's distress—the state of the labourers—the loans to farmers—the promotion of public works—the encouragement of fisheries—the promotion of emigration—each and every one of these questions has a sting, and the sting can only be taken out of it by our treating it in correspondence with a popular and responsible *Irish* body—competent to act for its own portion of the country.

GG2, II, 10

305. John Morley's summary of the Home Rule Bill of 1886

One of the cardinal difficulties of all free government is to make it hard for majorities to act unjustly to minorities. You cannot make this injustice impossible but you may set up obstacles. In this case, there was no novelty in the device adopted. The legislative body was to be composed of two orders. The first order was to consist of the twenty-eight representative peers, together with seventy-five members elected by certain scheduled constituencies on an occupation franchise of twenty-five pounds and upwards. To be eligible for the first order, a person must have a property qualification, either in realty of two hundred pounds a year, or in personalty of the same amount, or a capital value of four thousand pounds. The representative peers now existing would sit for life, and, as they dropped off, the crown would nominate persons to take their place up to a certain date, and on the exhaustion of the twenty-eight existing peers, then the whole of the first order would become elective under the same conditions as the seventy-five other members.

The second order would consist of 206 members, chosen by existing counties and towns under the machinery now operative. The two orders were to sit and deliberate together, but either order could demand a separate vote. This right would enable a majority of one order to veto the proposal of the other. But the veto was only to operate until a dissolution, or for three years, whichever might be the longer interval of the two.

The executive transition was to be gradual. The office of viceroy would remain, but he would not be the minister of a party, nor quit office with an outgoing government. He would have a privy council; within that council would be formed an executive body of ministers like the British cabinet. This executive would be responsible to the Irish legislature, just as the executive government here is responsible to the legislature of this country. If any clause of a bill seemed to the viceroy to be *ultra vires*, he could refer it to the judicial committee of the privy council in London. The same reference, in respect of a section of an Irish Act, lay open either to the English secretary of state, or to a suitor, defendant, or other person concerned.

Future judges were to hold the same place in the Irish system as English judges in the English system; their office was to be during good behaviour; they were to be appointed on the advice of the Irish government, removable only on the joint address of the two orders, and their salaries charged on the Irish consolidated fund. The burning question of the royal Irish constabulary was dealt with provisionally. Until a local force was created by the new government, they were to remain at the orders of the lord lieutenant. Ultimately the Irish police were to come under the control of the legislative body. For two years from the passing of the Act, the legislative body was to fix the charge for the whole constabulary of Ireland.

In national as in domestic housekeeping, the figure of available income is the vital question. The total receipts of the Irish exchequer would be £8,350,000, from customs, excise, stamps, income-tax, and non-tax revenue. On a general comparison of the taxable revenues of Ireland and Great Britain, as tested more especially by the property passing under the death duties, the fair proportion due as Ireland's share for imperial purposes, such as interest on the debt, defence, and civil charge, was fixed at one-fifteenth. This would bring the total charge properly imperial up to £3,242,000. Civil charges in Ireland were put at £2,510,000, and the constabulary charge on Ireland was not to exceed £1,000,000, any excess over that sum being debited to England. The Irish government would be left with a surplus of £404,000. This may seem a ludicrously meagre amount, but, compared with the total revenue, it is equivalent to a surplus on our own budget of that date of something like five millions.

The true payment to imperial charges was to be £1,842,000 because of the gross revenue above stated £1,400,000 though paid in Ireland in the first instance was really paid by British consumers of whisky, porter, and tobacco. This sum, deducted from £3,242,000, leaves the real Irish contribution, namely £1,842,000.

A further sum of uncertain, but substantial amount, would go to the Irish exchequer from another source, to which we have now to turn. With the proposals for self-government were coupled proposals for a settlement of the land question. The ground-work was an option offered to the landlords of being bought out under the terms of the Act. The purchaser was to be an Irish state authority, as the organ representing the legislative body. The occupier was to become the proprietor, except in the congested districts, where the state authority was to be the proprietor. The normal price was to be twenty years' purchase of the net rental. The most important provision, in one sense, was that which recognised the salutary principle that the public credit should not be resorted to on such a scale as this merely for the benefit of a limited number of existing cultivators of the soil, without any direct advantage to the government as representing the community at large. That was effected by making the tenant pay an annual instalment, calculated on the gross rental, while the state authority would repay to the imperial treasury a percentage calculated on the net rental, and the state authority would pocket the difference, estimated to be about 18 per cent. on the sum payable to the selling landlord. How was all this to be secured? Principally, on the annuities paid by the tenants who had purchased their holdings, and if the holdings did not satisfy the charge, then on the revenues of Ireland. All public revenues whatever were to be collected by persons appointed by the Irish government, but these collectors were to pay over all sums that came into their hands to an imperial officer, to be styled a receiver-general. Through him all rents and Irish revenues whatever were to pass, and not a shilling was to be let out for Irish purposes until their obligations to the imperial exchequer had been discharged.   Morley, *Gladstone*, III, 559–61 [corrected]

306. John Bright on Home Rule, May 1886
[John Bright to W. E. Gladstone, 13 May 1886]

I feel outside all the contending sections of the liberal party—for I am not in favour of home rule, or the creation of a Dublin parliament—

nor can I believe in any scheme of federation as shadowed forth by
Mr. Chamberlain.

I do not believe that with regard to the Irish question 'the resources
of civilisation are exhausted'; and I think the plan of your bill is full
of complexity, and gives no hope of successful working in Ireland or
of harmony between Westminster and Dublin. I may say that my
regard for you and my sympathy with you has made me silent in the
discussion on the bills before the House. I cannot consent to a measure
which is so offensive to the whole protestant population of Ireland,
and to the whole sentiment of the province of Ulster so far as its loyal
and protestant people are concerned. I cannot agree to exclude them
from the protection of the imperial parliament. I would do much to
clear the rebel party from Westminster, and I do not sympathise with
those who wish to retain them, but admit there is much force in the
arguments on this point which are opposed to my views upon it.

Up to this time I have not been able to bring myself to the point of
giving a vote in favour of your bills. I am grieved to have to say this.
As to the Land bill, if it comes to a second reading, I fear I must vote
against it. It may be that my hostility to the rebel party, looking at
their conduct since your government was formed six years ago, disables
me from taking an impartial view of this great question. If I could
believe them loyal, if they were honourable and truthful men, I could
yield them much; but I suspect that your policy of surrender to them
will only place more power in their hands, to war with greater effect
against the unity of the three kingdoms with no increase of good to the
Irish people....

The various reform bills, the Irish church bill, the two great land
bills, were passed by very large majorities. In the present case, not
only the whole tory party oppose, but a very important section of the
liberal party; and although numerous meetings of clubs and associations
have passed resolutions of confidence in you, yet generally they have
accepted your Irish government bill as a 'basis' only, and have admitted the need of important changes in the bill—changes which in
reality would destroy the bill. Under these circumstances it seems to
me that more time should be given for the consideration of the Irish
question. Parliament is not ready for it, and the intelligence of the
country is not ready for it. ...

For thirty years I have preached justice to Ireland. I am as much in
her favour now as in past times, but I do not think it justice or wisdom

for Great Britain to consign her population, including Ulster and all her protestant families, to what there is of justice and wisdom in the Irish party now sitting in the parliament in Westminster.

Morley, Gladstone, III, 327–9

307. Gladstone prepared for a long struggle over Home Rule, 1887
[W. E. Gladstone to Sir T. D. Acland, June 1887]

This is a great battle. Shall I, or will even you...see the end of it? When I look at the reason and the strength of the case the feeling rises up—that 'surely this contest cannot be long'—but when I recollect on the other hand that the *minor* battle of R.C. emancipation lasted for twenty-nine years after the Union, and that English obstinacy only yielded *then* to the fear of Civil War, a darker view asserts itself.

Acland, Memoir of Sir T. D. Acland, p. 384

308. Gladstone dissociates himself from Parnell after the O'Shea divorce case, 1890
[W. E. Gladstone to John Morley, 24 November 1890]

. . . While clinging to the hope of a communication from Mr. Parnell, to whomsoever addressed, I thought it necessary, viewing the arrangements for the commencement of the session to-morrow, to acquaint Mr. McCarthy with the conclusion at which, after using all the means of observation and reflection in my power, I had myself arrived. It was that notwithstanding the splendid services rendered by Mr. Parnell to his country, his continuance at the present moment in the leadership would be productive of consequences disastrous in the highest degree to the cause of Ireland. I think I may be warranted in asking you so far to expand the conclusion I have given above, as to add that the continuance I speak of would not only place many hearty and effective friends of the Irish cause in a position of great embarrassment, but would render my retention of the leadership of the liberal party, based as it has been mainly upon the prosecution of the Irish cause, almost a nullity. This explanation of my views I begged Mr. McCarthy to regard as confidential, and not intended for his colleagues generally, if he found that Mr. Parnell contemplated spontaneous action; but I also begged that he would make known to the Irish party, at their meeting to-morrow afternoon, that such was my conclusion, if he should find that Mr. Parnell had not in contemplation any step of the nature indicated. I now write to you, in case Mr. McCarthy should be unable to communicate with Mr. Parnell, as I understand you may possibly have an opening to-morrow through another channel. Should you have such an opening, I beg you to make known to Mr. Parnell the conclusion itself, which I have stated in the earlier part of this letter. . ..

Morley, Gladstone, III, 437

309. The Cabinet on Irish representation at Westminster, 1893

[W. E. Gladstone to Queen Victoria, 13 January 1893]

Mr. Gladstone submits his humble duty to your Majesty and reports that the Cabinet has this day proceeded with the consideration in detail of the Government of Ireland Bill.

They examined the difficult subject, which the Government has so reluctantly approached, of the retention of Irish Members at Westminster, a retention involving, when the manner of it comes to be discussed, serious difficulties and inconveniences, as to which all that judgment and care can effect is to choose the smaller among them in preference to the greater.

Acting in this spirit the Cabinet came to the conclusions that Irish Members should be retained in just proportion to the relative population of the Kingdom of Ireland, which would give them the number of eighty or thereabouts. But also that Irish Members so retained should, to speak in general terms, be excluded from voting on questions exclusively British.

The Cabinet do not view with favour on its merits the creation of a class of members disabled from voting on a portion of the business of Parliament; but they think the inconvenience less than that which would arise from a proposal to admit their votes as of equal authority on British questions under the new arrangement.   LQV, 3rd ser. II, 201–2

310. Asquith on the Government of Ireland Bill, 11 April 1912

AUTHORITY OF IMPERIAL PARLIAMENT

The supreme power and authority of the Imperial Parliament is to remain unimpaired and unchallenged. We mean this Bill to confer upon Ireland, in regard to Irish concerns, local autonomy, subject only to such reservations and safeguards as the peculiar circumstances of the case require. The Bill, therefore, proceeds in the first Section and first Clause to declare that—

after the appointed day there shall be in Ireland an Irish Parliament, consisting of His Majesty the King, and two Houses, namely, the Irish Senate and the Irish House of Commons.

What are to be the legislative powers of that body? It is to have power to make laws for the peace, order, and good government of Ireland. That is the general position. Now I come to consider and ask the House to consider what are the limitations of that general grant of legislative powers. In the first place it is limited by territorial limitations by the words I have quoted—

power to make laws for the peace, order, and good government of Ireland.

The Bill goes on to say that they shall only have power to make laws in respect of matters exclusively relating to Ireland or some part thereof. You start with a territorial limitation: that is perfectly clear. In the next place we have excluded—and here we follow the precedent of the Bill of 1893—we have excluded certain matters which, although they may fall within the territorial limit, are matters which everybody will admit it is desirable should not be dealt with by the new body. These are substantially the same as the matters enumerated in the Bill of 1893— matters affecting the Crown, the making of peace and war, the Army, the Navy, treaties, dignities, treason, and a number of other matters as hon. Members will readily recognise by referring to the two Bills. We have found it necessary to-day, in consequence of legislation which has taken place between that time and this—or partly in consequence of that legislation—to propose the exclusion of certain Irish services— described in this Bill as reserved services—services reserved for the Imperial Parliament and the Imperial Executive.

First, and in some ways the most important, is the subject matter of the Irish Land Purchase Act. It is, we think, of the utmost importance, in view of the history of this legislation and of future progress in its application and administration, that it should be made perfectly clear that the security of this system, which has been set up on the basis of Imperial credit, is not to be in any way affected.... That is the first of the reserved services, together with the Old Age Pensions Acts, 1908 and 1911, and the National Insurance Act, 1911. The second of the reserved services is the Royal Irish Constabulary. The third is the Post Office Savings Banks; next, Public Loans, as far as respects loans made in Ireland before the passing of this Act; and finally, the collection of taxes other than duties of postage....

While we have treated these as reserved services, in regard to which the Irish Parliament will have neither the power of legislation nor of administration, we have provided in the Bill that in regard to some of them there shall be either an automatic transfer or a transfer at the option of the Irish Parliament. In regard to the Constabulary there will be automatically, in consequence of the provisions of the Bill itself, a transfer of that force after the expiration of six years from the passing of the Act. In regard to Post Office Savings Banks, after ten years there may be a transfer at the wish of the Irish Parliament, after an adequate notice—a notice of six months—which will enable all depositors who are so minded to make their arrangements accordingly. I do not suppose for a moment that they will feel any disposition or temptation to do so. In regard to old age pensions and national insurance, we also give a power to the Irish Parliament to demand the transfer of those services after a year's notice.... In addition to these excluded topics embraced in the reserved services, we provide in the Bill that the Irish Parliament cannot repeal or alter any provision of the Act itself, except in regard to certain subsidiary matters which are specially dealt with. Neither will it have the power to affect the right of appeal, which, as I shall presently show, we are going to give to the Judicial Committee of the Privy Council in all the questions which may arise as to the validity of the laws passed by that Parliament itself. I come now to a further limitation. This, I think, vitally affects the main ground of the objection which is taken to the inclusion of Ulster, or certain parts of Ulster, at any rate, within the ambit of the authority of the new legislative body.

RELIGIOUS EQUALITY

The Bill of 1893 contained, in its fourth Clause, a number of restrictions upon the powers of the Irish legislature, which we do not in this Bill repeat. We do not do so for the reason, which we think is a good and sufficient reason, first of all that they were very vague in their terms, next because we believe them to be absolutely unnecessary so far as we can foresee the course of events; further, because they would give rise to infinite opportunity for litigation upon matters which are not very fit to be subject to the cognisance of the Courts of Law, and finally, because we believe that in so far as they were directed against real dangers, those dangers are amply provided against by the other safeguards provided in our Bill. We thought, and do think it right, to make special provisions for the protection and preservation of religious equality. I will read the exact terms of the Clause—it is Clause 3 in the Bill—which we shall submit for the consideration of the House:—

In the exercise of their power to make laws under this Act, the Irish Parliament shall not make a law so as either directly or indirectly to establish or endow any religion

—that was in the Bill of 1893—

or prohibit the free exercise thereof, or to give a preference, privilege or advantage, or impose any disability or disadvantage on account of religious belief or religious or ecclesiastical status, or to make any religious belief or religious ceremony a condition of the validity of any marriage....

We go on to provide, in order that the Irish Parliament may not transcend its constitutional limits, two additional safeguards.

In the first place there is the veto of the Lord Lieutenant under the Seventh Clause of the Bill, which provides that he shall give or withhold his consent to Bills passed by the two Houses of the Irish Parliament subject to two limitations—namely, first, he shall comply with any instructions given by His Majesty—that means by the Imperial Executive of this country—in respect of any such Bill; and next, he shall, if so directed by His Majesty—that again refers to the Imperial Executive here—postpone giving the assent of His Majesty to any such Bill for such period as His Majesty—that is the Executive—may direct. So we reserve completely unimpaired, subject to the responsibility of the Executive here, the Imperial Parliament, the power of vetoing or postponing any legislation which the Irish Parliament may pass. Finally, there is and must remain, and it is expressly recognised, the over-riding force of Imperial legislation, which can at any time nullify, amend, or alter any Act of the Irish Parliament. To make that matter abundantly clear we have provided in the last Clause of the Bill in these terms:—

Where any Act of the Irish Parliament deals with any matter with respect to which the Irish Parliament have power to make laws, which is dealt with by any Act of the Parliament of the United Kingdom passed after the passing of this Act and extending to Ireland the Act of the Irish Parliament shall be read subject to the Act of the Parliament of the United Kingdom and, so far as it is repugnant to that Act, but no further, it shall be void.

So you have, first of all, in the veto of the Lord Lieutenant exercisable by the Imperial Executive, and subject to the control of the Imperial Parliament, and next in the inherent power expressly preserved in the Act of the Imperial Parliament itself, a complete and adequate safeguard for the maintenance of the ultimate sovereignty of the Imperial Parliament.

Now I come to the powers of the Legislature. If any question arise as to the validity of an Irish Act, as to whether it is or is not within the powers conferred by this Statute, the question will be settled—if it arise in the course of ordinary litigation which involves any such point—first of all by an appeal to the Irish Court of Appeal, and from it to the Judicial Committee of the Privy Council, and next—even if the matter does not arise at all in the course of litigation—at the instance either of the Lord Lieutenant or of the Secretary of State here by a special reference to the Judicial Committee, which shall determine the point even before the Act has come into operation at all.

CONSTITUTION OF THE IRISH PARLIAMENT

So much for the legislative powers of the new Parliament. I now come to deal with its constitution. As I have said, we propose that it shall consist of two Houses—one to be called the Senate and the other the House of Commons. The Senate is to consist of forty Members, and the question, of course, arises in what manner and by what process those forty Members are to be selected. It will always be recognised, I think, that they should not be simply elected by the constituencies who return Members to the Lower House. In the Bill of 1893, where the number was, I think, forty-eight, they were to be elected, but elected upon a restricted franchise—a franchise confined to owners and occupiers of property over a certain rateable value. We do not think on consideration that that is a satisfactory plan, and I believe that such is the opinion of Ireland.

We have come to the conclusion—and it is a conclusion the reasonableness of which will, I think, become more clear when I state what are the character, the numbers and the composition of the Lower House that the best mode of dealing with this matter will be that the Senate should be a nominated body. We think so in view of the special circumstances of Ireland. It is most desirable to get in your Senate, if you can, representatives of the minority, persons who will safeguard the interests of the minority, persons who will not or who might not have a fair chance of being elected in a popular election, and it is still more desirable perhaps in Ireland than anywhere else that you should be able to draw for the purposes of your Senate upon resources which are not available in the case of elections. We believe that on the whole the exigencies of the case and the peculiar conditions of Ireland will be best satisfied by a nominated body—a body nominated, in the first instance here by the Imperial Executive, the Members to hold office for eight years, and to retire by rotation, and as they retire their places to be filled up by the Irish Executive. In the Bill of 1893 the Lower House consisted of 103 Members, the same number of Members as are returned to this House by Ireland. Experience shows—and the analogy of other legislative bodies in our Dominions seems to point to that conclusion—that the Lower House should be of somewhat larger dimensions, and we propose that the numbers of the Lower House should be 164 elected by the existing Irish constituencies. The unit of population is to be 27,000. There will be no constituency with a population of less than 27,000 which will be entitled to return a Member. The effect will be this: Ulster will have 59 Members; Leinster, 41; Munster, 37; and Connaught, 25, and if you add the Universities, which we retain for this purpose—that makes a total of 164. If you divide that in another way it comes to this—Counties 128, Boroughs 34, Universities 2. The exact distribution is shown in a Schedule to the Bill. When there is disagreement between the two Houses, if such a contingency should arise, we have followed the precedent of the South African Constitution, and provided that the two Houses should sit together and vote together— that is to say, if the Lower House persists after the disagreement in its view on the particular measure in question. The House will now see that with an elected Chamber of 164 and a nominated Chamber of 40, sitting in joint session, there is every probability, at any rate, unless there be a very even division of parties, that full opportunity will be given for public opinion in Ireland to have effect.

So much for the composition of the Legislature. I now come to the position of the Executive. The head of the Executive will be, as now, the Lord Lieutenant, in whose appointment religious disability will no longer count. The office will be open to any of His Majesty's subjects without distinction of creed, and we propose, following the example of the Bill of 1893, that he shall hold his office for a fixed term of years. The Lord Lieutenant will be advised in regard to Irish matters by an Irish Executive, and I wish to make it perfectly clear that, as far as the Executive in Ireland is concerned, the area of its authority will be co-extensive with the legislative power of the Parliament—neither greater nor less. In other words, whatever matters are for the time being within the legislative competence of the Irish Parliament will, for administrative purposes, be within the ambit of the Irish Executive, and whatever matters are for the time being outside the legislative province of the Irish Parliament will remain under the control and subject to the administration of the Imperial Executive....

IRISH POWERS OF TAXATION

This brings me to explain what are the powers of taxation which, under the new state of things, will be exercisable in Ireland so far as taxation is concerned. First of all, the Imperial Parliament will continue to tax the whole of the United Kingdom. Next, the Irish Parliament will have the power, first, to reduce or discontinue for Ireland any Imperial tax, with the result that, if it does, the Transferred Sum will be correspondingly reduced—that is to say, reduced by the amount of the diminished yield. Next the Irish Parliament will have power to impose Irish taxes of their own, whether by way of addition to Imperial taxes or otherwise, with the result that the taxes will be collected, as I have said, by Imperial officers, and the transferred sum will be correspondingly increased, that is to say, increased by the amount that the new increased taxation will yield. This latter power, the power of the Irish Parliament to add to Imperial taxes or to impose taxes of their own, is subject to certain restrictions. In the first place they cannot impose any Customs Duty except upon articles which are for the time being dutiable by way of Customs in the United Kingdom. Further, the Irish Parliament will not be able to add to any Imperial duty of Customs except on beer or spirits, or of Income Tax, or of Estate Duty, more than will produce a 10 per cent. increase. With regard to Excise their hands will be free....

JOINT EXCHEQUER BOARD

Next, we propose to set up a Joint Exchequer Board, consisting of five persons, two to be appointed by the Imperial Government and two by the Irish Treasury, with the chairman nominated by the Crown, to adjust the accounts between the two Exchequers in accordance with the Act....

Now I come to the last point, that is, the future representation of Ireland in the Imperial Parliament. The House will remember that under

Mr. Gladstone's first Bill, in 1886, the Irish Members were entirely excluded from this House. In the Bill of 1893, they were retained, to the number of eighty, that number being fixed as Ireland's proportion, according to the population, comparing Ireland with the other parts of the United Kingdom. They were retained, as those who are familiar with the history of this legislation will know, in the first instance, with powers only to vote on matters of general concern. That was called the 'in and out' Clause. Then, when that Clause was withdrawn, as it was in deference to criticism in the course of the debates, they were given power to vote on all subjects. That is the history. We regard the retention of the Irish Members at Westminster as essential..., but in regard to numbers, our proposal differs widely from that of 1893.

IRISH REPRESENTATION AT WESTMINSTER

We do not think that where Ireland has obtained full control of her own affairs, either justice or policy requires Ireland to continue to be represented here on the same footing in regard to population as the other component parts of the United Kingdom, for whom this House will still continue to be the organ of legislation; nor do we believe that the Irish people, themselves, are prepared to advance any such claim. Under our plan, the Irish representation at Westminster will be reduced to forty-two; in other words, Ireland will have a Member here, roughly, for every 100,000 of her population. This arrangement does not necessitate any general redistribution: but it involves the merger of some of the Irish boroughs and counties, and the grouping together of some counties which at present have separate representations. Three boroughs will be left: Belfast will have four Members, Dublin three, and Cork one. The Universities for this purpose will cease to be represented.

There will be eight borough Members and thirty-four county Members. 5 *Hansard (Commons)* XXXVI, 1408-22

LIST OF WORKS CITED

The place of publication is London unless otherwise indicated.
Official publications are listed separately at the end.

Acland, A. H. D. (ed.) *Memoir and Letters of the Right Honourable Sir Thomas Dyke Acland*. Privately printed, 1902.

Arnstein, W. L. *The Bradlaugh Case: a Study in late Victorian Opinion and Politics*. Oxford, 1965.

Aspinall, Arthur (ed.) 'Extracts from Lord Hatherton's Diary', *Parliamentary Affairs*, XVII, 15–22, 131–41, 254–68, 373–88. 1963–4.

   The Formation of Canning's Ministry, February to August, 1827. Camden 3rd ser. LIX. 1937.

   Three Early Nineteenth-Century Diaries. 1952.

Aspinall, Arthur and Smith, E. Anthony (eds.) *English Historical Documents: XI, 1783–1832*. 1959.

Asquith, H. H. (Earl of Oxford and Asquith) *Fifty Years of Parliament*. 2 vols. 1926.

   Memories and Reflections, 1852–1927. 2 vols. 1928.

Astley, Sir J. D., Bt. *Fifty Years of My Life in the World of Sport at Home and Abroad*. n.d.

Austin, John. *A Plea for the Constitution*. 1859.

Bagehot, Walter. *The English Constitution*. World's Classics edn. 1928.

Balfour, A. J. (Earl of Balfour) *Chapters of Autobiography*. Ed. by Mrs Edgar Dugdale. 1930.

Bealey, F. 'Negotiations between the Liberal Party and the Labour Representation Committee before the General Election of 1906', *Bull. Inst. His. Res.* XXIX, 261–74. 1956.

Belloc, Hilaire. 'The Liberal Tradition' in *Essays in Liberalism*, pp. 1–30. Ed. by J. S. Phillimore and F. W. Hirst. 1897.

   and Chesterton, Cecil. *The Party System*. 1911.

Birmingham Daily Post

Boulger, John. *The Master-Key to Public Offices, and Candidate's Complete Instructor.* . . . 1860.

Bridges, Lord. *The Treasury*. New Whitehall Series No. 12. 1964.

Bright, John. *The Public Letters of the Right Hon. John Bright*. Ed. by H. J. Leech. 2nd ed. 1895.

Brodrick, W. St. J. 'The Functions of Conservative Opposition', *Nineteenth Century*, XIII, 155–65. 1883.

Bulwer, Sir Henry Lytton. (Lord Dalling and Bulwer) *The Life of Henry John Temple, Viscount Palmerston: with Selections from his Diaries and Correspondence*. 3 vols. 1870–4.

Campbell-Bannerman, Sir Henry. *Speeches from his election as Leader of the Liberal Party to his Resignation of Office as Prime Minister, 1899–1908.* Reprinted from *The Times.* n.d.

Carlyle, Thomas. *Latter-Day Pamphlets.* 1850.

Cecil, Lady Gwendolen. *Life of Robert, Marquess of Salisbury.* 4 vols. 1921–32.

Chadwick, Edwin. *On the Evils of Disunity in Central and Local Administration....* 1885.

Chamberlain, Sir J. Austen. *Politics from Inside: an Epistolary Chronicle, 1906–1914.* 1936.

Chilston, Viscount (E. A. Akers-Douglas). *Chief Whip: the Political Life and Times of Aretas Akers-Douglas, 1st Viscount Chilston.* 1961.

Cobbett's Weekly Political Register

Cole, G. D. H. and Filson, A. W. *British Working Class Movements: Select Documents, 1789–1875.* 1951.

Cowan, Charles. *Reminiscences.* Privately printed, 1878.

Cox, Homersham. *The Institutions of the English Government; being an account of the Constitution, Powers and Procedure of its Legislative, Judicial and Administrative Departments.* 1863.

Devonshire Papers. Unpublished papers at Chatsworth House.

Dicey, A. V. *Lectures Introductory to the Study of the Law of the Constitution.* 1885.

Disraeli, B. *Lord George Bentinck: a Political Biography.* New ed. 1858.

Disraeli Papers. Unpublished papers at Hughenden Manor.

Donaldson, Frances. *The Marconi Scandal.* 1962.

Ensor, R. C. K. (ed.) *Modern Socialism as set forth by Socialists in their Speeches, Writings and Programmes.* 3rd ed. 1910.

Esher, Viscount. *Journals and Letters of Reginald, Viscount Esher.* Ed. by M. V. Brett. 4 vols. 1934–8.

Eyck, Frank. *The Prince Consort, a Political Biography.* 1959.

Fabian Society. *Fabian Tract No. 70. Report on Fabian Policy....* 1896.

Ferguson, William. 'The Reform Act (Scotland) of 1832: Intention and Effect', *Scottish Historical Review*, XLV, 105–14. 1966.

Finer, S. E. 'The Individual Responsibility of Ministers', *Public Administration*, XXXIV, 377–96. 1956.

Fitzmaurice, Lord Edmond. *The Life of Granville George Leveson-Gower, Second Earl Granville, K.G., 1815–1891.* 2 vols. 1905.

FitzRoy, Sir Almeric W. *Memoirs.* 2 vols. [1925.]

Foster, B. W. (Lord Ilkeston) *The Political Powerlessness of the Medical Profession, its Causes and its Remedies.* 1883.

Freeman, E. A. *The Growth of the English Constitution from the Earliest Times.* 1872.

Gardiner, A. G. *The Life of Sir William Harcourt.* 2 vols. 1923.

Gash, N. *Politics in the Age of Peel. A Study in the Technique of Parliamentary Representation,* 1830–1850. 1953.

Gladstone Papers. Unpublished papers in the British Museum.

Gladstone, W. E. *Gleanings of Past Years.* 7 vols. 1879.

Goodwood MSS. Unpublished papers of the Duke of Richmond at the County Record Office, Chichester.

Gorst, H. E. *The Fourth Party.* 1906.

Gorst, J. E. 'Elections of the Future', *Fortnightly Review*, new ser. XXXIV, 690–9. 1883.

Grey, Third Earl. (Henry George Grey) *Parliamentary Government Considered with Reference to a Reform of Parliament: an Essay.* 1858.

The Reform Act, 1832: the Correspondence of the late Earl Grey with His Majesty King William IV, and with Sir Herbert Taylor, from Nov. 1830 to June 1832. 2 vols. 1867.

Guedella, P. (ed.) *The Palmerston Papers: Gladstone and Palmerston.* 1928.

The Queen and Mr. Gladstone. 2 vols. 1933.

Hallam, Henry. *View of the State of Europe during the Middle Ages.* 2 vols. 1818.

Hamburger, Joseph. *James Mill and the Art of Revolution.* New Haven. 1963.

Handbook to Government Situations, or the Queen's Civil Service . . . 1866.

Hanham, H. J. *Elections and Party Management: Politics in the Time of Disraeli and Gladstone.* 1959.

'The First Constituency Party?', *Political Studies,* IX, 188–9. 1961.

'Political Patronage at the Treasury, 1870–1912', *Historical Journal,* III, 75–84. 1960.

Hankey, Lord. *Diplomacy by Conference: Studies in Public Affairs, 1920–1946.* 1946.

Hardcastle, Mrs Mary S. (ed.) *Life of John, Lord Campbell, Lord High Chancellor of Great Britain.* 2 vols. 1881.

Hare, Thomas. *A Treatise on the Election of Representatives, Parliamentary and Municipal.* 1859.

Harrison, Frederic. 'The Deadlock in the House of Commons', *Nineteenth Century,* X, 317–40. 1881.

'The Monarchy', *Fortnightly Review,* XI, 613–41. 1872.

Hart, Jennifer. 'The County and Borough Police Act, 1856', *Public Administration,* XXXIV, 405–17. 1956.

Haxey, Simon. *Tory M.P.* Left Book Club. 1939.

Henry Roberts MSS. Unpublished papers in Warrington Municipal Library.

Hewett, O. W. (ed.) '. . . and Mr. Fortescue': a Selection from the Diaries from 1851 to 1862 of Chichester Fortescue, Lord Carlingford, K.P.* 1958.

Hicks Beach, Lady Victoria. *Life of Sir Michael Hicks Beach, Earl St. Aldwyn.* 2 vols. 1932

Holdsworth, Sir William S. *A History of English Law*. 16 vols. 1903–66.

Hughes, Edward. 'Postscript to the Civil Service Reforms of 1855', *Public Administration*, XXXIII, 299–306. 1955.

'Sir Charles Trevelyan and Civil Service Reform, 1853–5', *English Historical Review*, LXIV, 53–88, 206–34. 1949.

'Sir Erskine May's Views on Parliamentary Procedure in 1882', *Public Administration*, XXXIV, 419–24. 1956.

Hutcheon, William (ed.) *Whigs and Whiggism: Political Writings by Benjamin Disraeli*. 1913.

Hylton Papers. Unpublished papers in the possession of Lord Hylton.

Jennings, Louis J. (ed.) *The Croker Papers: the Correspondence and Diaries of the late Right Honourable John Wilson Croker....* 3 vols. 1884.

Jennings, W. Ivor. *Cabinet Government*. Cambridge. 1936.

Kebbel, T. E. (ed.) *Selected Speeches of the late Earl of Beaconsfield*. 2 vols. 1882.

Keeton, G. W. *A Liberal Attorney General: being the Life of Lord Robson of Jesmond, 1852–1918....* 1949.

Lambert, Royston. *Sir John Simon, 1816–1904, and English Social Administration*. 1963.

Lathbury, D. C. (ed.) *Correspondence on Church and Religion of William Ewart Gladstone*. 2 vols. 1910.

Leighton, Baldwyn. *A Brief Record: being Selections from Letters and other Writings of the late Edward Denison, M.P. for Newark*. Privately printed. 1871.

Letters of Queen Victoria: a Selection from Her Majesty's Correspondence.
1st series (1837–61). Ed. by A. C. Benson and Viscount Esher. 3 vols. 1907.
2nd series (1862–85). Ed. by G. E. Buckle. 3 vols. 1926–8.
3rd series (1886–1901). Ed. by G. E. Buckle. 3 vols. 1930–2.

Leveson-Gower, Sir George. *Years of Endeavour, 1886–1907*. 1942.

Liberal Secretaries' and Agents' Association. *Report of its Formation, Rules and Conferences....* Liverpool, 1883.

Lloyd George, D. *War Memoirs*. 6 vols. 1933–6.

Long, W. H. (Viscount Long). *Memories*. 1923.

Lowell, A. L. *The Government of England*. 2 vols. New York, 1924.

'The Influence of Party upon Legislation in England and America', *Annual Report of the American Historical Association for the Year 1901*, I, 321–542. Washington, 1902.

Macaulay, T. B. (Lord Macaulay). *The Works of Lord Macaulay Complete*. Ed. by Lady Trevelyan. 8 vols. 1866.

MacDonagh, O. O. G. M. *A Pattern of Government Growth, 1800–60: the Passenger Acts and their enforcement*. 1961.

Mackenzie, W. J. M. and Grove, J. W. *Central Administration in Britain*. 1957.

Mackintosh, Sir James. 'Universal Suffrage', *Edinburgh Review*, XXXI, 165–203. 1818–19.

MacLeod, R. M. 'Law, Medicine and Public Opinion: the Resistance to Compulsory Health Legislation, 1870–1907', *Public Law*, XII, 107–28, 189–211. 1967.

Maine, Sir Henry J. S. *Popular Government: Four Essays.* 1885.

Manchester Liberal Union. Unpublished papers in the possession of the Manchester Liberal Federation.

Maxwell, Sir H. E., Bt. *The Creevey Papers: a Selection from the Correspondence & Diaries of the late Thomas Creevey, M.P. Born 1768 Died 1838.* 2 vols. 1903.

Miall, Arthur. *The Life of Edward Miall....* 1884.

Mill, J. S. *On Liberty: Representative Government: the Subjection of Women.* World's Classics ed. 1912.

Monk, C. J. *Reminiscences of Parliamentary Life.* Privately printed, 1901.

Morley, John (Viscount Morley). *The Life of William Ewart Gladstone.* 3 vols. 1903.

Walpole. 1889.

Morning Chronicle

Nash, T. A. *The Life of Richard Lord Westbury, formerly Lord High Chancellor.* 2 vols. 1888.

National Liberal Federation. *Proceedings attending the Formation of the National Federation of Liberal Associations.* Birmingham. 1877.

Proceedings at the Annual Meeting. 1891, 1898.

National Union of Conservative and Constitutional Associations. *The Principles and Objects of the National Union....* 1872.

Newton, Lord. *Lord Lansdowne: a Biography.* 1929.

Nicolson, Harold. *King George the Fifth, his Life and Reign.* 1952.

Noel, Hon. Baptist W. *Essay on the Union of Church and State.* 1848.

O'Brien, C. C. *Parnell and his Party, 1880–90.* Oxford. 1957.

Oldfield, T. H. B. *The Representative History of Great Britain and Ireland....* 6 vols. 1816.

Ostrogorski, Moisei. *Democracy and the Organization of Political Parties.* Trans. F. Clarke. 2 vols. 1902.

Parker, C. S. (ed.) *Sir Robert Peel from his Private Papers.* 3 vols. 1891–9.

Peel, George (ed.) *The Private Letters of Sir Robert Peel.* 1920.

Peel, Sir Robert. *Memoirs.* Ed. by Lord Stanhope and E. Cardwell. 2 vols. 1856–7.

The Speeches...delivered in the House of Commons. 4 vols. 1853.

Pollock, Sir Frederick. *The Land Laws.* 2nd ed. 1887.

Prentice, Archibald. *History of the Anti-Corn-Law League.* 2 vols. 1853.

The Radical Programme. With introduction by Joseph Chamberlain. 1885.

Ramm, Agatha (ed.). *The Political Correspondence of Mr. Gladstone and Lord Granville, 1868–1876.* Camden 3rd ser. LXXXI–LXXXII. 2 vols. 1952.

The Political Correspondence of Mr. Gladstone and Lord Granville, 1876–1886. 2 vols. Oxford. 1962.

[Roebuck, J. A.] 'Extracts from the Diary of an M.P.', *Tait's Edinburgh Magazine*, III, 409–16. 1833.

Rosebery, Earl of. *Lord Rosebery's Speeches (1874–1896)*. 1896.

Salisbury, Third Marquess of (Lord Robert Cecil). 'Parliamentary Reform', *Quarterly Review*, CXVII, 540–74. 1865.

Salisbury papers. Unpublished papers of the third Marquess of Salisbury at Christ Church, Oxford.

Smith, J. Toulmin. *Local Self-Government and Centralization: the Characteristics of each....* 1851.

Spencer, Herbert. 'The Great Political Superstition', *Contemporary Review*, XLVI, 24–48. 1884.

Over-Legislation. 1854.

Spender, J. A. *The Life of the Right Hon. Sir Henry Campbell-Bannerman, G.C.B.* 2 vols. [1923.]

and Asquith, Cyril. *Life of Herbert Henry Asquith, Lord Oxford and Asquith.* 2 vols. 1932.

Stanmore, Lord. *Sidney Herbert, Lord Herbert of Lea: a Memoir....* 2 vols. 1906.

Stansky, Peter. *Ambitions and Strategies: the Struggle for the Leadership of the Liberal Party in the 1890s.* Oxford, 1964.

Taylor, Sir Henry. *The Statesman.* Ed. Leo Silberman. Cambridge, 1957.

The Times

Todd, Alpheus. *On Parliamentary Government in England: its Origin, Development and Practical Operation.* 2nd ed. 2 vols. 1887–9.

Trollope, Anthony. *An Autobiography.* Ed. by Henry M. Trollope. 2 vols. 1883.

The Three Clerks. 3 vols. 1858.

Wagner, Leopold (ed.), *Modern Political Orations.* 1896.

Wallace, Robert. 'Single Chamber "democrats"', *Nineteenth Century*, XXXVII, 177–94. 1895.

Walpole, Sir Spencer. *Life of Lord John Russell.* 2 vols. 1889.

Wellington, Duke of. *Despatches, Correspondence, and Memoranda of Field Marshall Arthur Duke of Wellington, K.G.* Ed. by his son. 8 vols. 1867–80.

Winmarleigh Papers. Unpublished papers of Lord Winmarleigh in the possession of the Earl of Scarbrough.

Young, G. M. and Handcock, W. D. (eds.). *English Historical Documents XII (1), 1833–1874.* 1956.

OFFICIAL PUBLICATIONS, &c.

Cabinet Papers. Unpublished papers in the Public Record Office.

Hansard. Hansard's and later series of parliamentary debates.

Journals of the House of Commons

Journals of the House of Lords

London Gazette

Public General Acts

Public General Statutes

Standing Orders of the House of Commons.

Report from the Select Committee appointed to Inquire into the Present State of the Affairs of the East India Company.... H.C. 644 (1830). v, 1. *Second report.* H.C. 655 (1830). v, 675.

Report from the Select Committee on Official Salaries. H.C. 611 (1850). xv, 179.

Census of Great Britain, 1851. Religious Worship. England and Wales. Reports and Tables. [1690] H.C. (1852–3). LXXXIX, 1.

Report from the Select Committee on Dockyard Appointments. H.C. 511 (1852–53). xxv, 1.

Northcote, Sir Stafford H. and Trevelyan, Sir Charles E. *Report on the Organisation of the Permanent Civil Service* [1713]. H.C. (1854). xxvII, 1.

Papers relating to the re-organization of the Civil Service. [1870]. H. C. (1854–55). xx, 1

Correspondence between the Treasury and the Board of Trade relative to the Establishment of the latter office, including a Report by the Right Honourable Stephen Cave and Mr. G. Ward Hunt. H.C. 47 (1867). xxxIx, 213.

Report from the Select Committee on Parliamentary and Municipal Elections. H.C. 115 (1870). vI, 131.

Report of the Commissioners appointed . . . to inquire into the existence of Corrupt Practices in the Borough of Sandwich. [C. 2796]. H.C. (1881). xLV, 1.

Preliminary and Further Reports of the Royal Commissioners appointed to inquire into the Civil and Professional Administration of the Naval and Military Departments.... [Chairman: Marquess of Hartington] [C. 5979]. H.C. (1890), xIx, 1.

Report of the War Office (Reconstitution) Committee [Chairman: Viscount Esher]. Pt. 1. [Cd. 1932] H.C. (1904), vIII, 101.

Report of the Committee appointed to consider the Position and Duties of the Board of Trade and of the Local Government Board [Cd. 2121]. H.C. (1904). LXXVIII, 439.

Royal Commission on the Civil Service [Chairman: Lord MacDonnell] *Fourth Report.* [Cd. 7338]. H.C. (1914). xvI, 1.

INDEX